England's Queens

About the Author

Elizabeth Norton gained her first degree from the University of Cambridge, and her Masters from the University of Oxford. She is the author of nine books on the Tudors. She lives in London.

Praise for Elizabeth Norton

Catherine Parr
'Norton cuts an admirably clear path through tangled Tudor intrigues'
JENNY UGLOW
'Scintillating' *FINANCIAL TIMES*
'Eminently readable' SARAH GRISTWOOD
'Norton's strength is in her use of original sources' *BBC HISTORY MAGAZINE*
'Wonderful... a joy to read' *HERSTORIA*

Bessie Blount: Mistress to Henry VIII
'Secret of the queen Britain lost' *THE SUN*
'A lucid, readable, intelligent account of the life of a woman who might have been queen' *THE GOOD BOOK GUIDE*

Anne Boleyn: Henry VIII's Obsession
'Meticulously researched and a great read' *THEANNEBOLEYNFILES.COM*

Anne Boleyn in Her Own Words & the Words of Those Who Knew Her
'A very useful compilation of source material on Anne Boleyn... a well produced book' ALISON WEIR

Margaret Beaufort: Mother of the Tudor Dynasty
'Portrait of a medieval matriarch' *THE INDEPENDENT*

England's Queens: The Biography
'A truly enlightening read... introduced me to a whole host of women who are deserving of my admiration' *THEANNEBOLEYNFILES.COM*

England's Queens

THE BIOGRAPHY

ELIZABETH NORTON

AMBERLEY

For my son, Dominic

This edition first published 2012

Amberley Publishing
The Hill, Stroud
Gloucestershire, GL5 4EP

www.amberleybooks.com

British Library Cataloguing in Publication Data.
A catalogue record for this book is available from the British Library.

ISBN 978 1 4456 0904 1

Typeset in 10pt on 11.5pt Adobe Caslon Pro.
Typesetting and Origination by Amberley Publishing.
Printed in the UK.

Contents

1

The Early & Mythical Queens

England has always been a place of queens. The earliest known lived nearly 2,000 years ago. Early queens, such as Boudica and Cartimandua, are historical figures, whilst others, such as Cordelia and Guinevere, are mythical. In both historical documents and romantic legends, the early queens of Britain played a prominent role. With the coming of the Anglo-Saxons in the fifth century, England itself came into existence. At first, the English were divided into a number of smaller kingdoms, all of which had queens of their own, before finally, in the ninth century, the kings of Wessex triumphed, uniting the country of England as it still exists today.

From the period before the ninth century, numerous queens are known, some merely as a name and some in more detail. The first Anglo-Saxon queen, for example, can be considered to be the legendary Rowen, the daughter of Hengist, one of the first Saxon settlers. Rowen married the British king, Vortigern, in return for the grant of the kingdom of Kent to her father, and she later assisted her countrymen in obtaining more of the island at the expense of the British. A more significant queen is Sexburga, Queen of Wessex, who, in 672, on the death of her husband, ruled the kingdom as a reigning queen. It would be impossible to detail the lives of every early and mythical queen. Several queens did leave a tangible record, and whilst not queens of England as such, as the country of England did not exist in their time, their stories are remarkable.

The earliest named queens are the contemporaries BOUDICA and CARTIMANDUA, two queens who lived shortly after the Roman conquest of Britain. Boudica, or Boadicea as she is sometimes incorrectly known (*c.* AD 30-60/61), is the better known of the two women.

Britain was conquered by the Emperor Claudius in AD 43, making much of southern and eastern Britain part of the Roman Empire. Before the conquest, Britain had been divided into a number of tribal groups or kingdoms. Following the conquest, some tribes were placed under direct Roman control. Others remained in the hands of their existing rulers, who were friendly to Rome and became client kings. One such client king was Prasutagus, leader of the Iceni, a tribe based in East Anglia. Prasutagus remained on good terms with Rome throughout his life, and according to his near contemporary Tacitus, on his death, he

had made the emperor his heir along with his two daughters, under the impression that this token of submission would put his kingdom and his house out of reach of wrong. But the reverse was the result, so much so that his kingdom was plundered by centurions, his house by slaves as if they were the spoils of war. First, his wife Boudicea was scourged, and his daughters outraged. All the chief men of the Iceni, as if Rome had received the whole country as a gift, were stripped of their ancestral possessions, and the king's relatives were made slaves.

Prasutagus had expected his friendly relationship with Rome to continue after his death, but the conquerors had other ideas and decided to take the kingdom back into direct control.

If the Romans had assumed that the Iceni would simply accept this treatment, they had reckoned without Boudica, Prasutagus's widow. According to the chronicler Cassius Dio, Boudica was a particularly terrifying specimen and 'in stature she was very tall, in appearance most terrifying, in the glance of her eye most fierce, and her voice was harsh; a great mass of the tawniest hair fell to her hips; around her neck was a large golden necklace; and she wore a tunic of divers colours over which a thick mantle was fastened with a brooch'. Boudica was outraged at the whipping she had received at the hands of the invaders, the rape of her daughters and the attack on her kingdom, and setting herself up as the ruler of her people, she exploded out of her territory, intent on driving the Romans from Britain.

The Iceni were not alone in their hatred of Rome, and Boudica was joined by a neighbouring tribe, the Trinovantes, and other disaffected Britons. The Trinovantes had been driven from their lands so that a new city of Camulodunum (modern Colchester) could be built for Roman settlers. It was to Camulodunum that Boudica and her army went first. Boudica was fortunate in the timing of her rebellion, as the Roman governor of Britain, Gaius Suetonius Paullinus was far away, campaigning against the Druids on Anglesey. This meant that Britain was largely undefended; the inhabitants of Camulodunum begged for aid from Catus Decianus, a procurator stationed nearby, but he sent them only 200 troops with which to defend the town. The Romans were completely unprepared for any attack and the city had no walls or defences. As Tacitus put it, 'surprised, as it were, in the midst of peace, they were surrounded by an immense host of barbarians'. On reaching Camulodunum, Boudica's forces stormed the city, burning and plundering, before destroying the hated symbol of Roman rule, the Temple of Claudius. To the terror of the Roman settlers, Boudica's forces also routed a legion commanded by Petilius Cerialis, which arrived to try to restore order.

Boudica showed the Romans at Camulodunum no mercy, and flushed with success, she and her army moved on towards a second large Roman settlement, Londinium (modern London). The Roman governor, Paullinus, had, by that time, marched with a small number of troops to Londinium, ahead of Boudica's forces. On arrival, he realised that it would be impossible to defend the town and 'he resolved to save the province at the cost of a single town'. As the townspeople wept and implored him to stay, Paullinus marched away, taking with him anyone who was able to fight and leaving everyone else to Boudica's fury. Londinium suffered the same fate as Camulodunum, and in both cities, archaeological excavations often reveal a burned layer that testifies to the completeness of the city's destruction. Tacitus did not give a detailed description of the attack on Londinium, but Dio, writing what is likely to be a considerably embellished account, claimed that, in both cities, Boudica's treatment of the inhabitants was terrible:

They hung up naked the noblest and most distinguished women and then cut off their breasts and sewed them to their mouths, in order to make the victims appear to be eating them; afterwards they impaled the women on sharp skewers run lengthwise through the entire body. All this they did to the accompaniment of sacrifices, banquets, and wanton behaviour, not only in all their other sacred places, but particularly in the grove of Andate. This was their name for Victory, and they regarded her with most exceptional reverence.

With the destruction of Londinium, Boudica moved northwards, destroying the town of Verulamium (modern St Albans) before setting off in pursuit of Paullinus.

Tacitus claimed that 70,000 people were killed by Boudica's forces in the three cities; whilst this is almost certainly an exaggeration, the numbers involved were immense. Dio claimed that Boudica's army numbered 120,000 people, and again, whilst this is likely to be exaggerated, her forces considerably outnumbered Paullinus's. This discrepancy in numbers made Boudica believe that she was invincible, and she made the grave mistake of allowing Paullinus, with his well-trained Roman army, to select the place where their battle would take place.

Boudica's force was confident of victory, and her soldiers brought their families to watch the expected slaughter, with women and children sitting in wagons positioned behind the British lines. According to Tacitus, before the battle began, Boudica, riding in a chariot with her daughters, moved up and down the line declaring,

> It is not as a woman descended from noble ancestry, but as one of the people that I am avenging my lost freedom, my scourged body, the outraged chastity of my daughters. Roman lust has gone so far that not our very persons, not even age or virginity, are left unpolluted. But heaven is on the side of righteous vengeance; a legion which dared to fight has perished; the rest are hiding themselves in their camp, or are thinking anxiously of flight. They will not sustain even the din and the shout of so many thousands, much less our charge and our blows. If you weigh well the strength of the armies, and the causes of the war, you will see that in this battle you must conquer or die. This is a woman's resolve, as for men, they may live and be slaves.

Boudica's words were stirring, and in order to further encourage her troops, she released a hare from the folds of her dress in divination, which everyone watched run in an auspicious direction. This was enough for Boudica's troops, and they marched against the Romans. Whilst the Britons had superiority in numbers, they were undisciplined and untrained and no match for the highly organised Romans. The result was a dramatic defeat, and when the Britons attempted to flee, they found themselves hemmed in by their own wagons, leading to a bloodbath where even the women, children and horses were brutally killed. According to Tacitus, 80,000 Britons died that day and only 400 Romans. The numbers may not have been quite so dramatic, but it was a heavy defeat and the end for Boudica. Tacitus claims that she killed herself soon afterwards by poison, whilst Dio suggested that she escaped and was attempting to build a new army when she fell ill and died.

Whilst Boudica's revolt ended in defeat and her death, she made her point, and her rebellion was considered a terrible disaster by Rome. Dio claimed that 'moreover, all this ruin was brought upon the Romans by a woman, a fact which in itself caused them the greatest shame'. For the Romans, the idea of a female ruler was unnatural, but this was not so for the Britons. Whilst Boudica's queenship was conferred on her through marriage, her contemporary, Cartimandua, was a queen in her own right.

Cartimandua was the queen of the Brigantes, a tribe who occupied land that extended north to Dumfriesshire and south to Derby. As the hereditary ruler, it was Cartimandua with whom the Romans dealt following their conquest of Britain, and she came to terms with them, ruling as a client queen. Cartimandua is known only from Tacitus's works. She first came to his attention due to her somewhat notorious role in the capture of the British leader Caratacus, the son of King Cunobelinus of the Catuvellani tribe.

At the time of the Roman invasion, Caratacus refused to surrender and eventually joined with the warlike Silures, in what is now modern Wales, in order to wage a guerrilla campaign against the Romans. In AD 51, he was defeated in battle and fled. Forced to enter Cartimandua's territory, he appealed to her for aid. According to Tacitus, this was a near-fatal error of judgement. Cartimandua, eager to please her Roman friends, had him put in chains and handed over to Rome. Caratacus was taken to Rome to feature prominently in a victory parade but escaped execution by persuading the emperor to release him. He retired to a prosperous existence in Rome, a fate that Cartimandua may also have eventually enjoyed.

A few years later, Cartimandua faced a threat to her throne. She had been sharing power with her husband, Venutius, a famous warrior, but in AD 57, the marriage failed:

> A quarrel broke out between them, followed instantly by war, and he [Venutius] then assumed a hostile attitude also towards us [Rome]. At first, however, they simply fought each other, and Cartimandua by cunning stratagems captured the brothers and kinsfolk of Venutius. This enraged the enemy, who were stung with shame at the prospect of falling under the dominion of a woman. The flower of their youth, picked out for war, invaded her kingdom. This we had foreseen; some cohorts were sent to her aid and a sharp contest followed, which was at first doubtful but had a satisfactory termination.

Cartimandua had relied on Roman military aid before, when there had been an earlier disturbance amongst the Brigantes, and she had no qualms in appealing for aid again following her split with her husband. Venutius had a following amongst the Brigantes, but it was Cartimandua, with Roman assistance, who won the day.

Cartimandua was not so fortunate in AD 69. At some point after her divorce from Venutius, she replaced him with a second husband, Vellocatus, who had been Venutius's armour-bearer. This marriage increased hostility towards Cartimandua amongst the Brigantes, and in AD 69, Venutius once again invaded her territories. The Romans came to Cartimandua's aid, and though they managed to rescue her, they were unable to maintain her rule. With her flight, Cartimandua lost control of her kingdom and disappears from history. As a loyal ally of Rome, it is possible that she ended her days in the capital of the empire itself, but this can only be speculation. Boudica and Cartimandua, in spite of information about their lives being limited, are very much historical figures. Other early queens of Britain can only be considered legendary.

One mythical queen is CORDELIA, the youngest daughter of the famous King Lear. William Shakespeare immortalised Cordelia as Lear's loyal daughter, but the main details of Cordelia's life come from the twelfth-century writer Geoffrey of Monmouth, who created so much of the folklore that has been passed down in England.

According to Geoffrey of Monmouth, Lear was one of the great early kings of Britain, ruling the country for sixty years. He had no sons, but three daughters 'of whom he was dotingly fond': Goneril, Regan, and Cordelia. Cordelia, as the youngest, was her father's favourite. As he grew old, Lear decided to divide his kingdom between his three daughters in accordance with a trial of his own devising. He asked each of his daughters in turn which of them loved him the most. When his eldest two daughters answered that they loved him more than life itself and more than any other living thing, he immediately granted them each one third of his kingdom and the promise of good husbands. He then turned to his youngest daughter:

> But Cordeilla, the youngest, understanding how easily he was satisfied with the flattering expressions of her sisters, was desirous to make trial of his affection after a different manner. 'My father,' said she, 'is there any daughter that can love her father more than duty requires? In my

opinion, whoever pretends to it, must disguise her real sentiments under the veil of flattery. I have always loved you as a father, nor do I yet depart from my purposed duty; and if you insist to have something more extorted from me, hear now the greatness of my affection, which I always bear you, and take this for a short answer to all your questions; look how much you have, so much is your value, and so much do I love you.'

Cordelia's answer was honest, but it was not wise. Lear, furious, declared that he would give his youngest daughter no part of his kingdom and expend no efforts in securing an honourable husband for her. He then married his elder daughters respectively to the Dukes of Cornwall and Albany and gave them each one half of the kingdom. Cordelia was very beautiful and able to find a husband for herself, marrying Aganippus, King of the Franks, soon afterwards, without receiving any dowry from her father.

Cordelia's two sisters loved their father rather less than they had claimed. In his old age, Lear decided to stay with his eldest daughter, taking with him sixty servants. Lear's household was a source of great annoyance to Goneril, and after two years, she had had enough, demanding that Lear reduce his household by half. Enraged, Lear went to stay with Regan, only to find that she too demanded a reduction in his household, ordering him to retain only five men. Lear then tried to return to Goneril, but she refused to receive him unless he dismissed all but one of his servants. With this, Lear finally realised how unjustly he had treated his youngest daughter and travelled to Francia to be with her.

When Lear arrived in his daughter's kingdom, Cordelia was shocked to hear how low he had fallen and provided him with clothes and money and a retinue of forty servants. She and her husband invaded Britain on Lear's behalf, installing him again as king, where he reigned for a further three years until his death. Cordelia was widowed during this time and, following her father's death, took the throne alone as the sole ruler of Britain. She ruled peacefully and well for five years, but her two nephews resented being ruled by a woman and rebelled against her, imprisoning Cordelia in one of their fortresses and dividing the kingdom between themselves. In grief, Cordelia, seeing that all was lost, killed herself. The story of Cordelia is a myth, and it is unlikely that there ever was a historical King Lear, or his daughter, Queen Cordelia. Guinevere, who, according to legend, would have been one of the last British queens, is also mythical.

GUINEVERE, the famous wife of King Arthur, was developed as a character in the Arthurian romances over the medieval period. Her husband was a historical figure, and the early British chronicler Nennius noted that, at the time of the Anglo-Saxon incursions in the fifth century, 'the magnanimous Arthur, with all the kings and military forces of Britain fought against the Saxons. And though there were many more noble than himself, yet he was twelve times chosen their commander, and was as often conqueror.' According to Nennius, the real Arthur was a military commander of some strength, winning his twelfth and final victory at the hill of Badon, where he killed 900 Saxons with his own hand. Little more is known about the historical Arthur, but the fictional Arthur and his queen are well developed. By the late medieval period, Arthur was always depicted as a romantic and chivalrous figure, presiding over his Knights of the Round Table from his capital at Camelot.

Geoffrey of Monmouth provided the first full details of the legendary King Arthur. There is little information about Guinevere, although he notes that, once Arthur had taken control of his kingdom, 'he took to wife Guanhumara, descended from a noble family of Romans, who was educated under duke Cador, and in beauty surpassed all the women of the island'. All accounts of Guinevere note her beauty and, also, her treacherous conduct towards Arthur. Geoffrey states that Arthur resolved to leave Britain in order to carry out a military campaign. Before he sailed, he appointed his nephew, Mordred, as regent of Britain and committed Guinevere to his governance. As he was approaching Rome itself, Arthur heard that Mordred 'by tyrannical and treasonable practices set the crown upon his own head; and that queen Guanhumara, in violation of her first marriage, had wickedly married him'. On hearing this, Arthur returned to England, where he met Mordred in battle. Mordred was killed, and Arthur, mortally wounded, was forced to resign his crown and travel to the Isle of Avalon to seek a cure. Guinevere, in despair, ended her life as a nun.

By the late medieval period, Guinevere was renowned as an adulteress who became the lover of the famous Sir Lancelot. Sir Thomas Malory in his *Morte d'Arthur* provided one of the fullest depictions of the relationship between the queen and her lover. According to Malory, Lancelot rescued Guinevere when she was kidnapped by a knight whilst out riding. One night, following this,

> Sir Launcelot took his sword in his hand and privily went unto a place whereas he had espied a ladder toforehand, and that he took under his arm and bare it through the garden, and set it up to the window. And there anon the queen was ready to meet him. And then they made either to other their complaints of many divers things. And then Sir Launcelot wished that he might come in to her. Wit ye well, said the queen, I would as fain as ye that ye might come in to me. Would ye, madam, said Sir Launcelot, with your heart that I were with you? Yea, truly said the queen. Now shall I prove my might, said Sir Launcelot, for your love.

Lancelot spent some time that night with the queen and the affair between the couple was passionate. Arthur's nephews, Mordred and Agravaine, learned of the affair some time later, and since both hated Guinevere and her lover, they watched the couple closely. Finally, Agravaine brought the matter to the King's attention, and Arthur, devastated by the news, declared that he would only believe it if he had proof. Arthur resolved to lay a trap for the couple, informing them both that he was going hunting and would be out all night. That night, as expected, Lancelot went to Guinevere's chamber. Agravaine, Mordred, and twelve other knights tried to arrest him. Fearing that he would be killed, Lancelot 'took the queen in his arms, and kissed her, and said, Most noble Christian queen, I beseech you, as ye have ever been my special good lady, and I at all times your true poor knight unto my power, and I never failed you in right nor in wrong, since the first day that king Arthur made me knight, that ye will pray for my soul if that I here be slain'. Guinevere declared that she did not wish to live if Lancelot were dead.

Lancelot escaped from the trap laid for him. Arthur, however, furious at the betrayal, ordered that Guinevere be burned as a traitor. On the appointed day, Guinevere was led out to die. As she prepared for death, Lancelot rushed forward and killed a number of knights before carrying her away to safety. Arthur immediately declared war on Lancelot, attacking his castle in an attempt to take both Guinevere and her lover. It was only with the Pope's intervention that matters were resolved, and Lancelot brought Guinevere out to her husband with the promise that she would be safe and not shamed. Lancelot then travelled to the Continent and was followed by Arthur, intent on continuing their war. Whilst abroad, Arthur learned that Mordred had seized his crown and had attempted to marry Guinevere, who had remained in Britain. He returned to confront him, killing him before being mortally wounded himself. Guinevere was devastated when she heard of Arthur's death and, eschewing a possible future with Lancelot, became a nun, spending the rest of her life attempting to atone for her sins.

Guinevere, the sinful queen of King Arthur, is a mythical rather than a historical figure. In both Geoffrey of Monmouth's account and the *Morte d'Arthur*, Guinevere was the cause of the final confrontation between Arthur and Mordred. She turned to religion as a way of expiating her guilt. Early queens were often associated with religious devotions; for example, Bertha, Queen of Kent, who, unlike Guinevere, is very much a historical figure.

BERTHA (539-*c.* 612), the wife of King Ethelbert of Kent, is usually credited with having brought Christianity to England. She was the daughter of Charibert I, King of Paris, and his wife, Ingerberg, and the great-granddaughter of the great King Clovis of the Franks, who, at the instigation of his wife, Clotild, had converted to Christianity. Whilst Bertha was raised as a Christian, her father was rather less committed to piety than his grandmother had been. According to the historian Gregory of Tours, Bertha had a disturbed childhood, and her father's marital troubles led to him being the first Frankish king to be excommunicated:

> King Charibert married a woman called Ingoberg. He had by her a daughter, who eventually married a man from Kent and went to live there. At that time Ingoberg had among her servants two young women who were the daughters of a poor man. The first of these, who wore the habit of a religious, was called Marcoverfa, and the other Merofled. The king fell violently in love with the two of them. As I have implied, they were the daughters of a wool-worker. Ingoberg was jealous because of the love which the king bore them. She made a secret plan to set their father to work, in the hope that when Charibert saw this he would come to despise the two girls. When the man was working away Ingoberg summoned the king. Charibert came, hoping to see something interesting, and, without approaching too near, watched the man preparing wool for the royal household. He was so angry at what he saw that he dismissed Ingoberg and took Merofled in her place.

Charibert later tired of Merofled and married her sister instead, leading to the couple's excommunication. According to Gregory, he also had a further wife called Theudechild. Betha must have been glad that her own marriage, which was an arranged one, proved more lasting than that of her parents.

By the time of Charibert's death in 567, Ethelbert and Bertha were married. From Ethelbert's point of view, it was an excellent match, and it provided him with links to the prestigious Merovingian kings of Francia. Bertha's religion was important to her, and her father secured a promise that she be allowed to practice Christianity before she sailed to Kent. Once in Kent, she was given a converted Roman building to use as a chapel, and she and her chaplain, Bishop Liuthard, set about trying to convert the King. Bertha saw the conversion of England as her duty. According to the Anglo-Saxon historian Bede, in 596, Pope Gregory decided to begin the conversion of England by sending a churchman, Augustine, and some monks to preach in England. They arrived in Ethelbert's kingdom of Kent, an ideal landing place given the queen's Christian beliefs:

> On receiving this message, [that Augustine and the monks had arrived] the king ordered them to remain in the island where they had landed, and gave directions that they were to be provided with all necessaries until he should decide what action to take. For he had already heard of the Christian religion, having a Christian wife of the Frankish royal house named Bertha, whom he had received from her parents on condition that she should have freedom to hold and practice her faith unhindered with Bishop Liudhard, whom they had sent as her helper in the faith.

Ethelbert agreed to meet with Augustine's embassy, and it is likely that Bertha influenced this decision. She certainly allowed Augustine to use her chapel to perform Mass, preach, and baptise those that he managed to convert. Finally, Ethelbert, who had at first been highly wary of Christianity, came to be baptised, no doubt, to Bertha's pleasure.

She still wished to convert England to Christianity and was instructed to attempt this in a letter that she received from Pope Gregory in 602:

> We bless Almighty God, who hath graciously vouchsafed to reserve for your reward the conversion of the people of the Angles. For, as through the memorable Helena, the mother of the most pious Constantine, Emperor of the Romans, the hearts of the Romans were kindled to the Christian faith; so, by the zeal of your glory, we are confident the mercy of God is operating among the people of the Angles.

Bertha died some years before Ethelbert, and her husband had remarried by the time of his death in 616. He chose to be buried with Bertha in the Church of St Peter and St Paul that had been built in his kingdom. Bertha will always be remembered as prominent in the conversion of England, and whilst her own son, Eadbald, turned his back on his mother's religion for a time and even married his stepmother after his father's death, he was soon re-converted. Both Bertha and her daughter Ethelberga, who was responsible for the conversion of Northumbria through her marriage to the Northumbrian king, can be considered the first of a long line of pious and evangelical Anglo-Saxon queens. St Etheldreda is another.

ST ETHELDREDA, or Ethelthryth, (*c.* 636-679) was the daughter of King Anna of East Anglia. According to Bede, her father was pious and sent his stepdaughter, Sæthryd, and his daughter Ethelberga to be educated at the Frankish monastery at Brie, where both eventually became abbesses. Anna was also renowned for his patronage of monasticism. Etheldreda showed evidence of her family's piety early in her life, as described in the *Liber Eliensis*:

> [She] was always pleasant, sweet and gentle to everybody. But something very wonderful and laudable is that, favouring sobriety and chastity from the very earliest stages of her infancy, she used to keep making her way to the thresholds of churches, sometimes following in her parents' footsteps, sometimes alone, and was happy to pray to God assiduously, while neglecting the pastimes of girls.

Etheldreda, like her eldest sister, who became queen of Kent, was not originally intended for the church, and her father arranged for her to marry Tondbert, a prince of the South Gyrwas. Etheldreda was furious when she heard of her betrothal and resisted for a long time, declaring that she wished to remain a virgin. Her parents insisted, and she reluctantly agreed. When he died shortly after the wedding, Etheldreda was married to King Egfrid of Northumbria. Etheldreda had no vocation for either marriage or queenship and, before her first marriage, had made a vow of perpetual chastity. Etheldreda was able to persuade both her husbands to respect this and, whilst she lived with Egfrid for twelve years, she remained a virgin.

Etheldreda was always unhappy in her second marriage, and according to Bede,

> for a long time Etheldreda begged the king to allow her to retire from worldly affairs and serve Christ the only true king in a convent. And having at length obtained his reluctant consent, she entered the convent of the Abbess Ebba, King Egfrid's aunt, at Coludesbyrig, where she received

the veil and clothing of a nun from the hands of Bishop Wilfrid. A year later she was herself made Abbess in the district called Ely, where she built a convent and became the virgin mother of many virgins vowed to God and displayed the pattern of a heavenly life in word and deed.

As a mark of her piety, Etheldreda refused to wear the expensive linen to which her rank entitled her and, instead, wore only woollen clothes. She refused to wash in hot water, except on the eve of great festivals. Etheldreda ate only one meal a day and remained in church praying for most of every night. She was believed to have the gift of prophesy and prophesied her own death.

Etheldreda's hard life affected her health and she developed a tumour in her jaw, which eventually caused her death. Bede claims she bore the pain of the tumour with good humour, often saying, 'I realise very well that I deserve this wearisome disease in my neck, on which, as I well remember, when I was a girl, I used to wear the needless burden of jewellery. And I believe that God in His goodness wishes me to endure this pain in my neck so that I may be absolved from the guilt of my needless vanity. So now I wear a burning red tumour on my neck instead of gold and pearls.'

Etheldreda lived with her tumour for some time before finally asking her physician, Cynifrid, to attempt to cure her. She seemed to improve for two days before dying suddenly. Etheldreda's death was lamented by her nuns, and she was succeeded as abbess by her sister, Sexburga, Queen of Kent. Sixteen years after her death, it was decided to open her grave and place her body in a fine white-marble sarcophagus. When her tomb was opened, her body was found to be perfectly preserved and the wound where her tumour had been opened entirely healed. This would have been proof of her sanctity enough, but more was to follow: as her body was prepared for its reburial, a voice called out from the sky, 'Glory to the Name of the Lord!' Etheldreda was also said to cure those who prayed to her, and she was declared a saint soon after her death, with Bede declaring that she was 'all the more a queen because a bride of Christ'.

Whilst the early Anglo-Saxon period produced a high number of deeply pious and saintly queens, not all queens are remembered as favourably. The most notorious of the early queens is Cynethryth, the wife of King Offa of Mercia.

CYNETHRYTH (died after 798) is the only Anglo-Saxon queen to have minted her own coins and must have been powerful, although no details of her family background survive. Offa came to the throne of Mercia in 757 and reigned for nearly forty years. He was a remarkable man and William of Malmesbury claimed that 'he was a man of a great mind, and one who would endeavour to effect whatever he had preconceived'. He was also formidable, and the chronicler Roger of Wendover stated that he was 'a terror and a fear to all the kings of England'. By the time of his death, Offa had established his authority over most of England. His prestige was so great that, during his reign, he entered into an alliance with the Frankish emperor, Charlemagne, and there was talk of marriages between the families of the two men in around 789 or 790.

Cynethryth had a great deal of influence over her husband, and her notoriety rests on her role in the murder of King Ethelbert of East Anglia. According to Roger of Wendover, Ethelbert visited Mercia hoping to marry one of King Offa's daughters:

Now Offa, who was a most noble king, and of a most illustrious family, on learning the cause of his arrival, entertained him in his palace with the greatest honour, and exhibited all possible courtesy, as well to the king himself as his companions. On consulting his queen Quendritha, and asking her advice on this proposal, she is said to have given her husband this diabolical counsel, 'Lo,' said she,

'God has this day delivered into your hands your enemy, whose kingdom you have so long desired; if, therefore, you secretly put him to death, his kingdom will pass to you and your successors for ever.' The king was exceedingly disturbed in mind at this counsel of the queen, and, indignantly rebuking her, he replied, 'Thou hast spoken as one of the foolish women; far from me be such a detestable crime, which would disgrace myself and my successors'; and having so said, he left her in great anger.

Offa left his wife to dine with his visitor, but Cynethryth had no intention of abandoning her plan. She caused a room to be prepared for Ethelbert and, next to the bed, had a deep pit dug over which she placed a fine chair surrounded by curtains. As Cynethryth had planned, when Ethelbert retired to bed, he sat on the chair and fell into the pit where the queen's followers waited. Covering him with pillows, clothes and curtains, the murderers smothered the King. Shortly afterwards, Offa annexed East Anglia to his own kingdom.

Whilst Cynethryth is remembered as Ethelbert's murderer, in reality, it was Offa who must have been primarily responsible for the deed, and he was certainly the one to benefit most from it. Cynethryth was, however, a powerful queen, and she witnessed a number of her husband's charters. Little else is known about her life. She bore her husband one son and at least four daughters, one of whom was Queen Edburga of Wessex, a woman as notorious as her mother. Cynethryth outlived Offa, retiring to become the Abbess of Cookham following his death.

In the period before the ninth century, England, and the area of Britain that would become England, had many hundreds of queens. In 802, Egbert became King of Wessex, and the dynasty that he and his wife Redburga founded ruled a united England for over 200 years. Their descendants still sit on the throne today, and it is from Redburga that an unbroken line of English queenship can truly be traced.

2

The Anglo-Saxon Queens

The early Anglo-Saxon period was characterised by a number of small competing kingdoms. The kingdom of Wessex began the process of creating a united England, and the ninth-century kings of Wessex can be considered the first kings of England.

In 802, Egbert came to the throne of Wessex. Whilst he never attained direct control over the whole of what is now known as England, he attained ascendancy over Cornwall, East Anglia, Mercia and Northumbria during his reign, as well as subduing the Welsh. Egbert was the overlord of most of what would become England, and he and his wife were the ancestors of all but four future monarchs of England.

According to the ninth-century writer Asser, the role of the queen was deliberately kept in obscurity during the ninth century:

The West Saxons did not allow the queen to sit beside the king, nor indeed did they allow her to be called 'queen', but rather 'king's wife'. The elders of the land maintain that this disputed and indeed infamous custom originated on account of a certain grasping and wicked queen of the same people, who did everything she could against her lord and the whole people, so that not only did she earn hatred for herself, leading to her expulsion from the queen's throne, but she also brought the same foul stigma on all queens who came after her.

The queen in question was Edburga, or Eadburh, daughter of Offa of Mercia and the wife of Egbert's predecessor, King Beohtric. Edburga was politically influential and ultimately murdered her husband, before fleeing the kingdom, leading the people of Wessex to reject the office of queen altogether.

There is no contemporary record of Egbert's queen, although one later medieval document suggests that he was married to a woman called REDBURGA, or Rædburgh, and that she was a kinswoman of the great Frankish emperor Charlemagne. This is possible, as Egbert was exiled to Francia in around 800, staying at Charlemagne's court before returning to Wessex to take the throne in 802. Egbert retained contact with the Frankish royal family, and according to the *Annals of St Bertin*, he corresponded with Charlemagne's son and successor, Louis the Pious, shortly after Easter 839. The most that can be said for Redburga is that it is not impossible that she was a kinswoman of Charlemagne who married Egbert during his exile.

Given the strength of feeling against her predecessor, Edburga, Redburga would never have used the title of queen and, instead, would have been called 'lady'. Redburga bore her husband children, although only one, Ethelwulf, survived to adulthood. She had little involvement in Ethelwulf's upbringing, which was entrusted by Egbert to Bishop Helmstan. Ethelwulf was not Egbert and Redburga's eldest son, and he was originally groomed for a career in the church. According to the chronicler William of Malmesbury, he had previously been subdeacon of Winchester, but the deaths of all other legitimate heirs led to him returning to the secular world with the agreement of the Pope. There is no evidence that Redburga survived her husband, who died in 839.

Redburga's successor as queen is equally shadowy. OSBURGA, or Osburgh, was the first wife of King Ethelwulf. Ethelwulf was a mature man at his accession in 839 and, given the likely date of his parents' marriage, may have been approaching forty. Osburga and Ethelwulf's marriage occurred some years before Ethelwulf's accession, and he immediately made their eldest son king of Kent, implying that he was nearing adulthood. Osburga bore Ethelwulf five sons and a daughter. Her youngest and favourite child, Alfred, was born in 849 at the royal manor at Wantage in Berkshire. This date suggests that she was of a similar age to her husband, reaching the menopause shortly after this time.

Osburga was the daughter of Oslac, Ethelwulf's butler. The office of butler was not as lowly as it sounds to modern ears, and Oslac was an important nobleman at court, retaining his position after his son-in-law's accession to the throne. Oslac was a kinsman of two legendary chieftains of the Isle of Wight, the brothers Stuf and Wihtgar, who were famous for their extermination of the last native Britons on the island.

In addition to her noble birth, Osburga was renowned for her piety and her near-contemporary Asser, recorded that she was 'a most religious woman, noble in character and noble by birth'. Ethelwulf shared his wife's interest in religion, and their youngest son was sent on two pilgrimages to Rome in his early childhood. Unusually for a woman of her time, Osburga was educated and was given some responsibility for the upbringing and education of her children. According to a famous story told by Asser, Alfred had a particular interest in English poetry, of which Osburga was aware:

1. Extract from the manuscript of the ninth-century writer Asser, who recorded details of Queen Edburga, wife of King Beohtric.

One day, therefore, when his mother was showing him and his brothers a book of English poetry which she held in her hand, she said 'I shall give this book to whichever one of you can learn it the fastest'. Spurred on by these words, or rather by divine inspiration, and attracted by the beauty of the initial letter in the book, Alfred spoke as follows in reply to his mother, forestalling his brothers (ahead in years though not in ability): 'Will you really give this book to the one of us who can understand it the soonest and recite it to you?' Whereupon, smiling with pleasure she reassured him, saying: 'Yes, I will'. He immediately took the book from her hand, went to his teacher and learnt it. When it was learnt, he took it back to his mother and recited it.

The absence of Osburga's daughter, Ethelswitha, from the family group in this story implies that it took place after 853 when the princess married Burgred, King of Mercia, at Ethelwulf's manor at Chippenham. The wedding may have been Osburga's last public appearance as the King's wife, and she disappears from the records soon afterwards. By 853, Osburga was approaching fifty, elderly for the ninth century, and it is likely that she died before her husband made his second marriage to Judith of Francia.

JUDITH OF FRANCIA (b. 843/44) was the daughter of Charles the Bald, King of the Franks, and his wife, Ermentrude. Judith's parents were married on 13 December 842, and Judith, the eldest of the couple's eleven children, was born around a year later. In order to preserve the royal bloodline, it was very unusual for Carolingian princesses to be allowed to marry, and from her infancy, Judith knew that her likely future lay in a nunnery. She was not particularly pious, and this fate may have alarmed her. Her actual fate was no less terrifying, and it was only due to exceptional circumstances that Charles the Bald was prepared to make his daughter available for marriage.

In 851, Viking raiders landed in Devon. Later that year, the Vikings spent the winter in England, setting up camp on the Isle of Sheppey. Shortly afterwards, a great Viking army, with 350 ships, entered the mouth of the River Thames and ravaged Canterbury, putting the King of Mercia to flight. The attacks continued throughout the year. In 855, the Vikings returned and overwintered at Sheppey, demonstrating that they were likely to remain a threat for some time. The Vikings induced horror in England and on the Continent, and the fury and violence of the raids was the worst that anyone could remember. In spite of this, Ethelwulf coped with the early Viking raids and enjoyed an impressive military reputation. During the summer of 856, the Vikings attacked the Seine valley in Francia, the first raid in a decade of attacks on Charles the Bald's kingdom. Charles was eager to ally himself with the powerful King Ethelwulf. In 855, Ethelwulf passed through Francia on his way to Rome on a pilgrimage with his youngest son, Alfred. On his return in 856, he was invited to visit Charles's court, spending three months in the company of his fellow monarch whilst an alliance was negotiated. During his negotiations with Charles, Ethelwulf made it clear that the price of his support would be a marriage with Judith. By 856, Ethelwulf was at least fifty years old. Charles had misgivings about the match and insisted on a number of safeguards intended to secure his daughter's position as the child bride of an elderly king.

According to the *Annals of St Bertin*, Judith and Ethelwulf were married at Charles's palace at Verberie on 1 October 856. Whilst Ethelwulf had been able to insist upon the marriage, it was Charles who dictated the terms, and in the days before the wedding, he took the unusual step of ordering Bishop Hincmar, one of his advisors, to devise a marriage ceremony in which a coronation could be incorporated. Immediately after the marriage, a crown was placed on Judith's head by Ingmar, Bishop of Reims, who then honoured her as queen. Even more unusually, Judith was anointed with consecrated oil, something that was

2. Viking warriors. Scene from a viking-age picture stone from Stenkyrka, Gotland, Sweden.

designed to enhance her status as Ethelwulf's wife and prioritise her children over those of the unconsecrated Osburga following Ethelwulf's death. As far as Charles was concerned, this was the best safeguard that he could give his daughter, but it was viewed very differently when the ceremony was reported in England.

Ethelwulf and Judith set out for England soon after their marriage. According to the chronicler William of Malmesbury, on their return, they found Ethelbald, Ethelwulf's eldest son in revolt against his father. The revolt was due to Ethelwulf's marriage and the status that had been given to Judith and her future offspring. Ethelbald refused to receive his father in Wessex, and in order to avoid further conflict, it was agreed that the kingdom would be divided, with Ethelbald taking the richer western section of the kingdom, relegating his father to the eastern and central portions. This was a major blow to Ethelwulf, but he treated Judith kindly, and 'although the whole dispute was on account of his foreign wife, he [Ethelwulf] treated her with the greatest deference, and even defied the tradition of the West Saxons and set her beside himself on the throne'. Ethelwulf died in 858, leaving Judith a widow at the age of fourteen.

Judith must have expected to be summoned back to her father, where a lifetime in a nunnery awaited her, but within weeks of Ethelwulf's death, her life had taken a very different course, and she married her eldest stepson, Ethelbald. For Ethelbald, marriage to an anointed queen conferred additional throneworthiness on his future sons. Judith was given more prominence in her second marriage than in her first, and she witnessed a surviving charter from the reign, named only behind her second husband and his younger brother, Ethelbert, who was sub-king of Kent. In the charter, Judith was described as queen and signed her name above the bishops and other noblemen in attendance at her husband's court, a prominence unheard of in a ninth-century queen of Wessex.

Both Ethelbald and Judith were aware of hostility towards their marriage. Whilst Judith was some years younger than Ethelbald, she was still his stepmother and, in the eyes of the church, effectively his mother. Judith's contemporary Asser voiced the disgust felt by many when he recorded that Ethelbald, 'against God's prohibition and Christian dignity, and also contrary to the practice of all pagans, took over his father's marriage-bed and married Judith, daughter of Charles, King of the Franks, incurring great disgrace from all who heard of it'. Such a marriage was incestuous, and Asser believed that it was the reason for the troubles and lawlessness of Ethelbald's reign. In any event, Judith's second marriage lasted no longer than her first as Ethelbald died in 860, leaving the throne of Wessex to his brother, Ethelbert.

Soon after Ethelbald's death, Judith sailed for Francia, immediately finding herself immured in the nunnery at Senlis by her father, who had no plans for her to make a further marriage. After her freedom as Ethelbald's wife and as a powerful English queen, the nunnery must have felt like a prison, and in 862, Judith eloped with Count Baldwin of Flanders. The circumstances surrounding Judith's third marriage do not survive. It is likely that Baldwin was politically motivated, hoping both to secure access to Judith's cross-channel contacts and to make an alliance with her powerful father.

Charles was furious when he discovered his daughter's actions and ordered the Archbishop of Reims to excommunicate them. The pair travelled to Rome to ask for the intercession of Pope Nicholas I himself. The church generally disapproved of the remarriage of widows, but Nicholas, charmed by Judith and her husband, reversed the sentence of excommunication and granted them his personal protection. This forced Charles to recognise his daughter's marriage. Judith's third marriage proved longer than her first two, and she bore her husband children, disappearing into obscurity as Countess of Flanders. It is likely that she lived to see her children reach adulthood because, in 884, Judith's eldest surviving son, Baldwin II, married the daughter of her stepson and brother-in-law, Alfred the Great, a match that was almost certainly arranged using Judith's English connections.

King Ethelbert died unmarried in 871 and was succeeded by his brother, Ethelred I. Ethelred's accession coincided with a major upsurge in Viking attacks, and whilst they had previously consisted of a series of isolated raids, in the autumn of 865, a Viking army landed in East Anglia intent on conquest. By 867, the Vikings had subdued Northumbria and had forced the Mercians to buy peace. By the winter of 871, they had turned their attention towards Wessex, and they spent that winter in Reading, in the heart of Ethelred's kingdom. Ethelred spent most of his brief reign fighting against the Viking onslaught and, early in 871, met the Vikings in battle at Ashdown, winning a major victory. Two weeks later, Ethelred was defeated in the battle at Basing. He died suddenly soon afterwards and was buried at Wimbourne.

Very little is known about Ethelred's queen. A charter of Ethelred's for 868 was witnessed by a 'Wulfryth Regina', and this Queen Wulfthryth, or WULFRIDA, is likely to have been his wife. The fact that Wulfrida was described as a queen and witnessed a charter suggests that she had some political prominence; of her ninth-century predecessors, only Judith of Francia was similarly described in such a document. It has also been suggested that the use of the title of 'Queen' hints that Wulfrida may have been crowned. It is not impossible that Ethelred would have wanted his own children to enjoy the status of having a crowned mother, as his father and eldest brother had done. However, no details survive of any such ceremony, and this can only be speculation.

With the exception of the charter, Wulfrida is completely obscured. Wulfrida is an English name, and she was presumably the daughter of an Anglo-Saxon nobleman, perhaps, given the similarity in their names, the sister of Wulfhere, ealdorman of Wiltshire. Wulfhere witnessed immediately after Wulfrida in the charter and was given a position of prominence in other charters of Ethelred's reign, implying that he was held in high regard by the King. He was also the only one of Alfred the Great's ealdormen to defect to the Vikings, perhaps an attempt to assert his nephews' rights over their uncle.

If Wulfrida survived her husband, she would have seen her two young sons passed over in the succession in favour of their adult uncle, Alfred. Alfred, who sought to promote the claims of his own children, was suspicious of his nephews, and in his Will, he bequeathed them only estates in the eastern and less important portion of his kingdom, leaving the crown to his eldest son, Edward the Elder. In 902, Wulfrida's eldest son, Ethelwold, landed in Essex and persuaded the Vikings to attack Wessex, in the hope of gaining the throne for himself. He was killed in battle in Kent, and his younger brother later came to terms with the King.

The descendants of Ethelred and Wulfrida remained at the forefront of the Anglo-Saxon nobility and they were the ancestors of a number of later Anglo-Saxon queens.

The life of Wulfrida's successor as queen, EALSWITHA, or Eahlswith, (d. 902) is better documented. Ealswitha, the wife of Alfred the Great, was the daughter of Ethelred, known as Mucil, ealdorman of the Gaini. The Gaini was an old tribal group absorbed into the kingdom of Mercia, and Mucil was an important figure at the Wessex court, attesting two charters of King Ethelred I in 868. Ealswitha's maternal lineage was even more impressive, and her mother, Edburga, was a member of the Mercian royal family. According to Asser, Ealswitha's mother was a 'notable woman, who remained for many years after the death of her husband a chaste widow, until her death'.

Alfred married Ealswitha due to her prominent family and royal connections, and at the same time as their betrothal in 868, he was also created heir apparent by his elder brother, Ethelred I. At around the same time, Ethelred and Alfred received an appeal from their brother-in-law, King Burgred of Mercia, for aid against the Viking army, and the marriage was celebrated during this campaign. According to Asser, the ceremony was held in the presence of a number of witnesses and accompanied by feasting that lasted both day and night. It is possible that Ealswitha met her husband for the first time at her wedding, and if this is the case, the omens were not good. Following the feasting, Alfred 'was struck without warning in the presence of the entire gathering by a sudden severe pain that was quite unknown to all physicians'. Alfred's illness continued, on and off, for twenty years.

Alfred became king of Wessex in 871. In accordance with tradition, Ealswitha was never called queen, instead being referred to by the title 'lady'. In spite of this, Ealswitha was a prominent figure, and during the reign of her son, she was referred to as 'the true lady of the English' in order to emphasise her high rank. Ealswitha played no political role during Alfred's reign and was content to remain in a domestic sphere, accompanying her husband and children into exile in January 878 in order to avoid capture by the Vikings. This was a traumatic time for Alfred and Ealswitha, as the Viking leader, Guthrum, declared that Alfred had abandoned his kingdom and forfeited his crown. Alfred spent the first half of 878 as a fugitive on the Isle of Athelney. From here, Alfred carried out guerrilla attacks on Guthrum, defeating him in battle at Edington later that year.

3. Head of Alfred the Great from a silver penny.

4. A passage from a letter from Alfred the Great to Bishop Werferth.

Ealswitha returned to Wessex with Alfred when he regained his throne. There is little record of her activities during Alfred's reign, and she may have devoted her energies to the Church. Certainly, she had the pious example of her own mother to draw upon, and Alfred was also deeply religious, founding two religious houses during his reign: Athelney for monks and Shaftesbury Abbey for nuns. That Ealswitha was involved in the foundation of these houses is suggested by the fact that her daughter, Ethelgiva, was appointed abbess at Shaftesbury and lived there with other nuns of noble status. Ealswitha's piety can also be seen after Alfred's death, as she founded the Convent of St Mary at Winchester (known as Nunnaminster) during her widowhood. Asser referred to Ealswitha as Alfred's 'excellent wife', suggesting that she conformed to contemporary ideals of queenly piety.

There is little evidence to show the nature of the relationship between Alfred and Ealswitha. According to Asser, Alfred's mysterious illness plagued the first two decades of their marriage, and he did not 'have even a single hour of peace in which he does not either suffer from the disease itself or else, gloomily dreading it, is not driven to despair'. Alfred's illness, coupled with the ever-present threat of Viking invasion, cannot have made him a cheerful man to live with. Ealswitha bore a number of children, with five surviving to adulthood. Ethelfleda, Ealswitha's eldest child, married Ealdorman Ethelred of Mercia, succeeding as ruler of Mercia herself after her husband's death. The couple's second daughter, Ethelgiva, as previously mentioned, became the Abbess of Shaftesbury, whilst the youngest, Elfrida, married Count Baldwin II of Flanders. Ealswitha also bore two surviving sons, Edward, who succeeded his father as king, and Ethelweard.

Asser informs us that Edward and Elfrida were raised at court under the care of tutors and nurses and were a credit to their parents:

To the present day they continue to behave with humility, friendliness and gentleness to all compatriots and foreigners, and with great obedience to their father. Nor, amid the other pursuits of this present life which are appropriate to the nobility, are these two allowed to live idly and indifferently, with no liberal education, for they have attentively learned the Psalms, and books in English, and especially English poems, and they very frequently make use of books.

Alfred insisted on an education akin to that which he received in his mother's household during his childhood, and Edward and Elfrida's curriculum was focused both on religious instruction and works of English literature. Although not raised at court, Ealswitha's other children also received good educations and Ethelweard could read English and Latin.

Alfred and Ealswitha were married for over thirty years. Alfred died in 899 and, in his Will, paid Ealswitha the tribute of leaving her three estates and a share of £400 to be divided between her and her daughters. Ealswitha often visited her son's court and witnessed a charter in 901. She died on 5 December 902 and was buried in the New Minster at Winchester beside her husband. It was rare for Anglo-Saxon queens to be buried with their husbands, and this is a further indication that Ealswitha enjoyed a happy life and a long and contented marriage, in spite of the turbulent times in which she lived. Her relationship with Alfred was more lasting than the marriage of Ealswitha's successor as queen, Egwyna.

EGWYNA is sometimes referred to as the concubine of Edward the Elder, rather than his first wife. In the ninth and tenth centuries, marriage had not been entirely formalised and the repudiation of wives was common. It was also possible for a relationship that had not been officially sanctioned by the Church to have the status of a marriage, and it is likely that Egwyna and Edward were married, although not in any religious ceremony.

Few details about Egwyna survive. The later medieval chronicler Florence of Worcester claimed that she was of noble birth, although no details of her parentage survive. William of Malmesbury recounted a romantic legend to explain the attachment between Edward and Egwyna:

> There was in a certain village a shepherd's daughter, a girl of exquisite beauty, who gained through the elegance of her person what her birth could never have bestowed. In a vision she beheld a prodigy: the moon shone from her womb, and all England was illuminated by the light. When she sportively related this to her companion in the morning, it was not so lightly received, but it immediately reached the ears of the woman who used to nurse the sons of the king. Deliberating on this matter, she took her home and adopted her as a daughter, bringing up this young maiden with costlier attire, more delicate food, and more elegant demeanour. Soon after, Edward the son of king Elfred, travelling through the village, stopped at the house which had been the scene of his infantile education; indeed, he thought it would be a blemish on his reputation to omit paying his salutations to his nurse. Becoming deeply enamoured of the young woman from the instant he saw her, he passed the night with her. Pregnant from this single intercourse, she realised her dream when she brought forth her son, Ethelstan.

William of Malmesbury also recorded that, when Egwyna's son, Athelstan, claimed the throne, he met opposition on the grounds that he was born of a concubine. This, along with the story that Egwyna was a lowly born shepherd's daughter, sounds like slander, designed to debase Athelstan's claims in favour of another candidate. Egwyna and Edward's relationship was more lasting than a single night, and it is more plausible that she was a noblewoman, perhaps selected by Edward as a suitable bride whilst he was still some way off inheriting the crown. The marriage took place before 893, and Edward's father, Alfred the Great, considered it a valid relationship and delighted in his grandson.

Athelstan was knighted in his youth by his grandfather, Alfred the Great, and was sent to be raised in Mercia by his aunt, Ethelfleda. Egwyna also does not appear to have participated in the upbringing of her second child, a daughter who was married to King Sihtric of Northumbria. This daughter has been identified as St Edith of Polesworth, a queen who retired to a Mercian nunnery when she was widowed. The choice of a Mercian religious house suggests that she may have been raised in the kingdom by her aunt alongside her brother. Egwyna's fate is not known. It is possible that she died young. Alternatively, she may have been repudiated by Edward. What is certain is that he took a second wife shortly after coming to the throne. Egwyna played no role in the reign of Athelstan and was almost certainly dead by 925 when he became king.

Edward the Elder's second marriage was made entirely for political reasons. Within months of his accession, he had married ELFLEDA, or Ælfflæd, the daughter of Ealdorman Ethelhelm. Ethelhelm was the youngest son of Ethelred I and his wife, Queen Wulfrida, and the marriage was arranged in order to neutralise support for Elfleda's uncle Ethelwold's rebellion. Edward considered his second marriage to be more legitimate than his first, and he designated Elfleda's eldest son, Elfweard, as his successor in Wessex, allocating the lesser kingdom of Mercia to his eldest son, Athelstan. It was only Elfweard's death within days of his father that left Athelstan as king of Wessex. In 933, Elfleda's younger son, Edwin, also rebelled against Athelstan, an event that again supports the assumption that Elfleda's marriage was more legitimate that Egwyna's. There is some evidence that Elfleda was crowned at the same time as her husband on 8 June 900. Elfleda's family were prominent enough to insist on this, and an English coronation *ordo* (essentially, an order of service) from around this period includes the coronation of both a king and a queen, suggesting that this might have been for Edward and Elfleda.

Elfleda and Edward were married for around eighteen years and produced eight surviving children. Given the high infant mortality rates of the time, this implies that Elfleda may have borne almost a child a year during her marriage, suggesting that the couple were often together. Elfleda's eldest son, Elfweard, was Edward's favourite child. Elfleda spent the years of her marriage childbearing and raising her daughters, and four of her six surviving daughters made prestigious foreign marriages. Edward the Elder arranged the marriage of Elfleda's second daughter to Charles the Simple, King of the Franks, and her younger daughters were married respectively to Hugh, Duke of the Franks, Otto I, Emperor of Germany, and Conrad of Burgundy. Elfleda's remaining two daughters became nuns.

5. The coffin of St Cuthbert, one of the most important medieval saints of England, venerated by many English queens. Elfleda, Edward the Elder's queen, is known to have been pious, and at some point during her time as queen, she commissioned embroideries to adorn the tomb of St Cuthbert.

Around 919, Elfleda was repudiated by Edward in order to allow him to make a prestigious third marriage. She was sent to the nunnery at Wilton, where she became a nun, taking two of her daughters with her. Repudiation was a common way for a king to dispose of an unwanted wife, and Elfleda may simply have accepted her lot. Certainly, there is evidence that she was pious, and at some point during her time as queen, she commissioned embroideries to adorn the tomb of St Cuthbert.

Elfleda survived Edward, remaining at Wilton following his death. If she had harboured hopes of leaving her nunnery, these were dashed with the death of her eldest son, Elfweard, and the succession of Athelstan. It is possible that the rumours surrounding Athelstan's illegitimacy originated with Elfleda, and she undoubtedly supported the attempts of her second son, Edwin, to claim the crown in preference to his half-brother. With Edwin's murder on Athelstan's orders in 933, Elfleda lost any remaining hope of political power. The date of her death is not recorded, but she remained at Wilton, where she was buried.

Elfleda was not the only wife to survive Edward the Elder, and his third wife, EDGIVA, or Eadgifu, (c. 899-966/67) played a role in the succession dispute following his death. Edgiva was the daughter of the wealthy Kentish ealdorman Sigehelm, who was killed fighting the Vikings at the Battle of the Holme in 902. She may have been her father's heiress and, certainly, inherited estates from him in Kent. Edgiva's wealth and connections recommended her to Edward the Elder, and he married her in 919, shortly after his divorce from Elfleda. Edgiva was only around twenty years old, and Edward, who allowed her no political role during their brief marriage, was over twice her age. In spite of this, the couple spent much time together, and in a marriage of only around five years, Edgiva bore four children.

Edward died in July 924, and following the early death of his second son, Elfweard, he was succeeded by Athelstan, the son from his first marriage and a man several years older than Edgiva. Edgiva is all but invisible during the reign of her eldest stepson, and she may have devoted herself to raising her children: sons Edmund and Eadred, and a daughter, Edgiva, who married the continental nobleman Louis of Aquitaine. Edgiva's second daughter, Edburga, had been dedicated as an infant to the convent at Nunnaminster and was venerated as a saint following her death in around 950.

When Athelstan came to the throne, he had two living stepmothers with sons of their own. Following Elfweard's death, Edwin, Elfweard's younger brother, was Athelstan's most immediate threat, and it is not improbable that Athelstan sought to come to terms with Edgiva, whose sons were infants. It is possible that she secured Athelstan's promise to name her eldest son, Edmund, as his heir. Certainly, when Athelstan died in 939, Edmund's accession was undisputed, and Edgiva was finally able to come to prominence as the mother of the king.

During the reigns of both Edmund I and Edgiva's second son, Eadred, she was usually known by the title *Mater Regis*, mother of the king. As Edmund's mother, Edgiva entirely overshadowed both his queens. Edgiva witnessed a number of charters during the reigns of her sons and was always prominently placed, a further indication of her high status and power. Both of her sons made grants of land to her. In 943, for example, Edmund I granted Edgiva estates in Kent. In 953, Eadred granted his mother thirty hides at Felpham in Sussex. Eadred, in particular, was concerned for his mother's welfare, and in his Will, he bequeathed land to her at Amesbury, Wantage, and Basing, as well as other estates in Sussex, Surrey, and Kent.

Edmund died in 946 and was succeeded by Eadred, who never married and relied upon his mother as his leading councillor. Edgiva is remembered as a patron of the early religious reform movement in England, and under Eadred, she played a valuable role in assisting the leading churchmen in the kingdom. The Viking invasions of the late ninth century had impoverished the Church. Many monasteries had been burned or deserted during the period, and those that survived often failed to live up to the defining principles of monasticism: community life, celibacy, and personal poverty. Edmund I appointed a churchman called Oda as Archbishop of Canterbury in 942, and he immediately set about reforming the Church, advocating the strict observance of holy vows. Edgiva was very interested in this movement and was associated with another leading churchman, Dunstan, who came to prominence during Edmund's reign. According to the *Life of Dunstan*, Dunstan was in high favour at court under Edmund, and 'he dwelt a long time among the nobles in the royal palace, holding in holy governance a pair of reins, namely of the contemplative rule and of the practical life'. Dunstan's prominence led to jealousy amongst the noblemen at court, and they sought his ruin, persuading the King to strip him of his office. Edgiva may have played a role in persuading her eldest son to bring Dunstan back into favour and to appoint him as Abbot of Glastonbury. She certainly played a similar role in relation to another leading churchman, Ethelwold. Ethelwold was a monk of Glastonbury who expressed a desire to continue his studies at a continental monastery, petitioning King Eadred for his passport. Edgiva recognised the value of keeping him in England and persuaded her son to refuse. According to Ethelwold's biographer, Wulfstan of Winchester,

> Swayed by his mother, he [Eadred] decided to give the holy man a place called Abingdon. Here there had of old been a small monastery, but this had by now become neglected and forlorn. Its buildings were poor, and the estate consisted of only forty hides of land.

Ethelwold wanted to establish a strict monastic rule at Abingdon, as he had known at Glastonbury, and Edgiva was an enthusiastic patron:

> The king also gave his royal estates in Abingdon, the hundred hides, with excellent buildings, to the abbot and the monks to increase their everyday provisions, and he gave them much monetary help from his royal treasury; but his mother sent them presents on an even more lavish scale.

Edgiva spent much of Edmund and Eadred's reigns patronising the Church. Eadred was always willing to listen to his mother's advice, and Edgiva was one of the most powerful of the Anglo-Saxon queens. It is possible that ill health played a part in Eadred's reliance on his mother. He died in November 955.

The death of Eadred saw Edgiva's fortunes wane. Following a succession dispute between Eadwig and Edgar, the sons of Edmund I, Eadwig came to the throne. Edgiva, along with her ally Dunstan, supported her younger grandson, Edgar, and soon after Eadwig's accession, Edgiva was deprived of her lands and possessions. Dunstan was exiled to Ghent by the young king. Eadwig was not able to establish his authority as king for long, and by 958, Edgar had created his own kingdom north of the Thames. Eadwig died soon afterwards, and with the accession of her younger grandson, Edgar, Edgiva was once again restored to her lands and possessions. To Edgiva's satisfaction, Dunstan was appointed as Archbishop of Canterbury, and the religious reform reached its peak under King Edgar.

Edgiva was unable to return to a political position of prominence under Edgar. By the late 950s, she was elderly by the standards of her time and she retired to a religious life, rarely visiting court. She remained an important member of the royal family and, in 966, attended Edgar's refoundation of the New Minster at Winchester, a great ceremonial occasion. Edgiva was friendly with Edgar's wife, the equally reform-minded Elfrida, and in her Will, she bequeathed to her five hides of land in Essex to be presented on her behalf to the abbey at Ely. The date of Edgiva's death is nowhere recorded, but it appears to have been around 966 or 967, when she was approaching seventy.

The first of Edgiva's eclipsed daughters-in-law, the first wife of Edmund I, was ST ELGIVA, or Ælfgifu (d. 946). It is unclear when she married the King, but her eldest son, Eadwig, was born around 940/41. Elgiva's father's name is not recorded, but her mother was called Wynfleda. Nothing else is known of her background or of how she came to marry the King.

Throughout her marriage and even after her death, Elgiva was associated with holiness. According to Florence of Worcester, in 943, when Elgiva was pregnant with Edgar, St Dunstan heard voices on high praising the child that would be born. A second story, told by William of Malmesbury, implies that Elgiva had some role in the upbringing of her sons. Edgar was out hunting one day when he stopped to sleep under an apple tree, next to a river. He was woken by the sound of the puppies inside his pregnant dog barking whilst their mother slept. Edgar was astonished and looked up at the tree to see two apples fall, one after the other, into the river. He then heard a voice say 'well is thee' and two pitchers travelled past him down the river. Edgar was amazed by this and returned home to tell his mother what had happened. Elgiva offered to pray for guidance and, a few days later, came to Edgar with an answer to his vision. She told Edgar,

> 'The barking of the whelps while the mother was sleeping implies, that after your death, those persons who are now living and in power, dying also, miscreants yet unborn will bark against the church of God. And whereas one apple followed the other, so that the voice, 'well is thee', seemed to proceed from the dashing of the second against the first, this implies that from you, who are now like a tree shading all England, two sons will proceed. The favourers of the second will destroy the first, when the chiefs of the different parties will say to each of the boys, 'well is thee', because the dead one will reign in heaven, the living one on earth.'

Elgiva continued that the two pitchers symbolised the Viking attacks that would follow after Edgar's death. This story, with its reference to the Viking attacks and the succession dispute after Edgar's death, is unlikely to have occurred, and in any event, Edgar would only have been three at most when Elgiva died. However, it does demonstrate the holy way in which she was viewed in the medieval period.

William of Malmesbury described Elgiva as a saintly person during her lifetime, recording that 'she was devoted to good works and endowed with such piety and sweetness of temper that she would secretly redeem with her own money culprits who had been openly condemned by a strict verdict of the courts'. She also gave away her fine clothes to beggars. Elgiva was loved and 'with Ælfgifu [Elgiva] even the envious could only praise her physical beauty and her skill in handiwork, as there was nothing they could criticise'.

Elgiva and her husband Edmund died in the same year: 946. Edmund died on 26 May and had remarried by the time of his death, so Elgiva's death must have occurred in the early months of 946. She was buried at the royal nunnery at Shaftesbury and, according to the near-contemporary *Chronicle of Æthelweard*, was immediately considered a saint, and 'at her tomb, with the help of God, down to the present day, very many miracles take place in the monastery known by the common people as Shaftesbury'. St Elgiva made a deeper mark in England than her successor, Ethelfleda of Damerham, who, but for a reference in the *Anglo-Saxon Chronicle*, would be entirely forgotten.

The *Anglo-Saxon Chronicle* described ETHELFLEDA, or Æthelflæd, of Damerham, (died after 975) as Edmund's queen at the time of his death. Edmund and Ethelfleda must have married soon after St Elgiva's death, and Ethelfleda was married, at most, for a matter of weeks before she became a widow. Edmund probably selected Ethelfleda due to her wealth and family connections, as she was the daughter of Elfgar, ealdorman of Essex. On her father's death, her brother-in-law, Brihtnoth, became ealdorman in his place, and this, coupled with Ethelfleda's personal wealth and possession of a number of estates in Essex, suggests that she and her sister were their father's heiresses.

Ethelfleda first appears in the sources when, on 26 May 946, Edmund I was murdered at the royal manor of Pucklechurch in Gloucestershire. During the night, Liofa, a robber, entered the manor intent on plunder. Edmund came upon Liofa attacking his steward and, as he intervened, was stabbed to death. There is no evidence that Ethelfleda remarried, so she was a widow for at least thirty or forty years, making a Will some time after 975. In her Will, Ethelfleda left lands to the King, which may have been the return of her dower. She also left extensive bequests to her kin, including estates to her sister and brother-in-law. Ethelfleda's Will suggests that she, like the majority of her predecessors and successors as queen, was pious: many of her bequests were made to her family for life with the remainder passing to religious foundations. The date of Ethelfleda's death is nowhere recorded.

If Ethelfleda of Damerham is little recorded, her successor as queen enjoyed no such anonymity during her own lifetime, and she is amongst the most slandered of all queens of England: ELGIVA OF WESSEX, a descendant of Ethelred I and his wife, Wulfrida. The tenth-century chronicler Ethelweard is likely to have been her brother, and Elgiva's father was therefore Ealdorman Eadric, who died in 949. Elgiva's father died when she was still a small child and it was her mother, Ethelgiva, who was the dominant force in her upbringing. Like her husband, Ethelgiva was a descendant of King Ethelwulf, and she had a more immediate royal connection as a descendant of the niece of Queen Ealswitha. Elgiva was raised in the south of England, where her family had important connections and lands.

The death of King Eadred in 955 was due to a long illness, and his only close family were his nephews, Eadwig and Edgar. In 955, Eadwig was, at most, fifteen and Edgar was twelve. When Eadwig became king, factions had already split his court, with St Dunstan and Queen Edgiva openly in support of Edgar, and Elgiva and her family in support of Eadwig. This accounts for the hostility towards Elgiva and her mother in the *Life of St Dunstan*, and the chronicler claimed of Ethelgiva that 'a certain woman, foolish, though she was of noble birth, with her daughter, a girl of ripe age, attached herself to him [Eadwig], pursuing him and wickedly enticing him to intimacy, obviously in order to join and ally herself or else her daughter to him in lawful marriage'. It is not impossible that Ethelgiva sought to marry the King herself, but she was some years older than the teenage king, and it is unlikely. More plausibly, marriage to Elgiva was the price of her family's support.

St Dunstan and the other members of his faction considered Elgiva to be a dangerous influence on the King, and they were determined to blacken her name, refusing even to acknowledge her as Eadwig's wife. According to the *Life of St Dunstan*, Elgiva and her mother were nothing more than common harlots, and the chronicler claimed that, during Eadwig's coronation feast, it was noticed that the young king had disappeared. Dunstan and his kinsman, Bishop Cynesige, were asked to find him and bring him back. They went straight to Eadwig's bedchamber, where

they found the royal crown, which was bound with wondrous metal, gold and silver and gems and shone with many-coloured lustre, carelessly thrown on the floor, far from his [Eadwig's] head, and he himself repeatedly wallowing between the two of them [Elgiva and Ethelgiva] in evil fashion, as if in a vile sty. They said 'Our nobles sent us to you to ask you to come as quickly as possible to your proper seat, and not to scorn to be present at the joyful banquet of your chief men.' But when he did not wish to rise, Dunstan, after first rebuking the folly of the women, drew him by the hand from his licentious reclining by the women, replaced the crown, and brought him with him to the royal assembly, though dragged from the women by force.

It is highly unlikely that events happened as Dunstan described, as, by the time of the coronation, Elgiva and Eadwig were already married. In spite of this, even as late as the twelfth century, Eadwig was remembered as a 'wanton youth', and Elgiva as a harlot and a strumpet.

The picture painted of both Eadwig and Elgiva is not the entire story. Elgiva's brother, the chronicler Ethelweard, provided the only contemporary favourable account of Eadwig, claiming that 'he for his great beauty got the nick-name "All-fair" from the common people. He held the kingdom continuously for four years, and deserved to be loved.' Whilst the majority of leading churchmen supported Edgar and thus refused to recognise Eadwig and Elgiva's marriage, Ethelwold, Abbot of Abingdon, who would later work closely with Edgar's own queen, recognised Elgiva's position. In one charter of Abingdon, Elgiva witnessed as the King's wife, and in her Will, she left a number of bequests to Ethelwold's foundations and to the churchman personally, suggesting a debt of gratitude for his support during the troubled days of her marriage.

At first, Eadwig and Elgiva had the upper hand, exiling or seizing the goods of their enemies. However, in 957, Eadwig found himself deserted by the Northumbrians and Mercians, who chose Edgar as their king, dividing the kingdom at the Thames. Elgiva's family connections helped to secure the south for Eadwig, but the King's position was fatally weakened. The *Anglo-Saxon Chronicle* for 958 records that Archbishop Oda, an ally of St Dunstan, divorced Eadwig from his wife on the grounds of consanguinity. The couple were related at least three times, both with Elgiva's double descent from King Ethelred I and her relationship to Queen Ealswitha. However, the much closer marriage of Edgar's own grandfather, Edward the Elder, to Elfleda and, of course, the marriage of Elgiva's own parents were unchallenged, demonstrating that the consanguinity between Edgar and Elgiva should not, on its own, have been enough to warrant their separation. Elgiva was exiled to the Continent for the remainder of Eadwig's reign. Eadwig did not, in any event, have long to live, dying suddenly on 1 October 959 and leaving the remainder of his kingdom to Edgar.

Elgiva's thoughts on her separation from Eadwig are not recorded, but the fact that she never remarried suggests that she loved him. She made her peace with Edgar during her widowhood and returned to England by the mid-960s. In 966, she received two grants of land from her brother-in-law, which was, perhaps, the grant of her dower and an acknowledgement of her position as a former queen. As further proof of her rehabilitation, Elgiva attended the refoundation of the New Minster at Winchester in that same year. Elgiva remained on good terms with Edgar and her Will, which was made at some point between 966 and 975, included bequests to Edgar and one of his sons. Elgiva also made large grants to religious foundations, and it is not unlikely that she retired to a religious house for her last years. The date of her death is nowhere recorded, but she remained devoted to her husband until the end, requesting that she be buried with him.

As the examples of Elgiva and her earlier predecessors as queen, Egwyna and Elfleda, show, divorce was common amongst tenth-century kings. Elgiva's brother-in-law, King Edgar, was a serial monogamist, marrying three wives in quick succession. Around the time that he seized the throne of Mercia from his brother, he took his first wife, ETHELFLEDA, or Æthelflæd, the daughter of an ealdorman named Ordmer. Ethelfleda's nickname of *Eneda* translates as 'swan' or 'fair'. Edgar always had an eye for a beautiful woman, and Ethelfleda's charms recommended her to him. Edgar also sought an alliance with Ethelfleda's family in order to strengthen his position in Mercia.

No stories survive surrounding Ethelfleda *Eneda* and she played no political role. She bore one child, Edward, before Edgar's accession in 959. With his accession to the entire kingdom, the support of Ethelfleda's family was no longer required by Edgar, and the couple were divorced so that he could find a more politically prominent bride. Nothing more is heard of Ethelfleda, and it is likely that she died young. She played no role in her son's brief reign.

Once he had become King of England, Edgar looked for an alliance with an important noble family. His first choice was a beautiful young nun called Wulfhilde, who lived at Wherwell Abbey under the governance of her aunt, the Abbess. Edgar went to the Abbey and persuaded the Abbess to support his suit. Wulfhilde, who had no desire to marry the King, was tricked into a meeting with him by her aunt. When she entered the room, Edgar met her passionately, terrifying the girl, and she fled the room. Both Edgar and the Abbess were furious, and they locked her in her room until she would agree to marry. Wulfhilde managed to flee through the abbey sewers, forcing Edgar to abandon his suit and propose to her cousin, ST WULFRIDA OF WILTON, instead.

Wulfrida is almost certainly the young nun of Wilton Abbey who was mentioned in the *Life of St Dunstan*. According to the *Life*, Edgar fell in love with a young nun and made her his mistress. The *Life* does not consider Wulfrida to have been Edgar's wife, claiming that she was merely his concubine. However, there is evidence to suggest some sort of marriage, although it is unlikely to have been made with a church ceremony. It is possible that Wulfrida was not, at the time of her marriage, actually a nun, and William of Malmesbury claimed that Wulfrida 'had merely put on the veil as her own idea in her sudden fear of the king, before, as the story continues, the king snatched away the veil and dragged her to his bed'.

Nun or not, Wulfrida and Edgar were married by around 961, and she bore the King a daughter, Edith. According to William of Malmesbury, following this birth, 'Wulfthryth [Wulfrida] did not develop a taste for repetitions of sexual pleasure, but rather shunned them in disgust', retiring with her daughter to Wilton Abbey, where she became Abbess. It is indeed possible that Edgar and Wulfrida quickly found that they were not compatible and that their separation was mutually agreed. However, Wulfrida's retirement coincides with the beginnings of Edgar's relationship with his third wife, Elfrida, and it is more likely that she was divorced by the changeable king. Whether a voluntary exile or not, Wulfrida and Edith spent the rest of their lives at Wilton, with Edith succeeding her mother as Abbess before dying at the age of twenty-three. Both were venerated as saints after their deaths, a far cry from the reputation enjoyed by Edgar's third wife, Elfrida.

ELFRIDA, or Ælfthryth, (*c.* 940-1000/01) was the third wife of King Edgar, and whilst his other wives are shadowy and insignificant figures, Elfrida was a queen. She was the daughter of Ordgar, a West Country thegn. Her mother was of royal descent, and Elfrida, who was the family's only daughter, was born around 940. In 956, Elfrida made an advantageous marriage to Ethelwold, the eldest son of the powerful nobleman Athelstan Half-King. The Half-King had gained his nickname from his immense power, and he was the most prominent man in the country after the King. His prestige was so great that his wife was chosen as the foster mother for the young Edgar following the death of his mother, St Elgiva. In the summer of 956, the Half-King retired to Glastonbury Abbey to become a monk, allowing for the succession of Elfrida's husband to his father's lands and titles.

Elfrida bore her first husband two sons but played no role in their upbringing, and this may have been due to the frosty relations occasioned by the beginning of her relationship with Edgar. William of Malmesbury tells us that before Elfrida's marriage, Edgar heard reports of her beauty and sent Ethelwold to visit her and report if she was worthy of marriage to the King. Ethelwold, falling in love with her on sight, persuaded Elfrida to marry him, informing the King that she was very plain and not a suitable bride:

When Edgar's heart was disengaged from this affair, and employed on other amours, some tattlers acquainted him how completely Æthelwold had duped him by his artifices. Driving out one nail with another, that is, returning him deceit for deceit, he showed the earl a fair countenance, and, as in a sportive manner, appointed a day when he would visit this far-famed lady. Terrified almost to death with this dreadful pleasantry, he hastened before to his wife, entreating that she would administer his safety by attiring herself as unbecomingly as possible; then first disclosing the intention of such a proceeding. But what did not this woman dare? She was hardy enough to deceive the confidence of her miserable lover, her first husband, to adorn herself at the mirror, and to omit nothing which could stimulate the desire of a young and powerful man. Nor did events happen contrary to her design; for he fell so desperately in love with her the moment he saw her, that, dissembling his indignation, he sent for the earl into a wood at Warewelle, under pretence of hunting, and ran him through with a javelin.

A similar story is told by Gaimar, who recorded that Elfrida and Edgar began an affair before Ethelwold's death. Both stories imply that Edgar had already become king before Elfrida's first marriage, which was not correct, and must cast doubt on their truthfulness. Ethelwold died in 962 and Elfrida and Edgar only married in 964, again calling into question the claims that they organised Ethelwold's murder.

Elfrida played a much more political role as queen than either of Edgar's previous wives, and she received a dower from Edgar at the time of their marriage. Edgar's reign is remembered for religious reform and Elfrida played a prominent role in this movement. On his accession, Edgar appointed St Dunstan as his Archbishop of Canterbury and he quickly became his chief councillor. Other leading churchmen were prominent under Edgar, including Ethelwold, Abbot of Abingdon, who was appointed Bishop of Winchester. The tenth-century religious reform sought to regulate monasticism and bring it back to the stricter rule of St Benedict. Even before her marriage, Elfrida showed an interest in the reform and the *Liber Eliensis* claims that

a woman called Ælfthryth [Elfrida] pleaded with King Edgar that he sell to the blessed Æthelwold ten hides at Stoke, which is near Ipswich; and two mills which are situated in the southern part. Her entreaties availed with him. For the bishop gave the king one hundred mancuses for that land and the mills, [and] he afterwards presented [the same land and mills] to Æthelfryth.

This demonstrates both that, even before her marriage, Elfrida had an interest in the reform movement, and that she was already closely associated with Bishop Ethelwold.

In 964, shortly after their marriage, Edgar called a council which produced a famous document, the *Regularia Concordia*. This document set out the rules by which monks and nuns were expected to live. Elfrida, as queen, was given a specified political role, with Edgar declaring 'that his queen Ælfthryth, should be the protectress and fearless guardian of the monasteries; so that he himself helping the men and his consort helping the women there should be no cause for any breath of scandal'. Elfrida was placed in direct control of all the English nunneries.

Elfrida is remembered as one of the most prominent of all the Anglo-Saxon queens. Edgar made great efforts to assert the legitimacy of his third marriage over his two previous unions, and he always presented Elfrida as his queen rather than as merely his wife. Elfrida was a prominent figure at the great royal gathering at the New Minster at Winchester in 966. The charter drawn up to witness the event saw Edgar witness first, followed by the powerful St Dunstan. Immediately after Dunstan, witnessed Edgar and Elfrida's infant son, Edmund, who was strikingly described as the 'legitimate son of the king'. Edward, Edgar's son by Ethelfleda *Eneda*, witnessed next and was described only as the 'son of the king'. Elfrida was the fifth witness and described as the 'legitimate wife of the king'. It is obvious that Edgar intended to demonstrate that his third wife and her children were his legitimate family. Elfrida's eldest son by Edgar, Edmund, died in 971, and she transferred her ambitions to her youngest child, Ethelred, who was born between 967 and 969. Elfrida was crowned with Edgar at the Roman city of Bath in 973, a ceremony intended to highlight his imperial ambitions and dominance of the whole island of Britain.

Edgar was still a young man at the time of his coronation, and it was a shock to everyone when, on 8 July 975, he died suddenly. His only possible successors were his two young sons, Edward and Ethelred. Edward cannot have been more than fourteen or fifteen years old, and Ethelred around seven. Factions developed and Elfrida, naturally, supported her own child. St Dunstan settled on Edward. This led to the succession dispute allegedly foretold by Edgar's mother, St Elgiva, when she interpreted her son's childhood dream.

Dunstan won the succession battle and Edward was crowned king in around March 976, to Elfrida's fury. There was little she could do, except retreat with her son to her house at Corfe whilst Dunstan took over the governorship of England. In 978, matters suddenly changed, and when a meeting of Edward's council was called at Calne, the upper floor on which the councillors stood collapsed, causing everyone, except Dunstan, who was standing on a rafter, to fall to the floor below, killing or maiming the majority of the King's supporters. This was the opportunity that Elfrida had been waiting for.

On 18 March 978, King Edward happened to be in the area of Corfe Castle and decided to pay a visit to his stepmother and half-brother, attended by only a small escort. A number of different accounts describe the events at Corfe of that day. The fullest contemporary account is that contained in the *Life of St Oswald*, which claims that, when Edward arrived at Corfe,

> there came out to meet him, as was fitting, nobles and chief men, who stayed with the queen, his mother. They formed among them a wicked plan, for they possessed minds so accursed and such diabolical blindness that they did not fear to lay hands on the lord's anointed. Armed men surrounded him on all sides, and with them also stood the cupbearer to perform his humble office. The revered king indeed had with him very few thegns, for he feared no one, trusting 'in the lord and the might of his power'.

As Edward accepted a drink, one of Elfrida's thegns seized his hand, wounding him, as the King shouted, 'What are you doing – breaking my right arm?' Edward was then violently stabbed before his horse bolted, causing the King to fall from the horse with his foot trapped in the stirrup. Edward died as he was dragged along the ground behind his horse. The earliest accounts of the murder do not specifically accuse Elfrida of complicity, although one early version of the *Anglo-Saxon Chronicle* states that 'here King Edward was killed in the evening-time on 18 March at Corfe passage'. Elfrida was widely known to live at Corfe, and the fact that this was the scene of Edward's death is striking. By the early eleventh century, whilst Ethelred was still alive, the blame was already commonly attributed to those about the

Queen, and in the mid-eleventh century, the *Life of St Dunstan* by Osbern specifically laid the blame at Elfrida's door, declaring that Edward was 'killed by a stepmother's deceit'. It is impossible now to judge just what Elfrida's involvement in the murder was, but the surviving evidence is damning. It was also Elfrida and her young son who had the most to gain. Shortly after the murder, Ethelred was crowned king.

Ethelred II was no more than twelve years old at his accession, and Elfrida was the power behind the throne. She appears regularly on charters between 979 and 984, demonstrating that she attended councils during her son's minority. She generally witnessed using the title 'king's mother' and was placed directly below the King himself. Elfrida continued to co-operate with Bishop Ethelwold, and the pair kept the King under their control well past his fifteenth and sixteenth birthdays; ages at which an Anglo-Saxon monarch could expect to attain his majority. It was Ethelwold's death on 1 August 984 that finally allowed the King to assert his own authority, and by the end of the year, Elfrida had ceased to attend council meetings and had retired to her own estates, probably against her will.

Even in her old age, Elfrida remained a prominent political figure. At some point between 995 and her death, she became involved in a lawsuit over land. During Edgar's reign, Elfrida had persuaded him to return a large estate at Taunton to the see of Winchester. She also retained an interest in the business, as is recorded in her only surviving letter, written during her old age:

> Ælfthryth [Elfrida] sends humble greetings to Archbishop Ælfric and Earl Æthelweard. I bear witness that Archbishop Dunstan assigned Taunton to Bishop Æthelwold, in conformity with the Bishop's charters. And King Edgar then relinquished it, and commanded every one of his thegns who had any land on the estate that they should hold it in conformity with the bishop's wish or else give it up. And the king said that he had no land to grant out, when he durst not, for fear of God, retain the headship himself; and moreover he then put Ruishton under the Bishop's control. And then Wulfgyth rode to me at Combe and sought me. And I then, because she was my kinswoman, and Ælfsyth because he [Leofric] was her brother, obtained from Bishop Æthelwold that they [Wulfgyth and Leofric] might enjoy the land for their lifetime, and after their deaths the land should go to Taunton, with produce and men, just as it stood. And with great difficulty we two brought matters to this conclusion. Now I have been told that Bishop Æthelwold and I must have obtained the title deed by force. Now I, who am alive, am not aware of any force any more than he would be, if he were still alive. For Leofric had a new title deed; when he gave it up he thereby manifested that he would engage in no false dealings in the matter. The Bishop Æthelwold told him that none of his successors could dispossess him. He then commanded two documents to be written, one he kept himself, the other he gave to Leofric.

Whilst the outcome of the dispute is not recorded, it shows a touching loyalty to the memory of Bishop Ethelwold, Elfrida's greatest friend. As she aged, Elfrida continued to show an interest in the Church, founding two nunneries. Her name always remained linked to the death of Edward the Martyr, and it irked her to see him popularly honoured as a saint within months of his death. The exact date of Elfrida's death is not recorded, but she lived to a good age for the period, reaching around sixty. She died on 17 November in 1000 or 1001.

Elfrida will always be remembered as the murderer of Edward the Martyr. She was undoubtedly one of the greatest and most prominent of all Anglo-Saxon queens and one of the most powerful women in medieval England. This is in direct contrast to her first daughter-in-law, ELGIVA. The date of Ethelred's first marriage is not recorded, but his eldest four sons attested a charter in 993, suggesting that the marriage must have been by the mid-980s at the latest.

Elgiva is mentioned in no contemporary sources and attested no charters. Her existence can be glimpsed by the fact that four sons, Athelstan, Egbert, Eadred and Edmund had been born by 993, a fifth son, Eadwig, by 997, and a sixth, Edgar, by 1001. Two daughters, Elgiva and Edith, also survived to adulthood, and it is safe to assume that she was entirely occupied in childbearing during her marriage. Later records claim that Elgiva was either the daughter of Ealdorman Thored of York or, perhaps, an unidentified man named Ethelbert. No Ealdorman Ethelbert has been identified for the period and so Thored is more likely to have been her father. By 992, Thored had vanished from the sources, implying that he had died. In 1002, Ethelred remarried, and it is likely that Elgiva was repudiated in order to make way for a more prominent match. Alternatively, she may have died. Elgiva was entirely overshadowed by Elfrida, and she was never recognised as queen.

Whilst Ethelred II's first wife is entirely obscure, no such anonymity surrounds his second wife, EMMA OF NORMANDY (*c.* 980s-1052). She was the eldest of the nine children of Richard I, Duke of Normandy, and his second wife, Gunnor, and was born between 980 and 990. Emma's father died whilst she was still young, but her mother was a formidable woman. According to the chronicler Wace, Gunnor 'was very beautiful, well educated and very courtly. Her father and mother were Danish and she was born of noble Danes, with good lineage on both sides. She was kind and friendly, very generous and honourable; she knew all a woman could know about woman's work'. Richard was, at first, unwilling to marry Gunnor, and Emma was born of a union unsanctioned by the church. Gunnor was the dominant influence on her children's upbringing, and she imbued in Emma a love of Scandinavian culture, as well as ensuring that her daughter was fluent in her native language, Danish. Gunnor ruled as regent for her son Richard II following his accession as Duke of Normandy in 996.

Viking raids were a major concern to Ethelred II during his reign and this brought him into contact with Normandy. The Dukes of Normandy were descended from Vikings, and this, coupled with Gunnor's Danish origins, ensured that Normandy was largely sympathetic to the raiders. A letter from the Pope to Ethelred in 991 shows the strained relations between England and Normandy, and in it, the Pope stated the agreement that 'Richard is to receive none of the king's men, or his enemies, nor the king any of his, without their seal'. Normandy harboured Viking ships and the agreement of 991 failed to stop hostilities between the two countries. During the 990s, Ethelred carried out an unsuccessful raid on Normandy, presumably a reprisal for a Viking attack.

The death of Ethelred's mother, Elfrida, left the office of queen vacant, and in the hope of securing a more lasting peace with his troublesome neighbours, the King proposed a marriage alliance. England in the early eleventh century was a stable and wealthy country and the offer of marriage was a good one for the teenage Emma. In late 1001, Ethelred moved his court to Kent to await Emma's coming. She arrived a few weeks later, early in 1002, and the couple married that spring at Canterbury. From the first, it was intended that Emma would be treated as a queen, and she was crowned soon after her wedding. There is also some evidence that Richard II was able to insist on Emma's children taking priority over Ethelred's elder sons in the succession, as Charles the Bald had done in the ninth century with Judith of Francia. According to the *Life of King Edward who rests at Westminster*, when Emma was pregnant with her first child, 'all the men of the country took an oath that if a man child should come forth as the fruit of her labour, they would await in him their lord and king who would rule over the whole race of the English'.

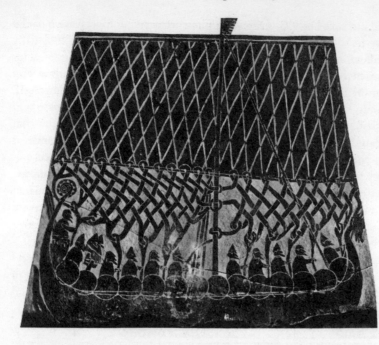

32. A Viking ship. Scene from a viking-age picture stone from Stenkyrka, Gotland, Sweden.

Ethelred was considerably older than Emma and had a number of adult children. The couple never became close and Emma bore her husband only three children in a marriage of fourteen years. She was based at Winchester, and she owned property there, living within her own household. She is likely to have been responsible for the upbringing of her stepdaughters, and also for raising her own children: Edward, born in 1004 or 1005, Godgiva, born in around 1007, and Alfred, born by 1013. Emma rarely appears in sources for Ethelred's reign, and with the large age gap between herself and her husband, it would have been difficult for her to establish herself politically. She was also perceived in England to have Danish sympathies. In 1003, the *Anglo-Saxon Chronicle* recorded that the city of Exeter was destroyed by the treachery of Emma's French reeve, who helped the Vikings gain access to the city. Emma did witness some of Ethelred's charters, an honour that was not granted to his first wife, but in the main, she had little public role.

Ethelred's long reign was continually troubled by Viking raids. The biggest crisis came in 1013, when Sweyn Forkbeard, King of Denmark, landed in England, intent on conquest. Ethelred sent Emma to Normandy with her daughter, Godgiva. This was both for Emma's own protection and in order to allow her to appeal personally to her brother for aid. Emma was soon joined by her sons, Edward and Alfred and, shortly afterwards, by Ethelred himself, who had abandoned his kingdom to Sweyn. It was a relief, in February 1014, when, following the sudden death of Sweyn, the family were invited to return to England and Ethelred recovered his throne. It cannot have been an easy homecoming, and within a year, Ethelred's eldest son, Edmund, was in open rebellion against his father. Sweyn's son, Cnut, was also active in the kingdom. Ethelred died quietly in London on 23 April 1016, beset on all sides. Emma was with him.

Ethelred's death left Emma in a perilous position, whilst Cnut and Edmund fought over the country. She, at first, threw in her lot behind her stepson, Edmund, who was immediately proclaimed king. In spite of this, she was under no illusions about the danger that she faced, and soon after Ethelred's death, her children returned to Normandy. Emma remained in

London and was horrified to find herself a prisoner of Cnut when he took possession of the city. Edmund's death late in 1016 left Cnut as king of the entire kingdom, and in mid-1017, he ordered Emma to be 'fetched' as his wife.

Emma provided her own account of her marriage to Cnut, and she sought to portray it as a marriage of equals. The *Encomium Emmae Reginae*, a book commissioned by Emma herself, provides an account of events once Cnut was secure in his new kingdom:

[He] lacked nothing except a most noble wife; such a one he ordered to be sought everywhere for him, in order to obtain her hand lawfully, when she was found, and to make her a partner of his rule, when she was won. Therefore journeys were undertaken through realms and cities and a royal bride was sought; but it was with difficulty that a worthy one was found, after being sought far and wide. This imperial bride was, in fact, found within the bounds of Gaul, and to be precise in the Norman area, a lady of the greatest nobility and wealth, but yet the most distinguished of the women of her time for delightful beauty and wisdom, inasmuch as she was a famous queen. In view of her distinguished qualities of this kind, she was much desired by the king, and especially because she derived her origin from a victorious people, who had appropriated for themselves part of Gaul in despite of the French and their prince. Why should I make a long story of this? Wooers were sent to the lady, royal gifts were sent, furthermore precatory messages were sent. But she refused ever to become the bride of Knutr, unless he would affirm to her by oath, that he would never set up the son of any wife other than herself to rule after him, if it happened that God should give her a son by him. For she had information that the king had had sons by some other woman; so she, wisely providing for her offspring, knew in her wisdom how to make arrangements in advance, which were to be to their advantage. Accordingly the king found what the lady said acceptable, and when the oath had been taken, the lady found the will of the king acceptable, and so, thanks be to God, Emma noblest of women, became the wife of the very mighty King Knutr.

This is how Emma wanted to present her marriage to the world. In reality, Emma never even left London, let alone returned to Normandy, and as Cnut's prisoner, she had little bargaining power. In spite of this, she was valuable to Cnut: marriage to the English queen helped cement his position as King of England. The marriage also neutralised Norman support for Emma's sons by Ethelred, and it is therefore not impossible that Cnut did agree to make any son born to Emma his heir in preference to his elder children by his first wife, Elgiva of Northampton. Elgiva was still living at the time of Cnut's second marriage to Emma, and unlike his predecessors as king, Cnut did not actually go to the trouble of repudiating his previous wife, instead, to both women's anger, maintaining them both as his wives throughout his reign.

Whilst Emma was not Cnut's only wife, she was his only queen, and in 1017, she shared his coronation. She quickly gained political power; aged around thirty at the time of their marriage, she was several years older than Cnut and was able to influence him. In Cnut's charters of 1018-19, Emma's name often appeared low down in the list of witnesses. After 1019, she tended to witness directly behind the King himself, demonstrating her rapidly increasing political power. A letter written by Wulfstan, Archbishop of York, addressed the couple jointly, highlights Emma's importance.

Emma bore Cnut two children, Harthacnut and Gunhild, between 1018 and 1020. Harthacnut, as the son of his legitimate wife, was Cnut's favourite child, and in 1023, he was sent to Denmark to be raised as the future king of his father's ancestral kingdom. Gunhild made an advantageous marriage to the eldest son of the Holy Roman Emperor. For Emma, her time as Cnut's queen was much more satisfying than her marriage to Ethelred, and she was given much more freedom to act. She and Cnut were often together and they jointly took part in conspicuous patronage, together presenting a shrine to Abingdon Abbey, for example. They are depicted as jointly presenting a cross to the New Minster, Winchester, on the frontispiece of the manuscript the *Liber Vitae*. In 1023, Emma was present at the most important church event of Cnut's reign, the reburial of St Alfheah at Canterbury. She and Cnut acted together throughout Cnut's reign in their attempts to establish a new Danish dynasty in England.

Emma also took political action without Cnut. She was always uncomfortably aware of the position of Cnut's other wife, Elgiva, and of her sons, Sweyn and Harold. When Harthacnut was sent to Denmark, Emma took steps to further secure his position. According to the chronicler Snorri Sturlsson, Harthacnut was placed under the guardianship of Earl Ulf before he sailed, and upon arrival in Denmark, Ulf produced a letter bearing Cnut's seal which stated that the King wished his son to become king of Denmark, to rule beside him. This was very far from Cnut's own intention, and according to the chronicler, 'it was Queen Emma who had been the originator of this plan, and it was she who had this letter written and sealed, having obtained the King's seal by trickery. But the King himself knew nothing about this'. Emma's plan was successful and she secured her son's election as king of Denmark during his father's lifetime, ensuring that Harthacnut's elder half-brothers were barred from asserting their own claims to the kingdom.

Emma was an active and visible figure throughout Cnut's reign and she was reluctant to relinquish power. She was at Winchester when Cnut died suddenly at Shaftesbury on 12 November 1035. She was entirely unprepared for the death of her still young and, apparently, healthy husband. Cnut's surviving son by Elgiva of Northampton, Harold Harefoot, was his only son present in England, and he took the initiative, rushing to Winchester and taking Cnut's treasure from Emma before attempting to secure the crown for himself. Emma immediately threw her support behind Harthacnut and a council at Oxford agreed that her son was Cnut's heir, offering the compromise that Harold should rule as regent until Harthacnut returned from Denmark. Emma set about trying to protect her own child's position, both by slandering Harold and his mother, Elgiva, and by buying support in England. Harthacnut, however, had no desire to leave his primary kingdom of Denmark and, by 1036, with Harold's position daily increasing in strength, Emma decided to take drastic action and recall one of her elder sons to England to take up the throne in their half-brother's stead.

A letter exists, summoning Edward and Alfred to England from Normandy. Emma herself, in the *Encomium Emmae Reginae*, maintained that this letter was a forgery produced by Harold in order to trick her sons into leaving the safety of Normandy. This is not impossible, but it is more likely that the summons came from Emma herself, desperate to maintain her position in England at any cost.

Emma, queen in name only, imparts motherly salutations on her sons, Edward and Alfred. Since we severally lament the death of our lord, the king, most dear sons, and since daily you are deprived of more and more of the kingdom, your inheritance, I wonder what plan you are adopting, since you are aware that the delay arising from your procrastination is becoming from day to day a support for the usurper of your rule. For he goes round hamlets and cities ceaselessly, and makes the chief men his friends by gifts, threats and prayers. But they would prefer that one of you should rule over them, than that they should be held in the power of him who now commands them. I entreat, therefore, that one of you come to me speedily and privately, to receive from me wholesome counsel, and to know in what manner this matter, which I desire, must be brought to pass. Send back word what you are going to do about these matters by the present messenger, whoever he may be. Farewell, beloved ones of my heart.

This was the first direct contact that Emma had had with her elder sons for twenty years. Whilst Emma requested that only one of her sons come to her, Edward and Alfred, who had spent their entire adulthoods in exile and as the penniless guests of their family in Normandy, were both determined to make an attempt on the English throne.

Edward set out directly from Normandy and arrived safely at Winchester for what must have been a difficult reunion with the mother that he had not seen for so long. Alfred, who, as the younger son, did not receive the financial backing of his Norman kin, took a more circuitous route, travelling first to Flanders before sailing for England. Upon arrival, he was intercepted by the powerful Earl Godwin, who had been Emma's strongest supporter in the days following Cnut's death. Godwin, who was well aware of Harold's increasing prominence in Harthacnut's absence, entertained the young prince at his house at Guildford before treacherously handing him over to Harold's men. Alfred was taken as prisoner to Ely where, on Harold's orders, his eyes were put out. He was then delivered to the monastery, dying soon afterwards. On hearing of his brother's murder, Edward returned to Normandy, leaving Emma alone in Winchester. Alfred's death and Edward's departure signalled the final blow for Emma's hopes, and in 1037, Harold seized the crown, exiling Emma to Flanders.

The fact that Emma chose to go to Flanders rather than Normandy suggests that relations between herself and her eldest son, Edward, and her Norman kin, were poor and that they objected to her marriage to Cnut and support for Harthacnut. Emma was made welcome in Flanders, although it was, perhaps, the most difficult time of her life. Whilst in exile, she received news that Gunhild, the only one of her five children that she had raised to adulthood herself, had died in Germany after only three years of marriage. Following her exile, Emma turned once again towards Harthacnut for support, and finally, in 1040, he sailed from Denmark, bringing a large fleet to Flanders.

Emma was overjoyed to see her youngest son, and the pair planned to mount an invasion of England. Whilst they were still in Flanders, word arrived that Harold had died and that Harthacnut had been proclaimed king. Harthacnut and Emma sailed at once, and Emma was able to establish herself as the power behind the throne, always witnessing immediately after the King in charters. Emma and Harthacnut also jointly issued a writ granting land at Hemingford to Ramsey Abbey, again demonstrating Emma's political prominence. During the reign, Emma commissioned what is, essentially, her autobiography, the *Encomium Emmae Reginae*, which she used to justify her actions throughout her lifetime. Emma became increasingly concerned about her youngest son's health, and loath to find herself alone and unprotected as she had been in 1035, in 1041, she persuaded Harthacnut to recall Edward to England to share in his rule. The *Encomium* presents this as a triumph of Emma's enlightened policy and ended with this comment:

> Obeying his brother's command, he [Edward] was conveyed to England, and the mother and both sons, having no disagreement between them, enjoy the ready amenities of the kingdom. Here there is loyalty among the sharers of rule, here the bond of motherly and brotherly love is of strength indestructible.

When Harthacnut died suddenly in 1042, Edward was proclaimed king in his place, just as Emma had hoped.

Edward the Confessor, who had spent most of his life waiting to become king of England, was in no mood to share his throne with his mother. Soon after his coronation in 1042, he deprived her of all her lands and treasures. According to William of Malmesbury, this was something that Edward had been planning for some time, and his 'royal spirit was woken to hostility against his mother by the memory of past events. She had not been very generous in her treatment of her son, while he was passing through his teenage years, and so he ordered all his mother's effects to be ransacked, down to the last pennyworth'. Emma was furious and, whilst she had not been entirely loyal to her son for much of his life, she had at least ensured his safety by arranging for him to leave for Normandy in 1016. She had also been instrumental in securing Harthacnut's recognition of him as his successor. Emma was powerless to act against her son, and Edward returned to her only those possessions that were sufficient to meet her needs. After 1043 Emma virtually disappears from the sources, and it is likely that she returned, defeated, to Winchester. Her last public appearance was at London in 1045, when she witnessed a charter granting privileges to Westminster Abbey. Emma died at Winchester on 14 March 1052 and was buried beside Cnut in the Old Minster there.

Emma of Normandy spent over fifty years as queen of England and is the most famous of all the Anglo-Saxon queens. Another woman who briefly became queen of England in between Emma's two marriages led an equally turbulent life, but unlike her famous contemporary, Aldgyth is barely remembered at all.

ALDGYTH has been described as a lady of 'distinguished lineage', although details of her parentage do not survive. Her family were based in the north Midlands and she was a kinswoman of Cnut's first wife, Elgiva of Northampton. Whilst she was still young, Aldgyth married Sigeferth, a Danish nobleman from the Five Boroughs. By 1015, King Ethelred, whose kingdom had been subject to Viking attacks for many years, was not feeling very favourable towards Scandinavians. William of Malmesbury states that, in 1015, he decided to take action against Aldgyth's powerful husband:

> A grand council of Danes and English was assembled at Oxford, where the king commanded two of the noblest Danes, Sigeferd and Morcard, accused of treachery to him by the impeachment of the traitor Edric [Eadric Streona], to be put to death. He had lured them, when deceived by his soothing expressions, into a chamber, and murdered them, when drunk to excess, by his attendants prepared for the purpose. The cause of their murder was said to be, his unjustifiable desire for their property. Their dependents, attempting to revenge the death of their lords by arms, were defeated, and driven into the tower of St Frideswide's church, where as they could not be dislodged, they were consumed by fire.

Aldgyth was present at the council, and she must have been terrified as events unfolded. Eadric Streona, her husband's murderer, was a favourite of the King, and there was nothing that any of Sigeferth's followers could do to avenge their lord. In order to obtain Sigeferth's lands, it was necessary to neutralise Aldgyth, and Ethelred had her taken by armed guard to Malmesbury Abbey, where she was to be imprisoned for life.

Sigeferth and Aldgyth were childless, and Aldgyth, as Sigeferth's widow, had a strong claim to both his property and to the loyalty of the people of his estates. She was also a famous beauty, and Edmund, the eldest son of Ethelred, who was already estranged from his father, resolved to visit her secretly. According to William of Malmesbury, Edmund immediately fell in love with Aldgyth and the couple married without the consent of his father. For Aldgyth, the marriage was an opportunity to regain all that she had lost, and

Edmund, 'at the instigation of his wife, he asked of his father the possessions of Sigeferth, which were of large extent among the Northumbrians, but he could not obtain them; by his own exertions, however, he procured them at last, the inhabitants of that province willingly submitting to his power'. By taking Sigeferth's lands for himself, Edmund showed himself in open rebellion to his father for the first time.

Aldgyth's connections were very important to Edmund in establishing his position in 1015. It is unlikely that the couple spent much time together following their wedding, and in the summer of 1015, Cnut, the son of Sweyn Forkbeard who had previously deposed Ethelred, landed in England and carried out raids in Kent and Wessex. Edmund made attempts to halt Cnut's progress, moving south from the Five Boroughs, leaving Aldgyth behind. With the death of Ethelred on 23 August 1016, the citizens of London chose Edmund as their king. He was immediately locked in a fight for his kingdom against Cnut and, whilst initially successful, he was defeated by the Danes at the Battle of Ashingdon. This defeat prompted Edmund to come to terms with Cnut, and at a meeting, it was decided that they would divide the kingdom amongst themselves, with Edmund taking Wessex and Cnut the rest of the country.

Aldgyth's whereabouts are not known during Edmund's brief reign, although it is likely that, following the agreement with Cnut, she took up residence in Wessex. She bore Edmund two sons during their brief marriage, Edward and Edmund, and they may have been twins. Edmund II's reign was very brief, and he died on 30 November 1016. It is possible that he died from wounds inflicted during his defeat at Ashingdon, but murder cannot be ruled out. William of Malmesbury, writing in the twelfth century, believed that the King was killed by Eadric Streona, the murderer of Aldgyth's first husband, on the orders of Cnut. If this is the case, then it appears that Edmund suffered a particularly horrifying death because, as he sat to answer a call of nature, assassins hidden in the privy 'drove an iron hook into his posteriors'.

With Edmund's death, Cnut became king of the whole of England. It is unclear what became of Aldgyth. Her two sons were considered a major threat by Cnut and, unwilling to be seen to be a murderer of infants, he sent them to the King of Sweden with secret instructions that they be put to death. The Swedish king took pity on them and spared their lives, allowing the boys to ultimately take refuge in Hungary. Aldgyth may perhaps have accompanied them. The children were taken in by the King of Hungary and raised as princes, with Edward marrying Agatha, sister of the Queen of Hungary. Whilst Aldgyth disappears from history, her son, Edward the Exile, remained a prominent figure, and during the reign of his childless uncle, Edward the Confessor, he was recalled with his family to England. Edward the Exile died soon afterwards, but following the Norman Conquest in 1066, his children found their way to Scotland, where the eldest daughter, Margaret, married the King of Scots. Their daughter, Matilda, married Henry I of England, and it was through this marriage that Aldgyth became an ancestress of future monarchs of England.

Aldgyth was not the only member of her family to become queen, and around the time of her marriage to Edmund II, her kinswoman, ELGIVA OF NORTHAMPTON, married his greatest rival, Cnut. Elgiva was born into a prominent and powerful Midlands family. He uncle, Wulfric Spot, was the founder of Burton Abbey. Her father was Ealdorman Elfhelm of southern Northumbria and her mother was a noblewoman called Wulfrun. Like their kinswoman, Aldgyth, Elgiva's family had Danish sympathies, and in 1006, when Elgiva was probably approaching twenty, her father was murdered and her two brothers blinded by Ethelred's great favourite, Eadric Streona, on the orders of the King.

Elgiva and Cnut, the son of the Danish king, Sweyn Forkbeard, began a relationship in around 1013. Sweyn invaded England in 1013, and he left his son at Gainsborough to guard the Danish fleet, whilst he attacked Mercia. For Cnut, a marriage with Elgiva, the daughter of a prominent local family, made political sense, and it provided him with kinship links across the local area. Elgiva and her surviving family, who had no reason to love King Ethelred, were happy to throw in their lot with the invaders. Elgiva bore Cnut two sons, and possibly also a daughter, and it is likely that she and her children remained in the Midlands during the events of 1016 as Cnut claimed the throne of England. Elgiva and Cnut's marriage was not sanctioned by the church, and she is often referred to as only the King's mistress. However, it is clear that the couple were committed to their relationship. Elgiva's eldest son was named Sweyn, after his paternal grandfather, and her younger son was named Harold, after Cnut's grandfather. The use of family names was important to Cnut, and his third son, by Emma, was left with only the name of Cnut's great-grandfather, Harthacnut.

There is no record of Elgiva's whereabouts between 1016 and 1029. She cannot have been happy to hear of Cnut's second marriage to Emma of Normandy. In spite of this, she was not actually repudiated by Cnut and his marital relations can be seen as something approaching polygamy. It is possible that Cnut brought Elgiva south following his accession, and a daughter of Cnut is supposedly buried in the church at Bosham in Sussex, not far from the royal court at Winchester. This daughter would have been Elgiva's, and it is not impossible that she was based at Bosham.

Cnut decided to make Sweyn, his eldest son by Elgiva, his successor in Norway, a recently conquered kingdom, and he sent them there to act as his regents in 1029. It was very unusual for a tenth-century woman to receive an official appointment as regent, and Elgiva's role is a demonstration of Cnut's confidence in her. Unfortunately, Elgiva's regency was not a success, and in Norway, 'Ælfgifu's time' is remembered as an age of wretchedness and oppression. This was not entirely Elgiva's fault, as her rule coincided with a period of poor harvests and famine, though she is remembered in Norway for her harsh and autocratic behaviour. She and Sweyn arrived with a large force of Danes and used them to ensure obedience to their rule. The chronicler Snorri Sturlsson commented that Elgiva 'instituted new laws in the land concerning many matters. They were patterned after Danish laws, but some were much harsher'. Elgiva's laws were bitterly resented, and they caused an upsurge of nationalism in Norway.

The previous king of Norway, Olaf Tryggvason, had begun to attract a cult by the time that Elgiva and Sweyn arrived in Norway. Elgiva was well aware of the dangers of this cult, and she sought to dispel it, attending the ceremonial exhumation of Olaf's body in 1031 to determine whether or not the deceased king was indeed a saint. According to Snorri Sturlsson, the coffin appeared brand new and the body smelled fresh:

> Then the bishop bared the countenance of the king and its aspect had changed in nowise, and there was a ruddiness on his cheeks as though he had only recently fallen asleep. Those who had seen King Olaf when he fell now saw a great change in that his hair and nails had grown almost as much as they would have if he had been alive all the time since he fell. Then King Svein [Elgiva's son] approached to view the body of King Olaf, and so did all the chieftains present.
>
> Then Alfifa [Elgiva] said, 'mighty little do bodies decompose when buried in sand. It would not be the case if he had lain in earth.' Then the bishop took a pair of sheers and cut the king's hair and trimmed his whiskers. He had had long whiskers as people in those days used to have.
>
> Then the bishop said to the king and Alfifa, 'now the hair and the beard of the king are as they were when he died, but it had grown as much as you can see here cut off.'
>
> Then Alfifa replied, 'that hair would seem to me a holy relic only if fire does not burn it. We have often seen wholly preserved and undamaged hair of persons who have lain in the ground longer than this man has.'

Therefore the bishop had fire put in a censer, blessed it, and put incense on it. Then he laid King Olaf's hair into the fire, and when all the incense was burned, the bishop took the hair out of the fire, and it was not burned. The bishop had the king and the other chieftains view it. Thereupon Alfifa bade him lay the hair into fire that had not been blessed. Then Einar Thambarshelfir bade her be silent and used hard language against her. So then, by the bishop's pronouncement, the consent of the king, and the judgment of all the people, King Olaf was declared a true saint.

The recognition of Olaf as a saint was the beginning of the end of Elgiva's rule in Norway. In 1032, Olaf's son entered Norway with an army to challenge Sweyn. When Sweyn and Elgiva attempted to raise an army, many of the leading men of the country refused to join, and it was only with difficulty that they defeated their rival. By winter 1033, Elgiva and Sweyn found it impossible to remain in Thrandheim, the centre of their administration. For nearly two years, they clung on to power in southern Norway, but in 1035, they were finally forced to flee to Denmark with Olaf's son, Magnus, being proclaimed king in Sweyn's place.

Soon after Elgiva arrived in Denmark, she heard that Cnut had died in England. This loss was shortly followed by the death of Sweyn, and Elgiva returned to England to support her surviving son, Harold. Emma's son, Harthacnut, was designated as Cnut's successor but Harold had designs on the crown. Although it was agreed that Harold would rule England as regent for Harthacnut until he could return from Denmark, Elgiva was desperate for her son to win the crown, and she began working on his behalf soon after her arrival in England. She held feasts and gave gifts to the leading men of England in return for their support of Harold's candidacy. Her rival, Emma of Normandy, was working equally hard in support of her own son, and it is likely that the rumours spread about Elgiva and her sons stemmed from Emma. The later chronicler Florence of Worcester, for example, had heard that Elgiva was a concubine of Cnut's and that 'this same Ælfgifu wished to have a son by the king, but could not, and therefore ordered to be brought to her the newly born infant of a certain priest, and made the king fully believe that she had just born him a son'. This story refers to the birth of Sweyn and Harold was accused of being the son of a shoemaker. The stories were slander, but Elgiva's efforts paid off, and in 1037, Harold was declared King of England.

Harold I's brief reign is poorly recorded, and he is an obscure figure. It is possible that Elgiva, who already had experience of ruling through one son, was the power behind the throne and, in the Will of Bishop Elfric of Elmham, Harold was referred to as 'my royal lord' and Elgiva as 'my lady', suggesting some sort of joint rule. Elgiva's time as queen mother was short-lived, as Harold died on 17 March 1040. Harthacnut and Emma sailed for England to claim the throne, and Elgiva made herself scarce. England would not have been a comfortable place under the rule of the son of her rival, and it is possible that she ended her life in Denmark.

Like Elgiva of Northampton, many of the eleventh-century English queens were Anglo-Danish in sympathy or origin, and the last powerful Anglo-Saxon queen, EDITH GODWIN (*c.* 1020s-1075) was no exception. She was one of the nine children of the powerful Earl Godwin, a self-made man who appears to have been a descendant of Ethelred I and who came from minor Sussex nobility. Through both intelligence and good fortune, he rose to power under Cnut, becoming a leading advisor to the King and his sons. By 1018, he had been made an earl and been given Cnut's sister-in-law, Gytha, as his wife. Edith was the couple's eldest daughter. The date of her birth is nowhere recorded, but it must have been between 1020 and 1030.

Edith was educated at the royal nunnery at Wilton, which provided her with a privileged lifestyle and a first-class education. At Wilton, Edith was educated with the daughters of other noble houses and prepared for a prestigious marriage rather than the life of a nun. She is described in contemporary sources as having been skilled in Latin prose and verse and fluent in French, Irish and Danish. William of Malmesbury described Edith as 'a woman whose bosom was the school of every liberal art, though little skilled in earthly matters: on seeing her, if you were amazed at her erudition, you must admire also the purity of her mind, and the beauty of her person'.

When Edward the Confessor succeeded his half-brother, Harthacnut, as King of England in 1042, he was around forty years old and, having spent most of his life in Normandy, was an unknown quantity in England. Whilst for Edward, Earl Godwin would always be the murderer of his brother, Prince Alfred, he was forced to rely on him as the leading man in the kingdom, and in 1045, Godwin persuaded the King to marry Edith. That this was not the King's free choice would later become apparent, but in 1045, Godwin and his sons were at the height of their power, with Edith's two eldest brothers, Sweyn and Harold, receiving earldoms in 1043 or 1044. There was little Edward could do but take Edith as his wife. William of Malmesbury claimed that Edward always kept Edith at a distance and refused to consummate the marriage, due to his hatred of her family. Edith also claimed that her marriage was not consummated in order to portray Edward as a saint and, also, to explain away her childlessness. It seems unlikely that Edward, who, as the last male member of his immediate family, badly needed an heir, would have ignored this consideration simply out of a dislike of his wife, and it is apparent that one party was simply infertile. The fact that Edward had no recorded illegitimate children, unusual for a medieval king, also points towards this conclusion.

Edith found Edward's court uncultured compared to her comfortable life at Wilton. In the *Life of King Edward who rests at Westminster*, which she commissioned, it was claimed that Edward spent most of his time hunting. Edith's husband was a disappointing specimen, and she took steps to make him appear more kingly:

> Moreover, it was quietly, and only for the occasion – in any case, it should be distinctly said with no mental pleasure – that he displayed the pomp of royal finery in which the queen obligingly arrayed him. And he would not have cared at all if it had been provided at far less cost. He was, however, grateful for the queen's solicitude in these matters, and with a certain kindness of feeling used to remark on her zeal most appreciatively to his intimates.

Edith loved finery and selected expensive clothes for Edward. She also made the royal palaces appear more regal, ordering a throne draped in gold fabrics and covering the floors in Spanish carpets.

In the *Life*, Edith was determined that she should be presented as a queen and her chronicler obliged:

> [Edward] stooped with great mercy to the poor and infirm, and fully maintained many of these not only daily in his royal court but also at many places in his kingdom. Finally, his royal consort did not restrain him in these good works in which he prepared to lead the way, but rather urged speedier progress, and often enough seemed even to lead the way herself. For while he would give now and then, she was prodigal, but aimed her bounty to such good purpose as to consider the highest honour of the king as well. Although by custom and law a royal throne was always prepared for her at the king's side, she preferred, except in church and at the royal table, to sit at his feet, unless perchance he should reach out his hand to her, or with a gesture of the hand invite or command her to sit next to him. She was, I say, a woman to be placed before all noble

matrons or persons of royal and imperial rank as a model of virtue and integrity for maintaining both the practices of the Christian religion and worldly dignity.

Although the *Life*, on its surface, is intended to glorify the memory of Edward the Confessor, in reality, Edith wanted to safeguard her own reputation. As queen, she had little political power and was only kept in place by the position of her kin, her childlessness making her particularly vulnerable.

Edith's fortunes during Edward's reign were closely linked to those of her family. In 1051, Edward finally felt strong enough to depose the Godwins. He publicly accused Godwin of the murder of his brother, Alfred. The crime had been preying on Edward's mind since his accession, and whilst Edith, in the *Life*, sought to lay the blame for Edward's suspicions on the Norman influence at court, it was well known that Godwin was involved in Alfred's murder. With the King and the nobility against him, Godwin fled to Bosham in Sussex and, taking his wife and younger children with him, sailed to exile in Flanders. Godwin's second son, Harold, took ship to Ireland.

With the removal of the Godwins, Edward was free to act against Edith. In the *Life*, Edith claimed that Edward was persuaded by his Norman Archbishop of Canterbury, Robert of Jumierges, to separate from her:

> For, in order that not a single member of the earl's family should remain at the king's side to provide for the country's well-being, he used every device to secure that even the queen herself, the earl's daughter, should be separated from the king, against the law of the Christian religion. This plan the king, although not opposing, yet did mitigate, giving out as reason for the separation this honourable pretext, that she was to await the subsidence of the storms over the kingdom in the monastery of Wilton, where she had been brought up. And so, with royal honours and an imperial retinue, but with grief at heart, she was brought to the walls of Wilton convent, where for almost a year in prayers and tears she awaited the day of salvation. Such grief more deeply moved and wounded the crowd of courtiers than even the departure of the earl himself. And no wonder! For she was in all the royal counsels, as we might say, a governess and the fount of all goodness, strongly preferring the king's interests to power and riches.

Edith's account of her exile from court is very far from the truth, and it is clear that Edward wanted to divorce her. Florence of Worcester claims that Edith was repudiated due to Edward's hatred of her father. Far from being sent with queenly honours to the comfortable Wilton Abbey, she was unceremoniously evicted from the palace and sent on foot with only one female attendant to Wherwell Abbey, where she was placed in the custody of the abbess, Edward's half-sister. Edward confiscated Edith's property and had no intention of ever taking her back. It is no wonder that Edith spent a whole year weeping.

In spite of his hopes of divorcing Edith and making a new marriage, Edward was forced to take her back the following year when Godwin returned to England with an army. This was a triumph for Edith, although relations must have been frosty between her and Edward following her return. From the mid 1050s, Edith was in a much stronger position at court, and she witnessed fourteen of the twenty-two charters surviving from the period. In the charters, Edith always witnessed immediately after Edward and always as queen. Even the sudden death of her father at Easter 1053 did not alter her position, and her brothers, Harold and Tostig, filled their father's place as Edward's chief advisors.

With the exception of providing an heir, Edith fulfilled most of the duties expected of her as queen. She was conspicuously pious and was involved in good works, rebuilding Wilton Abbey in stone towards the end of the reign, an action intended to complement Edward's building of Westminster Abbey. In spite of her good works, Edith's piety generally appears to have been coupled with her own self-promotion, and in the *Life*, she had it recorded that Wilton was more prudently and modestly planned than Westminster, ensuring that it was finished more quickly. Edith also became more political and had strong links to her brothers, who virtually ruled England during the 1050s and 1060s. Tostig was Edith's favourite brother and it was rumoured that in 1064, at his request, she arranged the murder of Gospatric, a rival to Tostig's position as Earl of Northumbria.

Edith was present at Edward's death on 4 January 1066, and she later claimed that he commended her and the kingdom to her brother Harold's protection. She was careful never to say that the King named her brother as his heir. The chronicler William of Poitiers later claimed that Edith, 'a woman of manly wisdom, loving good and eschewing evil, wished to see the English governed by William [of Normandy] whom her husband, King Edward, adopted as a son and made his heir'. This was the Norman viewpoint, attempting to justify Edward's cousin, William, Duke of Normandy, as his legitimate heir. The fact was that Edward the Confessor had no certain heir. His nephew, and closest male relative, Edward the Exile, had died some years before, leaving a young son, Edgar Ætheling, who was far too young to have built up his own party. In 1066, Edith's own brother, Harold, claimed the throne. In October 1066, William of Normandy defeated and killed Harold at the Battle of Hastings, and it was William who ended the year as King of England. For William, it was of paramount importance to present himself as Edward's legitimate heir, and he came to Edith at Winchester soon after his victory. Edith was determined to maintain her position as queen, and she submitted to William. This had tangible benefits as, in 1066, according to the Domesday Book, she was the richest woman in England. Edith retained most of her lands following the Conquest.

Edith lived at Winchester after the Conquest and played no part in her family's continued struggle against Norman rule. She was welcome at court and, in March 1071, attended the consecration of the Bishop of Durham. She enjoyed a comfortable retirement, dying at Winchester on 19 December 1075. In accordance with his desire to honour the widow of the Confessor, William arranged for her to be buried with great ceremony beside her husband in Westminster Abbey.

Edith Godwin was the last prominent Anglo-Saxon queen, and the last to retain her status in England, but she was not quite the last Anglo-Saxon queen. The first of Edith's two successors as queen was her sister-in-law and namesake, Edith Swanneck.

EDITH SWANNECK was the first wife of Harold II, the last Anglo-Saxon king of England. She is often called Harold's mistress rather than his wife, and the relationship was not solemnised in church. In spite of this, as with many earlier Anglo-Saxon queens, she can be considered Harold's spouse rather than simply a concubine.

Few details of Edith Swanneck's parentage or background survive, but she was apparently a great heiress, and according to the Domesday Book, in 1066, she held nearly 280 hides of land in eastern England worth over £520 a year. Edith's mother was a woman named Wulfgyth, who made her Will in 1046, but no other details of her family survive. It is likely that Harold and Edith formed a relationship around 1044, when Harold was created Earl of East Anglia by Edward the Confessor. A primary consideration for Harold would have been to secure good local connections. Edith's beauty also recommended her to him, and her nickname 'Swanneck' implies great beauty. She was described in the Domesday Book as 'Edith the Fair' and 'Edith the Beautiful', further testaments to her good looks.

Edith and Harold were married for over twenty years and had six surviving children: Godwin, Edmund, Magnus, Wulf, Gytha and Gunhild. The names show a marked Scandinavian bias, and it is possible that Edith, like Harold, came from an Anglo-

Scandinavian family. Edith was based in Canterbury during her marriage and, according to the Domesday Book, possessed four dwellings there. An unbaptised infant of Edith and Harold's was also buried in the cathedral there, close to the tomb of St Dunstan.

Harold and Edith were probably still married in January 1066 when he became king. Shortly afterwards, Harold married Edith of Mercia, repudiating Edith Swanneck. Edith Swanneck sought sanctuary at Waltham Abbey during the turbulent days of her ex-husband's reign, when he was faced first with an invasion by Harold Hardrada, King of Norway, and then by William of Normandy. On 14 October 1066, Harold was killed at the Battle of Hastings and a number of sources attest that it was Edith Swanneck who was summoned to the battlefield in order to identify the King's body. This must have been a deeply traumatic task for Edith, but she did as she was asked, identifying Harold's mutilated corpse through certain 'intimate' marks on his body. Once he had been identified, he received an honourable burial in Waltham Abbey.

Following the Battle of Hastings, Edith Swanneck disappears from the records. She was dispossessed of her lands and most of her children fled abroad. There was very little left for Edith in England, and it is possible that she accompanied her sons to Ireland. Alternatively, she may have joined Harold's mother, Gytha, at Exeter, and assisted the older woman in rebellion against the new Norman rule. Edith's children led adventurous lives across Europe. Her sons, Godwin, Edmund and Magnus, fled to Dermot, King of Ireland. With the Irish king's support, they launched unsuccessful raids on Somerset in 1068 and 1069 before disappearing from history. Edith's final son, Wulf, is recorded as a hostage in Normandy on the death of William I, and it is likely that he was captured soon after the Conquest. Edith's daughter, Gytha, came under the protection of her cousin Sweyn, King of Denmark, and married Vladimir II, Grand Prince of Kiev. Edith's second daughter, Gunhild, was left behind at Wilton Abbey when her family fled and forced to become a reluctant nun. In 1093, she was abducted by the Norman Count Alan the Red, marrying him shortly afterwards. Count Alan had been granted a number of Edith's estates after the Conquest, and it is possible that he sought marriage to her daughter in order to impose his authority there. The date of Edith Swanneck's death is not known. A similar obscurity shrouds the later life of the woman who supplanted her as Harold's wife.

EDITH OF MERCIA was queen of England for only a few brief months and left little mark on the kingdom. She was the daughter of the powerful Earl Elfgar of Mercia. Her grandmother was the famous Lady Godiva, who reputedly rode naked through the streets of Coventry. Little is known of Edith's early life, but it must have been turbulent. Her father was exiled in 1055. He returned soon afterwards with an army and raided Hereford before being reinstated to his earldom. In 1058, Elfgar was expelled again. On this occasion, Edith travelled with him, and during the exile, she was married to her father's ally, Gruffydd, King of Wales. This was a political match, and following its celebration, Elfgar returned once again to his earldom with Welsh help. He died around 1062.

Edith bore her husband a daughter, Nest, but no other children are recorded. Gruffydd was considered a major threat to England, and Edward the Confessor was determined to destroy him. In 1063, the brothers, Harold and Tostig Godwin, invaded Wales. They won a major victory over the Welsh, and Gruffydd was killed by his own men on 23 August 1063. Harold had his head brought to him and then sent to King Edward. At some point following Gruffydd's death, Edith returned to her family, bringing her daughter with her.

Edith's brother, Morcar, succeeded their father as Earl of Mercia, and following a rebellion in Northumbria, her second brother, Edwin, became earl there. Edith's brothers were powerful men, and their support was vital for Harold when he became king following the death of Edward the Confessor. Within weeks of his accession, he had married Edith in order to cement the political alliance. It is likely that Edwin and Morcar insisted on a full church marriage ceremony and a consecration for Edith as queen, and she was always referred to as Harold's queen during his reign.

Edith was in London at the time of the Battle of Hastings, and according to Florence of Worcester, as soon as they heard of Harold's death, Edwin and Morcar withdrew from the battle and travelled to London to find her. They hurried her to the safety of Chester, in the heart of Mercia, and it was there, shortly afterwards, that she bore a son named Harold. Edith spent some years at Chester, and during this time, her brothers continued to oppose William the Conqueror, first proclaiming Edward the Confessor's great-nephew, Edgar Ætheling, as king before abandoning him. It is likely that they hoped to set young Harold up as king, but in 1072, Edwin was killed by his own men and Morcar was captured by William.

In 1069-70, William occupied Chester and Edith fled. She left her daughter, Nest, behind, and the Welsh princess married Osbern, son of Richard FitzScrob, a French nobleman living in the Welsh Marches. In 1098, young Harold reappears in the sources as a follower of King Magnus Olafsson of Norway, who accompanied him on expeditions to the Orkneys and Mervanian Isles. Nothing more is known of Edith's son and he never attempted to reclaim his father's throne.

Edith must have spent the remainder of her life in exile. It is possible that she ended her days as a pilgrim in southern France. Sources at the Abbey of La-Chaise-Dieu in the Auvergne region of France record that an English 'Queen Edith' was cured of leprosy by the abbot there. In gratitude, this queen paid for the construction of the monastic dormitory and was annually commemorated by the monks. She was buried there in the 1070s or 1080s. This Queen Edith may have been Edith of Mercia, and it is possible that she was on a pilgrimage to Rome when she stopped at the abbey by chance. Alternatively, the fame of the abbey's founder, St Robert of Turland, or the growing monastic community there may have attracted her in her search for a cure. If the mysterious woman was indeed Edith, it demonstrates that she was able to retain her wealth following her flight from Chester and was free to travel as an independent woman.

Edith of Mercia was the last of the Anglo-Saxon queens of England, and like so many before her, she is a shadowy figure who made little impact on the records of her time. In spite of this, all the Anglo-Saxon queens helped to contribute to the development of the role of the queen in England, and their successors, the Norman queens, actively sought to maintain this. Just as William the Conqueror wanted to portray himself as the legitimate heir to the Anglo-Saxon kings, so his wife and her immediate successors wanted to show that they were the legitimate inheritors of English queenship.

3

The Norman Queens

William, Duke of Normandy, claimed the English crown through an English queen. According to the chronicler William of Poitiers, 'if it be asked what was his hereditary title, let it be answered that a close kinship existed between King Richard and the son of Duke Robert whose paternal aunt, Emma, was the sister of Duke Richard II, the daughter of Duke Richard I and the mother of King Edward himself'. Queens were important to the Norman kings, and the Norman period in England saw a number of prominent queens, culminating in the rivalry between the cousins Matilda of Boulogne and the Empress Matilda. The office of queenship remained remarkably stable, and Matilda of Flanders, the wife of William I, made a conscious effort to present herself as an English queen, in order to emphasise the continuity of her dynasty from what had gone before.

MATILDA OF FLANDERS (*c.* 1031-83) was the daughter of Baldwin V, Count of Flanders, and his wife, Adela, daughter of Robert II, King of France. On her father's side, she was descended from Alfred the Great. Little evidence survives of Matilda's upbringing, but the chronicler Orderic Vitalis claimed that 'the queen herself was endowed with fairness of face, noble birth, learning, beauty of character, and – what is and ever will be more worthy of praise – strong faith and fervent love of Christ'. William of Malmesbury also noted that Matilda 'was a model of wisdom and exemplar of modesty without parallel in our time'. This suggests that Matilda was educated, and it is likely that she could read and write. Religion was important to her, and she distributed alms to the poor every day, as well as giving extravagant gifts to the church throughout her lifetime.

Matilda had a number of suitors. One story claims that, during her youth, she fell in love with a young English nobleman who had been sent as an ambassador to her father's court. Matilda's passion was unrequited and the young nobleman refused to marry her, returning to England in something of a hurry. Matilda was furious at this rejection and, when she became queen of England years later, used her influence to have her former love imprisoned for life and confiscated his property. This story is almost certainly fanciful and, in reality, most unmarried young noblemen in Europe would have been pleased to marry Matilda.

Matilda's family connections recommended her to William, Duke of Normandy. William was born a few years before Matilda in around 1027. His childhood could not have been more different from the stable upbringing that Matilda received in Flanders because, whilst he was the only acknowledged son of Duke Robert I of Normandy, his mother was merely the duke's mistress, Herleva, the daughter of a tanner of Falaise. William succeeded his father as Duke of Normandy at the age of seven. As a result of his illegitimate birth, he wanted to marry a woman of good lineage, and as early as 1047, his attention focused on Matilda, who he tried to abduct. In around 1049, William made a more formal proposal and Count Baldwin, who, by then, looked more favourably on the young Duke, agreed to the match.

The marriage occurred in around 1050, when Matilda was nineteen and William twenty-three. At first glance, the couple must have appeared somewhat ill-matched, as William was a tall man, approaching six feet in height, and Matilda was unusually short even for the eleventh century, never reaching five feet. In spite of this, the couple fell in love. Matilda's near-contemporary Orderic Vitalis later referred to her as William's 'beloved wife'. Another near-contemporary, William of Malmesbury, wrote that William was devoted to her and that 'he had many children by Matilda, and she, with her willingness to please her husband and her ability to bear him children, kindled a passionate attachment in the spirit of that great man'.

Whilst the marriage brought personal happiness to the couple and, also, provided the young Duke with a boost to his international prestige, their union was not without controversy. When the couple's betrothal had first been announced in 1049, Pope Leo IX called a Church council at Reims in which he expressly forbade the marriage. The Pope's opposition was on the grounds of consanguinity, as the couple were both descended from Rollo, the first Duke of Normandy. A much closer link had also been provided by the betrothal of Matilda's mother, Adela, to William's uncle, Richard III, Duke of Normandy, which had ended with his death in 1027. This was not an actual blood tie between Matilda and William, but it was enough, from the Church's point of view, for them to be considered to be first cousins. In any event, Pope Leo IX was hostile to William and had no desire to see him make an advantageous marriage.

Both Matilda's father and William were prepared to ignore the hostility of the Church, and the marriage occurred without the required dispensation. This was a very dangerous position for the couple to be in, and William was forced to depose his uncle, Mauger, Archbishop of Rouen, for his opposition to the marriage, as William of Malmesbury explains:

> Some say there was a secret reason for this deposition: Matilda, who William had taken as his wife, was a near relation, and in his zeal for the Christian faith Mauger had found it intolerable that two blood-relations should share the marriage-bed and had aimed the weapons of *excommuni* against his nephew and his nephew's consort.

The threat of excommunication was a terrifying one and would have meant that the couple would no longer be able to participate in the services of the Church. They were forced to wait until the death of Leo IX in 1059 to make their union official, receiving a retrospective dispensation from the new pope, Nicholas II, who was anxious to be on friendlier terms with William. In order to atone for marrying without the Church's sanction, the couple built two religious houses in Caen: William, the monastery of St Stephen's for monks, and Matilda, Holy Trinity for nuns.

It must have been a great relief to Matilda to have her marriage recognised by the Church, as, by 1059, she had already borne William several children. The exact number of children born to the couple is not recorded. Orderic Vitalis believed that it was eight: Robert, Richard, William, Henry, Adelaide, Constance, Cecilia and Adela. Robert was the eldest son and always Matilda's favourite. William's own favourite was their second son, Richard, who, to his parents' grief, was killed in a hunting accident in the New Forest in 1075. The third and fourth sons, William and Henry, would become kings of England. Of their daughters, Constance, who was named after Matilda's grandmother, Constance of Arles, Queen of France, married the Duke of Brittany in 1068, and Adela, the youngest daughter, married the Count of Blois. Cecilia was dedicated in her childhood to Matilda's foundation of Holy Trinity, and Matilda spent a considerable amount of time with her in the abbey over the years. Adelaide, the last daughter named by Orderic Vitalis, also became a nun, and a further daughter, Matilda, who is named in other sources, appears to have died young. In another part of his history, Orderic Vitalis also noted that a daughter of William's, Agatha, had been betrothed to Harold Godwin when he visited Normandy during the reign of Edward the Confessor, and that, following the Battle of Hastings, she was sent to marry the King of Galica. This was a personal tragedy for Agatha, who was surely Matilda's eldest daughter, and 'she had seen and loved the Englishman, but she was terrified of the Spanish husband she had never seen'. Agatha never did see her Spanish husband, as she died on the journey.

Matilda and William were often in each other's company during the early years of their marriage, and their relationship underwent a fundamental change in 1066. William had always asserted that his cousin, Edward the Confessor, had named him as his heir, and given the English king's Norman upbringing and background, this is possible. However, Edward appears to have had second thoughts or, at least, did not specifically name William on his deathbed and, instead, his brother-in-law, Harold Godwin, took the crown. As soon as Harold's accession was known, William began to build an invasion fleet and Matilda played an important role in this, secretly fitting out a ship for William to use as his flagship. The ship was named the 'Mora' and the prow was fitted with a representation of their then-youngest son, William Rufus, with his right hand pointing towards England and his left holding an ivory horn to his mouth. This was an expensive gift, and William was so pleased that, following the conquest, he granted Matilda the revenues from the earldom of Kent.

William trusted Matilda's political judgement, and when he sailed for England, he left her to act as co-regent of Normandy with his friend, Roger of Montgomery. Matilda did a good job, and William repeated the compliment several times during their marriage. According to Orderic Vitalis, in 1069, for example, 'King William sent his beloved wife Matilda back to Normandy so that she might give up her time to religious devotions in peace, away from the English tumults and together with the boy Robert [her son] could keep the duchy secure.' Matilda spent a great deal of time in Normandy as regent following 1066, whilst William was occupied in England. She also, on occasion, acted as regent of England. When the couple were together in England, William accorded Matilda prominence, and she witnessed a number of charters during the reign. In the foundation charter for the priory at Lewes, for example, Matilda witnessed immediately after the King, taking a place higher than her sons.

Matilda was in Normandy when she heard the news of William's victory at the Battle of Hastings. He was crowned King of England at Christmas that same year, and it was not until March 1067, when William paid a brief visit to Normandy, that the couple were reunited. At Easter 1068, William sent ambassadors to Normandy to summon Matilda to England. She crossed the Channel triumphantly, accompanied by a great retinue of attendants, and upon her arrival in Winchester, she had a no-doubt-emotional reunion with William. William was determined that his wife should be officially recognised as queen, and on Whit Sunday, she was crowned by the Archbishop of York. William's coronation had been a hurried and tense affair, and he used Matilda's coronation as the first great state occasion of the Norman regime in England. William and Matilda quickly re-established the intimacy in their marriage, and Matilda bore her youngest child, Henry, at the end of 1068 or early in 1069.

Although their marriage was a happy one, as their children grew, Robert, the eldest, became a source of concern and disagreement for his parents. He was eager to attain his inheritance and was anxious to secure more authority for himself, placing himself in direct opposition to his father and allying himself with his cousin, Philip I of France. This caused the only known disagreement between Matilda and William as, according to Orderic Vitalis, Matilda was unable to cut all ties with her favourite child as William had done:

> Queen Matilda, feeling a mother's affection for her son, often used to send him large sums of silver and gold and other valuables without the king's knowledge. On getting word of it he [William] ordered her, in a passion, never to do such a thing again. When she recklessly renewed her offence, the king exclaimed in anger. 'How very true here and now is the maxim of a certain sage, "A faithless wife brings ruin to the state". After this who in this world shall ever find himself a trustworthy helpmate? The wife of my bosom, whom I love as my own soul, whom I have set over my whole kingdom and entrusted with all authority and riches, this wife, I say, supports the enemies who plot against my life, enriches them with my money, zealously arms and succours and strengthens them to my grave peril.' Whereat she replied, 'O my lord, do not wonder that I love my first-born child with tender affection. By the power of the Most High, if my son Robert were dead and buried seven feet deep in the earth, hid from the eyes of the living, and I could bring him back to life with my own blood, I would shed my life-blood for him and suffer more anguish for his sake than, weak woman that I am, I dare to promise.'

For Matilda, it must have been traumatic to find herself at odds with William, and she was horrified when he ordered that one of her messengers, Samson, should be blinded as a punishment. Samson was forewarned, perhaps by Matilda himself, and managed to flee before the punishment could be carried out, but the disagreement caused Matilda great grief. In spite of this, she was unable to stop herself from doing all she could to aid Robert. At some point after her disagreement with William, she heard of a hermit who lived in Germany and apparently had the gift of prophesy. She sent gifts to him and asked him to pray for both William and Robert. The response that Matilda received was not what she hoped for, as the hermit informed her that Robert would succeed his father in Normandy, but that he would give himself over to lust and indolence and govern poorly. Matilda was, perhaps, less than reassured when the hermit continued by saying that she would never see this, as she would die before William.

As the hermit predicted, Matilda did not survive William. She died suddenly of the plague in Caen in Normandy on 2 November 1083. She and William had become reconciled before her death, and according to William of Malmesbury, William's affection for his wife was clear both in the splendid funeral that he gave her at Holy Trinity in Caen 'and showed by many days of the deepest mourning how much he missed the love of her whom he had lost'. Following her death, William abandoned pleasure of every kind. He never contemplated marrying again, and he died, still grieving for Matilda, just under four years later in September 1087.

Matilda of Flanders was one of the luckier medieval queens of England, as she enjoyed a happy marriage with a man who loved her deeply. The marriage of her daughter-in-law, Matilda of Scotland, proved to be less happy, although Matilda of Flanders' successor as queen was every bit as capable as her mother-in-law.

William I bequeathed the English crown to his next surviving son, William Rufus, rather than his estranged eldest son, Robert. Rufus never married and England had been without a queen for nearly twenty years when, in 1100, the King was killed in a hunting accident in the

New Forest. Rufus's younger brother, Henry, who was conveniently close by when the accident occurred, hurried to have himself declared king, and it was Henry who provided England with the second Norman queen of England, MATILDA OF SCOTLAND (1080-1118).

Matilda of Scotland was an immensely important bride for Henry I. In spite of his father's claims to be the heir to Edward the Confessor, in reality, his title was based solely on conquest. At the time of Henry and Matilda's marriage, the *Anglo-Saxon Chronicle* enthused that she was 'of the rightful royal family of England' and the marriage went some way to healing the wounds created by the Conquest less than forty years before. Matilda of Scotland was the daughter of Malcolm Canmore, King of Scotland, who would later be immortalised by Shakespeare in *Macbeth*. It was Matilda's maternal family that was important to both Henry and to the people of England, as her mother was St Margaret, the daughter of Edward the Exile. Matilda was therefore the great-granddaughter of Edmund II and his wife, Aldgyth, and a great-great-niece of Edward the Confessor. St Margaret had been born during her father's exile in Hungary and she returned with the rest of her family to England when they were summoned to the court of Edward the Confessor. Although Edward the Exile died soon after his arrival, Margaret, her sister Christina and brother Edgar Ætheling were raised at court, and Edgar, as the last direct male-line descendant of Alfred the Great, was proclaimed king by some members of the nobility following the Norman Conquest. This came to nothing, and William the Conqueror tolerated the family for a time, although also viewing them with suspicion. In 1068, the family, headed by Margaret's mother, announced that they were returning to Hungary. Their ship was driven by storms to Scotland, forcing them to land in Lothian. Perhaps, unwilling to entrust their lives to the sea again, they remained in Scotland, and by 1070 or 1071, Margaret had married the Scottish king. Margaret's Anglo-Saxon descent was an important factor in the ambitious Malcolm's selection of her. This can be seen in the fact that their first five children were given royal English names: Edward, Edmund, Ethelred, Edgar and Edith. It was the couple's eldest daughter, Edith, who later took the name Matilda, who would unite the English and Norman royal houses. In spite of the political nature of their marriage, the couple were fond of each other, and the *Life of St Margaret* records that Malcolm was determined to please his wife and 'anything she rejected, he also rejected, and anything she loved, he loved because of his desire for her love. And for this reason, even though he was illiterate, he would hold the books that she used for reading or to assist in her prayers in his hands and look at them'.

Edith, or Matilda, was born in the late summer or early autumn of 1080, the fifth of the eight children born to her parents. Matilda's mother, St Margaret, was an exceptionally pious woman, and according to the *Life of St Margaret*, 'she was a very image of virtues'. Margaret played a major role in the upbringing of her children, and she was determined that they should be a credit to her, as this passage from the *Life* indicates:

> She poured out care to her children not less than to herself, seeing that they were nurtured with all diligence and that they were introduced to honest matters as much as possible. And because she knew the Scripture, 'who spares the rod hates the child', she had ordered her household steward that, whenever the children committed some childish mischief, as young children will, that they should be punished by him with threats and beatings. And because of the religious zeal of their mother, the children's manners were far better than those of other children older than they. And they never fought amongst themselves, and the younger children always displayed respect to the elder ones. For this reason, during solemn mass, when they followed their parents up to the altar, the younger never tried to outdo the elder but went up by age, oldest first. Margaret had her children brought to her very often, and she taught them about Christ and faith in Christ, using words suitable to their age and understanding. She admonished them diligently 'Fear the

Lord,' she said, 'O my children, because those that fear him will not be in need, and if you delight in him, O my flesh, he returns goodness to you through prosperity in the present life and by giving you a happy afterlife with all the saints.' This was the desire of the mother, these were the admonishments, this was the prayer that she prayed day and night, with tears on behalf of her offspring, so that they might come to know their Creator in faith which works through love, and knowing, that they might worship, worshipping, that they might love him in everything and above all things, loving, that they might arrive at the glory of the heavenly kingdom.

Margaret was literate and loved holy books, and it is likely that she supervised the early education of her daughter.

Matilda did not spend her entire childhood in Scotland. In 1086, her mother's sister, Christina, left Scotland to become a nun at Romsey Abbey in England, taking Matilda and her younger sister Mary with her. Matilda and Mary spent some time at Romsey before moving to the royal nunnery of Wilton to continue their education. Wilton was still famous as a centre of learning and Matilda received an education fitting for a royal princess. It is possible that, in sending her daughters to Romsey with her sister, St Margaret intended that they would both become nuns. This was certainly Christina's hope, and she put considerable pressure on her young nieces to take the veil. According to Matilda's own account, given to Archbishop Anselm, Christina was convinced that the veil was the only way to protect her young charges:

> For when I was quite a young girl and went in fear of the rod of my Aunt Christina, whom you knew quite well, she to preserve me from the lust of the Normans which was rampant and at that time ready to assault any woman's honour, used to put a little black hood on my head and, when I threw it off, she would often make me smart with a good slapping and most horrible scolding, as well as treating me at being in disgrace. That hood I did indeed wear in her presence, chafing at it and fearful; but, as soon as I was able to escape out of her sight, I tore it off and threw it on the ground and trampled on it and in that way, although foolishly, I used to vent my rage and the hatred of it which boiled up in me. In that way, and only in that way, I was veiled, as my conscience bears witness.

Whilst it is possible that Margaret hoped that her daughters would follow a religious life, Malcolm had no such intentions for them.

Malcolm Canmore had married Margaret for her grand lineage, and he was anxious to ensure prestigious marriages for his daughters. Orderic Vitalis claimed that Count Alan the Red of Richmond and the Earl of Surrey both asked for Matilda's hand in marriage. The King, William Rufus, was also rumoured to have been her suitor. According to William of Malmesbury, Matilda would wear the veil in order to reject unworthy suitors who came to her at the nunnery and this is borne out by Matilda's own account of one such occasion: in 1093, her father arrived unexpectedly at Wilton with Count Alan, intending that he should marry her. Malcolm, 'when by chance he saw me veiled snatched the veil off and tearing it to pieces invoked the hatred of God upon the person who had put it on me, declaring that he had rather have chosen to marry me to Count Alan than consign me to a house of nuns'. Malcolm was so furious that he took Matilda back to Scotland without taking the time to arrange her marriage.

Matilda did not spend long in Scotland. In November of that same year, her father was killed in a raid on Northumbria and her mother died only three days later following a long illness. To find herself so suddenly an orphan must have been a shock for Matilda and, with older half-brothers from their father's previous marriage, Matilda and her siblings were in a very difficult position. Matilda's uncle, Edgar Ætheling, was concerned about the danger and hurried his sister's younger children south to England immediately upon hearing the news of St Margaret's death. There is no evidence for Matilda's whereabouts between 1093 and 1100, but she may perhaps have returned to either Wilton or Romsey to finish her education.

Although William Rufus had earlier shown an interest in Matilda, he was not eager to embark on matrimony with anyone and was happy to let the matter rest. In 1100, soon after becoming king, Rufus's younger brother, Henry I, proposed marriage to Matilda. Henry had been born and raised in England and he was much more in tune with the political situation in the country than his two predecessors as king. He understood that, given the fact that Edgar Ætheling was unmarried and childless, as far as most people were concerned, the true heirs of Edward the Confessor were the children of St Margaret. The alliance was entirely political on both Matilda's and Henry's parts, and for Matilda, it was a way to ensure that she finally escaped the veil. The couple did at least have some common interests as both were noted for their scholarly pursuits.

The marriage plans did not run entirely smoothly. Many people, including Anselm, Archbishop of Canterbury, believed that Matilda was a nun and the Church forbade the marriage and ordered her to return to the convent. Matilda went personally to Anselm to ask for his help. She vehemently denied that she was a nun and set out the full story of her childhood with her aunt, Christina, and the pressure that had been put upon her. Anselm, to Matilda's relief and gratitude, believed her story and called a Church court at Lambeth, which investigated her claims. Matilda attended the council, and according to the report of Eadmer, a follower of Anselm, she offered to swear that she was free to marry. This was enough for the Archbishop, and he declared that she had never been a nun, allowing the couple to marry a few days later on 11 November 1100. Soon after the ceremony, Anselm consecrated Matilda as queen.

Matilda's contemporary William of Malmesbury characterised her as the ideal medieval consort. According to the chronicler, 'she was a woman of exceptional holiness, and by no means negligible beauty, in piety her mother's rival, and in her own character exempt from all evil influence, outside the royal marriage-bed of unblemished chastity, and untouched even by the breath of suspicion'. Matilda fulfilled her primary role as queen, bearing two children within three years of her marriage: Matilda in 1102 and William in 1103. According to William of Malmesbury, 'the bearing of two children, one of either sex, left her content, and for the future she ceased either to have offspring or desire them, satisfied, when the king was busy elsewhere, to bid the court goodbye herself, and spent many years at Westminster'. Henry acknowledged over twenty illegitimate children, and whilst most were born before his marriage, some were born after 1105. Given the fact that Matilda produced two healthy children so soon after her marriage, and the evidence of her husband's notorious fertility, it seems likely that the couple ceased to have a sexual relationship as soon as Matilda had fulfilled her primary duty and produced a son. William of Malmesbury, a great admirer of Matilda, suggested that this was Matilda's own choice, although it was rumoured that Henry, disgusted by Matilda's habit of kissing the sores of lepers, was unwilling to live too closely to her for fear of infection. Henry always showed respect for Matilda, but it appears that, after 1103, they came to an agreement to share the rule of the kingdom without living as man and wife.

In spite of the failure of the physical side of their marriage, Matilda had a great deal of influence over Henry. She was affectionate to Archbishop Anselm, presumably due to his assistance concerning her marriage. Anselm, following a disagreement with Henry, left

England in April 1103. He corresponded with Matilda throughout his two and a half years of exile, and during the period, Matilda witnessed at least one charter as 'Matilda, daughter of Anselm', a clear statement of her allegiance. Matilda worked on Anselm's behalf with Henry, and in one surviving letter to Anselm, she spoke both of her devotion to the archbishop and her efforts to secure his return:

> I give unnumbered thanks to your unceasing goodness, which, not unmindful of me, has condescended, by your letters presented to me, to shew forth your mind, though absent. The clouds of sadness in which I was wrapped being expelled, the streamlet of your words had glided through me like a ray of new light. I embrace the little parchment sent to me by you, as I would my father himself: I cherish it in my bosom, I place it as near my heart as I can; I read over and over again the words flowing from the sweet fountain of your goodness; my mind considers them. My heart broods over them; and I hide the pondered treasures in the very secret place of my heart. Yet, while I praise all you have said, at one thing alone I wonder; that is, at what your discreet excellency has said about your nephew. Yet I do not think I can deal otherwise with your friends than my own. I might say with 'mine' than my own, for all who are yours by kindred are mine by love and adoption. Truly the consolation of your writing strengthens my patience, gives and preserves my hopes, raises me when falling, sustains me when sliding, gladdens me when sorrowful, softens me when angry, pacifies me when weeping. Farther, frequent though secret, consultation promises the return of the father to his daughter, of the lord to his handmaiden, of the pastor to his flock. I am encouraged to hope the same thing from the confidence which I have in the prayers of good men, and from the good will which, by skilfully investigating, I find to be in the heart of my lord. His mind is better disposed towards you than many men think; and I, favouring it, and suggesting wherever I can, he will become yet more courteous and reconciled to you. As to what he permits now to be done, in reference to your return, he will permit more and better to be done in future, when, according to time and opportunity, you shall request it. But even though he should persist in being an unjust judge, I entreat the affluence of your piety, that, excluding the bitterness of human rancour, which is not wont to dwell in you, you turn not from him the sweetness of your favour, but ever prove a pious intercessor with God for him and me, our common offspring, and the state of our kingdom. May your holiness ever fare well.

It is clear, in the dispute between Anselm and Henry, where Matilda's sympathies lay and it was not with her husband.

Matilda was very politically influential and issued thirty-three surviving charters, as well as attesting a large number of Henry's. Henry spent much of his reign in Normandy whilst Matilda made only one brief visit there in 1106. It appears that Matilda, who had been largely raised in England, preferred to remain there and Henry made use of this preference, often requiring her to act as regent in his absence. In September 1114, Henry spent ten months in Normandy with Matilda remaining in England as regent. She was called upon to act as regent again in April 1116 and remained as England's ruler until her death in 1118. During her last period as regent, Matilda was assisted by her son, William, and she began to train him for his future role as King of England. She also played a prominent role in justice. In spring 1116, she became involved in the case of Bricstan of Chatteris, an unjustly condemned prisoner. According to reports, Bricstan, who had hoped to take holy vows before being arrested for some unknown offence, repeatedly called upon St Benedict and St Etheldreda for assistance. The saints tore his chains from him before throwing them against the wall with such force that the guards went rushing to the Queen. Matilda sent an investigator and, when convinced that a miracle had indeed occurred, she ordered

Bricstan's release, as well as ordering the bells in London to be rung in celebration and special Masses heard.

In spite of her abilities as regent, Matilda is chiefly remembered for her piety and, to her contemporaries, her charity work with the poor and sick led to her being known as 'Good Queen Matilda'. William of Malmesbury tells us that Matilda wore a hair-cloth shift under her royal robes and went barefoot to church in Lent. She had a particular interest in lepers, perhaps seeking to imitate Christ in his own favourable treatment of the marginalised group. She washed and handled the feet of lepers, as well as kissing their hands and feeding them herself. Matilda founded a leper hospital dedicated to St Giles, which was located just outside London and endowed with some of her revenues as queen. She was also a benefactress of the leper hospital at Chichester in West Sussex. Matilda tried to follow her mother's example in her piety, and she worked to improve the lives of her poorest subjects. She patronised the Augustinians and founded a priory in Aldgate in 1107 or 1108. Matilda had an interest in holy men and gave generously to them, in one case meeting with a former knight who had vowed always to wear his mail shirt next to his skin so that he would be armed to fight against Satan. Matilda was so impressed with this man's piety that she asked to feel his mail shirt and, as she did so, slipped a purse of gold inside.

Matilda died during her last regency on 1 May 1118, at the age of thirty-seven. The cause of her death is not recorded, but it may have been unexpected, as Henry did not travel back from Normandy. Matilda's daughter was absent in Germany, where she had married the Holy Roman Emperor, and of her two children, it is likely that it was to her son, William, that Matilda was closest. If this is the case, then she was, at least, spared the news of his drowning, in 1120, in the wreck of the White Ship. This was a calamity for Henry I and was a major catalyst in his decision to take a second wife, Adeliza of Louvain.

ADELIZA OF LOUVAIN (*c.* 1103-51) was the eldest daughter of Godfrey, Count of Louvain, and his first wife, Ida of Namur. She had one of the grandest lineages of any queen of England and was a descendant of Charlemagne on both sides of her family. Adeliza was born in around 1103, and whilst it is unclear whether she received any formal education, she was skilled in embroidery and, during her childhood, produced a standard for her father in silk and gold. She was a great beauty and was nicknamed 'the fair maid of Brabant' by her contemporaries. Another contemporary, John of Worcester, declared that she was 'a maiden of great beauty and modesty'. Adeliza's father was a vassal of the Holy Roman Emperor, Henry V, and it is likely that she would have had some contact with her future stepdaughter, the emperor's wife and King Henry I's daughter, the Empress Matilda. In February 1110, Count Godfrey met the Empress at Liege, when she agreed to intercede for him in relation to a dispute. It is not inconceivable that Adeliza was present. In any event, a common fondness for Germany provided a bond between Matilda and Adeliza in later years.

In December 1120, William, the only son of Henry I, drowned in the wreck of the White Ship whilst on his way home to England from Normandy. Henry I had been a widower for over two years by 1120 and had shown no real inclination to remarry. The loss of his only legitimate son made a new marriage a matter of urgency, and he swiftly began the search for a new bride. Adeliza was chosen in order to strengthen his alliance with the Holy Roman Empire, which had first come into effect with the marriage of his daughter. For Adeliza, it was a prestigious match, and she arrived in England in January 1121.

According to the *Anglo-Saxon Chronicle*, Henry spent Christmas 1120 at Brampton before travelling to Windsor, where he and Adeliza were married on 24 January. The next day, Adeliza was crowned as queen. Both ceremonies were marred by a farcical dispute between the Archbishop of Canterbury and the Bishop of Salisbury, within whose diocese

Windsor fell. The aged Archbishop claimed the right to conduct royal ceremonies anywhere in England, and he therefore conducted the marriage ceremony. He was so slow with age that Henry ordered the Bishop of Salisbury to conduct the coronation. The following day, everyone entered the church where the Bishop of Salisbury crowned Henry. Before he could reach Adeliza, the Archbishop strode in, all his infirmities forgotten in his fury. He promptly removed the crown from Henry's head before crowning him again. He then crowned and anointed Adeliza as Queen of England.

The thirty year age gap between the couple must have seemed large to Adeliza at the time of her marriage. In spite of this, she made attempts to share Henry's interests and affection developed between the couple. Henry had an interest in exotic animals, creating a zoo at Woodstock Palace. Adeliza commissioned the first known French bestiary, a work by Phillippe du Thuan, and this was, perhaps, an attempt to involve herself in pursuits enjoyed by the King. Due to the desperate need for an heir, Adeliza spent most of her marriage with Henry and the couple travelled together, in stark contrast to his first marriage. Surviving charters show that Adeliza was with Henry consistently until 1131. For example, the couple were at Winchester at Easter 1123, Normandy in 1125, England between 1126 and 1127, and Normandy again between 1129 and 1131.

Adeliza stopped travelling with Henry in 1131, and it is likely that it was at that point that the couple accepted that their marriage would produce no child. There is no evidence that Adeliza ever conceived during her marriage to Henry, to her great distress. She is known to have written to the churchman Hildebert of Lavardin for advice and comfort in relation to her childlessness. It is possible that her apparent barrenness also caused Adeliza to take an increasing interest in the traditional queenly pursuits of piety and patronage. She maintained a correspondence with Hildebert of Lavardin and one of his surviving letters granted her request to become a lay daughter of St Vincent's Abbey. He also praised her dedication and support of the monks of St Vincent and her visits there. Adeliza maintained friendly relations with several bishops. She warmly addressed Alexander, Bishop of Lincoln, in one charter, and William, Bishop of Hereford, later donated land in memory of Henry and Adeliza for 'nurturing' him. Adeliza made gifts to Waltham Abbey and Reading Abbey, and whilst her piety attracted less attention than that of her predecessor, Matilda of Scotland, she was devout.

Adeliza played a very limited political role during her time as queen. She was never named as regent, as her predecessor had been, a fact that can be attributed to Henry's need to keep her with him in the hope of conceiving a child. She was allowed some role in government and was present at several councils during Henry's reign. She is known to have been present at the great councils in May 1121 and Easter 1123, and she was present in the council chamber at Christmas 1126 when Henry named his daughter, Matilda, as his heir. She also participated in crown-wearing ceremonies, designed to emphasise the importance of the monarchy.

Adeliza worked to advance her countrymen. When she arrived in England, she brought a number of her compatriots with her, and her first chancellor was a Lotharingian called Godfrey, who was appointed Bishop of Bath by Henry in 1123. Godfrey took several of his countrymen with him to Bath, and a Chamberlain called Rothardus witnessed charters by him in 1135, as well as being present when Adeliza issued charters following Henry's death. Adeliza's second chancellor, Simon, who was also a Lotharingian, became Bishop of Worcester. He remained in contact with Adeliza and witnessed several of her grants. The evidence of her chancellors suggests that Adeliza used her influence with Henry to advance the careers of the Lotharingians who travelled to England with her. She was also accompanied by a number of Lotharingian ladies and helped them make advantageous marriages, with Juliana, the wife of the nobleman Jordan of Auffay, recorded as having arrived in England with the Queen. Adeliza's cousin, Melisende of Rethel made two English marriages, receiving a dowry on her second from Adeliza. Following Henry's death, Adeliza's half-brother, Jocelyn, arrived from Louvain and was prominent in her household.

Henry I died near Rouen in Normandy on 1 December 1135. Although he was in his late sixties, his death was unexpected, and Adeliza was not with him, although she attended his burial at Reading Abbey on Christmas Day. Adeliza and Henry had been married for fifteen years and she grieved for him, giving the manor of Eton in Hertfordshire to Reading Abbey on the first anniversary of Henry's death in exchange for prayers to be said for his soul. She gave one hundred shillings for a lamp to burn perpetually at his tomb. Adeliza continued to style herself as queen in charters, but retired from court, moving to Arundel Castle in Sussex, one of her dower properties.

Adeliza did not entirely shut herself away from the world and, around 1139, she married William d'Aubigny, a royal butler. It is likely that the couple had known each other at court during Henry's lifetime, and there is every reason to assume that it was a love match. William held lands in Norfolk and Suffolk and was made Earl of Lincoln by King Stephen early in 1139, although he later exchanged this earldom for the earldom of Arundel. Although no evidence of the couple's relationship survives, it must have been happy, and in spite of the childlessness of her first marriage, Adeliza bore her second husband at least seven children. William d'Aubigny was a supporter of Stephen throughout the civil war that wracked England following Henry's death, and the impetus for Adeliza's last public role came from her rather than from her husband.

Adeliza had maintained contact with her stepdaughter Matilda following Henry's death. The two were very close in age and, with their shared interest in Germany, had much in common. When Henry's nephew Stephen, the son of his sister Adela, seized the English crown, Matilda was, at first, unable to do anything to assert her claim but, by 1139, she had gained enough strength to take action. Adeliza offered her stepdaughter Arundel as a base from which to establish her claim to the throne, and later that year, Matilda arrived at the castle to stay with her. Adeliza had underestimated just what the backlash to her hospitality would be, and according to William of Malmesbury, she, 'with a woman's fickleness, in despite of the undertakings she had given via the many messengers she had sent to Normandy, broke the faith she had sworn'. In reality, Adeliza was in a very difficult position. She wanted to assist her stepdaughter and knew that Henry would have wanted her to provide Matilda with all the support that she could. However, as soon as Stephen heard of his cousin's arrival, he immediately moved to besiege Arundel, terrifying Adeliza. Rather than betraying Matilda, she took the only steps that she felt were possible and negotiated with Stephen for her stepdaughter to be given a safe-conduct to join her half-brother, Robert, Earl of Gloucester, in Bristol. Whilst Adeliza was not able to offer Matilda a refuge in the long-term, she helped her travel to her supporters in the South West, and she therefore played a role in ensuring that Matilda remained at liberty to pursue her claim.

Adeliza all but disappears from the sources following the events of 1139. It is unclear whether she had any further contact with Matilda, and she certainly played no further role in the civil war. It is likely that she spent most of her time at Arundel, creating her half-brother, Jocelyn, castellan there in the 1140s. She also granted him the honour of Petworth, which formed a substantial part of her income and was intent on furthering his career. Following Adeliza's death, Jocelyn continued to work closely with her husband.

By 1150, Adeliza had retired to the continental monastery of Affligham in Flanders, which had been founded by her father and uncle. Her retirement perhaps signified a decline in her health, and she died there on 24 March 1151. Her body was taken to Reading, where she was buried beside Henry I. At her burial, Jocelyn confirmed gifts to the abbey in her memory, and later, William d'Aubigny made a religious gift for the good of Adeliza's soul.

Adeliza of Louvain seems, for the most part, to have had a happy life. Family was important to her, and she was loved by both her own family and the family she acquired through marriage. In spite of this, she was grieved by her childlessness in her first marriage, and in her last years, she was painfully aware that if she had only provided Henry with a son, the turmoil that engulfed England following his death could have been avoided.

MATILDA OF BOULOGNE (*c.* 1103-52), the wife of King Stephen, is one of England's lesser-known queens, and she has always been overshadowed by her more famous cousin and namesake, the Empress Matilda. In spite of this, Matilda of Boulogne was a prominent political figure and one of the few women of her time to conduct a military campaign and lead her own troops as she sought to support her husband's debateable right to the English crown.

Matilda of Boulogne was the only child and heiress of Count Eustace of Boulogne and his wife, Mary, the younger sister of Matilda of Scotland. Matilda of Boulogne was always close to her English family and she was named after her aunt, the queen. She spent her childhood in England and was well known to her English family, including her uncle, Henry I. She is likely to have been educated at Bermondsey Abbey, of which her mother was a major benefactor, and she may have been present when her mother died there suddenly in 1115 during a visit.

Matilda was the heiress to the counties of Boulogne and Lens, as well as to extensive estates in England, making her one of the greatest heiresses in Europe. Henry I had always favoured his nephew, Stephen, the son of his sister, Adela, and, in 1125 he arranged for Stephen to marry Matilda. Stephen was around seven years older than Matilda and, as a younger son, could expect little inheritance of his own. Henry had raised Stephen in England, creating him Count of Mortaine in 1115, and he was described by the *Gesta Stephani* as the dearest of Henry's nephews. This is likely and, certainly, Henry's bestowal of Matilda on Stephen was a mark of great favour. It is also not impossible that the couple already knew and liked each other. Stephen was a kindly and affable man, with the *Gesta Stephani* describing him as 'rich and at the same time unassuming, generous, courteous; moreover, in all the conflicts of war or any siege of his enemies, bold and brave, judicious and patient'. The couple quickly became devoted to each other, and Matilda spent the rest of her life trying to protect her husband and children. Stephen was faithful to his wife, and his only recorded illegitimate child was born before his marriage.

As well as wanting to advance his favourite nephew, it is likely that Henry I had another motive for arranging the marriage. By 1125, he had come to terms with the probability that he would die without a male heir and Stephen, who had already sworn to support the claims of Henry's daughter, the Empress Matilda, may have been advanced as a reward for his compliance. If Henry hoped that the marriage would buy Stephen's support for his daughter, he was to be disappointed. Stephen and Matilda of Boulogne were together in Boulogne in December 1135 when word reached them of Henry's death in Normandy. Matilda must have been aware of her husband's intentions, and it is clear that his actions on his uncle's death had been planned for some time. According to the chronicler Henry of Huntingdon, as soon as word reached Stephen of Henry's death, he left his wife to sail to England:

For without delay came Stephen, younger brother of Theobald, count of Blois, a man of great resolution and audacity, who, although he had sworn an oath of fealty for the realm of England to the daughter of King Henry, trusting in his strength, shamelessly tempted God and seized the crown of the kingdom. William, archbishop of Canterbury, who had been the first to swear allegiance to the king's daughter, alas! crowned Stephen king, wherefore God visited him with the same judgment which he had inflicted on him who had stricken Jeremiah, the great priest; namely, that he should not live out the year. Roger, the great bishop of Salisbury, who had been the second to take the aforesaid oath and had ordered all the others to do likewise, contributed everything in his power to secure for him the crown. He, too, by the just judgment of God was afterwards taken captive by him whom he had made king and in dire torments came to a wretched end. But why tarry? All those who had sworn fealty, whether prelates, earls or magnates, offered to accept Stephen and paid homage to him. This indeed was an evil sign, that the whole of England should so suddenly and without delay or struggle, and, as it were, in the twinkling of an eye, submit to Stephen. So, after his coronation at Christmastide, he held his court at London.

In the early twelfth century, the English succession was far from settled, and Henry I himself had always maintained his claim to the kingdom in preference to his eldest brother, Robert, and Robert's son. However, the fact that Stephen, along with much of the English nobility, had sworn an oath to support the Empress as Henry's heiress was uncomfortable for the new king. Matilda of Boulogne never appears to have doubted her husband's title to the throne and she always regarded Stephen as the rightful king, perhaps considering that the crown belonged to its first successful claimant.

Matilda had joined her husband in England by Easter 1136 and she was crowned at Westminster on 22 March of that year before the court moved to Oxford. Matilda used her role as queen to support her husband throughout his reign and their marriage continued to be a happy one, in spite of the difficulties he faced as king. Stephen and Matilda were often described as a partnership in sources, and it appears that their characters complemented each other. Whilst Stephen was kindly and generous, Matilda was described in the *Gesta Stephani* as 'a woman of subtlety and a man's resolution'. Matilda bore Stephen five children and Eustace, William and Mary survived to adulthood. Eustace, the eldest son, was a favourite of his mother, but Matilda loved all her children and her grief at the deaths in infancy of her children Baldwin and Matilda can be seen in the gifts she gave to Holy Trinity, Aldgate, in their memory once she had become queen of England.

Matilda played a major political role during Stephen's reign. Soon after Stephen's coronation in December 1136, David of Scotland, the uncle of both Matilda of Boulogne and the Empress Matilda, invaded England in support of the Empress's claim. Peace was made between the Scottish king and Stephen in February, and it appears that this was linked to Matilda's influence and her imminent coronation. David of Scotland perhaps reflected that he would gain more from favouring Matilda of Boulogne over the Empress at that time, as, in 1136, the Empress was in no position to come to England and claim her crown. The Empress had also been raised in Germany, and David is likely to have had considerably more contact with Matilda of Boulogne over the years and to have been fond of her. Matilda played a significant role in the later peace negotiated between David and Stephen between September 1138 and Easter 1139, and she acted for her husband in the negotiations, being present in person when the terms were ratified at Durham on 9 April 1139. She then personally escorted David's son, Henry, south to London to be invested with the title of Earl of Northumbria by Stephen.

Stephen's reign has been referred to as a period of 'anarchy', and it was certainly a time of turmoil. Although the Empress was initially unable to lay claim to the crown, the threat that she might one day assert her rights hung over both Stephen and Matilda of Boulogne during the last years of the 1130s. With a disputed entitlement to the crown, Stephen found that he could not always rely on the loyalty of his vassals in England, and in 1138, he occupied Hereford in an attempt to assert his authority there. At the same time, Matilda of Boulogne took steps of her own to help secure her husband's crown, and according to Orderic Vitalis,

> The queen besieged Dover with a strong force on the land side, and sent word to her friends and kinsmen and dependants in Boulogne to blockade the foe by sea. The people of Boulogne proved obedient, gladly carried out their lady's commands and, with a great fleet of ships, closed the narrow strait to prevent the garrison receiving any supplies.

Matilda was present at the siege and co-ordinated the attack on the town herself. Faced with attacks on both sides, the castle surrendered, and Matilda entered the town in triumph. In order to ensure that the port remained in Stephen's hands, Matilda appointed her cousin, Pharamus of Boulogne, as castellan of Dover, before hurrying back to join her husband.

The Empress finally arrived in England in September 1139. Matilda of Boulogne immediately began working to secure her husband's grip on the throne, and she used her children's marriages to secure support for the King. It was Matilda who arranged the marriage of her second son, William, to Isabella, the heiress of the Earl of Surrey, a key ally for Stephen. She also personally oversaw the negotiations for the marriage of Eustace to Constance, the sister of Louis VII of France. In February 1140, Matilda and Eustace travelled together to France for the betrothal. At the same time, in return for a large sum of money paid by Matilda, Louis VII invested Eustace as Duke of Normandy. Matilda was too important to Stephen to remain long in France, and in August 1140, she attended a conference at Bath designed to negotiate peace with the Empress. As a mark of his respect for her, Stephen appointed Matilda, along with his brother, the Bishop of Winchester, as his representatives at the conference. Unfortunately, the two opposing parties were unable to agree terms, and both Stephen and Matilda of Boulogne were disappointed as the civil war continued to drag on.

The Empress and Stephen remained fairly evenly matched during the first few years of the civil war, with the Empress controlling the west of England and Stephen the remainder of the country. Early in 1141, however, disaster struck for Stephen at the Battle of Lincoln. According to Henry of Huntingdon, Stephen decided to besiege Lincoln Castle, which belonged to Ranulf, Earl of Chester, an important ally of the Empress. Ranulf was joined by the forces of Robert, Earl of Gloucester, an illegitimate son of Henry I, and the Empress's greatest supporter. On his arrival, it became clear that Stephen would have to give battle, and 'overwhelmed with a flood of cares', he heard Mass before entering into battle with the Empress's army. Early in the battle, the troops on Stephen's flanks fled, leaving him alone with his infantry. According to Henry of Huntingdon, Stephen was encircled and attacked from all sides:

> Thenceforth the battle was seen to rage horribly around the royal defences, helmets and swords gleamed as they clashed, and the dreadful noise re-echoed from the hills and the walls of the city. The cavalry, furiously charging the royal column, slew some and trampled down others, while yet others were dragged away captive. No respite, no breathing-space was given, except in the quarter where the most valiant king had taken his stand and the foe recoiled from the incomparable ferocity of his counter-strokes.

Stephen fought bravely, but his forces were inferior to those of the Empress, and by the end of the day, he was a prisoner, being carried as a captive to Bristol in chains. Matilda of Boulogne recognised that Stephen was unlikely to recover his crown, and the *Gesta Stephani* claims she 'sent envoys to the Countess [of Anjou, i.e., the Empress] and made earnest entreaty for her husband's release from his filthy dungeon and the granting of his son's inheritance, though only that to which he was entitled by her father's will'. Unsurprisingly, given the fact that she had been deprived of her own inheritance by Stephen, the Empress was not disposed to grant him his own lands, nor to suffer the release of a known oath-breaker in return for his promise not to challenge her title to the throne. There was no love lost between Matilda of Boulogne and her cousin, the Empress, and the only response she received to her message was abuse in 'harsh and insulting language'. Matilda of Boulogne also petitioned a number of the leading noblemen in England who, according to the chronicler, John of Worcester went to the Empress and 'offered to give her many hostages, castles, and great riches, if the king were to be set free and allowed to recover his liberty, though not his crown'. This approach also failed, and Matilda of Boulogne set about rebuilding the King's forces. According to Henry of Huntingdon, only Matilda of Boulogne and the captain of her troops, William of Ypres, 'continued to fight against the empress with all their might'. Stephen's cause must have looked hopeless to Matilda, as even her brother-in-law, the Bishop of Winchester, submitted to the Empress as the victor of the civil war.

Matilda retained some support in Kent and Surrey following her husband's imprisonment, and she raised an army there in Eustace's name as heir to the throne. In April 1141, at the Council of Winchester, the Empress was declared ruler of England and made her way slowly towards London, where she intended to be crowned. Whilst she was waiting at Westminster for her ceremonial entry to the city, she became on increasingly bad terms with the Londoners, and Matilda of Boulogne moved her army up the Thames to London. There, she set about negotiating with the Londoners and allied herself with them, causing them to expel the Empress from the city on 24 June 1141. This was a major victory for Matilda of Boulogne, and on her triumphant entry to the capital, she 'bore herself with the valour of a man; everywhere by prayer or price she won over invincible allies'.

Stephen's brother, Henry, Bishop of Winchester, had changed his allegiance to the Empress following his brother's capture at Lincoln. The bishop was the most powerful churchman in England, and whatever her personal opinion of the man who had abandoned his own brother, Matilda of Boulogne was determined to win him back to Stephen's cause, going in person to him at Guildford. According to the *Gesta Stephani*, Matilda 'humbly besought the Bishop of Winchester, legate of all England, to take pity on his imprisoned brother and exert himself for his freedom, that uniting all his efforts with hers he might gain her a husband, the people a king, the kingdom a champion'. Matilda's appeal touched the bishop, who was already contemplating returning to his brother's cause, and he wept as he declared that he would assist her. Following the meeting, the bishop returned to his see at Winchester.

The Empress was furious when she heard of the bishop's betrayal, and she took an army to Winchester in an attempt to capture him, besieging him in his castle. The Empress's forces were led by her leading supporters, King David of Scotland and her half-brothers, Robert of Gloucester and Reginald of Cornwall. When Matilda of Boulogne heard of the siege, she moved her army, augmented with almost one thousand Londoners, to besiege the besiegers at Winchester. Matilda of Boulogne's actions took the Empress by surprise, and whilst she was able to flee, her greatest supporter, Robert of Gloucester, was captured and brought to Matilda of Boulogne. Matilda was jubilant at her victory and had Robert imprisoned in

Rochester Castle whilst she set about negotiating a prisoner exchange. The Empress knew that her cause was lost without her half-brother, and on 1 November 1141, Stephen was finally released from Bristol Castle, leaving Matilda of Boulogne and Eustace behind as sureties for Robert. Stephen then rode to Rochester, where Robert was released after leaving his son as a surety. Robert rode to Bristol, where Matilda of Boulogne and her son were freed. Finally, Matilda and Eustace travelled to Rochester to secure the release of Robert's son, and it was there that Matilda was finally reunited with Stephen.

No record survives of the reunion between Stephen and Matilda, but it must have been an emotional one. Certainly, Stephen appreciated his wife's efforts on his behalf, and soon after he was released from his imprisonment, he bestowed a number of honours on Eustace, something that was designed to please his son's doting mother. According to the *Gesta Stephani*,

> The king, in the presence of the magnates, ceremonially girded with the belt of knighthood his son Eustace, a young man of noble nature, and after most bountifully endowing him with lands and possessions, and giving him the special distinction of a most splendid retinue of knights, advanced him in rank to the dignity of count [of Boulogne].

Stephen also set about trying to recover his position as king, but whilst, at Christmas, he and Matilda were crowned again by the Archbishop of Canterbury, he was never able to assert his authority over the whole of England. Matilda continued to work for Stephen after his release, and in 1142, she held a court at Lens, which suggests that she was visiting her continental lands in order to recruit foreign mercenaries. She was the driving force behind attempts to have Eustace crowned as king during his father's lifetime in order to further secure his succession. From 1150, Stephen made strenuous efforts to achieve this, even sending the Archbishop of York to Rome to obtain papal support for the coronation. This mission was unsuccessful, but Stephen tried again in April 1152 during a Church council in London, attended by Matilda herself. Once again, the bishops refused to recognise Eustace as heir to the throne, to Matilda's disappointment.

As well as being politically ambitious, Matilda became increasingly devoted to the Church as she aged. It was Stephen and Matilda's patronage that led to the establishment of the Templar movement in England, and in 1137, they jointly founded a monastery at Cressing for the order, endowing it with lands inherited by Matilda in England. The couple founded several other religious houses, including one at Longvilliers in 1135, Cowley in 1138 or 1139, and Faversham in 1148. In 1148, Stephen and Matilda established the convent at Lillechurch in order to allow their daughter, Mary, who had been dedicated as a nun in childhood, to become its first abbess. In addition to this, Matilda founded the Hospital of St Katherine by the Tower. Genuine piety played a major role in Matilda's activities, but she also used her gifts for political purposes, and Faversham, for example, was intended to be the family's mausoleum and was part of the conscious promotion of their dynasty, which had also prompted the attempts to crown Eustace as king during his father's lifetime.

Matilda was worn down by the continuing struggle to maintain Stephen's throne, and from around 1147, she went into semi-retirement, basing herself away from Stephen at Canterbury. She may also have been in ill health by this time, as she frequently stayed at St Augustine's Abbey in the city. Matilda remained an important figure, and she attended councils in London in 1151 and April 1152. On her way home from the second of these councils, she stopped to visit her friend Euphemia, Countess of Oxford, at Hedingham in Essex. Whilst there, Matilda suddenly became unwell, and she died on 3 May 1152. As she would have wanted, she was buried at her new foundation of Faversham.

Matilda's death caused Stephen great grief, and it was followed, on 10 August 1153, by the death of the couple's favoured eldest son, Eustace, who was buried beside his mother. Eustace's death saw the end of Stephen and Matilda's dynastic hopes, and the King gave up his attempts to retain the English crown for his own offspring, instead coming to terms with Henry of Anjou, the son of the Empress. Stephen died early in 1154. Stephen and Matilda's second son, William, who made no attempt on the English crown and may have been in ill health, inherited Matilda's county of Boulogne on Eustace's death, but died soon afterwards himself. This left only Abbess Mary to continue Stephen and Matilda's line, and with her accession as Countess of Boulogne, she was abducted from her convent and forced to marry the nobleman Matthew of Flanders. Marriage was not something that Mary desired, and after bearing her husband two daughters, she returned to her convent. Matilda of Boulogne was as powerful and dominant a personality as her cousin and rival, the Empress Matilda, but it was the Empress who would ultimately find herself the victor in the civil war.

The EMPRESS MATILDA (1102-67) was England's first potential queen regnant. She was never crowned but was acknowledged as ruler of England between February and November 1141 and ruled the west of the kingdom for a number of years. She was born on 7 February 1102 at Sutton Courtenay, near Abingdon. She was the eldest child of Henry I and Matilda of Scotland, and her birth was followed a year later by that of William, her only legitimate sibling. Matilda, as the King's only daughter, was a great diplomatic asset to him. According to the *Anglo-Saxon Chronicle*, in 1109, Henry I swore at Westminster to marry his daughter to the Holy Roman Emperor, Henry V. This was an extremely prestigious marriage and the initiative came from Henry V, who was in urgent need of funds. Henry I was excited at the prospect of his daughter becoming an empress, and he provided a large dowry of around 10,000 marks in silver. Matilda left for Germany the following year shortly before her eighth birthday. She must have been apprehensive, and she would have been aware that she was unlikely ever to see her homeland again. According to the chronicler Robert of Torigni, the emperor, 'who having won her hand welcomed her, escorted by famous men, bishops and counts acting as envoys, laden with innumerable presents from both her parents, to his realm, where at Utrecht the following Easter they were betrothed. After the betrothal she was crowned on St James' Day at Mainz by the archbishop of Cologne'. Matilda was still too young for a full marriage, and so, after her arrival in February 1110, she was sent away from her husband to learn the German language and customs.

Matilda, at the age of only eight, is unlikely to have had much idea about what to expect from her husband, and he must have seemed a daunting figure. Henry V was then aged twenty-four and had ruled much of modern Germany since 1106. During his lifetime, he had a rather sinister reputation. Whilst Henry V was still a very young child, his elder brother, Conrad, had rebelled against their father, Henry IV. This had led to Henry IV naming his younger son as his heir in 1098, in exchange for 'a solemn vow, specifically that he would never intrude himself either into the royal power or into the lands of his father while he [the father] was living, except, perchance, by his consent'. This oath meant little to Henry V, and by 1106, the younger man was in open rebellion against his father. The account of Henry IV himself discusses this:

All these oaths were cast aside and handed over to oblivion on the advice of treacherous perjurers and of our mortal enemies. So he was separated from us so completely that, wishing in every way to attack us in our holdings as well as in our person, he made it his constant goal from that hour to deprive us of kingship and life.

Through both military strength and treachery, Henry V secured the throne for himself in his father's lifetime, forcing the older man to abdicate. Henry V's reputation, as a usurper, was in no way helped by his father's suspicious death in captivity later in 1106. In spite of this, he always treated Matilda kindly. In 1114, she was deemed old enough for marriage, and the couple were married at Worms. The wedding ceremony was magnificent and was intended to reflect the glory of both the groom and his young bride. Matilda herself was described at the marriage as beautiful and distinguished, and she rapidly became popular in Germany, being remembered long after her death as 'the good Matilda'. She received a second coronation as empress at St Peter's in Rome in 1117.

During her time in Germany, Matilda gained practical experience of government, and her husband trusted her to act as regent for him on a number of occasions. In 1117, for example, Henry V left Matilda to rule over Italy, and she retained this position until summoned to rejoin him in Lotharingia in 1119. In spite of her abilities as regent, Matilda failed in her primary duty as empress. In the eleven years of her marriage, she bore only one child, a baby that died in its infancy and when Henry V died on 23 May 1125, he left Matilda a childless widow at the age of twenty-three.

By the time she was widowed, Matilda had spent over fifteen years in Germany, and the country had become her home. It is unlikely that she had much memory of England, and her wealth and status in the Holy Roman Empire made her the object of interest of a number of German princes who sought her hand in marriage. Following the death of her brother William in 1120, and her father's subsequent childless marriage to Adeliza, Henry I was adamant that Matilda should return home. She was, at first, reluctant to heed her father's summons, but, eventually, she submitted, perhaps reasoning that the position of heir to England and Normandy was preferable to that of a wealthy, but politically powerless, widow in Germany. No details of Matilda's reunion with her father survive, but it must have been satisfactory, and at the Christmas court at Windsor in 1126, Henry made all those present swear an oath to Matilda, recognising her as his successor. Anxious that Matilda should provide him with grandsons, the following spring, Henry opened marriage negotiations for her with Geoffrey, the fifteen-year-old son of the Count of Anjou.

Matilda, who was eleven years older than Geoffrey and had been the wife of the greatest ruler in Europe, was furious when she heard of the proposed marriage. Henry was determined that the marriage would go ahead and locked her in her room until she submitted. Matilda and Geoffrey were married on 17 June 1128 at Le Mans, but it quickly became apparent that the union was not a success, and in July 1129, after only one year of marriage, Matilda returned to her father in Rouen, seeking a divorce. Personally, the couple were entirely incompatible and they loathed each other, with Matilda always refusing to use the title of 'Countess of Anjou'. Henry I was uncertain about just what to do with his daughter, and in 1131, she accompanied him back to England, where a council was held at Northampton to debate her future. The council decided to send Matilda back to Anjou, and she set out once again to join her husband. This time, the couple were determined to make their marriage work, and both perhaps reasoned that they were unlikely to be granted a divorce and needed to make the best of things instead. The reunion was a partial success, and though the couple always disliked each other, their first son, Henry, was born at Le Mans in March 1133. A second son, Geoffrey, was born in Rouen in 1134, and a third son, William, in 1136. Matilda wept throughout the baptism of her eldest son, and his birth finally took away the stigma of her childlessness. Between 1133 and 1135, Matilda spent most of her time with her father and children in Normandy, receiving only occasional visits from Geoffrey. Later, following the birth of their third son, both felt that they had done enough for the succession and permanently separated.

In spring 1135, Henry quarrelled with Geoffrey and Matilda, who, in spite of her dislike of Geoffrey, knew that she was bound to him and took her sons to join him in Anjou. This proved to be a disaster for her cause in England and Normandy, and she was still in Anjou and heavily pregnant with her third son when word reached her in December 1135 of her father's death. On his deathbed, Henry confirmed Matilda as his heir and she took steps to occupy the Norman border castles that comprised her dowry, remaining on the edge of Normandy whilst she awaited the birth of her son. There was little else that Matilda could do, and within three weeks of her father's death, she had heard that her cousin, Stephen of Blois, had usurped the English throne and had had himself crowned. Matilda was in no position to invade England and was forced to bide her time. In September 1136, Geoffrey invaded Normandy on her behalf and Matilda arrived with troops to join him at Le Sap. Geoffrey's invasion was not a success, and it took him nearly nine years to conquer Normandy and restore Matilda's rights there.

Matilda spent four years in Normandy, biding her time. Finally, in 1139, she was joined by her half-brother, Henry I's favourite illegitimate son, Robert, Earl of Gloucester, who offered her his support. Robert had initially acquiesced to Stephen's accession to the throne but was uncomfortable with the King's treatment of his sister and, by 1139, was ready to act. His support was a godsend for Matilda, and she accepted his aid willingly, always relying on him as her greatest councillor. Matilda and Robert sailed to England in October 1139, landing at Portsmouth with a large army. On their landing, Robert travelled to Bristol whilst Matilda journeyed to visit her stepmother, Adeliza, at Arundel. Following Stephen's siege of the castle, Matilda was given a safe-conduct to travel to Bristol, and she joined her brother there, spending two months in the city receiving homage and dispensing laws as the ruler of England. For fifteen months, there was a war of sieges with little gain on either side. Whilst Stephen controlled the bulk of the kingdom, Matilda was the ruler in the west of England, spending most of 1140 at Gloucester. The turning point came in 1141, when Stephen quarrelled with the powerful Earl of Chester and his brother. They immediately turned towards Matilda, swearing fealty to her as queen. On 2 February 1141, they were attacked by Stephen at Lincoln. Stephen was captured in battle and taken to Matilda, who ordered him to be imprisoned in chains in Bristol Castle.

According to John of Worcester, Matilda 'was ecstatic at this turn of events, having now, as she thought, gained possession of the kingdom, which had been promised to her by oath'. Within weeks of Stephen's capture, Matilda had made a pact with his powerful brother, Henry, Bishop of Winchester, as recorded in the *Gesta Stephani*:

> When they had jointly made a pact of peace and concord he came to meet her in cordial fashion and admitted her into the city of Winchester, and after handing over to her disposal the king's castle and the royal crown, which she had always most eagerly desired, and the treasure the king had left there, though it were scanty, he bade the people, at a public meeting in the market-place of the town, salute her as their lady and their queen.

The council at Winchester was the moment of Matilda's greatest triumph, and the following day, 3 March, 'she was received in Winchester cathedral in ceremonial procession, with the bishop who was also legate, escorting her on the right side and Bernard, Bishop of St David's, on the left'. A few days later, whilst she was staying at Wilton, Matilda received a visit from the Archbishop of Canterbury, who recognised her as England's ruler.

At Winchester, the Bishop and other assembled dignitaries, recognised Matilda as the 'Lady of England'. This title was a recognition of Matilda's right to the throne, and it is unclear whether she ever actually used the title of queen. Matilda usually preferred to be addressed as 'Empress' but, on the majority of her charters between 1141 and 1148, she used the title of 'Lady of the English'. There are two extant charters from 1141 in which Matilda apparently referred to herself as Queen of England. However, these are both copies and must be treated with suspicion. There is evidence that Matilda commissioned a seal calling herself Empress of the Romans and Queen of England. It seems likely that Matilda intended to delay declaring herself Queen of England until after her coronation. In spite of this, during 1141, she was the ruler of England and a queen in all but name.

It took Matilda two months to persuade the Londoners to receive her for her coronation. Whilst she was waiting at Oxford, she was visited by her uncle, King David of Scotland, who came to see his niece crowned. According to the admittedly biased *Gesta Stephani*, Matilda began to allow her position to go to her head, and she arbitrarily annulled any grant that had been made by Stephen, as well as receiving Stephen's erstwhile supporters ungraciously. It was not unnatural for Matilda to wish to punish those who had supported the usurper, but it was not the most tactful approach to take. As a woman in what had always been a man's office, she was at a disadvantage and behaviour that would have been seen as kingly in a man was, in Matilda, considered arrogant. The *Gesta Stephani* claims that, when the King of Scotland, Bishop of Winchester and Robert of Gloucester came to Matilda on bended knee, she refused to rise respectfully, instead receiving them sitting down. She apparently 'repeatedly sent them away contumely, rebuffing them by an arrogant answer and refusing to hearken to their words; and by this time she no longer relied on their advice, as she should have, and had promised them, but arranged everything as she herself thought fit and according to her own arbitrary will'. Matilda's behaviour was heavily censured, and she continued to distance people throughout 1141.

Matilda was finally admitted to London in June 1141, arriving at the head of a large army to a rather muted welcome. She made Westminster her base as she prepared for her coronation. Matilda badly misjudged the mood of the Londoners. According to the *Gesta Stephani*, she alienated the Londoners by making demands for large sums of money. When the representatives of the city refused to pay, Matilda, 'with a grim look, her forehead wrinkled into a frown, every trace of a woman's gentleness removed from her face, blazed into unbearable fury. Saying that many times the people of London had made very large contributions to the king, that they had lavished their wealth on strengthening him and weakening her'. Matilda was furious at the Londoners' years of support for Stephen, but her reaction was counterproductive, and the leading men of the city began to correspond with Stephen's queen, Matilda of Boulogne, in Kent. On 24 June, as Matilda was sitting down to dinner, a mob came streaming out of the city, and she was forced to flee to Oxford, leaving her possessions behind. This was the end of Matilda's hopes of securing a coronation and, soon afterwards, with the capture of Robert of Gloucester at Winchester, she was forced to release Stephen from captivity and retreat to her powerbase in the west. Following 1141, the aim of Matilda's campaign changed markedly, and she came to accept that she was never likely to win the crown for herself, instead focusing her efforts on keeping her claim alive for her young son, Henry.

During Lent 1142 Matilda held a council at Devizes with her supporters, and it was agreed that she would have to send to Geoffrey in Normandy for aid. Geoffrey sent a response saying that he would deal only with Robert of Gloucester in person, and Matilda's half-brother crossed the Channel to confer with her husband. This was the opportunity that Stephen had been waiting for, and whilst Matilda was staying in Oxford castle, he moved to besiege her. During the three month siege, supplies ran dangerously low, and this led to one of the most famous incidents of Matilda's career. The *Gesta Stephani* records that, as winter set in and the people in the castle grew increasingly hungry and desperate, Matilda 'left the castle by night, with three knights of ripe judgement to accompany her, and went about six miles on foot, by very great exertions on the part of herself and her companions, through the snow and ice'. Matilda and her companions wore white cloaks as camouflage against the snow as they slipped past the lines of Stephen's soldiers, and it must have been a tense and exhausting journey as they crossed the frozen Thames before reaching Wallingford that night.

Matilda returned to Devizes following her escape from Oxford. Robert of Gloucester, who had returned from Normandy with nothing from Geoffrey but Matilda's nine-year-old son Henry, settled in Bristol with the boy whilst Matilda continued to use Devizes as her base and ruled the west of England from there. Matilda minted coins in her name at Bristol and Cardiff, as well as intermittently at Oxford and Wareham. She controlled the appointments of sheriffs in her Gloucestershire heartland and made grants of royal lands. In spite of this, Matilda knew that she was fighting a cause that she could not win, and finally, in 1148, judging her son old enough to take on her claim, she sailed to Normandy, never to return to England.

Matilda settled in Rouen in Normandy, taking an active interest in the politics of the duchy. In 1151, Geoffrey died suddenly, leaving Matilda a widow for the second time. The couple had learned to tolerate each other, but it is unlikely that she mourned his loss. In November 1153, the civil war finally came to an end with Stephen's recognition of Henry as his heir, and Matilda must have been jubilant: she had spent nearly twenty years working for the recognition of her rights in England, and the succession of her son had finally been secured. When Stephen died early the following year, Matilda did not accompany Henry to England for his coronation, perhaps aware of her controversial reputation there.

Matilda spent the rest of her life in Rouen, acting as Henry's unofficial regent in Normandy. Henry respected his mother's political judgement, and she had a great deal of influence over him. She is known to have dissuaded him from invading Ireland in order to provide his brother William with a kingdom, and in joint charters issued by Henry and Matilda, Henry always allowed his mother to be named first, in recognition of her prior rights to Normandy and England. Matilda was acknowledged as ruler of Normandy in a letter from Louis VII of France in 1164.

As Matilda aged, her influence over Henry began to wane. She advised against Thomas Becket's appointment as Archbishop of Canterbury but was overruled by Henry. She was still known for her power to persuade Henry, and in 1164, when Becket was exiled by the king, he appealed to Matilda to intercede for him. A surviving letter of Matilda's outlines her response to this request, and it is clear that she was no friend of the Archbishop:

My lord Pope sent to me, enjoining me, for the remission of my sins, to interfere to renew peace and concord between you and the king, my son, and to try to reconcile you to him. You, as you well know, have asked the same thing from me; wherefore, with the more goodwill, for the honour of God and the Holy church, I have begun and carefully treated of that affair. But it seems a very hard thing to the king, as well as to his barons and council, seeing he so loved and honoured you, and appointed you lord of his whole kingdom and of all his lands, and raised you to the highest honours in the land, believing he might trust you rather than any other; and especially so, because he declares that you have, as far as you could, roused his whole kingdom against him; nor was it your fault that you did not disinherit him by main force. Therefore I send you my faithful servant, Archdeacon Laurence, that by him I may know your will in these affairs, and what sort of disposition you entertain towards my son, and how you intend to conduct yourself, if it should happen that he fully grants my petition and prayer on your behalf. One thing I plainly tell you, that you cannot recover the king's favour; except by great humility and most evident moderation. However what you intend to do in this matter signify to me by my messenger and your letters.

Matilda, reluctantly, attempted to heal the rift between her son and his erstwhile friend, but she was unsuccessful, and the conflict led ultimately to the Archbishop's murder.

As well as maintaining her political interests, Matilda became increasingly pious in her later years, and most of her charters after 1154 were made in favour of Norman monastic houses. Her main patronage was reserved for the monks of Bec, and she was a great benefactor to them. She died in Rouen on 10 September 1167, having remained active to the end and, in accordance with her last wishes, was buried in the abbey of Bec-Hellouin.

Matilda is remembered as the woman who so nearly won the English crown, and she can be considered, to some extent, England's first queen regnant. She was unable to subvert the usual role accorded to women, and her famous epitaph 'great by birth, greater by marriage, greatest in her offspring, here lies the daughter, wife and mother of Henry' sums up the way that she continued to be viewed in relation to her male kin. Matilda's greatest achievement was in keeping her claim to the English throne alive, and the succession of Henry II and his Plantagenet dynasty in England was due to her persistence. Every reigning monarch of England after 1153 has been a direct descendant of the Empress Matilda and she, and her fellow Norman queens, helped shape the role of queen as it developed into the later medieval period.

4

The Plantagenet Queens

Henry II, the first Plantagenet king, claimed the throne through his mother, the Empress Matilda. She, in turn, was the daughter of Matilda of Scotland, the woman who brought the blood of the Anglo-Saxon kings into the Norman royal family. Henry II and his sons ruled over a territory larger than any other English kings either before or after them: the Angevin Empire. The early Plantagenet kings found themselves constantly drawn into continental wars or otherwise busy on the Continent. As a result of this, the office of queen consort during the period reached the pinnacle of its power, and queens were frequently called upon to rule as regents. Between 1154 and 1399, whilst the Plantagenet kings sat on the throne, there were no English queen regnants, but there were many powerful and prominent queens.

The first Plantagenet queen was one of the most prominent women of the medieval period, and she was easily a match for her husband, Henry II. ELEANOR OF AQUITAINE (1122-1204) was the wife of two kings, the mother of a further two, and an important hereditary ruler in her own right. She was the most famous woman of her day and is still widely known and remembered today.

Eleanor of Aquitaine was the heiress of one of the richest fiefdoms of medieval Europe, the duchy of Aquitaine and the county of Poitou. Eleanor's grandfather, Duke William IX, had created a cultured and literary court, and he dominated Eleanor's early childhood. Some years before Eleanor's birth, he had caused a scandal by abducting the beautiful Viscountess of Châtellerault and installing her as his official mistress, forcing his wife to enter a nunnery. The Viscountess persuaded her lover to marry his son to her daughter and William X and Aénor of Châtellerault were married in 1121. They had three children: Eleanor, born in 1122, followed by Petronilla and William Aigret. In 1130, both Eleanor's mother and her brother died suddenly. These deaths were followed in 1137 by William X, and Eleanor became Duchess of Aquitaine and Countess of Poitou.

On his deathbed, William X placed his daughters under the guardianship of Louis VI of France. This was a great opportunity for Louis, and on 18 June 1137, his sixteen-year-old son, also named Louis, set out with a large escort for Aquitaine to marry Eleanor. Eleanor had no input into the choice of her husband. Politically, the match was a good one, but personally, the couple were ill-suited. Eleanor completely dominated her husband after their marriage on 25 July 1137. Louis had been born a second son and raised for a career in the Church, something that had left him deeply pious, but entirely unprepared for the political world that he was forced to enter on the death of his elder brother. Eleanor was deeply unimpressed with her young husband, although Louis was overawed by his fiery and beautiful wife.

Louis VI died on 1 August 1137, leaving the throne to Eleanor's husband and obliging the couple to travel at once to Paris. Eleanor found Paris a very poor substitute for the opulence that she had known in her childhood, and the royal palace, in particular, was in a bad state of disrepair. She was crowned queen of France at Christmas 1137, although she was given little role in government, appearing only rarely in the charters of Louis's reign.

Whilst she had no defined political role, Eleanor was able to influence Louis. In 1141, for example, he invaded the county of Toulouse on her behalf, a territory claimed by her family. The campaign was a disaster, but it was not the last military exploit that the French king carried out for Eleanor. In 1142, Eleanor's sister, Petronilla, caused a scandal by marrying the nobleman Raoul de Vermandois, who then sent his existing wife, the niece of the Count of Champagne, home to her family in disgrace. The Count of Champagne appealed to the Pope for his niece's reinstatement, and Eleanor, who threw her support behind her sister, persuaded Louis to invade Champagne in January 1143. This campaign proved to be not just a military disaster, but also a personal one for Louis: when his army reached the town of Vitry in Champagne, the church there was accidentally set alight, burning those who had taken shelter inside to death. Following the disaster, Louis's captains found him in a trance-like state. A further breakdown in the summer of 1143 caused him to begin wearing monastic habits and spend hours at prayer. The trouble in Eleanor's marriage dates to this time, and she declared that 'she had married a monk, not a king'.

Eleanor already had reason to feel discontented with her marriage. By 1144, she had become worried by her failure to conceive a child. In June, she met with the churchman Bernard of Clairvaux privately to ask for his assistance in lifting the sentence of excommunication that hung over Petronilla and Raoul de Vermondois. Instead of offering to help, Bernard criticised Eleanor for involving herself in politics, and she promptly burst into tears, saying that she did so only because she had no child. Bernard then offered a deal: if she stopped interfering in politics, he would ask God to send her a child. Eleanor duly did as she was asked, and in 1145, she bore a daughter, Marie. The child's sex was a disappointment, but she was, at least, proof that Eleanor could bear a child. Her difficulties in conceiving appear to have been due more to her husband than to herself with Louis able to consummate his three marriages only rarely, and then often only after pressure from the Church.

Louis's piety increased, and at Easter, the court gathered at Vezelay, where he promised to undertake a crusade. His decision to take the cross was intended to be a great ceremonial occasion, and according to the chronicler Odo of Deuil, Bernard of Clairvaux 'mounted the platform accompanied by the king, who was wearing the cross; and when heaven's instrument [Bernard] poured forth the dew of the divine word, as he was wont, with loud outcry people on every side began to demand crosses'. Eleanor also did her bit for recruitment; as soon as her husband had taken the cross, she and her ladies appeared, dressed as Amazons, and rode through the crowd, encouraging those assembled to join the crusade. The recruitment drive continued right up to the moment of departure, and before the army set out, there was a great ceremony at St Denis at which Louis received a banner and a pilgrim's wallet, accompanied by a personal blessing from the Pope. Eleanor was once again right in the centre of events, and Odo of Deuil tells us that 'the crowds and the king's wife and his mother, who nearly perished because of their tears and the heat could not endure the delay'.

Eleanor's enthusiasm for the crusade was as genuine as Louis's, although, unlike her pious husband, it is likely that she saw it as a means to escape the tedium of her daily life in Paris.

It was not unusual for women to accompany their husband's on crusade and the chronicler William of Newburgh believed that the impetus behind Eleanor's participation came from Louis himself:

> Initially she had so emmeshed and captivated the heart of the young man with the charm of her beauty and that when he was about to embark on that most celebrated expedition his over-urgent longing for his young wife led him to decide that she should certainly not be left at home, but should set out with him to the wars.

It is difficult to imagine Louis VII having an over-urgent longing for anything other than the Church, and it was also cruelly suggested that he did not trust his wife enough to leave her behind.

Louis and Eleanor followed the route that their ally, the Holy Roman Emperor Conrad, had taken some months before, breaking their journey in Constantinople. Eleanor and the Byzantine Empress Irene corresponded during the journey to Constantinople and, upon their arrival there, Eleanor and Louis were entertained lavishly. They were taken to visit shrines and other sites, as well as invited to banquets in their honour. Eleanor was impressed by the city. Odo of Deuil comments on Constantinople:

> In every respect she exceeds moderation; for, just as she surpasses other cities in wealth, so, too, does she surpass them in vice. Also, she possesses many churches unequal to Santa Sophia in size but equal to it in beauty, which are to be marvelled at for their beauty and their many saintly relics. Those who had the opportunity entered these places, some to see the sights and others to worship faithfully.

The presence of an army encamped outside his capital was not entirely to the taste of the Byzantine emperor, and he made it clear that his guests were expected to leave as soon as possible. The French set out in high spirits and were disconcerted to hear, soon after leaving Constantinople, that the German army had been decimated in the Holy Land. In November 1147, the Holy Roman Emperor, fleeing the ruins of his army, joined the French, and Louis and Eleanor had no choice but to continue onwards towards Antioch.

In order to reach Antioch, it was necessary to cross Mount Cadmos, where the Germans had sustained their heavy defeat. Eleanor rode separately from Louis, in the vanguard of her army, which was led by one of her own vassals. On the day of the crossing, the vanguard, which carried little luggage, quickly reached the proposed campsite. Anxious to cross the mountain as quickly as possible, they decided to press on. This proved to be a disaster for the rear of the army, which was led by Louis. His soldiers, arriving at the original campsite only as night was falling, were horrified to find that the vanguard was nowhere in sight. As darkness set in, they were attacked by the Turks, causing heavy losses. The royal guard was killed and Louis, who fought bravely, only escaped because he was not recognised in his simple clothes. He spent the night hiding in a tree, before limping over the mountain to join the vanguard in the morning. Eleanor was later blamed for the ambush, with claims that her luggage hampered the army's progress.

Eleanor was relieved to finally reach Antioch on 19 March 1148 and spent ten days there in luxury. Antioch was ruled by her uncle, Raymond of Aquitaine, her father's younger brother, who had married the heiress to the principality. Raymond, like all the male members of Eleanor's family, was tall and handsome and, unlike Louis, had a reputation as a soldier. Eleanor found him fascinating, spending a great deal of time in his company. This caused comment, and according to one contemporary, John of Salisbury, whilst the French remained in Antioch

> to console, heal and revive the survivors from the wreck of the army, the attentions paid by the prince to the queen, and his constant, indeed almost continuous, conversation with her, aroused the king's suspicions. They were greatly strengthened when the queen wished to remain behind, although the king was preparing to leave, and the prince made every effort to keep her, if the king would give him consent. And when the king made haste to tear her away, she mentioned their kinship, saying it was not lawful for them to remain together as man and wife, since they were related in the fourth and fifth degrees.

It is not impossible that Eleanor and her uncle were lovers, and the scandal remained with her throughout her lifetime. However, she stayed in Antioch for only ten days, and it seems more likely that she found a sympathetic confidant in her uncle and finally decided to end her loveless marriage. The consanguinity between Eleanor and Louis had already been mentioned before they left France, and it had been suggested that this could be the reason for their lack of sons. Eleanor, who had no desire to continue following Louis's disastrous crusade, or even remain as his wife, seized upon this as a way of securing a divorce. Louis did not know how to respond to Eleanor's request, but his servants persuaded him that it would shame him if he left Antioch without her, and when it was time to travel to Jerusalem, she was bundled along against her will.

Eleanor remained in disgrace throughout her time in Jerusalem. It is a measure of the estrangement between her and Louis that, when they finally set sail for France, in April 1149, they sailed in separate ships. Louis, faced with Eleanor's coldness towards him, agreed to consider the state of their marriage, and both he and Eleanor broke their journey to visit the Pope at Tusculum. To Eleanor's horror, the Pope dismissed her concerns about the marriage, taking it upon himself to reconcile them. According to John of Salisbury, 'this ruling plainly delighted the king, for he loved the queen passionately, in an almost childish way'. The Pope even went so far as to prepare a special bed in which the couple were to cement their reunion, leading to the birth of a second daughter, Alix, in the summer of 1150. Eleanor was nonplussed by the Pope's enthusiasm for her marriage, but the birth of another daughter did prove something of a blessing to her, as, soon after Alix's birth, even Louis's council began to suggest that he take a new wife who could give him a son.

For Eleanor, the situation in Paris remained unsatisfactory until August 1151 when Geoffrey, Count of Anjou, and his son, Henry FitzEmpress, arrived to perform homage for Normandy. Henry was over ten years younger than Eleanor and he was not handsome, being stocky with a large head and a reddish, freckled, complexion. He compared favourably to Louis though, being an active and energetic ruler, unlike the monkish Louis. It is improbable that Eleanor and Henry had the privacy to commit adultery in Paris, but during the visit, they agreed to marry once Eleanor was free. A contemporary, Gerald of Wales, commented that Henry 'basely stole Queen Eleanor from his liege lord, Louis, king of the French, and then married her'.

Following Henry's departure from Paris, Eleanor again requested a divorce. After fifteen years of sonless marriage, Louis was prepared to consider the matter, and on 21 March 1152, their marriage was annulled on the grounds of consanguinity. The separation was amicable, with Louis retaining custody of their two daughters. He was entirely oblivious to Eleanor's plans for the future and allowed her to return home to Aquitaine without attempting to assert any control over her lands or freedom.

Henry arrived secretly in Poitiers in mid-May, and he and Eleanor were married. The marriage was not a love match and was solely based on political considerations: Eleanor was the greatest heiress in Europe, and Henry, who had already conquered Normandy, was close to victory in the civil war in England. The marriage was soon successful, and on 17 August 1153, Eleanor gave birth to her first son, William. For Eleanor, at thirty-one, this was a major triumph and further joy followed soon after with the death of King Stephen. Eleanor and William joined Henry in Rouen in June 1154, sailing for England in December. The couple were crowned together at Westminster on 19 December 1154, and in February 1155, Eleanor bore her second son, Henry. Henry II, who was often absent from England, relied on Eleanor to fulfil a political role, leaving her as regent in 1156 when he crossed to Normandy. Eleanor performed the role again in 1158, and Henry had full confidence in her abilities.

Although Eleanor was allowed a defined political role for the first time in her life during her marriage to Henry, her main activity was childbearing. To his parents' grief, William died in 1156, but in June of that year, Eleanor bore a daughter, Matilda. Her birth was followed at Oxford in September 1157 by that of Richard, with Geoffrey being born in September 1158. Daughters, Eleanor and Joanna were born in 1161 and 1165 respectively, and Eleanor's last child, John, was born on Christmas Eve in 1166. After years of childlessness and disappointment, Eleanor was delighted in her children, and of the eight she bore Henry, only William died in infancy. Richard was always Eleanor's favourite and she named him as the heir to Aquitaine at his birth.

In the early years of their marriage, Eleanor and Henry worked together as an effective team in ruling their empire but personal relations between them soured quickly. Henry was unfaithful and began his most long-lasting affair, with Rosamund Clifford, in around 1165. That Christmas was the first of their marriage that Eleanor and Henry spent apart, with Eleanor at Angers and Henry at Oxford. There was something of a reconciliation at Easter 1166, when Eleanor conceived her youngest child. She was again alone at Christmas 1166. There were no further reconciliations between the couple, and from mid-1166, they lived apart.

Eleanor spent 1167 preparing for her daughter Matilda's marriage to the Duke of Saxony, and in September, she escorted her to Dover. That Christmas, Eleanor informed Henry that she had decided to return to Aquitaine, a move that was, in effect, an informal separation. Henry agreed to this and Eleanor departed for Poitiers, accompanied by several of her children. She spent the years 1168 to 1173 ruling Aquitaine personally, and this may have been the happiest time of her life. She was visited by all her children except Alix and John, and even her eldest daughter, Marie, Countess of Champagne, spent time with her mother, with an affection developing between the two women, who were virtual strangers.

In spite of her personal happiness, animosity continued to grow between Eleanor and Henry. In 1170, Henry succeeded in having their eldest son, young Henry, crowned as his heir at Westminster, an event to which Eleanor was not invited. Like Eleanor, Henry was very fond of their children, but he was unable to see that they were growing up and needed their independence. This led to a growing resentment between Henry and his elder three sons, and in April 1173, they rose against him. Eleanor was the ringleader in this revolt, and when Henry summoned her to join him, at Easter 1173, she refused to come. The Archbishop of Rouen threatened Eleanor with excommunication if she persisted in her refusal, but she remained in Aquitaine. By June, the rebellion had spread throughout Henry's French lands. In August, he struck back, and Eleanor found herself cut off from her sons and other allies at Poitiers as Henry marched towards her. A few weeks later, she was captured trying to escape to France dressed as a man. Henry brought Eleanor back to England as a prisoner, ordering that she be kept closely confined at Salisbury castle.

Eleanor's fortunes reached their lowest ebb in 1173, and she spent the rest of Henry's reign as a prisoner: sixteen long years. Though some news reached her in her prison, she was effectively cut off from the world. In 1179, Louis died. Whilst Eleanor is unlikely to have grieved for him, news of his death must have reminded her of her own mortality. A bigger blow came in June 1183 with the death of her eldest surviving son, Henry, the Young King. According to the chronicler Roger de Hoveden, the Young King had remained in rebellion against his father, and in 1183, finding himself short of funds, he stripped the tomb of St Andemar at the monastery of Saint Mary de Roche Andemar and carried away the treasures for his own personal use. The Young King's contemporaries saw his death as the judgement of God, as he fell dangerously ill soon after his attack on the tomb. Aware that he was dying, he sent for his father, but Henry refused to come, understandably fearing treachery. As a sign of his repentance, he confessed his sins and put on a hair shirt before ordering that a cord be tied around his neck. As a final act of penitence, he was laid on a floor strewn with ashes before dying. When Henry heard the news of his son's death, he burst into tears and threw himself on the ground with grief. Eleanor and Henry's grief was further increased in 1186 when their third surviving son, Geoffrey, was killed in a tournament in Paris.

The Young King's last request was that his father show his mother mercy. Henry heeded this, and the conditions of Eleanor's imprisonment eased somewhat as the years went on. In October 1183, for example, Eleanor was brought to Normandy to take possession of certain castles that were disputed by France. Although she remained a prisoner, she was able to spend six months in the company of her daughter, Matilda, and on her return to England, her daughter visited her. At Lent 1185, Eleanor was again summoned to Normandy by Henry in order to receive the surrender of Aquitaine from Richard. Henry, bewildered by the hostility directed at him by his sons, was by then already worn down by the years of struggle, and during the winter of 1188 and 1189, Richard was in open rebellion with Philip Augustus, the young king of France. By July 1189, Henry was finally defeated by his son. He was also in ill health, and when, as part of the terms of his surrender, he received a list of those who had rebelled against him, he was heartbroken to see his youngest, and favourite son, John, at the top of the list. With this revelation, Henry II turned his face to the wall and died.

Eleanor did not mourn Henry, and she welcomed his death for the change that it brought to her circumstances. Her favourite son, Richard, succeeded unchallenged and immediately sent word to England that Eleanor should be set free and appointed to act as regent. Eleanor immediately went on a progress throughout the kingdom, promoting her son's rule, as Roger de Hoveden recounts:

[She] moved her royal court from city to city, and from castle to castle, just as she thought proper; and sending messengers throughout all the counties of England, ordered that all captives should be liberated from prison and confinement, for the good of the soul of Henry, her lord; inasmuch as, in her own person, she had learnt by experience that confinement is distasteful to mankind, and that it is a most delightful refreshment to the spirits to be liberated therefrom.

This was a cause close to Eleanor's heart, and it also made Richard, who was something of an unknown quantity in England, very popular.

Richard landed at Portsmouth on 13 August 1189 and met Eleanor at Winchester. They travelled slowly towards London, where Eleanor had arranged a grand coronation at Westminster Abbey, which was held on 3 September. Richard had little knowledge of England, and he relied upon Eleanor to help govern his new kingdom. He also had no intention of remaining in England for long and quickly set about raising money to fund his plans to go on crusade.

Eleanor's release also saw her reunited with her youngest son, John, whom she had not seen since his infancy. When Richard was ready to leave for the crusade, he obtained an oath from John that he would not enter England for three years. Eleanor was determined that John should not be disadvantaged, and at her express request, Richard agreed that John could be released from his oath. Soon after Richard left for the Holy Land in December 1189, Eleanor set out for Navarre to fetch a bride for Richard. She and the selected bride, Berengaria of Navarre, travelled together to Sicily, where Eleanor left her new daughter-in-law with her son before hurrying back to England, where her presence was badly needed.

Eleanor's appeal for Richard to release John from his oath proved to be a costly mistake, as, soon after Richard left, John began to call himself the king's heir and had himself appointed as the supreme governor of England. Eleanor landed at Portsmouth on 11 February 1192. As soon as he heard of her arrival, John ordered that a ship be prepared so that he could flee to Philip Augustus in France, but Eleanor swiftly prevented him. According to Richard of Devizes,

> His mother, however, fearing that the light-minded youth might be going to attempt something, by the counsels of the French, against his lord and brother, with an anxious mind tried in every way she could to prevent her son's proposed journey. Her maternal heart was moved and pained when she called to mind the condition of her older sons and the premature deaths of both of them because of their sins.

Eleanor continued saying 'with all her strength she wanted to make sure that faith would be kept between her youngest sons, at least, so that their mother might die more happily than had their father, who had gone before them'. She called four great councils, at Windsor, Oxford, London and Winchester and, with tears and pleas to the noblemen assembled, obtained John's promise to remain in England whilst Richard was away.

Eleanor took control of the government on her return to England. She hoped that Richard's absence would only be brief, so the news, in January 1193, that Richard had been captured on his way home from the crusade was devastating. Eleanor dispatched the Abbots of Boxley and Robertsbridge to Germany to find out where Richard was being held, and from them, she learned that he had been handed over to the Holy Roman Emperor, Henry VI. Eleanor called a council at St Albans in June 1193 to discuss the terms of Richard's release and to appoint officers to collect the ransom demanded. She threw herself into securing Richard's release and personally selected hostages from amongst the nobility to be sent to Germany.

Eleanor also directly appealed to the Pope for help. Two of her letters survive, and they show just what a remarkable character the queen was:

> To the reverend Father and Lord Celestine, by the Grace of God, the supreme Pontiff, Eleanor; in God's anger, Queen of England, Duchess of Normandy, Countess of Anjou, begs him to show himself to be a father to a pitiable mother. I had decided to remain quiet in case a fullness of heart and a passionate grief might elicit some word against the chief of priests which was somewhat less than cautious, and I was therefore accused of insolence and arrogance. Certainly grief is not that different from insanity while it is inflamed with its own force. It does not recognise a master, is afraid of no ally, it has no regard for anyone, and it does not spare them – not even you.
>
> So no-one should be surprised if the modesty of my words is sharpened by the strength of my grief – I am mourning for a loss that is not private; but my personal grief cannot be comforted

– it is set deep in the heart of my spirit. The arrows of the Lord are truly directed against me, and their anger will drain my spirit. Races which have been torn apart, peoples which have been shattered, provinces which have been stripped, in general the whole western church which is worn out with deep sorrow, they are all beseeching you in a spirit which has been ground down and humiliated, you whom God established above the races and kingdoms in the fullness of His power.

Please listen to the cry of the afflicted, for our troubles have multiplied beyond number; and you cannot conceal those troubles in as much as they are a mark of criminality and disgrace, since you are the Vicar of Christ Crucified, Peter's successor, the Priest of Christ, the Lord's Anointed one, even a God over Pharaohs. Father, may your face provide a judgement, may your eyes see impartially, the prayers of the people depend on your decision and on the mercy of your see; unless your hands seize justice more quickly, the complete tragedy of this evil event will rebound on to you.'

Eleanor's first letter continued at length, using allusions from the Bible and from history to demonstrate both her grief and her need for the Pope to intervene and help secure Richard's release. When her first letter failed to have the desired effect, she drafted a second, speaking of the conflict and misfortune that had afflicted her sons:

My insides have been torn out of me, my family has been carried off, it has rolled past me; the Young King and the earl of Brittany [Eleanor's son, Geoffrey] sleep in the dust – their mother is so ill-fated she is forced to live, so that without cure she is tortured by the memory of the dead. As some comfort, I still have two sons, who are alive today, but only to punish me, wretched and condemned. King Richard is detained in chains; his brother John is killing the people of the prisoner's kingdom with his sword, he is ravaging the land with fires.

Eleanor received little help from the Pope, but by 1194, the ransom had been raised and she and the Archbishop of Rouen were summoned by the Emperor to bring the ransom to Speyer. In late January 1194, Richard was released, and Eleanor and her son returned home in triumph. It was around this time that Eleanor also began to feel her age, and content that Richard was secure on his throne, she retired to Fontrevault Abbey in Aquitaine, where she hoped to live quietly in retirement. Eleanor rarely appears in sources between 1194 and 1199, and she lived a secluded and religious life.

Even at the age of seventy-eight, Eleanor did not entirely cut herself off from the world, and in April 1199, when she received word that Richard was lying dangerously wounded at Chalus, she travelled day and night to be with him. He was beyond help when she arrived, and he died in her arms on 6 April 1199, having named John as his successor. This was the biggest blow of Eleanor's life, but she did not allow herself to collapse with grief and, instead, threw herself into securing the throne for John. Eleanor's son, Geoffrey, had left a son, Arthur of Brittany, and Arthur, as the son of the elder brother claimed the throne in preference to his uncle. Eleanor, who supported her youngest son, advised him to go at once to Chinon to secure the royal treasury. John then crossed to England, where he was crowned on 27 May, whilst Eleanor remained on the Continent, making a tour of her lands. In mid-June 1199, she travelled to Tours, where she did homage in person to Philip Augustus for Aquitaine in order to ensure that Arthur could make no claim to her duchy.

Eleanor was deeply involved in the negotiations for a truce between John and Philip Augustus shortly after Christmas 1199. As part of the terms of the truce, it was agreed that John would provide a bride for Philip's son and Eleanor accordingly set out on the long journey to Castile to select one of the daughters of her daughter, Eleanor, the Queen of Castile. This was an arduous journey for a woman approaching her eightieth birthday, but she was at least able to spend some months in Castile meeting her grandchildren and reacquainting herself with her daughter. Eleanor selected her youngest granddaughter, Blanche, and the pair set off towards Normandy. Age finally caught up with Eleanor, and whilst she had hoped to escort her granddaughter all the way to Normandy for her marriage, she was forced to admit defeat, leaving Blanche with her escorts and travelling instead to Fontrevault for some much needed rest.

Eleanor's story did not end with her return to Fontrevault. Whilst John had secured his throne through his alliance with Philip, Arthur of Brittany remained a threat. In May 1202, Eleanor decided to travel to Poitiers to aid John in his war against his nephew. When Arthur learned that his grandmother had left Fontrevault, he pursued her, and Eleanor found herself besieged in the flimsy Castle of Mirebeau. By the time John reached Mirebeau, Eleanor and her retinue were trapped in the keep with the rest of the castle occupied by Arthur and his men. John swept into Mirebeau, capturing Arthur and winning what was to be his only victory on the Continent. Eleanor was relieved to see her son, and they had a conference together before she gladly returned to Fontrevault. Given Arthur's attack on her, it is unlikely that she was sympathetic about his fate. He disappeared into John's dungeon and was probably murdered soon afterwards.

Eleanor never emerged from her third period of retirement at Fontrevault, and at some point in 1204, she slipped quietly into a coma, dying on 1 April 1204 at the age of eighty-two. She was one of the longest-lived and most active of all the English queens, and she became a legend in her own lifetime. She entirely overshadowed her daughter-in-law, Berengaria of Navarre.

With the exception of Sophia Dorothea of Celle, who was never recognised as queen, BERENGARIA OF NAVARRE (c. 1165/70-1230) was the only English queen never to actually visit England. Though she was the wife of Richard I 'the Lionheart', her marriage, which began with such great promise, was a failure. Berengaria was the eldest daughter of King Sancho VI of Navarre, a kingdom that lay to the south of Aquitaine, and his wife, Sanchia of Castile. Her date of birth is nowhere recorded, but an analysis of her skeleton suggested a date of around 1165-1170. Berengaria was educated and was good at languages, speaking Castilian, Basque and Latin. Following her mother's death in 1179, Berengaria took on something of the queen's role at court, and this may account for the fact that no marriage was, at first, arranged for her. In recognition of this, in 1185, Berengaria's father gave her independent standing at court with the grant of a fiefdom.

Richard I succeeded his father as king of England in 1189. He had been betrothed since childhood to Alais of France, but both he and his mother, Eleanor of Aquitaine, were determined not to allow the marriage. Contemporary sources suggest that Richard was suspicious of Alais's virtue, and there were rumours that she had been his father's mistress. Whatever the truth of this, Richard had no intention of marrying Alais, and it fell to his mother to organise an alternative marriage. Eleanor's choice of Berengaria made sound political sense, guaranteeing a friendly neighbour to Aquitaine during Richard's absence on crusade. There were also links between the two families. Richard was a good friend of Berengaria's brother, and her father had been entertained by Henry II at Limoges in 1172.

Berengaria's father was flattered at the suggestion of the match, and he entertained Eleanor lavishly when she arrived in Navarre in September 1190. Eleanor was in a hurry to supply Richard with a bride before he sailed for the Holy Land, and after only a short visit, she and Berengaria set out to join him. Berengaria's thoughts on the betrothal do not survive, but she must have been in awe of her famous mother-in-law, and she was never able to move out of Eleanor's shadow. The *Gesta Regis Ricardi* states that Richard 'was attracted by her graceful manner and high birth, he had desired her very much for a long time – since he was count of Poitou'. Richard competed in a tournament in Navarre before he became king, and the couple may have met then. According to legend, Richard was captivated by Berengaria but was unable to marry her at the time due to his engagement to Alais. Given the later disinterest shown by Richard towards Berengaria, a love affair seems unlikely, and Berengaria was apparently no beauty, with one contemporary, Richard of Devizes, commenting that she was 'a maiden more prudent than pretty'. Richard was probably bisexual, with a preference for male partners, and Berengaria was never able to capture his interest.

After leaving Navarre, the party set out across the Alps and travelled through Italy towards Sicily. They arrived in Brindisi in March 1191, where Richard sent ships to bring his mother and fiancée to Reggio. Richard travelled in person to meet them and escorted them to Messina. He was satisfied with Berengaria, and his mother left soon afterwards, leaving Berengaria under the chaperonage of Richard's widowed sister, Joanna, Queen of Sicily. Since Berengaria's arrival coincided with Lent, it was decided that the marriage would occur after Easter, when the couple had reached the Holy Land.

Richard was eager to set out for the Holy Land, and on 10 April 1191, his two-hundred-strong fleet set sail. According to Richard of Devizes, in the first rank of the fleet sailed three ships, 'in one of which were the queen of Sicily and the Navarrese maiden, perhaps still a virgin'. The crossing was an ordeal and a number of ships were driven by storms onto the coast of Cyprus. Berengaria's own ship, which was driven into the port of Limassol, cast anchor and waited for Richard, with everyone on board uncertain as to whether it was safe to land. The *Gesta Regis Ricardi* explains that they 'had not dared to go on shore because they did not know the state of the country and they were afraid of the cruelty and treachery of the emperor'. They were right to be concerned. News of their presence reached the Emperor of Cyprus, who resolved to seize the ship and take the occupants captive. The emperor sent a message to the two queens, telling them that they could come to shore in safety and sending them presents of food and wine in an attempt to tempt them to land. Joanna and Berengaria were troubled and 'they began to waver, anxious that if they submitted to the emperor's persuasions they would be taken captive. On the other hand, they were afraid that he would attack them in their refusals'. Finally, on the third day, the two women sent a message to the emperor saying that they would disembark the next day, in order to buy themselves some time. Their ruse paid off and 'on that same Sunday, while they were gloomily discussing and bewailing their situation to each other and gazing out across the sea, two ships appeared in the distance'. They were overjoyed when gradually more ships appeared and they realised that it was the royal fleet. In anger at the emperor's treatment of his ships, Richard attacked the island and conquered it.

Berengaria was widely considered an excellent choice of a bride for Richard, and the *Gesta Regis Ricardi* commented that she was 'very wise and of good character'. Due to the delay occasioned by Richard's conquest of Cyprus, the couple were finally married at Limassol on 12 May 1191, with Berengaria being crowned Queen of England at the same time. Richard was reported to have been very merry at the ceremony, and whilst no record of Berengaria's demeanour or dress survives, Richard arrived for his marriage splendidly dressed. For Berengaria, her marriage was perhaps the happiest moment of her life, and it was as a bride that she was portrayed in her tomb effigy many years later. Within a month of the wedding, Richard set sail for the Holy Land with Berengaria and Joanna, who had been joined by a captured Cypriot princess, travelling together in their own ship.

Berengaria played no part in the military campaigns of the crusade. Soon after her arrival, the crusaders secured the fall of Acre, and Richard had the royal palace there fitted out for his wife and sister. Whilst Berengaria lived in some luxury during the crusade, she was not sheltered from all its horrors, and it is likely that she witnessed the slaughter of prisoners ordered by her husband before he left Acre. In August, Richard headed south with his army, leaving Berengaria, Joanna, and the Cypriot princess under a protective guard in Acre. The three royal women spent an isolated month in the palace before Richard returned and instructed them to follow him to the newly captured city of Jaffa. Richard then moved on towards Jerusalem and Berengaria and Joanna joined him for Christmas at his camp. They spent the rest of the crusade in various strongholds, then sailed for home from Acre on 29 September 1192. Richard sailed separately the following month.

Berengaria and Richard spent little time together during the crusade, and it appears that they quickly found themselves to be incompatible. There is no evidence that Berengaria ever conceived a child. and there have been suggestions that the marriage was never consummated. This is possible, but it seems unlikely, as Richard's need for an heir was the main reason behind his marriage. Once it became clear that there would be no child, the King had little use for his marriage or for Berengaria.

The years between 1192 and 1199 are the most obscure of Berengaria's life. She and Joanna arrived in Rome after leaving the crusade and spent six months there. It was there that they learned of Richard's capture in Austria, and Berengaria appealed to the Pope for aid in securing her husband's release. A romantic legend claims that it was Berengaria herself who first raised the alarm about Richard's capture. According to the story, she was shopping in the market when she saw a jewelled belt for sale that she recognised as belonging to Richard. This story is merely part of the legend that has built up around the capture of the famous king, but it is clear that Berengaria was distressed by her husband's imprisonment. Berengaria and Joanna left Rome in June 1193 and Berengaria played no further part in securing Richard's release. She remained quietly on the Continent, perhaps waiting for a summons, but on his return to England in 1194, Richard made no attempt to send for his wife. It was his mother, Eleanor of Aquitaine, who was present at his ceremonial second coronation, not Berengaria.

In 1195, Berengaria and Richard were finally reconciled. The sources differ as to the reason for the reconciliation, although it was Richard who took the initiative. One story claimed that Richard met a hermit whilst out hunting who admonished him for his sexual sins. Richard ignored this warning but fell ill soon afterwards and, seeing this as God's anger at his conduct, sent for Berengaria. Another version holds that the famous Bishop Hugh of Lincoln rebuked Richard, saying that 'concerning you, indeed, and I speak in sorrow, it is generally reported that you are not faithful in your marriage bed, and do not keep inviolate the privileges of the church, especially in the matter of the appointment or election of Bishops'. Bishop Hugh had little respect for Richard and his siblings, claiming, on his deathbed, that it was better to die than to see how the English Church would fare under Angevin rule, claiming,

The words of the Bible must inevitably be fulfilled in the case of the descendants of King Henry. 'Bastard shoots will not have deep roots' and 'the offspring of an adulterous union shall be destroyed'. The present king of the French will avenge his pious father Louis on the sons of the adulteress [Eleanor of Aquitaine] who forsook her lawful husband shamelessly for his rival.

Bishop Hugh publicly censured the King for his abandonment of his wife, and chastened, Richard recalled Berengaria. Berengaria was given a more public role after 1195, and she was present at Joanna's second marriage in 1196. In 1199, she also gave judgement with Eleanor of Aquitaine and Richard's brother, John, in a dispute concerning the see of St David. She was not invited to visit the kingdom of which she was queen, however, and she still spent little time with Richard. She was not summoned to his deathbed in April 1199.

Berengaria was at Beaufort Castle in Anjou when word reached her of Richard's death. There is no evidence that she ever contemplated a new marriage, and this, and the fact that her funeral effigy was that of a bride, may suggest that she grieved for her husband, in spite of their estrangement. A few days after Richard's death, she visited Fontrevault Abbey, where Richard's body had been taken for burial, before travelling on to Chartres in order to escort her sister, Blanche, to her wedding with the Count of Champagne. Almost immediately after Richard's death, Berengaria displayed the strong streak of independence that she would demonstrate throughout her widowhood, entering into a dispute with Richard's successor, King John, over her dower rights, which were her only source of income. In 1200, she was driven by poverty to seek refuge with her sister in Champagne.

John had no desire to make the payments that Berengaria was entitled to as part of her dower. As a consequence of this, Berengaria spent over twenty years battling first with King John and then with the minority council of his son, Henry III. She was able to enlist the support of Pope Innocent III, who, along with her sister, was her greatest supporter. A number of papal letters survive concerning Berengaria's dower. The first, dated March 1200, shows that Berengaria was denied her dower soon after Richard's death. In that same month, the Pope also sent two letters offering to relax the Interdict he had imposed on John if he would do justice to Berengaria. In a letter to John in 1204, Innocent again threatened the King with papal censure if he would not carry out his obligations towards Berengaria, and in September 1207, the King was ordered to appear personally before the Pope to answer to the Queen. The Pope's continuing interest was maintained by Berengaria's repeated appeals. By January 1204, she was in desperate straits, once again being compelled to seek aid from her sister. John was already in dispute with the Pope on other matters and had little regard for the threats made by Innocent. Finally, on 25 September 1215, he agreed to pay Berengaria a settlement, but her joy was short-lived, as, in 1216, her brother-in-law wrote to inform her that he could not, in fact, afford to pay her any money at all.

John died in 1216, and his successor, Henry III, proved to be more amenable to papal pressure. In spite of this, Berengaria still found herself without funds, and in 1220, she wrote to the Bishop of Winchester to ask for his assistance in the matter:

> We send to you our well-beloved Friar Walter, of the Cistercian order, the bearer of these presents, beseeching you humbly and devotedly with all the humility that we can, that, in reference as well to this present feast of All Saints as to other terms now past, you will cause us to be satisfied about the money due to us according to the composition of our dower, which, by your mediation, we made with our brother John, of happy memory, formerly king of England.

Henry III finally agreed to settle the debt owed to Berengaria in 1225-26. She still had to fight for the payment, writing personally to Henry III in 1225:

> We requested you by our letters patent, sent to you by Brother Walter de Persona, our chaplain of the Cistercian order, that you would send to us by the said Brother Walter and Master Simon, our clerks, 1,000 marks sterling, which you owe us at this feast of All Saints, according to the composition of our dower solemnly drawn out between us and you. But since the said Master

Simon, being detained by sickness, cannot come to you, we send in his stead our servant Martin, the bearer of these presents, earnestly requesting you to send us the thousand marks by the said Brother Walter, and by this Martin, or by one of them, if by any chance impediment both cannot come to you.

It must have been a relief to Berengaria, after years of fighting for her funds, that she finally received them. In the intervening years, however, when the English royal family had effectively washed its hands of her, she had been forced to rely on the French royal family for support.

In 1204, the French king, Philip Augustus, had taken Normandy from John. Later that same year, he granted Berengaria the city of Le Mans and 1,000 marks in exchange for the renunciation of her dower rights in Normandy. Since Berengaria had never actually received her dower, this was an excellent exchange, giving her financial security for the first time since Richard's death. Berengaria moved her household to Le Mans and she came to love the city, staying there for the rest of her life. She had a reputation for good works there and gave money to the Abbey of La Couture and the hospital of Coeffort. Berengaria also gave land in 1215 to the Franciscans to build a convent. She always wanted to build her own religious foundation, and in recognition of this, in 1228, Richard's great-nephew, Louis IX of France, granted her land at L'Epau near Le Mans. Berengaria spent the last years of her life engaged in the foundation of the abbey, with the monks arriving in May 1230. She died in Le Mans in December 1230 and was buried in her new foundation, one month before it was consecrated.

The marriage of Richard and Berengaria was not a success, and Berengaria was allowed no role in politics or even the opportunity to assert herself a queen. During her long widowhood, she showed that she had the strength and tenacity to take on the English crown and enlist papal support, and once she had the funds to support herself, she lived a life of great independence. John's first wife, Isabella of Gloucester, was not so lucky.

ISABELLA OF GLOUCESTER (*c.* 1160-1217), the first wife of King John, was never acknowledged as queen. She is often mistakenly called Hawise or Avice, which is probably the result of sources confusing her with her mother. It is as Isabella that John's first wife described herself in charters. She was the third and youngest daughter of William, Earl of Gloucester, and his wife Hawise, the daughter of Robert, Earl of Leicester. Isabella's father was the first cousin of Henry II as the son of the Empress Matilda's illegitimate half-brother, Robert of Gloucester, and Isabella was therefore the great-granddaughter of Henry I. Isabella's father was a magnate of some standing, but at her birth in around 1160, she must have seemed of little importance and nothing of her childhood is recorded. In 1166, her only brother died, leaving Isabella and her sisters as co-heiresses to their father's estates.

Whilst, in the medieval period, the eldest son would inherit the entire patrimony, where a landowner left only daughters, his estates were split equally between them rather than passing only to the eldest. Isabella's father was anxious to keep his estates together in order to maintain the power of his earldom and his house. In 1176, he entered into an agreement with Henry II. Henry II had been looking to provide his youngest son, John, with an inheritance for some time, and it was agreed that John should marry a daughter of Earl William in exchange for being named as the earl's heir. Isabella's two elder sisters, Mabel and Amica, were already married, and so it was decided that Isabella would become her father's sole heiress. Isabella's sisters were compensated with an income of £100 whilst John, through Isabella, succeeded to the titles and lands.

Isabella's father died on 23 November 1183. Instead of pressing for the marriage, Henry II took Isabella into his wardship and appropriated the Gloucester income for himself. Henry, who had endured years of rebellion from his elder sons, wanted the funds from Isabella's estates and, in spite of his fondness for John, was not prepared to simply hand over such a rich revenue stream to him. John, who had been born at the end of 1166, was some years younger than Isabella, and Henry may also have felt that his son was not yet ready for marriage. He had felt no such compunction about marrying his eldest son, young Henry, in his infancy, however, so it is likely that he was motivated by financial considerations.

Henry II died in July 1189 and was succeeded by his son, Richard I. On 13 August 1189, Richard arrived in England and was soon joined by John. The royal party moved on to Marlborough, where, on 29 August, John and Isabella were finally married. At the same time, Richard created John Count of Mortaine, endowing him with rich lands in England. For Isabella, the marriage represented a release from royal wardship, which, for a woman of nearly thirty, must have been irksome.

Due to the fact that both John and Isabella were the great-grandchildren of Henry I, a dispensation from the Pope was required in order to authorise the marriage. John did not bother to wait for this, marrying Isabella without papal sanction. This was to prove to be the first of John's many disputes with the Church and papacy, and Archbishop Baldwin of Canterbury summoned him to account for the marriage. John failed to appear before the Archbishop, and an interdict was laid over John and Isabella's lands, banning church services and other ceremonies there. This was a serious penalty and one that could not be ignored, leading John to appeal to the papal legate. To John and Isabella's relief, the legate cancelled the interdict following assurances from John that he would apply for a dispensation. There is some confusion over the result of John's application. It has been claimed that a dispensation was awarded with the bizarre condition that, whilst the couple were legally married, they could no longer have sexual relations with each other. The childlessness of the marriage has been given as evidence of this condition and is portrayed as the reason for John's divorce once he became king and needed an heir. However, it would be an extremely odd condition for the Pope to impose on a married couple, and dispensations for consanguinity were easy to obtain at the time. It, therefore, seems more likely that no dispensation actually arrived, perhaps because it became unnecessary when John and Isabella ceased to co-habit in their loveless marriage. Equally, John, who was never a friend of the Church, may simply not have bothered to apply for one.

Little evidence survives concerning John and Isabella's marriage. Charters issued by the couple suggest that they made at least one progress to Normandy together. By 1193, they appear to have become estranged from each other, with Isabella presumably retiring to live on her estates. The reason behind the estrangement is not clear and it may be that the couple simply found themselves to be incompatible.

During Richard I's absence on crusade, John set up a court of his own in England. He also made an alliance with Philip Augustus, King of France, around that time, promising to marry Philip's sister, Alais, in return for Richard's French lands. John was about to sail to France to carry out the terms of the alliance when his mother, Eleanor of Aquitaine, arrived, and he was forced to remain in England. In 1193, when news reached England of Richard's imprisonment, John travelled to Paris to do homage for Richard's French possessions and once again promised to marry Alais. The fact that John entered into negotiations for another marriage implies that he did not consider himself bound to Isabella. Divorce in 1193 was averted only by Richard's impending return. On his return, Richard held a council at Nottingham in March 1194 at which, as a punishment, John's lands were confiscated. These included Isabella's own lands, and she must have resented deeply her husband's actions. John behaved more loyally to his brother for the remainder of the reign and, in 1195, he was restored to the honour of Gloucester and his own county of Mortaine.

John was on the Continent when word reached him of Richard's death, and he returned to England in May 1199 to be crowned king at Westminster Abbey. Isabella did not share his coronation, and there was no suggestion that she would do so. Within months of his accession John had begun to look around for another bride, and in the summer of 1199, he sent envoys to the King of Portugal regarding his daughters. Due to the lack of a dispensation, it was an easy matter for John to annul his marriage, and he achieved this shortly after his accession. It is possible that Isabella objected to this, as, throughout her life, she continued to use a seal calling herself Countess of Gloucester and Mortaine.

Divorce failed to free Isabella from John, as he took her into his custody in order to prevent her from making a new marriage and bestowing her lands on her second husband. John already had other plans for Isabella's lands. In October 1199, he entered into a treaty with Philip Augustus, which included the marriage of his niece, Blanche of Castile, to Philip's son. Blanche's dowry included the rich city of Evreux, which belonged to Isabella's nephew, Amaury, Count of Evreux. In compensation, John granted to Amaury Isabella's earldom of Gloucester, and he issued a number of charters as earl until his death in 1213. Isabella deeply resented the loss of her lands, but as John's prisoner, there was nothing she could do. She spent her imprisonment in a number of places, including Sherborne Castle in Dorset, where she made her Will in 1213.

Isabella resigned herself to a life in captivity and the fact that she made her Will suggests that she was in ill health. In 1214, her fortunes changed again. In late 1213, John found himself in need of funds for an expedition to Poitou, part of the duchy of Aquitaine that he had inherited from his mother. He returned the earldom of Gloucester to Isabella before selling her, with her lands and titles, to Geoffrey de Mandeville, Earl of Essex. For the honour of marrying Isabella, Geoffrey paid 20,000 marks, the highest known sum paid for an English medieval heiress. Geoffrey and Isabella were married in January 1214, and whilst Isabella was undoubtedly forced to make her second marriage, it also meant a release for her. Isabella and Geoffrey acted jointly together during their marriage, which implies that they spent time together. The couple made a gift of land to Bassaleg Priory, for example.

The price agreed for Isabella was apparently too high even for the wealthy Earl of Essex, and he missed the first instalment of the money promised to John in early 1215. John responded in February 1215 by confiscating the Gloucester estates. This action drove Geoffrey towards the baronial opponents of King John and he was prominent at Runnymede when John was forced to sign the Magna Carta, setting down in writing the rights of the English nobility for the first time in history. It is not impossible that Isabella encouraged Geoffrey's participation in the rebellion, as there is unlikely to have been any love lost between her and her former husband. The success of the rebellion led to Geoffrey's reinstatement to the Gloucester lands in June 1215.

On 23 February 1216, Geoffrey died from wounds received in a tournament in London. The death ushered in the only period of independence that Isabella ever knew and, as a statement of her relief at finally being granted her freedom, she issued charters during the period with the words 'in my free widowhood'. Isabella had little time to enjoy her freedom. John died later in 1216 and was succeeded by his nine-year-old son, Henry III. In September 1217, Hubert de Burgh, one of the regents of the young king became Isabella's third husband. Once again, her wealth and status were the motivating factors and she had no choice in the matter. The marriage was destined to be brief, as Isabella died on 14 October 1217. She was buried at Christ Church, Canterbury, and was succeeded to her earldom by her sister Amica, Countess of Hertford.

Isabella of Gloucester has one of the unhappiest stories of any queen of England or king's wife. Her successor as John's wife, Isabella of Angoulême, enjoyed an equally turbulent and unhappy relationship with the King, but she at least was able to escape this with John's death and assert her own independence in later life as an autonomous European ruler.

ISABELLA OF ANGOULÊME (c. 1188/92-1246) was the only child and heiress of Aymer, Count of Angoulême, and his wife, Alice de Courtenay, a cousin of Philip Augustus of France. Her mother had been married twice before, and her parents cannot have been married before 1184. They are first recorded as married in 1191, and it is likely that Isabella was very young at the time of her marriage to John in 1200. She was frequently described as twelve years old in 1200, but this may have been because this was the legal earliest age for marriage, and she may have only been around eight or nine years old.

Isabella's father technically held Angoulême as a vassal of the duchy of Aquitaine, but, in reality, he had a great deal of independence. He had caused trouble during Richard I's reign by paying homage directly to Philip Augustus. Count Aymer entered into a more formal alliance with the French king soon after John's accession to the throne. As part of this agreement, he abandoned his claims to the neighbouring county of Le Marche in favour of his rival, Hugh de Lusignan. In early 1200, Isabella was betrothed to Hugh de Lusignan, a man more than old enough to be her father, and sent to live in his household until she was ready for marriage. A marriage between Isabella and Hugh posed a serious political threat to John, and the merger of their lands would have split the duchy of Aquitaine in half. It was very much in John's political interest to stop the marriage.

In the summer of 1200, John set out on a progress through Poitou. During this progress, he visited the Lusignans at Le Marche, meeting Isabella there for the first time. Soon afterwards, he spoke to Count Aymer discreetly about the match. Aymer, keen to see his daughter become a queen, agreed to recall her. John then sent Hugh to England on official business before returning secretly to Angoulême. On 23 August 1200, Isabella was informed by her parents that she was to marry John the next day. Some sources suggest that she wept and protested at the thought of marrying John, but others claim that she wished to become a queen. Whatever her personal feelings, Isabella and John were married the following day at Bordeaux.

Following their marriage, the couple made a leisurely progress through Normandy. They then crossed the Channel and were crowned together at Westminster Abbey on 8 October 1200. They spent the winter travelling around England, spending Christmas at Guildford. Isabella was never given any political role, and whilst this initially may have been due to her age, it is possible that John also did not trust his wife. John was not faithful to Isabella and had a number of illegitimate children. In 1214, he abducted and raped a noblewoman, Matilda FitzWalter, something that must have both been humiliating for Isabella and increased hostility towards John from the nobility. Isabella bore John five children during their marriage, and the couple did, at least, continue to live together as husband and wife. There is, however, some evidence that Isabella took lovers of her own, with the chronicler Matthew Paris claiming that Isabella was guilty of adultery, sorcery and incest. Whatever the truth of this, the marriage was not a close one, and John did not bother to mention Isabella in his Will.

Politically, John also appears to have come to regret his marriage, in spite of the fact that he obtained possession of Angoulême in 1202 on the death of Isabella's father. The Lusignans initially accepted Isabella's marriage, but in 1201, trouble broke out in Poitou, and John accused the family of treason. In response to this, they turned to Philip Augustus for support, and in 1202, the French king declared that John had forfeited Aquitaine, Poitou and Anjou and bestowed them upon his nephew, Arthur of Brittany. John blamed Isabella for this, telling her so in 1205. Isabella was also popularly held partly responsible for the loss of

Normandy, which fell to the French in 1204, with one source claiming that, following their marriage, the couple lay in bed together all morning rather than attending to business.

The last few years of John's reign were racked by civil war in England. It has been suggested that Isabella was imprisoned by John during these years, but references to her being under guard are more likely to have been for her own protection, as she was as deeply unpopular as John. Isabella was constantly on the move throughout her marriage, spending most of her time in the west of England. In early 1216, John's relations with his barons took a turn for the worst and they held a council in which it was decided to elect the French Dauphin, Louis, as king. Louis landed at Thanet on 20 May 1216 and quickly took Rochester castle. He was received with joy in London and, by the autumn, controlled most of southern England. In the midst of this turmoil, John died suddenly at Newark on 18 October 1216 and was buried at Worcester.

Isabella was in Bristol when word reached her of John's death. She travelled to Gloucester, where her nine-year-old son had been brought and had him hastily crowned on 28 October as Henry III. It is an indication of the impromptu nature of the ceremony that there was no crown available for the coronation, and Henry had to be crowned with one of Isabella's gold collars. In spite of this decisive action, Isabella was not permitted any role in the regency. She also had difficulty in securing her own property and this, and her lack of political power, lay behind her decision to return to Angoulême in June 1217, leaving her children in England.

On her return to Angoulême, Isabella was finally able to assert her own independence, and she established her authority in the county, even winning back control of the Cognac region, which had been lost to Angoulême in the 1180s. She still maintained contact with her son in England and wrote to him in around 1218 or 1219, requesting aid both in securing her position in Angoulême against hostile neighbours and in obtaining her English dower:

> Your Grace knows how often we have begged you that you should give us help and advice in our affairs, but so far you have done nothing. Therefore we attentively ask you again to despatch your advice quickly to us, but do not just gratify us with words. You can see that without your help and advice, we cannot rule over or defend our land. And if the truces made with the king of France were to be broken, this part of the country has much to fear. Even if we had nothing to fear from the king himself, we do indeed have such neighbours who are as much to be feared as the said king of France. So without delay you must formulate such a plan which will benefit this part of the country which is yours and ours; it is necessary that you do this to ensure that neither you nor we should lose our land through your failure to give any advice or help. We even beg you to act on our behalf, that we can have for the time being some part of those lands which our husband, your father, bequeathed to us. You know truly how much we owe him, but even if our husband had bequeathed nothing to us, you ought by right to give us aid from your resources, so that we can defend our land, on this your honour and advantage depend.

This is the first indication that the relationship between Isabella and her eldest son was troubled, although, after being granted no role in his upbringing by John, it is hardly surprising that the pair were not close. The English minority council expected Isabella to govern Angoulême for Henry's benefit, and it caused consternation in England when Isabella once again demonstrated her independence, surprising everyone in 1220 by marrying Hugh de Lusignan, the son of her former fiancé.

Isabella knew that news of her marriage would be greeted with hostility in England, particularly as her new husband was, at that time, betrothed to her own daughter Joanna, who was living in his household. Isabella sought to limit any retaliation by writing swiftly to Henry III, setting out her motives for the marriage:

> We hereby signify to you that when the Counts of March and Eu departed this life, the lord Hugh de Lusignan remained alone and without heirs in Poitou, and his friends would not permit that our daughter should be united with him in marriage, because her age is so tender, but counselled him to take a wife from whom he might speedily hope for an heir; and it was proposed that he should take a wife in France, which if he had done, all your land in Poitou and Gascony would be lost. We, therefore, seeing the great peril that might accrue if that marriage should take place, when our counsellors could give us no advice, we ourselves married the said Hugh, count of March; and God knows that we did this rather for your benefit than our own. Wherefore we entreat you, as our dear son, that this thing may be pleasing to you, seeing it conduces greatly to the profit of you and yours; and we earnestly pray you that you will restore to him his lawful right, that is, Niort, the castles of Exeter and Rockingham, and 3,500 marks, which your father, our former husband, bequeathed to us; and so, if it please you, deal with him, who is so powerful, that he may not remain against you, since he can serve you well – for he is well-disposed to serve you faithfully with all his power; and we are certain and undertake that he shall serve you well if you restore to him his rights, and, therefore, we advise that you take opportune counsel on these matters; and when it shall please you, you may send for our daughter, your sister, by a trusty messenger and your letters patent, and we will send her to you.

Isabella sought to explain her actions as being in her son's best interests, but in reality, she married for her own advancement, intent on creating the very political crisis that John had sought to avert in 1200. Isabella and Hugh's combined lands split the duchy of Angoulême in half.

Isabella's attempts to put a positive spin on her marriage fooled nobody in England, and Henry III's minority council confiscated her dower. Isabella retaliated by refusing to release her daughter until her rights were reinstated. The dispute dragged on until October 1220, when Henry finally agreed to pay Isabella the sums outstanding to her. In return, Hugh escorted Joanna to La Rochelle, where she was taken back into English custody. Isabella always had a troubled and manipulative relationship with her English children. In 1225, she and Hugh defected to the French, abandoning Henry's interests in return for a pension from the French king. In 1230, Isabella entered into another agreement with France at Henry's expense, in order to increase the size of her pension. Her actions infuriated Henry and his council, and from 1228, the English government was actively petitioning the Pope to annul her second marriage.

Isabella enjoyed a more equal relationship with Hugh than she had with John, and the couple were close in age. She was able to influence her second husband politically, and when, in June 1241, Hugh swore allegiance to Louis IX's brother as Count of Poitou without consulting her, Isabella packed up her household and left her husband. Hugh followed Isabella to Angoulême, begging forgiveness, and when she finally agreed to see him, she attacked him for supporting an alternative Count of Poitou to her own son. The couple were soon reconciled, and at Christmas 1241, Hugh declared against the French and persuaded Henry to join him on an expedition to Poitou.

The English army, led by Henry III and his brother, Richard, sailed on 9 May 1242. No evidence survives of Isabella's reunion with her two English sons, but it is likely to have been tense, as she had not seen them for twenty-five years. Relations between the three became frostier during the campaign, and Hugh almost immediately abandoned Henry for the French. The English campaign was a disaster, and Henry barely escaped with his life. Isabella then decided to take matters into her own hands, hiring assassins in 1244 to poison the French king. The assassins were discovered in the royal kitchens and confessed to Isabella's involvement. Aware that she was doomed if the King of France captured her, Isabella fled to Fontrevault Abbey to claim sanctuary, dying there on 4 June 1246.

Isabella was little lamented in England, and Henry ordered only a brief display of mourning for his distant and unreliable mother. He did extend a warm welcome to Isabella's children by Hugh, who arrived in England in 1247. The eight children that Isabella bore her second husband proved to be a major source of tension in England during the reign of their half-brother, and they caused particular difficulties for Isabella's successor as queen, Eleanor of Provence.

ELEANOR OF PROVENCE (1223-91) was the second of four daughters born to Raymond Berengar, Count of Provence, and his wife, Beatrice of Savoy. All four sisters were famed for their beauty, and all eventually became queens. This reputation and the marriage of Eleanor's eldest sister, Margaret, to Louis IX of France greatly improved Eleanor's chances of making a grand marriage. Eleanor was born in 1223 and little is known about her childhood, but the close relationship that she had with all her family in adulthood suggests that it was happy.

Henry III had great difficulty in finding a bride and spent ten years in futile negotiations. He succeeded in becoming betrothed to one lady, Jeanne of Ponthieu, only for her to marry Ferdinand III of Castile instead. A legend has built up around the betrothal of Henry and Eleanor, and it has been claimed that Eleanor composed an epic poem about a Cornish hero and sent it to Richard, Earl of Cornwall, as a compliment. Richard was impressed and recommended Eleanor to his elder brother, Henry III. This story is unlikely to be true and it is more likely that Henry selected Eleanor due to her relationship to the Queen of France.

Eleanor and Henry were betrothed on 23 November 1235 when Eleanor was twelve. Henry was twenty-eight, and Eleanor must have been nervous as she set out for England accompanied by her uncle, William of Savoy, and an escort of 3,000 horsemen. She landed at Dover in January 1236 and journeyed to Canterbury, where Henry was waiting. The couple were married on 14 January before setting out for London, where Eleanor was crowned six days later. The couple quickly became close, and a letter written by Eleanor to Henry a decade after their marriage shows her devotion to him, with Eleanor writing that 'we inform your lordship that by the grace of God we and our children are safe and well, which we lovingly hope you are also with our heart and soul'.

Eleanor brought a large train with her to England and many of her attendants chose to stay, hoping to receive rewards from Henry. Eleanor's uncle, William of Savoy, became one of Henry's chief counsellors and attempts were made to make him Bishop of Winchester, although he was eventually forced to settle for the see of Liege instead. Eleanor's mother came from a large family, and Eleanor had eight maternal uncles with limited resources of their own. At least 170 Savoyards visited England as a consequence of Eleanor's marriage and seventy chose to settle. Henry provided pensions for Eleanor's mother and her uncles Thomas and Amadeus of Savoy in the 1240s. A further uncle, Boniface of Savoy, was appointed as Archbishop of Canterbury in 1244. Eleanor's favourite uncle, Peter of Savoy, was created Earl of Richmond at Eleanor's request. Peter and Eleanor collaborated throughout her marriage, and together they led the Savoyard faction at court. The influx of foreigners greatly damaged Eleanor's reputation in England, especially as she and Peter pursued a policy of marrying their relatives to rich lords and heiresses in England.

Despite Eleanor's unpopularity, personally, she was very happy and bore five children. The eldest, Edward, was born at Westminster on 16 June 1239, and his birth was followed by those of Margaret in 1240, Beatrice in 1242, Edmund in 1244, and Catherine in 1253. Eleanor and Henry were fond parents. The couple's youngest child, Catherine, was born with an unspecified disability, and her parents were deeply distressed by her condition. Henry had an image of Catherine placed on the shrine of Edward the Confessor in the hope that she would be healed, and he also richly rewarded a messenger from Eleanor when she brought him news of an improvement in Catherine's condition. Catherine died young, and her parents grieved deeply for her, commissioning a fine tomb.

Whilst the happy family atmosphere created by Eleanor and Henry was beneficial to their children in their childhoods, in adulthood, they occasionally found it cloying. The couple were unwilling to let go of their children, and when their eldest daughter, Margaret, married Alexander III of Scotland, Eleanor and Henry continued to actively involve themselves in her welfare. In 1255, for example, when they received word that she was being mistreated by the Scottish regents, they set off north with an army, taking Margaret south to stay in Northumberland with Eleanor whilst Henry dealt with the political situation. When Henry went on campaign to Gascony in 1253, he wrote to Alexander asking that Margaret be allowed to come to England to keep her mother company. Margaret came south in 1260 in order to give birth to her first child under her mother's supervision at Windsor. Eleanor also played a significant role in the life of her second daughter, Beatrice, following her marriage to the Duke of Brittany, and she was entrusted with the couple's children when they went on crusade.

Eleanor and Henry desperately wanted to provide for their second son, Edmund, a policy which only served to increase their unpopularity. In early 1254, the Pope offered the crown of Sicily to Edmund on the condition that Henry conquered the island. Henry accepted the offer, agreeing to the enormous financial conditions imposed by the Pope, and the couple became deeply committed to what became known as the 'Sicilian Business', placing the negotiations in the hands of Eleanor's Savoyard uncles. The huge cost of the scheme made it deeply unpopular in England, and it ultimately ended in disaster when Eleanor's uncle, Thomas of Savoy, was captured and imprisoned in Turin. Eleanor was upset by the loss of Sicily, and she was also concerned about her uncle's imprisonment, jointly raising the ransom with Peter of Savoy.

The Sicilian business was not Eleanor's first foray into politics, and throughout her lifetime, she was a political force to be reckoned with. Formal recognition of her political role came in 1253, when she was made joint regent with her brother-in-law, Richard of Cornwall, whilst Henry campaigned in Gascony. Eleanor spent her time as regent raising men and money for Henry, and she had an excellent grasp of affairs in England. One surviving letter written jointly by Eleanor and Richard to Henry shows that they were firmly in control of matters:

We had been treating with your prelates and the magnates of your kingdom of England before the advent of the said Earl and John, on the quinzaines of St Hilary last past [27 January] about your subsidy, and after the arrival of the said earl and John, with certain of the aforesaid prelates and magnates, the archbishops and bishops answered us that if the King of Castile should come against you in Gascony each of them would assist you from his own property, so that you would be under perpetual obligations to them; but with regard to granting you aid from their clergy, they could do nothing without the assent of the said clergy; nor do they believe that their clergy can be induced to give you any help. Unless the tenth of clerical goods granted to you for the first year of the crusade, which should begin in the present year, might be relaxed at once by your letters patent, and the collection of the said tenth for the said crusade, for the two following years, might be put in respite up to the term of two years before your passage to the Holy Land; and they will give diligence and treat with the clergy submitted before them, to induce them to assist you according to that form with a tenth of their benefices, in case the King of Castile should attack you in Gascony; but at the departure of the bearer of these presents no subsidy had yet been granted by the aforesaid clergy.

Eleanor's measures as regent proved to be effective, but they were not popular, and she further damaged her relationship with the Londoners by rigidly enforcing a tax on boats unloading at Queenhithe. She also had two sheriffs of London imprisoned for failing to co-operate with her demands, and the Lord Mayor was punished for refusing the provide aid for Henry. In April 1254, Henry sent for Eleanor to join him in Gascony, and she resigned her regency to Richard of Cornwall.

Eleanor sailed to Gascony in the company of her two sons before journeying to Castile with her eldest son, Edward, for his marriage to Eleanor of Castile. After the wedding, Eleanor rejoined Henry and the couple travelled to visit the French court. To Eleanor's joy, her mother and sisters were present in Paris and Henry and Louis IX formed a firm friendship. It was a pleasant break for Eleanor and Henry before they returned to England, in December 1254, to face increasing baronial hostility.

Eleanor's Savoyard faction was not the only politically influential group of foreigners in England. In 1247, Henry's half-brothers Guy de Lusignan, William of Valence, the cleric Æthelmar, and his half-sister Alesia arrived in England. Henry received his mother's children joyfully and, in 1250, attempted to make Æthelmar Bishop of Winchester. The Savoyards resented the arrival of a competing group seeking patronage from the King. There was rivalry between the two groups from the first, and the Lusignans were always actively hostile to Eleanor.

The Savoyards were not the only party hostile to the Lusignans, and at parliaments in April and June 1258 at Oxford, the barons, led by the King's brother-in-law, Simon de Montford, forced a number of provisions on Henry III, including the acceptance of a council appointed by the barons and the exile of the Lusignans. Both Eleanor and Henry were alarmed by the Provisions of Oxford and the limits that they placed on royal authority. In spite of this, Eleanor did allow herself some triumph at the expulsion of her rivals, the Lusignans, and when they sought safe conduct from Louis IX to journey to France during their exile, this was refused, as the French king was 'exasperated by a complaint made against these Poitevins by the queen of France to the effect that they had shamefully scandalised and defamed her sister, the queen of England'. The triumph Eleanor felt at the expulsion of the Lusignans was short-lived, as she and Henry were forced to take oaths to uphold the Provisions of Oxford. Matters remained tense for the next few years, but by 1261, Henry finally felt strong enough to move against the barons and dismissed his council.

England erupted into civil war in 1263, when Henry refused to renew his commitment to the Provisions of Oxford. Eleanor and the Savoyards were a particular focus for attack, and in June, the Savoyard Bishop of Hereford was captured by the barons and imprisoned. Eleanor's lands were ravaged, and Henry and Eleanor withdrew to the Tower for their own protection. Frustrated by Henry's lack of positive action, Eleanor felt drawn towards her more proactive son, Edward. According to the *Annals of Dunstable*, Henry and Eleanor in the Tower and Edward, who was at Clerkenwell, were all in dire financial straits:

As they were all short of money and there was no one in London who would give them a halfpennyworth of credit, the lord Edward, not wishing to be disgraced, went on the feast of the apostles Peter and Paul, along with Robert Walerand and many others to the New Temple when the gates were closed; and when at his request he was given the keys, he said he wished to see the jewels of his mother, the queen, and summoning the keeper, he by this deceit entered with his men the Temple treasury and there, breaking open with iron hammers that they had brought with them the chests of certain people, he took and had carried away a large sum of money to the amount of a thousand pounds.

Edward's actions caused outrage, but Eleanor approved. She and Henry quarrelled over the best approach to take, and shortly afterwards, Eleanor resolved to leave the Tower and join Edward at Windsor. This proved to be nearly disastrous for her. According to the *Annals of Dunstable*,

The same year, on St Mildred's day, the queen left the Tower by the Thames on her way to Windsor by boat and came to London Bridge; when the Londoners assailed her and her men shamefully with foul and base words and even casting stones; so that freed with difficulty by the mayor of London and driven by necessity she went back to the Tower. The king would not let her enter, but she was conducted by the mayor of London safely to St Paul's and lodged in the house of the bishop.

This was a terrifying experience for Eleanor, and she would have fared considerably worse if she had not managed to escape from under the bridge. She and Henry were soon reconciled, and Eleanor rejoined her husband, abandoning her plans to go to her son.

Eleanor was with Henry when he surrendered to Simon de Montford on 16 July 1263 and handed over the government to him. This was humiliating, and Eleanor was soon plotting to restore Henry to power. It is likely that it was she who persuaded her brother-in-law, Louis IX, to mediate in the matter, and in October, Henry, Eleanor and their sons, along with Simon de Montford and his own party, crossed the Channel for a meeting with the French king. There they underwent mediation, and when, in January 1264, Louis found for Henry, civil war once more flared up in England. Henry, Edward, and De Montford returned to England before Louis gave his judgement, but Eleanor and her younger son remained in France, refusing to return.

Eleanor had no intention of returning to England whilst civil war raged and, instead, travelled to Paris to take control of Henry's treasury there. She set about raising money by any means possible, including pawning the English crown jewels. Whilst in France, she received the devastating news that Henry and Edward had been defeated at the Battle of Lewes in May 1264 and that both had been captured. In spite of her grief, this spurred Eleanor on, and both she and Peter of Savoy stepped up their efforts to obtain funds.

By the summer of 1264, Eleanor and Peter were ready with an army on the French coast. Eleanor's force was formidable, and the English barons, fearing her arrival, had already fortified the coast of England. Bad weather prevented Eleanor's army from sailing, and by October, her army had dispersed. This was a major blow to Eleanor, but she continued to work for her husband, jointly petitioning the Pope with her sister, the Queen of France, for a new papal legate to be sent to England. By February 1265, Eleanor had taken possession of Gascony, and she was there in May 1265, when she heard that Edward had escaped from captivity. On 4 August, Edward won a decisive victory against the barons at Evesham, killing Simon de Montford and restoring his father to power. Eleanor was jubilant and immediately made preparations to rejoin her family, landing in England on 1 November.

Eleanor returned to an England very different from the country she had left, and her Savoyard faction was never able to re-establish itself as the power that it had been. Eleanor occupied herself with several interests. She is known to have loved gardens and had a number of them laid out near her apartments at various royal palaces. In 1245, a new walled garden was made for her at Clarendon, and at Guildford, her wardrobe was situated above the garden steps so that she was able to access her outside space easily. Eleanor also had gardens at Kempton and Windsor, which she used for recreation in fine weather. She enjoyed reading and a work on the life of Edward the Confessor was dedicated to her. Like most of her predecessors as queen, she was pious, and both she and Henry were devoted to the cult of his canonised predecessor, Edward the Confessor. Eleanor and Henry gave very generously to the Franciscans, and during her widowhood, Eleanor founded a house for the Dominicans in memory of her grandson.

Eleanor remained influential in England, and when Henry died, on 16 November 1272, whilst Edward was away on crusade, she was instrumental in having her eldest son proclaimed king. Eleanor and Henry had been married for over thirty-five years and were devoted to each other. Eleanor, grieving deeply for her husband, focused all her attention on her children and grandchildren. In August 1274, she took Edward's children to Canterbury to meet their parents on their return from the Holy Land. Edward's coronation was a source of great pride for her, but she faced further grief when her eldest daughter, Margaret, died in February 1275, with her younger daughter, Beatrice, following her elder sister to the grave the following month.

Eleanor retired from court during her widowhood, but she remained in touch with affairs. Although, by the time of his accession, Edward was a mature man, Eleanor was unable to let him go, and her letters were filled with personal news and advice for her son:

> Know, dear sire, that we are most desirous to have good news of your health and how things have been with you since you left us. We are letting you know that we are in good health, thanks be to God. We have left Gillingham sooner than we expected, because of the noisomeness of the air, and the thick clouds of smoke which rise in the evenings and have come to Marlborough, arriving on the Friday after Michaelmas. Thanks be to God we are in good health, and we greatly desire to know the same of you.

Edward always treated his mother kindly, although, in spite of her best efforts, he allowed her no role in political affairs in England.

Eleanor became increasingly religious in her old age, and she developed an attachment to Amesbury Abbey, dedicating her granddaughters, Eleanor of Brittany and Mary of England, as nuns there. The two girls were placed in the abbey in order to provide company for their grandmother, and on 7 July 1286, Eleanor herself took the veil, always referring to herself from then onwards as 'Eleanor, humble nun of the order of Fontrevault of the Convent of Amesbury'. She did not entirely follow the life of a nun and retained an interest in the outside world, as well as securing a papal dispensation that allowed her to retain her dower. She continued to advise and cajole Edward, writing to him at one point to ask that he safeguard her Abbey's interests in France from the greed of her brother-in-law, the King of Sicily. More poignantly, she wrote to her son on behalf of one Margaret de Nevile:

> Sweetest son, we know well how great is the desire that a mother has to see her child when she has been long away from him, and that dame Margaret de Nevile, companion of Master John Giffard, has not seen for a long time past her child, who is in the keeping of dame Margaret de Weyland, and has a great desire to see him. We pray you, sweetest son, that you will command

and pray the aforesaid Margaret de Weyland, that she will suffer that the mother may have the solace of her child for some time, after her desire.

Eleanor placed a great deal of importance on family, and it is easy to imagine the sympathy that she felt when the mother presented her petition to her. It may also have been a veiled hint that she would like a visit from her own son, Edward I.

Eleanor spent the rest of her life at Amesbury, and she died there on 24 June 1291. At her request, her heart was buried with her daughter, Beatrice, with the rest of her body interred at Amesbury. Eleanor of Provence lived in turbulent times, and she was, perhaps, the most unpopular queen of England. Her daughter-in-law and successor as queen, Eleanor of Castile, was to find that she too was deeply unpopular.

ELEANOR OF CASTILE (1241-90) enjoyed as contented a marriage as her mother-in-law, Eleanor of Provence. She was born in 1241, the daughter of Ferdinand III of Castile and his second wife, Jeanne of Ponthieu. Jeanne was an indomitable figure and had experience of English kings. She was the daughter of Richard I's discarded fiancé, Alais of France, and had herself abandoned her betrothal to Henry III to marry Ferdinand. As the heiress to the county of Ponthieu, Jeanne was an important political figure in her own right, and she was largely responsible for Eleanor's upbringing. Eleanor was the only daughter in a family of seven half-brothers and four full brothers, and she was a valuable asset to her family. Very little is known of her childhood. She appears to have been present at her father's deathbed in Seville in May 1252 and remained in the city with her mother until shortly before her marriage in 1254. She was educated and fond of reading.

The death of Eleanor's father in 1252 had a profound effect on her childhood. Her eldest half-brother, Alfonso X, who succeeded their father as king of Castile, was a considerably more martial ruler. Castile had laid claim to English-held Gascony since the marriage of Alfonso VIII to Eleanor, the daughter of Henry II and Eleanor of Aquitaine. The claim had lain dormant for several years, but following his accession, Alfonso X invaded Gascony in order to claim it for Castile. Unlike his Castilian counterpart, Henry III of England had no taste for war, and he was eager to come to an agreement, opening negotiations for his eldest son, Edward, to marry Eleanor. Arrangements for the marriage were concluded in March 1254.

Eleanor may have been glad to escape a tense situation at home, as, shortly before her marriage, her mother left Castile for Ponthieu following the discovery of her involvement in a rebellion led by her stepson, Henry. The absence of her mother did not delay the arrangements for Eleanor's marriage, and in late 1254, she travelled with Alfonso to Burgos to meet Edward and his mother. Even at fifteen, Edward was strong and handsome, and he caused a stir by competing in a tournament before being knighted by Eleanor's half-brother. Edward and Eleanor were married at the convent of Las Huelgas near Burgos on 1 November 1254 before travelling to Gascony, which had been made over to Edward at Alfonso's insistence.

Edward and Eleanor always enjoyed a close marriage, and Eleanor bore a daughter at Bordeaux in May 1255 who died soon after birth, demonstrating that the marriage was very rapidly consummated. Even in the thirteenth century, fourteen was young to be a mother, and it is possible that Edward's parents kept the couple separate following the death of their first child, in order to ensure that Eleanor did not bear a second child until she was older and physically better able to cope with childbirth. Certainly, it was some years before her second pregnancy.

In late 1255, Eleanor travelled to England for the first time. Henry III had taken care to ensure that she would be comfortable in England's cold climate, fitting out rooms for her with glazed windows, a raised hearth and a wardrobe. The floors were also carpeted, a feature unknown in England at the time. Eleanor appreciated this thoughtfulness, but it was seen in England as further evidence of the King's favouritism towards foreigners. There was a real fear in England that Eleanor would bring a wave of followers with her as her mother-in-law had done, and the tensions surrounding her arrival did not help the troubled situation faced by the King.

Eleanor was, on the whole, careful to avoid the problems that her mother-in-law had faced, and she was discreet in the advancement of her family. She was young when she came to England, but whilst she had no political role, it was impossible for her to be sheltered from the political turmoil faced by Henry III. On 17 June 1264, following Henry and Edward's capture at the Battle of Lewes, she was ordered to leave Windsor with her baby daughter, Catherine, to join her father-in-law in London. The year that Eleanor spent as the barons' prisoner must have been bleak: her daughter died in September 1264 and a further daughter, Joan, who was born in January 1265, also soon died.

Eleanor's spirits were lifted by news of Edward's escape in May 1265, and in August of that year, following his victory over the barons at the Battle of Evesham, the couple were finally reunited. Eleanor bore her first son, John, in July 1266. His birth was followed by a second son, Henry, in May 1268, and a daughter, Eleanor, in June 1269.

Even before she became queen, Eleanor kept a close eye on her own property, and the acquisitive streak that would make her deeply unpopular during Edward's reign was already apparent in 1265 when she wrote to one of her officers, John of London:

> Know that our lord the king gave us the other day the manor of Berewic with its appurtenances, at the solicitation of Sir Roger de Leyburn, and because it is appurtenant to the guardianship of Cantilupe, my lord has given it to another, so that nothing of it is remitted to us, but there is another manor close by in the county of Somerset, which is at the town of Heselbere, which belonged to Sir William the Marshal, who is dead and held it of the king in chief. Wherefore we would desire that you should ask of Sir John de Kyrkbi if the guardianship of that manor is granted, and if it is not then that you should pray Sir Roger de Leyburn and the Bishop of Bath on our behalf that they should procure from our lord the king that he grant us the manor until the coming of age of the heir of Sir William. And, if it is given, there is another manor in the county of Dorset which is called Gerente, which belonged to Sir William de Keenes, who is dead, and he held it in chief of the king, wherefore we would that if we cannot have the other, you should pray them on our behalf that these should apply to the king to allow us this one; the manor of Heselbere is worth less. And if neither, pray Sir Roger in this way. Tell him that the manor of Berewic that the king gave us at his suggestion has been taken from us, for this will tend to make us seem less covetous; and say the same to the bishop of Bath. And if the letters which you have concerning it can profit nothing for this affair, give them to the bearer of this letter, for he will carry them to Walter of Kent, our clerk. Be careful to dispatch this affair, for it will be to our profit, and so suitably procure the affair that they shall not set it down to covetousness.

Eleanor had carried out detailed research to ensure that she received adequate compensation for the loss of the manor. She was right to be wary of appearing to be covetous, and this was how the majority of people in England later came to view her.

Henry III lived to a venerable age for his time, and he is still one of England's longest reigning monarchs. This longevity had its cost, and though Edward was undoubtedly fond of his father, he felt that there was little role for him in England whilst his father was alive. In 1270, Edward decided to join the crusade led by his uncle, Louis IX of France. Like her namesake and predecessor, Eleanor of Aquitaine, Eleanor of Castile insisted on accompanying her husband, declaring that a married couple should not be parted and that Syria was as close to Heaven as England or Castile. Eleanor's words were persuasive, and she and Edward set out for the Holy Land in 1270. On the way, they learned that Louis IX had died at Tunis, but they decided to continue, with Edward's army capturing Nazareth.

The crusade was not a success and disease took its toll on the crusaders. Daily life must have been hard for Eleanor, and she bore two daughters in Palestine, although only the second, Joan of Acre, survived. Eleanor was involved in one of the most dramatic events of the crusade, when an intruder attempted to assassinate Edward in his tent. Edward was stabbed twice before he managed to wrestle the knife away from his attacker, killing him. The attack left Edward gravely ill, and it was generally believed that he would die. A romantic legend survives of Eleanor's reaction when she discovered her husband's grave condition, recorded by the chronicler William Camden:

> When her husband was treacherously wounded by a Moor with a poyson'd sword, and rather grew worse than receiv'd any ease by what the Physician apply'd to it, she found out a remedy, as new and unheard of, as full of love and endearment. For by reason of the malignity of the poison, her husband's wounds could not possibly be clos'd: but she lick'd them dayly with her own tongue, and suck'd out the venomous humour, thinking it a most delicious liquor. By the power whereof, or rather by the virtue of a wife's tenderness, she so drew out the poisonous matter, that he was entirely cur'd of his wound, and she escaped without catching any harm.

This story shows great love and devotion. Sadly, it is unlikely to be true, and sources more contemporary to Eleanor claimed that Edward's life was saved by his surgeon and that Eleanor had to be carried, weeping, from his room. In spite of this, Eleanor probably did help to nurse Edward and in that way contributed to his recovery.

The assassination attempt dulled Edward's enthusiasm for the crusade, and he and Eleanor set out for home as soon as he was well enough. Edward's recovery took a considerable amount of time and they made slow progress on their journey home, sailing for Italy in late September 1272 and stopping to visit Edward's uncle, Charles of Anjou, King of Sicily, in his kingdom. During the visit, Eleanor and Edward received news that both their eldest son, John, and Henry III were dead. Charles was amazed by Edward's grief for his father compared to the philosophical way in which he took the news of his son's death and questioned his nephew on it. Edward replied that it was easy to beget sons, but that he would never have another father. It seems doubtful that Eleanor, who, after bearing at least eight children, had only one living son, felt the same way.

Edward and Eleanor were in no hurry to return to England, and in February 1273, after passing through Rome, stopped to visit the Pope at Orvieto. By the summer of 1273, they had reached Gascony, where Eleanor bore her third son, Alfonso. In November, she was visited in Gascony by her half-brother, Alfonso X, who stood as godfather to the prince, and she and Edward then travelled to Ponthieu to visit Eleanor's mother. As a mark of her affection for her mother, Eleanor left her youngest daughter, Joan, in Ponthieu to be raised by Jeanne. The couple then finally crossed to England to be welcomed as king and queen. They were crowned together in August 1274.

Life for Eleanor went on very much as before upon her return to England. Edward, conscious of the dominance that his mother had exerted over his father, was determined to keep his own wife in the background, and Eleanor never obtained a political role. In a Will made by Edward in 1272, for example, Eleanor was to be left wealthy, but she was not appointed as either regent or as guardian of her children. In March 1279, on the death of her

Above left: 6. Queen Bertha in stained glass at Canterbury Cathedral. Bertha has been credited with bringing Christianity to England, and her family insisted that she be granted the freedom to practise her faith in Kent.

Above right: 7. Queen Bertha from Canterbury Cathedral. The Frankish princess founded the first Anglo-Saxon Christian church in England.

Right: 9. A folio from the manuscript by the early British chronicler Nennius (*Historia Brittonum*) and the earliest mention of King Arthur, who was a real historical figure, unlike his queen, Guinevere, who was purely mythical.

8. The ruins of St Augustine's Abbey, Canterbury. Little now remains of the earliest Anglo-Saxon monastery. Bertha allowed Augustine to use her chapel to perform Mass, preach, and baptise those that he managed to convert.

Above: 10. Offa's Dyke. The great barrier built between England and Wales stands today as a testament to King Offa's power.

Left: 11. Etheldreda was always unhappy in her second marriage to King Egfrid of Northumbria according to Bede. A folio from Bede's *An Ecclesiastical History of the English People* completed in about 731 and which sketches the history of England from Caesar's invasion in 55 BC to the Synod of Whitby in 664.

Opposite: 12. Offa from a thirteenth-century English manuscript.

Incipit historia de Offa primo. q̄ strenuita-
te sua anglie marina p̄ce sbeg. Cui similium
Iter occidentalium Anglorum reges illuf sut
trissimos preceptu comendauerunt laude cele-
bratur rex Warmundus ab hiis qui historia
Anglorum no solum relatu proferre solet etiam
scriptis miserere consueuerunt. Si fundator
erat cuidam urbis a seipso denominate. Que
lingua Anglicana Warwic. adest curia War-
mundi nuncupatur. Qui usq̄ ad annos se-
niles absq̄ liberorum p̄mienum filiu
ch̄m ut estimabat regni sui heredem ⁊ succes-
sorem. pueris debilitatis incomodo laboran-
tem constituere non ualebat. licet enim
idem unu filium eius offa uel offanus nole
statura fuisset procem. corpore integer. ⁊ ele-
gantissime forme iuuenis existeret. pernia-
sit eum a natiuitate usu priuatus usq̄ ad an-
ni septimum. Mutus autem ⁊ illa h̄mana n̄
proferens usq̄ ad annu etatis sue tricesimum.
Huius debilitatis incomodum no solum rex
sed etiam regni proceres supra ch̄m dici potest mo-
leste sustinuerunt. Cum eius imminere p̄ri eta-
somnis. ⁊ ignoraret diem mortis sue. nesciebat
ch̄m alium sibi p̄stitueret sibi heredem ⁊ regni successore. Quidam ati p̄mari regni cui
nomen riganus. cu qrodá suo cōp̄lice nimi-
nio noie. ambiciosus ⁊ ambicioso. seductor cu
proditore. uidens regem decrepitu. ⁊ sine spe

prolis procreande somno katiscente. de se p̄
simens. cepit ad regie dignitatis culmen
aspirare. contemptis aliis regni p̄uinatib₂
se solum p̄ cetis ad h̄ dignu reputando. Se
ideo diebus singulis regi molestus nimis
proterue eum aggreditur. ut se sedili loco
adoptaret. Aliq̄ndo eor regi blande allicien-
inter asperie minis ⁊ terroribus prouocan-
persuadere no cessat regi q̄ optabat. Sugge-
rebat etiam regi per uiros potentes⁊plice cupi-
ditatis malicie sue. se regni sui s̄tmu apicē
uiolentia ⁊ terroribz. et in extrinqueter: nisi
arbitrio uoluntatis sue rex ipe parere fa-
cier do uirtute de necessitate. Super h̄ itaq̄
⁊ aliis regni negoens. eu ordro semel couetio
proterius ille a rege reprobatus discessit a
curie p̄sentia. iracundie calore frendes in se-
met ch̄o. pro repulsa ch̄m sustinuit. Hec mora
acerbat iustis qui cont̄ regis ipsum partē sua
p̄ouebant. infra paucos dies copiosum imo
infinitum exercitu ẜgregauit. ⁊ sub spe medii¹e
uulie optineude. regem ⁊suos ad hostile p̄
lium prouocauit. Rex ati confestus semo-
met rebellarē declinauit aliquoties imp̄d
aduersarios. Tandem uero conuocatis Tunum
p̄ncipibz. ⁊ uisignacis suis: delibare cēp q̄
kto opuf h̄ret. Dum igt̄ t̄ctar eunt commu-
ue per aliqt dies secu deliberantes instantis-
sime necessitatis Articulu: affinere int̄ simoet

Huc librum dedit
th̄s deo ⁊ ecc̄e scī Alb
Quem qui abstulit
titulu deleuerit: ana
Huna eiusde ecc̄ia
anime omniu fidel
sunctoꝝ req̄escat i

Above: 13. Sutton Hoo, considered to be the burial ground of one of the earliest Anglo-Saxon royal dynasties, the Wuffingas of East Anglia.

Left: 14. King Eadbald from Canterbury Cathedral, who married his stepmother. The Kentish king was initially reluctant to embrace his wife's faith, before becoming the first Christian Anglo-Saxon king.

Below: 15. Silver penny of Cynethryth. Cynethryth was the most notorious of the early queens. The wife of King Offa of Mercia, Cynethryth (died after 798) is the only Anglo-Saxon queen to have minted her own coins.

Above: 16. The tomb of King Eadbald at St Augustine's Abbey, Canterbury.

Below right: 17. A statue of King Alfred at Winchester. Alfred is remembered as having been one of the greatest kings England ever had, and most of the later kings and queens of England were his descendants.

Below: 18. Alfred the Great's preface to the English translation of *Pastoral Care*. This treatise on the responsibilities of the clergy written by Pope Gregory I around the year 590 was taken to England by Augustine, who was sent to Ethelbert and Queen Bertha's kingdom of Kent by Gregory in 597.

20. Winchester Cathedral. Winchester was the capital of the Anglo-Saxon kingdom of Wessex, and a number of early queens are associated with the cathedral and monasteries there. Alfred the Great's wife, Queen Ealswitha, is buried here in the New Minster beside her husband. It was rare for Anglo-Saxon queens to be buried with their husbands, and this is a further indication that Ealswitha enjoyed a happy life and a long and contented marriage.

19. The Tribal Hidage. This was a list of territorial assessments in Anglo-Saxon England which lists regions and the number of hides those regions contained, in what is in essence 'a tribute-taker's survey' and dates from the eleventh century. Bede makes passing references to hide assessments in his *Ecclesiastic History*, written in 731. Anglo-Saxon kings must have utilised assessments to extract labour and resources for the creation of projects such as Offa's Dyke and Alfred the Great used a similar hide assessment system.

22. The ruins of St Oswald's Minster, Gloucester. The original church was built on the orders of Ethelfleda of Mercia, the daughter of King Alfred and an important Anglo-Saxon ruler in her own right.

Above left: 21. The Lindisfarne Gospels. An illuminated manuscript of the gospels of Matthew, Mark, Luke and John it was produced on Lindisfarne in the Kingdom of Northumbria in around 715, and it is believed they were produced in honour of St Cuthbert, one of the most important medieval saints of England, venerated by many English queens.

Above right: 23. The *Anglo-Saxon Chronicle*. The *Anglo-Saxon Chronicle* mentions Ethelfleda of Damerham as Edmund I's queen.

25. Queen Emma's Mortuary Chest at Winchester Cathedral. The Queen shares her grave with her second husband, King Cnut, and son, King Harthacnut.

26. A statue of King Edgar at Powis Castle. Like many Anglo-Saxon kings, Edgar was a serial monogamist and married three wives.

27. The Anglo-Saxon coronation stone at Kingston upon Thames. Many of the Anglo-Saxon kings were crowned at Kingston, including Ethelred II, whose accession was engineered by his mother, Queen Elfrida.

Opposite: 24. The coronation of King Edgar at Bath Abbey. Unusually for the Anglo-Saxon period, Elfrida, Edgar's queen, shared his coronation.

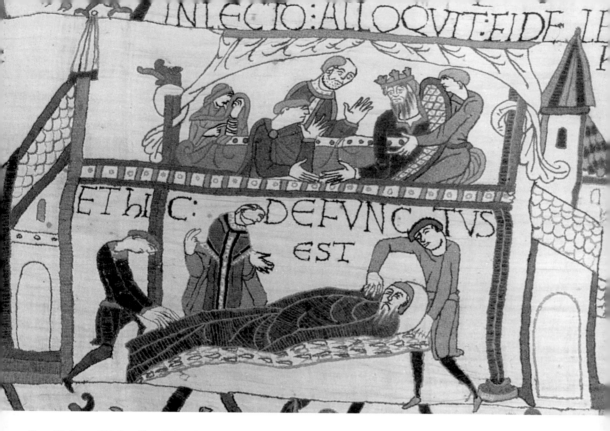

Above: 28. Queen Edith at King Edward the Confessor's deathbed from the Bayeux Tapestry.

Below: 29. The death of King Harold II. Edith Swanneck came to the site of the battle in person to identify the body of her ex-husband, King Harold II.

Opposite: 30. Edward the Confessor.

33. The tomb of Robert Curthose at Gloucester Cathedral. Matilda of Flanders' favourite son was passed over in the succession in favour of his younger brother.

Above left: 31. The coat of arms of Matilda of Flanders, the first Norman queen of England, from Lincoln Cathedral. Matilda's descent from the English royal family and close relationship with the kings of France was a deciding factor in William the Conqueror's choice of her as a bride.

Above right: 34. A page from a gospel book belonging to St Margaret, a descendant of the Anglo-Saxon royal dynasty and the mother of Matilda of Scotland.

35. Duke William (the future William the Conqueror) and Earl Harold (the future Harold II) from the Bayeux Tapestry.

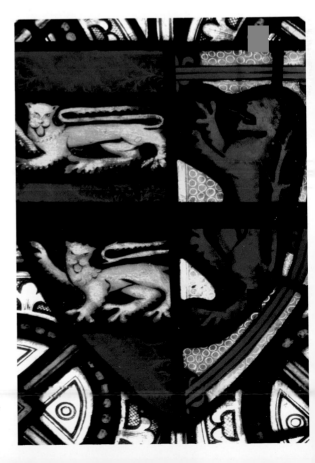

36. Coat of arms of Queen Matilda of Scotland, wife of Henry I, Lincoln Cathedral.

37. The coat of arms of Matilda of Boulogne, the wife of King Stephen, from Lincoln Cathedral. Stephen relied on his wife to aid him in his war with his cousin, the Empress Matilda, and Matilda of Boulogne proved herself to be an effective military commander.

38. A depiction of St Catherine in a stained-glass window from the church at Deerhurst in Gloucestershire. The saint is depicted in the dress of a medieval queen.

39. Isabella of Angoulême from her tomb at Fontrevaud.

40. Eleanor of Aquitaine from her tomb at Fontrevaud Abbey. The abbey became the mausoleum of the early Plantagenet kings and queens and was the place of both Eleanor of Aquitaine and Isabella of Angoulême's retirement and death.

41. Medieval Chronicler Matthew Paris, kneeling before the enthroned Virgin and Child. Matthew Paris claimed that Isabella of Angoulême was guilty of adultery, sorcery and incest. From Matthew Paris *Historia Anglorum* 1250-9.

42. A medieval king and queen embracing from an thirteenth-century English manuscrpt.

43. Coat of arms of Isabella of Angoulême, wife of King John, Lincoln Cathedral

Next page: 44. Matthew Paris described and portrayed many of the events of Henry III's life. A page from Matthew Paris's *Historia Anglorum* 1250-9.

nicorum anglie ab anno incarna
cionis dominice millesimo. Reg
nante etheldredo tre sci edwardi
Regis et martiris · · · · · anno · · ·

Millesimo Rex etheldredus duxit in
uxorem emmam filiam con
sulis normannorum. quem du
cem appellant. Regum pussim' et
belli prole feliciss'mi.

M · p'mo Inuentus est scs iuo epe
in partibus orientalibus ori
undus. in loco qui no multu
distat ab huntendonia. et
eius latum est scm corp' ei ad
nobile cenobium Ramesei
puncto abbe illepido p ocueam.
Hui tuba ultro recepit oblacom
ignotas suor miraclose apta.

M · ii· Angli die uno · hora una ipe
oppressiones scs sustinuerut
intolerabiles· duces q erat i
anglia tirannizantes tru
cidauerut immunitos· s. daco

M · iii· Wilfridus epe vir eximie
sctitatis cenobium de Bur
tona fundauit. Daci quoq
ira succensi venerut i angl
am. Multi daci z angli i pre
lio ceciderunt. Rex angl Athel
dred ducatu michor cadrico pdi
tor cognomito strone dedit

M · iiii· Suein dacus uenit cu inu
mera multitudie barbaror

qui omia terrauit uastaui i an
glia ferro z flamma · iram dei
z sci edmundi Regis z martiri
sibi coacuauit prout rei euetus
comprobauit. Joh sedit i cathed
ro · annis v.

M · v· Hug romanu adept' ipin' ipsu ann
Daci marti' iterata sollicitudi
nibus· repatriarunt. Famel q
maxima angliam inuasit qua
se nullus meminit p'uidisse

Eadem pditor ducm nobile ethelstanu
M · vi· Rex etheldredus pacificus z im
bellis a dacis pecunia pacem re
demptam optinuit. Iussu regis duo
filii dci pditoris iuleone pini facino
ris· execcant

M · vii· Angli cum dacis conuencone
fecerunt. et ad pacis obseruaconem
triginta milia librar esterligor
sunt statuta. Venat naq suam'
rex danor omia eximias. Q tade
ultore vo edmudo rex z iir pntciepe

M · viii· Rex etheldredus anno Regni su
decesimo fecit parari per totam
angliam ex trecentis z decem hidis
unam nauc. Et ex octo hidis lori
cam et galeam i spem aiatus

Annis duob; z mesibus nouem·
M · ix· Sergius sedit in cathedra roma
na. Defucto Sireburnesi epo· Al
mar successit.

M · x· Hounis danor exercitus i angli
am ueniens· icndis uacat z rapini

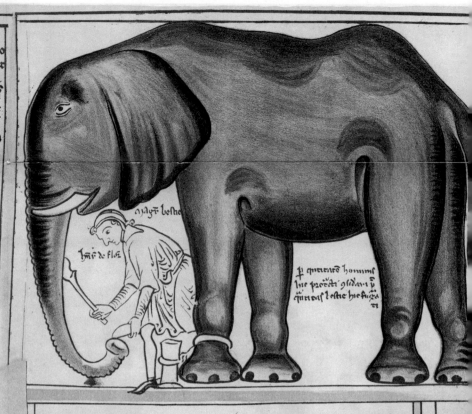

Animal huiusmodi secundum pur scientiam exercitia figuratur. elephas dicitur. Et est rex omnium iumentorum sicut leo bestiarum aqla auium. balena siue cetus uel cetus piscium. et draco serpentium. Iumenta dicuntur a domora que dantur ab co hominum in iuuamen laborum ut equi asinus et similia. et quo est maximum eorum elephas. Quem qui inscripturis frequenter de eo sit sermo rarus in istis uidetur occidentis. pa in hoc pagina figurata et figuram pre describentium.

sub niger. suligines siue terestris coloris est. nisi eorum pilorum instar aliorum animalium ornatus tegmine uel munit. Nullus uero unquam albus elephas uisus est sicut nec cornus albus uel cignus niger. Unde orati in explanaitionem penultima. Siue elephas albus uulgi conterret ora. Speraret populus ludis attentius et e. Secundum autem plinius. ysidorum et alios naturales filosophos. india et eis partes continens elephantes producit. Qui in aquis sunt draconum insidias ignitorum pariunt. Dracones enim elephantinum sanguine ad eos auide siciunt refrigerii. Quando autem draco ipsum elephantem cupit occupare. illaquat et concludit pedes ei cauda sua. ut sic spiris intricatii prosternat et interficiat morsib; uenenosis. et supra abintecto sanguinem geniciut. Est elephas atal ponderosum. terestre ac robustu. Qui cum necesse habeat a dracone saucius et mortuus cadere. cadit ultro super draconem. ut sic dum premens. forsan mortuus triumphet de inimico. sicut legitur de sansone. Et cum sit inter omnia gressibilia maximum atal est et deforme. unde lepra morbus elephantinus qp sui insanitatem et deformitate. Animal eo ad pugnandum docibile est et obediens. Et si leo prouocatur ad iram et pugnam propria cauda flagello. sic elephas uiso sanguine proprio maximo uel succo a moris et uius expressioq; sanguis protendit similitudine sophistice cheritis. ad euirand bellum et ad iram prouocatur. et hostes acerbius erigitur. Pond iuuanie portat ita ut expugnacitata machinam cum uiginti armatis et cor bauilet necessarius. et serpm loricatii. Magni fortes et adulti plerique triginta prout legit in libro machabeorum primo capitulo nono decimo de elephante regalis loricato quin eleazar fortissimus et audacissimus peremit ab eodem pemptus et oppressus. Implio uero existit ele

46. The Eleanor Cross at Geddington. Only three of the monuments to Queen Eleanor of Castile now survive.

Above & below left: 47. and 48. The Eleanor Cross at Hardinstone. The Eleanor Crosses provided a lasting testament to Edward I's devotion to his wife, Eleanor of Castile.

49. The Eleanor Cross at Waltham Cross. During her lifetime, Eleanor of Castile's reputation was poor, but the crosses served to create a posthumous reputation for queenly virtue.

Previous page: 45. A page from Matthew Paris's *Chronica Majora*.

50. Eleanor of Castile, effigy on monument, Lincoln Cathedral.

51. Berkeley Castle. Edward II was imprisoned and murdered in the castle on the orders of his wife, Isabella of France, and her love, Roger Mortimer.

52. Edward II's tomb at Gloucester Cathedral. The murdered king was provided with a fine tomb by his son, Edward III.

53. The tomb of Edward, the Black Prince, at Canterbury Cathedral. Philippa of Hainault did not live to see her beloved son's early death or the accession of her grandson, the troubled Richard II.

Opposite: 54. Actual portraits of Richard II and Anne of Bohemia, though the results may be affected to some extent by their conformity to the type of features from which artists found it difficult to escape. From *Liber Regalis* (Coronation Book of Richard II) executed in 1377 or 1378.

55. Richard II and the Duke of Gloucester (who plotted against the king) at Pleshy Castle in Essex from Froissart's *Chronicles*.

Above left: 56. One panel from the Wilton Diptych, an extremely rare survivor of a late medieval religious panel painting from England. Painted for Richard II *c.* 1395–99 he is shown kneeling in front of Edmund the Martyr, Edward the Confessor, and St John the Baptist.

Above right: 57. The medieval palace at the Tower of London reconstructed to how it would have looked in the thirteenth century.

Above left: 58. Richard II depicted with John the Baptist in stained glass at Winchester College. Richard established personally happy relations with both his queens, but his autocratic rule meant that his reign was politically troubled and he was ultimately deposed and murdered.

Above right: 60. Henry IV in stained glass at Canterbury Cathedral. The first Lancastrian king usurped the throne from his cousin, Richard II, and ushered in the Wars of the Roses.

Above left: 61. The tomb of Joan of Navarre at Canterbury Cathedral. Joan and Henry IV made a love match, but Joan's time in England was far from easy, and she was the only queen to be punished for witchcraft.

Above right: 62. The coronation of Joan of Navarre, Westminster Abbey February 1403.

Above left: 63. Joan of Navarre at a joust on the occasion of her marriage to Henry IV in 1403.

Above right: 64. Catherine of Valois, Henry V's queen, giving birth to Henry VI.

Above left: 65. The marriage of Catherine of Valois to Henry V in the parish church of St John, Troyes, 2 June 1420, a direct result of the Treaty of Troyes ratifed less than a fortnight earlier on 21 May.

Above right: 66. A queen depicted in a window in Fromond's Chantry, Winchester College. Work on the building was carried out during Catherine of Valois' time as queen and queen dowager. It is possible that the queen with her blond wavy hair was based upon Catherine, who was often depicted in a similar manner.

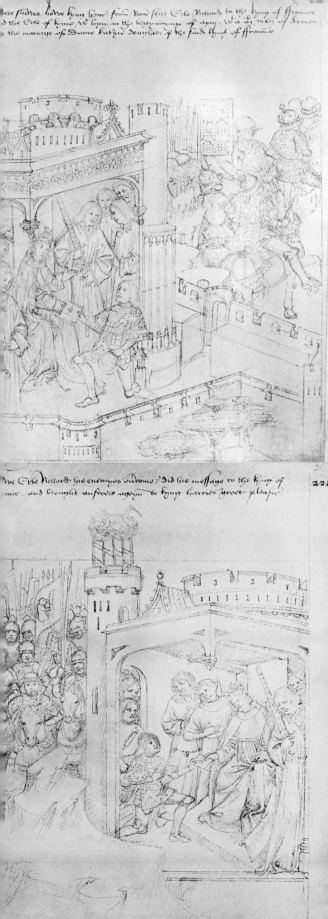

67, 68 and 69. This fifthteenth-century manuscript shows the process by which coutiers of Henry V brokered his marriage to the daughter of the King of France, Catherine of Valois. In the first image Henry V passes a letter to Richard Beauchamp, the Earl of Warwick, and on the right we see him riding away with his entourage to relay the message. In the second image Richard Beauchamp, the Earl of Warwick, delivers the message to the King of France. Note the stork on top of the tower – an omen of fertility. In the third image the Earl of Warwick presents the King of France's reply to Henry V.

Right: 70. Henry VI depicted in this screen at Ludham church in Norfolk.

Below left: 71. Elizabeth Woodville.

Below right: 72. Richard III. The last Yorkist king married Anne Neville, the widow of the Lancastrian Prince of Wales, in order to secure a share of the great Warwick inheritance.

Above: 73. Warwick Castle. One of the residences of Anne Neville, the wife of Richard III.

Left: 74. The White Tower. This late fifteenth-century manuscript illumination shows the Tower of London much as it was in 1483.

Right: 75. Margaret Beaufort from Christ's College, Cambridge. Margaret Beaufort passed her claim to the throne to her son, Henry Tudor, who took the crown as Henry VII.

Below: 76. Anne Neville (centre), her first husband Prince Edward of Lancaster (left) and her second husband, Richard III (right). Anne and Richard are depicted with crowns and sceptres.

77. Henry VII. The first Tudor king was always sensitive to claims that he wore the crown in right of his wife.

78. Elizabeth of York was the daughter, sister, niece, wife and mother of kings of England, and it was through her that the Tudor dynasty gained its legitimacy.

79. This richly illuminated psalter belonged in turn to Elizabeth of York, then Catherine of Aragon. It notes the birth of Henry VII and Elizabeth of York's eldest son, Arthur. Marked in the psalter are the precious statements: 'Thys boke ys myn Elisabeth ye quene' and 'Thys boke ys myn Katherina the quene'.

mother, Eleanor became Countess of Ponthieu. Whilst this role meant that she was involved in some administration work and diplomacy, she was never responsible for actually ruling Ponthieu, and she never used her title in England. She appears to have been happy with this state of affairs, and her time was almost completely occupied in childbearing and in her land acquisitions.

It is unclear exactly how many children Eleanor bore during her lifetime, although there must have been at least eleven daughters and four or five sons. Neither Edward nor Eleanor had much contact with their children whilst they were young, and this has been interpreted as evidence of a lack of affection for them. Certainly, it does appear callous that neither Edward nor Eleanor visited their dying son Henry at Guildford in October 1274 when they were nearby in London. It was also left to the boy's grandmother, Eleanor of Provence, rather than his parents, to commemorate him. Edward and Eleanor commissioned no memorial Masses for their heir, Alfonso, when he died in 1284, a fact unusual for the time.

There is no doubt that Eleanor and Edward were distant parents, but it is possible that, having lost all but six of her children in infancy or childhood, Eleanor was unwilling to commit herself emotionally to children who were unlikely to survive. There is also evidence of affection towards her children, and Eleanor objected to her daughter, Mary, becoming a nun at Eleanor of Provence's request, arguing that her daughter was too young to be committed in this way. On another occasion, Eleanor worked with her mother-in-law to convince Edward that their thirteen-year-old daughter was too young for marriage and that the ceremony should be delayed for eighteen months. This was obviously based on Eleanor's own experience of early marriage and shows a concern for her daughter. Eleanor's accounts for 1290 show that her eldest surviving daughters, Eleanor, Joan and Margaret, travelled with her for much of the time, and that at Easter, all her children were with her at Woodstock.

Eleanor's greatest interest was land acquisition, and she was perceived by her contemporaries to be hungry for land, making her deeply unpopular during her lifetime. She purchased some land legitimately, but she was also involved in a number of more controversial acquisitions. In 1275, Edward granted her the right to take over the debts owed to Jewish moneylenders. Eleanor would take over a debt and then appropriate the land that had been given as surety. Her association with the hated moneylenders badly damaged her reputation, and the Archbishop of Canterbury wrote to her to warn her that Edward's harsh policies were being blamed squarely on her influence, and that by dealing in debts, she was committing the mortal sin of usury. This did not deter Eleanor, and her accounts from the last year of her life show that she continued to acquire land.

Taking over debts was not the only underhand means that Eleanor employed to gain more land. In 1283, she acquired one manor and promptly ordered her bailiffs to dispute the boundaries, taking 100 acres from neighbouring land. Eleanor's bailiffs and other officials were notoriously corrupt, and Eleanor did nothing to stop them. It is likely that she was not directly responsible for some of their excesses, such as the eviction of a couple from their house, their subsequent imprisonment, and the dumping of their baby in its cradle in the middle of the road. She was, however, aware of what was going on, and she did not punish her officials for their actions. On her deathbed, she requested that compensation be paid for wrongs that had been committed in her name.

Eleanor had a reputation for having a quick temper, and she was not a woman to cross. She liked to involve herself in marriages within her household and, on one occasion, reacted angrily when her wardrobe-buyer's daughter refused to marry the son of Edward's physician at her command. Eleanor felt slighted and, in revenge, confiscated money belonging to the girl. In 1283, Eleanor pursued the Bishop of Worcester for a debt that she claimed was owed to her. The bishop denied that such a debt existed, but Edward's chancellor advised him to pay it rather than anger Eleanor. Such behaviour did not make Eleanor popular, and a contemporary rhyme shows the depth of public feeling against her: 'The king he wants our gold, the queen would like our lands to hold.'

Eleanor's greed and acquisitiveness was not the only side to her character, and both she and Edward were visible presences in their subjects' lives, travelling around the country constantly. Eleanor's accounts show that ordinary people felt able to approach her personally, and she was often given gifts of food by poor women. Eleanor involved herself in the lives of the poor, and between 1289 and 1290, she gave meals to over 9,000 of her poorest subjects. She widely patronised the Dominicans and founded priories for them in London and Chichester. As well as these charitable interests, Eleanor had an interest in learning, and she commissioned a book on a legendary Count of Ponthieu. She was a patron of both Oxford and Cambridge universities and left money to poor scholars in her Will.

Eleanor and Edward were frequently together, and the couple were devoted to each other, with Eleanor often accompanying her husband on his military campaigns. She was in Wales on campaign when she bore both her daughter Elizabeth in 1282 and her youngest child, Edward, in 1284. Eleanor travelled with Edward to Gascony in 1286, and the couple spent three years there whilst Edward administered his continental lands. Whilst she was in Gascony, Eleanor contracted malaria, and from 1287, she was frequently unwell. In November 1290, she and Edward set out from Clipston for Lincoln, a journey of only fifteen miles. They made little progress, only reaching Harby, still some distance from Lincoln, after nine days on 20 November. Harby was a tiny village with few facilities, and the stay was occasioned by a rapid deterioration in Eleanor's health. She died there in the evening of 28 November 1290.

Edward was grief-stricken at Eleanor's death, and he was determined that she should be commemorated. He ordered that her body be embalmed and placed in a litter for the journey to London. She was given a grand funeral cortege, which took twelve days to reach London. In memory of his beloved wife, Edward ordered that a stone cross be erected at every place that Eleanor's body stopped, with the first at Lincoln and the last at Charing Cross in London, which is a corruption of the French for 'dear queen'. Eleanor was given two fine tombs: one in Lincoln, where her bowels and other internal organs were buried, and the other at Westminster, where her body was interred. No other English queen received as extravagant a memorial as Eleanor, and Edward's actions on her death had a profound effect on her reputation. In the seventeenth century, William Camden wrote of the cross at Charing Cross that 'there stands a monument which King Edward I erected in memory of Queen Eleanor, the dearest husband to the most loving wife, whose tender affection will stand upon record for all posterity'. Posthumously, Eleanor was able to obtain a reputation for queenly virtue purely based on her husband's devotion to her. Edward I, in spite of his harsh military reputation, was a man who liked being married, and nine years after Eleanor's death, he took a second wife, Margaret of France.

MARGARET OF FRANCE (*c.* 1279-1318) is little remembered today and was, even in her own time, overshadowed by her more famous predecessor as Edward's wife, and by her successor as queen, the notorious Isabella of France. She played an important role in keeping the royal family together, and her life appears, in the main, to have been a happy one. She was the youngest child of Philip III of France and his wife, Marie of Brabant, and was born around 1279. In 1285, her father died, and she was raised under the guardianship of her brother, Philip IV.

In 1296, Philip invaded Gascony and took control of the duchy. Edward I was already committed to his war in Scotland and was unable to defend both areas. He had already made one marriage in order to safeguard Gascony from foreign attack, and he was therefore eager, in 1298, to adopt the Pope's suggestion of a marriage between himself and a sister of Philip IV, and for his eldest surviving son, Edward, to marry Philip's daughter, Isabella. At first, it was suggested that Edward marry Margaret's elder sister, Blanche, who was a renowned beauty. At some stage in the negotiations, Margaret's name was substituted for Blanche's. Margaret came from a good-looking family, and her brother was always known as 'Philip the Fair'. Whilst Margaret was always rather overshadowed by her brother and elder sister, she was an attractive woman in her own right, and according to the chronicler Peter Langcroft, she was 'the Lady Margaret, in whose least finger there is more goodness and beauty, whoever looks at her, than in the fair Idione whom Adamas loved'. Edward had no reason to feel short-changed by the substitution of Margaret in place of the fair Blanche.

Margaret must have been apprehensive, as she was, at most, twenty at the time of her marriage whilst Edward was sixty. She arrived at Dover in September 1299 and was taken straight to Canterbury, where she and Edward were married on 8 September. No record of the couple's first meeting survives, but Edward was apparently delighted with his young bride, and the couple, against expectations, became close. Margaret was presented to the people as a peacemaker for her role in ending the conflict in Gascony, and this made her popular, with the contemporary *Song of the Scottish Wars* commenting of the marriage that 'next the king returns, that he may marry Queen Margaret, the flower of the French; through her the kingdoms receive a more complete peace. Anger begets slaughter, concord nourishes love – when love buds between great princes, it drives away bitter sobs from their subjects'. Unusually, Margaret was not crowned, and instead, shortly after the wedding, Edward returned to his campaign in Scotland.

It must have been daunting for Margaret to meet her new husband only for him to rush away, but she continued to make a good impression in England, spending three weeks at the monastery at St Albans shortly after her wedding, where she gave generous charitable gifts. Margaret also joined the fraternity of the monastery. Religion was important to Margaret, and she often chose to stay in monasteries when she travelled.

Margaret regularly accompanied her husband on his campaigns, just as his first wife had done. She quickly fell pregnant following her marriage, and both she and Edward found they missed each other, in spite of the brief time that they had been together. According to the chronicler Peter Langcroft, soon after Easter 1300,

> Queen Margaret, by command of her lord the king, proceeds towards the North; she was advanced in pregnancy; by will of God Almighty at Brotherton on the wharf she is safely delivered of a son who is named Thomas at his baptism. King Edward receives information of it, prepares quickly to visit the lady, like a falcon before the wind. After her purification made solemnly the king resumes his road towards Scotland; the queen with her son waits at Cawood, on the River Ouse, much at her ease.

Given that Margaret had only arrived in England in September 1299 and her first son was born on 1 June 1300, coupled with the fact that Brotherton contained no royal residence, it is clear that Margaret's first child was premature. In spite of this, her son was healthy and as soon as she was well enough to travel she moved to Cawood which had been prepared for her lying-in. Margaret's other deliveries went more smoothly, and she bore Edward two further children: Edmund at Woodstock in August 1301, and Eleanor at Winchester in May 1306. It is a testament to Margaret's good nature that her only daughter was named after her predecessor as Edward's wife.

Like Eleanor of Castile, Margaret spent most of her time travelling with Edward, and she was a distant mother to her children. She did involve herself in their upbringing as much as possible, however, and whilst they had their own household, she is known to have personally selected Thomas's wet nurse. She gave her two sons the gift of an iron birdcage and grieved for her daughter when she died young. Edward was also interested in his children, and a letter survives from him to the steward of his sons' household, telling him to ensure that they attended Mass at Canterbury Cathedral and asking for a report on their conduct during the service. Edward asked for them to be brought to St Radegunds in September 1302 so that he could visit them. In a further letter to the children's household after the birth of Margaret's daughter, Edward asked for details of what the baby was like. It is obvious that both Margaret and Edward attempted to stay involved in their children's lives, and Edward treated the children of his second family with more indulgence than the strict upbringings imposed on his first.

Margaret made an effort to be on good terms with Edward's children from his first marriage. She had considerable contact with the future Edward II, and even though she was only a few years older than him, she filled the role of a mother to him. In 1305, the young Edward and some other youths invaded the estates of the Bishop of Chester, pulling down fences and allowing his game to escape. Edward I was furious with his son and sent him to Windsor, where he spent six months in disgrace. He was only released through a reconciliation engineered by Margaret when she convinced her husband not to punish his son further.

Edward I was faithful to both his queens, and he and Margaret enjoyed a loving relationship. There is evidence that he was anxious about Margaret's health and happiness, as a series of surviving letters show. Margaret was diagnosed with measles in 1305, and Edward was very concerned for her health, cancelling arrangements that had been made for her to travel to see him. In a letter to her physician, Edward told him not to let her travel until she was fully recovered or he would suffer for it.

In a letter written in May 1305 to Margaret's confessor, Brother Henry, Edward showed a desire to spare Margaret's feelings, albeit in a rather tactless way. Edward wrote to instruct Brother Henry to break the news to Margaret of her sister Blanche's death. He suggested that, to comfort her, the confessor might like to point out that she should not grieve too much for her sister, since Blanche had been as good as dead to her anyway since the elder sister had left her family in France for her marriage in Austria. It has been suggested that this callousness was due to a personal grudge against Blanche, as he had wanted to marry her. It seems more likely that Edward was simply trying to think of ways to console his wife.

Margaret was an exemplary queen, and her only recorded vice was a failure to control her finances. She was very extravagant, and by 1302, Edward had had to give her £4,000 out of wardships and marriages so that she could pay her debts. In 1305, her lands had to be increased by £500 a year, again in order to service her debts. Margaret spent the money on luxuries: in 1302, she owed £1,000 to an Italian merchant for fine clothes and other extravagant goods. She was left richly provided for in Edward's Will but died heavily in debt.

In spite of these debts, Margaret was a kind-hearted woman, and she interceded with Edward on a number of occasions on behalf of people who petitioned her. She saved the life of a Godfrey de Cogners, who had unwisely fashioned the crown with which Robert the Bruce was crowned in Scotland. Margaret was kind-hearted even to her opponents. In 1303 or 1304, she issued a writ against two men for trespass in her park in Camel in Somerset. Since both of the accused were in Scotland when the writ was issued, she agreed to postpone her action against them so that they would not be prejudiced by their absence. In a letter to Edward's chancellor, Margaret wrote,

> Because we have granted, at the request of our dear cousin, Sir Aymer de Valence, that the exigence [writ] which is running upon Sir Alexander Cheverel and Roger Parker (who remain in the service of our said lord the king in Scotland) in the county of Somerset by the order delivered to the sheriff of the same place by our said cousin, Sir Hugh le Despenser and Sir Henry le Spigurnel, justices assigned to hear and determine the trespass which was committed against our said lord the king and against ourself in our park of Camel, should be adjourned until the feast of St Hilary next coming, we command and request you that you hereupon make the said Sir Alexander and Roger have our lord the king's writ to the aforesaid sheriff in due manner, so that they in the meantime do not incur damage or danger by it for this reason.

In any event, at least in relation to one of the trespassers, Margaret did not have to wait too long for justice, writing again to the chancellor within a month to inform him that

> because Roger le Parker, who has recently done right concerning the trespass committed in our park of Camel, has paid to us into our Wardrobe his fine which he made for us, for this reason we request and command you that you hereupon cause him to have writs of our said lord the King to the sheriff of Somerset, that he should suffer him to be quit of all manner of exigencies and other demands that he made against him by reason of the before mentioned trespass.

Margaret was less dangerous in her protection of her lands and revenue than her predecessor, Eleanor of Castile, had been.

Margaret was not with Edward when he died on 7 July 1307 at Burgh-by-Sands on his way to yet another campaign in Scotland. Edward's death was unexpected, and Margaret grieved for him deeply, never contemplating a second marriage, in spite of being only in her late twenties at the time. She did not contemplate retiring from public life and, on 22 January 1308, sailed to Boulogne with her stepson, Edward II, for his marriage to her niece, Isabella of France. It had been nearly ten years since Margaret had last seen her homeland and family, and she quickly established a close relationship with her niece.

The royal party returned to England soon after the wedding for Edward and Isabella's coronation. Margaret's brothers, the Counts of Valois and Evreux publicly voiced their disapproval at the prominence given to Edward II's favourite, Piers Gaveston, at the ceremony, and it is likely that Margaret also disapproved. Certainly, she retired from court soon after the coronation. She may also have voiced her concerns to her brother, Philip IV, and in May 1308, it was reported that both Philip and Margaret had sent funds to the Earls of Lincoln and Pembroke to finance their campaign to oust Gaveston from power. She had reason to dislike Gaveston, as, at Easter 1308, Edward took Berkhamstead Castle from her and bestowed it on his favourite. Margaret played only a small role in the campaign against Gaveston, and it was the only foray into politics that she ever made.

Margaret's last public appearance was as a witness to the birth of the future Edward III at Windsor in 1312. She joined her niece, Isabella, two months before the birth and stayed until after the christening before returning to her own estates. She lived quietly for the rest of her widowhood and died at Marlborough Castle in February 1318 of some unspecified illness. At her request, she was buried at Greyfriars church in London, next to the altar in the choir that she had built. In spite of her brief life and even briefer marriage, Margaret of

France appears to have been content, and she enjoyed a happier marriage than her niece and successor as queen, Isabella of France.

ISABELLA OF FRANCE (*c.* 1295-1358) is one of the most famous queens of England. She also had one of the most prestigious backgrounds and, with the exception of the later Catherine of Aragon, was the only English queen to be the daughter of two reigning sovereigns. She was the only daughter of Philip IV of France and his wife, Jeanne, Queen of Navarre. Her mother died when she was around ten years old, but she was thoroughly spoiled by her adoring father. Isabella was first betrothed to the future Edward II in her infancy, at the same time that her aunt, Margaret, married Edward's father. Isabella, as the only daughter of the powerful King of France, was the most eligible princess of her generation, and according to the chronicler Froissart, she was also 'one of the feyrest ladyes of the worlde'. She was a member of a very good-looking family, and throughout her lifetime, she was known as 'Isabella the Fair'.

Edward I died in 1307, and Edward II decided to delay his coronation until he could share it with Isabella. Shortly after his accession, Edward crossed to France in the company of his stepmother, Margaret of France. He was met at Boulogne by Isabella and her father, Philip, as well as by other members of her family and the French nobility. Philip had provided Isabella with a magnificent trousseau, including seventy-two headdresses and two gold crowns. Edward and Isabella were married with great ceremony at Boulogne on 25 January 1308. Isabella is likely to have been pleased with Edward when she met him, as he was, by all accounts, a handsome and charming man. It is unlikely that, at first, she noticed anything unusual in his behaviour towards her, although the fact that he sent his wedding presents to his favourite, Piers Gaveston, in England, did not go unnoticed by Isabella's relatives.

Piers Gaveston had been a member of Edward's household since 1300. The relationship had caused Edward I much concern, and in February 1307, he had banished Gaveston, only for Edward II to immediately recall him on his accession. Edward II had an illegitimate son who was born before 1307, and so he clearly did have some attraction to women. They were not his primary interest, however, and several contemporary sources hint at an intimate relationship with Gaveston. Edward II is commonly believed to have been homosexual, and he is very likely to have had sexual relationships with both Gaveston and a later favourite, Hugh Despenser the Younger. Gaveston was also Edward's closest friend and confidant, and he was left as regent by the devoted King when he journeyed to France for his marriage.

Edward and Isabella sailed for England shortly after their marriage, in the company of Isabella's two uncles, the Counts of Valois and Evreux. Both Isabella and her uncles were shocked when, as soon as the ship docked, Edward flew to embrace Gaveston, who was waiting at the harbour. Isabella's uncles wrote indignantly to Philip in France, and Edward's conduct over the next few weeks made them increasingly concerned. The royal couple travelled to London and were crowned together at Westminster in a grand ceremony planned by Gaveston. He had ensured that he played a prominent role in the ceremony, and he caused indignation amongst the assembled English and French nobility by carrying the royal crown before the King. Edward also chose to sit beside Gaveston at the coronation banquet, relegating Isabella to an inferior seat. For Isabella, the daughter of two sovereigns, this rankled, and it was around this time that she noticed Gaveston wearing the jewels that her father had given to Edward as a wedding present.

Soon after the coronation, Isabella's two uncles returned to France bringing their own reports of Isabella's reception and the King's relationship with Gaveston. Edward also faced opposition in England for his conduct, as recorded by the *Chronicle of Lanercost*:

The people of the country and the leading men complained loudly at his [Edward's] coronation against the aforesaid Piers, and unanimously wished that he should be deprived of his earldom; but this the king obstinately refused. The rumours increased from day to day, and engrossed the lips and ears of all men, nor was there one who had a good word either for the king or for Piers. The chief men agreed unanimously in strongly demanding that Piers should be sent back into exile, foremost among them being the noble Earl of Lincoln and the young Earl of Gloucester, whose sister, however, Piers had received in marriage by the king's gift.

Edward had given his niece, Margaret de Clare, the daughter of his sister, Joan of Acre, in marriage to Piers, and this proved to be the final straw for much of the nobility. By June 1308, the King had been compelled to send Gaveston into exile.

Isabella spent more time with Edward during Gaveston's absence, with the couple spending Christmas together at Windsor. The time that they were able to spend together alone led to the couple coming to an understanding with each other, and even after Gaveston's return, they spent time together, with Isabella securing some political influence for herself. In an early letter to Edward, she wrote,

My very dear and dread lord, I commend myself to you as humbly as I can. My dear lord, you have heard how our seneschal and our controller for Ponthieu have come from Ponthieu concerning our affairs; the letters they had to bring can remain in the state they are at present until the parliament – except one which concerns you inheritance in Ponthieu and the Count of Dreux, which should be acted upon immediately in order to keep and maintain your inheritance. I beg you, my gentle lord, that by this message it may please you to request your chancellor by letter that he summon those of your council to him and take steps speedily in this matter according to what he and your said council see what is best to do for your honour and profit. For if action is not speedily taken, this will do you great harm and be of much benefit to the said count your enemy, as I have truly heard by my council. May the Holy Spirit keep you, my very dear and dread lord.

Isabella played an increasingly prominent role as queen, and by 1311, she controlled a household of over 200 people. She also developed an intimate relationship with Edward, and by early 1312, she was pregnant.

Although Edward was able to recall Gaveston to England, his presence was still deeply resented by the English nobility. By 1312, the barons, led by the Earls of Lancaster and Leicester, were actively working against the favourite. The two earls were the maternal half-brothers of Isabella's mother, and it has been suggested that they acted as their niece's champion in their actions against Gaveston. Whilst they certainly resented the slights done to Isabella by Gaveston in the early days of her marriage, by 1312, Isabella was on reasonable terms with the favourite, and she was not actively working against him.

Edward, Gaveston, and Isabella set out north in the early summer of 1312, aware of the hostility that was building towards Gaveston. Whilst they were staying at York, they heard that Lancaster had begun to march north with an army, intent on the favourite's destruction. Terrified, the three fled to Newcastle. Edward and Gaveston then sailed to Scarborough, leaving Isabella to travel to Tynemouth Castle to await the outcome of events. Soon after their voyage to Scarborough, Edward and Gaveston separated. They never saw each other again. Gaveston was captured by Lancaster and turned over to the custody of the Earl of Pembroke. On 19 July 1312, he was taken out to the crossroads at Blacklow Hill, near Warwick, and beheaded by the barons without trial. Edward was furious at the death of his favourite but powerless to take any immediate action in revenge. Isabella's feelings on the favourite's death are not recorded, but it is likely that she was not displeased by Gaveston's removal from Edward's side. Some time after the murder, she travelled slowly south towards Windsor to await the birth of her child.

Isabella bore her first child, a son, on 13 November 1312. According to the chronicler John Capgrave, there was some controversy over the choice of name for the new heir to the throne, and 'many Frensch lordis, that were aboute hir, wold a clepid him Philippea, aftir the kyng of Frans: the Englisch lords wold have him Edward. The king had so grete joy of this child new born, that his heavinesse for Petir [Gaveston] cesed some'. The King won the day, naming his son after himself rather than Isabella's father. Isabella and Edward's personal relationship continued to improve in the years following young Edward's birth, and between 1315 and 1321, Isabella bore a further three children. Whilst the frequency of these births does not suggest regular intimacy, it is obvious that the couple attempted to make their marriage work. Edward placed his trust in Isabella during the period, and the couple travelled to Paris together in 1313. The following February Isabella returned to France alone to negotiate a treaty with her father.

Isabella was probably always aware that there was a danger of Edward acquiring a new favourite to overshadow her. By the time of the birth of her youngest child, Joan, in 1321, Edward was noticeably fond of a father and a son, both called Hugh Despenser. Once again, surviving sources hint at the homosexual nature of the relationship between Edward and the younger Despenser, and Isabella, who would tellingly later have the younger Despenser castrated, was convinced that he and her husband were lovers. According to the chronicler Froissart, Edward was fully in thrall to the younger Despenser, and 'the sayd kyng governed right diversly his realme by the exortatcion of Sir Hewe Spencer, who had been norisshed with hym syth the begynnyng of his yougth; the which Sir Hewe had so enticed the kyng, that his father and he were the greatest maisters in all the realme, and by envy thought to surmount all other barons in Ingland'.

Whilst Isabella had been able to come to terms with Gaveston and tolerate his relationship with her husband, she and the Despensers were always implacably opposed. Froissart claims that 'the sayd sir Hewe Spencer achieved great hate in all the realme, and specially of the quene, and of the erle of Cane [Kent], brother to the kyng. And whan he perceived the displeasure of the quene, by his subtile wytte he set great discord bitwene the kyng and the quene, so that the kyng wold nat se the quene, nor come in her company; the whiche discord endured a long space'. The two Despensers were determined to crush any influence that Isabella had over Edward, and they showed their contempt for her in a number of ways. In 1320, for example, the elder Despenser refused to pay Isabella sums owed to her from her manor of Lechlade, and in 1321, the younger Despenser failed to pay the Queen rents that he owed her from the city of Bristol. When Isabella complained of this to Edward, she found that he supported his favourites over her.

In late 1321, Isabella decided to go on a pilgrimage to Canterbury, and on 2 October, she went to spend the night at Leeds Castle, one of her dower properties. As she approached the castle, her stewards were denied entry, and when they persisted, the castle guards opened fire, killing a number of Isabella's attendants. The castellan supported the barons who had once again risen to attack Edward due to the rise of the Despensers, and it is probable that Isabella's visit to Leeds was intended by Edward to trigger an attack on his opponents. As soon as Edward received word of what had happened at Leeds, he set out towards the castle with an army of Londoners, rapidly bringing it to submission. Edward then marched north to meet the barons in battle and achieved a great victory at Boroughbridge, ordering Isabella's uncle, Thomas of Lancaster, to be executed in the same manner in which Gaveston had died. Isabella's feelings are likely to have been mixed, but both she and her brother-in-law and cousin, Edmund of Kent were anxious at the power of the Despensers and, shortly after Lancaster's death, 'it was shewed to the quene secretly, and to the earl of Cane [Kent], that withoute they toke good hede to them selfe, they were likely to be destroyed; for sir Hewe Spencer was about to purchase moch trouble to theym'.

Isabella had reason to complain of her treatment in the years following her uncle's death, and with growing hostilities between England and France, she found that she was under increasing suspicion from Edward and the Despensers. In 1324, Isabella's uncle, Charles of Valois, invaded Gascony, and Edward retaliated by seizing Isabella's lands and those of foreign monasteries. Isabella's allowance was cut and her children removed from her custody. She was actively spied upon, and the younger Despenser's wife was 'appointed as it were, guardian of the queen, and carried her seal; nor could the queen write to anybody without her knowledge: whereat my lady the queen was equally indignant and distressed, and therefore wished to visit her brother in France to seek a remedy'. For Isabella, the opportunity to free herself from this scrutiny came in March 1325, when Edward, unwisely, agreed to send her to France to act on his behalf in peace negotiations with her brother, Charles IV, who had succeeded Isabella's father and then her two eldest brothers as king of France.

Edward and the Despensers were eager to get Isabella away from England, and they do not appear to have considered that she could be capable of taking independent action against them. According to the *Chronicle of Lanercost*, whilst Isabella was in France, the younger Despenser sent agents to the Pope to attempt to procure a divorce for Edward, and it is possible that it was intended that Isabella should not return. Isabella landed at Boulogne and immediately made her way towards Paris. According to Froissart, at her very first meeting with her brother, Isabella poured out her heart to him:

> She answered hym right sagely, and lamentably recounted to hym all the felonyes and injuries done to her by syr Hewe Spencer, and required hym of his ayde and comfort. Whan the noble kyng Charles of Fraunce had harde his suster's lamentation, who wepyngly had shewed hym all her need and besynesse, he sayd to her, Fayre suster appease your selfe, for by the faith I owe to God and to saynt Denyce, I shall right well purvey for you some remedy. The quene than kneled downed, whether the kyng wold or nat, and sayd, Y right dere lord and fayre brother, I pray God reward you.

Charles agreed to support Isabella in her dispute with Edward and the Despensers. Edward still suspected nothing, and shortly after her arrival, Isabella persuaded him to allow their eldest son to join her in Paris so that he could do homage for Gascony. Isabella was overjoyed to see her son and knew that, with him in her possession, she had a powerful bargaining counter to use against her husband. The possession of her son caused a number of the English nobility who were hostile to Edward and the Despensers to look towards her as their leader, and several English exiles joined her in Paris, including Edmund, Earl of Kent, and Roger Mortimer, a nobleman who had escaped from imprisonment in the Tower of London some years before.

Once she had secured her son's arrival and her brother's aid, Isabella finally declared her intentions and refused to return to England when summoned. The news of the Queen's defiance spread, and there were 'contradictory rumours in England about the queen, some declaring that she was the betrayer of the king and kingdom, others that she was acting for peace and the common welfare of the kingdom, and for the removal of the evil counsellors from the king'. The younger Despenser was concerned about the threat posed by Isabella, and he sent bribes of gold, silver and jewels to Isabella's brother in an attempt to persuade him to expel her from France. Edward petitioned the Pope, asking him to order Isabella to return to England.

Isabella did have plans to return to England, but not to her role as Edward's wife, and within months of her arrival in Paris, her brother was actively seeking to distance himself from her and her conduct. During their time together in Paris, Isabella and Roger Mortimer became lovers. Isabella remained devoted to Mortimer for the rest of his life, and it is clear that she was in love with him. Mortimer's feelings are less obvious, and certainly, a relationship with the Queen was to his advantage. However, the couple do appear to have had a passionate attachment to each other, to the horror of Isabella's family in France. Finally, embarrassed by all that was happening, Charles asked Isabella to leave, and she, Mortimer, young Edward and their supporters travelled to Hainault, where Isabella's cousin was countess. The exiles were given a warm welcome, and Isabella agreed a treaty, betrothing her eldest son to one of the count's daughters in exchange for ships and men for her invasion of England.

Isabella set sail from Hainault with a large fleet of ships and landed at Harwich on 24 September 1326. Aware of the danger of being perceived as foreign invaders, Isabella, her brother-in-law, Kent, and her son issued a proclamation when they arrived at Wallingford, determined to set out the righteousness of their cause:

Whereas it is well known that the state of the Holy Church and the Kingdom of England is in many respects much tarnished and degraded by the bad advice and conspiracy of Hugh le Despenser; whereas, through pride and greed to have power and dominion over all other people, he has usurped royal power against law and justice and his true allegiance, and through the bad advice of Robert de Baldock and others of his supporters, he has acted in such a way that the Holy Church is robbed of its goods against God and Right and in many ways insulted and dishonoured, and the Crown of England brought low in many respects, through the disinheritance of our lord the king and of his heirs; the magnates of the kingdom, through the envy and wicked cruelty of the said Hugh have been delivered to a shameful death, many of them blamelessly and without cause; others have been disinherited, imprisoned, banished or exiled; widows and orphans have been unlawfully deprived of their rights, and the people of this land much hurt by many taxes and held to ransom by frequent unjust demands for money and by divers other oppressions without any mercy, by virtue of which misdeeds the said Hugh shows himself to be a clear tyrant and enemy of God and the Holy Church, of our very dear lord the king and the whole kingdom.

Edward had made himself very unpopular in England, and Isabella was joined by her uncle Henry, Earl of Leicester, who, on his brother's death, had taken the title of Earl of Lancaster, and other members of the nobility. Isabella moved towards London with her forces and was glad to hear on her approach that the city had risen to support her. She stayed for only a few days in London before setting out in pursuit of Edward and the Despensers, who had fled.

Edward had left the elder Despenser in command at Bristol, and Isabella went there first, winning the town after a short siege. The elder Despenser must have known that he was doomed, and Isabella ordered him to be executed in front of Bristol Castle. Mortimer and Henry of Lancaster then set off in pursuit of Edward and the younger Despenser, who had fled towards Wales. The pair were soon captured and Edward was sent as a prisoner to Kenilworth Castle. Whilst Isabella may not at that point have decided just what to do with Edward, she was determined to have her revenge on the younger Despenser, and he was brought before her at Hereford. According to Froissart, Isabella sentenced her rival to a deeply unpleasant death:

> Fyrst to be drawen on an hyrdell with trumpes and trumpettis through all the cite of Herford, and after, to be brought into the market place, where as all the people were assembled, and there to be tyed on high upon a ladder that every man might se hym: and in the same place ther to be made a great fier, and ther his privy members cut from hym, because they reputed hym as an heretyk, and sodomite, and so to be brent in the fyre before his face: and than his hart to be drawen out of his body, and cast into the fyre, bycause he was a false traytour of hart, and that by hys traytours counsel and extorcion, the kyng had shamed his realme, and brought it to great mischief, for he had caused to be behedded the greatest lords of his realme, by whom the realme ought to have been susteyned and defended: and he had so enducd the kyng, that he wolde nat se the quene his wife, nor Edwarde his eldest son, and caused hym to chace them out of the realme for fere of theyr lyves: and than his heed to be stryken of and sent to London. And accordiyng to this judgement, he was executed.

The circumstances of the younger Despenser's death were particularly horrible, and it is a mark of Isabella's belief in his relationship with her husband that she ordered him to be castrated as a sodomite.

Isabella and Mortimer spent Christmas at Wallingford, and in January 1327, they arrived in London, where Isabella called a parliament. As she hoped, parliament agreed that Edward II should abdicate in favour of his son, and that Isabella 'for the great anxiety and anguish she had suffered' should be granted the title of queen for life.

Due to Edward III's youth, the real power behind the throne remained Isabella and Mortimer, something that the young king keenly resented. When Edward II had been asked to abdicate, he had wept and begged to receive visits from his wife and children. Isabella had no wish to see her estranged husband, and when he requested that she visit, she refused, saying that the lords would not allow her to see him. She did send him presents and clothes, although this is more likely to have been to ensure that she maintained the appearance of a dutiful wife rather than because she felt any fondness for her husband. For Isabella and Mortimer, Edward's continued existence was a threat, and he did not long survive his deposition. Late in 1327, he was taken as a prisoner to Berkeley Castle in Gloucestershire, and he died on the night of 1 September. The exact cause of death was not recorded, but it has been rumoured that he was killed by a red-hot spit inserted into his rectum. There is no contemporary evidence for this, but it is certain that Edward was murdered and that Isabella, even if she did not give the order herself, was complicit in the death of her husband. Whilst Mortimer was the dominant force in his relationship with Isabella, it is impossible that he would have acted without her authority.

The rumours surrounding Edward II's death reflected badly on Isabella, and she and Mortimer made themselves unpopular in other ways, too. Edward III and much of the nobility disapproved of their policies, such as the decision to make peace with Scotland. Isabella also caused anger by assigning herself the largest dower ever known for a queen of England, ensuring that she had access to a vast revenue source. Mortimer became increasingly domineering, and in 1329, the couple took steps to neutralise Edmund of Kent when he began to waver in his support for them. Kent was wracked with guilt at his involvement in the deposition of his half-brother, and in 1329, he was informed secretly that his brother was still alive. It is possible that this rumour was spread by Mortimer in order to test Kent's loyalty or to incriminate him, and when Kent responded by sending a friar to enquire into his brother's whereabouts, Mortimer struck. At a parliament later in the year, Kent was accused of plotting to restore Edward II and sentenced to death, with the sentence being carried out against the wishes of his nephew, Edward III. The execution of the son of a king shocked the nobility and undermined any vestige of support for Isabella and Mortimer's rule.

By 1330, Edward III was approaching eighteen, and he resented the dominance of his mother and her lover. He also resented the rumours about Isabella and Mortimer's relationship that were prevalent in England, and Froissart, for example, recorded in his chronicle that Isabella was believed to be pregnant by Mortimer. This rumour was untrue, but it angered the King, and there were also claims that Mortimer wished to depose him and become king himself. In 1330, Mortimer and Isabella called a parliament at Nottingham, and Edward decided to act, entering Nottingham Castle one night with a group of attendants through a secret tunnel. According to the Chronicle of Geoffrey Le Baker,

> Having rushed out of the underground passage and subterranean route, the king's friends advanced with drawn sword to the queen's bedroom, the king waited, armed, outside the chamber of their foes, lest he should be seen by his mother. As the conspirators charged in, they killed Hugh de Turpinton, knight, as he tried to resist them, Lord John de Neville of Hornby directing the blow. Then they found the queen mother almost ready for bed, and the Earl of March [Mortimer] whom they wanted. They led him captive into the hall, while the queen cried 'fair son, fair son, have pity on gentle Mortimer'; for she suspected that her son was there, even though she had not seen him.

Edward had no intention of showing mercy towards Mortimer, and he was executed. Isabella's life was never in danger, but immediately after his coup, Edward placed her under strict house arrest and seized her lands and goods. Isabella spent two years confined at Castle Rising in Norfolk, grieving for Mortimer and her lost liberty.

Edward retained affection for Isabella, and he gradually allowed her to be rehabilitated back into the royal family. She was never given any political role, however, and Edward never learned to trust her again. She spent the rest of her life quietly, mainly living at Castle Rising. She fell ill on 22 August 1358, apparently due to taking an overdose of medicine, and died later the same day. Edward III gave his mother a royal funeral, which he attended himself, and according to legend, Isabella was buried in her wedding dress, clutching Edward II's heart in a silver casket. This may suggest that she felt remorse for the murder of her husband, but it is more telling that she asked to be buried at Greyfriars in London, the burial place of her true love, Mortimer.

Isabella of France is the most notorious of any post-conquest queen of England, and she is remembered today as the 'She-Wolf of France', thanks to a reference to her role in Edward's murder in a poem by Thomas Grey:

> The shrieks of death, thro' Berkeley's roofs that ring,
> Shrieks of an agonising king!
> She-wolf of France, with unrelenting fangs,
> That tear'st the bowels of thy mangled mate,
> From thee be born, who o'er thy country hangs
> The scourge of Heav'n what terrors round him wait!'

Isabella sought to extend her power as queen beyond the death of her husband and the marriage of her son, and for the first few years of Edward III's marriage to Philippa of Hainault, she refused to yield any power or status to her young daughter-in-law.

PHILIPPA OF HAINAULT (1310-69) was the daughter of William III Count of Hainault and his wife, Jeanne of Valois. She was born in 1310 and was one of a family of four daughters and one son. In December 1325, Philippa's grandfather, the Count of Valois, died, and her mother travelled to Paris for the funeral. It is uncertain whether she brought any of her daughters with her to meet her French kin, but certainly, whilst in Paris, Jeanne met with her cousin, Isabella of France, and suggested a marriage alliance between one of her daughters and Isabella's eldest son. By late 1325, Isabella was badly in need of allies, and it was to Hainault that she and her supporters travelled in July 1326 when they were forced to leave France.

Isabella and her son, Edward, journeyed to Valenciennes in Hainault, where they were warmly received by the townspeople. According to Froissart, Philippa's parents were anxious for such a prestigious match for one of their daughters.

> [Isabella] was brought before the erle Guyllaume of Heynaulte, who receyved her with great joye, and in lyke wyse dyd the countesse his wife, and feasted her ryght nobly. And as than this erle hadde foure fayre daughters, Margaret, Philyppe, Jane, and Isabell; amonge whome the yong Edwarde sette moost his love and company on Phylyppe; and also the yong lady in al honour was more conversaunt with hym than any of her susters.

Isabella and Edward remained with Philippa's family for eight days, and during that time, Edward was given the opportunity to select which of the four sisters he would prefer as a wife. His preference for Philippa soon became clear, and whilst she was no beauty, Edward was pleased with the devotion that she showed towards him. Whilst the choice of bride had not been finalised by the time Edward and his mother left Valenciennes, it was clear that it would be Philippa, and as she said goodbye to her English cousin, she burst into tears.

On 27 August 1326, Isabella and Count William agreed a marriage treaty between Edward and one of the count's daughters. It was agreed that the marriage would take place within two years, and that, in return, William would supply a dowry of troops, ships and money in advance of the wedding. Given the fact that Isabella and Philippa's mother were first cousins, it took some time to secure the necessary dispensation from the Pope, but finally, on 3 September 1327, it was granted, with the document naming Philippa as the intended bride for the first time.

In December 1327, Philippa's uncle, John of Hainault, arrived from England to fetch her for her marriage. Philippa landed in England on 23 December and made her state entry to London the following day. She was lodged at Ely Palace and spent the Christmas period there, feasting and dancing. After Christmas, she set out north to join Edward, who was busy campaigning against the Scots, and they met at York, where they were married on 30 January. The marriage was conducted in the freezing cold, but it was a lavish ceremony and Philippa and Edward found their feelings for each other unchanged after so many months apart. In spite of this, Philippa cannot have failed to notice the prominence of Isabella of France in the young king's affairs, and she may have felt uneasy about the precedence that Isabella enjoyed over her. Unusually, Philippa was granted no dower or independent household at her wedding, and Isabella, anxious to be the only anointed queen in England, refused to allow her daughter-in-law to be crowned.

The first few years of Edward's reign were dominated by Isabella and her lover, Roger Mortimer. Edward keenly resented this and the forced subordination of Philippa, and he had hoped that his marriage would be the occasion at which he was able to assert his authority as an adult. Philippa's lack of a coronation rankled with Edward, especially as by late 1329 she was pregnant. It was unthinkable that an heir to the throne should be born without his mother being crowned, and Isabella finally consented to the ceremony taking place on 4 March 1330. Shortly afterwards, Philippa bore her first son, Edward, who would later be known as the Black Prince. Philippa had no involvement in the coup against Mortimer and Isabella, but she benefited from Isabella's forced retirement and was finally able to take up her position as queen of England.

Philippa and Edward's long marriage proved to be extremely close, and Edward was very protective of her. On 21 September 1331, Philippa and her ladies assembled to watch Edward take part in a tournament at Cheapside. As the tournament began, the wooden stand on which Philippa and her ladies sat collapsed, causing Edward to be thrown from his horse and knocking all the ladies to the ground. No one was badly hurt, but Edward, in a rage, swore that the carpenters who built the stand would be put to death. Philippa, although still shaken from her fall, threw herself on her knees before Edward and begged that the workmen's lives be spared. This appeal softened Edward's mood, and he agreed to her request. This is the first incident of many during their marriage where Philippa calmed her husband and protected those who angered him.

Another indication of the close relationship between Edward and Philippa is their large family. Philippa gave birth to seven sons and five daughters during her marriage, five of whom outlived her. This was a large number of children even in the medieval period, and few queens have equalled Philippa's record. Edward and Philippa were indulgent parents. This can be seen in their treatment of their eldest daughter, Isabella, who went through a number of broken betrothals before finally, in 1350, being sent to France to marry. A few days before the wedding, Isabella changed her mind and promptly sailed for home. Edward and Philippa accepted her decision and she remained unmarried with a generous annual income until 1365 when she eloped with a French hostage imprisoned in London. Again, Edward and Philippa accepted their daughter's choice, and they remained on excellent terms with her. They also allowed their eldest son, Edward, the Black Prince, to make a love match with his cousin, the divorced Joan of Kent, and Philippa was present at their wedding at Windsor on 10 October 1361.

The preoccupation of Edward's life was his invasion of France. Edward's uncle, Charles IV of France, had died in 1328 and was succeeded by his cousin (and Philippa's uncle), Philip V. Edward, as the grandson of Philip IV, believed that he had a better claim to the French throne than his grandfather's nephew and he decided to press his claim through force. He hoped to build an alliance through his and Philippa's family connections, and in August 1336, he banned the export of English wool to the Low Countries in order to persuade them to join with him. English wool was essential to the cloth industries there, and the export ban soon had an effect. This policy damaged Hainault's economy, and Philippa took steps to mitigate the suffering of her countrymen, encouraging foreign weavers to settle in England and using her influence with Edward to assist them in establishing themselves.

By late 1337, Edward's export ban had had an effect, and on 7 October, he felt strong enough to declare himself king of France. He and Philippa sailed on 16 July 1338 to meet with their allies and discuss the proposed invasion. They spent Christmas at Antwerp, where Philippa had given birth to her second surviving son, Lionel, in November. Edward's preparations continued throughout the next year, and in early 1340, he returned to England to raise further funds, leaving Philippa, her daughter Isabella and son Lionel as surety for his good faith to his allies in Ghent. This must have been a lonely few months for Philippa, and it is notable as one of the few occasions when the couple were apart during their marriage. She bore a third surviving son during her stay in Ghent, John of Gaunt. By June 1340, Edward had the money he needed and rejoined Philippa. Given the conflict of interest that Edward's war with her uncle placed her in, she may also have been secretly relieved when her mother, the sister of the French king, negotiated a truce between England and France, allowing Philippa and Edward to return home to England.

The next few years may have been the happiest of Philippa's life. She was extravagant and loved finery and luxuries. For example, in 1335, she ordered a bed of green velvet embroidered with gold, and a velvet robe costing £700, a vast sum. In 1344, Edward founded the Order of the Garter, which entailed an annual celebration on St George's Day at Windsor. According to Froissart, Philippa played a prominent role in the first celebration, appearing richly dressed and attended by 300 ladies.

Whilst Philippa was happiest in England, the peace with France did not last long, and in 1346, Edward left England to invade France, taking his eldest son with him. Philippa remained in England as co-regent with her young son Lionel. Philippa's time as regent was not without drama, as King David of Scotland invaded the country and burned the suburbs of York. According to Froissart, Philippa responded quickly:

> [She] got together all the forces she was able, and marching to Newcastle, gave the Scots battle at a place called Neville's Cross, where she took King David prisoner. The capture of the king gave the queen of England a decided superiority over her enemies; they retired and when she had sufficiently provided for the defence of the cities of York and Durham, as well as for the borders generally, she herself set out for London; and shortly after, having confined her royal prisoner in the Tower, joined the king, her husband, at Calais.

Although Philippa did not personally lead her army, she was present in the area throughout the campaign and issued personal instructions to her commanders. Her great victory confirmed Edward's trust in making her regent, although she missed her husband too much to continue with the role and travelled to join him at Calais.

Edward had begun a siege of Calais soon after winning a great victory at the Battle of Crecy in September 1346. According to Froissart, the siege took longer than Edward had planned, and he grew increasingly impatient. Finally, the six principal citizens of Calais came out to meet him wearing ropes around their necks to symbolise their submission and carrying the keys to the castle and the town. Edward was in no mood to be merciful:

> [He] loked felly on theym, for greatly he hated the people of Calys, for the gret damages and displeasures they had done hym on the see before. Than he commaunded their heedes to be stryken of. Than every man requyred the kyng for mercy, but he wolde here no man in that behalfe. Than sir Gaultier of Manny sayd, A noble kyng, for Goddessake, refrayne your courage; ye have the name of soverayne nobles. Therefore nowe do nat a thing that shulde blemysshe your renome, nor to gyve cause to some to speke of you villainy; every man woll say it is a great cruelty to put to deth suche honest persons, who by their owne wylles putte themselfe into your grace to save their company. Than the kyng wryed away fro hym, and commanded to sende for the hangman, and sayd, They of Calys had caused many of my men to be slayne, wherefore these shall dye in likewyse. Than the quene beynge great with chylde, kneled downe and sore wepyng, sayd, A gentyll sir, syth I passed the see in great parell, I have desired nothing of you; therefore nowe I humbly require you, in the honour of the Son of the Virgyn Mary and for the love of me that ye woll take mercy of these sixe burgesses. The kyng

59. Queen Philippa (left) and her headstrong eldest daughter, Princess Isabella. Drawings of scenes depicted in tapestries made during the reign of Edward III and which hung in St Stephen's Chapel, Westminster, until they were destroyed when the old Palace of Westminster burned down.

behelde the quene and stode styll in a study of space, and than sayd, A dame, I wold ye had ben as nowe in some other place, ye make suche request to me that I can nat deny you; wherefore I gyve them to you, to do your pleasure with theym. Than the quene caused them to be brought into her chamber, and made the halters to be taken fro their neckes, and caused them to be newe clothed, and gave them their dyner at their leser; and than she gave ech of them sixe nobles and made them to be brough out of thoost in savegard and set at their lyberte.

Only Philippa had the influence over Edward to save the six men, and he trusted and relied on her judgement. Soon after the fall of Calais, Philippa bore a daughter, Margaret, before returning home to England with Edward and the infant.

The advent of the Black Death in the late 1340s led to a truce between England and France, as neither country had the men to field an army. The plague touched Philippa and Edward personally, as their daughter Joan, who was on her way to marry the King of Castile, caught the plague at Bordeaux and died within a few hours. For a fond mother like Philippa, this was devastating. She may, however, have found some consolation in her remaining children, and she continued to bear children for several years after Joan's death. Philippa's youngest child, Thomas, was born at Woodstock in 1355, when she was in her mid-forties.

Philippa's interests mainly focused on her family and her enjoyment of fine clothes and entertainments. She was also a patron of learning and is remembered as the foundress of Queen's College, Oxford. She provided the majority of the funds for her college and, in 1342, obtained a confirmation of the foundation from the Pope. She continued to show an interest in her foundation, granting an annual sum for the sustenance and aid of the provost and scholars of the college in July 1347. Philippa was the first queen to found or patronise a college, although most later medieval queens followed her example. She was also the patron of the chronicler Jean Froissart, and he personally handed her a copy of his chronicle when it was completed.

The sources are largely silent on Philippa's whereabouts during the last years of her life, and it is likely that she lived quietly, accompanying Edward on his travels and devoting herself to her family. In the summer of 1369, she fell ill at Windsor, as documented by Froissart:

> Whanne she knewe and perceyved that there was with her no remedy but dethe, she desyred to speke with the kynge her husbande, and whan he was before her, she put out her bedde her right hande, and toke the kynge by his right hande, who was right sorrowfull at his hert; than she said, Sir, we have in peace, joye, and great prosperyte, used all oure tyme toguyder: Sir, nowe I pray you at our departing, that ye wyll graunt me thre desires. The kynge, ryght sorrowfully wepyng, sayd, Madame, desire what ye wyll, I graunt it.

Philippa first asked Edward to pay her debts. She then requested that he honour any promises that she had made to the Church. Finally, and touchingly, she said, 'Thirdely, sir, I requyre you that it may please you to take none other sepulture, whan soever it shall please God to call you out of this transytorie lyfe, but beside me in Westmynster.' Edward agreed to Philippa's requests, and she made the sign of the cross before commending her youngest son, Thomas, who sat weeping at her side, to her husband. Philippa of Hainault then 'yelded up the spiryte, the whiche I believe surely the holy angels received with great joy up in heven, for in all her lyfe she dyd neyther in thought nor dede thing, wherby to lese her soule, as ferr as any creature coulde knowe'.

Edward was devastated by Philippa's death and the whole country grieved for a woman who had been queen for thirty-nine years and who had never been touched by scandal or accusation of wrongdoing. Philippa was a quiet, happy woman who was devoted to her husband and children, and Edward relied on her. With her third request, that Edward should share her tomb, Philippa appears to have feared that Edward might remarry and forget her. She was aware that the King had been discreetly unfaithful to her throughout their marriage and that he was involved in an affair with one of her maids, Alice Perrers. Following Philippa's death, Perrers came to dominate the King, helping to decide policy and controlling access to him. In 1376, the Black Prince died, leaving his young son as heir to England. The following year, Edward III also died, and his body was stripped of its jewels by Alice Perrers before he was even cold. Philippa of Hainault's death left a void in England, and the office of queen was left vacant for nearly twenty years until the arrival of Anne of Bohemia, the first wife of Richard II.

ANNE OF BOHEMIA (1366-94) had great influence over her devoted husband, Richard II, and she was also an important figure in the early religious reform movement. Whilst most of the Plantagenet kings drew their wives from France, Anne of Bohemia's origins were exotic and she was born in Prague in May 1366, the eldest daughter of the Holy Roman Emperor, Charles IV, and his fourth wife, Elizabeth of Pomerania. Anne was very well educated and could speak several languages. Whilst she was still young, her father died and was succeeded by his son, Wenzel. It was Wenzel who negotiated Anne's marriage to Richard II.

Richard II would probably have looked for a bride in France if it had not been for the Great Schism in the Church. In 1376, Urban VI was elected as pope by a conclave in Rome. This appointment was controversial, and shortly afterwards, a further group of cardinals elected a second man as pope. France, Spain, Naples and Savoy supported the second pope, Clement, whilst England and the Holy Roman Empire supported Urban. On the death of Edward III in 1377, his ten-year-old grandson succeeded to the throne as Richard II, and almost immediately, the King's guardians began to search for a suitable bride for him. There appears to have been something of a shortage of eligible ladies, as Froissart comments:

Ther was great counsaile in Englande amonge the kynges uncles and the prelates and barons
of the realme, for to mary ther yonge kyng Richarde of England. And thenglysshmen wolde
gladly have had hym to ben maryed in Heynalt, for love of the good lady queen Philyp, wife to
kyng Edwarde the Thirde, who was so good and so gracyous a lady, for all the realme large and
honourable, who was come out of Heynaulte; but as than the duke Aubert had no daughters to
mary. The duke of Lancastre wolde have hadde the king his nephew to have hadde his eldest
doughter, my lady Blanche of Lancastre, to his wife: but the realme wolde in no wyse consent
therto, for two reasons: the first, bycause the lady was his cosyn germayne, the whiche was to nere
of blode to mary toguyder; the other cause was, they wolde the kynge shulde marry without the
realme, to have therby more alyaunce.

The council settled on a daughter of the Duke of Milan, and later that year, envoys were sent
to Italy to negotiate the match. Pope Urban, anxious to bind his allies more closely together,
summoned the English envoys to Rome where he proposed a marriage between Richard
and Anne. English interest was pricked and one of the King's advisors, Sir Simon Burley,
was sent to negotiate with Anne's brother. Wenzel was eager for the marriage, and Anne's
mother, who commissioned a report to discover whether England was a suitable home for
her daughter, also gave her consent.

By late 1381, negotiations were complete and Anne was ready to set out for England.
Although the marriage had been favourably received in both England and the Holy Roman
Empire, it was not treated so positively amongst the supporters of Pope Clement. Anne set
out for England accompanied by a great train of ladies and gentlemen, travelling overland to
Brussels, which was ruled by her uncle, the Duke of Brabant. According to Froissart, Anne
was forced to spend a month in Brussels waiting to continue her journey to England:

> It was shewed her that ther was on the see a xii. Vessels of Normayns bytwene Caleys and
> Hollande, and they robbed and pylled on the see, they cared nat who. And so they kepte the
> boundes of the see about Flaunders and Zelande, abyding the coming of this yonge lady. For the
> French kyng wolde gladly have broken that maryage, for he greatlye douted the alyaunce bytwene
> Englande and Almayne.

Whilst it was 'nat honourable to take ladyes in warre', the French were determined to capture
Anne. Anne's uncle, the Duke of Brabant, took the initiative himself, sending messengers to
the King of France and insisting that a safe-conduct be granted. Anxious to remain on friendly
terms with the duke, the French king relented, and Anne continued her journey, travelling
overland through Flanders and on to Calais, where she was welcomed by a deputation of English
noblemen. Anne spent only a short time in the English-held town before sailing to Dover.

Even Anne's sea crossing did not go smoothly, and according to the sixteenth-century historian
John Hayward, 'she had no sooner set foote within this land but such a tempest did forthwith
arise as had not bene seene many yeares before, whereby divers ships within the haven were
quashed to peeces, but especially, and first of all, the ship wherin the quene was carried'. Anne
was met at Dover by the King's uncle, John of Gaunt, and taken to Leeds Castle to celebrate
Christmas. She then journeyed to Westminster, where she met her future husband for the first
time. The couple were very close in age, with Richard only a year younger than Anne, and they
rapidly became close, suggesting that their first impressions of each other were favourable.

Anne and Richard were married in the chapel at Westminster Palace on 14 January 1382.
The wedding was a small, intimate occasion with the major ceremony being reserved for
Anne's coronation. On 18 January, Anne rode on horseback to Westminster. Several days of

festivities followed and she was crowned on 22 January. Large crowds turned out to see her, although, according to the Westminster chronicler, she was not received wholly favourably and 'to those with an eye for the facts it seemed that she represented a purchase rather than a gift, since the English king laid out no small sum to secure this tiny scrap of humanity'. Richard himself was never displeased with the bargain he had made for Anne, in spite of the fact that her brother offered no dowry. Soon after their marriage, the couple went on progresses together to the West Country and East Anglia. They fell in love and were inseparable throughout their marriage.

Anne travelled almost constantly with Richard but had little interest in politics. Instead, she became a leader of fashion and is attributed with having introduced both the side-saddle and the high-peaked horn headdress into England. She and Richard loved luxury and enjoyed attending the theatre and pageants. The couple fitted a bath with taps for hot and cold water at their favourite palace of Sheen, and at Eltham, another palace of which they were fond, Richard had a garden laid out and a bathhouse built. In 1390, he held a grand tournament and feasts in London, and Anne and her ladies attended to select the winners and award the prizes. Both Richard and Anne were determined to enjoy themselves, and the couple had many similar interests.

Anne also had a more serious side, and she was devoted to learning. She took a keen interest in Queen's College, Oxford, and wrote a letter on the subject of education. Anne was very well educated and brought copies of the New Testament in Latin, Czech and German with her to England. Soon after she arrived in England, she ordered an English translation of the Gospels: something that was both an attempt to learn English and which demonstrates her interest in religious reform. The Archbishop of Canterbury spoke of her Biblical study in her funeral oration and William Wycliffe, the first person to translate the Bible into English, mentioned Anne's gospels in his writings. Anne's interest in the Bible helped to publicise Wycliffe's translation, and the English Bible was a major focus of the religious reform movement of the sixteenth century. Anne brought a number of Bohemian book illustrators with her to England, and English manuscripts from the period show their distinctive style.

Anne and Richard went on another progress together in 1383, making a pilgrimage to the shrine at Walsingham during their journey. This pilgrimage may have been intended to seek divine intervention for their childlessness. The couple spent time at Ely during their progress, and there, according to the *Westminster Chronicle*, a royal favourite, Sir James Berners, was struck by lightning and blinded. Anne and Richard witnessed him being healed at the tomb of St Etheldreda in the town, and this merely served to reinforce their own deeply pious beliefs. The progress continued north to Nottingham and York before returning to London again.

In spite of his happy domestic life with Anne, Richard's reign was troubled. Anne had brought a large train with her from Bohemia, and Richard made himself unpopular by arranging marriages between Anne's countrywomen and noblemen in England. The biggest scandal of the reign centred on one of Anne's Bohemian ladies. Richard II's most prominent favourite was Robert de Vere, Duke of Ireland. According to John Hayward, 'Robert Duke of Ireland forsooke the companie of his lawfull wife, whose mother, Lady Isabel, was daughter of King Edward the third, and in steede of her he tooke unto him a base Bohemian, a taverner's daughter. The king little regarded this indignitie done unto his cosin'. Richard and Anne supported de Vere, and Anne went so far as to write to the Pope on his behalf, seeking his divorce. This brought the couple into direct conflict with Richard's uncles, who were angry at the treatment meted out to their discarded niece.

Richard's uncles were a thorn in his side. In 1385, his most senior uncle, the domineering John of Gaunt, left England in order to press his claims to the throne of Castile. Richard was, initially, glad to see the back of him, but he came to regret his absence. In 1386, a hostile parliament assembled and forced Richard to dismiss his chancellor. At the parliament, it became clear that Richard's youngest uncle, Thomas, Duke of Gloucester, was in open opposition to his nephew. By 1387, Gloucester controlled London, and he and the Earls of Warwick and Arundel, who were collectively known as the Lords Appellant, accused Richard's friends of treason at Westminster in November 1387. They were joined in their rebellion by the Earl of Derby (the future Henry IV) and the Earl of Nottingham, who defeated the King's army, led by de Vere, in December.

It is probable that Gloucester had designs on the throne, and this period was one of intense worry for Richard and Anne. The couple were present in February 1388 when the 'Merciless Parliament' was assembled by the Lords Appellant and Richard was forced to dismiss his remaining supporters. Sir Simon Burley was arrested and Anne, who was fond of the man who had negotiated her marriage, threw herself on her knees before Gloucester to beg for his life. This did not have the desired effect, and Gloucester merely told her curtly to pray for her husband and herself. Burley was executed a few months later. The Appellants remained in power throughout 1388, although their popularity began to wane. Finally, on 3 May 1389, Richard confronted them at a council meeting and wrested power back from his opponents.

Anne's intercession on behalf of Sir Simon Burley was not her only attempt to obtain mercy for accused and convicted people in England, and like her predecessor as queen, Philippa of Hainault, she was famed for her good works as a mediator. Intercession was always an important part of medieval queenship, and Anne fulfilled the role to perfection, becoming known as 'Good Queen Anne'. At her request, a general pardon was granted at her coronation, and she interceded successfully for a convicted felon in 1384 by throwing herself at Richard's feet.

Anne's most famous intercession was on behalf of the city of London. In July 1392, Richard called representatives of London to him at Windsor in order to extract a loan from them. When they refused, he swore revenge on the city, to the Londoners' terror. According to the *Westminster Chronicle,* this revenge never occurred:

> At length through the intercession, on behalf of the Londoners, of friends, conspicuous among them the queen (who more than once, indeed on many occasions, both at Windsor and at Nottingham, prostrated herself at the king's feet in earnest and tireless entreaty for the city, and the welfare of its citizens that he would cease to direct his anger against them and would not let so famous a city and its teeming masses perish without due consideration simply because of the burning passion of its enemies), the king's mild and kindly nature was moved by pity, and persuaded by the queen and by others among his nobles and prominent men he forgave the Londoners all their offences against him on condition that within the next ten years they paid him or his unquestionable attorneys £40,000 in real terms of jewels or species and that on the day appointed for his progress, which was 21 August they should come out to meet him and receive him at Wandsworth with appropriate pomp.

On the day of their entry into London, the couple set out from Sheen and were met by thousands of riders and men on foot. The Londoners presented Richard with a sword, the keys of the city and a horse. They gave Anne a horse with a golden saddle. The streets of London were decorated with banners and crowded with people and a number of pageants were staged, including one where a choir of boys, dressed as angels, placed crowns on

Anne and Richard's heads. The couple then processed to Westminster Abbey, where they dismounted and ceremonially performed their devotions. At Christmas 1393 the couple were again entertained by the Londoners, who presented Anne with 'a large and remarkable bird with an enormously wide gullet'. This was possibly a pelican and Anne's reaction to the gift unfortunately does not survive. Thanks to Richard's favourable reaction to the show put on for him by the city, Anne was able to persuade him to remit some of the £40,000 owed to him by the Londoners.

Anne did not long survive Richard's reconciliation with his capital city. Whilst staying at her favourite palace of Sheen, she fell ill suddenly with the plague and died on 7 June 1394 at the age of just twenty-eight. Richard was grief-stricken and he ordered that Sheen, the palace where they had been happiest, be demolished so that he would never have to visit it without her. Richard gave Anne a grand funeral in Westminster Abbey and commissioned a fine double tomb for Anne and himself which showed the couple's effigies, touchingly, holding hands. Anne of Bohemia and Richard II were devoted to each other and Anne brought out the best in the King. After her death, Richard's hold on his throne rapidly spiralled out of his control and his second queen, Isabella of Valois, never exercised any authority over the increasingly autocratic and unpredictable king.

The marriage of ISABELLA OF VALOIS (1389-1410) and Richard II was one of the strangest royal marriages and caused comment by contemporaries. In June 1393, a peace treaty with France was drawn up, but Richard's parliament refused to ratify it. Richard II, who was very far removed from his martial father and grandfather, remained anxious to make a lasting peace with France, and his second marriage was a substitute for this aborted treaty. In spite of his grief on the death of Anne of Bohemia, Richard needed a new wife so that he could father an heir. Within months of Anne's death, he sent envoys to ask for the hand of Yolande of Aragon in marriage. He was persuaded to break off negotiations when Charles VI of France offered his own daughter, Isabella, as a bride.

Isabella of Valois, the eldest child of Charles VI of France and his wife, Isabella of Bavaria, was born in 1389. Richard was attracted to marriage to Isabella primarily due to the promise of peace that it offered. It is also possible that the bride's extreme youth appealed to him, as it would give him time for his grief for Anne of Bohemia to mellow. Certainly, when challenged on the wisdom of marrying a bride so far from being old enough for childbearing, Richard contended that she would become older with every day that passed. This was a clever response but one that satisfied no one, and the marriage was deeply unpopular in England. Richard was the only surviving child of the Black Prince and had no direct or obvious successor, meaning that there was a great urgency for him to father an heir. The marriage was not universally unpopular and the scholar Philippe de Mézières wrote an open letter to Richard setting out the benefits of the marriage and pointing out that Richard had no guarantee of issue with an adult queen. He highlighted the benefits of being able to train Isabella as an English queen from an early age, suggesting that a camel had to be trained from infancy to obey man. He concluded that 'would it not be better that the lady he chooses as helpmeet and wife, from her childhood, before reaching the age of discretion and before acquiring harmful habits of mind, should be well instructed under the prudent and wise guidance of the royal majesty'. It is unlikely that this letter dispelled many doubts about the marriage, but Richard himself remained committed to the match.

Negotiations for the marriage proceeded slowly, but Richard and Charles eventually agreed a twenty-eight-year truce in March 1396. According to Froissart, at the same time, the English ambassadors requested that they be allowed to see Isabella, in order to report on her appearance and conduct to their master. This was granted, although the French, concerned by Isabella's extreme youth, pointed out

> that they muste be content howe so ever they founde her, for they sayde she was but a yonge chylde of eyght yere of age, wherefore they sayd, there coulde nat be in her no great wysdome nor prudence; howbeit, she was indoctryned well ynough, and that the lords founde well whan they sawe her. The erle Marshall, beynge on his knees, sayde to her: Fayre lady, by the grace of God ye shall be our lady and quene of Englande. Than aunswered the yonge lady well advisedly, without counsayle of any other persone: Syr, quod she, and it please God and my lorde my father that I shall be quene of Englande, I shall be glad therof, for it is shewed me that I shall be than a great lady.

The ambassadors left convinced that Isabella 'was lykely to be a lady of hygh honoure and great goodnesse'.

Richard sailed to Calais in 1396 for a meeting with the French king. The two kings had much in common, and the visit was a cordial one. Over dinner one night in a rich tent, Charles commented to Richard that he wished Isabella was older, so that she would love Richard more. To this, Richard replied that he was pleased with her as she was. Froissart recorded the couple's first meeting: immediately after dinner, Isabella was led in accompanied by a great number of ladies and was ceremonially handed over to her new husband, receiving English attendants, led by the Duchesses of Lancaster and Gloucester, in place of her French ladies. She was seated in a rich litter and, together with Richard and the English nobility, travelled back towards Calais. For Isabella, at the age of only seven, this must have been a bewildering experience, but her first meeting with her husband went well. The couple were married in Calais and then sailed for England. The crossing was marred by storms and many of Richard's ships were lost. According to the sixteenth-century historian John Hayward, many people in England saw the stormy arrival of Richard's second queen as a bad omen. Other bad omens were also seen at the time, including a plank of wood that bled and flies swarming thickly in one of Richard's palaces. In a superstitious age, this did not augur well for either Richard's marriage or his reign.

Richard gave Isabella a grand entry into London. This must have been a terrifying experience for her, as the people of the town, eager to catch a glimpse of their young queen, crowded thickly around her. Isabella was unscathed, but at least nine people were crushed to death on London Bridge, a tragedy that marred the occasion. Isabella's coronation at Westminster Abbey went ahead as arranged. At only seven years old, it was never intended that she would be ready for either marriage or queenship, and she was sent with her own household to Windsor in order to grow up. Isabella was allowed to keep some of her remaining French attendants and her countrywoman, Lady de Coucy, was appointed as her governess.

Due to Isabella's youth, she played no role in the politics of Richard II's troubled reign. Richard was fond of his young bride and visited her regularly. Isabella was glad of this attention, and she became devoted to him. It is likely that she was not aware of the growing resentment towards him in England. Richard had been slowly working towards revenge against the five Lords Appellant since he had wrested control back from them. Soon after his marriage, he heard of a plot by his uncle, the Duke of Gloucester, and the Earl of Arundel to imprison him and Isabella and rule England as regents. Richard, who was with Isabella when he heard of the plot, left her at Eltham and made a pretence of going hunting. He then rode to Havering where Gloucester was staying and asked him to come with him to London.

Gloucester was surprised but obeyed and rode to London with the King. As they entered the city, the duke was accosted by a large group of armed men. Richard rode away from the trap, leaving Gloucester to be arrested and taken to Calais, where he was murdered. Richard saw this as just revenge against his troublesome uncle, but there were murmurings amongst the other noblemen in England. Richard failed to heed this and, soon after Gloucester's arrest, had the Earl of Arundel executed. A further Appellant, the Earl of Warwick, was also arrested, although his death sentence was commuted to life imprisonment following a plea for mercy from Isabella.

The remaining two Appellants, Henry, Earl of Derby, and the Earl of Nottingham, gave Richard the opportunity he needed to complete his revenge when they quarrelled in 1398. Both accused the other of treason, and it was agreed that the dispute should be settled by combat. On 16 September 1398, as the two men prepared to do battle, Richard dramatically stopped the proceedings and exiled Nottingham for life and Derby for six years. The lenience of Derby's sentence was due to the powerful position of his father, John of Gaunt, in Richard's government. By September, John of Gaunt was already ailing, and in February 1399, he died. Richard immediately seized John of Gaunt's extensive lands and declared that Derby, who was still in exile on the Continent, could never return to England. Richard felt that that was the end of the matter and made plans for an expedition to Ireland.

Before he left for Ireland, Richard held a grand tournament and feast in London. The tournament was intended to highlight the splendour of Richard's reign, and Isabella was present. In spite of the expense laid out in the tournament, it was poorly attended, and according to Froissart, this was due to Richard's treatment of the Earl of Derby. Isabella played the part of queen well, but soon after the tournament, she returned to Windsor, where Richard took his leave of her. Neither can have realised that this would be the last time that they would meet.

Soon after Richard left for Ireland, Derby sailed from France in order to claim his inheritance as Duke of Lancaster. He received a rapturous reception in England and decided to make an attempt on his cousin's crown. Richard had left his remaining uncle, the Duke of York, as regent of England in his absence, and as soon as he heard of Derby's plans, York had Isabella conveyed to the safety of Wallingford Castle. Richard made an attempt to regain his throne and sailed home from Ireland. He was deeply unpopular however and, on 20 August 1399, was captured attempting to seek refuge in Wales and taken to the Tower of London on the orders of the triumphant Earl of Derby. He was soon compelled to abdicate, and Derby took the throne as Henry IV.

The deposition of her husband left Isabella in a difficult position, and she was moved by Henry from Wallingford to Havering-at-Bower, where she could be kept under close watch. According to Froissart, her state was 'tourned and broken', and she was stripped of the French and English ladies of her household with whom she was familiar and furnished with an entirely new household loyal to Henry. This must have been an unsettling time for Isabella, especially as her new servants were ordered to provide no information about Richard's whereabouts or mention his name. The French ambassadors received a similar prohibition when they were permitted to visit Isabella shortly after Richard's capture. Froissart records that the ambassadors travelled to see the young queen in her household:

> [She] received them sweetly, and demaunded of them howe the Frenche kinge her father dyd and the quene her mother. They saide, Well, and so communed with her a great season. They kepre well their promesse, for they spake no worde of kynge Rycharde. Than they tooke leave

of the quene and retourned to London: than shortely after they wente to Eltham to the kynge, and there dyned and the kyng gave them fayre presents and jowelles, and right amiably they toke their leave of the kynge, who sayd to them: Syrs, ye may say whan ye come into Fraunce, that the quene of Englande shall have no hurte nor trouble, but shall always kepe her estate as to her belongeth, and shall enjoy all her right, for as yet she shall nat knowe the mutacyons of the worlde.

Henry's words satisfied the French ambassadors and her family as to her treatment, but for Isabella, the lack of news of Richard was alarming, and she determined to take action herself.

Whilst Isabella was staying at Sunning near Reading, a group of Richard's supporters obtained a man to impersonate the deposed King and spread rumours that he had escaped and was raising an army. These supporters came personally to Isabella and informed her that Richard already had 100,000 men and that he had good hopes of victory. According to John Hayward, Isabella was jubilant at this news:

> Shee defaced King Henries armes and plucked away his cognisance from those his servants that attended uppon her, and having in some sorte satisfied her womanish anger with this harmelesse spight, she and the lords departed together, first to Wallingforde, and from thence to Abington, stirring the people by the waye to take armour and to rise in ayde of King Richard, who was (saide they), and is, and should be their prince.

By the time that Isabella and the lords who accompanied her had reached Chichester in Sussex, they had amassed a large army. When they attempted to enter the city, they were attacked by the townspeople and heavily defeated. The false Richard, who attempted to flee to Scotland following news of the defeat, was captured and executed, and Isabella found herself once again a prisoner of Henry IV. Isabella's rebellion had far greater consequences, and soon afterwards, Richard was murdered at Pontefract Castle. Isabella was not, at first, aware that she had become a widow, and she continued to look towards Richard's restoration to the throne.

Isabella remained a prisoner during the early years of Henry's reign as the new King had no intention of allowing such a valuable bargaining counter to leave his kingdom. When her father heard of Richard's death, he demanded that Isabella be returned to France. Froissart claimed,

> The Englysshemen wolde in no wyse delyver her, but sayd she shulde lyve styll in Englande upon her dowrie; and that though she had lost her husbande, they wolde provide for her another, that shulde be fayre, yong, and gentyll, with whom she shuld be better pleased than with Richard of Burdeaux, for he was olde, and this shuld be the prince of Wales, eldest sone to kyng Henry.

When word reached Isabella that a new match had been proposed for her, she finally realised that her husband was dead. According to John Hayward, she plunged her household into mourning and 'estranged her selfe from all occasions of pleasure or comforte, and was accompanied with a heavy traine composed to sorrow both in behaviour and attire'. Isabella spent her time loudly lamenting her husband's fate and cursing Henry IV. She surprisingly requested an audience with Henry IV himself, which was granted, and she used this opportunity to attack him openly to his face. Upon being admitted to the King's presence, Isabella wept before declaring,

'In seeking to obtaine our purpose of others, it is an ordinarie endeavour to move ether by prayers pittie, or by promises hope, or by threats feare. But as with men cruell and ambitious and in theire owne opinion mightie, these meanes are of litle force, soe with them whose miserie is beneath all releife they cannot bee of any use. Being now therefore in that distresse that there remaineth to mee nether thing to desire nor thought to obtaine, I am come only to putt you in remembrance, what benefittes with what ingratitude you have required, that in my heaviest misshape, I may conceive this vaine satisfaction to have reproved you openly to your face.'

As the daughter of the King of France, Isabella knew that she had little to fear, and she gave vent to her anger and grief. She criticised Henry's ingratitude to Richard, accusing him of greed in seeking further honours. She ended saying,

'And albeit ambition (an unquiet humour) hath hitherto blinded your judgement, yet shame will shortlie cause you to discerne that you possesse onlie an appearance of honor sett upon you by a few flatterers which will easily bee escared [defaced] by those infamies which our just complaintes shall blazen through the world. Your owne conscience alsoe shall torment you and compel you to condemne your selfe to the severest punishments which treason and parricide cann deserve. And albeit it may seeme by successe that god in his secrett judgement hath furthered your proceedings, yet assure your selfe hee hath not favored them. But your dominion begunne with crueltie shall in you, or in your progenie, end with contempt. As for my dishonour, I will not offend the law of modestie in being overcarried with remembrance therof, being fullie purposed to make light accounte of any disgrace of fortune afterward, yet I make litle doubte but it shall alsoe appeare to be instantly recompenced with revenge.'

Isabella's speech appears prophetic, and the authenticity of her words is doubtful. It is clear that she revered Richard's memory and cursed Henry IV, and Hayward's account may record something of her own thoughts.

Isabella's hostility and her family's demands for her return finally convinced Henry IV that she would never marry his son. When she was still only twelve years old, Isabella was returned to France with all the jewels and plate that she had brought with her to England. For Isabella, it must have been a sombre homecoming to the country that she had left when barely out of her infancy. She quickly settled back into her life as a princess of France and, in 1407, married Charles, heir to the Duke of Orléans. Like her first, Isabella's second marriage was destined to be brief, and on 1 September 1410, she bore a daughter, before dying a few hours later. It was a sorry end for a queen who had shown so much promise.

Isabella of Valois was one of the most unlucky of any medieval queen, and her brief life, in which she was used as a pawn by male relatives and other figures, was a far cry from the powerful lives led by earlier Plantagenet queens, such as Eleanor of Aquitaine. With the usurpation of the crown in 1399 by Henry IV, the direct line of descent from the Empress Matilda came to an end. Henry IV was a direct male-line descendant of the Empress, but by seizing the crown, he founded his own Lancastrian dynasty, which saw four women married to the three Lancastrian kings.

5

The Lancastrian Queens

With his usurpation of the throne in 1399, Henry IV diverted the line of succession to the descendants of John of Gaunt, the third surviving son of Edward III, in preference to Richard II, the sole heir of Edward III's eldest son, and to the descendants of his second surviving son. The Lancastrian dynasty saw four women married to its kings, and whilst the first, Mary de Bohun, was never a queen, the remaining three women all helped to develop the role of queen in response to the very particular circumstances they faced. Henry IV's reign was dogged by rebellion as he sought to establish the legitimacy of his dynasty. His son, Henry V, was undisputed king as long as he lived, but the long reign of his son and successor, Henry VI, marked the end of the dynasty. The four Lancastrian kings' wives led very different lives, but each sought to maintain and extend the prestige of the Lancastrian dynasty in England.

MARY DE BOHUN (c. 1368-94), the first wife of Henry IV, was never queen and would have had no idea that her husband, and later her son and grandson, would wear the crown of England. Mary was the daughter of Humphrey de Bohun, Earl of Hereford, and his wife, Joan Fitzalan. Her mother was the daughter of the Earl of Arundel by his wife Eleanor of Lancaster. Mary and her elder sister Eleanor were their parents' only surviving children, and on their father's death in January 1373, they inherited his extensive estates. In 1376, Mary's elder sister married Thomas of Woodstock, Duke of Gloucester, the youngest son of Edward III and Philippa of Hainault.

Mary lived with her mother both before and in the early years of her marriage. There is evidence that she was educated and her family were patrons of a number of books produced during the fourteenth century. Both Mary and her sister continued this family tradition. Mary's family commissioned two psalters as wedding presents for her and Henry on their marriage, and it is likely that it was known that these gifts would be appreciated by the couple. Henry IV also loved learning. Before he became king, he attended lectures at the University of Paris, and once he became king, he commissioned a study to be built for him at Eltham Palace, with cupboards specifically built for his books. Their shared love of learning brought the couple together during their marriage.

As one of the greatest heiresses in England, Mary de Bohun was much sought after as a bride. According to Froissart, her brother-in-law, the Duke of Gloucester, wishing to keep Mary's inheritance to himself, attempted to force her to become a nun. Mary had no vocation, and in July 1380, whilst Gloucester was out of the country, John of Gaunt, the third surviving son of Edward III, purchased the right to her marriage from the King for 5,000 marks. This presented Gloucester with a *fait accompli*, and on or around 5 February 1381, Mary married John's eldest son, Henry, Earl of Derby, at her family's manor of Rochford Hall in Essex.

Mary was very wealthy, and this was part of the attraction for John of Gaunt in purchasing the rights to her marriage. John himself had taken the English heiress, Blanche of Lancaster, as his first wife, and he wanted to ensure that his son was similarly provided for. It has been suggested that Mary's wealth was not the only reason for the marriage. Whilst Mary's inheritance was extensive, she was not the only unmarried heiress in England. John of Gaunt was a product of the famously happy marriage between Edward III and Philippa of Hainault. His first marriage was also a fond one, and he is famous for marrying his long-term mistress and the mother of several of his illegitimate children, Catherine Swynford. It is possible that John chose Mary because Henry had already shown an interest in her. The couple's mothers were cousins and the pair knew each other in childhood. They shared a number of interests and enjoyed music, with both able to sing and play. Surviving depictions of Mary show that she conformed to the contemporary ideal of beauty, with fair skin, blond hair and delicate features. Henry was also personable enough, and according to his sixteenth-century biographer, John Hayward, 'he was verie courteous and familiar respectively towards all men, whereby hee procured great reputation and regarde'. Froissart considered that Henry, at the time of his marriage, 'though he were but yonge, yet he was of great wysdome, and likely to come to great honour'.

At the time of her marriage, Mary was too young to live with her husband and remained with her mother. On 10 March 1386, Henry officially received Mary's inheritance, and it is likely that the couple had begun to live together shortly before this. The couple travelled around together and spent a considerable amount of time in each other's company, with Mary bearing children frequently. Their eldest child, the future Henry V, was born at Monmouth Castle on 16 September 1386. Young Henry's birth was followed in late summer or autumn 1387 by that of a second son, Thomas, in London. A third son, John, was born on 20 June 1389, and a fourth, Humphrey, in the autumn of 1390. Mary's first daughter, Blanche, was born in the spring of 1392, and her youngest child, Philippa, in the early summer of 1394. Remarkably for the time, all six children survived to adulthood, and Mary de Bohun spent her brief life in a domestic sphere, devoting herself to childbearing.

Mary was anxious for the safety of her husband during the troubled years of the reign of Richard II. Henry left Monmouth shortly after the birth of his eldest son in order to attend a parliament at which he openly declared his opposition to the King. The opposition to Richard was led by Mary's brother-in-law, the Duke of Gloucester, who declared the King's favourites to be traitors. This caused the King to storm out of parliament in an attempt to dissolve it, only for the lords and commons to continue sitting. Richard re-entered parliament on 24 October and, around that time, declared his twelve-year-old cousin, Roger Mortimer, Earl of March, who was a grandson of the second surviving son of Edward III, to be his heir. This disappointed the hopes of John of Gaunt and Mary's own husband, and it was a melancholy and angry Henry who returned to Mary in late November 1386. The couple spent the summer of the following year together at Kenilworth before moving to London in the autumn to await the birth of their second child. Mary spent only a brief time in London, and as the political situation deteriorated, she and her children left the capital for the safety of the countryside.

Mary's constitution was weakened by her frequent childbearing, and in the early spring of 1394, whilst still only in her mid-twenties, she passed away either during or shortly after the birth of her youngest child, Philippa. Henry was not with Mary at the time, but he gave her a grand funeral on 6 July 1394 in the Lady Chapel at the Lancastrian Collegiate Church in Leicester. Mary's funeral was held the day after that of Henry's stepmother, Constanza of Castile, who had died at around the same time, and both events were attended by Henry and his father in an attempt to mark the prestige of the Lancastrian dynasty. Henry mourned Mary sincerely and wore black for an entire year as a mark of respect. Mary de Bohun was not the only love of his life, and he went on to make a second love match to Joan of Navarre.

JOAN OF NAVARRE (1368-1437), the second wife of Henry IV, came from a particularly noble background and was the daughter of Charles the Bad, King of Navarre, and his wife Joan, daughter of King John of France. Her father, as his nickname suggests, lived a turbulent life. He was the eldest son of Jeanne, Queen of Navarre, who had been the only surviving child of King Louis X of France, the eldest son of Philip IV. On her father's death, Jeanne had been passed over in the succession of France in favour of her two uncles and then her father's cousin, but had been allowed to inherit her father's second kingdom of Navarre.

Charles was frequently at war with France, and in 1381, his three children, who were lodged in one of his castles in Normandy, were captured by the regents of France in an attempt to ensure his good behaviour. Joan could have been in a very difficult position on finding herself as a hostage in Paris, particularly since Charles had no intention of being bound by any terms and, instead, tried to poison the regents. Joan and her two elder brothers did not suffer for their father's actions, and the French regents, who were their maternal uncles, treated them honourably. Charles was anxious to secure his children's return, and they were released on the intervention of the King of Castile, a man that Joan had been betrothed to in her childhood.

Joan did not spend long in Navarre because, on her return, her father opened negotiations for her to marry John IV, Duke of Brittany. John was nearly thirty years older than Joan and had been married twice before: first, to Mary of England, the daughter of Edward III, and then to Joan Holland, a half-sister of Richard II. Neither marriage produced children and, following the death of Joan Holland in 1384, John sought an urgent remarriage. In June 1384, Breton envoys arrived in Navarre to fetch Joan, and on 2 September, she and John were married by proxy. Joan sailed for Brittany immediately afterwards and was married in person to John at Saille on 11 September. She rapidly fulfilled her primary role as Duchess of Brittany, and whilst her first child, a daughter born in 1388, died in infancy, on 24 December 1389, she bore her first son. Joan bore her husband three further sons and three daughters, providing for the succession in Brittany.

Joan's time as Duchess of Brittany was dominated by childbearing, but she was also able to build some political role for herself. Shortly before her husband's death, she wrote to his brother-in-law, Richard II, on his behalf, regarding some lands that the English king had withheld:

I desire every day to be certified of your good estate, which our Lord grant that it may ever be as good as your heart desires, and as I should wish it for myself. If it would please you to let me know of it, you would give me great rejoicings in my heart, for every time that I hear good news of you I am most perfectly glad at heart. And if to know tidings from this side would give you pleasure, when this was written my lord, I and our children were together in good health of our persons, thanks to our Lord, who by his grace ever grant you the same. I pray you, my dearest and most redoubted lord, that it would ever please you to have the affairs of my said lord well recommended, as well in reference to the deliverance of his lands as other things, which lands in your hands are the cause why he sends his people so promptly towards you. So may it please you hereupon to provide him with your gracious remedy, in such manner that he may enjoy his said lands peaceably; even as he and I have our perfect surety and trust in you more than in any other. And let me know your good pleasure, and I will accomplish it willingly and with a good heart to my power.

The outcome of Joan's suit is unknown, but the fact that the letter was written shows the trust placed in her by her husband. John IV died on 1 November 1399, leaving Joan as regent of Brittany.

Joan's first marriage was an arranged one, and whilst she was fond of her husband, it is unlikely that she was in love with him. She had already met the man that would become her second husband, and she and Henry IV of England made a love match. The couple were almost exactly the same age, and the King, with his Plantagenet good looks, must have seemed like a welcome contrast to John IV when Joan first met him. No details of the first meeting between the couple exist, but they had probably already met by 1396 when both attended Richard II's marriage to Isabella of Valois at Calais. On that visit, Henry spent almost a month on the Continent, and the couple would have met frequently. Joan and her first husband also visited England in April 1398, and again, she would almost certainly have had an opportunity to renew her acquaintance with Henry. A letter written by Joan to Henry in 1400 suggests that the relationship was more than merely a formal one:

> Since I am desirous to hear of your good estate, which our Lord grant that it may ever be as good as your noble heart knows best how to desire, and, indeed, as I would wish it for myself, I pray you, my most dear and honoured lord and cousin, that it would please you very often to let me know the certainty of it, for the very great joy and gladness of my heart; for every time that I can hear good news of you, it rejoices my heart very greatly. And if of your courtesy you would hear the same from across here, thanks to you, at the writing of these presents, I and my children were together in good health of our persons, thanks to God, who grant you the same, as Johanna of Bavalen, who is going over to you, can tell you more fully, whom it please you to have recommended in the business on which she is going over. And if anything that I can do over here will give you pleasure, I pray you to let me know it, and I will accomplish it with a very good heart, according to my power.

Joan's concern for Henry's welfare and the personable tone in which she wrote makes it clear that the couple were fond of each other, and Joan gave up much to be with Henry.

Henry IV came to the throne following the deposition of his cousin, Richard II. His kingship was not universally recognised, and for the first few years of his reign, he was on the verge of war with France. As a result of this, the relationship between Joan and Henry was at first conducted with secrecy. Whilst Joan and Henry renewed their acquaintance shortly after her husband's death, it was only on 20 March 1402 that a papal bull permitting the marriage was obtained. On 2 April 1402, the couple were married by proxy at Eltham Palace. Joan was heavily censured when the match was publicised, and whilst she and her two daughters were allowed to sail to England in December 1402, she was forced by the nobles of Brittany to relinquish her regency and the custody of her sons.

Coupled with her grief at the loss of her sons, Joan's crossing must have been an ordeal, as John Hayward recounts:

> As shee crossed the seas for England, her passage was verie dangerous by reason of tempestuous wether, which accident was esteemed ominous in both King Richard's wives. The king received her at Winchester, and there having spent some time in devises of pleasures, upon the viith of

Februarie the marriage was solemnized between them, and upon the xxvith of the same moneth shee was with all ceremonies of state, crowned at Westminster.

Henry rushed to meet Joan as soon as she had landed, and they settled into married life together.

Henry was determined to ensure that Joan lived in some state, and on 8 March 1403, he granted her a dower of 10,000 marks. Coupled with her Breton dower, this made Joan an exceptionally wealthy woman. She also built a relationship with her stepchildren, and Henry's youngest sons, Humphrey and John, presented her with a rich pair of tablets as a wedding present. In a letter that Joan wrote to her stepson John in 1415, she referred to him as her 'dearest and best-beloved son', and Henry's children helped to fill some of the gap left by her separation from her own sons.

Joan and Henry's relationship was not without difficulties, as, whilst he was a kind and attentive husband, he cannot have been easy to live with. By around 1408, he had contracted a skin disease that appears to have been similar to leprosy, and he became a virtual recluse, shutting himself away with Joan. It must have been sad for Joan, who had known Henry in the prime of his life, to see him struck down with the disfiguring disease. According to John Hayward, Henry's troubles were compounded by his guilt at his usurpation of the crown, and his mind was 'perpetuallie perplexed with an endless and restless chardge, ether of cares, or greifes, or of suspicions and feares'. For Joan, it may perhaps have been a relief when he died in 1413.

Joan made no attempt to return to either Navarre or Brittany on Henry's death, as she considered England to be her home. She was often referred to as queen mother during her stepson Henry V's reign, and she continued to play a public role as a member of the English royal family, taking a prominent place in a procession from St Paul's to Westminster in celebration of Henry V's victory at Agincourt against the French. This went against Joan's personal feelings, as her son-in-law, the Duke of Alençon, and her brother, Charles of Navarre, were both killed fighting for the French. Joan's own son, Arthur, was captured and brought as a prisoner to England, although this did at least allow her to renew her acquaintance with him.

Henry V's French wars took a harsh toll on his finances, and he looked with interest at Joan's vast wealth. On 27 September 1419, the English council made an order depriving Joan of all her possessions and revenues, and four days later, she was arrested for witchcraft at her palace of Havering-atte-Bower. Joan had always been on good terms with Henry V, and her arrest must have been a terrible shock to her. The charges stemmed from a confession by her confessor, John Randolf, who claimed that he had tempted Joan to use witchcraft to try to kill the King. Joan had no reason to kill her stepson, and there is no doubt that the accusations were trumped up in order to allow the King to claim her wealth. This can be seen in the lenient treatment she received, and whilst a prisoner, she maintained a luxurious existence. Joan's household accounts survive and, in the first months of her imprisonment, she kept a stable, an indication that she was able to continue to ride. She also employed nineteen grooms and seven pages and lived in some state, purchasing expensive goods including furs, lace, gold chains and a gold girdle. She stocked a large wine cellar at Leeds Castle, where she was imprisoned, and entertained visitors. In spite of this, the stigma of being an imprisoned witch remained, and it cannot have been an easy period of her life.

Henry V did not believe in his stepmother's guilt, and whilst he was happy to keep her in prison and make use of her wealth during his lifetime, in 1422, as he lay dying of dysentery in France, he felt remorse and ordered that she be released and have her goods returned to her. This allowed Joan to resume her life as an independent and wealthy widow. She remained in contact with the English court, and in 1437, her step-grandson, Henry VI, made her a New Year's gift of a bejewelled tablet, suggesting that he was fond of her. She employed the renowned composer John Dunstable during the late 1420s and was in contact with her grandson Giles, who was present in England between 1432 and 1434. Joan became increasingly religious, and in 1427, she went on a pilgrimage to Walsingham. She virtually disappears from the sources following her release from prison, and she died at Havering in July 1437 and was buried with Henry IV at Canterbury. This would have been Joan's wish, as the early years of her marriage with Henry were probably the happiest times of her life.

Whilst Joan of Navarre made a love match with Henry IV, her successor as queen, Catherine of Valois, was married to Henry V for purely political reasons. Catherine brought the kingdom of France as her dowry, but her most lasting legacy is that she brought the Tudor dynasty to prominence and the connection with Catherine helped bring them the crown of England.

CATHERINE OF VALOIS (1401-37) was the youngest of the twelve children of Charles VI of France and Isabella of Bavaria. She was the younger sister of Richard II's second queen, Isabella of Valois, and was born on 27 October 1401 in Paris. Catherine had a troubled childhood, and by the time of her birth, her father was insane for long periods. Her mother was notorious for her lovers, and according to one story, Isabella and her lover, the Duke of Orléans, stole the King's revenues, leaving the infant Catherine and her elder sister Michelle so poor that they nearly starved. The sisters were housed in the same palace as their insane father and only survived thanks to the charity of their servants. When Charles returned to his senses, Isabella and Orléans fled to Milan. They attempted to abduct the royal children, and Catherine and her siblings were only saved by the Duke of Burgundy overtaking them on the road out of France.

Henry V had originally been suggested as a husband for Catherine's eldest sister, Isabella, whilst the widowed queen was held in England. This came to nothing, but in 1413, Henry himself suggested a marriage with Catherine. Initial overtures were unsuccessful, but the subject of the marriage was raised again in 1415 when Henry V demanded Catherine's hand in marriage along with a dowry of 2 million crowns and the return of the entire Angevin empire. These demands were extortionate and not intended to be accepted. Whilst the French attempted to negotiate, Henry would not budge, using the rejection of his demands as an excuse to invade France. He was rapidly successful and, on 25 October 1415, won his greatest victory at Agincourt. During the battle, the French suffered huge losses, and three French dukes, ninety counts, 1,500 knights, and between 4,000 and 5,000 men at arms are believed to have died. Catherine shared her family's alarm at Henry V's invasion, but there were also domestic issues to contend with.

In 1417, Charles VI entered a period of relative sanity. Isabella had begun a new love affair not long before, and this was reported to the King. He reacted angrily and had the lover tortured and killed before imprisoning Isabella at Tours. Isabella did not remain a captive for long, as, later the same year, the Duke of Burgundy rescued her, and she set herself up as regent of France at Troyes. She gained control over the once-more-mad Charles and her last unmarried daughter, Catherine.

Henry V always claimed to be King of France through his descent from Isabella of France, the daughter of Philip IV of France, and he continued his war over the next few years, inflicting huge losses on the French. After the fall of Rouen to the English, it was agreed that he would meet with Isabella and the Duke of Burgundy at Meulan. Catherine, who was the beauty of her family, was brought to the meeting, and according to *Hall's Chronicle*, when he arrived, Henry kissed and embraced both Catherine and her mother.

> The next day after they had assembled againe, & the Frenche part brought with them the lady Katherin, only to thentent that the king of Englnd seyng and beholding so fayre a lady and so minion a damsel, should so be inflamed and rapte in loye, that he to obtayne so beautiful an espouse should the soner agre to a gentle peace & louvyng [loving] composicion.

Henry was indeed eager to marry Catherine, but not, as the French hoped, without first being granted the crown of France.

Henry V arrived at the meeting at Meulan as a conqueror, and Isabella of Bavaria was in no position to bargain with him. It was agreed that Henry would marry Catherine and in return, Charles VI would make him his heir, disinheriting Catherine's brother, the Dauphin. In order to ensure that France remained firmly in English hands, it was also agreed that Henry would be appointed as regent of France for the remainder of Charles's life. On a personal level, the agreement may have been satisfying for both Catherine and Henry, and some reports claim that Henry had fallen in love with Catherine. This may be true, but the match was primarily political and essential to Henry's French ambitions. Shakespeare may well sum up Henry's true feelings for Catherine in his play *Henry V* with the line given to Henry that Catherine was 'our capital demand, comprised within the fore-rank of our articles'. Catherine's own feelings about the match are not recorded, but she does not appear to have been concerned about the disinheritance of her brother. Henry was a dashing figure, and the eighteen-year-old Catherine may have been pleased with the idea of marriage to him. She was, in any event, a dutiful daughter and did as her mother bid her.

In May 1420, Henry arrived in Troyes in order to seal his treaty with Isabella and marry Catherine. The couple were married in St Peter's church in the city, and they soon afterwards made a triumphant entry to Paris accompanied by Catherine's parents. Catherine and Henry kept a grand court at the Louvre, whilst Catherine's parents stayed, ignored, in the Hotel St Pol. The couple then travelled to Rouen, where they celebrated Christmas before travelling to Calais and sailing for Dover. They were greeted by jubilant crowds intent on celebrating Henry's victories. On 24 February 1421, Catherine was crowned at Westminster Abbey. It was at her coronation banquet that she made her only recorded act of queenly intercession, when she asked for the captive James I of Scotland to be released from his imprisonment.

Catherine spent little time with her new husband, as, immediately after her coronation, Henry set out on a progress around England, initially leaving her in London. The reason for this separation is not clear, and Catherine had rejoined him at Leicester by Easter 1421. Henry set off north, whilst Catherine moved on to Lincoln to await his return. The couple then returned to London, where they parted, with Henry returning to his wars in France. Catherine had conceived a child shortly after her arrival in England, and Henry's parting words to her were that she should, under no circumstances, bear their child at Windsor, a castle in which he believed no lucky king of England had been born. With Henry gone, Catherine chose to ignore this advice, and on 6 December 1421, she gave birth to the future Henry VI at the castle. Henry V was destined never to see his son, and Catherine spent some months recovering from the birth before sailing to join him in France in May 1422.

The couple spent a few weeks together in France before Henry set off to besiege the town of Meaux. Whilst in France, Catherine was reunited with her parents, and the three travelled to Senlis to await Henry's return. Whilst she was there, Catherine heard that Henry had contracted dysentery and had been taken by litter to Vincennes. She must have spent an anxious few weeks with her parents before news reached her that he had died on 31 August 1422. Catherine was further shocked by the news that Henry had left her with neither the regency of England nor France, nor custody of her son. Catherine joined Henry's funeral procession at Rouen and made the long sombre journey back to England.

Catherine rejoined her son upon her return to England, and she was still with him in September 1422 when news arrived that her father had died and that her son, Henry VI, had been proclaimed king of France. Catherine devoted the early years of her widowhood to her son's upbringing, despite not being named as his guardian. The *Chronicle of London* gives one example of Catherine's continuing association with her son in November 1423:

> The king and the queen his mother removed from Windsor towards the parliament at London, which began at Westminster on the 21st day of October before, and on the aforesaid 13th day of November at night the king and queen were lodged at Staines, and upon the morrow, which was Sunday, the king was borne towards his mother's chair, and he shrieked and cried and sprang and would not be carried further. Wherefore he was borne again into the inn, and there he abode on Sunday all day; and on the Monday he was borne to the chair, and then he was glad and happy in spirits. In the evening he came to Kingston and there rested the night, and on the Tuesday he came to Kennington and on Wednesday he came to London with a glad countenance and happy spirits, and was borne in his mother's bosom in a chair through London to Westminster, and on the morrow was brought into parliament.

This story was intended to show the piety of Henry VI, who, even as an infant, refused to break the Sabbath. It also demonstrates the close relationship between Catherine and her son in his early years.

Whilst she enjoyed playing a role in Henry VI's upbringing, Catherine had been only twenty-one at Henry V's death, and she was not prepared to shut herself away. Within a few years of Henry V's death, she became romantically involved with Edmund Beaufort, a cousin of her late husband. Whilst details of the relationship are scant, it is possible that the couple became lovers, and there is no doubt that they planned to marry. Any man that Catherine married would become the King's stepfather, and Henry's minority council were anxious that he would also seek to become regent. In 1426, parliament made a formal request to the regency council that they cease their refusals to allow Catherine to remarry. It is likely that Catherine petitioned parliament for their aid herself. Henry VI's council was determined to prevent Catherine from marrying, and in the parliament of 1429 to 1430, a statute was passed legislating on the remarriage of dowager queens. The new law ordered that anyone who dared marry the Queen without the King's express permission would have his lands and property confiscated and effectively meant that Catherine could not remarry until Henry VI obtained his majority. Further restrictions were placed on Catherine around this time, and between 1427 and 1430, her household was merged with that of her son.

The opposition of the regency council and the statute prohibiting her remarriage made it impossible for Catherine to marry someone as prominent and influential as Edmund Beaufort. She did not, however, abandon her desire to remarry. At some point around 1428 or 1429, Catherine, 'folowyng more her awne appetite, then frendely counsaill and regardyng more her priuate affeccion, than her open honour, toke to husband priuily'. The object of Catherine's affection was Owen Tudor, a Welshman in her household. Despite later attempts by the Tudor dynasty to present Owen as of noble lineage, he was of low birth and may have been the keeper of Catherine's household or of her wardrobe. The origins of their love affair are obscure but one legend claims that Owen fell into Catherine's lap during a dance. Few details of the marriage survive, and it was not common knowledge until after Catherine's death. Catherine bore Owen four children: Edmund, Jasper, Owen, and a daughter who died in infancy.

Catherine apparently found happiness in her second marriage, but this did not last long. According to some accounts, Henry VI's governors discovered the marriage in the late summer of 1436 and sent Catherine, under restraint, to Bermondsey Abbey. Alternatively, Catherine, already in ill health, may have decided to retire to the abbey to die. Whatever the reason for her stay at Bermondsey, she did not long survive and died on 3 January 1437 aged just thirty-five. On Catherine's death, Owen Tudor was arrested and imprisoned in Newgate in accordance with the statute of 1430. He was finally released in July 1439, when he was pardoned by Henry VI and taken into his household. Henry VI was fond of his half-brothers, Edmund and Jasper, and he created them, respectively, Earls of Richmond and Pembroke. He arranged for Edmund to marry the royally descended Margaret Beaufort, a union which produced the future King Henry VII. It was through Catherine that the Tudor family gained its closeness to the throne of England and the status with which to claim it.

Catherine's story does not quite end with her death. She was buried in Westminster Abbey with Henry V, but at some point, her mummified body was disinterred and put on display. On 23 February 1669, the diarist Samuel Pepys visited the abbey and recorded that 'here we did see, by particular favour, the body of Queen Katherine of Valois, and had her upper part of her body in my hands. And I did kiss her mouth, reflecting upon it that I did kiss a Queen, and that this was my birthday, 36 years old, that I did first kiss a Queen'. This was a bizarre postscript to the life of an extraordinary queen. Both during and after her life, Catherine was essentially a cipher through which the crowns of England and France were transmitted. Catherine of Valois was a politically important figure who wielded little power herself. This was in stark contrast to her successor, Margaret of Anjou, who was amongst the most politically influential of all English queens.

MARGARET OF ANJOU (1430-82) has one of the worst reputations of any queen of England. She was the fourth child of Rene of Anjou and his wife, Isabel, Duchess of Lorraine. Margaret had little contact with either of her parents in her early childhood, and on 2 July 1431, her father was captured at the Battle of Bulgneville and spent some years in prison. In November 1435, Rene's elder brother died, and he inherited the county of Anjou, as well as the titles to the crowns of Jerusalem and Naples. He was already titular King of Sicily. In spite of this wealth of titles, Rene only controlled Anjou and Lorraine, which he ruled on behalf of his wife. Margaret's mother was determined to increase the family's prestige, and in 1435, she set out with an army to conquer Naples, leaving her children in the care of their paternal grandmother, Yolande of Aragon. Yolande was an example to Margaret of the power that a woman could wield, and she had already ruled Anjou for several years by the time she took custody of her grandchildren. She had also raised the French king, Charles VII, marrying him to her daughter, Marie. Margaret lived with Yolande until her death in November 1442. By that time, both her parents had returned to Anjou, and Margaret returned to her mother's care.

The war between England and France continued throughout Margaret's childhood, with the English losing much of what they had won under Henry V. In 1444, a meeting was held at Tours in an attempt to agree a peace. According to *Hall's Chronicle*, it was suggested at the meeting that a marriage between Henry VI and a French princess be arranged. Charles VII had no intention of allowing his English nephew to marry any of his daughters, and Margaret, as the niece of the Queen of France, was nominated. Margaret's father was happy with the match, and he was badly in need of funds, 'callyng himself kyng of Sicile, Naples, and Hierusalem, hauyng onely the name and stile of the same, without any pay profite, or fote of possession'. The English agreed to surrender lands in Anjou and Maine to Rene in return for Margaret's hand in marriage. To his embarrassment, Rene was unable to pay for Margaret's journey to England, and 'Kyng Reyner her father, for all his long stile, had to short a purse, to sende his doughter honourably, to the kyng her spouse'. Henry and Margaret were married by proxy at Tours on 23 May 1444, with the Earl of Suffolk playing the role of Henry VI. This was followed by celebrations before Margaret returned home with her mother to prepare for her journey. In March 1445, she set out for England accompanied by an escort of 1,500 people, paid for by Henry VI.

Henry VI had requested a portrait of Margaret as soon as marriage negotiations opened, and he was eager to meet her when she landed in England. According to the report of the Milanese ambassador to England, Henry rushed down to see Margaret unofficially as soon as she arrived:

> When the queen landed in England the king dressed himself as a squire, the Duke of Suffolk doing the same, and took her a letter which he said the King of England had written. While the queen read the letter the king took stock of her, saying that a woman may be seen very well when she reads a letter, and the qyeen never found out it was the king because she was so engrossed in reading the letter, and she never looked at the king in his squire's dress, who remained on his knees all the time. After the king had gone the Duke of Suffolk said: 'Most serene queen, what do you think of the squire who brought the letter?' The queen replied: 'I did not notice him, as I was occupied in reading the letter he brought'. The duke remarked: 'Most serene queen, the person dressed as a squire was the most serene King of England', and the queen was vexed at not having known it, because she had kept him on his knees.

The couple's first meeting was not encouraging, but their official meeting soon afterwards was more successful. Margaret was a beauty, with the Milanese ambassador commenting that she 'is a most handsome woman, though somewhat dark'. Whilst he has a reputation for being somewhat simple, Henry was a kindly man. The historian Polydore Vergil summed up his character:

> King Henry [VI] was a man of mild and plain dealing disposition who preferred peace before wars, quietness before troubles, honesty before utility, and leisure before business; and, to be short, there was not in this world a more pure, more honest and more holy creature. There was in him honest reproachfulness, modesty, innocence, and perfect patience, taking all human chances, miseries, and all afflictions of this life in so good part as though he had justly by some offence deserved the same. He ruled his own affections so that he might more easily rule his own subjects; he hungered not after riches, nor thirsted for honour and worldly estimation, but was careful only for his soul's health.

Henry was also described as 'tall of stature, slender of body [and] of comely visage', and Margaret must have felt that she had done well in her husband. The couple were married at Tichfield Abbey on 22 April before travelling up to London, where Margaret was crowned.

Margaret was a much more forceful personality than Henry, and she rapidly gained influence over him, persuading him in December 1445 to surrender the county of Maine to France. The loss of any territory won in Henry V's wars was deeply unpopular in England and created hostility towards Margaret. This increased when, in July 1449, her uncle, Charles VII, declared war on England, ending the truce sealed by her marriage. Margaret worked closely with the Duke of Suffolk, Henry's hated chief minister, and there were rumours that the pair were lovers, with *Hall's Chronicle* referring to him as 'the Quenes dearlynge'. This was slander, but it was widely believed.

Whilst Margaret was never popular in England, she was able to carry out the traditional role of queen during the early years of her marriage. Henry had founded Eton College in September 1440 and King's College, Cambridge, in February 1441, and following his example, Margaret founded Queen's College, Cambridge. She was conventionally pious and made two pilgrimages to Becket's shrine at Canterbury. She made a further pilgrimage of thanksgiving to Walsingham in the spring of 1453, shortly after she discovered that she was pregnant for the first time.

Margaret had little time to enjoy her pregnancy, as, on 16 July 1453, the English army was decisively defeated in France at the Battle of Castillon, leaving England in control only of Calais on the Continent. Henry was devastated by the news, and it triggered an attack of the mental disorder that had so plagued the life of his maternal grandfather, Charles VI of France. On 15 August 1453, the King felt unusually tired and went to bed early. According to Whethamstead's Register, during the night 'a disease and disorder of such a sort overcame the king that he lost his wits and memory for a time, and nearly all his body was uncoordinated and out of control that he could neither walk, nor hold his head upright, nor easily move from where he sat'. Whilst seemingly conscious, he was unable to take in anything around him. On 13 October 1453, whilst Henry was still unresponsive, Margaret gave birth to her only child in London, a son whom she named Edward.

From the moment of Edward of Lancaster's birth, he became Margaret's focus, and she sought to ensure his inheritance at all costs. As soon as he was born, the old rumours surfaced that Margaret had been unfaithful to the King, and in 1460, Margaret's enemy, the Earl of Warwick, wrote that 'our king is stupid and out of his mind; he does not rule but is ruled. The government is in the hands of the queen and her paramours'. According to *Hall's Chronicle*, many people in England believed that Edward was either a changeling, introduced into the Queen's bedchamber because she could not conceive a child of her own, or that he was Margaret's son by the Duke of Somerset, a cousin of Henry VI's. These rumours had no basis in fact, but they were damaging, and Margaret immediately attempted to secure Henry's recognition of her son. Once she had recovered from the birth, she moved her household to Windsor, where Henry was staying. According to a newsletter written by John Stodeley in January 1454,

> As touchyng tythynges, please it you to write that at the Princes coming to Wyndesore, the Duc of Buk' toke hym in his armes and presented hym to the Kyng in godely wise, besechyng the Kyng to blisse hym; and the Kyng gave no answere. Natheless the Duk abode stille with the Prince by the Kyng; and whan he coude no maner answere have, the Quene come in, and toke the Prince in hir armes and presented hym in like forme as the Duke had done, desiryng that he shuld blisse it; but alle their labour was in veyne, for they departed thens without any answere or counteaunce saving only that ones he loked on the Prince and caste doune his eyene ayen, without any more.

Henry's lack of response to his son was disastrous for Margaret's reputation, and the rumours about her son's birth persisted. In February 1454, she decided to act, and presented a bill of five articles to parliament in London, claiming the regency of England for herself. Even in this she was unsuccessful, and Henry's cousin, the Duke of York, was named as Protector of England on 27 March 1454. Margaret was firmly allied with York's enemy, the Duke of

Somerset, and this appointment horrified her, but there was nothing she could do except rejoin Henry at Windsor and await the outcome of events. Once at Windsor, Margaret renewed her efforts to wake Henry, and in late December 1454, he suddenly recovered. Margaret brought their son to him 'and then he askid what the Princes name was, and the Queen told him Edward; and than he hild up his hands and thankid God thereof. And he seid he never knew til that tyme, nor wist not what was seid to him, nor wist where he had be whils he hath be seke til now'. Margaret was overjoyed that Henry finally recognised their son, and the couple travelled to London, where they relieved York of his protectorate. Henry's recovery was only partial, and it was Margaret who emerged as the real power behind the throne.

The Duke of York had no intention of surrendering power, and following Henry's return to London, he moved north to raise troops. In late May 1455, Henry set out from London to attend a parliament at Leicester, whilst Margaret remained behind in London. On 21 May, Henry's men were attacked by an army led by York at St Albans. This was the first battle of the Wars of the Roses and saw the beginning of a civil war that would nearly bring the crown and nobility to its ruin. During the course of the battle, Somerset and other leading Lancastrians were killed, and Henry was taken prisoner by York and escorted back to London. Margaret withdrew with her son to the Tower, but she was powerless to do anything to stop York, and on 17 November 1455, his second period of protectorate was declared. Margaret continued to build up her own powerbase, and in October 1458, an attempt was made to assassinate York's nephew, the powerful Earl of Warwick, at Westminster. Warwick fled to Calais, where he began raising troops. His father, the Earl of Salisbury, raised an army in the north and York began recruiting in Wales. Margaret herself, alarmed by the sudden activity of the Yorkist party, travelled to Cheshire to raise troops in her son's name. She won a victory over the Yorkists in October 1459 when they fled in the face of her army in the Welsh Marches. In June 1460, the tide turned again, and Margaret's army was defeated by Warwick and Salisbury at Northampton. During the battle, Henry was taken prisoner and Margaret and her son were forced to flee to the safety of Harlech Castle.

The recapture of Henry VI emboldened the Duke of York, and on 10 October 1460, he arrived at a parliament in London and sat down in the King's empty throne, signalling his decision to claim the crown of England. York had a strong claim to the throne because, when Henry IV had usurped the crown from Richard II in 1399, he had ignored the rights of Edmund Mortimer, the great-grandson of Edward III's second son, Lionel of Clarence. Edmund Mortimer died childless and his claim passed to the Duke of York himself, the son of Mortimer's sister, Anne. York was therefore a descendant of Edward III's second son, whilst Henry VI was only a descendant of his third. York set out his claim to parliament, and it was agreed that, whilst Henry would retain the throne for the remainder of his life, York would be acknowledged as his heir, in preference to Edward of Lancaster. This was something to which Margaret could never agree, and she marched north with 20,000 men. On 31 December 1460, she met an army commanded by York and Salisbury at Wakefield where she won a decisive victory. York was killed in battle, and Salisbury, who was captured, was summarily executed on Margaret's orders. Margaret was determined to have her revenge, and according to *Hall's Chronicle*, her men 'came to the place wher the dead corps of the duke of Yorke lay, and caused his head to be stryken of, and set on it a croune of paper, and so fixed it on a pole, and presented it to the Quene'. Margaret had York and Salisbury's heads set on poles above the gates of York before marching south in triumph.

Margaret met a second Yorkist army at St Albans soon after Wakefield and was once again victorious, rescuing Henry VI, who had been brought out of London to lead the Yorkist forces. Whilst Margaret and Henry had initially had a fond marriage, following the birth of Edward of Lancaster and Henry's acquiescence to his disinheritance, Margaret became more ambivalent towards her husband and he was no longer the focus of her efforts. In spite of this, he was an important figurehead and possession of the King was crucial to her efforts to ensure her son's position. Margaret continued her journey south towards London, and once outside the city, she issued a manifesto to the citizens, demanding entry to the capital:

> And whereas the late Duke of York of extreme malice, long hid under colours, imagined by divers and many ways and means the destruction of our lord's good grace, whom God of his mercy ever preserve, hath now late, upon an untrue pretence, feigned a title to my lord's crown, and royal estate, and pre-eminence, contrary to his allegiance and divers solemn oaths of his own offer made, uncompelled or constrained, and fully proposed to have deposed him of his regality, ne had been [had it not been for] the sad [firm], unchangeable and true dispositions of you and others, his true liegemen, for the which your worshipful dispositions we thank you as heartily as we can. And howbeit, that the same untrue, unsad and unadvised person, of very pure malice, disposed to continue in his cruelness, to the utterest undoing, if he might, of us, and of my lord's son and ours the prince, which, with God's mercy, he shall not be of power to perform, by the help of you and all my lord's faithful disposed subjects, hath thrown among you, as we be certainly informed, divers untrue and feigned matters and surmises; and in especial that we and my lord's said son and ours should newly draw toward you with an unseen power of strangers, disposed to rob and to despoil you of your goods and havings [property]; we will that you know for certain that, at such time as we or our said son shall be disposed to see my lord, as our duty is and so binds us to do, you, nor none of you, shall be robbed, despoiled, nor wronged by any person that at that time we or our said son shall be accompanied with, or any other sent in our or his name, praying you, in our most hearty and desirous wise, that above all earthly things you will diligently intend [attend] to the surety of my lord's royal person in the mean time; so that through malice of his said enemy he be no more troubled, vexed, nor jeoparded. And, so doing, we shall be unto you such lady as of reason you shall be largely content.

The Londoners were not convinced by Margaret's promise, and they sent out a delegation headed by the Duchesses of Bedford and Buckingham and Lady Scales to beg her not to allow her army to enter. Margaret made the greatest error of her life in agreeing, and she took her army back towards the north without securing the capital. A few days later, the Duke of York's eldest son, Edward, Earl of March, entered the city, and on 4 March, he was proclaimed king as Edward IV. On 29 March, Margaret's army was decisively defeated by the new King at Towton, leaving Margaret, Henry and their son as fugitives.

Margaret waged a campaign from Scotland against Edward IV for the next two years, even visiting France in an attempt to secure aid. In May 1464, she was defeated in battle on the edge of Hexham Forest. This was the final straw for Margaret, and she and her son abandoned their army, and Henry VI himself, and sailed to France. Whilst she had abandoned her husband's kingdom, Margaret had not abandoned the cause, and she continued to seek aid in France for some years. In 1465, she was dealt another blow when news arrived that Henry had been captured hiding in northern England and that he had been taken as a prisoner to the Tower of London.

For Margaret, the turning point came in 1470. Relations between Edward IV and his closest ally, the Earl of Warwick, had become increasingly strained throughout the 1460s, and in 1470, Warwick fled to France. Margaret's cousin, Louis XI, had been looking for an opportunity to attack Edward IV, who had allied himself with the French king's rival, the

Duke of Burgundy, and he offered to reconcile Margaret and Warwick so that they could launch a joint attack on England. For Margaret, negotiations with her opponent were a bitter pill to swallow, but she was a pragmatist. On 22 July 1470, the pair underwent a formal reconciliation. It was agreed that Warwick would restore Henry to the throne with French aid and that, in return, Edward of Lancaster would marry Warwick's daughter, Anne Neville. True to his word, Warwick sailed to England and caused Edward IV to flee, restoring Henry VI to the throne. Margaret was jubilant at the news, and she and her son and daughter-in-law prepared to sail to England, only to find themselves delayed by bad weather.

Margaret and her party finally landed in England on 18 April 1471. On the very day that Margaret landed, Warwick fought a battle with the recently returned Edward IV at Barnet. The Lancastrians suffered a heavy defeat, and Warwick was killed. Edward IV returned to London in triumph and moved Henry VI from the palace rooms of the Tower back to the prison. Margaret was devastated, and Polydore Vergil documents her reaction:

> When she heard these things the miserable woman swooned for fear, she was distraught, dismayed and tormented with sorrow; she lamented the calamity of the time, the adversity of fortune, her own toil and misery; she bewailed the unhappy end of King Henry, which she believed assuredly to be at hand, and, to be short, she behaved as one more desirous to die than live.

Margaret had no alternative but to continue her fight. She raised an army in the West Country before marching to Tewkesbury to confront Edward IV. According to *Hall's Chronicle*, as they prepared for battle, Margaret and her son rode amongst their troops to encourage them. Margaret then retired from the battlefield to await news of the day's events. Her hopes were dashed later that day when she heard that her army had been destroyed and that her son was amongst the Lancastrian dead. With the loss of her only child, Margaret was entirely broken, and she was captured by Edward IV at a religious house near the battlefield. She was led back to London as the prize prisoner in Edward IV's victory parade before being imprisoned in the Tower. On the very night of her arrival in the ancient fortress, Margaret was also widowed, as Henry VI was quietly murdered. With the deaths of her husband and son, Margaret had no relevance in English politics and nothing to fight for. After a few months, Edward IV, recognising her powerlessness, turned her over to the custody of her friend, the Duchess of Suffolk, at Wallingford.

At a meeting between Edward IV and Louis XI at Picquigny on 25 August 1475, in which a truce was agreed between the two monarchs, Louis agreed to ransom Margaret for the sum of 50,000 crowns. In late January 1476, Margaret left England for the last time. It was a broken woman who returned to the land of her birth, and after receiving the promise of a modest pension from her father, she retired to his castle at Reculee. In July 1480, Margaret's father died, and she found herself entirely dependent on the grudging generosity of the French king. She died miserable and poor on 25 August 1482 at Dampierre Castle.

The four queens of the House of Lancaster enjoyed varying fortunes as the dynasty came to prominence in a wave of popular support and, ultimately, suffered an ignominious end. Of the four women, only Margaret of Anjou asserted political dominance, and she was amongst the unhappiest of any English queen. As the Wars of the Roses continued to cause devastation and havoc in England, the successors to the Lancastrian queens, the queens of the House of York, fared little better as their fortunes, and those of their dynasty, ebbed and flowed.

6

The Yorkist Queens

The fortunes of the Yorkist dynasty proved to be as turbulent as those of the preceding House of Lancaster. Edward IV, the first Yorkist king, spent the first few years of his reign in uncertainty, due, to a large extent, to his marriage to the commoner, Elizabeth Woodville. His short-lived successor, Edward V, failed to establish himself and was deposed by his uncle, Richard III. Richard had great difficulty in establishing his regime, and at the Battle of Bosworth in 1485, he was killed by the forces of Henry VII, the first Tudor king.

The three Yorkist queens faced many of the concerns that had plagued their Lancastrian predecessors as the Wars of the Roses came to a close. Elizabeth Woodville, the first Yorkist queen, endured her husband's deposition in 1470 before his triumphant return and then found that her unpopularity brought her children and family to near ruin. Her sister-in-law, Anne Neville, who had previously almost been a Lancastrian queen due to her marriage to Edward of Lancaster, was marginalised by her childlessness and is an obscure figure. Finally, Elizabeth of York, the daughter of Edward IV and Elizabeth Woodville, whilst in truth the first Tudor queen, had a life entirely dominated by her father's dynasty and her position as the heir to the House of York.

ELIZABETH WOODVILLE (1437-92) was the first Englishwoman to be acknowledged as queen of England since Edith of Mercia in the eleventh century. She was the daughter of Jacquetta de St Pol, Duchess of Bedford. Jacquetta came from an ancient family in Luxembourg and could trace her descent back to Charlemagne. In 1433, she had married Richard, Duke of Bedford, the younger brother of Henry V. After her husband's death, Jacquetta caused a scandal, which *Hall's Chronicle* describes, when she married Richard Woodville, a lowly member of her household:

> The duchesse of Bedford sister to Lewes, erle of Sainct Paule, myndyng also to marye rather for pleasure than for honour, without counsayl of her frenders, maryed a lusty knight, called Sir Richarde Wooduile, to the great displeasure of her vncle the bishop of Tyrwyne, and the erle her brother: but they now coulde not remedie it, for the chauce was cast and passed.

Regardless of the scandal, it was a very happy union, and Elizabeth, who was born at Grafton in Northamptonshire in 1437, was the eldest child of thirteen.

No details survive of Elizabeth's childhood. By the mid-1450s, she had married Sir John Grey, the son of Sir Edward Grey and his wife, Lady Ferrers. Elizabeth bore two children in quick succession: Thomas in around 1455 and Richard in the late 1450s. Sir John Grey was the heir to both his parents and the marriage was a good match for Elizabeth. On 17 February 1461, however, he was killed fighting for the Lancastrians at the second battle of St Albans.

The loss of her husband was devastating. Her family were staunchly Lancastrian in their sympathies, and within weeks of being widowed, Elizabeth was dealt a further blow with the capture of her father and eldest brother by the Yorkists at the Battle of Towton. With her fortunes at their lowest ebb, she returned to her mother at Grafton whilst her estates were confiscated by the new Yorkist king, Edward IV. Elizabeth resolved to personally approach the King to petition for the return of her lands, positioning herself and her sons under an oak tree that she knew the King would pass whilst he was out hunting. Elizabeth's surviving portraits show that she was both blond and beautiful. Edward was smitten with the young widow and fell in love with her at first sight.

Whilst Edward IV was very taken with Elizabeth, he had no intention of marrying her, as recounted by a contemporary, Dominic Mancini:

> When the king first fell in love with her beauty of person and charm of manner, he could not corrupt her virtue by gifts or menaces. The story runs that when Edward placed a dagger at her throat, to make her submit to his passion, she remained unperturbed and determined to die rather than live unchastely with the king. Whereupon Edward coveted her much the more, and he judged the lady worthy of a royal spouse, who could not be overcome in her constancy even by an infatuated king.

Although of lowly birth herself, Elizabeth was descended from noble ancestors, and she had a high opinion of her honour. She was determined not to become the King's mistress, even when he threatened to rape her at knifepoint, instead telling him plainly 'that as she wist herself too simple to be his wife, so thought she herself too good to be his concubine'. When she made this comment, Elizabeth can never have expected that Edward would marry her, and at most, she may have hoped for an introduction to a more suitable second husband. Edward was, however, besotted with her, and on or around 1 May 1464, the couple were married in a secret ceremony.

Edward's decision to marry Elizabeth was impulsive, and he did not think through the consequences of his hasty action. Whilst the couple enjoyed the first few days of their married life, Edward's cousin and chief advisor, the Earl of Warwick, was in France attempting to arrange a marriage between Edward and the sister-in-law of the King of France. Following Warwick's return, Edward was forced to admit at a council meeting that he was already married. Edward's mother, Cecily Neville, was aghast and publicly declared that Elizabeth was not good enough for her son. More damagingly, in a fit of pique, she also claimed that Edward was not the son of her husband and was instead the product of an adulterous affair. There was no truth to this, but it demonstrates the fury with which news of Edward's marriage was greeted. Edward's brother, George, Duke of Clarence, objected to the marriage, saying that Edward should have married a virgin rather than a widow with children. It was Warwick's opposition that was most damaging to Edward and Elizabeth.

Elizabeth was secure in Edward's devotion to her, and aware that there was little her enemies could do to change the situation, she was not unduly concerned. Once news of their marriage became public, Edward was determined to promote his wife, and he gave her a grand coronation on 26 May 1465, a ceremony that was delayed in order to give Elizabeth's grand maternal relatives time to arrive from Luxembourg. Elizabeth intended that her family should benefit from her good fortune, and she arranged marriages for her many siblings. Elizabeth's sisters married the Earls of Essex and Kent, the wealthy Lord Strange and the heir to Lord Herbert. Elizabeth's youngest sister, Catherine, made by far the grandest match when she married the Duke of Buckingham. Elizabeth also arranged rich marriages for her brothers, with the marriage of one brother causing particular comment. According to the *Annales Rerum Anglicarum*, in January 1465, 'Catherine, Duchess of Norfolk, a slip of a girl of about eighty years old, was married to John Woodville, the queen's brother, aged twenty years, a diabolical marriage'. In February 1467, Elizabeth obtained the marriage of Edward's niece, Anne Holland, for her eldest son, Thomas Grey. The rise of the Woodvilles was resented in England, but Elizabeth ploughed on regardless, persuading Edward to ennoble her father as Earl Rivers and her eldest son as the Marquis of Dorset.

Elizabeth kept a tight control over her household and finances during her time as queen, and she was a very effective manager. Her household was smaller than Margaret of Anjou's, and she was less extravagant in her spending. She had an income of £4,500 and made a point of living within her means, appointing only seven maids instead of Margaret of Anjou's ten. In spite of this economy, Elizabeth enjoyed luxury goods and sums spent on furs and goldsmith's works are noted in her accounts for 1466-67. She guarded her rights, as can be seen from a letter that she wrote to Sir William Stoner, threatening him for exploiting one of her forests:

Trusty and well beloved, we greet you well. And whereas we understand, by report made unto us at this time, that you have taken upon you now of late to make masteries within our forest and chase of Barnwood and Exhill, and there, in contempt of us, uncourteously to hunt and slay our deer within the same, to our great marvel and displeasure; we will you wit that we intend to sue such remedy therein as shall accord with my lord's laws. And whereas we furthermore understand that your purpose, under colour of my lord's commission, in that behalf granted unto you, as you say, hastily to take the view and rule of our game of deer within our said forest and chace; we will that you show unto us or our council your said commission, if any such you have, and in the mean season, that you spare of hunting within our said forest and chace, as you will answer at your peril.

Elizabeth had suffered poverty following the death of her first husband, and this coloured her management of her affairs once she became queen.

Elizabeth also found time to carry out acts of patronage. In 1465, she was granted a licence by Edward to patronise Queen's College, Cambridge. Elizabeth proved enthusiastic in her support of the college and was often referred to as the college's true founder in documents of the period, reflecting the size of her contribution. She had strong religious beliefs and founded a chapel in Westminster Abbey. In March 1546, she obtained a royal licence to support sixty priests at Leadenhall in London. As a further demonstration of their faith, Edward and Elizabeth went on pilgrimages to Walsingham and Canterbury. They named their youngest child Bridget after a popular Swedish saint and Elizabeth saw charitable and religious patronage as part of her duty as queen.

Elizabeth fulfilled another aspect of the role of queen admirably. She bore her first child by Edward, a daughter named Elizabeth, on 11 February 1465, and this was soon followed by the births of two further daughters. Elizabeth was a fond mother and raised all her children in her household, with the exception of her eldest son by Edward. Both Elizabeth and Edward were pleased with their daughters, but they required a son, and

Elizabeth was pregnant again in 1470 when Edward was forced to abandon his kingdom and his throne.

Both the Earl of Warwick and Edward's brother, the Duke of Clarence, had been furious when they heard of Edward's marriage, and by 1469, their hostility had turned into rebellion. Elizabeth was visiting Norwich with her daughters when Warwick and Clarence launched their attack on Edward. The rebellion was intended as an attack on Elizabeth's family, as a proclamation made by Warwick, Clarence and the Archbishop of York on 12 July 1469 made clear:

> The king our sovereign lord's true subjects of divers parts of this his realm of England have delivered to us certain articles [remembering] the deceitful, covetous rule and guiding of certain seditious persons, that is to say, the Lord Rivers, the Duchess of Bedford his wife, William Herbert, Earl of Pembroke, Humphrey Stafford, Earl of Devonshire, Lord Scales [Elizabeth's eldest brother] and Audley, Sir John Woodville and his brothers, and others of this mischievious rule, opinion and assent, which have caused our sovereign lord and his realm to fall into great poverty and misery, disturbing the administration of the laws, only tending to their own promotion and enrichment.

Edward's forces were no match for Warwick's, and he was defeated at the Battle of Edgecote on 26 July and captured soon afterwards. Elizabeth was terrified and worse news followed when she heard that her father and brother John had been captured by Warwick's forces near Coventry and executed without trial. The Woodville family were always particularly close and Elizabeth plunged into mourning. Warwick was unable to hold the King for long, and Edward and Elizabeth were soon reunited, but any joy was short-lived. After a brief exile, Warwick and Clarence returned to England allied with Margaret of Anjou and the Lancastrians in September 1470, and deposed Edward IV, reinstating Henry VI as king of England.

Edward did not have the military strength to give battle against the Lancastrians and, instead, fled to Burgundy on hearing of Warwick's landing. Elizabeth was in London at the time of Warwick's invasion, and she immediately began to provision the Tower for a potential siege. As news reached her of Warwick's strength, it was obvious that she could not hold the Tower, and Elizabeth, her mother and daughters entered the sanctuary at Westminster Abbey. Soon afterwards, Warwick entered the city in triumph. It must have been a miserable party who awaited the outcome of events in sanctuary in late 1470, although the mood was lightened somewhat on around 1 November when Elizabeth gave birth to her first son by the King, whom she named in honour of his father.

On 11 March 1471, Edward sailed for England with an army. He had always been popular in London, and on 11 April, he was admitted to the city and promptly re-proclaimed as king, removing Henry VI from the royal apartments of the Tower and returning him to his prison rooms. Elizabeth was overjoyed by Edward's return, and she left sanctuary for what must have been an emotional reunion. Edward did not remain in the city for long and soon marched out at the head of an army to meet Warwick at the Battle of Barnet. Edward won the day and, on 4 May 1471, obtained his final victory over the Lancastrians, defeating the forces of Margaret of Anjou at Tewkesbury. With this victory, Edward was finally secure on his throne, and Elizabeth was equally secure in her position as his queen.

On her release from sanctuary, Elizabeth showed Edward their infant son for the first time, and his father declared him Prince of Wales. In 1473, Elizabeth accompanied the prince to Ludlow, where she was to rule Wales on his behalf for a time. She was responsible for appointing her son's council whilst at Ludlow, and she appointed both her eldest brother, who had succeeded their father as Earl Rivers, and her second son, Sir Richard Grey, to prominent posts. Elizabeth was back in London by 1475, and that summer, when Edward set out to invade France, he paid her the compliment of naming their four-year-old son regent, a move that made Elizabeth the effective ruler of England. Edward IV was notoriously unfaithful to Elizabeth throughout their marriage, something that she always pretended to ignore. The couple remained in love, and young Edward's birth was followed by the births of Margaret in 1472, Richard in 1473, Anne in 1475, George in 1477, and Catherine in 1479. Elizabeth bore her youngest child, Bridget, in November 1480, when she was forty-three years old. Elizabeth's youngest son, George, died in infancy, but her second son by Edward was created Duke of York.

Edward was some years younger than Elizabeth, but throughout his reign, he enjoyed fine food and drink and overindulged himself, growing immensely fat. By Christmas 1482, his health had begun to fail, and on 9 April 1483, he died, shortly before his forty-first birthday. This was devastating for Elizabeth, but she was forced to ignore her grief in order to ensure the succession of her twelve-year-old son, Edward V. According to the *Crowland Chronicle Continuations*, Elizabeth met with her late husband's council at Westminster soon after his death and, in order to allay fears about Woodville dominance, agreed to instruct her son to bring no more than 2,000 men with him to London. At the time, she must have felt that she had nothing to fear.

Edward V set out from Ludlow accompanied by his uncle, Earl Rivers, and half-brother, Sir Richard Grey, soon after news of Edward IV's death reached him. Unbeknownst to Elizabeth, Edward V's paternal uncle, the Duke of Gloucester, and his friend, the Duke of Buckingham, who fiercely resented his marriage to Elizabeth's sister Catherine, set out to meet the young king at around the same time, arriving at Northampton as the King reached Stony Stratford. Out of politeness, Rivers and Grey met with the two dukes, and they spent the evening together, feasting and drinking. It was late before the feasting came to an end, and Elizabeth's two kinsmen agreed to spend the night at the dukes' residence. They were horrified to find, in the morning, that they had been placed under arrest as they slept whilst the two dukes rode to intercept the young king. Edward V, who was fond of his mother and maternal family, put up a spirited defence when his paternal uncle informed him that his uncle and two half-brothers had intended to rule the country through him. He declared that 'what my brother Marquis has done I cannot say. But in good faith I dare well answer for mine uncle Rivers and my brother here, that they be innocent of any such matters'. Edward's loyalty to the Woodvilles deeply troubled the two dukes as they accompanied the King to London.

According to Dominic Mancini, Elizabeth heard the news of Gloucester's actions just after midnight the next day, and she and her eldest son, Dorset, immediately 'began collecting an army, to defend themselves and to set free the young king from the clutches of the dukes. But when they exhorted certain nobles who had come to the city, and others, to take up arms, they perceived that men's minds were not only irresolute, but altogether hostile to themselves'. With no other option, Elizabeth, Dorset, and her five daughters and youngest son, Richard, Duke of York, fled once again to the sanctuary at Westminster. Elizabeth must have felt very alone, and her contemporaries believed that she was overreacting, with the chancellor visiting her at Westminster to give her the great seal as a demonstration that she had nothing to fear. This did little to reassure her, and soon afterwards, the chancellor came to her again on the orders of Gloucester to obtain the surrender of her youngest son.

Elizabeth had no intention of handing over her youngest son without a fight, and she was very concerned about what Gloucester intended towards her family. On his second visit to Elizabeth, the chancellor informed her that her younger son, Richard, Duke of York, should be with his elder brother to provide the young king with a companion. Elizabeth retorted that it would be better for both children to be with their mother. The chancellor, believing that he was dealing with a hysterical and melodramatic woman, offered a pledge for her youngest son's safety, to which Elizabeth replied that 'each of these children is the other's defence while they be asunder, and each of their lives lie in the other's body. Keep one safe and both be sure, and nothing for them both more perilous than to be both in one place'. Alone and friendless, Elizabeth knew that it was only a matter of time before she would be forced to comply, and shortly afterwards, when Gloucester surrounded the abbey with soldiers, she tearfully gave in, relinquishing her youngest son.

Elizabeth was right to be uneasy about Gloucester's intentions towards her sons. Six days after she surrendered her youngest son, on 22 June, a sermon was preached at Paul's Cross claiming that Edward IV was a bastard born as a result of an adulterous affair and that he and Elizabeth had never been married. The assertion that Edward IV was illegitimate was quickly dropped, perhaps due to the outrage of his mother, Cecily Neville, and instead, the focus of Gloucester's attack was that Elizabeth had never truly been the King's wife. According to the chronicler, Philippe de Commines, the Bishop of Bath 'revealed to the Duke of Gloucester [in 1483] that King Edward, being very enamoured of a certain English lady, promised to marry her, provided that he could sleep with her first, and she consented. The bishop said that he had married them when only he and they were present'.

The lady in question was Eleanor Butler, a noblewoman who had died in 1468. If the claims that Edward had secretly married her were true, then his later marriage to Elizabeth would be invalid and their children illegitimate. It seems very unlikely that Edward ever did enter into a full marriage with Eleanor, and a precontract with her, which, once consummated, could be as valid as a marriage is also debateable. Few people in England believed the claim, and most saw it for the pretext that it was, a device used by Gloucester to claim the throne as Richard III. Soon after his accession, Elizabeth's two sons disappeared into the Tower and were never seen again. Their fate is fiercely debated, although, at the time, it was widely believed that they were murdered by their uncle. Elizabeth is likely to have believed this, and the fact that she later came to terms with Richard is no indication that she believed her sons to be still alive. She already knew that he was the murderer of her second son, Sir Richard Grey, and her eldest brother, Earl Rivers, who were executed by the new king on trumped up charges.

With the accession of Richard III, Elizabeth was demoted from Queen Dowager to merely Dame Elizabeth Grey. For a woman as proud as Elizabeth, this rankled, and she began plotting against the new king, conspiring from sanctuary with Margaret Beaufort, the mother of Henry Tudor, the leading Lancastrian claimant to the throne. The two women shared a physician, who passed messages between them, and within months of the deposition of her son, Elizabeth had agreed that, if Henry Tudor promised to marry her eldest daughter, Elizabeth of York, she would support his bid for the throne. Both Elizabeth and Dorset were heavily involved in a rebellion that broke out in October 1483, which was intended to support an invasion by Henry Tudor from Brittany. Richard's decisive action brought matters under control, and Elizabeth, faced with the defeat of her Lancastrian ally, instead made terms with the King, agreeing to come out of sanctuary with her daughters in return for a promise from Richard that he would do her and her family no harm. This is surprising, as Elizabeth had every reason to hate Richard. However, she was several years older than him and must have felt that she was unlikely to survive him. Elizabeth's ambition was also pricked by Richard's scheme to marry her eldest daughter, although this came to nothing.

Elizabeth was living in London when word reached her in August 1485 that Henry Tudor had launched a second invasion of England, having sworn that, if he was victorious, he would marry Elizabeth of York. With his victory over Richard III at Bosworth, he claimed the throne as Henry VII, something that, along with the death of Richard III in battle, must have been gratifying to Elizabeth. Soon after his accession, Henry VII repealed the Act declaring Elizabeth's marriage invalid and reinstated her as Queen Dowager. He married Elizabeth of York the following year.

Elizabeth was not on entirely good terms with Henry VII, and there is some evidence that she conspired against him, perhaps in the hope that her grandson, Prince Arthur, could become king in his father's place. According to the historian Francis Bacon, in the early years of Henry VII's reign, a pretender called Lambert Simnel emerged, claiming to be Edward IV's nephew, the Earl of Warwick. Simnel had been well-schooled in how to behave:

> So that it cannot be, but that some great person that knew particularly and familiarly Edward Plantagenet [Warwick], had a hand in the business, from whom the priest might take his aim. That which is most probable, out of precedent and subsequent acts, is, that it was the Queen Dowager, from whom this action had the principal source and motion. For certain it is, she was a busy negotiating woman, and in her withdrawing-chamber had the fortunate conspiracy for the king against King Richard the third been hatched; which the king knew, and remembered perhaps but too well; and was at this time extremely discontent with the king, thinking her daughter, as the king handled the matter, not advanced but displeased: and none could hold the book so well to prompt and instruct this stage-play as she could.

When news of the plot became known, Henry seized Elizabeth's property and sent her to Bermondsey Abbey, officially claiming that this was in punishment for her delivering her daughters to Richard III. Elizabeth was a spent force, and she remained at Bermondsey in forced retirement from May 1487 until her death on 8 June 1492. As befitted her status, she was given a grand funeral and was buried beside her second husband, Edward IV. Elizabeth Woodville lived a life of great turbulence, her fortunes greatly affected by the troubled times in which she lived. Her successor as queen, Anne Neville, lived an equally turbulent and tragic life.

ANNE NEVILLE (1456-85) was a figure of major importance in the Wars of the Roses. Married first to a Lancastrian prince and then to a Yorkist one, she participated in many of the major political events of the late fifteenth century. Anne was the daughter of the famous Richard Neville, Earl of Warwick, and his wife Anne Beauchamp, who was the heiress to the earldoms of Warwick and Gloucester, and the rich Despenser estates. Anne's father, who was known as 'The Kingmaker' for his role in bringing Edward IV to the throne and then deposing him in favour of Henry VI, had no male heir and was ambitious for his two daughters, Anne, who was born in 1456, and Isabel, who was five years older.

In May 1457, Warwick was appointed captain of Calais and moved his household to France. His wife accompanied him, and it is possible that the couple took their two daughters. The family returned to England in 1460. By 1465, Warwick's young cousin, Richard, Duke of Gloucester, had joined the household. Anne's feelings for the King's youngest brother are nowhere recorded, but he was only four years older than her, and she would have had some contact with him in childhood. Gloucester and his elder brother George, Duke of Clarence, were the most eligible men in England, and in 1464, Warwick suggested a double marriage between them and his two daughters. Nothing came of either match in 1464, perhaps because the scheme was vetoed by the King.

Whilst Anne's marriage was allowed to drop, Warwick was determined to secure Clarence for his eldest daughter, and the King's attempts to thwart him were another reason for the earl to be discontented. Clarence was also disillusioned with his brother, and in early July 1469, Warwick, Clarence and Warwick's wife and daughters crossed the channel to Calais in the company of Warwick's brother, the Archbishop of York. Safely out of the reach of Edward IV, Isabel and Clarence were married on 11 July. Soon after the ceremony, Warwick, Clarence and the Archbishop issued a proclamation opposing the King, before sailing for England to raise troops. Anne, her mother and sister probably remained in Calais during Warwick and Clarence's first invasion. At some point after Edward's defeat and capture, the three women returned to England, and they were present in London for the Christmas celebrations where Edward, Warwick and Clarence were publicly reconciled. The public show of unity convinced no one that the rivalry between Warwick and the King was at an end, and Anne and her family returned to Warwick soon after Christmas, deeply concerned about the future.

In early 1470, violence again erupted between Warwick and Clarence and Edward IV. Edward inflicted a heavy defeat on Warwick's forces at Stamford, and Warwick and Clarence fled. On their way to the coast, the fugitives passed through Warwick, where they were joined by Anne and her mother and sister. The family then took ship, intending to land at Calais. They were nonplussed on 16 April to find Calais defended against them. Unable to land, matters became worse the following day when Isabel went into labour with her first child. With few women present to attend her, it is likely that both Anne and her mother assisted in Isabel's labour. It must have been a major trauma for everyone present, and Isabel's child was either stillborn or died soon after birth.

Whilst they were considering their next move, the family remained at sea, engaging in piracy against Burgundian ships, the allies of Edward IV. They finally landed in France, where Warwick allied himself with the Lancastrians in an attempt to oust Edward IV. According to the *Crowland Chronicle Continuations*, Anne was central to her father's plans:

> King Louis received them with kindness and, in the end, they were reconciled with Queen Margaret and her son, Prince Edward, and promised, henceforth, fruitfully to support their cause and the cause of King Henry. Furthermore, so that their renewed love and faith might be made more certain in time to come, a marriage contract was made between the prince and Lady Anne, the Earl of Warwick's younger daughter.

It is likely that Warwick wanted to witness the marriage, as a token of Margaret's good faith, but the couple, who were both descended from John of Gaunt, were forced to wait for a dispensation from the Pope, which had still not arrived by 9 September when Warwick finally sailed.

Anne spent the weeks of her betrothal largely with her fiancé's mother, Margaret of Anjou. Margaret kept her word and, following the arrival of the dispensation, the couple were married on 13 December at Amboise. By then, news of Warwick's success in deposing Edward IV and reinstating Henry VI had reached France, and Anne and her new husband were fêted by Louis XI in a grand reception held in their honour in Paris. Anne and Edward spent some time getting to know each other, and then, in late March 1471, travelled, with their respective mothers, to Harfleur with the intention of sailing to England. They were delayed by bad weather, but finally sailed the following month, with Anne travelling in the ship carrying her husband and mother-in-law. Whilst the weather had calmed to some extent, it was still a dangerous crossing and the fleet was scattered at sea, with Anne's ship landing in Weymouth and her mother's at Portsmouth. Within days of landing, Anne was horrified to hear that her father had been killed by Edward IV at the Battle of Barnet. When Anne's mother heard the news, instead of joining her daughter at Weymouth as arranged, she fled to the sanctuary of Beaulieu Abbey. Anne remained with Margaret whilst the Battle of Tewkesbury was fought, and she must have been shocked to hear that she was widowed that day so soon after her marriage.

Edward IV captured Margaret and Anne near the battlefield and took them triumphantly back to London. Margaret was imprisoned in the Tower, but Anne was, instead, passed into Clarence's custody. Clarence had recently been reconciled with his brother, and a legend has grown up around Anne's time in his household. According to the *Crowland Chronicle Continuations*,

Richard, Duke of Gloucester, sought to make the same Anne his wife; this desire did not suit the plans of his brother, the Duke of Clarence (married previously to the earl's elder daughter) who therefore had the girl hidden away so that his brother would not know where she was, since he feared a division of the inheritance. He wanted it to come to himself alone, by right of his wife, rather than to share it with someone else. The Duke of Gloucester, however, was so much the more astute, that having discovered the girl dressed as a kitchen-maid in London, he had her moved into sanctuary in St Martin's.

Clarence had good reason for keeping Anne unmarried, and he vetoed any suggestion of a marriage between her and his brother.

It is unlikely that Richard and Anne made a love match, as is indicated by Richard's interest in her inheritance. There is no evidence of the date of Anne's second marriage, but by 16 February 1472, they were betrothed, and they married soon afterwards. The marriage brought Richard and his brother Clarence into open rivalry, with the elder brother refusing to give up any of Warwick's estates. A series of hearings were held in the early spring to decide the matter, and a settlement was agreed where Clarence gave up some lands in return for receiving the Neville titles of Earl of Warwick and Earl of Salisbury. Edward IV personally brokered the settlement, which disinherited Anne Beauchamp, who remained in sanctuary at Beaulieu. Anne's feelings on the treatment meted out to her mother are not recorded, but she was apparently happy to occupy her mother's estates. Neither Clarence nor Richard were entirely happy with the settlement, and the matter continued to fester.

Anne Beauchamp keenly resented her treatment, and a petition by her to parliament survives, protesting her innocence:

It hath pleased the king's highness, by some sinister information to his said highness made, to direct his most dread letters to the abbot of the monastery of Beaulieu, with right sharp commandment that such persons as his highness sent to the said monastery should have guard and strait keeping of her person, which was and is to her great heart's grievance, she specially fearing that the privileges and liberties of the church, by such keeping of her person, might be interrupted and violated, where the privileges of the said sanctuary were never so largely attempted unto this time, as is said; yet the said Anne and Countess, under protestations by her made, hath suffered strait keeping of her person and yet doth, that her fidelity and liegeance to the king's highness the better might be understood, hoping she might the rather have had largess to make suits to the king's highness in her own person for her livelihood and rightful inheritance, with all revenues and profits thereto pertaining, with her jointure also, and dower of the earldom of Salisbury, fully and wholly hath been restrained from her, from the time of the death of her said lord and husband unto this day.

Anne Beauchamp's claims were a threat to both Clarence and Richard. Early in June 1473, Richard's agents removed Anne Beauchamp from Beaulieu and took her to his castle at Middleham. She probably thought that she was being offered her freedom and the return of her status and estates, but in reality, she was imprisoned by her son-in-law. The extent to which Anne Neville was involved in this is unclear, but both she and Richard feared the possibility of Anne Beauchamp remarrying. Anne may well have been complicit in the imprisonment of her mother in order to safeguard her inheritance. There is no record of any protest by her when her mother, who was still very much alive, was declared legally dead by Act of Parliament in May 1474, in order to allow her sons-in-law to inherit her property.

Anne Neville virtually disappears from the sources during her time as Duchess of Gloucester, and she spent most of her time on her estates in the north. On 22 December 1476, her sister died in childbirth, and Clarence, who had never fully regained the King's trust, was executed in the Tower just over a year later. Anne and Richard rarely visited court, and Anne's time was occupied in running her household. At some point during the 1470s, she bore her only child, Edward of Middleham. He is first recorded in contemporary records in February 1478, when he was created Earl of Salisbury, and it is likely that he was born between 1473 and 1476. There is no evidence that Anne ever conceived another child, and it is likely that she was in ill health by the late 1470s. By 1484, when she was still only in her twenties, she was popularly considered to be past childbearing.

Richard and Anne were together at Middleham on 9 April 1483 when Edward IV died. On hearing the news, Richard acted decisively, travelling to intercept his nephew, Edward V's, journey from Wales. Anne joined her husband in London on 5 June 1483. Officially, she was there to attend Edward V's coronation, but it is likely that she had some idea of her husband's real intentions. Anne and Richard stayed at Baynard's Castle whilst they were in London, and the couple were both there when Richard accepted the throne on 26 June, becoming king as Richard III. Anne shared Richard's coronation on 6 July, in which the couple processed through the streets of London, with Anne attended by a great train of ladies and wearing a coronet of gems in her hair. Once they had been crowned, the couple attended a grand banquet, and sitting as an anointed queen, Anne may have felt that her father's hopes for her had finally been fulfilled.

Richard III's usurpation of the crown did not have universal public support, and immediately following his coronation, he went on a progress to show himself to the people. He set out on 20 July, travelling first to Windsor. Anne did not set out with Richard, and she may have been delayed by ill health. She had rejoined him at Warwick by August, and the pair travelled slowly northward through Coventry, Leicester and Nottingham. On 24 August, they were joined at Pontefract by their son. The royal party reached York on 29 August, where they found cheering crowds waiting for them and the city decorated in celebration of their visit. Richard was so delighted with this that he decided to create his son Prince of Wales in the city. Following the ceremony, Richard, Anne and Edward of Middleham walked in procession through the streets of York with Anne holding her son's hand. The couple were fond parents to their only child, and as they slowly moved southwards again, Anne decided to remain at Middleham with him.

Anne had rejoined Richard by March 1484 when the couple set out on another progress. During their journey, they visited Cambridge, where Anne made a generous endowment to

Queen's College. They then travelled to Nottingham, where they received devastating news, as recorded in the *Crowland Chronicle Continuations*:

> In the following April, on a day not far off King Edward's anniversary, this only son, on whom, through so many solemn oaths, all hope of the royal succession rested, died at Middleham Castle after a short illness, in 1484 and in the first year of King Richard's reign. You might have seen the father and mother, after hearing the news at Nottingham where they were staying, almost out of their minds for a long time when faced with sudden grief.

The couple attempted to comfort each other in their grief, suggesting that they were close. However, the loss of their only son and Anne's inability to bear more children caused a rift between them that eventually drove them apart.

Anne spent Christmas 1484 at court in increasingly bad health. It cannot have been a happy occasion for her, and she suffered from comparisons with Richard's young niece, Elizabeth of York, who appeared wearing the same dress as Anne. Over Christmas, rumours arose that Richard wished to marry Elizabeth, intending to either divorce Anne or await her death. *Hall's Chronicle*, which, as a Tudor source, is admittedly hostile to Richard, claimed that Richard intended to hasten Anne's death. He complained publicly that she was barren, and around that time, ceased to sleep with her. He also apparently spread a rumour that she had already died, hoping that the shock of hearing it would hasten her death. *Hall's Chronicle* states that

> when the quene heard tell that so horrible a rumour of her death was sprong emongest the comminallie she sore suspected and judged the world to be almost at an ende with her, and in that sorofull agony, she with lamentable countenaunce of sorofull chere, repaired to the presence of the kyng her husband, demaundynge of hym, what it should meane that he had judged her worthy to die. The kyng aunswered her with fake words, and with dissimulynge blandimentes and flattering lesynges comforted her, biddynge her to be of good comforte, for to his knowledge she should have none other cause.

Anne died on 16 March 1485 on the day of a total eclipse of the sun. She was still only twenty-nine years old and her last months were not happy, with the likelihood that Richard would have divorced her had she lived longer. By the time of Anne's death, Richard's kingship was already unstable, and he was forced, on 30 March 1485, to make a public denial that he had murdered Anne. The crown brought Anne Neville nothing but misery. Her successor as queen, Elizabeth of York, was happier.

ELIZABETH OF YORK (1466-1503) was, for much of her life, the most important political figure in England and crucial to the success of any man who claimed the English crown. Elizabeth was the eldest child of Edward IV and Elizabeth Woodville and was born at Westminster Palace on 11 February 1466. Her childhood was dominated by marriage negotiations, and she was first betrothed at the age of four to Warwick's nephew, George Neville, who was created Duke of Bedford for the occasion. This marriage came to nothing, but in 1475, it was instead agreed that Elizabeth would marry the Dauphin of France.

With the exception of her father's exile and her time in sanctuary with her mother in 1470 and 1471, Elizabeth had a happy and secure childhood. This came to an abrupt end in April 1483 with Edward IV's death, and following the seizure of Edward V by Richard III, she once again fled with her family to sanctuary. It was from sanctuary that Elizabeth watched the events that placed her uncle on the throne, and on 25 June 1483, Elizabeth and all her siblings were declared to be illegitimate by parliament. Elizabeth may have known something of her mother's plot with Margaret Beaufort to marry her to Margaret's son, Henry Tudor, if he was able to claim the throne. With the disappearance of her brothers into the Tower and their likely murders, Elizabeth was widely regarded as the heiress to the House of York, and there is evidence that she desired to become queen of England, presumably seeing it as her birthright. Henry Tudor's first invasion of England ended in failure, and Elizabeth Woodville gave up hope of the deposition of Richard III, instead moving the family out of sanctuary in March 1484 and entrusting her daughters to Richard III's care. Elizabeth met with Richard III soon afterwards and was placed in the household of his queen, Anne Neville.

Upon Elizabeth's arrival at court, rumours began to spread that Richard III intended to divorce his wife and marry his niece. By marrying Elizabeth, Richard hoped to have his kingship popularly recognised as legitimate. Elizabeth's feelings about the marriage are unclear. It is often claimed that she found the idea totally abhorrent, and certainly, this was the view that Tudor historians were keen to portray. However, a now lost letter supposedly written by Elizabeth to the Duke of Norfolk in February 1485 suggests a different story. In the letter, Elizabeth asked Norfolk to mediate with Richard for her on the subject of their marriage, and she wrote that she feared that Anne Neville would never die. This letter no longer exists and must be considered highly suspect. If it is genuine, it demonstrates an aspect of Elizabeth's character that has been lost to history, and she may have been as ambitious as her mother. Whether she welcomed the marriage to her uncle or not, it was not to be. Richard was forced to publicly deny that he had considered making an incestuous marriage after there were murmurs of rebellion in the country in disgust.

The last months of Richard III's reign were filled with suspicion, and Elizabeth's conduct was closely watched. During the summer of 1485, the country was poised for Henry Tudor's expected invasion, and Elizabeth was sent north to Sheriff Hutton with her cousin, the Earl of Warwick, the son of the Duke of Clarence, to ensure that they were out of Henry's reach. On 22 August 1485, Richard was defeated and killed at the Battle of Bosworth and Henry Tudor was declared king as Henry VII. The new king sent Sir Robert Willoughby to Sheriff Hutton to bring Elizabeth and Warwick back to London. Warwick was sent as a prisoner to the Tower, whilst Elizabeth was lodged at her mother's house in the capital.

Henry VII claimed the crown through three separate titles: his maternal descent from the House of Lancaster, by right of conquest, and through his proposed marriage to Elizabeth of York. According to the historian Francis Bacon, his claim through Elizabeth was the one most favoured by the people of England. This unnerved Henry, and 'it lay plain before his eyes, that if he relied upon that title, he could be but a king at courtesy, and have rather a matrimonial than a regal power; the right remaining in his queen, upon whose decease, either with issue, or without issue, he was to give place and be removed'. Henry was anxious not to be seen only as a king through marriage and so delayed his marriage to Elizabeth, refusing to marry her until after his coronation on 30 October 1485.

Henry and Elizabeth began living together as husband and wife before their marriage, and she was in the early stages of pregnancy when they married on 18 January 1486. News of the marriage was received joyfully in England according to *Hall's Chronicle*:

> By reason of whiche marriage, peace was thought to discende oute of heuen [heaven] into England, considering that the lynes of Lancastre and Yorke, being both noble families equivalent in ryches, fame and honour, were now brought into one knot and connexed together, of whose two bodyes one heyre might succeed, whiche after their tyme should peaceably rule and enjoye the whole monarchy and realme of England.

The marriage was portrayed as bringing peace out of the turmoil of the Wars of the Roses, and Elizabeth, who had been deeply affected by the troubles, must have been proud of her role in bringing the civil war to an end.

There is some debate as to the relationship between Henry and Elizabeth. Francis Bacon believed that Henry 'shewed himself no very indulgent husband towards her, though she was beautiful, gentle, and fruitful. But his aversion towards the house of York was so predominant in him, as it found place not only in his wars and councils, but in his chamber and bed'. Bacon believed that Henry hated Elizabeth and was a cold and indifferent husband. It is certainly true that Henry gave Elizabeth no political role, and it was to his mother, Margaret Beaufort, that he turned for advice. However, throughout their marriage, the couple were rarely apart, and Henry was genuinely grief-stricken at her death. The marriage was political in origin, but it appears that affection developed between the couple.

The birth of Elizabeth's first child was greatly anticipated in England. Henry was acutely aware of the symbolic importance of the child who would be the heir to both Lancaster and York, and he asked Elizabeth to bear the child at Winchester, which was believed to have been King Arthur's capital. Through his grandfather, Owen Tudor, Henry claimed descent from Welsh royalty, and he was eager to stress his links with the mythical British king. On 20 September 1486, Elizabeth gave birth to a son who was named Arthur. The prince was given a grand christening in Winchester Cathedral with a great procession beginning and ending in Elizabeth's chamber. For Elizabeth, the birth was a triumph, and she had fulfilled her dynastic purpose. The christening was also a tribute to Elizabeth and her family, and her mother, Elizabeth Woodville, stood as godmother to the prince. Elizabeth's sister, Cecily, and her sister-in-law, the Marchioness of Dorset, carried the baby and his train.

The early years of Henry's reign were troubled by rebellions, and one of the most serious erupted in June 1487, when a rebel army landed in England led by Lambert Simnel, a boy who claimed to be Elizabeth's cousin, the Earl of Warwick. Elizabeth did not believe that Simnel was her cousin, and it is likely that she knew that the real Warwick was imprisoned in the Tower. For her safety, Henry sent Elizabeth to Greenwich whilst he marched north to confront the rebels, whom he crushed in battle at Stoke. With his victory, Henry finally felt secure enough to crown Elizabeth. On 23 November 1487, Elizabeth, Margaret Beaufort, and a company of ladies sailed from Greenwich in a procession of decorated boats, with one shaped like a red dragon. The procession docked at the Tower, where Henry met Elizabeth and escorted her inside. Two days of celebrations and feasting followed, and on 25 November, Elizabeth was crowned in Westminster Abbey, wearing a gown of purple velvet.

Much of Elizabeth's time as queen was spent in childbearing. She bore a daughter, Margaret, in 1489, followed by a second son, Henry, in 1491. Elizabeth was particularly fond of her second son, who she raised herself, and he bore a remarkable resemblance to her father, Edward IV. A second daughter, Elizabeth, was born the year after Henry's birth, and a further son in 1497. Mary was born in 1498 and Edmund in 1499. Elizabeth's eighth and last child, Catherine, was born in 1503. Elizabeth was a fond mother to her children, and it is possible that the death of her daughter Elizabeth in 1497 caused the premature birth of her third son, who died before he was given a name. Elizabeth grieved for both these children and went on a pilgrimage to Walsingham in their memory. When her fourth son, Edmund, died in infancy, he was given a grand funeral in London.

Elizabeth played an active role in the negotiation of her children's marriages. Both she and Henry were overjoyed in 1497 when they secured the betrothal of their eldest son, Arthur, to Catherine, the youngest daughter of Ferdinand, King of Aragon, and Isabella, Queen of Castile. This match was proof of the strength of the Tudor dynasty and provided international recognition of Henry's kingship. A letter from Elizabeth to Isabella of Castile survives in which Elizabeth sought to reassure Catherine's mother of the warm welcome her daughter could expect in England:

> Although we before entertained singular love and regard to your highness above all other queens in the world, as well for the consanguinity and necessary intercourse which mutually take place between us, as also for the eminent dignity and virtue by which your said majesty so shines and excels that your most celebrated name is noised abroad and diffused every where; yet much more had this our love increased and accumulated by the accession of the most noble affinity which has recently been celebrated between the most illustrious Lord Arthur, prince of Wales, our eldest son, and the most illustrious princess the Lady Catherine, the infanta, your daughter. Hence it is that, amongst all other cares and cogitations, first and foremost we wish and desire from our heart that we may often and speedily hear of the health and safety of your serenity, and of the health and safety of the aforesaid most illustrious Lady Catherine, whom we think of and esteem as our own daughter, than which nothing can be more grateful and acceptable to us. Therefore we request your serenity to certify of your estate, and of that of the aforesaid most illustrious Lady Catherine, our common daughter. And if there be any thing in our power which would be grateful or pleasant to your majesty, use us and ours as freely as you would your own; for, with most willing mind, we offer all that we have to you, and wish to have all in common with you.

Catherine of Aragon arrived in England in October 1501 and was placed in Elizabeth's care until her marriage. Catherine and Arthur were given a great state wedding before being sent to Ludlow to rule Wales. Disaster struck on 2 April 1502 when Arthur died suddenly. The news of his death was brought first to Henry, who sent for Elizabeth so that he could tell her himself. Both parents were grief-stricken, but Elizabeth tried to comfort Henry, pointing out that they were young enough to have more children and that they still had one son. Henry was calmed by Elizabeth's words, and she left him to return to her own chamber, where she gave way to her grief, falling on the floor and sobbing. Elizabeth's ladies rushed to Henry and he immediately joined his wife and comforted her in turn. No further proof of the close relationship that had developed between the couple is needed than their shared grief at the death of their eldest son.

Elizabeth conceived another child soon after Arthur's death and, on 10 February 1503, bore a daughter, whom she named Catherine. Elizabeth was a day short of her thirty-seventh birthday, an advanced age for childbearing at the time, and the labour was difficult. The next day, she quietly died, with her baby daughter following her to the grave shortly afterwards. Henry was devastated by Elizabeth's death, and he gave her a splendid funeral. In spite of the fact that she had played no political role, she was an admirable queen, and it was always through her that her son, Henry VIII, and her later descendants claimed their right to the crown.

The three Yorkist queens were all English by birth and upbringing, and whilst they sought to carry out the traditional role of queen, they also opened up the possibility of an Englishwoman becoming queen of England. This was a precedent followed in the Tudor dynasty, and of the six wives of Henry VIII, all but two were members of the English nobility.

7

The Six Wives of Henry VIII

Henry VIII, who came to the throne in 1509, was married to his first wife, Catherine of Aragon, for over twenty years. In the latter years of his life, Henry completely revolutionised English queenship, fitting five marriages into the space of fourteen years. Four of these women were Englishwomen. Whilst, at first, Catherine of Aragon was essentially a medieval queen, she and her successors as Henry's wives brought queenship into the early modern era.

CATHERINE OF ARAGON (1485-1536) was the daughter of two sovereigns, Isabella, Queen of Castile, and Ferdinand, King of Aragon. She was the couple's youngest child and was born on 16 December 1485 whilst her mother, the redoubtable Isabella, was undertaking a military campaign in southern Spain. Catherine's sex was a disappointment to her parents, and of the family's five children, only one was a son. In September 1496, Catherine's brother, Juan, died, and his widow bore a stillborn son a few months later. The next heir, Catherine's eldest sister, Isabella, Queen of Portugal, died in childbed, and her only child, Manuel, Prince of Portugal, died aged two. These disasters devastated Catherine's family and drove her mother to seek solace in the Church. It was the second sister, Juana, who ultimately succeeded their parents, only to be declared insane and unfit to rule. Catherine cannot have realised that her mother's misfortunes in losing her children would be mirrored, even more unhappily, by herself.

At the age of three, Catherine was betrothed to Arthur, Prince of Wales, and she spent her childhood preparing for her future as queen of England. Catherine was particularly close to her mother, and Isabella was unwilling to part with her youngest child. Catherine finally left her mother in Granada on 21 May 1501 and set out for England. The first part of her journey was overland across Spain, and Catherine made slow progress, only sailing in late September. She landed at Plymouth on 2 October 1501. The arrival of the daughter of the famous 'Catholic Kings of Spain' enhanced the prestige of the English royal house, and Henry VII was determined to demonstrate to the world that his son was the equal of his Spanish bride. Catherine spent the days before her wedding in the company of Arthur's mother, Elizabeth of York, and his grandmother, Margaret Beaufort. On 14 November, she was escorted along a six-foot-high wooden stage in St Paul's Cathedral, erected for her marriage, to where Arthur was waiting. The young couple wore white, and following their marriage, Catherine was escorted to the Bishop's Palace by Arthur's younger brother, the ten-year-old Henry, Duke of York. The wedding was followed by great feasting and dancing, and that evening, the couple were ceremonially put to bed together naked.

Neither Catherine nor Arthur can have realised the importance that would later be attached to their wedding night. Catherine was fifteen and Arthur a year younger and both were considered ready to live together as husband and wife. George, Earl of Shrewsbury, who was present when Arthur was conducted to Catherine's bedchamber, later testified that he had always assumed that the marriage was consummated. Sir Anthony Willoughby, a friend of Arthur's, also claimed that the prince called for him the morning after the wedding, saying, 'Willoughby, bring me a cup of ale, for I have been this night in the midst of Spain.' He later boasted to his friend that 'it is good pastime to have a wife', again implying that the couple had a sexual relationship. Catherine always swore that her first marriage remained unconsummated, and whilst it is possible that this was a lie, it seems unlikely given her deep religious faith. More likely, Arthur's comments were the boasts of a youth aware of what had been expected of him on his wedding night.

Regardless of what happened on the wedding night, publicly, Catherine and Arthur fulfilled their roles as Prince and Princess of Wales, and in December 1501, they travelled to Ludlow to rule their principality. In late March, both fell ill with the dangerous sweating sickness, and on 2 April 1502, Arthur died, leaving Catherine a widow at the age of sixteen. Catherine was too ill to attend Arthur's funeral, but as soon as she was well, she was brought to London and kept under observation until it was certain that she was not pregnant. Once this had been ascertained, Arthur's brother, Henry, was created Prince of Wales.

Catherine had been raised to become queen of England, and Arthur's death threw her hopes into disarray. On her arrival in London, she was installed in Durham House on the Strand whilst her future was decided. When word reached Spain of Arthur's death, Ferdinand and Isabella instructed their ambassador to seek the return of Catherine and her dowry. Such an outcome was not in the interests of either set of parents, and the Spanish ambassador was instructed to discreetly suggest a marriage between Catherine and the new Prince of Wales. This solution suited Henry VII, and on 23 July 1503, Catherine's new betrothal was agreed. From a political perspective, the new match made perfect sense, and there was a precedent in Catherine's own family, as her sister Maria had married the widower of their eldest sister, Isabella. Personally, Catherine cannot have been entirely happy, as Henry's youth meant that she would have to wait several years for marriage. More immediately, the marriage treaty also required that she renounce her widow's dower, forcing her to rely on the charity of Henry VII.

The death of Isabella in October 1504 was a personal blow to Catherine, and it had consequences for her own future prospects. Castile was the more powerful of the two kingdoms ruled by her parents, and on Isabella's death, it passed to Catherine's sister, Juana, and her husband, the Archduke Philip of Austria. Catherine was reduced to merely being the daughter of the King of Aragon. On 27 July 1505, Henry VII made his son secretly renounce his betrothal to Catherine before the Bishop of Winchester. Catherine was unaware of this, but she did notice a change in the King's conduct towards her. Soon after Isabella's death, he stopped her allowance, arguing that it was her father's responsibility to provide for her. Ferdinand was just as determined that Catherine's upkeep was Henry's responsibility, and between 1502 and 1507, she received no money from either king. Her desperate letters to her father indicate the difficulties she was in, as she was unable to pay the wages for her household or buy clothes or food. In one letter, Catherine wrote,

Now I supplicate your highness, for the love of our Lord, that you consider that I am your daughter, and that after Him I have no other good nor remedy, except your highness; and how I am in debt in London, and this is not for extravagant things, nor yet by relieving my own [people], who greatly need it, but only for food; and how the king of England, my lord, will not cause them [the debts] to be satisfied, although I myself spoke to him, and all those of his council, and that with tears: but he said that he is not obliged to give me anything, and that even the food he gives me is of his goodwill; because your highness has not kept promise with him in the money of marriage portion. I told him that I believed that in time to come your highness would discharge it. He told me that that was yet to see, and that he did not know it. So that, my lord, I am in the greatest trouble and anguish in the world. On the one part, seeing all my people that they are ready to ask for alms; on the other, the debts which I have in London; on the other, about my own person, I have nothing for chemises; wherefore, by your highness' life, I have now sold some bracelets to get a dress of black velvet, for I was all but naked; for since I departed thence [from Spain] I have nothing except two new dresses, for till now those I brought from thence have lasted me, although now I have nothing but the dresses of brocade. On this account I supplicate your highness to command to remedy this, and that as quickly as may be; for certainly I shall not be able to live in this manner.

Catherine's complaints eventually had some effect, and Ferdinand sent her the formal credentials to act as his ambassador in England. Catherine took this role seriously and had her own cipher for coded dispatches. Her new role improved her position somewhat and she was still acting in this capacity when Henry VII died on 21 April 1509.

Catherine cannot have been sorry to hear of the death of her father-in-law, but she must have been amazed at just how suddenly her position in England improved. Her marriage to Prince Henry had originally been meant to take place when he turned fifteen, but this birthday had come and gone with no talk of a wedding, and at the time of his accession, Henry VIII was nearly eighteen years old. He had lived a secluded existence and was anxious to prove his maturity to the world. One way of demonstrating this was to marry, and for Henry, Catherine was a conveniently available princess. The couple knew each other well, and Henry, who was always a romantic at heart, believed himself in love, seeing her as a princess in distress. Catherine cannot have believed her good fortune, as Henry was known as the most handsome man in Europe. According to the report of a Venetian diplomat who met the king in 1515, he was

the handsomest potentate I ever set eyes on; above the usual height, with an extremely fine calf to his leg, his complexion very fair and bright, with auburn hair combed straight and short, in the French fashion, and a round face so very beautiful, that it would become a pretty woman, his throat being rather long and thick.

Henry was a fine physical specimen, and he and Catherine made a good-looking couple at their marriage at Greenwich on 11 June 1509. In spite of the five-year age gap between them, they had a number of interests in common and, for Catherine, Henry was the love of her life. The couple were crowned together shortly after their marriage.

The early years of her marriage were the best years of Catherine's life, and both she and Henry took part in dancing and other entertainments and presided over a glittering court. Henry loved to appear in Catherine's apartments in disguise, believing that she did not recognise him, and the Queen always played along. A particular highlight for Catherine was the meeting between Henry and Francis I of France outside Calais in 1521, which became known as the Field of the Cloth of Gold. This was one of the most splendid events of Henry's reign, as both kings attempted to outdo each other, and Catherine was a major participant, entertaining the French king on a number of occasions.

The early years of Catherine's queenship were not entirely given over to pleasures, and she was acutely aware of her duties as a princess of Spain. She always promoted her father's interests in England, a fact she set out in a letter to Ferdinand soon after her marriage: 'As to the king my lord, amongst the reasons that oblige me to love him much more than myself, the one most strong, although he is my husband, is his being the so true son of your highness, with desire of greater obedience, and love to serve you than ever son had to his father.' Catherine found her inexperienced husband easy to influence, and in the summer of 1512, Henry invaded Gascony jointly with Ferdinand. Catherine genuinely believed that an alliance with her father was in England's best interests, but Ferdinand proved an unreliable ally, using the English invasion as a pretext for him to occupy Navarre. The campaign of 1512 was a success from Ferdinand's point of view, but for the English, it was an unmitigated disaster.

In June 1513, Henry decided to mount a further campaign against France in person. Catherine accompanied Henry to Dover, and he paid her the compliment of naming her as regent of England. Catherine's regency was eventful, as, soon after Henry left, the Scots invaded northern England. Catherine was not the martial Isabella's daughter for nothing, and she raised an army, travelling north as far as Buckingham before leaving the defence of England to her commanders. Catherine had an anxious wait for news, and she was jubilant when word reached her that her army had won a decisive victory at Flodden in which James IV of Scotland and much of his nobility were killed. Catherine was proud of her triumph and sent the Scottish king's bloodstained coat to Henry in France, writing that 'I thought to send himself unto you, but our Englishmen's hearts would not suffer it'. Catherine's achievements rather overshadowed Henry's own mediocre French campaign.

Catherine miscarried a daughter a few months after her marriage. This was a disappointment, but neither she nor Henry was unduly alarmed. She was soon pregnant again, bearing a son on New Year's Day 1511. Henry held a grand tournament in celebration, jousting under the name of Sir Loyal Heart. The joy proved to be short-lived, as, on 22 February 1511, the little prince died at Richmond. *Hall's Chronicle* recounts his parents' response:

> The kyng lyke a wyse prynce, toke this dolorous chaunce wonderous wisely, and the more to comfort the Quene, he dissimiled the matter, and made no great mourning outwardely: but the Quene lyke a naturall woman, made much lamentacion, how be it, by the kynges good persuasion and behauvious her sorowe was mitigated, but not shortlye.

Catherine was devastated, but both she and Henry believed that they would soon have more children. Catherine became pregnant again in early 1513, although, like her first, this pregnancy ended in miscarriage. In February 1515, Catherine bore a second son at Greenwich, but he was either stillborn or died soon after birth. On 18 February 1516, both were overjoyed when Catherine bore a healthy daughter. Whilst the sex of the child, whom they named Mary, was a disappointment, Henry saw her as the promise of healthy sons to follow. This was not to be, and Catherine's last pregnancy ended with the birth on 18 November 1518 of a stillborn girl. Within a few years of Mary's birth, it was clear that she would be Catherine's only surviving child, and she focused on preparing her for her likely future as queen of England, commissioning a book on the education of girls by the Spanish scholar, Juan Luis Vives. Catherine, as the daughter of a female sovereign, was unconcerned by the prospect of Mary's accession, but for Henry, it was deeply worrying.

Like her mother, Catherine became increasingly religious and came to be regarded as something of a living saint. According to the *Life of Jane Dormer*, which chronicled the life of a friend of Catherine's daughter,

[Catherine] rose at mid-night to be present at the matins of the Religious. At five o'clock she made herself ready with what haste she might, saying that the time was lost which was spent in apparelling herself. Under her royal attire she did wear the habit of St Francis, having taken the profession of his Third Order. She fasted all Fridays and Saturdays and all the Eves of our Blessed Lady with bread and water'.

By the mid-1520s, Catherine was following a punishing daily regime of religious devotions, and she and Henry had grown apart. She had always ignored Henry's infidelities, but in 1527, he began a relationship with one of her ladies, Anne Boleyn, which was to prove very different from any of his earlier affairs.

Anne, unlike Henry's earlier loves, refused to become the King's mistress, insisting on marriage. Henry was besotted with her, and by spring 1527, the couple had vowed to marry. On 5 May 1527, Henry led Anne out as his dancing partner for the first time, a public statement of his relationship, and twelve days later, an ecclesiastical court opened to try the validity of Catherine's marriage. Henry argued that the marriage was invalid due to Catherine's earlier marriage to his brother. He was unable to keep the court secret, and Catherine knew of it within hours. As Henry had feared, she appealed to her powerful nephew, the Holy Roman Emperor, Charles V, who was the son of her sister Juana, and asked him to alert the Pope. On 16 June 1527, Charles, who was determined to uphold his aunt's honour, sacked Rome and imprisoned the Pope, making it a virtual impossibility for Henry to obtain a divorce.

Catherine was devastated when, following the failure of the ecclesiastical hearing, Henry took her aside privately and informed her of his doubts about the marriage. She burst into tears, leaving Henry to retreat impotently from the room. Henry continued to petition the Pope, and with Anne Boleyn still in her household, it was a difficult time for Catherine. The sixteenth-century historian George Wyatt recorded a story that confirmed the rivalry between the two women:

And in this entertainment of time they had a certain game that I cannot name then frequented, wherein dealing, the king and queen meeting they stopped, and the young lady's hap was much to stop at a king; which the queen noting, said to her playfellow, My lady Anne, you have good hap to stop at a king, but you are not like the others, you will have all or none.

Both Henry and Anne were determined to be rid of Catherine. In April 1528, the Pope agreed to send a legate, Cardinal Campeggio, to England to hear the case. Henry and Anne were jubilant at the news, unaware that Campeggio had been given secret instructions to delay matters as much as possible to ensure that Catherine's nephew was not offended.

Campeggio made slow progress to England, only arriving in October 1528. He promptly took to his sickbed, where he remained until early 1529, when he finally set about trying to 'perswade the Queen to a Divorce; and disswade the King from it, as having either way the end he propos'd: yet he fail'd in both'. For the Pope, the ideal solution was for Catherine to enter a nunnery, allowing her to retire with honour and the King to remarry. This solution did indeed have its merits, and Catherine would have been able to live in some comfort as an abbess. She would also have been able to safeguard the position of her daughter, and it is likely that, had she agreed to retire, Henry would have confirmed Mary's legitimacy and her position as heir apparent. Whilst this solution might have been the most beneficial to Catherine and her daughter, it was not something that Catherine could countenance, as she loved her husband, declaring to Campeggio that she had no vocation for the religious life. Campeggio had no better luck with Henry, commenting that the King was so convinced of the invalidity of his marriage that 'if an angel was to descend from heaven he would not be able to persuade him to the contrary'.

Campeggio was left with no option but to try the matter, and he and Cardinal Wolsey opened a legatine court at Blackfriars on 18 June 1529. When Catherine was called to speak, she walked to the King and knelt at his feet. She then made a direct appeal, begging her husband in broken English for justice. Catherine's plea was recorded by her contemporary, George Cavendish, in his *Life of Cardinal Wolsey*:

> I beseech you for all the love that hath been between us, and for the love of God, let me have justice and right, take of me some pity and compassion, for I am a poor woman and a stranger born out of your dominion. I have here no assured friends, and much less impartial counsel. I flee to you as to the head of justice within this realm. Alas! Sir, wherein have I offended you, or what occasion of displeasure have I deserved against your will and pleasure – now that you intend (as I perceive) to put me from you? I take God and all the world to witness that I have been to you a true, humble and obedient wife, ever comfortable to your will and pleasure, and never said or did anything to the contrary therof, being always well pleased and contented with all things wherein you had any delight or dalliance, whether it were in little or much. I never grudged in word or countenance, or showed a visage or spark of discontent. I loved all those whom ye loved only for your sake whether I had cause or no, or whether they were my friends or enemies. This twenty years or more I have been your true wife and by me ye have had divers children, although it hath pleased God to call them out of this world, which hath been no default of me.

Catherine continued, insisting that she had been a virgin at her second marriage. Once she had spoken, Catherine stood and left the hall, saying when she was ordered to return that 'it makes no matter, for it is no impartial court for me therefore I will not tarry'. Catherine maintained her refusal to return to court throughout the duration of the hearing and insisted that only the Pope had the power to hear her case. Whilst the hearing continued, she was visited by Wolsey, who asked to speak to her in private. Catherine, who hated the chief minister and believed that he was responsible for the divorce, ordered him to speak his business in front of her household. When he spoke in Latin, she stopped him, insisting that he speak in English so that everyone assembled could hear, something that he did not dare do. Finally, Campeggio, aware that he could delay no more, declared before a furious Henry that he could give no judgement and that he had to refer the case to Rome.

Henry was furious at the failure of the Blackfriars trial, and whilst it was a victory for Catherine, it was a hollow one. Throughout the early years of the divorce, Catherine and Henry had continued to live in the same household, and Henry, on occasion, had continued to dine with his wife. On 11 July 1531, however, he rode away from Windsor without saying goodbye to Catherine: she never saw him again. More cruelly, shortly afterwards, she was ordered to separate from her daughter, and the pair were kept apart until Catherine's death.

Following her separation from Henry, Catherine was ordered to go to the More, one of his smaller and more isolated palaces. Catherine spent the remainder of her life in isolation, moving from one house to another as her household was gradually reduced in size. At Easter 1533, she received a deputation headed by the Dukes of Norfolk and Suffolk and other lords, who informed her that Henry had married Anne Boleyn earlier in the year and that Catherine would now be known as Princess Dowager of Wales, the title she was entitled to as Arthur's widow. Anne was publicly proclaimed queen soon afterwards, and on 23 May, the new Archbishop of Canterbury, Thomas Cranmer, declared Catherine's second marriage invalid on the basis that her marriage to Arthur had been consummated.

Catherine had been staying at the manor of Ampthill when she was informed of Cranmer's verdict on her marriage, but in July, she was ordered to move again, this time to Buckden, a property that was considerably more remote. Catherine and Mary enjoyed immense public support in England, and Henry feared that they might mount a rebellion against him. Wherever Catherine travelled, she was greeted by cheering crowds, and by sending her to the damp and unhealthy Buckden, Henry hoped to keep her out of the public's mind. Both Henry and Anne were exasperated by Catherine's defiance and her insistence that she remained the true queen, and the couple reacted with petty bullying. In late 1532, Anne Boleyn demanded Catherine's jewels, and in anticipation of the birth of her own child in the summer of 1533, she also ordered that Catherine hand over a christening gown that she had brought with her from Spain, something that she indignantly refused to do.

Catherine's health was broken by the years of struggle and by her unsanitary living conditions, and by December 1535, she was gravely ill. One of Catherine's greatest friends during the years of the divorce was Eustace Chapuys, the Imperial ambassador. Henry, pleased to hear of Catherine's illness, granted the ambassador permission to visit her, and he rushed to Kimbolton, where he found her in bed. His report of his final visit to Catherine survives:

> After I had kissed hands she took occasion to thank me for the numerous services I had done her hitherto and the trouble I had taken to come and see her, a thing that she had very ardently desired, thinking that my coming would be salutary to her, and at all events, if it pleased God to take her, it could be a consolation to her to die under my guidance and not unprepared, like a beast. I gave her every hope, both of her health and otherwise, informing her of the offers the king had made to me of what houses she would, and to cause her to be paid the remainder of certain arrears, adding, for her further consolation, that the king was very sorry for her illness, and on this I begged her to take heart and get well, if for no other consideration, because the union and peace of Christendom depended upon her life.

Chapuys stayed with her for four days, and she gradually improved, appearing to be out of danger.

Catherine suffered a relapse on the night that Chapuys left. She had brought a number of high-born Spanish maids with her to England in 1501, and one of these, Maria de Salinas, had married an Englishman, becoming Lady Willoughby. When she heard that Catherine was dying, she set out for Kimbolton and forced her way into the house. She went straight to Catherine, and it was in her friend's arms that the former queen died on 7 January 1536 at the age of fifty.

Before she died, Catherine dictated one last letter to Henry, setting out her continuing love for him:

> My most dear lord, king and husband,
> The hour of my death now drawing on, the tender love I owe you forceth me, my case being such, to commend myself to you, and to put you in remembrance with a few words of the health and safeguard of your soul which you ought to prefer before all worldly matters, and before the care and pampering of your body, for the which you have cast me into many calamities and yourself into many troubles. For my part, I pardon you everything, and I wish to devoutly pray to God that He will pardon you also. For the rest, I commend unto you our daughter Mary, beseeching you to be a good father unto her, as I have heretofore desired. I entreat you also, on behalf of my maids, to give them marriage portions, which is not much, they being but three. For

all my other servants I solicit the wages due them, and a year more, lest they be unprovided for. Lastly, I make this vow, that mine eyes desire you above all things.

Far from grieving for his first wife, Henry celebrated Catherine's death by wearing yellow and, on hearing the news, exclaimed, 'God be praised that we are free from all suspicion of war.' When Catherine's body was examined, her organs were all found to be healthy save her heart, to which a black mass was attached. This immediately gave rise to suspicions that the queen had been poisoned, and whilst this had no basis in fact, the prime suspect was her rival, Anne Boleyn.

ANNE BOLEYN (*c.* 1501-36) was not born to be a queen. Her date of birth was not recorded, but it was most likely 1501. She was the second of the three surviving children of Sir Thomas Boleyn and his wife, Elizabeth Howard, and spent her childhood at Blickling Hall in Norfolk and Hever Castle in Kent. Anne's mother was the daughter of the second Duke of Norfolk, and Anne's father, whilst less well born, was the grandson of the Earl of Ormonde. With the exception of her first cousin, Catherine Howard, Anne was the most nobly born of Henry's English wives.

Anne's father, Thomas Boleyn was an ambitious man. He was the best French speaker at the English court and, in 1512, was sent as ambassador to Margaret of Austria, the regent of the Netherlands, in Brussels. By the time he left Brussels, Thomas had secured Margaret's promise of a place in her household for one of his daughters. Anne joined Margaret's household in 1513 and set about learning French, making an excellent impression on the regent, who wrote to Thomas saying that she found his daughter 'so pleasing in her youthful age'. When Anne arrived in Brussels, England was allied with Margaret and her father, the Emperor Maximillian. In August 1514, this alliance foundered, and Henry VIII became allied with Louis XII of France, arranging for his sister, Mary, to marry the elderly French king. Mary required Englishwomen to serve her, and Thomas Boleyn secured a place for his eldest daughter, Mary Boleyn in the French queen's household. Anne's presence was also required, and she travelled from Brussels to France to join the new queen's household. Mary Tudor's time as queen of France was brief, as her husband died on 1 January 1515, after only a few short months of marriage. Anne then transferred to the household of Claude, the new queen of France.

Anne developed a love for France, and she became French in all but birth, appearing exotic when she returned to England in 1522. It was not her choice to return, and she would probably have been happy to remain in France. However, in 1515, her great-grandfather, the Earl of Ormonde died. The earl had no sons and expressed the wish that Thomas Boleyn, his favourite grandson, should succeed him. In spite of this, the earldom was seized by his cousin, Piers Butler. Thomas appealed to the King, and the dispute dragged on for some time. In 1522, Cardinal Wolsey suggested that Piers Butler retain the title and his eldest son, James, marry Thomas's only unmarried daughter, Anne. As a result of this, Anne was recalled and took up a position in Queen Catherine's household whilst the marriage was negotiated.

Whilst the Butler marriage was a neat solution to the problem of the Ormonde inheritance, Anne was not entirely happy with the match and looked around for something better. Anne was never described as a beauty, and her sympathetic biographer, George Wyatt, admitted that 'in beauty she was to manie inferior, but for behaviour, manners, attire and tonge she excelled them all. For she had bene brought up in France'. Anne did not conform to contemporary ideals of beauty, and she had a dark complexion with black hair and eyes. Later sources, such as the hostile Nicholas Sander, have claimed that she was deformed in some way, most notably that she had an extra finger on one hand. George Wyatt, who was favourable to Anne and had access to people who knew her, stated,

There was found, indeed, upon the side of her nail upon one of her fingers, some little show of a nail, which yet was so small, by the report of those that have seen her, as the workmaster seemed to leave it as occasion of greater grace to her hand, which, with the tips of one of her other fingers, might be and was usually by her hidden without any least blemish to it.

Anne's blemish did not have an effect on her attractiveness to men, and within months of arriving at court, she had attracted the interest of Henry Percy, heir to the earldom of Northumberland. This was an excellent prospect for Anne, and according to her contemporary, Cavendish, 'there grew such a secret love between them that at length they were engaged together, intending to marry'. Anne may have been in love with Percy. The couple were a similar age, and he was the first man with whom Anne was romantically linked. It was the loss of Percy that led to Anne's enmity towards Cardinal Wolsey, as, when the Cardinal discovered the betrothal, he summoned Percy's father, who indignantly removed his son from court and married him to a more suitable bride. Anne was sent home from court in disgrace.

Anne returned to court in late 1525 or early 1526, and once again took up a position in the Queen's household. During her time at Hever, Anne may have become acquainted with a Kentish neighbour, Thomas Wyatt. They certainly enjoyed a flirtation following Anne's return to court. Anne features in a number of Wyatt's poems as 'Brunet'. It was through Wyatt that Anne came to the attention of the King, and one poem sets out the relationship between Anne and Wyatt once Henry's interest was known:

Whoso list to hunt: I know where is an hind
But as for me, alas I may no more
The vain trevail hath wearied me so sore,
I am of them that farthest come behind
Yet may I by no means be wearied mind
Draw from the deer, but as she fleeth afore
Fainting I follow. I leave off therefore,
Sithens in a net I seek to hold the wind
Who list her hunt, I put him out of doubt,
As well as I may spend his time in vain,
And graven with diamonds in letters plain
There is written her fair neck round about
Noli me tangere, for Caesar's I am,
And wild for to hold, though I seem tame.

Henry, at first, looked upon Anne only as a potential mistress, but Anne, who had witnessed her own sister being discarded after several years as Henry's mistress, refused to countenance such a suggestion.

A number of Henry's letters to Anne survive. In 1526, Henry VIII was in his mid-thirties and, whilst not the handsome youth he had been, still close to his prime. He was unused to a woman refusing him, and as the months passed and Anne continued to elude him, he became increasingly besotted. One letter from Henry to Anne early in their relationship shows something of the depth of his feelings:

For although by absence we are parted it nevertheless keeps its fervency, at least in my case and hoping the like of yours; assuring you that for myself the pang of absence is already too great, and when I think of the increase of what I must needs suffer it would be well nigh intolerable but for my firm hope in your unchangeable affection; and sometimes to put you to mind of this, and seeing that in person I cannot be with you, I send you now something most nearly pertaining thereto that is at present possible to send, that is to say, my picture set in a bracelet with the whole device which you already know; wishing myself in their place where it shall please you.

Anne continued to be unresponsive to the King's pleas to consummate their relationship, and finally, he came up with a radical solution, offering her an entirely new role in England and writing,

If it please you to give yourself body and heart to me, who have been, and will be, your very loyal servant (if your rigour does not forbid me), I promise you that not only the name will be done to you, but also to take you as my sole mistress, casting off all others than yourself out of mind and affection, and to serve you only.

The offer to make Anne his official mistress was a radical one and is a testament to Henry's devotion, but Anne still refused. Finally, desperate, Henry offered Anne the only thing that she would accept from him, and by spring 1527, the couple had decided to marry.

An early letter from Anne to Henry survives that suggests that she returned at least some of the King's feelings:

It belongs only to the august mind of a great king, to whom Nature has given a heart full of generosity towards the sex, to repay her favour so extraordinary an artless and short conversation with a girl. Inexhaustably as is the treasure of your majesty's bounties, I pray you to consider that it cannot be sufficient to your generosity; for if you recompense so slight a conversation by gifts so great, what will you be able to do for those who are ready to consecrate their entire obedience to your desires? How great soever may be the bounties I have received, the joy that I feel in being loved by a king whom I adore, and to whom I would with pleasure make a sacrifice of my heart, if fortune had rendered it worthy of being offered to him, will ever be infinitely greater.

The warrant of maid of honour to the queen induces me to think that your majesty has some regard for me, since it gives me the means of seeing you oftener.

Henry's love for Anne Boleyn was the most passionate of his life, and once the couple had decided to marry, he began his long struggle to divorce Catherine of Aragon.

The long years of the divorce were particularly trying for Anne, who received much of the blame from contemporaries. She had a fiery temper and frequently quarrelled with Henry and made verbal attacks against Catherine of Aragon. Anne's main ire was reserved for Cardinal Wolsey, who had been her enemy since the loss of Henry Percy. When he first decided to divorce Catherine, Henry trusted Wolsey to arrange matters for him, and Anne was prepared to work with the Cardinal if he could secure her desires. After the failure of the Blackfriars trial, Anne turned on the Cardinal, intent on securing his ruin. According to Cavendish, who was a member of Wolsey's household, Wolsey nicknamed Anne the 'Night Crow'. Following the Blackfriars debacle, this enmity finally came out into the open, with Anne writing to Wolsey, all pretence of friendship gone:

Though you are a man of great understanding, you cannot avoid being censured by everybody for having drawn on yourself the hatred of a king who had raised you to the highest degree to which the greatest ambition of a man seeking his fortune can aspire. I cannot comprehend, and the king still less, how your reverent lordship, having allured us by so many fine promises about divorce, can have repented of your purpose, and how you could have done what you have, in order to hinder the consummation of it. What, then, is your mode of proceeding? You quarrelled with the queen to favour me at the time when I was less advanced in the king's good graces, and after having therein given me the strongest marks of your affection, your lordship abandons my interests to embrace those of the queen. I acknowledge that I have put much confidence in your professions and promises, in which I find myself deceived. But, in future, I shall rely on nothing but the protection of Heaven and the love of my dear king, which alone will be able to set right again those plans which you have broken and spoiled, and to place me in that happy station which God wills, the king so much wishes, and which will be entirely to the advantage of the kingdom.

Anne was determined to bring Wolsey down, and she used her influence with Henry to turn his doubts about the Cardinal's loyalty into hatred. Finally, in October 1529, Henry charged the Cardinal with taking orders from the Pope and brought about his ruin. The following year, Anne secured her final revenge, arranging for Henry Percy to arrest Wolsey and bring him to London for trial. Wolsey died a broken man during the journey.

With the failure of the Blackfriars trial, Henry and Anne looked for a more radical solution, and it was Anne who first suggested the possibility of breaking with Rome. Anne was a great patron of the religious reform, and this solution appealed to her. In 1531, Henry declared himself Supreme Head of the Church of England. In August 1532, the conservative Archbishop of Canterbury finally died, allowing the appointment of Thomas Cranmer, a Boleyn family chaplain and a man who shared Anne's reformist views. By the end of 1532, when it was clear that Anne, who had already been created Lady Marquis of Pembroke, would soon be queen, she and Henry consummated their relationship. They married secretly on 25 January 1533 when Anne was already in the early stages of pregnancy, and at Easter, she was acknowledged as queen. Her coronation followed in the summer.

Anne adopted the motto 'The Most Happy' to signify her joy to the world. Both Anne and Henry were confident that their child would be Henry's longed-for son, and it was with disappointment that the couple greeted the birth of their daughter, Elizabeth, on 7 September 1533. Elizabeth was immediately declared heir to the throne, and her parents were confident that she would soon be followed by brothers. Anne was a fond mother to her daughter, and whilst Elizabeth was given her own household in her infancy, Anne visited her regularly and supervised her upbringing and welfare. She was ambitious for her daughter and, according to her chaplain, William Latymer, was anxious for Elizabeth to learn Latin, Hebrew, Greek, Italian, Spanish and French. The birth of her daughter made Anne fiercely protective, and this brought out the less attractive side of her character in her conduct towards Henry's elder daughter, Mary, with one recorded comment that she 'intended to bring down the pride of this unbridled Spanish blood'. She also claimed publicly that both Mary and her mother were 'rebels and traiteresses deserving death'. The most charitable thing that can be said of this is that Mary, as the King's elder daughter, was a threat to Anne's own child.

Anne also faced difficulties in her marriage. After only a few months of marriage, she and Henry quarrelled when he took a mistress during Anne's pregnancy. In early 1534, Anne was once again pregnant, and on discovering that Henry had taken a new lover, she railed against him. She was horrified when Henry replied that 'she had good reason to be content with what he had done for her, which he would not do now if the thing were to begin and that she should consider from what she had come'. Anne was forced to hold her tongue, and in the summer

80. Ludlow Castle. Catherine of Aragon and Prince Arthur spent their brief marriage at the castle.

81. Jousts at Westminster Abbey held to celebrate the birth of Henry VIII and Catherine of Aragon's eldest son. The King jousted as 'Sir Loyal Heart' as a compliment to his wife, but the prince died in early infancy.

Left & Below: 82. & 83. Real Alcazar in Seville. The favourite palace of Catherine of Aragon's mother, Isabella of Castile.

Above: 84. Cardinal Wolsey, drawing from *c.* 1510; he is not the obese figure of the more familiar likenesses.

Above: 85. Letter from Catherine of Aragon.

Above right: 86. Bull of Pope Clement VII against Henry VIII's divorce. Whilst the Pope was under the control of Catherine of Aragon's nephew, Emperor Charles V, it was impossible that he would even consider granting Henry VIII a divorce.

Below right: 87 Bessie Blount, one of Henry VIII's mistresses (whilst he was married to Catherine of Aragon) and the mother of Henry Fitzroy (the Duke of Richmond and Somerset, Henry VIII's bastard son). Detail from the side of her parents tomb in Kinlet church, Shropshire.

Below: 88. Catherine of Aragon's Tomb at Peterborough Cathedral. Many years after her death, Catherine was finally accorded the status of queen that was denied her during the last years of her life.

Left: 91. Anne Boleyn. Henry VIII's second wife was no beauty, but she was exotic with captivating dark eyes.

Below left: 92. Hever Castle, Kent. The childhood home of Anne Boleyn.

Below right: 93. Letter written by Anne Boleyn.

Above: 89. Catherine of Aragon. Henry VIII's first wife always ignored his infidelities, but she was unable to compete with his love for Anne Boleyn.

*Above righ*t: 90. Henry VIII by Holbein.

Right: 94. Henry VIII.

Above left: 95. Holbein Pageant for the coronation of Anne Boleyn.

Above right: 96. Mary ('Madge') Shelton, by Holbein. If the label is correct, then this is Mary Shelton, later Lady Heveningham, thought to have been one of Henry's later mistresses.

Below: 97. Thomas Wolsey depicted shortly before his fall from power.

Left: 98. Stained glass from Wolf Hall in Wiltshire showing Jane Seymour's emblem of a phoenix with a Tudor rose and the feathers of the Prince of Wales. Nothing else now survives of Jane's childhood home.

Above: 99. Anne Boleyn's execution, 19 May 1536.

Below: 100. The entwined initials of Henry VIII and Jane Seymour (H & I) at Hampton Court.

Edward Prince of Wales.

Left: 101. Jane Seymour's son, Edward VI.

Right: 102. Jane Seymour by Hans Holbein. Henry VIII's third wife. Jane was always aware of the dangerous precedent set by her predecessor and was determined not to follow her to the block.

Below: 103. Anne Zouche, one of Jane Seymour's ladies-in-waiting.

A Souch

Top left: 104. The Chapel Royal at Hampton Court. Jane's son was christened in the chapel and her body was placed there whilst a solemn vigil was kept.

Top right: 105. Windsor Castle, where Henry VIII is buried longside Jane Seymour.

Right: 106. Henry VIII.

Above: 107. The Chapel at Windsor Castle. Jane and Henry are buried together in a vault beneath the choir.

Above Left: 108. The gatehouse at Richmond Palace. Little else remains of the great Tudor palace that Anne of Cleves made her home.

Above: 109. Anne of Cleves' House in Lewes. Anne was granted the house following the annulment of her marriage, and it now houses a museum.

Left: 110. Anne of Cleves, the painting by Holbein that persuaded Henry she was a beauty.

Below: 111. Westminster Abbey where Anne of Cleves is buried.

Left: 112. Catherine Howard as the Queen of Sheba from a stained-glass window at King's College Chapel, Cambridge.

Above: 113. Traitor's Gate, through which both Anne Boleyn and Catherine Howard passed on their entry to the Tower of London.

Left: 114. Catherine Parr depicted in stained glass at Sudeley Castle.

Above: 115. Catherine Parr's badge as queen showing a maiden emerging from a Tudor rose from stained glass at Sudeley Castle.

Above: 116. The tomb of Catherine Parr at Sudeley Castle. Catherine was the last queen consort for over fifty years, and the late Tudor period was dominated by queen regnants.

Right: 117. Catherine Willoughby, Duchess of Suffolk. Court rumour suggested that Henry VIII considered making the widowed duchess his seventh wife.

Below: 118. Sudeley Castle. Catherine and Thomas saw the castle as the seat of the dynasty that they hoped to found and Catherine died there after giving birth to her only child.

Top: 119. Henry VIII's will.

Left: 120. Lady Shelton, Princess Mary's governess, appointed by Anne Boleyn.

Above: 121. Interior view of Gainsborough Old Hall. The Hall has been reconstructed to be shown as it appeared at the end of the fifteenth century, shortly before it became Catherine Parr's home.

Above left: : 139. The coat of arms of the Dudleys carved as graffiti into the wall of the Beauchamp Tower at the Tower of London. The verse carved below refers to Lady Jane Grey's husband, Guildford Dudley, and his brothers.

Above right: 141. Lady Jane Grey depicted in stained glass at Sudeley Castle. Henry VIII's great-niece was surprised to find herself proclaimed queen of England on the death of Edward VI.

140. The chapel of St Peter ad Vincula in the Tower with the scaffold site in the foreground. Three queens of England – Anne Boleyn, Catherine Howard, and Lady Jane Grey – died on Tower Green and were buried in the chapel.

Above left: 142. Mary Queen of Scots.

Above right: 143. Holbein's design for a jewelled pendant for Princess Mary, probably done during his first visit to England (1526-28), when Mary was still in favour and was perhaps even being groomed for possible succession to the throne.

Below left: 144. Mary I as princess. Mary had a happy early childhood, but her parents' divorce blighted her life.

Below right: 145. Mary I as queen. Mary's reign began to popular acclaim, but it quickly proved to be a disaster.

Above: 146. Framlingham Castle. Mary I chose Framlingham as her base from which to launch her attempt to claim the English throne.

Right: 147. The memorial to John Hooper, Bishop of Gloucester, one of the 'heretics' burned by Mary I.

Bottom left: 148. Philip II of Spain. Mary I dearly loved her husband, but he was indifferent to her, spending much of their marriage abroad.

Bottom right: 149. Manuscript owned by Mary I

Below: 150. Great Seal of Mary I.

Above: 151. Hatfield House, the childhood home of Elizabeth I.

Left: 152. Queen Elizabeth's Oak Tree at Hatfield. A modern tree now grows on the spot where Elizabeth I learned of her accession to the throne.

Below: 153. Elizabeth I's seal.

Left: 154. Elizabeth I at prayer is the frontispiece to *Christian Prayers* (1569), which reputedly was for the Queen's private use. It was printed by John Day, whose print works were at Aldersgate.

Above spread: 155. London Bridge. Unable to force London Bridge on 3 February 1554, the rebel Sir Thomas Wyatt and his Kentish followers had to go upstream to Kingston in order the cross the Thames (6 February). Note the heads of traitors displayed on poles at the gate of the city, a familiar sight in Tudor times.

Below left: 156. The figure of Elizabeth I above the entrance to the vestry porch of the church of St Dunstan-in-the-West came from Ludgate, rebuilt in 1586 and demolished in 1760.

157. View of the Tudor palace at Greenwich. Within easy reach of London and Westminster by water, it was a favourite residence of all the Tudors. Henry VIII was born here (1491), as were his daughters Mary (1516) and Elizabeth (1533). It was here, at the end of April 1536, that the infant Elizabeth saw her mother, Anne Boleyn, for the last time before she was rowed away to the Tower and her death.

158. Whitehall Palace was one of the main royal residences. The 'tiltyard' at Whitehall was the arena for a particularly splending jousting tournament held in 1581 to celebrate the anniversary of Elizabeth's accession.

Above left: 159. Great Seal of Elizabeth I. Beneath her feet is a plinth with the motto 'Pulchrum pro patria pati' ('it is sweet to suffer for one's country'), perhaps an allusion to her experiences under Mary, which were recorded as 'virtual martyrdom' in Foxe's *Book of Martyrs*.

Above right: 160. Letter written by Elizabeth I in her own hand to Emperor Ferdinand I. Note Cecil's signature in the right-hand lower corner. From the Vienna State Archives.

Below: 161. Signature of Elizabeth.

Right: 162. Robert Dudley, the Earl of Leicester. Robert Dudley was a favourite of the Queen's from the start of the reign, and was given the prestigious Court position of Master of the Horse. In the early 1560s Elizabeth was widely reckoned to be in love with him, even though he was already married. Although his wife died in 1560, the suspicion that her death was too timely to be an accident made any idea of a royal marriage impossible. As a Privy Councillor he was a close and loyal servant for many years, and he was by her side at Tilbury in 1588 as the commander of her army. He died shortly afterwards.

Above: 163. The Tower of London. Lady Jane Grey was immured here from July 1553 until her execution in February 1554.

A Gentleman Vsher of the privy Chamber.

The Lady Marchiones of Northampton Principall mourner assisted by the Lord Buckherst Lord Thresorer & the Erle of Nottingham lord Admirall

William Dethick Garter principall Kinge of Armes.

Her Trayne Assisted by two Countesses. & Sr John Stanhop vicechamberlaine

Opposite Bottom left: 164. Elizabeth I in old age.

Above 165. Helena, Marchioness of Northampton, as the chief mourner for Elizabeth I. It was the Marchioness's relationship to Catherine Parr that led to her being selected for the important office of chief mourner at the funeral of Catherine's stepdaughter, Elizabeth I, in 1603.

Below: 166. The Queen's House at Greenwich was begun for Anne of Denmark but only completed during Henrietta Maria's time as queen.

Opposite top: 167. James I, his queen, Anne of Denmark (also known as Anna, Queen of Scots), and their eldest son, Prince Henry.

Opposite bottom right: 168. Anne of Denmark from a manuscript *c.* 1623.

JACOBUS

HEN PRINC S

UXI ANNA DINMAR

The Queenne of England.

Above: 169. Charles I on campaign during the English Civil War.

Below left: 170. Letter of Henrietta Maria to Charles I.

Below right: 171. Queen Henrietta Maria.

Above: 206. Carisbrooke Castle on the Isle of Wight. Charles I was imprisoned in the castle during the Civil War.

Above right: 207. Charles I's chamber at Carisbrooke Castle. The King attempted unsuccessfully to escape from this room.

Below: 208. Charles I.

Below right: 209. Henrietta Maria by Van Dyck.

Above left: 210. Catherine of Braganza, wife of Charles II.

Above: 211. Charles II miniature by Samuel Cooper.

Left: 212. St Paul's Cathedral. Catherine of Braganza was consulted on the rebuilding of London following the Great Fire in 1666. Sir Christopher Wren's great cathedral was the most ambitious part of the design.

Opposite top row left: 213. Anne Marie Louise D'Orléans. Charles II proposed to her in 1659 but was rejected.

Opposite top row right: 214. Lucy Walters, who had a brief affair with Charles II.

Opposite centre row left: 215. Barbara Villiers, mistress of Charles II, miniature by Samuel Cooper.

Opposite centre row right: 216. Nell Gwyn, long-standing mistress of Charles II, by Peter Lely.

Opposite bottom row left: 217. Louise de Kerouaille, mistress of Charles II, by Pierre Mignard.

Opposite bottom row right: 218. Hortense Mancini, mistress of Charles II, by Pierre Mignard.

Top left: 219. Anne Hyde, first wife of King James II of England, by Peter Lely.

Top right: 220. Mary of Modena, wife of King James II of England.

Above left 221. Queen Mary II, wife of King William III of England, by Peter Lely.

Above right: 222. The entrance to the Queen's Apartments at Kensington Palace. Kensington was Mary II's favourite residence, and she died there in 1694.

Left: 223. A statue of Queen Anne outside St Paul's Cathedral. Although dominated by her female favourites, Anne was a successful monarch and held her throne in spite of the claims of her half-brother, the Old Pretender.

Below left: 224. Caroline of Brunswick and George, Prince of Wales (the future George IV). The couple loathed each other from their first meeting, and George spent their wedding night in a drunken stupor lying in the fire grate.

Above: 225. Mary II loved gardening and helped to plan the formal gardens at Hampton Court.

Below right: 226. William III and Mary II carried out major building works at Hampton Court in an attempt to rival Louis XIV's Palace of Versailles.

Above left: 227. Queen Victoria's bathing machine at Osborne House. The bathing machine would be wheeled into the sea to allow the Queen to enter the water without being observed in her bathing costume.

Above: 228. A satirical cartoon depicting the morning after the wedding of Mrs Fitzherbert and Prince George. Although denied by the prince, news of the marriage quickly spread.

Below: 229. Osborne House on the Isle of Wight. Victoria and Albert bought the house as a place of retreat and they spent as much time as possible there with their children.

Below left: 230 Victoria as queen from stained glass at Canterbury Cathedral.

Opposite page top: 231. Queen Victoria.

Opposite page bottom left: 232. Elizabeth Bowes-Lyon as Duchess of York.

Opposite page bottom right: 233 Elizabeth Bowes-Lyon with her daughter, the future Elizabeth II.

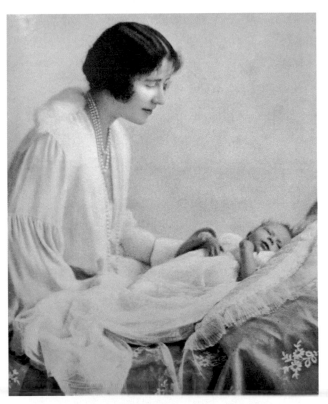

INSTRUMENT OF ABDICATION

I, Edward the Eighth, of Great
Britain, Ireland, and the British Dominions
beyond the Seas, King, Emperor of India, do
hereby declare My irrevocable determination
to renounce the Throne for Myself and for
My descendants, and My desire that effect
should be given to this Instrument of
Abdication immediately.

In token whereof I have hereunto set
My hand this tenth day of December, nineteen
hundred and thirty six, in the presence of
the witnesses whose signatures are subscribed.

SIGNED AT
FORT BELVEDERE
IN THE PRESENCE
OF

Above left: 234. Abdication letter from Edward VIII.

Above: 235. King George VI and Queen Elizabeth, to become better know in the late twentieth century as the Queen Mother. The future Elizabeth II is next to her mother.

Left: 236. The procession of Princess Diana's funeral.

of 1534, she miscarried. It took her until the end of 1535 to conceive again, but on the very day of Catherine of Aragon's funeral, in January 1536, she miscarried a son. Anne and Henry quarrelled over the cause of their loss, with Anne blaming both her fright at the news that Henry had fallen from his horse and the shock of seeing Henry with a new love, Jane Seymour. Henry stalked out of the room, muttering that 'he would have no more boys by her'.

Without a son, Anne was as vulnerable as Catherine of Aragon had been, and she had made many enemies. One of Anne's maids, Jane Seymour, had caught Henry's eye, and by spring 1536, Henry was considering marrying her. Jane was an ally of Princess Mary, who gave her support to Anne's rival. Even more dangerously, in early 1536, Anne quarrelled with the King's chief minister, Thomas Cromwell, and threatened him with death. This was enough for Cromwell to join with the other parties seeking Anne's ruin.

It would have been impossible for Anne's enemies to act without the King's consent, but he was eager to rid himself of the wife who he felt had promised so much and delivered so little. For Anne, the end came quickly. On 30 April 1536, Mark Smeaton, a young musician in Anne's household, was arrested by Cromwell and tortured. By the following morning, he had confessed to committing adultery with Anne. On 1 May, Anne and Henry attended a tournament at Greenwich. During the jousting, Henry suddenly rose to his feet and, without saying a word, rode to Westminster with only six attendants. On the journey, he repeatedly questioned Henry Norris, one of his attendants, on his relationship with Anne. According to Norris's servant, George Constantine, 'all the waye as I heard saye, had Mr Noryce in examinacyon and promised hym his pardon in case he wolde utter the trewth. But what so ever could be sayed or done, Mr Norice wold confess no thinge to the Kynge, where vpon he was committed to the towre in the mornynge'.

The following morning several members of the King's council came to arrest Anne at Greenwich, and after being interrogated for much of the day, she was taken to the Tower. Anne, who was usually so composed, was terrified and, on her arrival at the fortress, 'fell downe on her knees before the said lords, beseeching God to help her as she was not giltie of her accusement, and also desired the saide lords to beseech the kinge's grace to be good unto her, and so they left her prisoner'. Anne was accused of adultery with a number of men of the court: Mark Smeaton, Henry Norris, Francis Weston and William Brereton. She was also accused of incest with her brother. Anne, who, as queen, was very rarely alone, would never have had the privacy to commit adultery on the occasions and with the number of men with whom it was alleged. She had strong religious beliefs and, before her death, swore her innocence on the sacrament, something that is testament to her freedom from guilt. In spite of this, she, along with the accused men, was tried and condemned to die, with Anne being sentenced to be burned or beheaded at the King's pleasure.

Anne had entirely lost her composure on arriving in the Tower and appeared hysterical, at times laughing and then breaking down into tears. She had also spoken unguardedly, and it was her own words that had caused Francis Weston's arrest when she told the lieutenant of the Tower that 'she spoke to hym by cause he dyd love hyr kynswoma[n Mrs Shelton and that s]he sayd he loves not hys wyf and he made anser to hyr [again that he] loved won in hyr howse better then them bothe[; she asked him who is that? To which he answered] that it ys your selfe; and then she defied hym'. By 17 May, Anne had composed herself, and on hearing of the executions of the men with whom she was accused, she merely commented of Smeaton's death, 'Did he not exonerate me, before he died, of the public infamy he laid on me? Alas! I fear his soul will suffer for it.' Later that day, Anne heard that her marriage to the King had been annulled.

As a concession to the woman he had once loved so dearly, Henry delayed Anne's execution so that a swordsman could arrive from Calais, a more merciful death than beheading by axe. On the morning of 19 May, Anne made her way to a scaffold that had been erected on Tower Green. She turned to the crowd and made a carefully planned speech, recorded in *Hall's Chronicle*:

> Good Christen people, I am come hether to dye, for according to the lawe and by the lawe I am judged to dye, and therefore I wyll speke nothing against it. I am come hether to accuse no man, nor to speake any thing of that wherof I am accused and condemned to dye, but I pray God save the king and send him long to reigne over you, for a gentler nor a more mercyfull prince was there never: and to me he was ever a good, a gentle, and sovereigne lorde. And if any persone will medle of my cause, I require them to iudge the best. And thus I take my leve of the worlde and of you all, and I heartely desire you all to pray for me. O Lorde have mercy on me, to God I commende my soule.

Anne knelt on the scaffold and said loudly 'to Christ I commend my soul' as the headsman stepped up behind her and severed her head with a sword.

Before her death, Anne was aware that Henry had already selected his third wife and that her rival was waiting to assume her place. Anne Boleyn showed that it was possible for an Englishwoman to aspire to the throne. Unfortunately, in doing so, she laid the foundations for her own ruin by showing how to win the King and induce him towards marriage, an example that Henry's third wife, Jane Seymour, followed in her own pursuit of the King.

JANE SEYMOUR (*c.* 1508-37), the third wife of Henry VIII, is often considered to be the wife that he loved best. Whilst, during her lifetime, Jane found her position as unstable as any of Henry's later queens, she died giving the King what he most ardently desired, and posthumously, in Henry's eyes, she became his favourite wife. She was not born to be a queen and came from fairly humble origins. Jane was born around 1508 and was the eldest daughter of Sir John Seymour of Wolf Hall in Wiltshire and his wife, Margery Wentworth. Jane's father came from a family of local gentry, but her mother was more distinguished, being a descendant of Edward III. More immediately, Margery's mother, Anne Say, had been the half-sister of Elizabeth Tylney, Countess of Surrey. Elizabeth Tylney was the mother of the third Duke of Norfolk and also of Elizabeth Howard, the mother of Anne Boleyn, and of Edmund Howard, the father of Catherine Howard. Nothing is recorded of Jane's childhood, although she is likely to have been able to read and write. There is also evidence that she knew some French and that she was accomplished at needlework. At some point, she joined the household of Catherine of Aragon.

It was from her service to Catherine that Jane gained her lifelong devotion to Princess Mary. Catherine retained a royal household until after her divorce in May 1533 and it is likely that Jane remained with her until then, missing out on an appointment with Anne Boleyn, who had assembled her own royal household before April 1533. Around the middle of 1534, Jane's kinsman, Sir Francis Bryan, suggested a marriage for her with William Dormer, the only child of Sir Robert Dormer of Eythrope in Buckinghamshire. The Dormers were prominent and wealthy, and it would have been a good match for Jane. According to the *Life of Jane Dormer*, a work commissioned by William's daughter, the Dormer family were less happy, and whilst Sir Robert was prepared to negotiate with Bryan, his wife was determined that the match would not take place:

> The mother, detesting the conditions of the knight [Bryan], took her son and rode up to London to Sir William Sidney's house, having before made an overture to the Lady Sidney, who was

well pleased. There the two ladies made up the match between the son of the one and the eldest daughter of the other. Which when Sir Francis Bryan understood, seeing his pretence deluded, was ill-pleased, but the lady took the business and blame upon herself, assuring him that she had treated the matter before with Lady Sidney and could not go back.

William Dormer's hurried marriage with Mary Sidney took place on 11 January 1535. Bryan, who felt some sense of responsibility for his Seymour kin, arranged another future for Jane, securing a place for her with Anne Boleyn.

Jane did not have wealth, status or looks to recommend her to a husband, and the Imperial ambassador, Eustace Chapuys, described her as 'of middle stature and no great beauty, so fair that one would call her rather pale than otherwise'. Whilst blond hair and pale skin was the contemporary ideal of beauty, Jane's surviving portraits do not compare favourably to those of other members of Henry's court. In spite of this, she was obviously comely enough to attract the King as a potential mistress, and it is probable that both Sir Francis Bryan and Jane's eldest brother, Edward Seymour, an experienced courtier, had this in mind for her. During Anne Boleyn's time as queen, a number of women had been introduced to the King by the different factions at court in the hope that they would become his mistress. In the summer of 1534, the so-called 'Imperial Lady', whose identity is unknown, had enjoyed some success after becoming the King's mistress and obtained better treatment for the King's eldest daughter, of whose party she was a member. Anne Boleyn's party had retaliated with a mistress of their own, Margaret Shelton. Sir Francis Bryan had previously been a partisan of Anne's, but the pair had quarrelled. Jane was willing to put herself forward as Henry's mistress, and by January 1536, she and Anne Boleyn were rivals. According to the historian Thomas Fuller,

> It is currently traditional that at her first coming to court, Queen Anne Boleyn, espying a jewel pendant about her neck, snatched thereat (desirous to see, the other unwilling to show it) and casually hurt her hand with her own violence; but it grieved her heart more, when she perceived in it the king's picture by himself bestowed upon her.

The *Life of Jane Dormer* suggests that Jane gave as good as she got, and 'there was often much scratching and bye blows between the queen and her maid'. The crisis came in late January, when Anne came upon Henry with Jane sitting on his knee, a sight that she blamed for her final miscarriage. This worked to Jane's advantage, and whilst she had been happy to become the King's mistress, the relationship was in its early stages, and she was still a virgin. With Anne's miscarriage, Jane and her supporters changed their objective, and as Anne had done before her, Jane made it clear that her price was marriage or nothing.

The first indication that Henry had of Jane's change of policy was when he sent her a purse of gold with a letter, which perhaps contained an invitation for her to join him in his bed.

> [Jane,] after kissing the letter, returned it unopened to the messenger, and throwing herself on her knees before him, begged the said messenger that he would pray the king on her part to consider that she was a gentlewoman of good and honourable parents, without reproach, and that she had no greater riches in the world than her honour, which she would not injure for a thousand deaths, and that if he wished to make her some present in money she begged it might be when God enabled her to make some honourable match.

Henry was smitten and vowed not to see her unchaperoned. Shortly afterwards, Edward Seymour and his wife were moved into apartments adjoining Henry's own so that he could regularly visit Jane. Jane was coached in how to behave by her supporters, but she also greatly desired to be a queen herself and presented an appearance of quiet virtue to the King – the opposite of Anne Boleyn. By the end of April 1536, Henry and Jane had decided to marry, and she was sent away from London to ensure that she was not implicated in Anne's fall. The day after Anne's death, the couple were betrothed, marrying on 30 May 1536.

Jane had come to prominence as part of an alliance between her family and the supporters of Princess Mary, and Jane was fond of her unfortunate stepdaughter. Mary had been declared illegitimate with the divorce of her parents and banished from court. Even before her marriage, Jane had attempted to persuade Henry to recall Mary, as Eustace Chapuys records:

> [She] proposed to him to replace the Princess to her former position; and on the king telling her that she must be out of her senses to think of such a thing, and that she ought to study the welfare and exaltation of her own children, if she had any by him, instead of looking for the good of others, the said Jane Seymour replied that in soliciting the Princess's reinstatement she thought she was asking for the good, the repose, and tranquillity of himself, of the children they themselves might have, and of the kingdom in general.

Jane raised the matter again once she had become queen, claiming that she needed someone of her own status to keep her company at court. Henry was more receptive, but he was determined to humble his daughter first and insisted that the price of her reinstatement was an acknowledgement of the invalidity of her parents' marriage and her own illegitimacy. Mary at first refused, but on hearing that Henry intended to try her for treason, she finally relented, agreeing to all he asked. For Jane, who was genuinely fond of Mary, this was excellent news and Mary was soon writing to her stepmother as 'the Queen's grace my good mother'.

Jane and Mary had much in common, and in spite of the rise of the religious reform and the changes to the Church that Henry had wrought with the break with Rome, both remained staunchly attached to traditional religion. The seminal religious reformer Martin Luther referred to Jane as 'an Enemy of the Gospel', and she was known to be no friend to reform. Henry was determined that Jane should not acquire political influence as his two previous wives had done, and he did not look kindly on any intervention by her. In October 1536, a great rebellion against the religious changes broke out in Lincolnshire and soon spread to Yorkshire, where it was known as the Pilgrimage of Grace. This was the greatest threat to Henry's throne of his reign, and he was furious when Jane threw herself onto her knees before him and begged him to restore the religious houses that he had dissolved, suggesting that 'perhaps God permitted this rebellion for ruining so many churches'. Henry was furious at Jane's intervention and roared that 'he had often told her not to meddle with his affairs', before pointedly referring to the fate of Anne Boleyn. For Jane, the idea that she might go the same way as her predecessor was terrifying, and she made no further public political interventions during her time as queen.

When Jane attempted to intercede for the rebels in late 1536 she had been married to Henry for six months and still showed no signs of being pregnant. This was worrying for her, and there were rumours that her coronation was delayed until she had proved that she could bear a son. Finally, early in 1537, Jane realised that she was pregnant, to both her and Henry's joy. With her pregnancy, Henry could not do enough for his third wife, obtaining the quails that she craved to eat from France and vowing to remain close to her side so that she was not frightened by any rumours. Jane went into confinement at Hampton Court in September 1537 to await the birth of her child, and finally, after a labour that lasted three days, she bore a healthy son on 12 October. The whole country erupted in rejoicing with news of the birth, and for Henry, who had waited nearly thirty years for a male heir, Jane had fulfilled everything that was required of her. Jane was well enough to play a role in the christening of her son, who was named Edward, on 15 October, but, soon afterwards, she fell ill with a fever. Thomas Cromwell later blamed those about her for her illness, claiming that 'our Maistres through the faulte of them that were about her which suffred her to take greate cold and to eat things that her fantazie in syknes called for'. It was actually puerperal, or childbed, fever that killed her. Jane became increasingly weak, and by 24 October, she was barely conscious. She died that night, only twelve days after the birth of her son.

Jane's death was greeted with sorrow in England, and her stepdaughter, Mary, acted as chief mourner at her funeral. Henry was also devastated, as Jane had died giving him his greatest desire. For a man who liked being married, Jane's death also created a void in his life, and within weeks of her death, he had begun his search for a fourth bride.

ANNE OF CLEVES (1515-57) was not Henry VIII's first choice of bride. The death of Jane Seymour took him by surprise, and aware that England was dangerously isolated in Europe, he wanted a foreign bride. His first choice was a French alliance, but when this came to nothing, he turned to the Imperial royal family, his choice settling on Christina of Denmark, the niece of the Emperor Charles V. Christina was unenthusiastic, and by the end of 1538, negotiations had ended unsuccessfully. Dangerously, France and the Empire had by then concluded an alliance. Henry decided to approach the Protestant Schmalkaldic League of Germany, whose founder, the Elector of Saxony, had an unmarried sister-in-law: Anne of Cleves.

Anne of Cleves was the second of four children born to John, Duke of Cleves, and his wife, Maria of Juliers. She was born at Dusseldorf on 22 September 1515. Anne's lineage was noble, and she was descended from Edward III of England, as well as being closely related to Louis XII of France and to the Imperial royal family. Anne's father ruled the German dukedoms of Cleves and Mark, and her mother was the heiress of the duchies of Juliers and Berg. The marriage of Anne's parents created a strategically important territory on both sides of the Rhine, and this prestige was further increased by the acquisition of the dukedom of Ghelders by Anne's brother, William, an inheritance that was disputed by the Emperor Charles V and brought the two into conflict. Contrary to common belief, Anne's family were not Protestants, and whilst Anne's father had some interest in reform and did not recognise the authority of the Pope, Anne's mother had raised her daughters to be staunchly Catholic. Anne's eldest sister, Sibylla, was married to John Frederick, Elector of Saxony, one of the founders of the Schmalkaldic League, a Protestant defensive league in opposition to the Holy Roman Empire.

Anne's upbringing was strict, according to the report of Nicholas Wotton, an English ambassador to Cleves:

[Anne] hathe from her childehode (lyke as the ladye Sybille was, tyll she wer maryed, and the ladye Amelye hathe ben and is) ben brought up withe the ladye Duchesse her mother, and yn maner never from her ellebow, the ladye Duchesse being a wysse ladye, and one that verye streytelye lookithe to her children. All the gentylmenne of the courte, and other that I have askyd of, rapport her [Anne] to be of verye lowlye and gentyll condicions, by the whiche she hathe so muche wonne her mothers favour, that she is verye lothe to suffer her to departe from her.

She received a very limited education. She could read and write but knew no language other than German. She was skilled in needlework but knew nothing of music. In spite of this, the English ambassador in 1539 noted encouragingly that 'her witte is so goode, that no doubte she wille in a short space lerne th'Englissh tongue, when so ever she puttithe her mynde to hit'. Politically, Anne was a highly suitable bride, and the match was first suggested at the end of 1537. Negotiations began in earnest in early 1539, and the marriage treaty had been agreed by the end of September. After a long journey, Anne arrived in England at the end of December accompanied by a large retinue. By New Year's Day, she had reached Rochester, where Henry, impatient to see his new bride, decided to visit her.

Henry VIII enjoyed being married, and by the time of Anne's arrival in England, he imagined that he was already in love with her. With the exception of one report by his ambassador to Brussels at the end of 1537 in which the ambassador commented that 'there is no great praise either of her personage or beauty', Henry had received nothing but good reports on Anne. A portrait produced by Hans Holbein on Henry's instructions during the marriage negotiations looks comely enough. A description of Anne at the time of her marriage by Marillac, the French ambassador, suggests that she was no great beauty:

> The queen of England has arrived who, according to some who saw her close, is not so young as was expected, nor so beautiful as everyone affirmed. She is tall and very assured in carriage and countenance, showing that in her turn and vivacity of wit supplies the place of beauty. She brings from her brother's country 12 or 15 damsels inferior in beauty even to their mistress and dressed so heavily and unbecomingly that they would be thought ugly even if they were beautiful.

Marillac further commented that Anne 'looks about 30 years of age, tall and thin, of medium beauty and of very assured and resolute countenance'. Henry's chief minister, Thomas Cromwell, thought that she had a queenly manner. She was also considered more beautiful than Catherine Parr, Henry's sixth wife. In spite of her reputation, Anne was very far from ugly, but she was no beauty. By 1540, Henry VIII was approaching fifty and was grossly overweight with an ulcered leg, and of the pair, it was Anne who received the worst surprise in her spouse.

There is much speculation regarding the first meeting between Anne and Henry. In accordance with romantic tradition, Henry visited Anne in disguise, dressed as a messenger. He entered the chamber to find Anne standing at a window. According to the account of Henry's companion, Sir Anthony Browne, Henry kissed and embraced Anne:

> [She] regarded him little, but always looked out of the window of the bull beating, and when the king perceived she regarded his coming so little, he departed into [an]other chamber and putt of his cloke and came in againe in a cote of purple velvet; and when the lords and knightes did see his Grace they did him reverence; and then she, perceiving the lords doeing their dewties, humbled her Grace lowlie to the kinges Majestie, and his Grace saluted her againe, and so talked together lovinglie, and after tooke her by the hand and leed her into another chamber, where they solaced their graces that night and till Fridaie at afternoune; and then his Grace tooke his leave and departed thence to Gravesend, and there tooke his barge.

The meeting was a disaster, and to Henry's dismay, Anne failed to recognise him. This was not the loving meeting that he had hoped for. Henry also immediately showed a dislike of Anne's appearance, and the eighteenth-century historian Smollett claimed that Henry complained that he had been brought a 'Flanders Mare'. Henry was so dismayed that he forgot to give Anne the rich furs and sables that he had brought as a New Year's present and, in the boat back to Greenwich, complained loudly that 'I see nothing in this woman as men report of her; and I mervail that wise men would make such report as they have done'. Anne was oblivious to his reaction to her, and she continued her journey to London, being received publicly by the King at Blackheath on 3 January.

In public, Henry, terrified about offending Anne's brother, continued to show his commitment to the marriage. In private, he instructed his councillors to find some way out of the match, and in the days before the wedding, they were frantically busy. The council focused on a childhood betrothal between Anne and the son of the Duke of Lorraine, but when the ambassadors from Cleves swore that it had been broken off and Anne herself gave an oath that she was free to marry, there was nothing more that could be done. Henry went to the wedding on 5 January with bad grace, complaining to Cromwell that 'I must nedes agenst my will put my neck in the yoke'. Attempts to consummate the marriage were disastrous, with Henry finding himself impotent on the wedding night and every subsequent night that they spent together.

For Henry, the marriage was an absolute disaster, but Anne's thoughts are less clear. In June 1540, three of Anne's ladies, Ladies Rutland, Rochford and Edgecombe, reported a conversation that they had apparently had with Anne around Midsummer:

> First, al they being together, they wished her Grace with child. And she answered and said, she knew wel she was not with child. My lady Edgecombe said, how is it possible for your Grace to know that and ly every night with the king? I know it wel I am not said she. Then said my lady Edgecombe, I think your Grace is a mayd stil. With that she laughed. And than said my lady Rocheford, by our lady, Madam, I think your Grace is a mayd stil, indeed. How can I be a mayd, said she, and slepe every night with the king? There must be more than that, said my lady Rocheford, or els I had as leve the king lay further. Why, said she, when he comes to bed he kisses me, and taketh me by the hand, and byddeth me, Good night, swete hart: and in the morning kisses me, and byddeth me, Farewel, darling. Is not thys enough? Then said my lady Rutland, Madam there must be more than this, or it wil be long or we have a Duke of York, which al this realm most desireth. Nay, said the Quene, is not this enough? I am contented with this, for I know no more.

This is usually taken as evidence that Anne was unaware of the troubles in her marriage, but it must be considered suspect. As late as July 1540, Anne's chancellor, Lord Rutland, required an interpreter to speak to Anne, and it is unlikely that she had a sufficient command of English for such an intimate conversation. More likely, the conversation was fabricated at the time of Anne's divorce in order to support the King's position. The couple's marital difficulties were well known, and Cromwell, whose own fall was caused by his promotion of the marriage, begged Anne's servants to make her appear more pleasing to the King. Anne also desperately tried to speak to Cromwell, suggesting she was aware that something was very wrong.

By the end of June 1540, Henry had decided to end his marriage to Anne. He was, by that time, deeply involved in an affair with one of her ladies, Catherine Howard. The political situation in Europe made an alliance with Cleves much less favourable than it had been, and in June, Anne was sent to Richmond, ostensibly to keep her safe from the plague. In order to facilitate a divorce, Henry ordered a Church court to rule on the marriage's validity based on Anne's earlier betrothal to Francis of Lorraine, non-consummation, and Henry's own lack of consent to the match. In the early hours of 6 July, a messenger arrived at Richmond to speak to Anne. Anne sent for her brother's ambassador, Carl Harst, and around 4 a.m., she summoned her chancellor, Rutland. The King's message, which contained a request for her consent for her marriage to be tried, struck Anne speechless, and she meekly agreed to the trial. Whilst she is usually considered to have taken her divorce well, in reality, she was terrified, remembering the fates of Catherine of Aragon and Anne Boleyn.

The result of the hearing was a foregone conclusion, and on 7 July, the assembled clergymen ruled that 'the king and Anne of Cleves were nowise bound by the marriage solemnised between them'. Henry then sent commissioners to Anne in order to obtain her agreement to the annulment. The commissioners claimed that Anne took the news well, but according to the seventeenth-century historian Edward Herbert, on their arrival she fainted, perhaps fearing imminent arrest. Harst had also spoken to Anne shortly before the commissioners had arrived, and she had insisted that she would remain Henry's wife until death parted them. Harst claims Anne cried and screamed and it broke his heart to hear her. This was never communicated to the commissioners, but it accounts for Anne's later attempts to be reinstated as queen after Catherine Howard's death and to annul her divorce during the reign of Mary I.

Whilst Anne never privately accepted the divorce, she had no desire to be a second Anne Boleyn and agreed to write to the King, setting out her consent to all that happened:

It may please your majesty to know that, though this case must needs be most hard and sorrowful unto me, for the great love which I bear to your most noble person, yet, having more regard to God and his trust than to any world affection, as it beseemed me, at the beginning, to submit me to such examination and determination of the said clergy, whom I have and do accept for judges competent in that behalf. So now being ascertained how the same clergy hath therein given judgement and sentence, I knowledge myself hereby to accept and approve the same, wholly and entirely putting myself, for my state and condition, to your highness' goodness and pleasure; most humbly beseeching your Majesty that, though it be determined that the pretended matrimony between us is void and of none effect, whereby I neither can nor will repute myself your Grace's wife, considering this sentence (whereunto I stand) and your Majesty's clean and pure living with me, yet it will please you to take me for one of your most humble servants, and so to determine of me, as I may sometimes have the fruition of your most noble presence; which as I shall esteem for a great benefit, so, my lords and others of your Majesty's council, now being with me, have put me in comfort thereof; and that your highness will take me for your sister; for the which I most humbly thank you accordingly.

Anne tactfully signed her letter as 'Anne, the daughter of Cleves'. She acquitted herself cleverly in the divorce, and Henry was so relieved that he assigned her a huge divorce settlement, granting her the palaces of Richmond and Bletchingley, as well as a number of other properties and a generous annual allowance. For the remainder of Henry's life, Anne lived in comfort as a rich and independent single woman. Following the King's death, however, there was less necessity to ensure that she continued to accept the terms of her divorce, and Edward VI's council stripped Anne of many of her properties, including her two principal residences. She also found that, with high inflation, her pension was of little value, and she lived in poverty, desperate to return to Cleves. Anne's position improved somewhat in 1553 with the accession of her friend, Mary I, and she made her last public appearance at Mary's coronation, riding in the same chariot as Princess Elizabeth. She continued to live independently and was the last survivor of Henry VIII's six wives, dying on 15 July 1557.

Anne of Cleves is often called the luckiest of Henry VIII's wives. She used her intelligence to survive a very difficult situation, but her brief marriage blighted her life, and her craving to return to her homeland was never fulfilled. She was, however, certainly luckier than her successor as queen, the unfortunate Catherine Howard.

CATHERINE HOWARD (*c.* 1521/25-42) was the first cousin of Anne Boleyn, and she followed her cousin to the block. Catherine's date of birth is nowhere recorded, but she was young when she became queen, and it was probably between 1521 and 1525. She was the daughter of Lord Edmund Howard, a younger brother of the Duke of Norfolk and his wife, Joyce Culpeper. Catherine's mother died whilst she was still a young child, and her father died in 1539, having spent the previous two years absent from England as mayor of Calais. Catherine had little contact with either of her parents, and she was raised in the household of her father's stepmother, the dowager Duchess of Norfolk, at her home in Horsham.

The duchess's household was home to a number of young girls, and Catherine mixed with both gentlewomen, such as herself, and servants, sharing a dormitory room with the other unmarried women. She was taught to read and write, but received little further education. The duchess was, however, aware that Catherine, whose father was virtually penniless, needed to attract a rich husband, and she arranged for a neighbour, Henry Manox, to teach her to play the virginals. In spite of her pennilessness, Catherine was a member of one of the premier noble families in England, and Manox was far beneath her socially. He seduced the young girl, and according to his later testimony, the couple fell in love with each other, but the duchess found them alone together one day and, after beating Catherine, ordered them to separate. In spite of the duchess's prohibition, the relationship continued, and whilst it was never consummated, Catherine herself later admitted that 'at the flateryng and feire perswacions of Mannoke beyng but a yong gyrle suffred hym at soundry tymez to handle and towche the secret partz of my body whiche neyther became me with honesty to permytt nor hym to requyre'. Manox was dismissed when the duchess caught him and Catherine alone in her chapel chamber. Probably hoping to marry Catherine, he followed the household when it moved to Lambeth.

Catherine lost interest in Manox at Lambeth when she met a young kinsman of hers, Francis Dereham. Although not of equal status to Catherine, Dereham was higher born than the lowly Manox. He was also young and handsome and a particular favourite of Catherine's step-grandmother. Many of the girls in the duchess's household had lovers, and whilst the maidens' dormitory was locked at night, the key was easily stolen. The young men of the household were then free to come and go, and they entertained their lovers with picnics before sleeping with the girls. Catherine had been very young at the time of her flirtation with Manox, but when she met Dereham, she was ready for a full affair. Catherine later admitted that

> Frauncez Derame by many persuasuions procured me to his vicious purpose and obteyned first to lye upon my bedd with his doblett and hose and after within the bedd and fynally he lay with me nakyd and used me in suche sorte as a man doth his wyff many and sondry tymez but howe often I knowe not and our company ended almost a yere before the Kynges majestye was married to my lady Anne of Cleve and contynued not past oon quarter of a yere or little above.

Catherine and Dereham's relationship was consummated, and Dereham later claimed that the pair became engaged, although Catherine, aware of her higher status, denied this. The couple referred to each other as husband and wife and exchanged love tokens, with Dereham lending Catherine the substantial sum of £100.

There was little privacy in the duchess's household, and the affair was soon common knowledge. Henry Manox was jealous of the new relationship and wrote to Catherine's step-grandmother setting out the details of the affair. Rather than passing it directly to the duchess, Manox left it on her pew in the house's chapel, where Catherine found it and showed it to Dereham. The precaution of destroying the letter was perhaps not necessary, as the duchess already knew of the relationship. According to Katherine Tylney, one of the girls in the household, the duchess once 'found Dereham embracing Mrs Katherine Howard in his arms and kissing her, and thereat was much offended and gave Dereham a blow, and also beat the Queen [Catherine] and gave Joan Bowmar a blow because she was present. When Dereham was wanted the duchess would say, "I warrant you if you seek him in Katherine Howard's chamber you shall find him there"'. The duchess apparently felt that, providing Catherine's conduct did not disturb her peace, it was not her responsibility. She did, however, ask her son to speak to Catherine about what was expected of her as a Howard.

Catherine forgot all about her affair with Dereham when her uncle, the Duke of Norfolk, secured a place for her in the household of Anne of Cleves. Catherine arrived at court towards the end of 1539, and she quickly caused a stir. It is possible that Norfolk selected Catherine over her cousins and sisters for her beauty. Marillac, the French ambassador, described Catherine as 'a lady of great beauty', although he later qualified this by saying that she was more graceful than beautiful and very short. It is more likely that Norfolk intended Catherine to attract a high-profile husband rather than the King, as, in December 1539, Henry was still very much looking forward to the arrival of Anne of Cleves. With his disappointment in Anne, Henry began looking around the women of his court, and his eye was caught by Catherine. Once it became obvious to Catherine's family that Henry was interested in her, they coached her to present an air of youthful purity. Henry's infatuation with her was soon public knowledge at court. According to one report,

> This was first whispered by the courtiers, who observed the king to be much taken with another young lady of very diminutive stature, whom he now has. It is a certain fact, that about the same time many citizens of London saw the king very frequently in the day-time, and sometimes at midnight, pass over to her on the river Thames in a little boat. The Bishop of Winchester also very often provided feastings and entertainments for them in his palace; but the citizens regarded all this not as a sign of divorcing the queen, but of adultery.

Catherine was always in her element at court festivities, and she loved the attention that she received. In spite of the rumours about her relationship with Henry, it is unlikely that it was consummated, at least until he had promised to marry her, and Henry was convinced that Catherine was a virgin. The couple were married on 28 July 1540, shortly after the King's divorce.

Catherine was determined to enjoy herself as queen, and Henry showered her with presents. Over Christmas and New Year 1540/41, for example, she received many fine presents of jewellery, including a square containing twenty-seven table diamonds and twenty-six clusters of pearls and a muffler of black velvet covered in gems. That New Year, Henry and Catherine received a visit at Hampton Court from Anne of Cleves, and after some uncertainty over how Catherine should receive her predecessor, the pair got on well together. Catherine and Anne danced together, and when Henry sent Catherine a present of a ring and two small dogs, she presented them to Anne. Catherine had her own barge, which she made use of in her ceremonial entry to London in early 1541.

Henry's marriage to Catherine rejuvenated him, and he called her his 'jewel'. He could not stop time indefinitely, and in March 1541, his leg ulcer, which had troubled him since his marriage to Anne Boleyn, suddenly closed, putting him in danger of his life. Henry barred Catherine from his presence, the first sign of trouble in their marriage. In May 1541, Catherine complained to Henry that she had heard a rumour that she was to be set aside in favour of Anne of Cleves. He reassured her by saying that 'even if he had to marry again, he would never retake Mme. de Cleves', something that cannot have put her mind at rest.

Henry was over thirty years older than Catherine and a poor physical specimen. Although she was in awe of her husband, she was not in love with him and was, in fact, already in love with someone else at the time of her marriage. Catherine met Thomas Culpeper shortly after she arrived at court. He was a member of Henry's privy chamber and a man who would have been considered an entirely suitable husband for Catherine. He was young and handsome and the couple may already have been lovers before Catherine became queen. They certainly became lovers after her marriage, and Catherine's only surviving letter, written around April 1541, is a testament to her love for Culpeper:

> Master Culpeper, I heartily recommend me unto you, praying you to send me word how that you do. It was showed me that you was sick, the which thing troubled me very much till such time that I hear from you praying you to send me word how that you do, for I never longed so much for [a] thing as I do to see you and to speak with you, the which I trust shall be shortly now. The which doth comfortly me very much when I think of it, and when I think again that you shall depart from me again it makes my heart to die to think what fortune I have that I cannot be always in your company. It my trust is always in you that you will be as you have promised me, and in that hope I trust upon it still, praying that you will come when my Lady Rochford is here for then I shall be best at leisure to be at your commandment, thanking you for that you have promised me to be so good unto that poor fellow my man which is one of the griefs that I do feel to depart from him for then I do know no one that I dare trust to send to you, and therefore I pray you take him to be with you that I may sometimes hear from you one thing. I pray you to give me a horse for my man for I had much ado to get one and therefore I pray send me one by him and in so doing I am as I said afor, and thus I take my leave of you, trusting to see you shortly again and I would you was with me now that you might see what pain I take in writing to you. Yours as long as life endures, Katheryn.

Committing details of her affair to writing was not wise, and Catherine and Culpeper were incapable of allaying suspicions. Soon after her marriage, Catherine's maids noticed her giving loving glances to Culpeper out of the window. She also barred them from her chamber at certain times, admitting only her kinswoman, Lady Rochford.

Catherine relied on Lady Rochford to help her and Culpeper meet in secret throughout her marriage. In her own examination, Catherine confessed that 'my lady Rocheford wold at everey lodging serche the bak doors & tell hir of them if there were eny'. Henry and Catherine left London on 30 June 1541 for a progress to the north of England. Culpeper, as one of Henry's gentlemen, was present and the couple saw no reason to curtail their relationship. According, again, to Catherine's examination, in which she denied any impropriety, one night Culpeper met her in a chamber off the stairs at Lincoln, and on other occasions, the pair met in both Catherine and Lady Rochford's bedchambers. Whilst the couple met, Lady Rochford would sit apart with her back to them.

Catherine remained oblivious to any danger when the court returned to Windsor on 26 October 1541, and the affair continued with the pair meeting in a kitchen on one occasion. Catherine, as a Catholic, had many enemies, and soon after the court's return, Archbishop Cranmer was approached by John Lassells, an ardent religious reformer. Lassells' sister, Mary Hall, had been a member of the dowager Duchess of Norfolk's household at the same time as Catherine, and she told her brother that the Queen was 'light of living', giving him the details of Catherine's relationships with Manox and Dereham. Cranmer was shocked by this and put everything in a letter, passing it to Henry on 2 November. Henry was devastated and refused to believe it but, in order to clear Catherine's name, ordered that an investigation be carried out. Catherine knew nothing of the investigation, but under pressure, Manox confessed. On 4 November 1541, guards burst into Catherine's room as she was practising her dancing steps, telling her that 'it is no more time to dance'. Under interrogation, she confessed to her relationships with Manox and Dereham. Both the affairs ended before Catherine's marriage, and the duchess, for one, predicted that the worst that would happen would be that Catherine was divorced and sent home in disgrace. Within days, however, Culpeper's name had been mentioned, and on 11 November, Catherine was sent as a prisoner to Syon House.

The evidence of Catherine's relationship with Culpeper was much more dangerous than her earlier affairs, and adultery in a queen was high treason. Catherine always denied that she had committed adultery, and she, Culpeper and Lady Rochford all sought to blame each other in an attempt to save themselves. They were unsuccessful, and Dereham and Culpeper were executed on 10 December 1541. Catherine still hoped that she would escape with her life, but on 16 January 1542, parliament opened in London and condemned the Queen and Lady Rochford to death without trial. On 10 February, Catherine was taken by water to the Tower of London. On the evening of 12 February, she was told that she would die the next day. She had spent her time in the Tower weeping but, on hearing that she was soon to die, she composed herself and asked for the block to be brought to her so that she could practice for the morning. The next day, both Catherine and Lady Rochford were led to a scaffold on Tower Green. Catherine was so weak that she could hardly speak, and after being helped onto the scaffold, she made no speech, confessing only that she deserved to die. Still trembling with terror, she knelt and placed her head on the block before being beheaded with an axe a few minutes before her accomplice, Lady Rochford.

Catherine Howard almost certainly died before her twentieth birthday. Unlike Anne Boleyn, she was guilty of the crimes of which she was accused. She was entirely unsuited for the role of queen, and Henry VIII must bear much of the blame for Catherine's terrible end. In his sixth wife, Catherine Parr, he chose more wisely, as she was an eminently suitable queen.

CATHERINE PARR (1512-48) was the eldest surviving child of Sir Thomas Parr of Kendal and his wife, Matilda, or Maude, Green. She was born in 1512 and was named after Catherine of Aragon, who was probably her godmother. Catherine's parents enjoyed solid court careers and were in high favour with the King. The family was rocked by the sudden death of Thomas Parr on 11 November 1517, leaving Catherine's mother to raise three young children alone. Maude Parr was a remarkable woman and defied expectations that she would remarry, instead maintaining her position as a lady in waiting to the Queen. She was ambitious for her children and provided them with a good education, with a letter from Lord Dacre to his son-in-law Lord Scrope recommending that his son be raised in Maude's household, 'for I assure you he might lerne wt her as yn any place that I knowe, as well nature, as Frenche and other language, whiche me semes were a commodious thinge'.

Maude sought ambitious marriages for her children, and in 1523, she opened negotiations for Catherine to marry Henry Scrope, the son and heir of Lord Scrope. Maude, who was on friendly terms with the boy's grandfather, Lord Dacre, agreed the match with him before approaching Lord Scrope. Scrope, who apparently resented his father-in-law's interference, was not as enthusiastic about the marriage as Maude had hoped, and she wrote to Lord Dacre to complain:

Most honourable and my very good lord, I heartly rec'mend me vnto you. Where it pleased you att your last being here to take payn in the mater in consideracion of marriage between the Lord Scrop's son and my doughtor Kateryn, for the whiche I hertly thank you; at which time I thought the matter in good furtherance. Howe bee yt, I perceive that my said Lord Scrop is nott aggreable to that consideracyon, as more plainly may appere vnto you by certeyn articles sent to me from my seyd lord; the coppy of which articles I send you herein inclosyd. My lord's pleasour is to have a full answere from me before La'mas next coming, wherefore it may please you to bee so good to have this matter in your remembraunce, for I perceive well this matter is not lyke to take effecte except it be by your helpe.

Lord Dacre admired Maude and was enthusiastic about the match, persuading her to persevere. He also attempted to persuade his son-in-law:

I cannot see, w'ont that ye wold marry him to one heire of land, which wolbe right costly, that ye can mary hym to so good a stok as my lady Parr, for divers considerations, first, is remembering the wisdom of my seid lady, and the god wise stok of the Grenes whereof she is comen, and also of the wise stok of the Pars of Kendale, for al whiche men doo looke when they do mary their child, to the wisedome of the blood of that they do marry wt.

Lord Scrope still refused to countenance the match, and eventually, Maude admitted defeat. She continued to seek advantageous marriages for her children and, in 1527, secured Anne Bourchier, heiress to the Earl of Essex, for her son, William. Maude impoverished herself in purchasing William's marriage, and she was forced to lower her standards for Catherine. By 1529 at the latest, Catherine had married Edward Burgh, the son and heir of Sir Thomas Burgh of Gainsborough Hall in Lincolnshire. The marriage was brief, and there is little surviving evidence of Catherine's time in Lincolnshire. She was widowed in early 1533.

Catherine's second marriage was more lasting than her first. By the end of 1533, she had married John Neville, Lord Latimer, a widower in his forties. It was a good match for Catherine, and she became mistress of Snape Castle in Yorkshire, taking on the upbringing of her two stepchildren. Catherine's time in Yorkshire was not wholly happy, and she became personally caught up in the events of the Pilgrimage of Grace, the great northern rebellion against Henry VIII's changes to the Church. Catherine was an adherent of the reformed faith and is unlikely to have had any sympathies with the rebels. Latimer, however, was staunchly Catholic, and when a mob arrived at Snape Castle in October 1536 demanding that he become one of the rebellion's leaders, he went with them. Catherine quickly began to hear reports of her husband's conduct, and it must have been a very worrying time for her. Although Latimer joined the rebels under duress, once in command, he proved energetic, dangerously asking the Archbishop of York and clergy 'to show their learning whether subjects might lawfully move war in any case against their prince'.

Latimer's conduct sounded like treason to Henry VIII, and when the rebels dispersed, following the promise of a pardon from the King, Latimer attempted to hurry south to London to explain himself. Latimer's actions pleased no one, and the King ordered him to remain in the north until called for. More worryingly, the rebels saw Latimer's conduct as a betrayal. Latimer wrote a letter in early 1537 to the Lord Admiral of England:

I learn the Commons of Richmondshire, grieved at my coming up, have entered my house at Snape and will destroy it if I come not home shortly. If I do not please them I know not what they will do with my body and goods, wife and children. I beg to know the king's pleasure and shall follow the same whatsoever come of it, likewise as I advertised my coming up now. If it were the king's pleasure that I might live on such small lands as I have in the South, I would little care of my lands in the North.

Catherine and her stepchildren were at Snape Castle when it was attacked by the rebels, and they must have been terrified, effectively being held as hostages for Latimer's loyalty. Latimer rushed to Snape and persuaded the rebels to let his family go. He remained in disgrace with the King for some time but had returned to royal favour before his death in March 1543.

Lord Latimer left Catherine comparatively wealthy. It is unlikely that Catherine expected a lengthy widowhood, as she already had two suitors by the time of Latimer's death. In a letter written by Catherine in 1547, she wrote, 'I would not have you think that this mine honest goodwill towards you to proceed of any sudden motion of passion; for, as truly as God is God, my mind was fully bent, the other time I was at liberty, to marry you before any man I know'. The object of Catherine's affection was Thomas Seymour, the brother of Jane Seymour and a very substantial man. Seymour had spent much time on the Continent in the King's service but returned to court in January 1543. The only evidence for Catherine and Seymour's relationship in 1543 comes from their later letters, but it appears that they soon fell in love and decided to marry once Catherine was free. Thomas was only a few years older than Catherine and very handsome, and after two arranged marriages, Catherine looked forward to making her own choice.

Unfortunately for Catherine and Seymour, Catherine had another suitor in early 1543. Catherine's mother had served Catherine of Aragon, and Catherine was acquainted with Henry VIII's eldest daughter, Princess Mary, in her childhood. By 16 February 1543, Catherine had renewed her acquaintance with the princess. On that date, the King paid a tailor's bill addressed to Catherine for fabrics for Italian, French, Dutch and Venetian-style gowns, as well as pleats and sleeves, hoods and other items of clothing. The clothes were for both Catherine and Mary, and the fact that Henry settled the bill is the first indication of his interest in Catherine. Henry also became unusually attentive to his daughter at around the same time, and Chapuys noted that 'the king has shown the greatest possible affection and liberality to the Princess, and not a day passes but he goes to visit her in her chamber two or three times with the utmost cordiality'. The object of Henry's interest was not Mary, and to her horror, Catherine soon discovered that it was her. When Henry's interest became clear, Seymour took a step back from Catherine. Henry also wanted to keep the couple apart, and in May 1543, he appointed Seymour as his ambassador in Brussels.

By 1543, Henry VIII, with his disastrous marital history, was a terrifying figure, and Catherine was reluctant when she first received his proposal of marriage, replying boldly that 'it were better to be your mistress than your wife'. Henry was adamant that Catherine should become his sixth wife, and as she considered ways to avoid this fate, she had a religious experience, later writing, 'God withstood my will therein most vehemently for a time, and through his grace and goodness, made that possible which seemed to me most impossible; that was, made me renounce utterly mine own will, and to follow his will most willingly.' Catherine believed that she was called by God to become queen so that she could promote the religious reform. The couple were married on 13 July 1543.

In spite of her apprehension about her marriage, Catherine and Henry did become close, and Henry referred to Catherine as 'Kate' or 'Sweetheart'. Catherine grew fond of Henry, and in the summer of 1544, she wrote,

122. Henry VIII and Anne Boleyn at Hever Castle in the days of their courtship.

Above left: 123. Henry gave Anne Boleyn an elaborate clock during their courtship, as a symbol of his devotion. When she accepted him, she gave him a present designed to represent her troubled state of mind: a jewel fashioned in the image of a maiden in a storm-tossed ship.

Above right: 124. Title page of the first edition of the Great Bible, published in English in 1539. Anne Boleyn promoted the study of the scriptures and she owned a copy of the Bible in French. She also kept an English version on open display for her household to read. Anne had considerable influence over Henry and, some years after her death, an English Bible known as the 'Great Bible' was published with royal support.

125. The family of Thomas More. Thomas More, who was appointed as Lord Chancellor after Wolsey's fall, and his friend John Fisher, Bishop of Rochester, were the most outspoken critics of the break with Rome and Henry's divorce. When they refused to take the Oath of Succession, swearing to recognise Anne and her children as Henry's legitimate family, they were imprisoned and executed.

Above left: 126. Letter from Anne Boleyn to Cardinal Wolsey. Writing before her marriage to the King, she thanks Wolsey for his great services in her cause, and promises that if, after the attainment of her hopes, there is anything in the world she can do for him, 'you shall fynd me the gladdyst woman in the woreld to do yt'.

Above right: 127. A letter from Cranmer at Dunstable (17 May 1533), informing Henry VIII of the date when 'your graces grete matter' will be resolved, and apologising because the liturgical calendar for the week meant it could not happen earlier than Friday.

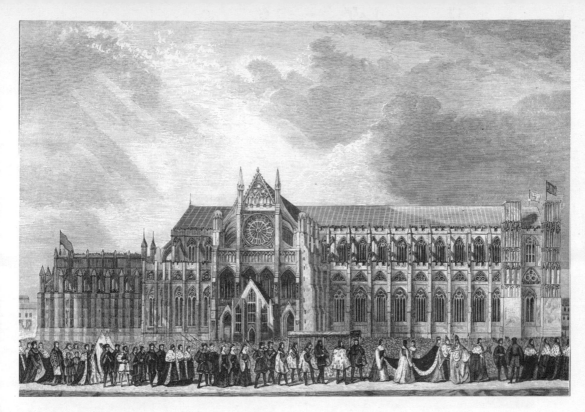

128. The coronation procession of Anne Boleyn to Westminster Abbey, 31 May 1533.

129. The Condemnation of Anne Boleyn. Anne quarrelled with the King's chief minister, Thomas Cromwell early in 1536, declaring that she would have his head. As a result, he joined with Jane Seymour and the supporters of Princess Mary in an attempt to bring about her ruin.

130. Pope Clement VII's judgement against Henry. The Pope's 'definitive sentence' issued on 23 March 1534 was in favour of Catherine of Aragon.

131. Catherine of Aragon spent the last years of her life in a number of unhealthy and isolated residences. She finally died in January 1536, still declaring her love for the King, her 'husband'.

Above left: 132. At Windsor Castle, Anne's ghost has been seen standing at this window in the Dean's Cloister.

Top right: 133. The Barn at Wolfhall. Legend claims that Henry and Jane were married in this barn before enjoying their honeymoon at the Seymour family home.

Above right: 134. Jane's signature as queen.

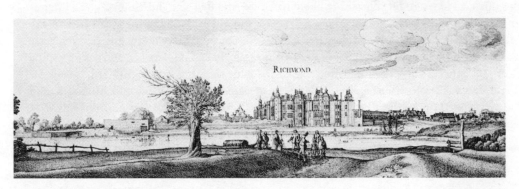

Above: 135. Catherine Parr's signature during her time as regent of England.

Right: 136. Sybille of Cleves. Anne of Cleves' older sister was a famous beauty, and it was hoped in England that Anne would resemble her.

137. Richmond Palace by Hollar *c*. 1650.

138. Oatlands Palace in Surrey, where Henry VIII and Catherine Howard were married in a private ceremony.

Although the discourse of time and account of days neither is long nor many of your Majesty's absence, yet the want of your presence, so much beloved and desired of me, maketh me, that I cannot quietly pleasure in any thing, until I hear from your Majesty. The time therefore seemeth to me very long with a great desire to know how your Highness has done, since your departing hence. Whose prosperity and health I prefer and desire more than mine own. And whereas I know your Majesty's absence is never without great respects of things most convenient and necessary, yet love and affection compelled me to desire your presence. And again, the same zeal and love forceth me also to be best content with that which is your will and pleasure, and to embrace most joyfully his will and pleasure whom I love. God, the knower of secrets, can judge these words not to be only written with ink, but most truly impressed in the heart.

Henry showed great trust in Catherine by appointing her to act as regent during his campaign in France in the summer of 1544. Catherine relished the challenge that this offered and played an active role in ensuring the security of the northern border of England, as well as arranging supplies for Henry in France.

Catherine is mainly remembered for her domestic role, and whilst the tradition that she nursed Henry in his illnesses is likely to be exaggerated, she did show a great interest in her three royal stepchildren: Mary, Elizabeth and Edward. Catherine was often in the company of Princess Mary, and they had a close relationship. Mary and Catherine regularly exchanged gifts and had a number of similar interests, including dancing and a love of fine clothes. Catherine also took an active role in the education and upbringing of her younger stepchildren, Elizabeth and Edward. Catherine became particularly close to Elizabeth, and the girl looked upon her as her mother. A letter of Elizabeth's to Catherine from July 1544 shows the princess's devotion:

Inimical fortune, envious of all good and ever resolving human affairs, has deprived me for a whole year of your most illustrious presence, and not thus content, has yet again robbed me of the same good, which thing would be intolerable to me, did I not hope to enjoy it very soon. And in my exile, I well know that the clemency of your highness has had as much care and solicitude for my health as the king's majesty himself. By which thing I am not only bound to serve you, but also to revere you with filial love, since I understand that your most illustrious highness has not forgotten me every time you have written to the king's majesty, which, indeed, it was my duty to have requested from you. For heretofore I have not dared to write to him. Wherefore I now humbly pray your most excellent highness, that, when you write to his majesty, you will condescend to recommend me to him, praying ever for his sweet benedicition, and similarly entreating our Lord God to send him best success, and the obtaining of victory over his enemies, so that you highness and I may, as soon as possible, rejoice together with him on his happy return. No less pray I God, that he would preserve your most illustrious highness, to whose grace, humbly kissing your hands, I offer and recommend myself.

Catherine was a great influence on Elizabeth, particularly concerning religion. She used her position as queen to publicise the reformed faith, and she published her own religious work, *Prayers and Meditations*, during her marriage. She also prepared a more radical work, *Lamentation of a Sinner*, although she was unable to publish this until after Henry's death. Catherine was the patron of a translation of Erasmus's *Paraphrases of the Gospel*, a work for which she obtained the Catholic Princess Mary's translation services. This was particularly impressive given the fact that the work was condemned as heretical in Mary's reign and shows Mary's love for her stepmother. Catherine was able to perform a service to both her stepdaughters by including them in the family circle, and in February 1544, the Third Act of Succession was passed, bringing both princesses back into the succession, although both still remained illegitimate.

Whilst Catherine had been fearful about marrying Henry, over time, she came to believe he was harmless and became bolder, seeking to convert him to the religious reform. Although Henry had engineered the break with Rome, he remained largely traditional in his religious beliefs and was by no means a Protestant. Catherine's religious beliefs earned her enemies at court, the most dangerous of which were Stephen Gardiner, Bishop of Winchester, and Thomas Wriothesley, Henry's Lord Chancellor. The first signs of a plot against Catherine can be seen in the arrest of Anne Askew, an evangelist with links to Catherine's ladies and to the Queen herself. By spring 1546, Catherine's enemies were ready to strike.

Henry was in increasingly ill health, and by early 1546, Catherine got into the habit of visiting him in his chamber and entering into religious debates with him. According to the sixteenth-century writer John Foxe, one day, as Catherine left the room, Henry remarked, "'a good hearing", quoth he, "it is, when women become such clerks; and a thing much to my comfort, to come in mine old days to be taught by my wife'". The Bishop of Winchester, who was present, used this opportunity to persuade Henry to order Catherine's arrest on a charge of heresy, and a warrant was drawn up. Catherine was oblivious to this and continued to debate with Henry. Shortly before the arrest was scheduled, Henry confided in his doctor, Dr Wendy, that he 'intended not any longer to be troubled with such a doctress as she was', before swearing the physician to secrecy. The arrest warrant was then found on the floor by a member of Catherine's household. Catherine was horrified when she saw the document and became hysterical, loudly bewailing her fate. Henry heard this and sent Dr Wendy to her, who, taking pity on Catherine, gave her the full details of the plot.

The next evening, Catherine went to visit Henry in his bedchamber. She found Henry talking to a group of gentlemen, and when she entered, he asked her to clear up a point of doubt he had over the correct interpretation of the scriptures. Recognising this for the trap it was, Catherine responded by saying,

'Your Majesty,' quoth she, 'doth right-well know, neither I myself am ignorant, what great imperfection and weakness by our first creation is allotted unto us women to be ordained and appointed as inferior and subject unto man as our head; from which head all our direction ought to proceed: and that as God made man to his own shape and likeness, whereby he, being endued with more special gifts of perfection, might rather be stirred to the contemplation of heavenly things, and to the earnest endeavour to obey his commandments, even so, also, made he woman of man, of whom and by whom she is to be governed, commanded, and directed; whose womanly weaknesses and natural imperfection ought to be tolerated, aided, and borne withal, so that, by his wisdom, such things as be lacking in her ought to be supplied.

'Since, therefore, God hath appointed such a natural difference between man and woman, and your majesty being so excellent in gifts and ornaments of wisdom, and I a silly poor woman, so much inferior in all respects of nature unto you, how then cometh it now to pass that your majesty, in such diffuse causes of religion, will seem to require my judgment? Which when I have uttered and said what I can, yet must I, and will I, refer my judgment in this, and in all other cases, to your majesty's wisdom, as my only anchor, supreme head and governor here in earth, next under God, to lean unto.'

Henry continued to press Catherine, but she was adamant, declaring that she had disputed with him to take his mind off his illness and learn from him. With that answer, Henry was entirely satisfied, saying, 'and is it even so, sweet heart!, and tended your arguments to no worse end? Then, perfect friends we are now again, as ever at any time heretofore', as he kissed and embraced her. The couple were walking in the gardens the following day when Wriothesley came to arrest Catherine, and Henry furiously turned on him, abusing him as a knave as the chancellor scurried away.

There are too many coincidences and strokes of good fortune for the plot against Catherine to be taken entirely at face value, and it seems likely that Henry had meant all along to bring about Catherine's submission rather than to actively rid himself of her. In spite of this, the danger was real, and Catherine was expected to change her conduct to ensure her survival. She was chastened and confined herself to a domestic sphere for the remainder of Henry's life, breathing a sigh of relief at his death on 28 January 1547.

Henry's death left her free to return to her true love, Thomas Seymour. Catherine retired with Elizabeth to her dower house at Chelsea, and she was quickly receiving secret visits from Seymour, the uncle of the new king, Edward VI. Seymour, who, in spite of his earlier love for Catherine, had already considered more advantageous marriages to either Princess Mary or Princess Elizabeth, was anxious to increase his prestige through marriage to Catherine. Catherine was deeply in love, as one letter to Seymour shows:

> I send you my most humble and hearty commendations, being desirous to know how you have done since I saw you. I pray you be not offended with me, in that I send sooner to you than I said I would, for my promise was but once in a fortnight. Howbeit the time is well abbreviated, by what means I know not, except weeks be shorter at Chelsea than in other places.

In spite of her doubts about the propriety of the marriage, Catherine could not resist Seymour, and they were married in secret by the end of May 1548.

Once the marriage had been celebrated, Catherine and Seymour were faced with the difficulty of publicising it. Seymour wrote to Princess Mary, asking for her support, and the couple were nonplussed when she wrote condemning any plan for the Queen to remarry so soon. Seymour next approached the young king, who was fond of both Seymour and Catherine, and to their relief, the boy wrote to Catherine on 25 June giving his blessing. Seymour's brother, Edward Seymour, Duke of Somerset, who was Edward's Lord Protector, took the news less favourably, but with the King's consent, there was little he could do, and Catherine and Seymour made their marriage public, setting up home with Elizabeth and Seymour's ward, Lady Jane Grey.

Whilst marriage to Seymour was Catherine's greatest desire, it did not bring her happiness. The Lord Protector's wife, Anne Stanhope, angered by the Queen's marriage to her husband's younger brother, considered that it reduced Catherine's status. When Catherine was at court, the duchess vied with her for precedence, physically pushing Catherine aside to pass through a doorway first in the place of honour. The Duke of Somerset showed his disapproval of the match by confiscating Catherine's jewels, and with these slights, Catherine spent less time at court, retreating to her household and focusing on the upbringing and education of her two royal charges, Elizabeth and Jane.

Unbeknownst to Catherine, Seymour had proposed marriage to Elizabeth early in 1547, and he and the girl had a mutual attraction to each other, carrying out a flirtation in Catherine's household, as Katherine Ashley, Elizabeth's governess, related:

> Incontinent after he was married to the Queene, he [Seymour] wold come many mornings into the said Lady Elizabeth's Chamber, before she was redy, and sometime before she did

rise. And if she were up, he would bid hir good morrow, and ax how she did, and strike hir upon the Bak or on the Buttocks famylearly, and so go forth through his lodgings; and sometimes go through to the Maydens, and play with them, and so go forth: And if she were in hyr Bed, he wold put open the Curteyns, and bid hir good morrow, and make as though he wold come at hir: And she wold go further in the Bed, so that he could not come at hir.

This was scandalous behaviour, but Catherine, when she was informed of her husband's conduct, believed it to be innocent, even participating in some of the romps herself. On one occasion, in the gardens at Hanworth, Catherine held Elizabeth whilst Seymour slashed the girl's gown into pieces.

As time went on, Catherine did begin to see that the relationship between her husband and her stepdaughter was unhealthy, and on one occasion, she rebuked Mrs Ashley after claiming to have seen Elizabeth embrace a man through the gallery window. Mrs Ashley believed that the Queen invented this in order to make her keep a better watch on her charge, but Seymour and Elizabeth still had ways to meet, and finally, when Catherine found the couple embracing, she sent Elizabeth away. Catherine must have been furious with both Seymour and Elizabeth, but she parted with her stepdaughter on good terms, as a later letter from Elizabeth suggests:

> Although I coulde not be plentiful in giuinge thankes for the manifold kindenis received at your highnes hande at my departure, yet I am some thinge to be borne withal, for truly I was replete with sorowe to departe frome your highnis, especially leving you undoubtful of helthe, and albeit I answered litel I arrayed more dipper whan you sayd you wolde warne me of all euelles that you shulde hire [hear] of me, for if your grace had not a good opinion of me you wolde not have offered frindeship to me that way, that al men iuge the contrarye, but what may I more say than thanke God for prouiding suche frendes to me, desiring God to enriche me with the long life, and the grace to be in hart no les thankeful to receyue it, than I now am glad in writing to shew it. And although I have plenty of matter, hire I will staye for I know you are not quiet to rede.

Unbeknownst to Catherine and Elizabeth, their parting in May 1548 was to be their last meeting. In spite of three childless marriages, Catherine had finally conceived, and on 30 August 1548, she gave birth to a daughter at Sudeley Castle. Catherine's health rapidly deteriorated after the birth, and in her delirium, she accused Seymour of wanting her dead, perhaps referring to his relationship with Elizabeth. She died on 5 September 1548 of puerperal fever.

After Catherine's death, Seymour, who had for months been plotting against his brother, became increasingly unstable, and after an attempt to abduct the King, he was executed for treason. Catherine's daughter, Mary Seymour, disappeared from the records in her infancy, suggesting that she did not long survive her parents.

The six wives of Henry VIII lived varied lives and had differing fortunes. The lives of all six were blighted by the terrifying King and his attempts to secure the succession of a male heir. Henry's only legitimate son, Edward VI, was not destined to become a great king, and he died aged fifteen after only six years on the throne. At the time of his death, there was only one other male descendant of Henry VII alive, Henry, Lord Darnley. All other Tudor claimants were female, and it was apparent to everyone that England would finally have its first effective queen regnant. The three Tudor reigning queens – Jane, Mary and Elizabeth – faced very different problems and constraints to their predecessors as queens of England. Their reputations are varied and rest on how successfully they negotiated the almost unprecedented position in which they found themselves.

8

Tudor Queen Regnants

Henry VIII's complicated marital career produced only one son, Edward VI. By the end of 1552, Edward was ailing. With no close male relatives, it was inevitable that England was to have its first effective queen regnant. The only question was who would it be? The struggle for the crown between Lady Jane Grey and Mary I provided the answer. It was to be Mary's successor, Elizabeth I, who showed just what a queen regnant could be, and she is remembered as one of the greatest rulers that England ever had.

LADY JANE GREY (1537-54) looked, for a few short days, as though she would be England's first effective queen regnant. She was the eldest surviving child of Henry Grey, Marquis of Dorset, and Frances Brandon and was born shortly before her second cousin, Edward VI, in 1537. Frances Brandon was the daughter of Mary Tudor, the younger sister of Henry VIII, by her second husband, Charles Brandon, Duke of Suffolk. Frances later came to bear an unnerving resemblance to her royal uncle and she raised her three daughters, Jane, Catherine and Mary, to be acutely aware of their royal status. This was confirmed in 1547 by the terms of Henry VIII's Will. Henry bequeathed the crown to his three children in turn. If they did not survive or leave heirs, he willed the crown to Frances and her heirs, overlooking the descendants of his elder sister, Margaret. Following Henry's death, Jane was fourth in line to the throne.

Jane's royal blood made her a very important figure, and soon after Henry VIII's death, the new king's uncle, Thomas Seymour, made overtures to her father for her wardship. According to Dorset's own report,

> Immediately after the king's death Hartington, the lord admiral's [Seymour's] servant, came to my house at Westminster and showed me that the admiral was highly likely to come to good authority and, as the king's uncle, he might do me much pleasure, advising me to report to him and enter more into his friendship. He advised me to allow my daughter Jane to be with the admiral, saying he would have her married to the king. Within a week I went to the admiral's house at Seymour Place where he persuaded me to send for my daughter, who remained there until the queens death.

Seymour promised the Dorsets that he would marry Jane to the King. Around the same time, Seymour married Queen Catherine Parr, and Jane was sent to be raised in her household.

Seymour had little official role in government, but as the King's uncle, he had access to him. He was obsessively jealous of his elder brother, the Duke of Somerset, who was the King's protector and tried to undermine him, attempting to 'allure the king with money and praise of his liberality, to make the king fond of him'. It appeared entirely likely to the Dorsets that Seymour would be able to do as he promised.

Jane became fond of Catherine Parr during her time in her household, and she was with her at her death in September 1548, acting as chief mourner at the funeral. Catherine's death was sudden, and Seymour was shocked, uncharacteristically offering to send Jane home to her parents and momentarily forgetting his ambitions. He soon regretted this and sent a hasty letter to Dorset to reclaim her:

> After my moste hastye commend unto your good lordship. Whereby my last letters unto the same, written in a Tyme when partelye with the Quene's Highnes Death, I was so amazed, that I had smale regard eyther for my self or to my doings; and partelye then thinking that my great house must be broken upp and dissolved my hole house I offred unto your lordship to sende my Lady Jane unto you, whensoever you wolde sende for her, as to him whome I thought wolde be most tender on hir.

Seymour requested that Jane remain with him and brought his mother up from Wiltshire to act as her chaperone.

With the Queen's death, Seymour had lost a great deal of his prestige, and the Dorsets, who were considering marrying Jane to the Protector's son, were no longer prepared to trust Seymour's promises. Dorset therefore requested Jane back:

> Nevertheless considering the state of my Doughter and hyr tender yeres, (wherin she shall hardlie rule hyr sylfe as yet without a Guide, lest she shuld for lacke of a Bridle, take to moche the Head, conceave such Opinion of hyr sylfe, that all such good behauvior as she heretofore hath learned, by the Quenes and your most holsom instructions, shuld either altogether be quenched in hyr, or at the leste moche diminished, I shall in most harties wise require your Lordeshippe to commit hir to the Governaunce of hyr Mother; by whom for the Feare and Duetie she owither hyr, she shall most easily be ruled and framd towards Vertue, which I wishe above all things to be most plentifull in hyr. And although your lordshypes good Mynd, concerning hyr honest and godlie education, ys so great, that myn can be no more, yet waying, that you be destitute of such a one as shuld correcte hyr as a Mystres, and monishe hyr as a Mother, I perswade my sylfe that you wyl think the Eye and Oversight of my Wife shalbe in thys respect most necessarie.

On receipt of this letter, Seymour rushed to see Jane's parents, and after negotiations, it was agreed that he should purchase Jane's wardship for £2,000, a substantial sum. At the same time, Seymour renewed his promise to marry Jane to the King. This promise was not in his power to grant, and when he attempted to abduct the King in January 1549, he was arrested for high treason and executed. When news of Seymour's arrest reached Jane's father, he hurried to London and took her back to the family seat at Bradgate.

The Dorsets had firm ideas about raising their daughters, and as Dorset's letter to Seymour shows, Jane was very strictly kept. In order to avoid her parents' company as much as possible, she retreated to her studies, at which she excelled. In 1550, the great scholar Roger Ascham visited Bradgate, and he was surprised to find Jane alone at her books whilst her family were out hunting. When Ascham questioned her about this, she replied,

I will tell you, quoth she, and tell you a trust, which perchance ye will meruell at. One of the greatest benefits, that euer God gave me, is, that he sent me so sharpe and seuere Parentes, and so ientle a scholemaster. For when I am in presence of either father or mother, whether I speake, hope, silence, sit, stand, or go, eate, drinke, be merie, or sad, be sowing, playing, dauncing, or doing anie thing els, I must do it, as it were, in such weight, mesure, and number, even so perfitelie, as God made the world, or else I am so sharplie taunted, so cruellie threatened, yea presentlie some tymes, with pinches, nippes, and bobbes, and other waies, which I will not name, for the honor I beare them, so without measure misordered, that I thinke my selfe in hell, till tyme cum, that I must go to Mr Elmer [Aylmer], who teacheth me so ientlie, so pleasantlie, with soch faire allurements to learning, that I thinke all the tyme nothing, whiles I am with him. And when I am called from him, I fall on weeping, because, what soever I do els, but learning, is ful of grief, trouble, feare, and whole misliking vnto me: And thus my booke hath bene so moch my pleasure, and bringeth dayly to me more pleasure and more, that in respect of it, all other pleasure in very deede, be but trifles and troubles vnto me.

Jane was unhappy at home, and she spent a great deal of time with her tutor, John Aylmer.

Jane's father, who became Duke of Suffolk in 1551, was an adherent of the religious reform, and both he and Jane corresponded with the Continental reformer Henry Bullinger. Jane, like her cousin, Edward VI, was a fanatical Protestant, and this brought her into conflict with the King's eldest half-sister, Princess Mary. Mary loved children, and she often invited Frances Brandon and her daughters to stay with her. Jane was something of a favourite of hers, and on one visit, Mary gave her a gold necklace with pearls. Jane made herself unpopular during another visit to Mary's house at Newhall in July 1552; according to *Holinshed's Chronicle*, when she was in the chapel there, one of Mary's ladies curtsied to the altar: a tradition of Mary's Catholic faith. Jane asked whether Mary was there and was informed that the curtsey was 'to him that made us all'. Jane then rudely replied, 'How can he be there that made us all, and the baker made him.' Mary was highly offended but continued to treat Jane kindly. According to Jane's tutor, John Aylmer,

A great man's daughter [Jane] receiving from Lady Mary before she was queen good apparel of tinsel, cloth of gold and velvet, laid on with parchment lace of gold, when she saw it, said, 'what shall I do with it?' 'Marry' said a gentlewoman, 'wear it'. 'Nay', quoth she, 'that were a shame, to follow my Lady Mary against God's word, and leave my Lady Elizabeth which followeth God's word'.

Unsurprisingly, as a result of these incidents, Mary 'did neuer love hir after'.

Edward VI had been raised to be a fanatical Protestant, and he was concerned about the prospect of his Catholic half-sister succeeding him. This was also a concern for John Dudley, Duke of Northumberland, who, following a coup against the Duke of Somerset, had emerged as Edward's chief councillor and, essentially, the ruler of England. At Easter 1552, Edward VI fell ill with what he himself described as 'the measles and the smallpox'. By October, he was coughing up blood, and his illness alarmed Northumberland and his supporters. Northumberland, who had played an active role in attacking Mary regarding her religion, knew that he could expect no mercy from her as queen. He therefore looked around for his own candidate as monarch, and his choice fell on Jane. In early 1553, he approached Jane's parents about the possibility of her marrying his youngest and only unmarried son, Guildford. In return, he promised that Jane would succeed to the throne. Jane's parents were thrilled, and whilst Jane attempted to refuse Guildford, her parents insisted, and the couple were married on 25 May 1553.

With his son safely married to Jane, Northumberland set about arranging for her accession. He discreetly raised the matter with Edward and was pleased to find that the King had already put his mind to the problem of Mary succeeding. Edward was entirely happy to disregard the prior claims of Mary, Elizabeth and Frances Brandon in order to secure the Protestant succession, and he drew up a document entailing the crown on Jane. Jane was staying at Chelsea when Edward died on 6 July 1553.

Northumberland kept Edward's death secret for some time whilst he worked to secure Jane's succession. Finally, on 9 July, his daughter, Lady Sidney, arrived at Chelsea and informed Jane that she had been summoned by the council. According to Jane's own account, on her arrival, she was informed of the King's death. To her horror, the assembled lords then began to do her reverence. Northumberland informed her that Edward had taken care of his kingdom and had ensured that it would be defended 'from the Popish faith and to deliver it from the rule of his evil sisters'. He continued, telling Jane that she was Queen of England. Jane was shocked and fell to the ground weeping before turning to God 'humbly praying and beseeching him, that if what was given to me was rightfully and lawfully mine, his divine majesty would grant me such grace and spirit that I might govern it to his glory and service, and to the advantage of the realm'. When Jane received no answer to her prayers, she took this as a sign of God's approval and, composing herself, accepted the crown. She travelled to the Tower of London the next day to await her coronation.

Soon after her arrival in the Tower, the Marquis of Winchester brought Jane the crown and other regalia. Holding out the crown, he asked her to place it on her head 'to try whether it really became me [Jane] well or no'. Jane, understanding the gravity of what she had done in accepting the crown, refused. Winchester reassured her 'that I [Jane] might take it without fear, and that another also should be made to crown my husband with me'. Jane thoroughly disliked her spoilt and childish husband, and Winchester's words concerned her. Later that day, when she was alone with Guildford, she summoned the Earls of Arundel and Pembroke:

> If the crown belongs to me, I should be content to make my husband a duke, but would never consent to make him king. Which resolution of mine gave his mother (this my opinion being related to her) great cause for anger and disdain, so that she, being very angry with me and greatly displeased, persuaded her son not to sleep with me any longer as he was wont to do, affirming me moreover that he did not wish in any wise to be a duke but a king. So that I was constrained to send to him the earls of Arundel and Pembroke, who had negotiated with him to come, from me, otherwise I knew that the next morning he would have gone to Sion.

Jane had no desire for her husband's presence, but it would have shamed her if he left. Guildford's reaction in rushing to his mother confirmed Jane's doubts about his suitability to be king, but it is likely that she would have been forced eventually to grant him the Crown Matrimonial.

Jane did not have time to carry out many actions as queen. Before Edward's death, Northumberland had sent messages to Princesses Mary and Elizabeth summoning them to London. Elizabeth, prudently, refused to come. Mary was equally concerned but set out warily. She reached Hunsdon in Hertfordshire on the night that Edward died and was informed secretly of the death. Alarmed, she rode to Kenninghall in Norfolk before moving on to the nearby Framlingham Castle, which could more easily be defended. Jane possessed London, and even the ambassadors of Mary's cousin, the Emperor Charles V, reported that her decision to claim the throne was hopeless. Mary would not abandon her rights, and on the evening of Jane's first night in the Tower, a letter arrived from Mary in which she expressed her amazement about not being officially informed of her brother's death and stating that the crown was hers according to 'Act of Parliament, and the Testament and last Will of our Dearest father'. Jane's council responded by setting out Jane's right to the crown and referring to Mary's illegitimacy. Whilst the reply was full of bravado, the council were worried, especially when news of Edward VI's death became known and people began flocking to Mary, who had always been highly popular in England. It became clear that it would be necessary for an army to be raised, and the council decided to send Jane's father, the Duke of Suffolk. When she heard this, Jane, who strangely believed that Northumberland was trying to poison her, absolutely refused to let her father go, and instead, it was agreed that Northumberland would lead the army. Once Northumberland left the Tower, support for Jane ebbed away, and she was forced to lock the gates to keep the council from fleeing.

According to the *Chronicle of Queen Jane and Two Years of Queen Mary*, Northumberland had difficulty in attracting troops to his cause, commenting as he passed through stony-faced crowds in Shoreditch that 'the people prece [press] to se us, but not one sayeth God spede us'. By the time Northumberland left London, Mary had been proclaimed queen in Buckinghamshire and Norfolk, and shortly afterwards, the crews of six royal ships anchored off Yarmouth mutinied in her favour. By 19 July, Mary had a substantial force assembled at Framlingham, whilst Northumberland's army had rapidly begun slipping away. Sensing defeat, Northumberland fled to Cambridge, and it was there, on the evening of 19 July, that he heard Mary had been proclaimed in London. Admitting defeat, he proclaimed her queen himself in the marketplace.

By 19 July, most of the council had managed to escape the Tower, leaving Jane with only a slender company. She had tried to carry on as normal and, that evening, was dining when her father entered the room and tore down the canopy above her head with his own hands, signifying that she was no longer queen. Jane was bewildered and asked her father if she could go home. Suffolk ignored her and went out to Tower Hill himself to proclaim Mary, before fleeing to his house at Sheen. For Jane, there could be no return home, and by nightfall, she, Guildford and the Duchess of Northumberland were all prisoners in the Tower.

Mary, who believed that her accession was a miracle from God, resolved to be merciful, and of the leading conspirators, only Northumberland was executed immediately. Jane had hopes for her life, and in the summer of 1553, she wrote a long letter to Mary setting out exactly what had happened and denying her guilt, arguing that she was 'deceived by the Duke [Northumberland] and the Council, and ill treated by my husband and his mother'. Mary believed her, and after Jane and Guildford were condemned to death on 13 November 1553, she privately informed them that they would be released once, politically, it was safe to do so. Jane's imprisonment was not onerous, and the anonymous author of the *Chronicle of Queen Jane and Two Years of Queen Mary* met her on 29 August 1553, when they were both invited to dine with the lieutenant of the Tower. The chronicler found Jane in good spirits, and she declared confidently that 'the queenes majesty is a mercyfull princes'. They spent a pleasant evening discussing religion, and Jane complained that Northumberland 'hathe brought me and our stocke in most miserable callamyty and mysery by his exceeding ambicion'.

Whilst Northumberland had brought Jane low by his ambition, it was her father who caused her death. In early 1554, a rebellion broke out against the Queen's proposed marriage to Philip of Spain, led by Sir Thomas Wyatt. Jane's father was one of the main conspirators, and there were rumours that, as he rode north to raise troops, he re-proclaimed his daughter as queen. This is unlikely, but Suffolk's actions demonstrated to Mary the dangers of keeping alive a woman who had been proclaimed queen. By his actions, Jane's father signed her death warrant, as she herself recognised in a letter that she wrote to him shortly before her death, saying, 'Father, although it hath pleased God to hasten my death by you, by whom my life should rather have been lengthened, yet can I so patiently take it, as I yield God more hearty thanks for shortening my woeful days unto my possession, with life lengthened at my own will.'

On the morning of 10 February 1554, Jane watched as Guildford was led out to his execution. She remained at the window as his lifeless body returned in a cart and she 'dyd see his ded carcase taken out of the cart, aswell as she dyd see him before an lyve going to his death, – a sight to hir no less than death'. It was then time for Jane to go to her own death, and dressed in black and accompanied by two of her women, she made her way to the scaffold. Jane's women were weeping, but she kept her composure as she addressed the crowd, saying,

> Good people, I am come hether to die, and by a lawe I am condemned to the same. The facte, in dede against the queens highnesse was unlawfull, and the consenting thereunto by me; but touching the procurement and desire therof by me or on my halfe, I doo wash my hands thereof in innocence, before God, and the face of you, good Christian people, this day.

Jane declared that she died in the reformed faith before turning to Master Feckenham, a Catholic chaplain Mary had provided in the hope that Jane would convert. The pair said a psalm together, Jane in English and Feckenham in Latin. Jane then looked at the scaffold and asked the executioner to dispatch her quickly:

> Then she kneeled down, saying, 'Will you take it of [i.e. her head] before I lay me down?' and the hangman answered her, 'No, madame' she tyed the kercher about her eyes; then feeling for the blocke, saide, 'What shall I do? Where is it?' One of the standers-by guyding her thereunto, she layde her heade down upon the block, and stretched forth her body and said: 'Lorde, into thy hands I commende my spirite!' And so she ended.

The execution of Lady Jane Grey was judicial murder, and the image of the blindfolded sixteen-year-old feeling helplessly for the block haunted Mary's reign. As one contemporary wrote, Jane 'was queen for only nine days, and those most turbulent ones'. Mary I endured a similarly turbulent reign, although hers was considerably longer.

MARY I (1516-58) was the first effective queen regnant of England. She was the only surviving child of Henry VIII and Catherine of Aragon. Mary was a pretty child, and her father loved to display her to visitors at his court. She later came to resemble her father, and in 1541, the French ambassador reported that she was 'of middle stature, and is in face like her father, especially about the mouth, but has a voice more manlike, for a woman, than he has for a man'. Henry used Mary as a diplomatic tool, and she had a number of childhood betrothals. In 1525, he arranged for her to be sent to Ludlow, something that suggested that he considered her to be Princess of Wales. Any idea that she was his heir was dropped with the divorce of her mother. In April 1533, Mary was informed that she was illegitimate, and early the following year, she was sent to serve her infant half-sister, Elizabeth. Her parents' divorce devastated Mary's life, and she endured particularly poor treatment during Henry's marriage to Anne Boleyn. She was rehabilitated in 1536 under the auspices of Jane Seymour, but only after she had been forced to confirm the invalidity of her parents' marriage, something that she always regretted as a betrayal of her beloved mother. Henry refused to legitimise Mary and, seeing her as a potential political threat, kept her unmarried and under his control. For Mary, this was devastating, as she greatly desired marriage and children.

On Edward VI's accession in January 1547, Mary became heir presumptive, and she was also a wealthy and independent landowner in her own right. No one seriously expected her to become queen because, at over twenty years older than her half brother, she was unlikely to survive him. Mary found her personal situation difficult under Edward, as, whilst she had always been an ardent Catholic, Edward's Lord Protector, the Duke of Somerset, was an adherent of the religious reform. Edward VI had been raised in accordance with the reform, and he was as fanatical a Protestant as his sister was a Catholic. Mary always made it clear that she disapproved of the changes made to religion, and as she was the heir apparent, this was a threat to Edward's council. During 1549, Mary was visited by two members of the council, who came to investigate her adherence to the new religious laws. Mary refused to recognise their authority and declared that 'she would have the old service until the king came of age'. Mary enlisted the aid of her powerful cousin, the Emperor Charles V, and he sent his ambassadors to demand an assurance that she be allowed to follow her faith. Somerset was terrified that any opposition could lead to war, and he gave Mary a verbal assurance that she could follow the Roman Catholic faith in her own household.

Mary was satisfied with her verbal assurance and made a point of opening her chapel to anyone who wished to hear Mass. Somerset, beset by his own political troubles, ignored this, but his successor as Edward's chief minister, John Dudley, Duke of Northumberland, was not so tolerant. Northumberland knew that the King was angered by Mary's defiance, and he sent commissioners to her at Kenninghall to attempt to force her to conform. Mary refused to listen, answering that she was not subject to the council and did not have to follow their religion. The pressure on her was intense, and whilst Northumberland knew that he could not risk offending Charles V by arresting Mary, he did take action against her household, imprisoning several of her servants for attending church services. By 1550, Mary was petitioning her cousin for help in escaping England, and whilst she eventually decided to stay, she remained under pressure for much of Edward's reign. It was Mary's intransigence that convinced Northumberland to seek an alternative candidate to succeed Edward VI.

Mary acted decisively when she heard that Edward had died on 6 July 1553, and she swept to power on a wave of public support, brushing Lady Jane Grey aside. She was still at Framlingham Castle when she heard of her accession on 19 July, and she saw her victory, which was won with no bloodshed, as a miracle from God. At thirty-seven, Mary suddenly found herself queen of England, and on 24 July, she set out for London to claim her throne. On her approach to the city, Mary was met by her half-sister Elizabeth, and in a jubilant mood, she welcomed her, allowing her to ride with her through the ecstatic crowds. Once she had arrived at the Tower, Mary released a number of prisoners, including Stephen Gardiner, Bishop of Winchester, and Edward Courtenay, a great-grandson of Edward IV, who had been imprisoned as a child by Henry VIII solely because of his royal blood. Mary was determined to be more merciful than either her father or her brother, and she even let it be known that she intended to pardon Lady Jane Grey.

Mary had a personal matter to settle once she became queen, and one of her first acts was to repeal her parents' divorce and declare herself legitimate. Another matter close to her heart was the restoration of traditional religion in England. Mary was particularly anxious about the fate of her brother, Edward VI, and wanted to give him a full Catholic funeral in order to save his soul. London had always been at the forefront of the religious reform and even Simon Renard, the Imperial ambassador, was horrified at the prospect of Mary so going against the wishes of the deceased king. Mary was eventually persuaded to accept a compromise, burying her brother in accordance with his Protestant faith, whilst, in private, she attended a Requiem Mass for his soul. This was one of the few compromises regarding religion that Mary could be induced to make, and she was unable to understand that Protestants could feel as strongly about their faith as she did about hers. There was an immediate backlash to the Mass held for Edward, and on the Sunday after his funeral, a Catholic priest was attacked in the pulpit at St Paul's. Before the end of July 1553, Mary had written to the Pope asking for England to return to his authority, and her changes came quickly, with Renard reporting in August that

> last Sunday a solemn predication was held at St Paul's by a doctor who has long been associated with the Bishop of Winchester. Several members of the queen's council were present, and the yeomen of the guard, for the protection of the said preacher, who discoursed pertinently on the holy sacrament. The sermon was well received, without murmurs or interruptions. Mass is sung habitually at Court; not one mass only, but six or seven every day, and the Councillor's assist. My ladies of Cleves and Elizabeth have not been present yet. On Saint Bartholemew's Day mass was sung at St Paul's; matins and vespers are already being recited there in Latin.

Mary believed that England would quickly return to the faith that she had known in her youth, and she was unprepared for the genuine popularity of Protestantism. She gradually resorted to increasingly vicious means to try to bring about her religious changes.

Mary was the first queen regnant of England to be crowned, and she was determined that the ceremony should be magnificent. On 28 September 1553, Mary, accompanied by most of the nobility, sailed to the Tower. As the procession sailed, they were met by the mayor and aldermen of London, who came out in boats decorated with streamers, and as they landed, a great peal of guns was fired from the Tower. The following day, Mary, following the custom of monarchs at their coronation, appointed fifteen new Knights of the Bath. The new knights then ceremonially served her at dinner on 30 September.

Once dinner was over, the party assembled to process through the streets of London. The *Chronicle of Queen Jane and Two Years of Queen Mary* records the event:

> [They] proceeded from the Tower through the city of London towards the palace of Westminster. The streets were well gravelled and railed on one side from Gracechurch [Street] to the little conduit in Cheapside, that the horses should not slide on the pavement. Within the rails the crafts of London stood in order to the conduit where stood the aldermen. There was presented to the queen by the chamberlain of London in the name of the mayor, aldermen and whole city 1,000 marks in gold, for which her highness gave thanks. On either side the windows and walls were garnished in tapestry, arras, cloth of gold and tissue, with cushions of the same, garnished with streamers and banners. In many places ordained goodly pageants and devices, and therein great melody and eloquent speeches of noble histories treating of the joyful coming of so noble and famous a queen.

Mary sat in a rich chariot drawn by six horses. She loved fine clothes, and for her coronation, she ensured that she looked splendid, wearing a dress of blue velvet trimmed with ermine. On her head, she wore a veil of tinsel decorated with pearls and stones and a gold circlet that was so heavy she was forced to hold her head up with her hands. It was the greatest ceremonial occasion of Mary's reign, and the following day, she was crowned queen in Westminster Abbey. For Mary, it was the moment of her greatest triumph, but she was also aware that the coronation of a single woman was an oddity and that she was expected to marry and provide England with a king.

Marriage was something that Mary desired above all else, but at thirty-seven, she was entirely inexperienced in the ways of the world. She had always relied on her cousin, Charles V, for advice, and soon after her accession, she informed Simon Renard, the Imperial ambassador, that she would be guided by Charles in the choice of a husband. As soon as she became queen, Mary was bombarded with suitors, but the only husband she wanted was Philip of Spain, Charles's son. Philip, who was a twenty-six-year-old widower, was the greatest prince in Europe, and as a member of Mary's beloved mother's family, seemed the perfect candidate. When Mary finally received his proposal, she attempted to be coy, protesting that she was too old for Philip. In reality, she already believed herself to be in love with him and accepted him gladly.

Whilst Mary was deliriously happy in the choice of Philip, there was a distinct lack of enthusiasm both amongst her council and in England. Much of her council had favoured the English Edward Courtenay, with her chancellor, Stephen Gardiner, Bishop of Winchester, telling Renard bluntly that 'it would be difficult to induce the people to consent to a foreigner'. This was indeed the view of many in England, and by the end of the year, a group of disaffected noblemen had come together to form a conspiracy with the aim of putting Elizabeth on the throne. On 25 January 1554, Wyatt rode into the marketplace at Maidstone and issued a proclamation:

Forasmuch as it is now spread abroad, and certainly pronounced by [Stephen Gardiner, Bishop of Winchester] the lord chancellor and others of the [Privy] Council, of the queen's determinate pleasure to marry with a stranger, &c. We therefore write unto you, because you be our friends, and because you be Englishmen, that you will join with us, as we will with you unto death, in this behalf; protesting unto you before God, that no earthly cause could move us unto this enterprise but this alone: wherein we seek no harm to the queen, but better counsel and councillors; which also we would have foreborne in all other matters, saving only in this. For herein hath the health and wealth of us all.

For trial hereof and manifest proof of this intended purpose, to now, even at hand, Spaniards be now already arrived at Dover, at one passage, to the number of a hundred, passing upward to London in companies of ten, four, and six, with harness harquebusses and moriass with match light[ed]; the foremost company whereof be already at Rochester.

We shall require you therefore to repair to such places as the bearers hereof shall pronounce unto you, there to assemble and determine what may be best for the advancement of liberty and common wealth in this behalf, and to bring with you such aid as you may.

Wyatt, who presented himself as a loyal subject of the Queen merely concerned by the influx of foreigners, was well received and built up a substantial following.

Mary was furious when she heard the news of Wyatt's rebellion and sent out an army to engage the rebels. Her troops met with little success, and Wyatt pressed on towards Dartford. Mary sent a deputation, but Wyatt refused to negotiate unless he was first given custody of both Mary and the Tower. This was obviously not something the Queen could agree to, and she abandoned attempts to negotiate, instead turning her attention towards defending London.

As the rebels approached London, Mary decided to take decisive action, and on 31 January, she went on foot to the Guildhall in the city in order to rally the populace. Here she made the speech of her life, and she declared that her marriage to Philip was only arranged with the consent and approval of her council before adding that it would only be her second marriage:

I am already married to the Common Weal and the faithful members of the same; the spousal ring whereof I have on my finger: which never hitherto was, nor hereafter shall be, left off. Protesting unto you nothing to be more acceptable to my heart, nor more answerable to my will, than your advancement in wealth and welfare, with the furtherance of God's glory.

The Londoners decided to support their queen, and when Wyatt reached Southwark, on 3 February, he found London Bridge defended against him. He spent the next two days trying to cross before marching his troops to Kingston and crossing the Thames there.

When Mary heard that Wyatt had entered London, she panicked and was unable to sleep that night, fearing the worst. By the morning, she had composed herself and sent out her infantry to meet the rebels. Wyatt's force was broken by the royal army, but he was able to push on towards Fleet Street. According to the *History of Wyat's Rebellion*, Mary was urged to flee, but she stood firm. She asked where the Earl of Pembroke was, and on being told that he was in the field, "'well then", quod her Grace, "fall to prayer and I warrant you, we shall hear better news anon. For my lord will not deceive me, I know well. If he would, God will not: in whom my chief trust is, who will not deceive me"'. Soon after, Mary received word that Wyatt had been captured and taken to the Tower. Mary was triumphant, and in order to safeguard her position, she ordered the executions of Lady Jane Grey and her husband, Guildford Dudley. Wyatt was tried for treason on 15 March 1554 and implicated Elizabeth, leading to her also being imprisoned in the Tower. Mary was unable to prove that her sister was involved in the rebellion, but she never trusted her again and was fond of stating that Elizabeth bore a distinct resemblance to Mark Smeaton, the lowliest of Anne Boleyn's supposed lovers. The thought that Elizabeth might succeed her filled Mary with dread, and she was anxious to marry and bear a child.

Philip finally landed at Southampton on 19 July 1554, and he met with Mary at Winchester where the couple spent over an hour talking to each other. Philip cannot have been pleased with his bride, and one of his attendants complained that Mary looked older than they had expected and dressed badly. Although young, Philip was a sober and dutiful man, and he hid any disappointment, marrying Mary in Winchester Cathedral on 25 July 1554. One touching detail of the ceremony suggests that it was the happiest day of Mary's life, and according to a report of the marriage written by one John Elder, 'the queens marriage ring was a plain hoope of gold without any stone in it: for that was as it is said her pleasure, because maydens were so married in olde tymes'. At Mary's request, Philip was also declared king of England, although it was stressed by the English council that this was only for the duration of Mary's life.

Mary confidently believed that God would give her an heir, and she was therefore unsurprised in September 1554 to discover that she was expecting a child. She showed all the signs of pregnancy, and at Easter 1555, she went into confinement at Hampton Court to await the birth. The child was expected in May, and according to John Foxe, in early June,

The time was thought to be nigh that this young master should come into the world, and that midwives, rockers and nurses with the cradle and all were prepared and in readiness, suddenly, upon what cause or occasion it is uncertain, a certain vain rumour was blown in London of the prosperous deliverance of the queen and the birth of her child; insomuch that the bells were rung, bonfires and procession made, not only in the City of London and in most other parts of the realm, but also in the town of Antwerp guns were shot off upon the river by the English ships, and the marines thereof rewarded with a hundred pistolets or Italian crowns, by the lady regent who was the Queen of Hungary. Such great rejoicing and triumph was for the queen's delivery and that there was a prince born; yea, divers preachers, namely one the parson of St Anne within Aldergate, after procession and Te Deum sung, took it upon him to describe the proportion of the child, how fair, how beautiful, and great a prince it was, as the like had not been seen.

Embarrassingly, Mary and her council were forced to publish that no child had, in fact, been born. Mary continued to wait at Hampton Court, and when she showed no signs of going into labour, her doctors recalculated, giving dates of June and then July. As time went on, people became increasingly sceptical, and there were rumours that Mary's agents had attempted to buy a child to pass off as the Queen's. By late May, Mary's stomach began to decrease in size, and eventually it was only Mary herself who continued to look for the birth of a child. Even she was forced to accept the truth in early August, and the court abruptly left Hampton Court: a public recognition that there would be no child. Mary, desperate for a baby, had suffered a phantom pregnancy, and she was devastated. Her distress was compounded on 29 August when Philip sailed for Flanders, and whilst Mary wrote to him every day, it became increasingly clear that he had deserted her.

Mary had always believed that God would provide her with a healthy son, and she saw the failure of her 'pregnancy' as evidence that she had incurred His displeasure in her failure to punish the Protestants in England. She had already begun to burn Protestants in early 1555, but the number dramatically increased following Philip's departure. Mary genuinely believed that she was saving her victims' souls, but it was a cruel policy and earned her the nickname 'Bloody Mary'. As well as ordinary people, she burned a number of high-profile figures, and the execution of Thomas Cranmer, Archbishop of Canterbury, may have given her particular satisfaction given that he was the man who had officiated over her parents' divorce. Mary was not the only Tudor monarch to burn heretics, but she was remembered as the cruellest, with the (highly biased) Protestant author John Foxe recording that 'before her was never read in history of any king or queen of England since the beginning of the kingdom, under whom, in time of peace, by hanging, heading, burning and prisoning, so many Englishmen's lives, were spilled within this realm, as Queen Mary, for the space of four years'.

Philip and Mary became king and queen of Spain in early 1556, and whilst Mary was never to leave England, it gave her some personal satisfaction to be queen of her beloved mother's homeland. The accession led to a reunion between the couple, as, when Philip requested that Mary support him in his war against France, she refused unless he made the request in person. Philip landed at Dover on 18 March 1557. Mary was overjoyed to see her husband, and she was devastated when, after a visit of less than four months, he sailed away, never to return. The loss of Philip broke Mary's heart, but she agreed to his demands that England declare war on France. On 7 January 1558, Calais, the final continental English possession, fell to the French. This was the moment when the great Angevin Empire was finally lost, and in England, it had a great psychological impact. Mary understood this and is reported to have said 'when I am dead and opened, you shall find Calais lying in my heart'.

Mary believed that she was pregnant following Philip's visit, and whilst no one else believed her, she made a Will in March 1558 in which she bequeathed the crown to her child. Once again, there was no child, and in late May, nearly ten months after Philip's departure, she finally admitted that she would bear no child. In November, Philip's ambassador, the Count of Feria, visited Mary and found her to be dying. According to Feria, Mary, still deeply in love with her husband 'was happy to see me, since I brought her news of your majesty, and to receive the letter, although she was unable to read it'. Touchingly, Feria discovered that Mary had kept every letter that Philip had sent her. On 13 November 1558, Mary was given the last rites. She rallied the next day, but it was obvious that her end was near, and as her council and other members of the court flocked towards Hatfield where Elizabeth was staying, Mary quietly passed away on 17 November 1558. Due to her deep unpopularity, in celebration of her death bonfires were lit and church bells rung in London.

With the exception of the early years of her childhood and the first few months of her marriage, Mary I led a bitter and unhappy life. Whilst she was intelligent, she was not suited to the role of queen regnant, and she sought to provide England with a king so that she could retreat to a more traditional role. Mary's half-sister and successor, Elizabeth I, whilst also blighted by an unhappy youth, was a very different proposition, and she is remembered not just as one of England's greatest queens but, arguably, the greatest monarch the country has ever had.

ELIZABETH I (1533-1603) was the daughter of Henry VIII and Anne Boleyn and was born on 7 September 1533. In her infancy, she was heiress of England. This changed with the execution of Anne Boleyn in 1536, and Elizabeth, like her older half-sister before her, was declared illegitimate and barred from succeeding to the throne. The loss of her mother also had more immediate consequences for Elizabeth, as Henry ignored her. As a growing child, Elizabeth soon had nothing to wear, and her governess, Lady Bryan, wrote to Thomas Cromwell, Henry's chief minister, begging for clothes. A major change for Elizabeth came with Henry's sixth marriage to Catherine Parr, as the new queen became a mother to her, supervising her education and exposing her to her Protestant religious beliefs. Elizabeth continued to live with Catherine after Henry's death on 28 January 1547, although she was sent away before Catherine's own death in 1548 following the discovery of her flirtation with Thomas Seymour. By that time, Elizabeth was old enough to live independently, and her father had left her well provided for. She was officially second in line to the throne, with an income of £3,000 a year and a dowry of £10,000.

Elizabeth was interrogated by the council of her half-brother, Edward VI, following Thomas Seymour's arrest in January over reports that she and Seymour had intended to marry. She answered so cleverly that nothing could be proved against her, but her reputation was tarnished, and she spent the remaining years of her brother's reign living quietly. She played no role in Lady Jane Grey's brief reign, riding to congratulate Mary I in London once she had safely attained the throne. Mary was determined to see her sister convert to Catholicism, and Elizabeth, who favoured Protestantism, finally agreed to attend Mass. She attended Mass for the first time on 8 September 1553 but complained loudly throughout the service that her stomach hurt, disrupting the service and angering the Queen. It was a relief to both women when Elizabeth finally left court in December 1553.

Elizabeth incurred Mary's anger with the outbreak of Wyatt's rebellion early in 1554. The extent of Elizabeth's involvement is not clear, but she almost certainly knew of plans for the uprising, perhaps intending to await the outcome of events. Following the defeat of the rebellion, she was brought to London on Mary's orders. Her situation became even more dangerous on 15 March 1554 when, at his trial, Sir Thomas Wyatt claimed that he had sent Elizabeth a letter and that she had thanked him for his warning. On 17 March, Elizabeth was informed that a barge was waiting to take her to the Tower. Terrified, she was determined to delay her departure, begging leave to write to the Queen. Elizabeth wrote,

If any ever did try this old saying, that a king's word was more than another man's oath, I beseech your majesty to verify it in me, and to remember your last promise and my last demand that I be not condemned without answer and proof; which it seems now I am, for without cause proved I am by your council from you commanded to go to the Tower. I know I deserve it not, yet it appears proved. I protest before God I never practised, counselled or consented to anything prejudicial to you or dangerous to the state. Let me answer before you, before I go to the Tower (if possible) – if not, before I am further condemned. Pardon my boldness. I have heard of many cast away for want of coming to their prince. I heard Somerset say that if his brother [Thomas Seymour] had been allowed to speak with him, he would never have suffered, but he was persuaded he could not live safely if the admiral lived. I pray evil persuades not one sister against the other. Wyatt might write me a letter, but I never received any from him. As for the copy of my letter to the French king, God confound me if I ever sent him word, token or letter by any means. I crave but one word of answer.

Elizabeth's letter did not change the Queen's decision, and she was taken by water to the Tower early the next morning. According to the *Chronicle of Queen Jane and Two Years of Queen Mary*, when she entered, Elizabeth declared, 'Oh Lorde! I never thought to have come in here as prisoner; and I praie you all goode frendes and fellows, bere me wytnes, that I come yn no traytor, but as true a woman to the queens majesty as eny is nowe lyving, and therone will I take my deathe.' She went a little further into the Tower, and, on seeing the guards, asked the Lord Chamberlain if they were for her. When he denied it, she said, 'I know yt is so; yt neded not for me, being, alas! but a weak woman.' Even in times of great stress, Elizabeth knew how to win the hearts of those around her. When she had entered the Tower, the Earl of Sussex, who was present, warned the gaolers not to treat her too harshly.

Elizabeth was not severely treated in the Tower, although she must have been terrified. She was interrogated, but did not incriminate herself, and Wyatt, who was executed on 11 April, denied on the scaffold that Elizabeth was involved in the plot. Eventually, Mary and her council were forced to admit that there was little evidence against Elizabeth, and in May 1554, she was moved from the Tower to Woodstock. Elizabeth spent a dull and uncomfortable year imprisoned there, but with her release from the Tower, she knew the danger had passed. On 17 April 1555, she received a summons to London to attend Mary in her confinement. Elizabeth arrived at court on 30 April, but Mary would not see her for several weeks. Mary's failure to produce a child that summer made Elizabeth's accession a virtual certainty, and she returned to her estates, spending her time consolidating support.

Mary fell ill in August 1558. In early November 1558, she was visited by her husband's ambassador, the Count of Feria, who found her dying. Feria summoned the council and told them that Philip favoured Elizabeth's succession to the throne. He found the councillors terrified of what Elizabeth would do to them, and he resolved to visit her himself to assure her of Philip's support. Elizabeth received Feria, but he did not find her as malleable as he had hoped, as he comments:

She is a very vain and clever woman. She must have been thoroughly schooled in the manner in which her father conducted his affairs, and I am very much afraid that she will not be well-disposed in matters of religion, for I see her inclined to govern through men who are believed to be heretics and I am told that all the women around her definitely are.

Elizabeth was indignant at her treatment by Mary and in no mood to give any credit to Philip for helping her win the throne, declaring that 'it was the people who put her in her present position and she will not acknowledge that your majesty or the nobility of this realm had any part in it'. Feria noted that Elizabeth was determined to be ruled by no one, least of all Philip. Feria's dispatch is the first indication of how Elizabeth intended to rule, and it is a model that she followed throughout her reign.

On the morning of 17 November 1558, Sir Nicholas Throckmorton set out from London for Hatfield bearing Mary's betrothal ring as proof that the Queen had died. He was overtaken on the road by the councillors, the Earls of Arundel and Pembroke, and it was they who came upon Elizabeth sitting in the garden at Hatfield under an oak tree, reading the New Testament in Greek. The two men approached her and informed her that she was now queen. Elizabeth was overcome with emotion and unable to speak for a few moments before praising God.

Elizabeth appointed her council whilst at Hatfield. A few days later, she set off for London, attended by her council, and was met by crowds. Catholics considered Elizabeth to be illegitimate, and following her accession, her Catholic cousin, Mary, Queen of Scots, was proclaimed queen of England in France. This was a source of anxiety for Elizabeth, and she set about arranging her coronation. According to the historian William Camden, Elizabeth was crowned in Westminster Abbey on 15 January 1559 by the Bishop of Carlisle, the only Bishop who would crown her:

> For the Archbishop of York and the rest of the Bishops refused to perform the Office, out of a suspicious and jealous fear of the Romish Religion, which both her first breeding up in the Protestant religion had stricken them into, and also for that she had very lately forbidden the Bishop in saying Mass to lift up the Host to be adored, and permitted the litany, with Epistle and Gospel, to be read in the vulgar tongue; which they held for most heinous sins.

Ignoring this slight, Elizabeth was triumphant and showed her delight to the crowds that lined the route of her coronation procession, laughing and speaking with those who wished her well.

On her accession, England was a Catholic country, something that was unacceptable to the Protestant Elizabeth. She was no religious fanatic and attempted to create a church incorporating aspects of both Catholicism and Protestantism with the monarch as its head. On 29 April 1559, Elizabeth's first parliament passed the Act of Supremacy, making her Supreme Governor of the Church of England. Whilst most people in England approved of Elizabeth's religious policy, it was widely criticised on the Continent.

Religion was not the only item of business at Elizabeth's first parliament. At the time of her accession, she was twenty-five years old and unmarried. In February 1559, parliament presented a formal petition, asking that she marry to settle the succession in England. Elizabeth responded with a long speech claiming that she had no inclination to marry and that she wished to remain a virgin. She ended this speech saying, 'Lastly, this may be sufficient, both for my memory and honour of my name, if when I have expired my last breath, this may be inscribed upon my tomb: Here lies interred Elizabeth, A virgin pure until her death.' This speech caused little stir for the simple reason that no one believed her. It was unthinkable for a queen to rule alone without a husband to guide her.

It was not the first time that Elizabeth had sworn never to marry, as, early in 1558, she had turned down an offer of marriage from the Prince of Sweden, claiming that she wished to remain a virgin. Although Elizabeth flirted with the idea of marriage, she never wavered in her refusal to marry, and it is likely that there were a number of reasons for this. In the sixteenth century, wives were subject to their husbands, a rule that applied even when one spouse was a reigning queen. This was perhaps not the only reason behind Elizabeth's aversion to marriage. There were no examples of happy marriages in her immediate family. Her mother, Anne Boleyn, had been put to death by her husband. She also remembered the fate of her stepmother Catherine Howard, and it was later claimed that she first vowed never to marry around the time of Catherine's execution. Thomas Seymour was executed, in part, for plotting to marry her, a further example of the dangers of matrimony.

Elizabeth was prepared to entertain proposals from foreign suitors when politically necessary. In January 1559, Philip of Spain, in spite of serious misgivings about Elizabeth, felt that it was his duty to maintain the Catholic religion in England and instructed his ambassador to propose marriage to her. Elizabeth kept negotiations open until 14 March 1559, by which time, England had concluded a peace with France and Philip's friendship was no longer so crucial.

Soon after she rejected Philip, Elizabeth received a proposal from his cousin, the Archduke Ferdinand. This match soon foundered, and Ferdinand's younger brother, the Archduke Charles, proposed marriage himself. Charles was a persistent suitor, and Elizabeth managed to drag negotiations out for over seven years until Charles, too, lost patience with her. Elizabeth always insisted that her suitors visit England, saying that she could not marry a man she had never seen. That this was a delaying tactic is clear from her alarm when she heard, in October 1559, that John of Finland had arrived in England to woo her. Elizabeth was relieved when marriage negotiations failed, although she professed herself insulted when the Archduke Charles married elsewhere after waiting for her for the best part of a decade. Elizabeth was courted by foreign princes until well into her fifties.

It was not only foreign princes who sought Elizabeth's hand in marriage. She received proposals from several English candidates. During the early years of her reign, the Earl of Arundel attempted to marry Elizabeth, showering her with gifts. Elizabeth never considered the elderly earl to be a serious suitor, nor the wealthy Sir William Pickering, who also sought her hand. She concentrated her affection on another Englishman, Robert Dudley.

Robert Dudley was almost exactly the same age as Elizabeth, and she had known him since childhood. As the son of the Duke of Northumberland, Dudley was a prisoner in the Tower whilst Elizabeth was there, and this forged a common bond between the two. On her accession, Elizabeth appointed Dudley as both her master of horse and a Knight of the Garter. This preference for Dudley mystified Elizabeth's contemporaries, and Camden sums up the general confusion, stating that people asked 'whether this [favour] proceeded from any vertue of his, wherof he gave some shadowed tokens, or from their common conditions of imprisonment under Queen Mary, or from his Nativity, and the hidden consent of the stars at the hour of their birth, and thereby a most strait conjunction of their minds, a man cannot easily say'. Dudley was tall and handsome, and Elizabeth was very attracted to him.

Dudley had been married for several years at the time of Elizabeth's accession. By early 1559, there were rumours that he and Elizabeth were lovers and that they were waiting for Dudley's wife to die in order to marry. Elizabeth was angry about the rumours, but her conduct only served to fuel them. Soon, foreign ambassadors courted Dudley openly as the future king, and he asked for the assistance of the Spanish in persuading Elizabeth to marry him. For Elizabeth, part of Dudley's attraction may have been that he was married and so could not expect to marry her.

Dudley's wife, Amy, was not encouraged to come to court by the Queen and stayed with friends near Abingdon. On the morning of 8 September 1560, Amy, who was in ill health, insisted that all her servants visit a fair, leaving only her and two other women in the house. When everyone returned that evening, they found Amy Dudley dead at the foot of a shallow flight of steps with a broken neck.

When news of Amy Dudley's death was brought to Elizabeth, she was so shocked that she was almost speechless. She immediately ordered Dudley to leave court whilst the death was investigated. Elizabeth knew that unless she fully investigated the circumstances of the death, both she and Dudley would be tainted with suspicion of murder. The enquiry returned a verdict of accidental death, holding that Amy had fallen down the stairs, but most people believed that Dudley arranged her murder. Amy Dudley's death has never been satisfactorily explained, but the evidence of her ladies and her own conduct point towards suicide. It has also recently been suggested that she may have suffered a spontaneous fracture due to breast cancer. Whatever the cause, the suspicion under which Dudley was held meant it was impossible for Elizabeth to ever contemplate marrying him, even if she wished to.

Dudley was not Elizabeth's only favourite and she attracted male attention throughout her life. She was never a beauty, but she knew how to make the best of herself and was considered to be pretty in the early years of her reign, as Hayward's description of her appearance at her accession shows:

> Shee was a lady, upon whom nature had bestowed, and well placed, many of her fairest favores; of stature meane, slender, straight, and amiably composed; of such state in her carriage, as ever motione of her seemed to beare majesty: her heire was inclined to pale yellow, her foreheade large and faire, a seemeing sete for princely grace; her eyes lively and sweete, but short-sighted, her nose somewhat rising in the middest; the whole compasse of her countenance somewhat long, but yet of admirable beauty.

Elizabeth was aware of her fading appearance as she grew older and took to wearing wigs and thick layers of make-up. Her clothes also became more elaborate, and she owned around 3,000 gowns. She attracted suitors into her old age, enjoying the fiction that they were in love with her. In 1581, the tall and handsome Walter Raleigh came to court and remained a favourite of Elizabeth's for several years. He was supplanted by the Earl of Essex, Robert Dudley's stepson, who was Elizabeth's last great favourite.

With her failure to marry, the English succession was uncertain throughout Elizabeth's reign. This was dangerously demonstrated in October 1562 when, one evening, Elizabeth felt unwell and decided to have a bath. It was soon clear that the Queen was suffering from smallpox, and after falling unconscious, she was thought to be dying. The council held an urgent meeting to decide the succession but were unable to agree, some choosing Catherine Grey and others the Plantagenet-descended Earl of Huntingdon. In the midst of these crisis talks, Elizabeth regained consciousness, and her council hurried to her. Although still dangerously ill, Elizabeth begged the council to make Robert Dudley Protector of England. She swore to the council that, although she loved Dudley, nothing improper had ever happened between them. Everyone was relieved when Elizabeth recovered.

The uncertainty over the succession had been further complicated by the return of Mary, Queen of Scots, to Scotland in 1560. Mary took Henry, Lord Darnley, as her second husband, a man who was both an English subject and the grandson of Elizabeth's aunt, Margaret Tudor. The marriage was a disaster, with events coming to a head on 9 March 1566 when Darnley accused Mary of having an affair with her secretary, David Rizzio. Darnley and his accomplices then stabbed Rizzio to death in Mary's presence. Mary did not take any action at first and, on 19 June 1566, bore a son whom she named James. Elizabeth reacted to James's birth with despair, falling to her knees and bewailing her childlessness. She also watched events in Scotland with growing unease. Darnley had made many enemies, including his wife. A few months after the birth of her son, Mary, and the rest of Edinburgh, were awoken by a large explosion. Upon investigation, the house in which Darnley was staying was discovered to have been blown up with gunpowder. Darnley was found in the orchard next to the house, strangled rather than killed by the explosion.

A few days after the murder, Elizabeth wrote to Mary expressing her condolences. Remembering the Amy Dudley affair, she also advised Mary on how best to protect her reputation, telling her that she must be seen to avenge the murder:

My ears have been so deafened and my understanding so grieved and my heart so affrighted to hear the dreadful news of the abominable murder of your mad husband and my killed cousin that I scarcely yet have the wits to write about it. And inasmuch as my nature compels me to take his death in the extreme, he being so close in blood, so it is that I will boldly tell you what I think of it. I cannot dissemble that I am more sorrowful for you than for him. O madame, I would not do the office of faithful cousin or affectionate friend if I studied rather to please your ears than employed myself in preserving your honour. However, I will not at all dissemble what most people are talking about: which is that you will look through your fingers at the revenging of this deed, and that you do not take measures that touch those who have done as you wished, as if the thing had been entrusted in a way that the murderers felt assurance in doing it. Among the thoughts in my heart I beseech you to want no such thought to stick at this point.

Mary failed to heed Elizabeth's warning, and on 15 May 1567, she married the Earl of Bothwell, the man commonly held to be responsible for Darnley's death.

Soon after her marriage, Mary was captured by rebel Scottish lords and imprisoned. Elizabeth was furious about this treatment of a fellow queen and sent ambassadors to try to secure Mary's release. The Scottish lords were determined to remove Mary, and she was forced to abdicate in favour of her infant son, who was crowned as James VI of Scotland. Elizabeth refused to recognise the new king and raged at the Scottish lords, but she was not prepared to reinstate Mary by force. She was nonplussed when Mary, who had escaped from her imprisonment, arrived in England on 17 May 1568. Elizabeth promised her protection, but she refused to meet her whilst she was suspected of Darnley's murder. Mary was placed under house arrest whilst Elizabeth decided what to do with her.

The presence of Mary, Queen of Scots, proved to be a major headache for Elizabeth. Mary was the leading Catholic claimant to the English throne. She was also a romantic figure and attracted interest amongst the nobility, most notably from Elizabeth's kinsman, the Duke of Norfolk. In late 1569, a rumour reached court that Norfolk wished to marry Mary in order to become king and return the English Church to Catholicism. Elizabeth summoned Norfolk, hoping to encourage him to confess, but he denied everything. In late 1571, Norfolk became involved in a plot to depose Elizabeth and replace her with Mary. Whilst Elizabeth was prepared to sentence Norfolk to death, she could not bring herself to sign the death warrant. She was always squeamish about ordering the deaths of her kin, and she spent several weeks wracked with uncertainty. According to a letter from John Lee to Lord Burghley, 'they say on 26 February last, was a warrant directed to the lieutenant for the execution of Norfolk on the following morning, but the queen, after she had signed the warrant, was so greatly disquieted in mind and conscience that she could not rest until she had sent to the lieutenant to return it'. Finally, Elizabeth was prevailed upon to sign, and Norfolk was executed on 2 June 1572. This decision caused Elizabeth a great deal of emotional turmoil and many people shared the view of the Earl of Sussex that she needed a husband to keep her safe.

As time went by, Elizabeth came under increasing pressure to marry and settle the succession. In 1571, she received an offer of marriage from the Duke of Anjou, the brother of the King of France. Anjou was over twenty years younger than Elizabeth and a fervent Catholic, but Elizabeth, needing a French alliance, informed her council in March that she intended to marry him. Neither Anjou nor Elizabeth were enthusiastic, and Elizabeth

Above left: 172. Lady Jane Grey (1537-54), eldest granddaughter of Henry VIII's younger sister Mary.

Above right: 173. Edward's 'Device' for the succession, naming Jane Grey as his heir. The document is in the King's hand throughout, except for the amendments, which make all the difference to its meaning.

Below: 174. Warrant of Queen Jane for the issue of letters patent appointing Edward Benarde to be sheriff of Wiltshire, 14 July 1553. This has the signature 'Jane the Quene' and is one of the very few documents signed by Jane during her nominal reign of nine days. The name 'Edwarde Benarde', the sheriff-designate, is also in her hand.

Above: 175. Lady Jane Grey refusing to accept the Crown.

Left: 176. The execution of Lady Jane Grey.

Opposite top left: 177. A page from Edward VI's Journal, for 18 March 1551, in which he refers to Mary and his dispute with her over the Mass.

Opposite top right: 178. John Fisher, Bishop of Rochester, by Hans Holbein. A fierce defender of Catherine of Aragon's marriage and of Mary I's legitimacy, he was executed by the King for treason in 1535.

Opposite centre: 179. Mary's instructions to John Russell, Earl of Bedford, sent to Spain in June 1555 to escort Prince Philip to England for his wedding. He is to brief Philip about the affairs of the kingdom.

Opposite bottom: 180. Passport for Richard Shelley to go into Spain, signed by both Philip and Mary. Shelley's mission was to have been to announce the safe arrival of Queen Mary's son, so the passport remained unused.

5. The L[ord] Mary ? Sister came to me to westminster whare after salutacions she was called to my counsel into a chambre, where was declared how long i had suffered her masse again... in hope of her reconciliation, and how now being no hope, wich i perceived by her letters except i sar some short amendement, i could not beare it she answered that her soul was god and her faith she wold not chaung, nor desemble hir opinion i conterary doings so was sayd her to her faith, but willed her not to ... as a subiect to obey... And that her exaumple might breed to much inconuenient.

9. The emprours embassadour came with short message frome his master of warre, if i wold not suffre his cosin the princesse to use her masse. To this was no answer given at this tyme, but the...

20. The b[ishop] of Canterbury, London, and Rochester did conclude to gyue licence to synne was synne to suffre and winke at it for a time, might be borne, so at last possible might bee used

---

Instructions for my ... prevised

Furste to tell the kyng the whole state of this Realme, and all thyngs appartayning to the same as muche as ye knowe to be trewe

Seconde to obey hys comandment in all thyngs

Thyrdly in all thyngs he shall aske your advise to declare your opinion as becometh a faythfull conceyllour to do
Marye the quene

Marye the quene

Whereas ... at this ... our trustie and right ... forward bedford ... into our good brother the king of ... to our dearest ... the prince of portingall ... in Spayn ...
... happy ... we that it hath pleased god to ... of a princ... we wyll commaund you not only to suffre hym quietly to passe by you in his ... ... money ... & all other his hors... baggage & ... ... you from let or molest... but also ... ... all ... nedefull by ... way ... for his ... money & by waye of a convenient ... for his transportation, wherof ... faile you not as you tender our pleasur & will answer for the contrary at your uttermost perill, and thes our l[ett]res shalbe your sufficient warrant in this behalf. Yoven under our Signet at our Manor of hamptoncourt the ... of ... the first and seconde yere of our reigne

To all mayors, shiryffs, baliffs, constables, custom-... comptrollers & officers & to all other our officers ministers & subiects to whom in this case shall apperteyne

181. The burning of John Hooper at Gloucester on 9 February 1555. Hooper, who was former bishop of Gloucester, was burned on a slow fire. He was one of the first victims to suffer.

182. The burning of Ridley and Latimer at Oxford on 16 October 1555. The sermon was preached by Richard Smith, who had been driven from his Regius Chair in Edward's time for his Catholic beliefs.

183. The burning of Thomas Tompkyns hand by Bishop Bonner. This example of Bonner's alleged cruelty was a part of Foxe's campaign against the Bishop. Whether the incident actually occurred is uncertain.

Above left: 184. Title-page of a volume of prayers or meditations written by Queen Catherine Parr, translated into French by Princess Elizabeth, and written with her own hand.

Above right: 185. George Gascoigne depicted presenting a book to Queen Elizabeth. She is seated in her Chamber of Presence on a throne beneath a 'cloth of estate', a formal sign of her royal status.

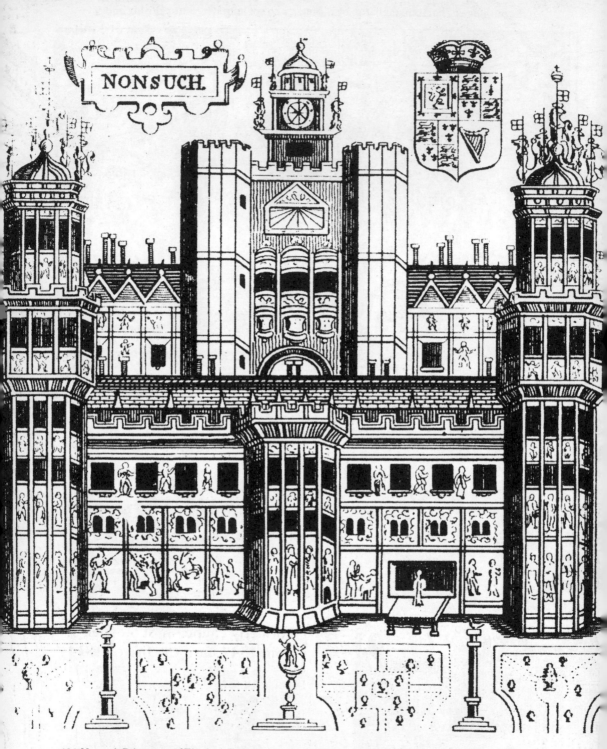

NONSUCH.

186. Nonsuch Palace, one of Elizabeth I's favourite residences. From an old English engraving in the late Emperor of Austria's private library.

Opposite: 187. Plan of the palaces of Westminster and Whitehall, from a later version of the 1578 map known as Ralph Agas's map (but not in fact by him). The Thames was in effect the main highway connecting London, Westminster, Lambeth, Southwark and Greenwich.

Great Hall,
by Wolsey, 1528

The pond

The Longe Gallery

F

The Court

Tennis court
G

Preaching
place

The Court

'Holbein' gate

H

Privy bridge

Court

F F

King St Gate

Kinges street

Channon row

C

B

Weomynster Hall (the seat of the law courts)

Starre Chamber

A

Abby

E

House of Commons
(formerly chapel of St Stephen's)
from 1547 until the fire of 1834

E

House of Lords

Court of Requests

The Queenes bridge

Henry VII's chapel

E

188. The Entrance of Queen Elizabeth. Queen Elizabeth's accession (or 'entrance') came to be celebrated as a religious festival. This allegorical representation of the accession, from a later work commemorating God's mercies to Protestant England, depicts the new queen bringing justice and piety (represented by the sword and the Bible) to her realm.

Above left: 189. Elizabeth's falcon downs a heron. Illustration from George Turberville, *The Book of Faulconrie or Hauking* (1575), p .81. Although the book does not explicitly state that the princely lady in the illustratrations is meant to be Queen Elizabeth, the Tudor roses on the liveried servants in the scenes makes her identity obvious.

Above right: 190. Francis, Duke of Alençon and later (once his elder brother Henri became Henri III of France in 1576) Duke of Anjou, came closer than anyone else to securing Elizabeth's hand in marriage.

191. 'A Hieroglyphic of Britain', which John Dee himself designed as the frontispiece to his *General and Rare Memorials Pertayning to the Perfect Arte of Navigation* (1577). John Dee (1527–1608), alchemist, geographer, mathematician and astrologer to the queen, wrote the *Arte of Navigation* as a manifesto for Elizabethan naval imperialism. He explains in the text (p. 53) that the frontispiece shows the British Republic (or commonwealth) 'on her Knees, very Humbly and ernestly Soliciting the most Excellent Royall Maiesty, of our Elizabeth, (Sitting at the helm of this Imperiall Monarchy; or rather, at the helm of this Imperiall Ship, of the most parte of Christendome...)', and that above is a 'Good Angell', sent by God to guard the English people 'with Shield and Sword'. Elizabeth steers her vessel towards the Tower of Safety, atop which stands Victory, ready with a wreath to crown her.

Babington with his Complices in S.t Giles fields.

192. In 1586, the Derbyshire gentleman Anthony Babington was the central figure in a plot to liberate Mary Queen of Scots and assassinate Elizabeth. The confidence in success which led him to commission a group portrait of the conspirators was misplaced. Sir Francis Walsingham's spies had penetrated the conspiracy and all the correspondence between the plotters and the captive queen passed across his desk. In due course Babington and the rest were rounded up. They were executed on 20 September 1586. The real significance of this plot was that it enabled the Privy Council to overcome Elizabeth's reluctance to sanction a definitive solution to the problem posed by Mary.

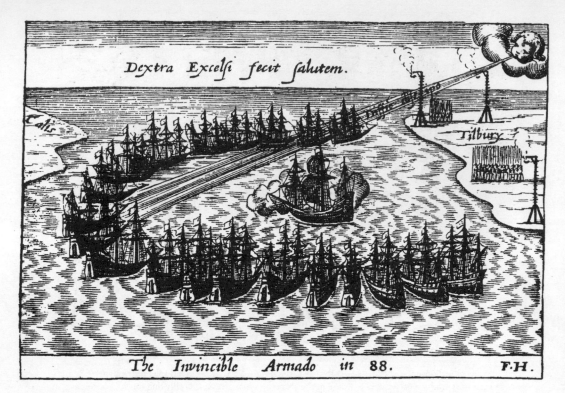

Dextra Excelsi fecit salutem.

Calis

Tilbury

The Invincible Armado in 88.   F·H·

193. The Spanish Armada off the French coast. From George Carleton's *Thankfull Remembrance* (1627). By the 1620s, when this pamphlet was published, the 'Protestant wind' here shown blowing along the Channel was already a fixture in the national mythology.

Yea, because of the house of the Lord our

God, I will seeke to do Thee good, Pf.122. 9.

Blessed is that Preacher bee,
That will pray and speake for mee.

194. Preaching at Paul's Cross, London. Londoners flocked to hear sermons at the open-air pulpit in the cathedral churchyard. On Sunday 24 November 1588, a stately procession escorted Elizabeth to the cathedral for an official service of thanksgiving for victory over the Armada, which included a sermon preached from this pulpit by John Piers, Bishop of Salisbury.

195. When Elizabeth visited the Earl of Hertford at Elvetham in 1591, he arranged splendid outdoor entertainments around a small ornamental lake in the shape of a half-moon, specially dug for the occasion. The entertainments, including pageants, songs, verses, fireworks and banquets, filled all three days of her visit. In this picture of the scene, Elizabeth is shown seated beside the left horn of the moon on a throne beneath a cloth of estate.

196. The 'Procession Picture', from Elizabeth's last years, is an idealised representation of one of her formal public appearances. Gentlemen Pensioners (her bodyguard) armed with halberds line the route, while other young gentlemen carry the Queen shoulder high on a litter beneath an exotic canopy. Before her walk senior courtiers, Knights of the Garter, while behind her follow ladies-in-waiting and maids of honour.

Next page: 197. Engraved portrait of Elizabeth I by William Rogers *c*. 1595.

employed her usual delaying tactics, insisting that the prince visit her before she would commit herself. Anjou disparagingly called Elizabeth an old woman with a sore leg, and by September 1571, negotiations had ground to a halt. The French queen mother, Catherine de Medici, then offered her youngest son, Francis, Duke of Alençon. Elizabeth allowed her ambassadors to open negotiations and, as usual, insisted on meeting him.

Alençon proved a more ardent suitor than Elizabeth's earlier admirers, and on 5 August 1579, he arrived in England. His arrival was a shock to Elizabeth, and although she insisted on meeting her suitors, she had never imagined that a foreign prince would actually arrive. Elizabeth was charmed by her guest, and the couple spent two weeks together, giving every indication that they intended to marry. Elizabeth may, at least in part, have attempted to make Robert Dudley jealous, as Alençon's representative had earlier informed her that Dudley had secretly married, something she saw as a betrayal. That Elizabeth did have genuine feelings for Alençon, however, is clear from the poem 'On Monsieur's Departure', which she composed when he returned to France:

> I grieve and dare not show my discontent;
> I love, and yet am forced to seem to hate;
> I do, yet dare not say I ever meant;
> I seem stark mute, but inwardly do prate
> I am, and not, I freeze and yet am scorned,
> Since from myself another self I turned.
>
> My care is like my shadow in the sun –
> Follows me flying, flies when I pursue it,
> Stands, and lies by me, doth what I have done;
> His too familiar care doth make me rue it.
> No means I find to rid him from my breast,
> Till by the end of things it be suppressed.
>
> Some gentler passion slide into my mind,
> For I am soft, and made of melting snow;
> Or be more cruel, Love, and so be kind.
> Let me float or sink, be high or low;
> Or let me live with some more sweet content,
> Or die, and so forget what love e'er meant.

Elizabeth and Alençon corresponded passionately, and the attraction between them was genuine. In one letter, Elizabeth wrote, 'For my part, I confess that there is no prince in the world to whom I would more willingly yield to be his, than to yourself.' Alençon's courtship of Elizabeth was the most intense that she experienced, and he was the man she came closest to marrying.

Alençon returned to England in late 1581. He continued to press Elizabeth for marriage and, finally, whilst they were walking together, 'discourse carried her so far, that she drew off a ring from her finger, and put it upon the Duke of Anjou's [Alençon's], upon certain conditions betwixt the two the standers-by took it, that the marriage was now contracted by promise'. Elizabeth agreed to marry Alençon, but she still had doubts, and that night,

The Queen's gentlewomen, with whom she used to be familiar, lamented and bewailed, and did so terrify and vex her mind, that she spent the night in doubts and cares without sleep amongst those weeping and wailing females. The next day she sent for the Duke of Anjou [Alençon], and they two, all by-standers being removed, had a long discourse together. He at length withdrew himself to his chamber, and throwing the ring from him, a while after took it again, taxing the lightness of women, and the inconsistency of islanders.

Alençon's pursuit of Elizabeth was her last courtship, and when he died only three years after leaving England, she was bereft.

Following Alençon's departure, it was clear that Elizabeth would never bear children to secure the succession. This left the Catholic Mary, Queen of Scots, as her most likely successor, a fact that worried Elizabeth's council. Mary had remained Elizabeth's prisoner since her arrival in England in 1568, with Elizabeth always refusing to meet with her. In May 1586, a young Catholic nobleman called Anthony Babington was contacted by John Ballad, a Catholic priest, who had obtained Spanish support for a plot to murder Elizabeth. Babbington became involved in the conspiracy and wrote to Mary, asking for her support. Mary wrote agreeing to Elizabeth's murder, unaware that the correspondence was monitored. Faced with the proof of Mary's involvement, Elizabeth ordered that she be tried for treason, and Mary was, accordingly, sentenced to death. This sentence sent Elizabeth into turmoil, and she pleaded with her council to find a way by which she might spare her cousin and fellow queen. She was angered when everyone insisted that the Scottish queen must die.

Elizabeth prevaricated for several months before finally signing the death warrant and handing it to her secretary, William Davison. Elizabeth's council acted quickly, fearing that she would recall the warrant on further thought. Elizabeth did indeed send for it to be returned to her the following morning. She was disconcerted to hear that it had already been dispatched to Fotheringay, where Mary was imprisoned. Mary was beheaded on the morning of 8 February 1587. Camden records the Queen's reaction:

> As soon as the report was brought to Queen Elizabeth's ears, who little thought of such a thing, that the queen of Scots was put to death, she heard it with great indignation, her countenance altered, her speech faultered her, and through excessive sorrow she stood in a manner astonished; insomuch as she gave herself over to passionate grief, putting herself in mourning habit and shedding abundance of tears.

Elizabeth wrote to James VI of Scotland, denying her guilt in the death of his mother. She always maintained that she had signed the warrant only for use in an emergency and that Davison had deliberately disobeyed her orders. In the days following Mary's execution, Elizabeth raged about Davison, threatening to have him hanged. She was restrained by her council but did order that he be fined and imprisoned. The truth of Elizabeth's feelings on the death of Mary, Queen of Scots, cannot be known. The fact remains, however, that she did sign the warrant and that Davison provided a useful scapegoat in mitigating Elizabeth's guilt.

Philip of Spain was not convinced by Elizabeth's protestations of innocence on the death of Mary, Queen of Scots. He had grown increasingly angry at Elizabeth's promotion of Protestantism and had begun building an invasion fleet even before Mary's execution. Elizabeth anxiously monitored progress in Spain and began preparing for war, placing the English fleet under the control of Lord Howard of Effingham and Francis Drake. On 29 May 1588, 130 ships holding 20,000 troops set sail to invade England. The Spanish Armada made slow progress, but on 19 June, it was sighted off Cornwall, and warning beacons were lit along the coast of England. Howard and Drake had assembled a large fleet, and they engaged the Spanish in the Channel. These encounters made little impact on the Armada, and it anchored off Calais whilst it waited for further troops from the Netherlands. The English fleet seized their chance by sending in fire ships during the night. This caused panic, and the Spanish ships cut their anchors and sailed out to sea to escape the flames. On 29 July, they were attacked by the English again, and the weakened Armada was scattered, the remnant of the fleet being chased as far north as the Firth of Forth.

This proved to be the final defeat of the Armada, but news of the scale of the English victory did not reach Elizabeth for some time. The Armada was merely the fleet that conveyed Spanish troops to England, and Elizabeth expected a land-based invasion. She was determined to play a part in the defence of her kingdom, and on 9 August 1588, she reviewed her troops at Tilbury, making one of the most famous speeches of her reign. Elizabeth's speech was stirring, and she declared, 'I know I have the body but of a weak and feeble woman, but I have the heart and stomach of a king and of a king of England too – and take foul scorn that Parma [the Armada's commander] or any other prince of Europe should dare to invade the borders of my realm.' Elizabeth was overjoyed to hear the news of the Armada's defeat, and she ordered public thanksgiving across England and went in procession through London in a chariot. For Elizabeth, the celebrations ended with the death of Robert Dudley on 4 September 1588.

Elizabeth grieved deeply for Dudley, who had been the love of her life, and, on hearing the news, shut herself in her chamber, refusing to see anyone or come out. Finally, her council ordered her door to be broken open. Elizabeth never had as close a relationship with any man as she did with Robert Dudley. She did, however, find some consolation in his stepson, the Earl of Essex, who had first come to court in 1585. Essex was young and handsome, and Elizabeth adored him, talking of him continually when he was away from court. She ignored the fact that he was also vain, arrogant and ambitious and appointed him to prominent posts, such as placing him in command of her army in Ireland.

As the years went by, the favourite's behaviour became increasingly outrageous. On 28 September 1598, Essex, who had returned to England from Ireland without Elizabeth's permission, arrived at court and burst into Elizabeth's chamber as she was dressing. Essex's intrusion shattered the myth that the passage of time had not touched Elizabeth, and he saw her wrinkled face and thin grey hair. She kept her composure and had a private interview with him, but was furious and never forgave him for his insolence.

Essex's behaviour continued to be erratic, and he gathered a party of disaffected lords around him. He and his followers conceived a plot to imprison Elizabeth, with Essex to rule in her place as lord protector. By February 1601, the conspirators were ready and Essex imprisoned several of Elizabeth's council in his house in London. Essex and 150 armed men then left his house, hoping to gain support from the people of London. He had badly overestimated his own popularity though and was unable to persuade the mayor of London or the people to join his coup. This lack of support finally showed him the folly of his actions, and his followers returned to Essex House to plan their next move.

On hearing of Essex's conduct, Elizabeth was furious, and according to reports, 'the Queen was so far from fear that she would have gone out in person to see what any rebel of them all durst do against her, had not the councillors with much ado stayed her'. She refused to sleep until Essex and his supporters had been arrested and ordered that canons be brought from the Tower to force him from his house. Essex, fearing that his house would be blown up, surrendered and was sent to the Tower. He was tried and sentenced to death, and Elizabeth showed him no mercy, ordering his execution on 25 February 1601. Essex was Elizabeth's last favourite, and she felt badly let down by him.

By the early 1600s, Elizabeth's health was failing and nobody in England expected her to live much longer. On 30 November 1601, she addressed parliament for the last time:

> There will never queen sit in my seat with more zeal to my country, care to my subjects, and that will soon with willingness venture her life for your good and safety, than myself. For it is not my desire to live nor reign longer than my life and reign shall be for your good. And though you have had and may have many princes more mighty and wise sitting in this seat, yet you never had or shall have any that will be more careful and loving.

Elizabeth's speech was recognised as the passing of an era, and few could remember a time before she had been queen.

In early 1603, Elizabeth's friend, the Countess of Nottingham, died, causing the queen to become depressed. Elizabeth seemed suddenly to age, and her memory deteriorated, meaning that she could no longer concentrate on political affairs. By March 1603, she was very ill and unable to either eat or sleep. She remained lucid to the end, dying on 24 March 1603 after finally falling asleep. As soon as she died, Lady Scrope took a ring from Elizabeth's finger and threw it out of the window to Robert Carey, who was waiting, on horseback, below. Carey rode to Scotland and, later that same day, James VI of Scotland was proclaimed king of England.

The three Tudor ruling queens enjoyed mixed fortunes. Lady Jane Grey was barely a queen at all and was never able to prove herself as a ruler. Mary I, on the other hand, was very much a reigning queen, being swept to the throne on a wave of popular support. Her reign was an abject failure, and she died, unlamented, just over five years later. In spite of the failures of her two predecessors, Elizabeth I is remembered as England's greatest monarch. She was a great survivor and one of the greatest politicians that England has ever known, demonstrating to all that a queen could reign successfully. By her good management of affairs, she also left her kingdom much more prosperous and stable than when she found it. In spite of her failure to ever name a successor, the succession of the first Stuart king was a smooth one, and the Stuart dynasty, which saw both queen consorts and queen regnants, was quickly established on the throne.

9

The House of Stuart

Throughout the reign of Elizabeth I, the English succession had been debated, and there were fears that her death would usher in a civil war as dangerous as the Wars of the Roses. Elizabeth always refused to name a successor, but as she aged, many of the leading claimants fell away. By the time of her death in March 1603, James VI of Scotland, the son of Mary, Queen of Scots, was the near-universal choice.

James was proclaimed king on the day of Elizabeth's death, and within months, both he and his queen, Anne of Denmark, were established in London. The Stuart dynasty had been luckless in Scotland, and this poor fortune intensified when they succeeded in England. The seven women who were either queens or married to the Stuart kings were ill starred.

ANNE OF DENMARK (1574-1619) was the second child of Frederick II, King of Denmark, and his wife, Sophia of Mecklenburg. Frederick was a fiery character and, on hearing that his second child, like his first, was a girl, he burst into the birthing chamber to remonstrate with his wife, insisting that he only wanted a son. Two years later, Sophia obliged, giving birth to the future Christian IV. All three children were sent to be raised by their maternal grandparents, the Duke and Duchess of Mecklenburg, in their duchy. They returned to Denmark when Anne was four, and she remained under her mother's care until her marriage. She was given a good education, and Anne's future husband, James VI of Scotland, later wrote to her father that he had been informed of 'the chaste and pious morals, the surpassing beauty, and truly royal education of your very sweet children'.

By the time that he wrote the letter to Anne's father, James had a very particular interest in the children of Frederick II. As early as 1586, there were rumours that James intended to marry a Danish princess. James first sent an embassy to Denmark the following year, ostensibly to discuss the future of the Orkneys and Shetland, which had been given to Scotland a century before as surety for the dowry of Margaret of Denmark when she married James III of Scotland. The ambassadors were also instructed to raise the possibility of a marriage between James and Frederick's eldest daughter, Elizabeth. Frederick, who was dying, showed little interest in the match, and the Scots went home empty-handed. They returned again in June 1689, and when they heard that Elizabeth had become betrothed to the Duke of Brunswick, the focus of Scottish interest shifted to Anne.

Negotiations for the marriage were concluded quickly, and the couple were married by proxy on 20 August 1589. Anne, who had a romantic nature, believed herself to be in love with the Scottish king, and she eagerly began to learn French so that she would be able to converse with her husband. Sixteen ships were prepared to take Anne to Scotland, and she was given a magnificent trousseau. James had originally shown little interest in his marriage, but a portrait of the blond and beautiful Anne caught his interest. This in itself was surprising, as James, who was almost certainly homosexual, had little interest in women. Nevertheless, he believed himself in love with Anne, using her as his inspiration for a number of romantic poems that he wrote as he awaited her arrival. He also wrote a letter to Anne's mother, shortly before the proxy marriage, setting out his eagerness to meet Anne 'since this relationship by marriage lies so close to our heart and mind, we have no higher desire than to behold in person this noble and lovable princess whose picture has fascinated our eyes and heart'.

Anne sailed from Denmark on 5 September. Almost as soon as they left, storms scattered the fleet, and Anne, who suffered severely from seasickness, found herself tossed about on the sea for some days. Eventually, the fleet was forced to return to Denmark, before setting out once more. The voyage from Denmark to Scotland was not a great distance, and by the middle of September, James had become worried at Anne's continued nonappearance. On 15 September, he received news that the Danish fleet had last been sighted off the Danish mainland, but he then heard nothing further. Frantic with worry, James ordered that 24 September be declared a public fast day in Scotland and that prayers be said for Anne's safe arrival. Anne had still not arrived by early October, and the difficulties that she experienced in her voyage were later attributed to witchcraft in both Scotland and Denmark. James decided to despatch a ship to look for Anne, and the captain, Colonel Stewart, found her in Norway. According to the Danish account of the marriage, Anne's ship was driven onto the coast and the princess was forced to disembark:

> When the admiral perceived that everything was going against them and the ship had even sprung a leak, all present decided it best for her grace to go ashore and lodge with a farmer on Flekkeroy until the ship was ready again. Her grace did this, and slept in a small farmhouse for two nights. King James also slept there when he landed on Flekkeroy later, saying that he desired to sleep in the same place as she had slept earlier.

The Danish fleet made further attempts to leave Norway, but they were always driven back by the storms and, eventually, the decision was taken to move on to Oslo to await the end of the winter. Norway was ruled by Denmark, and Anne was made welcome in the city, finding a comfortable lodging in the Old Bishop's Palace.

When James heard of Anne's plight, he decided to go in person to find her. James sailed in a small and overcrowded ship at the end of October, and whilst he also met storms, he soon landed in Norway. This was the bravest act of the naturally timid James's life, and it shows the devotion that he believed he felt for Anne. He travelled quickly to Oslo, and on his arrival, before even visiting his own lodgings, he rushed to meet his bride. The Danish account records that the couple spent only half an hour in each other's company, and it was not the romantic meeting either were expecting. According to a Scottish account of the meeting, 'his Majestie myndit to give the Queine a kisse after the Scotis faschioun at meiting, quhilk scho refusit as not being the forme of hir countrie. Marie, after a few wordis priuely spokin betwixt his Majestie and hir, their past familiarelie and kisses'. The real Anne could never meet up to the romantic ideal that James had built in his mind, and Anne also had cause to be disappointed. James was a poor physical specimen, with an overlarge tongue, which caused him to dribble food when he ate. He also, reportedly, had an aversion to washing.

In spite of the mutual disappointment, the couple soon became fond of each other, and they were married in Oslo on 23 November, holding hands as they listened to a sermon preached by one of James's Scottish chaplains. With the poor weather, they were in no hurry to leave for Scotland, and the couple travelled by sledge to Denmark in December. Anne was pleased to be reunited with her family, and she and James spent three months in Denmark being lavishly entertained. James had become so fond of Anne that he insisted on having a second wedding ceremony in early January, and the couple stayed for the wedding of Anne's elder sister before finally departing for Scotland in April 1590. For Anne, the second parting from her family may have been harder than her first, and she could never again bring herself to cross the North Sea for a visit to her native land.

Anne was well received in Scotland when she and James landed on 1 May 1590. She was given a grand ceremonial entry to Edinburgh and, on 17 May, was crowned as queen of Scotland. At her coronation, Anne made an oath that she would later break, much to James's horror:

> I, Anna, by the grace of God, Quene of Scotland, professe and befoir God and his angels haillelie [wholly] promise, that during the haille course of my lyffe, so farre as I can, sall sincerlie worshipe that same eternall God, according to his will revillit unto ws in his haillie scriptours, and according to thois preceptis quhills ar in the same scriptours commandit and derectit: That I sall defend the true religoun and worshipe of God, and advance the samyn, and sall withstand and dispys all papisticall superstitions, and quhatsumever ceremonies and rites contrair to the word of God.

Although details are sparse, within a few years of Anne's marriage, she had converted to the Catholic faith. James was shocked when he heard of his wife's conversion, and she agreed to keep it a secret, although it soon became widely known.

The selection of a Protestant bride had met with favour with Elizabeth I of England, and she was disapproving of Anne's conversion. In other respects, Anne proved an admirable queen and an asset to James's bid to obtain the throne of England, and she soon produced an heir, bearing Prince Henry Frederick in February 1594. Anne bore a daughter, Elizabeth, in 1596, and further children soon followed, although only her two eldest and her second son, Charles, survived to adulthood. Anne was a fond mother and Charles, in whose upbringing she was most involved, was her favourite. Whilst Anne was pleased with the birth of Henry, it also signalled the end of her marriage.

It is unlikely that Anne had expected to raise her eldest child, and certainly, she had not spent her early childhood with her mother. When Henry was born, however, she fell completely in love with him and was devastated when James informed her that it was the custom for the heir to the Scottish throne to be raised in Stirling Castle by the Earl of Mar. As well as a determination not to be parted from her son, Anne's anger was inflamed by the fact that she hated both the earl and the dowager countess, his mother. James's main objection to Anne being involved in Henry's upbringing was his fear that the boy could be used against him by his enemies. In 1595, while the quarrel with Anne raged, he wrote to the Earl of Mar:

> This I command you, out of my own mouth, being in company of those I like; otherwise, for any charge or necessity which can come from me, you shall not deliver him. And, in case God call

me at any time, see that, neither for the queen nor the estates their pleasure, you deliver him, till
he be eighteen, and that he command you himself.

Anne would not let the matter drop, and she became so hysterically upset that it caused a
miscarriage at the end of July.

James succeeded to the throne of England on 24 March 1603 and immediately headed
south to England, leaving Anne to follow more slowly. James's absence was the opportunity
that she had been waiting for, and together with a party of noblemen, she travelled to Stirling
and demanded to see her son. The Earl of Mar had gone to England with James, but his
mother refused to allow Anne entry, and after a furious quarrel, the Queen suffered another
miscarriage. For several days, it looked as though she might die, and James, anxious to have
Anne with him in London for appearance's sake, finally relented and allowed her to travel
south to London with both Henry and their daughter, Elizabeth.

England had not had a queen consort for over fifty years, and there was great excitement as
Anne moved south. Anne's contemporary, Lady Anne Clifford, recorded in her diary that she
and her mother killed three horses with exhaustion in their hurry to meet the Queen. By the
time she arrived at Windsor, Anne had an escort of 250 carriages and 5,000 horsemen. She
and James were crowned together in Westminster Abbey on 25 July 1603, a ceremony which
caused some comment both when Anne refused to take the sacrament and when James, who
received a kiss on the cheek from his favourite, the Earl of Montgomery, laughed and joked
during the paying of homage.

Anne found the opulent English court much more to her liking than Scotland, and she
set about indulging herself. She inherited Elizabeth I's fine wardrobe of over one thousand
dresses, and she loved to dress richly. Her main pastime in her early years as queen was in
producing and performing in masques, and she was a great patron of the playwright Ben
Jonson and the designer Inigo Jones, with whom she worked closely in her productions.
Anne's masques were extremely costly. The 'Vision of the Twelve Goddesses', which she
staged in January 1604, has been estimated to have cost between £2,000 and £3,000, and
Anne appeared in the lead role wearing jewellery worth around £100,000. Anne's masques
became steadily more lavish as the reign progressed, although they were not always well
received, and she caused a great deal of comment when she and her ladies appeared in the
'Masque of Blackness' in revealing costumes, their arms and faces blackened. Lady Anne
Clifford, for one, was shocked, recording that 'now there was much talk of a mask which the
queen had at Winchester, & how all the ladies about the court had gotten such ill names
that it was grown a scandalous place, & the queen herself was much fallen from her former
greatness and reputation she had in the world'. Anne continued to produce and appear
in masques until grief and ill health finally caused her to lose interest. She retained the
services of Inigo Jones however and commissioned him to build the fine Queen's House at
Greenwich.

Anne was grief-stricken in the summer of 1612 when her eldest son, Prince Henry, fell
ill. The prince was loved in England, and everyone had high hopes for his succession, but
as the months passed, he grew steadily worse. By November, Anne had been informed that
there was little hope for him, and he died on 12 November 1612. This was the greatest grief
of Anne's life, and she never recovered. She was further grieved the following year when her
daughter married the Count of the Palatinate and left for Germany. Shortly after her arrival
in England, Anne began to suffer from both gout and arthritis, writing to James of her
condition in one letter that 'I feare som inconvincens in my leggs' and in another that 'you
shall not feare the paine in my fingers'. Grief caused her health to deteriorate further, and

she relied on the company of her only surviving son, Charles, who often visited her when she was ill and wrote kind letters. In one, he wrote,

> Seeing I cannot have the happiness to see your majesty, give me leave to declare by these lines the duty and love I owe to you, which makes me long to see you. I wish from my heart that I might help to find a remedy to your disease; the which I must bear the more patiently, because it is the sign of a long life. But I must for many causes be sorry; and specially because it is troublesome to you, and has deprived me of your most comfortable sight, and of many good dinners; the which I hope, by God's grace, shortly to enjoy. And when it shall please you to give me leave to see you, it may be I shall give you some good recipe, which either shall heal you or make you laugh.

In her final years, Anne's relationship with James improved, and whilst they were rarely together, they were cordial to each other. James always had close male friends, and Anne was on poor terms with his first great English favourite, Robert Carr, but George Villiers, who would later become the Duke of Buckingham, charmed her, and she often wrote friendly letters to him, using her pet name for him of 'dog'. Anne and James settled comfortably into a marriage in which they rarely saw each other, with Anne writing on one occasion that 'as for the blame you charge me with of lassie [lazy] writing I think it rather rests on your self because you be as sloe in writing as my self. I can write of no mirth but of practise of tilting of riding of drumming and of musike which is all, wher with I am not a little pleased so wishing your Majesty perpetuale happiness'.

James was also, on occasion, prepared to listen to Anne's advice, and it was she who first secured an appointment for George Villiers as a gentleman of the bedchamber.

Anne's health continued to steadily deteriorate, and over Christmas 1618, she was too ill to join the court for the festivities, remaining at Hampton Court. James always had a horror of disease and refused to visit the Queen, but Charles remained with her until the end. She died in the early hours of 2 March 1619 at Hampton Court, in the same chamber as Jane Seymour, the last woman to die as queen consort. She was given a grand funeral by her husband and, with her death, the office of queen fell into abeyance until the marriage of Anne's son, Charles I, to Henrietta Maria of France over a decade later.

HENRIETTA MARIA OF FRANCE (1609-69) was the youngest child of Henry IV of France and his second wife, Marie de Medici. Although, at the time of her birth, Henrietta's parents had three sons, her sex was a disappointment to her father. When he received the news, he said coldly that he would have given 100,000 crowns for the child to have been a boy. Regardless of this disappointment, Henrietta was named after both her parents. She was not destined to ever know her father, as he was assassinated less than six months after her birth. Henrietta's mother, the indomitable Marie de Medici, became regent for her eldest son, Louis XIII, and she presided over a troubled regime until 1617, when she was forced out of Paris by her son. Henrietta continued to live with her mother after her fall, and the pair spent the next two years under house arrest in the Castle of Blois. To Marie's relief, she was finally reconciled with her son, allowing Henrietta to continue her education at court.

Marie de Medici had an ambition for all three of her daughters to become queens. She was successful in this ambition for her eldest daughter, who became queen of Spain, although her second daughter had to be content only with marriage to the Duke of Savoy. Henrietta's father, Henry IV had been a Protestant during his youth as king of Navarre and had famously converted to Catholicism when he succeeded to the French throne, declaring that Paris was worth a Mass. Marie ensured that her children were raised to be ardent Catholics. She was prepared to relax her principles somewhat in her pursuit of a crown for Henrietta when Charles, Prince of Wales, caught her attention.

It had always been the wish of Charles's mother, Anne of Denmark, that her son would marry into the Spanish royal family, and in January 1623, Charles and his dearest friend, George Villiers, Duke of Buckingham, set out on a romantic adventure to Spain in the hope of wooing the Spanish infanta. The pair travelled in disguise, and Lord Herbert, the English ambassador to France was entirely unaware of the prince's arrival when he passed through Paris. Charles was recognised in the street by a maid who sold linen in London, and she informed a Scot named Andrews, who immediately asked the ambassador if he had seen the prince. Herbert replied, 'What prince "for" said I, "the prince of Conde is yet in Italy"; he told me, the prince of Wales, which yet I could not believe easily.' Whilst Herbert found it hard to believe that Charles was present in France, the French government were certainly aware, and the two anonymous travellers were accorded preferential treatment, being given access to the French royal ladies. The anonymous author of the *Life and Death of Henrietta Maria* (the *Life*) later claimed that, when he saw her, Charles 'took in by the eye, that love which he preserved inviolable for her to his death; and she likewise entertained a love for him by the ear; for when she was told that he passed through Paris, it was then discoursed that she should say, that, if the Prince of Wales went into Spain for a wife, he might have had one nearer hand, and saved himself a great part of the labour'.

Henrietta hoped to make an impression on the heir to England, but Charles, by his own account in a letter written to his father with Buckingham, showed little interest in her:

> Since the closing of our last, we have been at court again (and that we might not hold you in pain, we assure you we have not been known). Where we saw the young queen, little monsieur, and madame [Henrietta], at the practising of a mask that is intended by the queen to be presented to the king; and in it there danced the queen and madame, with as many as made up nineteen fair dancing ladies, amongst which the queen is the handsomest, which hath wrought in me a greater desire to see her sister [the infanta].

Charles's visit to Spain proved fruitless, and he soon turned instead towards Henrietta.

Shortly after Charles returned to England from Spain, Viscount Kensington was sent to Paris to negotiate a marriage with Henrietta. According to the *Life*, Henrietta 'was reckoned then the loveliest creature in France, and the sweetest thing in nature', and Kensington wrote approvingly of her to England. Henrietta had little cause for complaint in Charles, as, whilst he was of below average height and had a slight build, he was very handsome in his youth. Once she was aware that negotiations were underway, she borrowed a portrait of Charles from Kensington and spent an hour with it alone in her closet. She also took a letter that she had received from Charles and, 'not without some tears of joy', placed it in her 'bosom'. News of Henrietta's eagerness for the match was well received in England, and James I commented that 'he would thank her, for lodging his son's letters so well'. The couple were married by proxy in Notre Dame in Paris on 11 May 1625, and three weeks later, Henrietta left Paris to travel to England, accompanied by her mother and a large train. Charles had become king of England three months before, and everywhere she went, Henrietta was addressed as queen.

Henrietta landed in England in the evening of 23 June and spent the night at Dover Castle. She was met there the following morning by Charles. Henrietta had been raised to understand that marriage was the purpose of her life, and this, coupled with leaving her family and her life in France, made for an emotional meeting, as demonstrated in the *Life*:

When the king her husband received her on the top of the stairs; she striving on her knees to kiss his hands, and he preventing her with civilities on her lips. Being retired, she wept, and he kissed off her tears, professing he would do so, till she had done, and persuading her that she was not fallen into the hands of strangers, as she apprehended tremblingly, but unto the wise disposal of God, who would have her leave her kindred, and cleave to her spouse, he professing to be no longer master of himself, than whilst he was a servant to her.

Whilst the first meeting between the couple went well, it soon became clear that there were problems in their relationship.

The couple were married in Canterbury and Henrietta was noted to seem uncomfortable the next morning. Once they had travelled to London, she found that the Duke of Buckingham was determined to stir up trouble, causing a number of misunderstandings between the royal couple. Henrietta's reliance on her French attendants also came between her and Charles, and according to the diarist John Evelyn, her ladies often upbraided the Protestant religion. Henrietta, under the influence of her attendants, refused to attend Charles's coronation on 2 February 1626, complaining that it was heretical, something that angered the King. When, three days later, Henrietta refused to attend the opening of parliament, she and Charles had a furious quarrel, after which they did not speak to each other for three days. Matters came to a head in July 1626, when Charles announced that he intended to send all her attendants back to France. Henrietta was so distraught that she smashed a window with her bare hands, calling out to her French servants in the courtyard below before Charles dragged her back. In spite of her grief, the return to France of her attendants did improve the relationship between the couple. The assassination of Buckingham in August 1628 cleared the last obstacle between them, and to the surprise of everyone, Charles and Henrietta fell in love.

After their initial troubles, Henrietta and Charles were always devoted to each other, and whenever Charles spent a night apart from the Queen, she kept his portrait propped up next to her in bed. Henrietta fell pregnant in late 1628, and whilst her first son died within hours of his birth, her second, who was born on 29 May 1630, proved to be incredibly robust. Henrietta was proud of her strong son, writing to her former governess, Madam St George, that 'he is so fat and so tall, that he is taken for a year old, and he is only four months: his teeth are already beginning to come: I will send you his portrait as soon as he is a little fairer, for at present he is so dark that I am ashamed of him'. To both Charles and Henrietta's surprise, their son, young Charles, did not resemble either of them and instead inherited the dark looks of Henrietta's Italian ancestors. In a later letter to Madam St George, Henrietta joked that her son 'is so ugly, that I am ashamed of him, but his size and fatness supply the want of beauty'. Henrietta bore a further six children over the decade following young Charles's birth: Mary in 1631, James in 1632, then Elizabeth, Anne, Catherine and Henry. Henrietta's children were mostly healthy, and whilst Anne died young and Catherine in infancy, the others survived at least until adolescence.

Henrietta spent much of her time, in her early years as queen, enjoying herself, and like her mother-in-law before her, she liked taking part in court masques, in 1632 acting in a pastoral that she prepared 'as well for her recreation as for the exercise of her English'. In 1638, she was pleased to receive a visit from her mother, who had been expelled from France, and in spite of being heavily pregnant, Henrietta rushed to meet her coach, kneeling with her elder children for her mother's blessing. Charles was less happy when it became apparent that his mother-in-law's visit was to be an indefinite one, but the presence of Marie de Medici in England was, by the late 1630s, the least of his troubles.

Charles believed that he had a divine right to the throne and that, as king, he was answerable only to God. This belief meant that, almost from the start of his reign, he had a difficult relationship with parliament, and by 1640, he had ruled without a parliament for eleven years. In 1637, Charles attempted to introduce a new prayer book to Scotland with the intention of bringing the Scottish Church into line with the Church of England. Many people in Scotland, observing Charles's relationship with the Catholic Henrietta Maria, feared that this would be the first step towards reinstating Catholicism, and when, in July 1637, the Dean of St Giles attempted to use the prayer book, there were riots. To Charles's fury, Scotland was soon in revolt against him, and by May 1639, he was present at the Scottish borders with an army. He did not have the funds to fight a prolonged war in Scotland, and he reluctantly summoned parliament, on 13 April 1640, to request that they vote him a tax subsidy. To Charles's anger, parliament, led by John Pym, refused absolutely to vote the subsidy until Charles had addressed a number of their concerns. Charles refused to even consider the points raised until he received the subsidy, and facing deadlock, he dissolved parliament after only three weeks, vowing to fight his war in Scotland alone. By the summer of 1641, Charles had been defeated in Scotland, and he returned to England to find discontent brewing. By the middle of 1642, relations between Charles and parliament had collapsed and both began to raise armies. On 22 August 1642, Charles raised his banner at Nottingham, and a victory by him in a skirmish outside Worcester was followed by a full-scale, and inconclusive, battle at Edgehill, marking the start of the English Civil War.

Henrietta and her mother, as prominent Catholics, were the focus of much of the discontent in England, and Marie de Medici, who frequently found St James's Palace, where she was lodged, surrounded by a mob, returned to the Continent. In 1641, Charles and Henrietta's friend, the Earl of Strafford, was arrested and executed on the orders of parliament. Marie de Medici had previously suggested a match between one of her granddaughters and the son of the Prince of Orange, and whilst both Charles and Henrietta felt that the match was beneath their daughter, the offer of Dutch assistance was too important to resist, and their eldest daughter, Mary, was married to William of Orange in London on 2 May 1641. Mary's marriage provided Henrietta with an excuse to escape the tense situation in England, and she escorted her daughter to the Hague the following year. Charles accompanied his wife and daughter to the coast, and the parting was emotional as the King kissed Henrietta repeatedly. As the ship sailed, Charles rode four leagues along the coast until it was no longer in sight, waving his hat in salute to his wife and daughter.

Henrietta and Charles had prepared a cipher to ensure that they could correspond with each other securely, and whilst she was absent from England, Henrietta had no intention of abandoning her husband's cause. She had smuggled many of the crown jewels, as well as personal valuables, out of England and set about trying to sell or pawn as many as she could in the Netherlands. Her letters to Charles set out the trouble she had in raising funds for him. In one, she wrote, 'The money is not ready, for on the jewels, they will lend nothing. I am forced to pledge all my little ones, for the great ones, nothing can be had here, but I assure you I am losing no time.' Parliament discovered Henrietta's actions and attempted to stop her, as she related to Charles:

After much trouble, we have at last procured some money, but only a little as yet, for the fears of the merchants are not yet entirely passed away. It was written from London, that I had carried off my jewels secretly, and against your wish, and that if money was lent me upon them, that would be no safety for them; so that all this time, when we were ready to conclude anything, our merchants always drew back. At last, it was necessary to show your power, signed under your own hand, about which I have written to you before, and immediately we concluded our business.

Henrietta was determined to do all she could to assist Charles, and when the Prince of Orange gave her seven fine horses, she sent them to Charles. She also retained an active interest in Charles's campaigns, often writing to him with advice.

By the end of 1642, Henrietta was ready to sail for England with a fleet of ships loaded with ammunition and supplies. Whilst it had been decided that she would land at Newcastle, in order to divert suspicion, she wrote a letter to Charles without using the cipher, intending that it should fall into the hands of parliament. In her letter, Henrietta declared that she intended to land at either Boston or Great Yarmouth, some distance from Newcastle. In an attempt to create dissent amongst the Parliamentarians, she also tried to cast suspicion on one of the leading Parliamentarians, writing that 'I received yesterday a letter from Pym, by which he sends me word that he fears I am offended with him, because he has not had a letter from me for a long time. I beg you tell him that this is not the case, and that I am as much his friend as ever.' Henrietta sailed on 19 January 1643, but her luck was against her, and after nine days at sea, she was forced back by storms to Holland. She sailed again eleven days later and was forced by the weather to land at Burlington Bay in Yorkshire.

The parliamentary forces moved quickly in an attempt to capture or kill Henrietta. According to one account, she spent the night after her landing in a house close to the port:

> Thir rebel ships are hastily advertised by a pinnace of her arrival, whereupon they hoist sail and come with shot of canon to the town, sends privately a pinnace ashore to design the house where the queen was lodged, whilk being done, her majesty, having mind of no evil, but glad of rest, now wearied by the sea, is cruelly assaulted, for this six rebel ships, ilk ane by course, sets their broadside to her lodging, batters the house, dings down the roof, ere she wist of herself; but she gets up out of her naked bed in her night walycoat, barefooted and barelegged, with her maids of honour, whereof one for plain fear went straight mad, being a nobleman of England's daughter. She gets safely out of the house, albeit the stones were falling about her head, yet courageously she goes out, they shooting still, and by providence of the Almighty she escapes, with all her company (except the maid of honour) and goes to a den which the canons could not reach, and on the bare fields she rested.

Henrietta provided her own account of her dramatic escape to Charles, writing that she was forced to hide in a ditch in the freezing cold whilst 'a serjeant was killed twenty paces from me'. Her ordeal only came to an end when the Dutch Admiral, who had been sent as a neutral escort, threatened to open fire on the parliamentary ships if they did not cease their attack. This had the desired effect, and Henrietta was able to return to her lodging. She was shaken by the attack, and it was certainly an attempt to murder her, with Henrietta herself pointing out that 'I am told that one of the captains of the Parliament ships had been beforehand in reconnoitre where my lodging was, and I assure you that it was well marked, for they always shot upon it'. Undaunted, Henrietta continued her efforts on Charles's behalf, bringing an army and ammunition to his base at Oxford, where the couple enjoyed an emotional reunion.

Henrietta remained with Charles until 17 April 1644, when the couple said their final farewells at Abingdon. Before she had even arrived at Oxford, Henrietta had been impeached as a traitor by parliament and she knew that, if she were captured, it was likely that she would be executed. By April 1644, she was heavily pregnant with her last child, and she resolved to return to her homeland, France. Unbeknownst to both Charles and Henrietta, their parting at Abingdon was to be their last meeting. Henrietta's final pregnancy was her most difficult, and she bore her ninth child, a daughter whom she named Henrietta Anne, at Exeter on 16 June 1644. Henrietta had been ill before the birth, and her sickness increased following her delivery. Believing that she would die, she wrote to Charles:

> Since I left you at Oxford, that disease which I began to feel there has constantly increased, but with attacks so violent as no one ever felt before. I bore it patiently, in hopes of being cured by my accouchement; but instead of finding relief, my disease has increased, and is so insupportable, that if it were not that we ought not to wish for death, it would be too much longed for, by the most wretched creature in the world. And to render my condition complete, from three days before my confinement to this present time, Essex has been threatening us with a siege, to which I cannot make up my mind, and would rather set out on the road towards Falmouth, to pass from thence into France, if I can do it, even at the hazard of my life, than stay here.

Henrietta was desperately ill, and she could take no more, leaving her infant daughter in the care of Lady Dalkeith before setting out secretly from Exeter fifteen days after the birth. Henrietta travelled disguised in humble dress and accompanied by only three companions. The journey, coupled with her illness, was the most traumatic of her life, and she was forced to hide in a hut for two days, crouched under a heap of litter. As parliamentary soldiers passed by her refuge, she could hear them speaking and was horrified to hear that a reward of 50,000 crowns would be paid to the man who brought her head back to London. As soon as the danger had passed, Henrietta was carried in a litter to Cornwall before sailing to Brittany, hotly pursued by parliamentary ships.

For Henrietta, the return to her homeland was a great relief, and once she had recovered her health, she was welcomed at the French court. She continued to work on her husband's behalf and was glad to welcome both her eldest son Charles, Prince of Wales, and her infant daughter, Henrietta Anne, to her household in France. For Charles I, the situation in England went from bad to worse, and in 1646, he was captured by the Scots and held as their prisoner for some time. He and Henrietta continued to correspond and, on 2 January 1647, he wrote, 'I must tell thee that now I am declared what I have really been ever since I came to this army, which is a prisoner (for the governor told me some four days since, that he was commanded to secure me, lest I should make an escape), the difference being only this, that heretofore my escape was easy enough, but now it is most difficult, if not impossible.'

Charles was handed over to the English parliament shortly afterwards. Parliament resolved to try the King for treason, and he was condemned on 27 January 1649, being granted a farewell interview with his two captive children, Henry and Elizabeth, two days later. In the morning of 30 January 1649, Charles stepped out of the Banqueting House at Whitehall onto a specially erected scaffold. He made a final speech before kneeling and placing his head on the block. He was beheaded with one blow of the axe.

Henrietta at first heard a rumour that, as Charles stepped out onto the scaffold, the crowd rose up and rescued him, and she was jubilant when a messenger from the French court arrived at her residence. When she was informed of Charles's death, she was, at first, disbelieving, before weeping uncontrollably. Charles and Henrietta were truly devoted to each other, and the King sent a final verbal message to Henrietta through their daughter Elizabeth, telling the girl to inform her mother that 'his thoughts had never strayed from her. And that his love should be the same to the last'. Henrietta always remained devoted to Charles's memory and her immediate reaction was to shut herself away from the world in a convent. She only emerged because of her desire to assist her children and, in particular, her eldest son in winning back the throne of England, and Charles, in an earlier letter, had enjoined his eldest son to listen to Henrietta, 'whom I command you to obey in everything, (except in religion, concerning which I am confident she will not trouble you)'.

Whilst Charles I had been confident that Henrietta would not try to influence the religion of their children, in reality, she had no intention of allowing them to remain Protestants. Before his death, Charles had confirmed to Henrietta that their youngest daughter, who he realised was likely to spend her life in France, could be raised in Henrietta's faith, but at his final meeting with Henry and Elizabeth, he pressed them to remain Protestants. Whilst Henrietta had hoped to be able to influence the affairs of her eldest son, who was immediately proclaimed as King Charles II on his father's death, she soon found that he allowed her little involvement. She therefore focused her energies on raising her younger children. Henrietta's second daughter, Elizabeth, died in captivity, but her youngest son, Henry, was released soon afterwards and returned to his mother's care. Henrietta always had a deeply troubled relationship with Henry, who she had not seen since his infancy. When he arrived with her in Paris, she was determined to convert him to Catholicism, and she arranged for him to study at a Jesuit school. Unlike Henrietta, Charles II was well aware that England would not accept a Catholic king, and he was not prepared to have his potential return to England jeopardised by a Catholic brother. Charles wrote sternly to Henry in November 1654, declaring that whilst he understood that it was 'ye Queenes purpose to do all shee can to change your religion', in the event that Henry did bow to pressure then he 'must never thinke to see England or mee againe'. Matters came to a head when Henry refused to listen to Henrietta further on religion. With that, the Queen swore that she would never see her youngest son again, something that proved true, and the pair were not reconciled before his early death in 1660.

Henrietta spent the years of her exile living quietly in France, and she was overjoyed to hear of her son's restoration to the throne in 1660. She was less than eager to return to the country that had executed her husband, and it was only in order to secure the payment of her dower that she returned in November 1660, accompanied by her youngest daughter. Henrietta had been absent from London for nineteen years, and the city found her much changed, with the diarist Samuel Pepys commenting, 'The queen a very little, plain old woman, and nothing more in her presence in any respect nor garbe than any ordinary woman.' Tragedy struck Henrietta again on Christmas Eve, when her eldest daughter, Mary, Princess of Orange, died of smallpox, only three months after Henry had died of the same disease. Her daughter's death caused Henrietta to look more favourably on Anne Hyde, who had secretly married her second son, James, Duke of York, who had spent time as a prisoner of parliament before escaping to France. Whilst before leaving France Henrietta had declared that she intended to 'unmarry her son', on New Year's Day, she and her daughter-in-law, who was considerably below James in rank, were publicly reconciled. Henrietta and her youngest daughter returned home to France soon afterwards. On 31 March 1661, to her mother's joy, Henrietta Anne married the Duke of Orléans, the younger brother of Louis XIV.

Henrietta returned to England for a second visit in July 1662 in order to meet her daughter-in-law, Catherine of Braganza. She missed her daughter and her life in France and finally, in 1665, she returned to her homeland. Henrietta lived out her last years in increasingly bad health, spending time with her daughter and her grandchildren, including the future Queen Anne of England, who was sent, in her infancy, to live with her. According to the *Life*, Henrietta died on 31 August 1669 'after a long disposition of body and decay of health'. She was given a grand funeral by her nephew, Louis XIV, as befitted a daughter of France.

Henrietta Maria of France's life was one of great extremes and whilst she had one of the happiest marriages of any English queen, her and her husband's lives were devastated by events for which they must, at least partially, be held responsible. Henrietta was fond of her daughter-in-law and successor as queen, Catherine of Braganza, who also suffered the uncertainties of leaving her homeland for an unknown husband.

CATHERINE OF BRAGANZA (1638-1705) was one of the least influential English queens, both politically and personally. She was born on 25 November 1638, the daughter of Joao, Duke of Braganza, and his wife, Louisa of Medina-Sidonia. At the time of Catherine's birth, Portugal was annexed to Spain, and her father, a member of the old Portuguese royal house, was viewed by many as the leading claimant to the throne. When Catherine was only two years old, her father received a summons to Madrid, something that he suspected would lead to his imprisonment. Instead of going, he accepted the crown of Portugal from a group of noblemen anxious to ensure independence and, in a bloodless coup, took possession of the country.

As the daughter of the King of Portugal, Catherine received a very cosseted upbringing. Charles II's chancellor, the Earl of Clarendon later lamented that

> though she was of years enough to have had more experience of the world, and of as much wit as could be wished, and of a humour very agreeable at some seasons; yet she had been bred, according to the mode and discipline of her country, in a monastery, where she had only seen the women who attended her, and conversed with the Religious who resided there, and without doubt in her inclinations was enough disposed to have been one of that number.

Catherine would later show that she had no desire to be a nun, but she was raised to be dependent on her mother and the women who served her. She did, however, know something of the way in which the royal court worked, not blushing when, after her arrival in England, Lord Clarendon commented that

> 'he knew well, that she had been very little acquainted with or informed of the world; yet he could not believe that she was so utterly ignorant, as to expect that the king her husband, in the full strength and vigour of his youth, was of so innocent a constitution, as to be reserved for her whom he had never seen, and to have had no acquaintance or familiarity with the sex;' and asked, 'whether she believed, when it should please God to send a queen to Portugal, she should find that court so full of chaste affections'.

A marriage between Catherine and the exiled Charles II of England had first been proposed in Catherine's childhood. In 1656, Catherine's father died and her mother became regent for her brother. Catherine's mother was eager to establish firmer ties with England, and when news reached Portugal of Charles II's restoration to the throne in 1660, she once again suggested that he marry Catherine.

Not everyone was happy with the match, and according to the account of the Earl of Clarendon, the Earl of Bristol and the Spanish ambassador both tried to dissuade Charles, telling him that Catherine was 'deformed, and had many diseases; and that it was very well known in Portugal and Spain that she was incapable to bear children'. They instead suggested that Charles select one of the 'many beautiful ladies in Italy, of the greatest houses', and in return, the King of Spain promised to dower Charles's choice as though she were a princess of Spain. Charles paid no attention to the comments about Catherine. Whilst Catherine did indeed prove unable to bear a child, there is no evidence that this was known before her marriage, and it is more likely that the earl and the ambassador resorted to slander to prevent an alliance with Spain's great enemy, Portugal. Charles was badly in need of funds, and to secure the match, Catherine's mother was prepared to offer a considerable sum as a dowry, as well as Tangiers and Bombay, and a guarantee of free trade with the Portuguese colonies in the Indies and Brazil. This was the deciding factor for Charles, and on 8 May 1661, he announced to parliament that he had contracted to marry Catherine.

Charles sent an embassy, headed by the Earl of Sandwich, to Lisbon in March 1662, together with a fleet to bring Catherine to England. On his arrival, Sandwich was disconcerted to be informed by Catherine's mother that she could only afford to pay half the promised dowry at that time. Anxious not to return home without Catherine, Sandwich reluctantly accepted, and he was further concerned when he found that Catherine's mother had no cash to offer at all, and instead, his ships were loaded with goods to be sold in London. There was nothing he could do, and after her final farewells to her family, Catherine boarded Charles's flagship, the *Royal Charles*, and sailed to England. Disastrously for Catherine, at her final interview with her mother, the Portuguese queen made her promise that she would, on no account, ever receive Charles's mistress, Lady Castlemaine.

Catherine had an uneventful voyage and landed at Portsmouth to be met by Charles's brother, James, Duke of York. A few days later, Charles himself arrived. In her innocence and her dependence on her Portuguese escort, Catherine did not immediately endear herself to Charles or the English people. According to Clarendon, Catherine was determined not to embrace anything English:

> There was a numerous family of men and women that were sent from Portugal, the most improper to promote that conformity in the queen that was necessary for her condition and future happiness, that could be chosen: the women for the most part old and ugly and proud, incapable of any conversation with persons of quality and a liberal education. And they desired and indeed had conspired so far to possess the queen themselves, that she should neither learn the English language, nor use their habit, nor depart from the manners and fashions of her own country in any particulars; 'which resolution' they told her, 'would be for the Dignity of Portugal, and would quickly induce the English ladies to conform to her Majesty's practice'.

Catherine listened to what her ladies told her and had already refused to see the tailor that Charles had sent to Portugal to prepare English fashions for her. She also refused to wear any of the English clothes that Charles provided. This was unfortunate, and whilst great farthingales were in fashion in Portugal, in England they were considered hilariously old fashioned. According to the diarist Samuel Pepys, Catherine obtained a reputation for meanness as soon as she landed, giving a present of money to be distributed amongst the crew of the *Royal Charles*, but nothing for the gentlemen who attended her. She apparently thought that they would see any gift as an insult. Catherine caused a stir by refusing to even greet the English ladies that had come to meet her until Charles himself arrived.

Catherine's first meeting with Charles went well. According to the diarist John Evelyn, Charles wrote to Clarendon, who had brokered the match, from Portsmouth to tell him that he 'was well pleased with her'. Evelyn also provided his own description of the Queen on her arrival in London:

> The queen arrived with a train of Portuguese ladies in their monstrous fardingales, or guard-infantes, their complexions olivader [i.e. dark olive] and sufficiently unagreeable. Her Majesty in the same habit, her foretop long and turned aside very strangely. She was yet of the handsomest countenance of all the rest, and though of low stature, prettily shaped, languishing and excellent eyes, her teeth wronging her mouth by sticking a little too far out; for the rest, lovely enough.

Catherine was generally considered pretty, particularly when she finally consented to wear English dress, and Charles found her attractive, particularly noticing her eyes. Catherine was also pleased with Charles, who Evelyn's account describes:

> [Charles] was then thirty years of age, and, as might have been supposed, past the levities of youth, and the extravagance of pleasure. He had a very good understanding. He knew well the state of affairs both at home and abroad. He had a softness of temper that charmed all who came near him, till they found how little they could depend on good looks, kind words, and fair promises, in which he was liberal to excess, because he intended nothing by them, but to get rid of importunities, and to silence all farther pressing upon him.

The couple were married publicly the next day in a Protestant ceremony at which Catherine caused offence by refusing to speak, viewing the ceremony as worthless. Catherine placed far more importance on the secret Catholic marriage ceremony that she and Charles had undergone earlier that day, which, according to Evelyn, was attended only by Charles's brother, the Duke of York, and a small number of Catherine's Portuguese attendants. Once they were married, the couple travelled to Hampton Court.

Catherine's mother had warned her never to receive Charles's mistress, Lady Castlemaine, and Catherine soon heard that the delay in Charles coming to meet her at Portsmouth had been occasioned by his desire to stay with Lady Castlemaine until she had given birth to his expected child, a son. According to Clarendon, Charles was entirely oblivious to the possibility of jealousy between the two women. He had promised Lady Castlemaine that she could be one of Catherine's ladies of the bedchamber, and shortly after he and Catherine arrived at Hampton Court,

> He led her [Lady Castlemaine] into her [Catherine's] chamber, and presented her to the queen, who received her with the same grace as she had done the rest; there being many lords and other ladies at the same time there. But whether her Majesty in the instant knew who she was, or upon recollection found it afterwards, she was no sooner sate in her chair, but her colour changed, and tears gushed out of her eyes, and nose bled, and she fainted; so that she was forthwith removed into another room, and all the company returned out of that where she was before. And this falling out so notoriously when so many persons were present, the king looked upon it with wonderful indignation.

Charles was furious with Catherine's refusal to meet Lady Castlemaine, and he responded by avoiding her and berating the Portuguese ambassador over the unpaid dowry. He and Catherine also had a very public row, in which each accused the other of unkindness, with Charles insisting that he intended to remain faithful to her if only she would do what he asked. He instructed Lord Clarendon to speak to Catherine on the issue, but Clarendon found her entirely firm, insisting that 'she did not think that she should have found the king engaged in his affections to another lady'. She further insisted that, if pushed to recognise Lady Castlemaine, she would return to Lisbon, something to which Clarendon responded by saying that 'she had not the disposal of her owne person, nor could go out of the house where she was without the king's leave'. Clarendon tried to protect Catherine as much as he could, telling Charles that 'her unwillingness to obey him in this one particular proceeded only from the greatest passion of love which she had for him, that transported her beyond the limits of her reason', but the damage was done, and for several months, the couple were barely on speaking terms.

Catherine finally capitulated to Charles's demands, agreeing to receive Lady Castlemaine as one of her ladies, but the relationship between the two women was never easy. Lady Castlemaine was often rude to Catherine, and on one occasion, the King happened to come in when his mistress spoke disrespectfully to Catherine, and he sent her from court for a time. Charles always insisted that Catherine be shown the proper respect due to her rank, and after the first few months of their marriage, he treated her kindly. He was not in love with her and enjoyed a succession of mistresses, abandoning Lady Castlemaine for Frances Stuart, another of Catherine's ladies, before turning his attentions to Louise de Kerouaille, a maid of his sister, Henrietta, Duchess of Orléans, and also the actress, Nell Gwynne. After her disastrous attempt to force Charles to abandon Lady Castlemaine, Catherine pretended to ignore his infidelities, treating his mistresses with respect, but they caused her nothing but grief.

Catherine knew that her primary purpose was to bear the King a son. According to Evelyn, who knew Charles personally, 'the king himself told me, she had been with child; and Willis, the great physician, told doctor Lloyd, from whom I had it, that she had once miscarried of a child, which was so far advanced, that, if it had been carefully looked to, the sex might have been distinguished. But she proved a barren wife.' Catherine conceived at least twice, and possibly three times during her marriage, but all her pregnancies ended in miscarriage. In January 1665, a letter from Thomas Salisbury to the Earl of Huntingdon records that Catherine was believed to be pregnant. A more definite report, written by Viscount Conway on 9 May 1668, claimed that 'the worst news I have to write is that for certain the queen miscarried upon Thursday morning last'. It took Catherine some time to conceive following her marriage, and on the advice of her doctors, she regularly took the waters at Tunbridge Wells and Bath. Her first pregnancy may have been at the end of October 1662, when Pepys noted, 'It is believed the queen is with child, for that the coaches are ordered to ride very easily through the streets.' For Charles, the miscarriages were at least proof that Catherine could conceive, but she was unable to carry a child to term. As the years passed and it became increasingly obvious that Catherine would bear no child, the couple continued to grow apart, with Charles lavishing affection on his illegitimate children.

Catherine's childlessness grieved her, and her misery was compounded by the fact that it was obvious that the problem lay with her. In October 1663, she fell dangerously ill with a fever, which she was not expected to survive. According to Hamilton, a contemporary of Catherine, 'the good nature of the king was much affected with the situation in which he saw a princess, whom, though he did not love her, yet he greatly esteemed'. Charles sat with Catherine during her illness and begged her not to die. Catherine's grief at her failure to bear a child poured out during her delirium, a fact that Pepys records:

Dr Pierce tells me that the queen is in a way to be pretty well again, but that her delirium in her head continues still; that she talks idle, not by fits, but always, which in some lasts a week after so high a fever – in some more, and in some for ever, that this morning she talked mightily that she was brought to bed, and that she wondered that she should be delivered without pain and without being sick, and that she was troubled that her boy was but an ugly boy. But the king being by, said, 'No, it is a very pretty boy' – 'Nay', says she, 'if it be like you, it is a fine boy indeed, and I would be very well pleased with it'.

To spare Catherine's feelings, Charles played along with her belief that she had borne a child. The following day, Pepys reported that

Mr Coventry tells me to-day that the queen had a very good night last night; but yet it is strange that still she raves and talks of little more than of her having of children, and fancys now that she hath three children, and that the girle is very like the king. And this morning, about five o'clock, the physician, feeling her pulse, thinking to be better able to judge, she being still and asleep, waked her, and the first word she said was, 'How do the children?'

Catherine's grief when she recovered and remembered that she had no children can only be imagined. Charles's attempts to spare her feelings are touching, and he remained Catherine's protector throughout her life, always refusing to divorce her when he was pressed to do so by his subjects in order to marry a more fertile wife.

Charles also came to Catherine's aid at the most dangerous time of her life. In 1678, Titus Oates, a former Jesuit, and his friend, Israel Tonge, reported that they had information about a Catholic conspiracy to assassinate the King and place his Catholic brother, James, Duke of York on the throne. There was no truth in the information supplied by Oates but it pandered to the anti-Catholic hysteria in England and was widely believed, becoming known as the 'Popish Plot'. The Duke of York was specifically named as an accomplice to the plot, and dangerously for Catherine, her physician, Sir George Wakeman, was also accused. As Oates found that his accusations were believed, they became more outlandish, and he claimed that the Catholics intended to exterminate every Protestant in England and burn the principal cities in England. France and Spain were reportedly ready to invade. Charles II was officially informed of the plot in August 1678 and declared it to be nonsense. However, his privy council firmly believed everything they were told, as did parliament, and arrests were swiftly made with many leading Catholics fleeing to the Continent. At the height of the hysteria, a magistrate, Sir Edmund Bury Godfrey, was found murdered, and to Catherine's horror, two of her chaplains were accused. In November 1678, suspicion firmly turned towards Catherine, and Oates claimed that he had overheard her plotting with her chaplains to poison Charles. Like the rest of the plot, this was plainly nonsense, but the danger to Catherine was real and, at the height of the crisis, her brother sent an ambassador to bring her safely back to Portugal, something that Catherine refused to countenance. Many people in England, Oates among them, were surprised that Charles did not leap at this opportunity to rid himself of his barren wife, but he resolutely refused to take any action against Catherine, publicly declaring her innocence. The danger was defused somewhat in July 1679 when Sir George Wakeman was tried and acquitted of any involvement. However, the shadow of the plot hung over Catherine for some time, and she was grateful for Charles's show of support.

In spite of the difficulties in the early years of their marriage, by the time of the Popish Plot, Charles and Catherine were genuinely fond of each other, and they lived comfortably together until Charles's death. On 2 February 1685, Charles suffered a stroke. According to Evelyn, Catherine was much on Charles's mind as he lay dying, and he sent a message to her in which 'he entreated the queen to pardon him (not without cause); who a little before had sent a Bishop to excuse her not more frequently visiting him, in regard of her excessive grief. And withal that his Majesty would forgive it if at any time she had offended him.' Charles asked his brother to be good to his illegitimate children and his mistresses, asking that 'Nelly [Gwynne] might not starve'. Catherine was too distraught to visit Charles, but she was aware of everything that was going on. The French ambassador's account records that Charles's mistress, Louise de Kerouaille, Duchess of Portsmouth, took him aside and informed him that Charles was truly a Catholic. The ambassador went immediately to the Duke of York, who confirmed this was true, and they resolved to bring a priest to Charles. None of Catherine's chaplains spoke English, but she took the precaution of bringing Father

Huddlestone, the only English Catholic priest officially allowed to live in the kingdom, to her chapel. He was summoned in great secrecy, and Charles converted to Catholicism shortly before his death. This pleased Catherine, but she was not with Charles when he died on 6 February 1685.

Catherine was devastated by Charles's death and immediately plunged her household into mourning. Soon afterwards she retired to Somerset House, where she spent long hours at prayer. She had never been happy in England and, almost immediately, requested an escort from James II to take her back to Portugal. Whilst this was granted, ill health forced her to remain in England, and she was still present at Somerset House when James was deposed in 1688 and replaced by his Protestant daughter, Mary II, and her husband, William III. William and Mary were less favourable to Catherine than James had been, and she immediately renewed her request to return to Portugal. This was finally granted in March 1692, and Catherine crossed the Channel, landing at Dieppe. She then made her way slowly overland to Lisbon.

Catherine received a rapturous reception in Portugal and, in 1704, was surprised to find herself appointed to act as regent of Portugal for her brother, Pedro II, due to his ill health. She acquitted herself well in this new role, winning a number of important victories over Spain. By the time of her appointment as regent, she was already elderly, and her health was frail. She remained in control until the end, dying suddenly, on 31 December 1705, whilst still the official ruler of her native land.

Catherine of Braganza suffered both humiliation and disappointment in her marriage, and politically, she was a nonentity in England. In spite of this, she developed a fond relationship with her husband, and she was loved in her own country. She was also loved by many who knew her personally, and her closest friend in England was her sister-in-law, Anne Hyde, who, whilst never queen of England, enjoyed as turbulent a marriage as Catherine's own.

ANNE HYDE (1638-71) was never queen of England. She had the most unlikely background of any king's wife, and at the time of her birth, her father, Sir Edward Hyde, was a lawyer in the service of the King. Edward Hyde came from a prominent gentry family in Wiltshire, and he married well, making his second marriage in 1632 to Frances Aylesbury, the daughter of the Master of the Mint. Anne was the family's eldest child, and in her early childhood, she was close to her father, with him later commenting that 'he had always had a great affection for her; and she, being his eldest child, he had more acquaintance with her than with any of his children'. Anne's father remained loyal to Charles I throughout the Civil War and, in 1646, left England for what would prove a fourteen year exile, going first to Jersey with Charles, Prince of Wales, before eventually travelling to France and then the Netherlands. Anne, her mother and younger siblings remained in England during the first part of Hyde's exile before joining him on the Continent.

Hyde was appointed as Charles II's chancellor during the exile in France. Anne also became something of a favourite of Charles II's aunt, Elizabeth of Bohemia, who was living in the Netherlands. In 1654, it was suggested that Anne should become a maid to Charles's eldest sister, Mary, Princess of Orange, and Elizabeth of Bohemia wrote approvingly that 'I heare Mrs Hide is to come to my Neece in Mrs Killegrews place, which I am verie glad of, she is verie fit for itt and a great faourit of mine'. Mary of Orange was eager to secure Anne's services, and whilst Hyde was against the appointment, fearing for his daughter's honour at court, his wife pushed him to accept. Anne was uncertain about the appointment, and on 19 October 1654, she wrote to her father stating that she would cheerfully submit to a life that she did not much desire, but that she was anxious about leaving her parents. As it happened, Anne had her mother with her, at least at first, and Elizabeth of Bohemia was soon able to send a message to Hyde to inform him that 'his ladie and my faourit his daughter came hither upon Saterday, and are gone this day to Teiling. I find my faourit growen euerie way to her aduantage'.

Anne was no beauty and the diarist Samuel Pepys, for one, considered her 'a plain woman, and like her mother, my lady Chancellor'. Another contemporary, Hamilton, recorded that she 'had a majestic air, a pretty good shape, not much beauty, a great deal of wit, and so just a discernment of merit, that, whoever of either sex was possessed of it, were sure to be distinguished by her: an air of grandeur in all her actions made her to be considered as if born to support the rank which placed her so near the throne'.

The company was somewhat limited in the Netherlands, and Anne stood out, with Elizabeth of Bohemia commenting approvingly that at a court masque Anne, who appeared dressed as a shepherdess, 'was verie handsome in it' and second only to the Princess of Orange in appearance. Anne certainly made an impression on the Princess of Orange's brother, James, Duke of York, when they met in February 1656 when the Princess brought her court to Paris to visit her mother, Henrietta Maria. James went out to meet his sister on her approach to Paris, and in his memoirs, he later commented that 'it was there that the Prince for the first time saw Mistress Hyde maid of honour to the Princess his sister, and whom he afterwards married'. James was notorious for his womanising, but Anne, who was highly intelligent, refused his advances. The couple finally consummated their relationship when James promised before witnesses to marry her, creating a binding union in the eyes of the Church. Anne was pregnant by the time Charles II was restored to the throne and, keeping her secret, returned with her parents to London.

James, Duke of York, was the second surviving son of Charles I and Henrietta Maria and was five years older than Anne. After escaping from England in 1648, he had spent much of his time on the Continent serving in the French army. Desperate to make Anne his mistress, he did not think through the consequences of his actions, but with Anne's advancing pregnancy, the gravity of the situation hit him. James was not the only one to panic, and according to Elizabeth of Bohemia, there were rumours that Anne had taken a potion to try to induce an abortion whilst still in the Netherlands. This was unsuccessful, and once in London, she called upon James to publicly acknowledge their betrothal, declaring that 'she was his wife, and would have it known that she was so, let him use her afterwards as he pleased'.

Whilst in the Netherlands, James had been happy in his relationship with Anne. However, according to Hamilton, his feelings changed following the restoration:

When he saw himself enjoying a rank which placed him so near the throne; when the possession of Miss Hyde affirmed him no new charms; when England, so abounding in beauties, displayed all that was charming and lovely in the court of the king his brother; and when he considered he was the only prince, who, from such superior elevation, had descended so low, he began to reflect upon it. On the one hand, his marriage appeared to him particularly ill suited in every respect.

Aware of his dignity as the heir to the throne, James was anxious to rid himself of Anne, and he stole the written evidence of the match that she had kept. More damagingly, his friend, Lord Falmouth, obtained the testimonies of four men who were prepared to swear that they had had love affairs with Anne. Once he had spoken to the men himself, James went to speak to his brother, the King. Charles, who was fond of Anne's father and would later create him Earl of Clarendon, was anxious not to offend his chief minister. According to Bishop Burnet, the King told his brother bluntly that 'he must drink as he brewed, and live with her whom he had made his wife'.

198. St James's Palace, London, the arrival of Queen Mary de Medici to visit her daughter, Henrietta Maria.

Left: 199. Charles II by Pieter Nason.

Centre: 200. Lord Mayor's Day 1683 by John Griffier.

Bottom: 201. The Fire of London, 1666, by Lieven Verschuur.

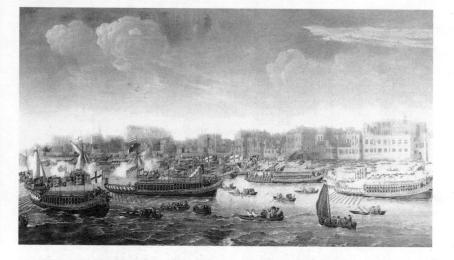

Above: 202. Coronation procession of Mary of Modena, Queen of James II.

Below: 203. Coronation in Westminster Abbey on 23 April 1685 of James II and Mary of Modena.

The Queen's Addres'd, and by new Senate told,
They'll Act with more Obedience than Her old.

Above: 204. Coronation in Westminster Abbey on 11 April 1689 of William III and Mary II, from a contemporary ballad, *c.* 1689. They were crowned together by Henry Compton, the Bishop of London. The crowning was normally the duty of the Archbishop of Canterbury, but the Archbishop at the time, William Sancroft, refused to recognise the removal of James II.

Left: 205. Contemporary depiction of Queen Anne, who ascended the throne in 1702.

Anne was fortunate in her husband, and whilst he at first sought to find a way out of the marriage, according to Hamilton, he was 'a scrupulous observer of the rules of duty and the laws of justice', and his conscience eventually got the better of him. Rather than publicly dishonour Anne, 'his morality and justice struggling for some time with prejudice, had at last triumphed, by his acknowledging for his wife Miss Hyde'. Once he had secured his brother's consent, James went in person to Anne's parents to inform them of what had happened. In spite of Anne's advancing pregnancy, her father was oblivious to all that had happened and was furious when he heard the news. In his anger, he declared that he would rather Anne was James's whore than his wife and said that, by rights, she ought to be sent to the Tower and beheaded for treason for daring to marry a member of the royal family. He then ordered that she keep to her room, but there was nothing he could do to prevent the match, and on 3 September 1660, the couple were privately married. Anne gave birth to a son, Charles, Duke of Cambridge, the following month.

As soon as her marriage was publicly known, Anne began to live as Duchess of York. According to Bishop Burnet, she 'soon understood what belonged to a princess; and took state on her rather too much'. This was a common criticism of the new duchess, and Pepys also commented on Anne's pride, calling her the 'proudest woman in the world'. Neither Anne nor James were able to live within their means, and by 1667, their annual expenditure exceeded their income by over £20,000, a vast sum. Anne received the blame for this bad management, and it was recognised at court that she was the dominant party in the marriage, with Pepys claiming 'that the duke of York, in all things, but in his amours, is led by the nose by his wife'.

Whilst Anne had a great deal of influence over James, she was unable to ensure that he was faithful to her, and within weeks of the wedding on 14 October, Pepys recorded that, at Whitehall, 'I also observed, how the Duke of York and Mrs Palmer did talk to one another very wantonly through the hangings that part the king's closet and the closet where the ladies sit'. Anne was furious at James's infidelities, and when, in November 1662, he was noted to be openly courting Lady Chesterfield, she complained to the King and her father, causing Lady Chesterfield to be sent away. James was furious, and in January 1663, Pepys commented that he had heard that Anne was 'very troublesome to him by her jealousy'. James was spectacularly unfaithful throughout his marriage, and in 1665, Anne began flirtations with Henry Sidney, the younger son of the Earl of Leicester, and Harry Saville, one of James's grooms of the bedchamber. The flirtation with Sidney proved the more serious, and Anne persuaded James to appoint him as her master of horse. It seems improbable that Anne ever consummated her relationships with her admirers, and given the dynastic importance of her children, it is very unlikely that she would have risked jeopardising their position. Anne wanted to make James jealous, and as a result of her actions, he secured Sidney's banishment from court in January 1666 and stopped speaking to her for several days. James continued to be unfaithful and, by the end of 1666, was involved with Lady Denham.

As well as her flirtations with Sidney and Saville, Anne also showed her frustration at James's behaviour in other ways, such as channelling her energies into eating, on which Hamilton commented:

The duchess of York was one of the highest feeders in England; as this was an unforbidden pleasure, she indulged herself in it, as an indemnification for other self-denials. It was really an edifying sight to see her at table. The duke, on the contrary, being incessantly in the hurry of new fancies, exhausted himself by his inconstancy, and was gradually wasting away; while the poor princess, gratifying her good appetite, grew so fat and plump, that it was a blessing to see her.

Frequent childbearing also did nothing to help Anne's figure, and she rapidly became enormous.

Anne and James's first son was born within weeks of their marriage, and whilst publicly acknowledged as legitimate, there was doubt about his status. According to Pepys, this difficulty was soon solved, and he wrote, on 6 May 1661, 'I hear to-night that the Duke of York's son is this day dead, which, I believe, will please everybody; and I hear that the duke and his lady are not much troubled by it.' Anne did not have a close relationship with any of her children, and both she and James reasoned that she would soon bear a second, unquestionably legitimate son. In April 1662, she gave birth to a second child, Mary. James, Duke of Cambridge, arrived in July 1663, followed by a second daughter, Anne, in 1665. A third son, Charles, Duke of Kendal, was born in 1666, although tragedy struck the following year when both Anne's young sons died within a month of each other. By the late 1660s, it had become obvious that Catherine of Braganza was unlikely to bear a child and that Anne's children were the future of the dynasty. It was, therefore, with rejoicing that, in September 1667, she bore her youngest son, Edgar, Duke of Cambridge, who seemed more likely to live than his brothers. Two further daughters followed in 1669 and 1671 respectively, neither of whom lived long.

Anne's marriage caused trouble for her father, Pepys commenting about him in 1667:

> The duke of York's marriage with her hath undone the kingdom, by making the Chancellor so great above reach, who otherwise would have been but an ordinary man, to have been dealt with by other people; and he would have been careful of managing things well, for fear of being called to account; whereas, now he is secure, and hath let things run to rack, as they now appear.

Anne's father was, in fact, very far from secure, and by 1664, there were rumours that he had selected Catherine of Braganza as a bride for the King either with the knowledge that she was incapable of bearing children or after arranging for her to be given a potion that would render her infertile and ensure that his own grandchildren succeeded. This was obviously nonsense, but by 1667, he was deeply unpopular, and in November of that year, he was impeached by parliament and forced to flee to France. Anne never saw her father again and, whilst they had once been close, they became estranged in the final years of Anne's life due to her religious interests.

Anne failed to recover from the birth of her youngest son, Edgar, in 1667, and over the next few years, she became increasingly unwell. With her illness, she turned to religion. During their years of exile before the restoration, both Anne and James had come into contact with the Roman Catholic Church. Burnet records that, from the last months of 1669, it began to be noticed that Anne refused to receive the sacrament in church and that she disputed with the Protestant clergy about the Roman Catholic faith, expressing an admiration for clergy who remained unmarried. Anne's confessor questioned her on this and later reported that 'he had spoken plainly to her about it, and told her what inferences were made upon it. She pretended ill health and business; but protested to him, she had no scruples with relation to her religion, and was still of the Church of England; and assured him, that no popish priest had ever taken the confidence to speak to her of those matters.'

Anne promised that she would speak to her confessor if she ever did have any concerns about her religion, but she and James had already converted to Catholicism. Both remained committed to their new faith, with Anne writing a paper setting out the reason for her conversion, which was published after her death.

Anne's health continued to steadily decline after 1667, and whilst she continued to endure annual pregnancies, it was clear that she did not have long to live. She suffered from breast cancer and, in March 1671, shortly after bearing her youngest child, she collapsed suddenly. Anne had always been friendly with Catherine of Braganza, and the Queen sat with her, ensuring that Anne's Protestant chaplain, who was with her, did not begin any Protestant ceremonies. At length, he told Anne that 'he hoped she continued still in the truth: upon which she asked, what is truth: and then, her agony increasing, she repeated the word truth, truth, often'. James was with Anne when she died, and as she slowly expired, she whispered 'duke, duke, death is terrible, death is very terrible', before passing away on 31 March 1671.

Anne Hyde was not loved in England, and her death was very little lamented. Her only surviving son, Edgar, died soon after his mother, leaving only Anne's two daughters – Mary and Anne – to continue the Stuart dynasty in England. The death of Edgar and the continuing infertility of Catherine of Braganza made it a certainty that James would marry again. Anne's younger daughter later commented that she could not remember what her mother looked like and it was James's second wife, Mary of Modena, who tried to fill something of the gap left by Anne Hyde.

MARY OF MODENA (1658-1718) was the second wife of James II. She was the only daughter of Alphonso IV, Duke of Modena, and his wife, Laura Martinozzi. Mary's father died whilst she was still young, and her mother was appointed as regent of the Italian duchy for her son. James, Duke of York, began to look for a new wife in 1672, a year after Anne Hyde's death, and as a convert to Catholicism, he sought a Catholic bride. Mary's mother first offered her twenty-nine-year-old sister-in-law, Leonora, but on further enquiries from the English, she was forced to admit that her own fourteen-year-old daughter was also available. James sent his friend, the Earl of Peterborough, to Modena to discuss a possible match with either Mary or Leonora, and the earl was taken with the younger princess, writing approvingly to his master:

> The Princess Mary of Este appear'd to be at this time about fourteen years of age; she was tall, and admirably shaped, her complexion was of the last fairness, her hair black as jet, so were her eyebrows and her eyes; but the latter so full of light and sweetness so they did dazzle and charm too. There seemed given unto them from nature, Sovereign Power; power to kill and power to save; and in the whole turn of her face, which was of the most graceful oval that could be framed, there was all the features, all the beauty, and all that could be great and charming in any humane creature.

James was smitten and asked for her hand in marriage. As well as beauty, Mary had received an excellent education and was particularly good at languages. As a kinswoman of Cardinal Mazarin, she was pious, something that suited James, although she caused consternation when, on being informed of her marriage, she insisted that she intended to become a nun.

Mary's decision threw James's embassy into confusion, and her mother, who was herself a pious woman, insisted that she had no intention of forcing her daughter to abandon her scruples. The marriage was looked upon as important in Italy as well as in England, and Pope Clement X, who hoped that James would be the man to bring England back to the Catholic Church, was anxious that it should go ahead, taking the unprecedented step of writing personally to Mary on 19 September 1673 and declaring that 'considering, in effect, the influence of your virtues, we easily conceived a firm hope that an end might come to the persecution still smouldering in that kingdom and that the orthodox faith, reinstated by you in a place of honour might recover the splendour and security of former days'. The Pope continued, speaking of the anxiety he felt at Mary's repugnance for marriage and effectively appointing her as a missionary for her faith in England. In the face of papal pressure, Mary had no choice but to capitulate, and she and James were married by proxy on 30 September 1673. Whilst Mary had submitted, she was still filled with anxiety at the prospect of travelling to a distant land and meeting a husband who was well over twice her age. She therefore insisted that her mother accompany her to England, and she set off on 5 October 1673, her fifteenth birthday, weeping as she left her homeland.

Whilst the marriage to a Catholic princess was personally satisfying to James, in England it caused a great deal of controversy, and parliament petitioned the King before Mary arrived, asking him to break off his brother's marriage and send the bride home. Charles II absolutely refused to countenance this, but he was unable to silence the mutterings, and it was to a muted reception at Dover that Mary arrived on 1 December. James waited for Mary as her yacht landed, and he was immediately taken with his young bride, conducting her to a house where the couple were formally married. Mary was terrified, but she was glad to find her new husband kind, and gradually, the couple fell in love. In January, she wrote to her friend, the mother superior of the Visitation at Modena, that, whilst she would not have chosen marriage if she had been at liberty,

> may it be a consolation to you, dear mother, to know (and I say it to the glory of God) that the Duke is a very good man and wishes me well and would do anything to prove it to me; he is so firm and steady in our holy religion (which as a good Catholic he professes) that he would not leave it for any thing in the world and in my affliction (which is increased by the departure of my dear Mama) this is my consolation.

Mary was received favourably at court, with Charles II commenting that his brother had done well in his marriage. She soon became close to her two stepdaughters, Mary and Anne, although, given the tiny age gap between them, she was always more of a sister than a mother to them.

Mary found that she enjoyed many of the pleasures available in England, and in 1675, for example, her friend Lady Bellasyse commented that she had visited a fair incognito. On Christmas Day the following year, the same friend recorded that 'the Dutchesse is much delighted with making and throwing of snow balls and pelted the D[uke] soundly with one the other day and ran away quick into her closet and he after her, but she durst not open the doore. She hath also much pleasure in one of those sledges which they call *Trainias*, and is pulled up and downe the ponds in them every day'. Mary enjoyed playing cards, although she was less happy when she lost, with the diarist John Evelyn commenting one evening that 'I observed that she was exceedingly concerned for the loss of £80'.

Whilst she was interested in pleasures and other diversions, Mary knew that her primary purpose was to bear a son. She fell pregnant within months of her marriage, and on 20 January 1675, shortly after dining with her two stepdaughters, she went into premature labour, bearing a daughter, Catherine Laura. The baby initially thrived, but in October 1675, she suddenly died, proving to be the first tragedy of many in Mary's difficult childbearing record. On 7 September 1676, Mary bore a second daughter, Isabel, who was again born so quickly that none of the required witnesses to the birth were able to get there in time. Once again, Mary was pleased with her daughter, who lived until the age of four. On 7 November 1677, only three days after her eldest stepdaughter's wedding, Mary, to the joy of nearly everyone, bore a son, who was given the name of Charles, Duke of Cambridge. Disaster struck in December, when Mary's younger stepdaughter Anne, who had been ill with smallpox, rushed to see her baby brother as soon as she was well enough. The princess was still infectious and passed the illness on to Mary's son, who died soon afterwards. Mary was grief-stricken at the loss of her child and wrote a despondent letter to her brother:

> With my eyes full of tears I write to give you the ill news of the loss of my dear son, whom it pleased God to take unto Himself yesterday: at mid-day. You can imagine in what affliction I am, and great as was my joy when he was born, so much the greater is my anguish at his loss, but we must have patience, God knows what He does; may His holy will be done. I should have been too happy if this child had escaped. I am well in health, and should be very well if this affliction had not befallen me. This is the first day I am capable of writing, not having written even to our lady mother before to-day.

Mary caused consternation in England when, soon afterwards, she declared that she had had a vision where Lady Frances Villiers, the Protestant governess of all James's children and the person who had passed smallpox on to Anne before dying of the disease, had appeared to her from Hell. Whilst personally popular in England herself, Mary spent much of her time as Duchess of York either in Scotland or on the Continent, as her husband was forced to leave the country due to distrust of his religion in England. Mary bore a further two daughters during Charles II's lifetime, but neither lived longer than a few months.

By the time of her arrival in England, Mary knew that it was a near certainty that James would one day become king, and with the death of Charles II on 6 February 1685, he took the throne as James II. He was the first openly Catholic sovereign since Mary I, and he was determined to assist the Catholics in England, hearing Mass openly with Mary at St James's Palace on the Sunday after his accession. James's accession was popular, and at their coronation in April, the couple were greeted by cheering crowds. He was also victorious later in the year against Charles's illegitimate son, the Duke of Monmouth, who claimed the crown in preference to his uncle. James saw this as a sign that he could more openly promote his religion and, against Mary's own advice, set about promoting Catholics, seeking a cardinal's hat for a particularly controversial Jesuit, Father Petre. As James himself recorded, in his memoirs, which are written in the third person, none of his measures in support of his religion were popular in England:

> It was impossible for the king to do the least thing in favour of Religion, which did not give disquiet, notwithstanding all his precautions not to break in upon his engagement; and that the liberties he permitted to Catholicks should no ways interfere with the possessions, priviledges, and immunities of the Church of England; however the kingdom was so generall prepossess'd that the king's intentions were otherwise, that nothing appear'd indifferent to them in that matter.

In the absence of surviving children by Mary, James's heir was his eldest daughter by Anne Hyde, who had been raised a Protestant and was married to his Protestant nephew, William of Orange. The people of England were prepared to tolerate a Catholic king for the duration of one lifetime, but when, at the end of 1687, it was publicly announced that Mary was pregnant, the prospect that she and James might found a Catholic dynasty filled both William of Orange and the majority of the people in England with dread.

James had never been on friendly terms with his nephew and son-in-law William of Orange, and he had been deeply opposed to his daughter's marriage. William had always hoped that his marriage would bring him the crown of England, and he was involved in attempts to suggest that Mary of Modena's pregnancy in 1682, which had resulted in the birth of a daughter, had been faked. As soon as Mary's next pregnancy was announced at the end of 1687, the rumours once again surfaced, with claims that, at twenty-nine, Mary was past childbearing age and that she was pretending to be pregnant in order to frustrate the Protestant succession of James's daughters. Mary had always been kind to her two stepdaughters but, whilst she was particularly friendly with her elder stepdaughter in the Netherlands, her relationship with Anne was more difficult, with the younger princess writing to her sister in May 1687:

> The Queen, you must know, is of a very proud and haughty humour; and though she pretends to hate all form and ceremony, yet one sees that those that make their court this way, are very well thought of. She declares always that she loves sincerity and hates flattery, but when the grossest flattery in the world is said to her face, she seems extremely well pleased with it. It really is enough to turn one's stomach to hear what things are said to her of this kind, and to see how mightily she is satisfied with it.

Mary's elder stepdaughter, Mary of Orange, was childless, and Anne had always been confident that she would eventually inherit the throne. With the prospect that she might be marginalised by a half-brother, she threw in her lot with William of Orange, and when James II requested that Anne attend the birth of Mary's child, she refused, insisting on travelling to Bath for her health.

James and Mary were disappointed in Anne's failure to attend the birth, but they ensured that there would be a large number of witnesses present, as was required at all royal births, and when Mary went into labour, on 10 June 1688, there were forty-two people present in the room, including Catherine of Braganza, Mary's ladies, and much of the privy council. As with all her labours, the birth was quick, and Mary bore a son who was named James Francis Edward and proclaimed Prince of Wales. Both Mary and James were overjoyed, but they quickly became aware that the rumours surrounding Mary's pregnancy had intensified. Princess Anne was one of the main rumourmongers, and she planted doubts about the birth in her elder sister's mind, as in this letter:

> My dear sister can't imagine the concern and vexation I have been in, that I should be so unfortunate to be out of town when the Queen was brought to bed, for I shall never now be satisfied whether the child be true or false. It may be it is our brother, but God only knows, for she never took care to satisfy the world, or give people any demonstration of it.

Anne continued, complaining that she had never been permitted to feel the child kick before it was born, something that both James and Mary vehemently denied, finishing with this comment:

> The thing which to me seems the plainest thing in the world, is her being brought to bed two days after she heard of my coming to town [i.e. about to return to London], and saying that the child was come at the full time, when everybody knows, by her own reckoning, that she should have gone a month longer. After all this, 'tis possible it may be her child; but where one believes it, a thousand do not. For my part, expect they do give very plain demonstrations, which is almost impossible now, I shall ever be of the number of unbelievers.

Anne was not the only one to claim that the birth was suspicious, and there were rumours that the baby had been smuggled into Mary's bed in a warming pan. There is no doubt that the prince was the son of James and Mary, and his resemblance to his mother was later commented upon by John Evelyn and others. In spite of this, the rumours were extremely damaging, and James was obliged to hold an enquiry, taking witness statements from all those who had been present at the birth. The child was a great inconvenience to both Mary's stepdaughters and to William of Orange, and Anne summed up their hopes when, in a letter to her sister in July, she commented that the prince was ill, 'and if he has been as bad as some people say, I believe it will not be long before he is an Angel in Heaven'. Mary of Orange pointedly omitted prayers for her brother in her chapel, claiming forgetfulness when her father challenged her.

William of Orange had no plans to see his wife's place in the succession taken by her infant half-brother, and by the summer of 1688, there were rumours that he was preparing a fleet with which to invade England. In late June, William received an invitation from a number of leading men in England, including the Bishop of London, asking him to liberate the country from its Catholic king. By 17 August, Mary was aware of this hostility, and she sent a hurt letter to her elder stepdaughter, who she had always viewed as her closest friend, complaining that Mary of Orange was indifferent to her new brother and did not wish him well. By September, both James and Mary knew that William would soon arrive, and James began to make preparations for the defence of his crown. By October, William was ready with a fleet of 300 ships, and he landed at Torbay on 15 November, quickly attracting local support. William carried a flag with English colours and bearing the motto 'The Protestant Religion and Liberties of England'. To much of the population, he was the saviour of the Church of England, and even as James and his army marched to confront him, his soldiers began to desert, with Anne's husband, George of Denmark, one of the first to flee. Unable to go further, James returned to London on 26 November to find that Anne had also abandoned him, leaving her house in secret one night. According to James's own report, Anne's conduct only served to inflame the situation:

> Her Nurs and my Lady Clarendon run about like people out of their sences, crying out, the Papists had murther'd her; and when they met any of the queen's servants, asked them what they had done with the Princess; which, considering the ferment people were in, and how susceptible they were to any ill impression against the queen, might have made her been torn to pieces by the rabble.

Anne soon turned up safe and sound in Oxford, where she had rejoined her husband and thrown her support firmly behind her brother-in-law.

As the son of the executed Charles I, James believed that William's invasion would end with his death, and in a panic, he made preparations for Mary's escape to France with their son, the details of which are recorded in his memoirs:

> [Mary] had a great reluctance to this journey not so much for the hazards and inconveniences of it as to leave the king in so doubtfull a situation; she haveing never done it hitherto in his greatest difficulties and dangers: and therefore when it was first proposed, her Majesty absolutely refused it in reference to herself; telling the king she was very willing the Prince her son should be sent to France, or where it was thought most proper for his security, that she could bear such a separation with patience, but could never endure it in reference to himself; that she would infinitely rather run his fortune whatever it should prove than abandon him in that distress.

Mary was finally persuaded when James promised that he would follow her within days, and at 2 a.m. on 10 December, she left Whitehall secretly with her son, accompanied by only two attendants and dressed as a servant. A carriage was waiting for them at the garden gate. The party drove through London unnoticed before transferring into a boat on the Thames. The journey must have been an ordeal, and according to Francesco Riva, one of Mary's attendants, the night was so dark that, as they sat huddled together, they could see nothing. Miraculously, the infant prince remained silent throughout the journey, and they were able to land, coming to an inn where a coach was waiting for them. They travelled to Gravesend and boarded a yacht, reaching Calais at 9 a.m. the next day.

As soon as she arrived, Mary wrote to James's cousin, Louis XIV, notifying him of her arrival and requesting his aid:

> Sire, a poor fugitive queen, bathed in tears, has not feared to brave the perils of the sea, to seek consolation and refuge from the greatest king and most generous monarch in the world. Her ill-fortune has procured her a happiness which the most distant nations have ambitioned. Necessity does not lessen it; since she has made the choice and with singular esteem desires to confide to him her most precious possession in the person of her son, the Prince of Wales, who is as yet too young to share her gratitude. It lies entirely in my heart, and it is a pleasure to me, in the midst of all my grief, to come under the shadow of your protection.

Louis offered Mary sanctuary, and when James joined her on 4 January 1689, having abandoned his kingdom, the couple moved to Paris and were granted the palace at St Germains where Henrietta Maria had previously lived. Mary's flight to France heralded thirty years of exile for her, and soon after James had joined her, the couple learned that William of Orange and his wife had accepted the English throne jointly as William III and Mary II. This was a major blow to James, and he never forgot the treachery of his daughters, going to Ireland in early 1689 in an attempt to reclaim his crown from there. In early 1692, it became clear that Mary was pregnant, and seeking to prove the truth of his son's birth, James sent messages to his eldest daughter and the English council, inviting them to come and witness the birth themselves. In the event, no one came, and Mary bore her youngest child, a daughter named Louise Marie, later that year. James always called his youngest child his consolation in exile.

James never gave up his attempts to regain his throne but met with little success, and on 4 March 1701, whilst attending Mass at St Germains, he suffered a seizure. He continued in ill health throughout the year and, in July, suffered a second stroke, which left his right side paralysed. He suffered a further stroke in chapel on 2 September 1701 and was left bedridden, with Mary staying, weeping, by his side. James had become increasingly pious as he aged and was regarded by many as a living saint. As he lay dying, he forgave his enemies, specifically naming both his elder daughters and William of Orange. He then commended his youngest children to Mary before dying at 3 p.m. on 16 September 1701.

Mary was inconsolable and retired to a convent for a time before emerging to assist her son, who had been proclaimed King James III in France, and was later remembered as the Old Pretender in England. The younger James's struggle to regain the crown proved as fruitless as his father's, and Mary was never able to return to England. In 1712, she suffered further grief when her daughter died of smallpox, and later that year, her son was expelled from France after the French king made a peace treaty with England. Mary remained living quietly at St Germains in increasingly ill health, and she died there on 7 May 1718.

Mary of Modena was queen of England for only a few short, troubled years, and whilst she found personal happiness with her husband and children, her life was blighted by the loss of her husband's crown. Mary's eldest stepdaughter, Mary II, who caused her father so much grief by her involvement in the invasion that ousted him, survived his flight by only six years, but for a few short years, she was England's third effective queen regnant.

MARY II (1662-94) was the eldest daughter of James II and Anne Hyde. She was born following the death of her eldest brother, Charles, Duke of Cambridge, and her sex was a disappointment. On the day after Mary's birth on 30 April 1662, Samuel Pepys commented that 'the duchess of York is brought to bed of a girle, at which I find nobody pleased'. In spite of this, Mary, who was the only one of her parents' children to be born healthy, was her father's favourite. When she was two, Pepys commented that, when he visited James, he 'saw him with great pleasure play with his little girle, like an ordinary private father of a child'. Mary was precocious, and in 1669, the diarist was again permitted to see her, commenting that 'I did see the young Duchess [Mary] a little child in hanging sleeves, dance most finely, so as almost to ravish me'. Mary always loved to dance, and she was taught by the same French dancing master who had taught her father and his siblings, as well as her grandmother, Queen Henrietta Maria.

Following Anne Hyde's death and the publication of James's conversion to Catholicism, Mary and her sister Anne were taken by the King to be raised away from their father in order to ensure that they retained their Protestant faith. This rankled with James, but there was little he could do, and the sisters, who received only a very limited education, were firmly schooled in the doctrine of the Church of England. Isolated from their family, the sisters looked for affection wherever they could find it, and shortly after her mother's death, Mary began to pour out all her love and affection to Frances Apsley, a girl five years older than her who had shared some of her lessons. Mary's correspondence with Frances endured until well into Mary's marriage, and it is clear that the princess had a schoolgirl crush on the older girl, writing as a wife to her 'dear husband'. In one early letter, she wrote, 'I have dear husband bestoed a new croe quil pen upon this letter which I did promise should be so full of secrets and so long,' before adding that 'I hope you will not show it mean my letter to any body but I think you never doe and so I may trust you as I doe and have done and shall doe ever while I am allife and am your friand and loving wife'. Mary's letters to Frances were full of extravagant expressions of love for her friend, with Mary in a later letter declaring,

> Two leters already you have had today dear Aurelia from me I hope you wil read the third tho you I suppose are tired with them now I hope my pardon is sealed by you dear dear dear dear Aurelia I may if I can tel you how much I love you but I hope that is not douted I have given you proves anufe if not I wil die to satisfie you dear dear husband if al my hares were lives I wold lose them al twenty times over to sarve or satisfie you in any doute of my love.

She finished, writing, 'I do love you I love you with a heart intire I am for you all one desire I love you with a flame more lasting then the vestals fire thou art my life my soul my al.' Frances's replies do not survive, but she must have responded in a tone loving enough to please Mary. It is unlikely that Mary had any romantic interest in Frances, but she was devoted to her, and she was irked when her sister also began writing to Frances, declaring her own love for the girl.

By the late 1660s, it had become clear that the Queen, Catherine of Braganza, was unlikely to bear a child, and with the deaths of their brothers and their stepmother's failure to produce an heir, Mary and Anne became politically very important. The sisters were closely observed when they made their court debuts on 15 December 1674, when they acted in a comedy performed by a number of court ladies. According to John Evelyn, the performance was a success, and it was repeated a week later with the leading participants again loaded down with jewels. Mrs Blagg, the lady given the principal part, wore £70,000 worth of jewels in her costume, an astronomical sum, although the evening was marred somewhat when she lost a gem worth £80, forcing the Duke of York to pay the sum to the gem's outraged owner, the Countess of Suffolk. Once Mary had been formally established at court, both her father and uncle began to look around for a husband for her.

William, Prince of Orange, visited England in November 1670 to see his uncle, Charles II, and it is possible that Mary may have seen him for the first time then, although the prince is unlikely to have made any impression on her. According to John Evelyn, William was favourably received in England and 'he has a manly, courageous, wise countenance, resembling his mother and the Duke of Gloucester, both deceased'. The prince was the son of Charles I's eldest daughter, Mary, Princess of Orange, who Mary II was named after, and the pair were first cousins. William, a posthumous child, had been prince of Orange since his birth, and by the late 1670s, he had a reputation as a military commander of some note. In spite of this and Evelyn's praise of his appearance, in reality, William cut a rather unprepossessing figure. In contrast to his two Stuart uncles, he was of only average height and was asthmatic with a large hooked nose. His preference for wearing plain, dark clothing also made him seem dowdy. He was, however, staunchly Protestant, and when the possibility of his marriage to Mary was first raised, early in 1677, he was looked upon very favourably in England.

Before he would commit to the marriage, William insisted that he wanted to see Mary for himself, and a visit was arranged. William was pleased with what he saw, commenting on both her beauty and good manners. Mary was renowned as a beauty, and at nearly six foot tall, towered above her suitor, resembling the famously beautiful Mary, Queen of Scots, in appearance. William asked for Mary's hand, and Charles willingly gave it, forcing his brother, James, who hated his Protestant nephew, to consent to the match. It was left to James to break the news to Mary, and he did so on 21 October 1677, apparently with such bad grace that he terrified his fifteen-year-old daughter. On hearing that she was to marry, Mary wept hysterically for two days, but there was nothing that she could do except sulk as she awaited her wedding.

William and Mary were married at 9 p.m. on 4 November 1677. With a weeping bride, the ceremony was a gloomy affair, and the King attempted to lighten the mood by first pointing to Mary's stepmother, the heavily pregnant Mary of Modena, and bidding the bishop to make haste in case she was delivered of a son before it was concluded. When, as part of the ceremony, William promised to endow Mary with all his worldly goods and placed some gold coins on the altar, Charles again made a joke, laughing 'put those in your pocket, niece, it's all clear gain'. William, who disliked both his English uncles, resented this intrusion. It was certainly pertinent that Charles commented that the birth of a son to Mary of Modena might scupper the marriage, and when she did, indeed, bear James a son a few days later, William was furious that Mary had lost place in the succession. He was also, by that stage, thoroughly annoyed with the whole business, and Mary spent the days following the marriage weeping, with even William's wedding present of £40,000 of jewels failing to pacify her. When Catherine of Braganza, seeking to comfort her niece, told her that she had also had to leave her homeland for marriage, Mary hysterically retorted, 'But you, madam, were coming to England, and I am leaving it!' As the Princess of Orange, Mary had no choice but to travel to the Netherlands with her husband, sailing on 28 November 1677 and landing the following day.

In spite of her terror at leaving England, Mary made an impression in Holland and immediately became very popular. She soon settled into life as Princess of Orange and found, to her surprise, that she liked the country. Away from her family and friends, Mary rapidly fell deeply in love with William, finding herself heartbroken when, early in 1678, he left her to rejoin his army. On 3 March 1678, Mary wrote a letter to Frances Apsley demonstrating that her husband had fully supplanted Frances in her heart:

> I suppose you know the prince is gone to the army but I am sure you can geuse at the troble I am in I am sure I could never have thought it half so much I thought coming out of my own country parting with my friands and relations the greatest that ever could as long as thay lived happen to me but I am to be mistaken that now I find till this time I never knew sorrow for what can be more cruall in the world then parting with what one loves and nott only common parting but parting so as may be never to meet again to be perpetually in fear for god knows when I may see him or wethere he is nott now at this instant in a batell I recon him now never in safety ever in danger oh miserable live that I lead now I do what I can to be mery when I am in company but when I am alone then tis that I remember all my grifes.

In spite of William's shy and reserved nature and the twelve-year age gap between the couple, Mary adored him. William soon took one of Mary's English attendants, Elizabeth Villiers, as his mistress – an affair that lasted until Mary's death – and also had a preference for male favourites, but he loved Mary deeply too. Soon after their marriage, William presented her with a diamond and ruby ring that she treasured for the rest of her life, and following William's own death, he was found to be wearing this, together with a lock of Mary's hair, close to his heart, proof of his quiet devotion to her. Mary fell pregnant soon after her marriage, but in the spring of 1678, she miscarried following a fall. She suffered a second miscarriage later that year, and this was the last time that Mary conceived, suggesting that she may have suffered an infection that rendered her infertile. The lack of children was a great grief to both William and Mary and brought them closer together.

Mary lived quietly in Holland with William, devoting herself to the Protestant religion. Her court was enlivened in 1684 by the arrival of her cousin, Charles II's illegitimate son, the Duke of Monmouth. Mary had known Monmouth from her childhood and was fond of him. In Holland, the pair went out walking and ice skating. Both William and Mary were aware that Monmouth's presence was an offence to her father, as many people in England viewed Monmouth as a Protestant alternative to the Catholic Duke of York. When news reached William of Charles II's death in 1685, he responded by asking Monmouth to leave, and the duke travelled to Brussels, from where he launched his invasion of England later that year. In spite of William's attempts to distance himself from Monmouth when James became king, Mary's father was furious and he ordered his agents in the Netherlands to bring William's relationship with Elizabeth Villiers to Mary's attention in the hope that it would break up her marriage. He also tried to convert both his daughters to Catholicism. According to Mary's memoir for 1688, he wrote, saying,

> That I understand controversies better than the most part of my sex, and that he hoped I shall use this capacity which God has given to carry me into the right way, and after several obliging expressions he added that he would send me some books and counselled me to read the papers of the late king and of the duchess my mother.

Mary agreed to read the papers but would enter into no theological debates with James's chaplains, instead remaining devoted to her faith.

In believing that she could be converted and that she would listen to him in preference to William, James had badly misjudged Mary, and her journal makes it clear that she was deeply opposed to his rule in England. When she heard in early 1688 that her stepmother, Mary of Modena, of whom she had always been fond, was pregnant, Mary was filled with misgivings, as her memoirs demonstrate:

> In brief, as far as regards myself only, I should wish as much as the king himself that he might have a son, but though I was thus indifferent for myself I found that I could not remain long indifferent to the interests of the Protestant Religion which depends on this; so that, though it is the duty of each member of his family to wish the king well one cannot do so without being necessarily alarmed by the thought of a Papist successor. This took from me, then, my sweet and satisfying tranquillity and made me see how I was obliged to wish that I might come to the crown.
>
> Besides the interest of the church, the love that I have for the Prince [William] made me wish him all that he merits, and though I regret not to have more than three crowns to bring to him, it is not my love that blinds me; no, I can see his faults, but I say this because I know also his merits.

Mary had always believed that she would become queen of England and when encouraged by her sister, Anne, to consider the Queen's pregnancy to be fictitious, she was prepared to believe the worst. Distanced from events in Holland, Mary genuinely believed that the Prince of Wales was indeed smuggled into his mother's chamber in a warming pan, and she lamented that her sister, Anne, had not been present at the birth. Following the announcement of the birth, Mary initially ordered that prayers be said in her chapel for her half-brother, but as her doubts increased, she ordered the prayers to cease, 'as I did not wish to be guilty of a dissimulation towards God'. William, who was better apprised of the news from England, saw no reason to disabuse her of her suspicions. Mary was fully behind William's invasion of England, stating in her journal after setting out her doubts about the birth,

> The consideration of this and the thought that my father was capable of a crime so horrible and that, humanly speaking, there was not any other means to save the Church and the State than that my husband should go to dethrone him by force, are the most afflicting reflections and would not be supportable without the assistance of God and a firm and unshakeable confidence in Him, His grace extending over all that He does.

Mary saw William off when he sailed to invade England, weeping at their final interview when he insisted that, if he died during the campaign, she should marry again, a thought that caused Mary to feel 'as if some one had torn my heart out'.

Mary spent the last months of 1688 nervously waiting for news. Her sympathies were fully with William, and she was overjoyed to hear that, by the end of December, her father had fled, and William was safe and in possession of the kingdom. She was less overjoyed at the thought of leaving Holland, where she had made her home, but at William's insistence, she sailed to join him, arriving at Whitehall on 12 February. For Mary, it was a difficult homecoming to England, and she was in turmoil, writing in her memoirs that 'on the other side I saw my husband in a prosperous way and blessed God for it, and was sorry I could not so much rejoice as his wife ought; neither was I so sad as became the daughter of a distressed king'. Mary was a dutiful wife, and William instructed her to appear joyful when she came to England – a request that she obeyed.

Mary rather overdid her appearance of happiness, to the cost of her reputation. According to the admittedly hostile account of the Duchess of Marlborough, on first arriving at Whitehall, Mary went up to the apartment assigned to her, which had recently been vacated by her father and stepmother, and 'she ran about it, looking into every closet and conveniency, and turning up the quilts upon the bed, as people do when they come into an inn'. The duchess voiced the thoughts of many when she complained that 'whatever necessary there was of deposing King James, he was still her father, who had been so lately driven from that chamber, and that bed; and, if she felt no tenderness, I thought she should at heart have looked grave, or even pensively sad, at so melancholy a reverse of his fortune'. William, who had no intention of being merely Mary's consort, insisted that he become king of England, a decision that Mary heartily agreed with. The couple were therefore proclaimed as joint sovereigns the day after Mary came to Whitehall to general public rejoicing, on which Evelyn reflects:

> It was believed that both, especially the Princess, would have shown some (seeming) reluctance at least, of assuming her father's crown, and made some apology, testifying by her regret that he should by his mismanagement necessitate the nation to so extraordinary a proceeding, which would have shown very handsomely to the world, and according to the character given of her piety; consonant also to her husband's first declaration, that there was no intention of deposing the king, but of succouring the nation; but nothing of all this appeared; she came into Whitehall laughing and jolly, as to a wedding, so as to seem quite transported.

Evelyn had further criticism for the new queen in that, within days of her accession, she was seen playing cards at Whitehall as Mary of Modena used to do. He also later commented that he was invited to see Mary's collection of china and other fine objects. On seeing a cabinet containing silver filigree which had previously belonged to Mary of Modena, he commented that the cabinet 'in my opinion, should have been generously sent to her [Mary of Modena]'. Mary was wounded by the criticism and toned down her behaviour, quickly regaining her popularity.

Whilst Mary was joint sovereign, the terms under which the crown was offered made it clear that it was William who was to exercise all sovereign authority. Mary was happy to retreat to a domestic sphere, but this was not always possible, as William was absent from England for more than half of Mary's six-year reign, leaving her as regent. Shortly after their accession to the throne, William and Mary heard that James had landed in Ireland in an attempt to re-establish his authority as king. William went personally to oversee the campaign against his father-in-law, leaving Mary behind to head a cabinet council in England. Mary was at first acutely aware of her inexperience, remaining silent in council meetings. She soon gained in authority and proved an effective ruler throughout William's absences.

Mary's letters to William during his Irish campaign in 1690 survive, and they demonstrate her desire to rule in a way that would be pleasing to him. Her first action as regent was to order the transportation of a criminal, commuting his sentence of death. As Mary assured William, she did so because she believed that this was what he would have done under the circumstances. Mary also took action against the queen dowager, Catherine of Braganza, who was found to have forbidden the official prayers for William's success in Ireland in her chapel at Somerset House. Mary was furious at this show of disloyalty by an aunt whom she had never liked and summoned Lord Feversham, who was in charge of Catherine's household, to explain himself:

He came yesterday to my bed-chamber, at the door there was a great deal of company (I mean then just before dinner) he seemed extremely concerned, lookt as pale as death, and spoke in great disorder; he said, he must own it a very great fault, since I took it so: But he begged me to believe 'twas not one out of any ill-intention, nor by agreement with any body: He assured me the Queen (Dowager) herself knew nothing of it; he said 'twas a fault, and a folly, an indiscretion, or any thing I would call it: I told him, after doing a thing of that nature, the best way was not to go about excusing it; that 'twas impossible, since to call it by the most gentle name I could give it, 'twas an unpardonable folly, and which I did not expect.

Mary received a personal visit from Catherine, and it was in this incident that Mary showed her independent authority for the first time. Throughout William's Irish campaign, Mary and her council were also concerned about the possibility of a French invasion and a French fleet menaced the south coast of England for some time, causing the English and Dutch fleets to engage it in battle. Once again, Mary rose to the occasion, although her letters reveal that she was anxious to ensure that she always acted in a way that William would approve and that she was eager for him to return home as soon as possible.

Mary had not wanted to leave her happy life in Holland for England, and even when William was present, she found herself lonely and isolated. She had been fond of her sister Anne during their childhood, and they had remained in contact whilst Mary was in the Netherlands. Mary therefore looked to her sister to provide her with companionship when she returned to England, but she was soon to find that they had grown very far apart. Anne had resented ceding her place in the succession to William, who was granted the crown for life, even in the event that Mary did not survive him. She was also fully under the influence of Sarah Churchill, the future Duchess of Marlborough, who was determined to stir up trouble between the sisters. The first disagreement came when Anne requested apartments that had recently been vacated by the Duchess of Portsmouth at Whitehall. Mary explained that these had already been promised to the Duke of Devonshire but promised that, if the duke was happy to relinquish them, Anne could have them. Anne was determined to take offence and, to Mary's frustration, declared that 'she would not have my Lord Devonshire's leavings'. She then requested Richmond Palace, which was also refused her, again causing anger. A further disagreement was occasioned when William and Mary discovered that Anne had petitioned parliament to increase her income. William was determined that any grant to Anne should be made by him alone, leaving Mary caught in the middle between her sister and her husband. When Mary questioned Anne on her dealings with parliament, she replied that 'she heard her friends had a mind to make her some settlement', to which Mary angrily replied, 'Pray what friends have you but the king and me?'

William despised Anne and always treated her husband, George of Denmark, with contempt, another cause of resentment between the sisters. At his own expense, George, who had been an experienced soldier in his youth, had joined William's Irish expedition, acquitting himself well on the field. William treated George with thinly veiled disdain throughout, refusing to make even a pretence of consulting him on military matters or to allow him to share his coach. George, who was a good-natured man, was upset by this and, instead, resolved to sail with the navy as a volunteer. When he informed William of this wish, the King merely embraced his brother-in-law, leaving George to assume that he had been given permission. He therefore loaded his belongings onto a ship ready to sail. William had no intention of allowing George to travel in his navy, and he instructed Mary that 'she should neither suffer the prince to go to sea, nor yet forbid him to go, if she could so contrive matters, as to make his staying at home his own choice'. This placed Mary in a difficult position, and in the hope of arranging the matter quietly, she approached Lady Marlborough to ask her to persuade Anne to request that George stay at home, telling her of William's orders. Lady Marlborough, who hated the Queen, refused and went straight to Anne. Anne, who deeply loved her husband, was furious, and George was concerned that 'to send for his things back, without giving any reason for changing his design, would be making a very ridiculous figure, and therefore he would not submit'. Anxious to obey William in everything, Mary then ordered George to remain at home.

The final break between the sisters came in February 1692, when William discovered that Lord Marlborough had been corresponding with James II in France. William ordered Marlborough to surrender his offices and leave the court, effectively also banning his wife from court. Mary assumed that, as a result of this, Anne would dismiss Lady Marlborough from her service but, instead, was horrified to find that her sister brought her friend to wait upon the Queen at Kensington Palace the following day. Anne was then pregnant and Mary did not want to upset her, but as soon as her sister had left, she sat down to write to her, informing her that 'I hope, you do me the justice to believe, it is as much against my will, that I now tell you, that, after this, it is very unfit Lady Marlborough should stay with you, since that gives her husband so just a pretence of being where he ought not'. Anne was furious and fired back a response, refusing absolutely to give up her friend. To this, Mary sent a written message forbidding Lady Marlborough from remaining with Anne at her house at the Cockpit, an order that Anne twisted to her own political advantage, claiming to everyone who would listen that Mary had forced her from her house.

Mary was not entirely ready to give up on her relationship with her sister, and when, shortly afterwards, Anne gave birth to a child that died within minutes of its birth, Mary came to visit her. According to Lady Marlborough,

> The Princess herself told me, that the queen never asked her how she did, nor expressed the least concern for her condition, nor so much as took her by the hand. The salutation was this: I have made the first step, by coming to you, and I now expect you should make the next by removing my Lady Marlborough. The Princess answered, that she had never in all her life disobeyed her, except in that one particular, which she hoped would, some time or other, appear as unreasonable to her Majesty, as it did to her. Upon which the queen rose up and went away.

Mary felt remorse for speaking so sharply to her sister when she had just lost a child, but neither sister was prepared to be the first to attempt a reconciliation. This was the last time that Mary and Anne saw each other, although Mary continued to show a fond interest in Anne's son, William, Duke of Gloucester, sending him presents of toys and arranging for him to visit her. She also sent her ladies to enquire after him when he was ill, although these messengers were instructed to studiously ignore Anne, 'passing by her, as she stood or sat, without taking more notice of her than if she were a rocker [i.e. a nursery servant]'.

Mary was grieved by the break with her sister, and by 1694, although she was only approaching her thirty-second birthday, she felt weary of life, writing to a friend that 'I believe that I am becoming old and infirmities come with age'. She was ill early in 1694, and in November 1694, she lost the stone from the ring that William had given her after their wedding, something that she saw as a bad omen. On 20 December 1694, Mary suddenly felt ill. Two days later, she was considerably worse, and she shut herself up in her apartments, burning her confidential and personal papers. She also wrote a paper detailing her plans for a funeral, as well as a final letter to William asking that he break off his relationship with Elizabeth Villiers. On 23 December, the eruptions characteristic of smallpox appeared on

Mary's skin and William hurried to be with her, weeping at her bedside as she grew steadily worse. By Christmas Day, it was clear that there was no hope for Mary. William remained by her side throughout her illness, ordering a camp bed to be set up in a side room on which he occasionally lay down for some rest. Anne, anxious to be reconciled with her sister, also sent messengers begging for a meeting, although this was denied her. It is unlikely that Mary was even informed of her sister's interest. Aware of the deadly nature of her sickness, Mary ordered that any of her servants who had not had smallpox leave the palace, and she then prepared for death. She died in the early hours of 28 December 1694 with William by her side.

Mary II had been loved by her husband, and he gave her a grand funeral, unaware of the paper that she had placed in her desk requesting that she be buried in as simple a manner as possible. He sincerely grieved for her, writing to his cousin within a week of her death that 'I know not how to dispense with letting you learn the extreme affliction which it has pleased God to visit on me by the death of the queen, my very dear wife'. As a more tangible expression of his love, on reading Mary's last letter, he broke off his relationship with Elizabeth Villiers, pensioning her off with a rich marriage. Anne also mourned her sister, and with Mary's death, she filled something of the role of queen at court until her own accession, following William's death, just over seven years later.

ANNE (1665-1714) was the youngest surviving daughter of James II and Anne Hyde and was born on 6 February 1665. She was never in robust health and suffered from an eye problem all her life, causing her to squint and be extremely short-sighted. By the time she was three, Anne's parents were sufficiently worried to send her to Paris to live with her grandmother, Queen Henrietta Maria, so that she could be treated by a French eye specialist. Anne lived with her grandmother until her death in August 1669 before passing into the household of her aunt, Henrietta Anne, Duchess of Orléans, to be raised with the duchess's two daughters. Her time with her aunt proved brief, as the duchess died suddenly on 20 June 1670. To the worry of Anne's father, Anne then passed into the custody of the duchess's husband, the unstable Duke of Orléans, who insisted on dressing Anne and her eldest cousin up in full court dress whilst the court came to pay them their condolences. By the end of June, Anne had been extracted from the Orléans household, and she was returned to England, bringing with her two fine jewelled bracelets as a farewell gift from Louis XIV.

On her return to England, Anne was raised with her elder sister, Mary. Anne always had a stubborn streak to her character, and this was manifested early in her childhood, as one incident shows:

> When they [Mary and Anne] were children, walking in the park together, a dispute was started between them, whether something they saw at a great distance were a man or a tree; her sister being of the former opinion, & she of the latter. When they came so near that their eyesight could convince them it was a man, the Lady Mary said, now sister, are you satisfied that it is a man? But Lady Anne, after she saw what it was, turn'd away, & persisting still in her own side of the question cried out, no, sister, it is a tree.

Anne's stubbornness was also demonstrated in her later belief that her half-brother, the Prince of Wales, was a changeling, in spite of all the evidence to the contrary.

Following Mary's marriage to William of Orange in 1677, Anne's father came under increasing pressure in England for his Catholic beliefs and was frequently forced into exile. In July 1681, Anne joined her father and stepmother in Scotland, spending ten months there until they were permitted to return to London. On her return to London, Anne spent more time at court, and it was there that she came across John Sheffield, Earl of Mulgrave, a bachelor nearly twenty years her senior. Details of Anne's relationship with Lord Mulgrave are vague, but it appears that the earl attempted to seduce her and that Anne was not an unwilling participant in the flirtation. By 1682, Anne was seventeen years old, and whilst she took after her mother's family in appearance and would later become grossly overweight, in her youth, she was considered pretty. The affair suddenly came to an end in November when some of Mulgrave's letters to Anne were discovered, and he was banished from court. The flirtation caused a great scandal, and news of it reached Anne's sister in Holland, who wrote disapprovingly to her friend, Frances Apsley:

> If I could love you better then I did before your last letter would make me do so, to see the consern you are in for my pore sister. I am sure all who are truelly her friands must be so, for my part I never knew what it was to be so vext & trobled as I am at it, not but that I believe my sister very innocent however I am so nice upon the point of reputation that it makes me mad she should be exposed to such reports, & now what will not this insolent man say being provokt, oh my dear Aurelia tis not to be imagined in what conserne I am that I should ever live to see the oneley sister I have in the world, the sister I love like my own life thus abused & wronged.

Anne's own feelings are not recorded, although she cannot have been happy with the gossip that circulated, claiming that the relationship had been consummated, or with the fact that Mulgrave became commonly known as 'King John' in reference to the affair. It is unlikely that Anne was in love with Mulgrave, and she showed no interest in him when she came across him later in life. The main consequence of the affair, from Anne's point of view, was that the King decided, finally, that it was high time that she was married.

A marriage between Anne and her cousin, and eventual successor, George of Hanover, had been suggested in 1680, and the prince visited England in December of that year, meeting with Anne. This came to nothing, and George married his cousin, Sophia Dorothea of Celle, in 1682 instead. With the loss of the Hanoverian match, Charles II instead opened negotiations for her to marry Prince George of Denmark in early 1683. George was the younger brother of King Christian V of Denmark and, through Anne of Denmark, a distant cousin of Anne's. Anne was lucky in her husband, as George, who was twelve years older than her, was a kindly, if ineffectual, man. John Evelyn saw George soon after he arrived in England, and the prince made a favourable impression on the diarist:

> I again saw Prince George of Denmark: he had the Danish countenance, blonde, of few words, spoke French but ill, seemed somewhat heavy, but reported to be valiant, and indeed he had bravely rescued and brought off his brother, the king of Denmark, in a battle against the Swedes, when both these kings were engaged very smartly.

The couple fell deeply in love, and George proved an attentive suitor, with Anne writing to Frances Apsley,

> Another thing you tax me of is never sending for you, which is a thing I have not done, I confess, this great [while] but has not been my fault, I assure you. For the Prince [George] stays with me every day from dinner to prayers, and by that time I come from prayers 'tis half an hour after four, and on my playing days from that time I am always in expectation of company. On those days that I do not play, I commonly go to Whitehall at six, so that that hour and a half which I have from prayers till I go to the Duchess I am glad sometimes to get a little of it alone, it being

the only time I have to myself, and for the other part of it the Prince either comes to me or I go to him, and we stay with one another till I go out.

The couple were married at St James's Palace on 28 July 1683 and, throughout their married life, were rarely apart, unusually for their time, sharing a bedroom. On her marriage, Charles II granted Anne a house at the Cockpit, which she used throughout the time before she became queen.

With her marriage, Anne was granted her own household, and she persuaded her father to allow her to take her friend, Sarah, Lady Marlborough, into her service. Anne first came across Sarah Jennings, who would later become Lady Marlborough, when she was around five years old and Sarah ten. The pair soon became friends, although it was not until Sarah was appointed to Anne's household that they became close. Sarah later wrote her own detailed account of her relationship with Anne, and whilst this is naturally heavily biased, it does provide a great deal of information on how their relationship developed. According to Sarah, she had a particular attraction for Anne, and 'young as I was, when I first became this high favourite, I laid it down for a maxim, that flattery was falsehood to my trust, and ingratitude to my greatest friend; and that I did not deserve so much favour, if I could not venture the loss of it by speaking the truth of it'. There has always been much speculation about the nature of the relationship between Anne and Sarah, and Sarah certainly appears to have believed that Anne was attracted to women. However, it is more likely that the friendship was platonic and what Anne really wanted was a friend. Sarah became the dominant influence on her life, far more than the weak but amiable George. According to Sarah,

[Anne] grew uneasy to be treated by me with the form and ceremony due to her rank; nor could she bear from me the sound of words which implied in them distance and superiority. It was this turn of mind, which made her one day propose to me, that whenever I should happen to be absent from her, we might in all our letters write ourselves by feigned names, such as would import nothing of distinction of rank between us. Morley and Freeman were the names her fancy hit upon; and she left me to chuse by which of them I would be called. My frank, open temper naturally led me to pitch upon Freeman, and the princess took the other; and from this time Mrs Morley and Mrs Freeman began to converse as equals, made so by the affection of friendship.

Sarah was a very intelligent woman, and Anne was completely under her thumb. Unfortunately for Anne, she was also quarrelsome and had an ungovernable temper.

With the accession of her father to the throne, Anne became the most senior Protestant member of the royal family in England, and she took steps to demonstrate this. According to Evelyn, in December 1685, 'Dr Patrick, Dean of Peterborough, preached at Whitehall, before the Princess of Denmark [Anne], who, since his Majesty came to the crown, always sat in the king's closet, and had the same bowings and ceremonies applied to the place where she was, as his Majesty had when there in person'. James remained close to Anne, providing her with a generous annual income. The relationship was somewhat troubled however, and the King was as anxious to convert his younger daughter to Catholicism as he was his elder. Anne also had a poor relationship with her stepmother, the Queen, writing to her sister that 'it is a sad and very uneasy thing to be forced to live civilly and as it were freely with a woman that one knows hates one, and does all she can to undo everybody; which she certainly does'. With her elder sister's childlessness, Anne knew that the crown was likely to come to her eventually, and she looked forward to that day, saying that the date of her accession would be her 'sunshine day'. Anne was furious to hear of Mary of Modena's pregnancy and the birth of the Prince of Wales in June 1688, and she resolutely refused to believe that the child was her half-brother. Anne insisted on going to Bath at around the time of Mary of Modena's confinement, in spite of her father's request that she remain to witness the birth, and, unfairly, later criticised the Queen when she lamented the doubts over her son, replying 'very coldly' that 'it was not so much to be wonder'd at, since such persons were not present, as ought to have been there'. Anne was one of the leading sources of the rumours about the prince's birth, and she persuaded her sister that the birth was doubtful.

Anne had nothing to gain in remaining loyal to her father during William of Orange's invasion in the autumn of 1688, and both she and George always intended to join William as soon as it was clear that he was likely to be the victor. George had originally gone with James and his army in order to confront William, but at Salisbury, he deserted, riding to join William. James was not unduly concerned by the loss militarily, writing in his memoirs that 'he was more troubled at the unnaturalness of the action than the want of his service, for that the loss of a good trooper had been of greater consequence'. George was not the only member of the army to desert, and aware that he did not have the strength to defeat William, James returned to London. This unexpected event threw Anne into a panic, and she escaped down the backstairs of the Cockpit at midnight into a waiting coach, rejoining George soon afterwards. It is unlikely that Anne had considered the possibility that William, who, by the laws of heredity, took his place after her in the succession, would insist on becoming king as William III, and she resented this, leading to her quarrelling with both her sister and her brother-in-law.

Anne's time during the reign of William and Mary was mostly taken up with childbearing, and she has the worst childbearing record of any English queen, eventually losing all eighteen of her children. Anne became pregnant soon after her marriage, giving birth to a stillborn daughter in May 1684. She was soon pregnant again, bearing a daughter, Mary, on 1 June 1685. She bore a third daughter, Anne Sophie, prematurely on 12 May 1686. Anne Sophie, in particular, seemed healthy and likely to live, but on 21 January 1687, Anne suffered her first miscarriage. Further disaster struck within days when both of Anne's daughters and George were struck with smallpox. Anne, who was a devoted wife and mother, nursed her family, but her two little girls died within days of each other. In October of that year, she bore a son who had been dead inside her womb for a month. Her sixth pregnancy ended in miscarriage in April 1688. Finally, on 27 July 1689, Anne bore a son who seemed likely to live, and he was named William, after the King, and immediately granted the title of Duke of Gloucester. Gloucester's birth made Anne and George hopeful that future children would live, but in spite of a further ten pregnancies, including one of twins, none of Anne's later children lived more than a few hours. According to Sarah, Anne was deeply concerned by her losses, and she took steps when pregnant to guard against miscarriages. In one pregnancy, she 'stayed constantly on one floor, by her physicians advice, lying very much upon a couch to prevent the misfortune of miscarrying'. This had no effect, and that pregnancy resulted in a stillborn son.

With the loss of so many children, Anne poured all her affection into her only child, Gloucester. In one letter to Sarah, she wrote, 'My boy is, God be thanked, very well, and in good humour, but I don't find any alteration in him since dear Mrs Freeman saw him; only I must say this for him, that the day you was here he neither looked so well nor was in so good humour as he used to be'. In another, she wrote of her desire to have him near her when she went to Bath, saying that 'I might have the child at a house within three miles of the Bath, for it would be more for my satisfaction than to leave him behind me'. She was not prepared to risk his health in any way, continuing,

[If] the journey was not too great for my boy, I should be mightily tempted to carry him, but since Campden House agrees so well with him, and that there is so much reason to believe people consider their own satisfaction more than mine or than they do the child's good, I think I had better be from him five or six weeks, than run the hazard of his meeting with an accident that one may have cause to repent of one's whole life.

It was soon clear that something was not entirely right with Gloucester. His balance was so poor that he was unable to use stairs without assistance, and he could not raise himself up from the floor when he lay down. He was a precocious child but had such a large head that only a man's hat could be found to fit him. On 24 July 1700, the duke celebrated his eleventh birthday at Windsor with a dinner and a fireworks display. That evening, he was put to bed with a sore throat that soon developed into something more serious, and he may have been suffering from scarlet fever or, perhaps, smallpox. Anne devotedly nursed her child, but there was nothing that could be done, and he died on 29 July 1700. Anne was devastated and, from that date, referred to herself in her letters to Sarah as 'your poor, unfortunate, faithful Morley'.

Anne's health was ruined by her frequent pregnancies, and by the time of Gloucester's death, she was grossly overweight and an invalid, barely able to walk across a room. She conceived for the last time in the year of Gloucester's death,and by the time of her accession to the throne, it was clear that she would leave no living child to succeed her. James II, in exile in France, heard about his grandson's death before it was officially announced, and it is possible that it was Anne herself who sent him the news. Unbeknownst to William, Anne was in some contact with her father, and in 1691, she had written him, expressing her repentance:

I have been very desirous of some safe opportunity to make you a sincere and humble offer of my duty and submission to you, and to beg that you will be assured that I am both truly concerned for the misfortune of your condition and sensible, as I ought to be, of my own unhappiness. As to what you may think I have contributed to it, if wishes could recall what is past, I had long since redeemed my fault. I am sensible it would have been a great relief to me if I could have found means to acquaint you earlier of my repentant thoughts, but I hope they may find the advantage of coming late, of being less suspected of insincerity than perhaps they would have been at any time before.

It will be a great addition to the ease I propose to my own mind by this plain confession if I am so happy as to find that it brings any real satisfaction to yours, and that you are as indulgent and easy to receive my humble submissions as I am to make them, in a free, disinterested acknowledgement of my fault, for no other end but to deserve and receive your pardon.

I have had a great mind to beg you to make one compliment for me, but fearing the expressions which would be properest for me to make use of might be perhaps the least convenient for a letter, I must content myself at present with hoping the bearer will make a compliment for me to the Queen.

James was suspicious of this letter, and it was written at around the time that Marlborough made contact with the former king, suggesting that Anne wrote merely to ensure that Marlborough's approaches were taken as sincere, when they were certainly not. However, in 1689, as she prepared for William and Mary's coronation, Anne does appear to have finally accepted the legitimacy of her half-brother. According to James II's memoirs, she summoned Mrs Dawson, a faithful old family retainer who had been present at the prince's birth and asked her whether he was really the son of Mary of Modena. Mrs Dawson replied 'that she could answer for it as much as she could, that she herself was the late Dutchesse's daughter, haveing seen them both born'. Mrs Dawson chided her mistress, pointing out that Anne herself had felt her stepmother's stomach and felt the child move. Anne had been able to ignore all the evidence for her own political gain, but with William's usurpation of her position in the succession, she did begin to feel some remorse for her treatment of her father.

Anne's repentance went only so far, and she had no intention of giving up the throne by recognising her half-brother as legitimate. When William III died on 8 March 1702, she happily accepted the crown. As queen, Anne sought to model herself on her great predecessor Elizabeth I, and she adopted the Tudor queen's motto, *Semper Eadem* or 'Always the Same', as her own. She sought to portray herself as the mother of her country in her first speech to parliament in March 1702. In spite of her personal invalidism, Anne was a largely successful queen, presiding over a country that became increasingly prominent in Europe following her great general the Duke of Marlborough's victories in the War of the Spanish Succession. Whilst Anne was happy to celebrate Marlborough's victories, she became increasingly frustrated by the dominance that his wife, Sarah, had over her.

By the time of her accession to the throne, Anne had relied on Sarah for advice and support for nearly twenty years. Once she became queen, Anne attempted to assert herself, and she became increasingly frustrated with the domineering Sarah. Anne also obtained a new favourite, Abigail Masham, who was a cousin of Sarah's. Sarah's memoirs make it clear that she was furiously jealous of Anne and Abigail's relationship, in which the two would spend at least two hours alone together every day. Sarah had always been blunt with Anne, and unable to control her jealousy, she wrote a letter to Anne accusing her and Abigail of lesbianism. In this, Sarah had gone too far, and Anne, who was devoted to her husband, was appalled by the accusation. Whilst Marlborough remained head of the army, Anne was unable to act against Sarah, but she no longer considered her as a friend. This estrangement was compounded in October 1708 when George died. Anne was devastated by the loss of her husband, and Sarah belittled the Queen's grief, mocking her when she asked that 'there may be a great many yeomen of the guards to carry the prince's dear body, that it may not be let fall, the great stairs being very steep and slippery'. Cruelly, she also took away a portrait of George that hung in Anne's bedchamber, complaining when Anne was forced to beg for its return that, if she had truly loved her husband, she would not have been able to bear seeing his portrait every day. Finally, when Sarah told Anne to 'be quiet' when she attempted to speak in public, Anne had had enough, and she broke with her former friend, refusing to speak to her at their final meeting in April 1710. As a parting shot, Sarah accused the Queen of 'inhumanity' before stripping all the moveable fixtures from her apartments at court. In retaliation, Anne stopped work for a time on Blenheim Palace, the lavish mansion she was funding as a reward to Marlborough for his victories.

With the loss of George, as well as Sarah's company, Anne became increasingly secluded, and in her last years, she spent much time with her final favourite, the Duchess of Somerset. The succession played much on her mind, but she always refused to recognise her half-brother as her heir. Following the death of the Duke of Gloucester, parliament had passed the Act of Settlement, settling the throne on Sophia, the dowager Electress of Hanover, and her descendants in the event that Anne died childless, and Anne remained committed to this until her death. Sophia was the twelfth of the thirteen children of Elizabeth of Bohemia, the daughter of James I, and as a Protestant, she was seen as a suitable monarch, in preference to her elder siblings, the children of Charles I's daughter, Henrietta Anne, and Anne's own half siblings. Anne had no desire to receive Sophia in England, as she feared that a rival party would build up around her heir as it had once built up around her in the reign of William and Mary. Throughout her reign, suggestions were frequently made that Sophia should be invited to England, and Anne always refused. In early 1714, they were raised again, and Anne, furious, fired off a rude letter to her cousin:

> Since the right of Succession to my Kingdom has always been declared to belong to you and your family, there have always been disaffected persons who by particular views of their own interests have entered into measures to establish a Prince of your blood in my Estates even whilst I am yet living. I have never thought till now that this project could have gone so far as to have made the least impression upon your mind, but as I have lately perceived by public Rumours which are industrially spread that the Electoral Prince is come into this Sentiment, it is of importance with respect to the Succession of your family that I should tell you such a proceeding will infallibly draw along with it some consequences that will be dangerous to that succession itself, which is not secure otherwise than as the Prince, that actually wears the Crown maintain her Authority and Prerogative. There are here (such is our misfortune) a great many people who are seditiously disposed, so I leave you to judge what Tumults they may be able to raise if they should have a Pretext to begin a Commotion. I persuade myself therefore you will never consent that the least thing should be done that may disturb the repose of me or my subjects. Open yourself to me with the same freedom I do to you and propose whatever you think may contribute to the security of the Succession. I will come into it with zeal, provided that it does not derogate from my dignity, which I am resolved to maintain.

The aged Sophia, who greatly desired to be queen of England, was devastated by Anne's letter, and according to popular reports, the shock killed her in June 1714 at the age of eighty-three. Anne did not long survive her cousin, as she suffered a series of strokes at the end of July 1714, dying on 1 August at the age of forty-nine.

Queen Anne was the last of the Stuarts, and with her death, the throne passed, in accordance with the Act of Settlement, to Sophia's son and Anne's own early suitor, George of Hanover. The Stuart dynasty in England was always an unlucky one, and this was reflected in the fates of many of its queens. The queens from the House of Hanover were generally happier, and the dynasty ended with a far greater queen regnant than Anne or Mary II. In spite of this, the first queen of the House of Hannover was probably the most miserable and unfortunate wife of a king of England that ever lived.

10

The Hanoverian Queens

The House of Hanover, which ruled from 1714 until 1901, saw a great variety in the lives and fortunes of the seven women who were either queens or the wives of kings. They varied from the powerless Sophia Dorothea of Celle and the unacknowledged Maria Fitzherbert to the powerful Caroline of Ansbach, with the dynasty ending in the triumphant reign of Queen Victoria. With the exception of Maria Fitzherbert, all the women were of German birth or descent, and they brought their own unique ideas and interpretation to the role of queen. For its first thirteen years, the dynasty had no queen, and the whereabouts of George I's wife was very much a mystery in England.

SOPHIA DOROTHEA OF CELLE (1666-1726) was a mysterious and tragic figure, and her life has developed into a romanticised legend over the centuries. With the exception of Isabella of Gloucester in the twelfth and thirteenth centuries, Sophia Dorothea had the most wasted and restricted life of any queen, and she shares the distinction only with Berengaria of Navarre of never actually having visited England. She was the only surviving child of George William, Duke of Celle, and Eleanor d'Olbreuse. Sophia Dorothea's parents had a complicated marital relationship, which impacted on her own status. George William had originally been betrothed to Sophia, the granddaughter of James I of England. He soon changed his mind about the match and suggested that his younger brother, Ernest Augustus, marry her instead. In return, George William contracted not to marry. At that time the duchy of Brunswick-Lüneburg, of which both Celle and Hanover were a part, was divided between the rule of various members of the family, and George William's promise ensured that his younger brother would, in due course, rule the entire duchy. George William had no taste for marriage, but this changed when he met Eleanor d'Olbreuse, the daughter of a French nobleman who had fled the persecution of Protestants in his native land. The couple fell in love, but Eleanor refused absolutely to become George William's mistress. He, in turn, could not offer her marriage, and a compromise was reached in the form of a morganatic marriage. This allowed for a union that was valid in the eyes of the Church but gave no change in status to the spouse or inheritance rights to the children. At the time of her birth, Sophia Dorothea was not a princess and her mother was not Duchess of Celle. This all changed in 1676, when, with the consent of the Holy Roman Emperor, George William raised Eleanor to the status of a full wife, and she was recognised as Duchess of Celle. At the same time, Sophia Dorothea's own prospects improved, as she was fully legitimised as a princess and as her father's heir.

Sophia Dorothea, as her parents' only child, was raised in a happy and loving household. Her parents began considering a marriage for her from an early age, and before she was legitimised, a match had been suggested by the wealthy Count Königsmarck with his son, a boy of sixteen, who was introduced to the seven-year-old Sophia Dorothea. With Sophia Dorothea's improvement in status, this match was abandoned, but it is clear that both Sophia Dorothea and her young suitor were fond of each other, and their relationship was later reignited to the ruin of them both. Shortly after her legitimisation, Sophia Dorothea was betrothed to Augustus Frederick, Crown Prince of Wolfenbuttel. He died in August 1676, and whilst his younger brother was offered as an alternative candidate, Sophia Dorothea's father had, by then, other plans for her.

George William's sister-in-law and jilted fiancée had always disapproved of his relationship with Eleanor, and according to a letter written to the future George II of England by a courtier, Sophia 'never countenanced the consort of George William, Duke of Zell, on account of the comparative obscurity of her family: and it was to that antipathy all the misery which befell her devoted daughter-in-law, Sophia Dorothea, might fairly be attributed'. Whilst Sophia never felt that Sophia Dorothea and her mother were truly legitimate members of the family, Sophia Dorothea's importance as the heiress of the elder brother was impossible to ignore, and in 1682, she came personally to Celle to arrange a match between the princess and her eldest son, George Louis. George Louis was six years older than Sophia Dorothea and had previously considered a match with the future Queen Anne of England. A marriage with his cousin made better territorial sense, and it was agreed that George Louis would inherit Celle on his father-in-law's death. Sophia Dorothea was not consulted, but she obeyed her parents, and soon after her betrothal, she wrote a dutiful letter to her future mother-in-law:

I have so much respect for my lord the Duke, your husband, and for my lord my own father, that, in whatever manner they both may act in my behalf, I shall always be very content. Your highness will do me, I know, the justice to believe so, and that no one can be more sensible than I am of the many marks of your goodness. I will with much care endeavour, all my life long, to deserve the same, and to make it appear to your highness, by my respect and very humble services; that you could not choose as a daughter, one, who knows better than myself how to pay you what is due. In which duty I shall feel very great pleasure, and also in showing to you, by my submission, that I am, Madam, Your Highness's very humble and very obedient servant.

The couple were married on 21 November 1682 and left Celle the following month.

Sophia Dorothea quickly settled into life in Hanover, and on 30 October 1683, she bore a son, George Augustus. A daughter, Sophia Dorothea, followed in March 1687. In spite of the births of their children, the couple were hopelessly ill-matched. George Louis took mistresses throughout his marriage, something which outraged his wife and which led to an estrangement between them. Dangerously, according to a near-contemporary, Horace Walpole, George Louis's conduct inspired Sophia Dorothea to seek revenge: 'Though she was very handsome, the Prince, who was extremely amorous, had several mistresses; which provocation, and his absence in the army of the confederates, probably disposed the Princess to indulge some degree of coquetry.'

Sophia Dorothea fixed her attention on the handsome Count von Königsmarck, a childhood friend. Königsmarck was a Swedish nobleman in the employ of Sophia Dorothea's father-in-law, the Elector of Hanover. He was probably, at first, drawn to Sophia Dorothea by virtue of their earlier acquaintance, but 'his vanity, the beauty of the Electoral Princess [Sophia Dorothea], and the neglect under which he found her, encouraged his presumption to make his addresses to her, not covertly; and she, though believed not to have transgressed in her duty, did receive them too indiscreetly'.

A great deal of mystery surrounds the relationship between Königsmarck and Sophia Dorothea, and it has been embellished over time. Whilst it is not certain that their relationship was consummated, from their surviving letters, it appears likely. The couple's letters show that they were passionate about each other, and on 1 July 1690, Königsmarck wrote,

> I am now desperate and only a letter from your incomparable hand can save me. If I were fortunate enough to receive one I would be at least somewhat consoled. I hope you will be charitable enough not to refuse me this favour, and because you are the cause of my affliction it is only fair that you should also comfort me. Thus it rests with you to console me for the grief that this sad absence is causing me, and I will see from this whether I can believe the things that you had the kindness to tell me sometimes. If I were not writing to a person for whom I have as much respect as love, I would find better words to express my passion, but as I fear to offend you I must end here and I beg you only to remember me a little bit and to believe that I am your slave.

That the passion was fully reciprocated is clear from Sophia Dorothea's own letters. She wrote in March 1692,

> If something can make me bear your absence without dying of grief it is the hope of showing you by my conduct that no one has ever loved as I love you and that nothing is the equal of my fidelity. It is proof against every test, and whatever may happen nothing in the world will be able to take me away from what I adore. Yes, my dear child, my passion can only end with my life.

The couple were besotted with each other, and they threw caution to the wind, trusting their letters to servants and appearing to be in love in public. George Louis noticed, and in her letter of March 1692, Sophia recorded that 'I was so changed and depressed today that the Reformer [George Louis] took pity on me and said that he could well see that I was ill and that I ought to take care of myself. He is right, but my illness comes only from loving, and I never want to be cured'. Neither Sophia Dorothea nor Königsmarck saw the warning signs and when, in June 1694, the Electress Sophia questioned her closely on Königsmarck, Sophia Dorothea saw it only as a sign that her mother-in-law was fond of the count and not that she suspected the relationship. Sophia Dorothea's parents, however, who heard the rumours of the relationship in Celle, were anxious. When she visited them in July 1692, they questioned her closely and sought to catch her out, with Sophia Dorothea writing to Königsmarck that 'I got into bed after finishing my letter. I was reading all of yours and I thought myself safe because I had left word that I was asleep. The Pedagogue [the Duchess of Celle] came to surprise me for the second time. All the Confidante could do was hide them under my blanket. I did not dare move for fear the paper would rustle'. Two weeks later, Sophia Dorothea's parents again came close to discovering her secret, and she wrote that 'I have just been interrupted by the Scold [the Duke of Celle] and the Peda[gogue]. All I could do was hide what I was writing. What a treat they would have had if they had seen it. They are very kind, but they are always preaching me to live on good terms with the Reformer [George Louis]'. A reconciliation with George Louis was certainly the last thing that Königsmarck wanted for Sophia Dorothea, as he was jealous of her husband, writing in one letter that 'I cannot sleep for rage that an Electoral Prince is depriving me of the pleasure of my charming mistress'. In another, he complained,

You say that you see no one, which is the most obliging thing in the world. But you see the Reformer [George Louis] all the more which makes me fear that you will little by little become accustomed to his mediocre caresses and that he will kiss you so often that I die of grief simply to think of it. For your own self respect don't become accustomed to it. Always think of the way he treats you – you who are worthy of all honest, obliging, and respectful behaviour.

The couple failed to understand the danger they were in and they underestimated everyone, including the Elector's powerful mistress, Countess von Platen.

Countess von Platen had shown a romantic interest in Königsmarck herself, and she was furious when she noticed the attention that he paid to Sophia Dorothea. Sophia Dorothea was concerned enough about the Countess to caution Königsmarck in July 1692 'don't be silly enough to stop going to Platen's. You absolutely must humour her and I beseech you with all my love to go there as before'. Countess von Platen was the couple's enemy, and when, in 1694, Königsmarck unwisely became drunk whilst visiting the Polish court and spoke of his affair with Sophia Dorothea, the news of this disclosure was swiftly brought to the Countess, who informed the Elector. Königsmarck's unwise comments, which included the disclosure that he and Sophia Dorothea were planning to flee to France together, marked the beginning of the end for the couple.

On remembering what he had said, Königsmarck hastened to Hanover to see Sophia Dorothea. She was overjoyed to see him and immediately granted him a private audience. Aware that it was only a matter of time until they were discovered, Königsmarck begged the princess to flee with him at once, but she refused, saying that she required one more day in which to see her children for the last time. This delay proved fatal for Königsmarck, as he disappeared that night. His fate has never been entirely explained, but it was assumed by contemporaries that he was murdered on the orders of the Elector and George Louis. According to one near-contemporary account, Königsmarck was set upon by a group of assassins on leaving Sophia Dorothea's room and cut to pieces with their swords. This is possible. Alternatively, he may have been strangled, and Walpole related that, in the reign of Sophia Dorothea's son,

> some alterations to the palace being ordered by him, the body of Königsmarck was discovered under the floor of the Electoral Princess's dressing-room; the Count having probably been strangled there the instant he left her, and his body secreted. The discovery was hushed up; George the Second intrusted the secret to his wife, Queen Caroline, who told it to my father.

Sophia Dorothea was soon aware that her lover was dead, and after his papers were searched and the couple's letters discovered, she was arrested.

Sophia Dorothea was informed that George Louis intended to divorce her, and she complied willingly, hoping to be allowed to retire quietly. On 28 December 1694, an ecclesiastical court pronounced a sentence of divorce on the couple, with the stipulation that, whilst George Louis was free to marry, Sophia Dorothea was not. Neither George Louis nor his father had any intention of allowing the princess to remarry, and rather than being freed as she had hoped, she was imprisoned in the Castle of Ahlden. Sophia Dorothea was never given a trial, but her imprisonment was always intended to be for life, and for the first few months, she was not even allowed outside the castle walls. From July 1695, the conditions were relaxed somewhat, and she was allowed out in her coach, although always surrounded by an armed troop of guards. She was permitted a limited household, but it was filled with spies reporting to George Louis. She also found that whilst her prison was in her father's duchy, he refused absolutely to see her, only softening his view of her in the last months of his life. Only Sophia Dorothea's mother continued to speak for her, and she was finally allowed to visit her daughter, something that was her daughter's only consolation in her imprisonment.

For Sophia Dorothea, the cruellest part of her imprisonment was that she was not allowed to see her children, and she begged George Louis for news of them. The children were forbidden to speak of their mother, although both thought of her. On her marriage to the Crown Prince of Prussia, the younger Sophia Dorothea took her mother's disgraced servant, Fräulein von dem Knesebeck into her service, in spite of the fact that she had been imprisoned for assisting Sophia Dorothea and Königsmarck in their affair. She also corresponded with her mother but was unable to assist her in any way. Sophia Dorothea's son, the future George II of England, was devoted to his mother, and as a child, he slipped away from his escorts whilst hunting in an unsuccessful bid to reach her prison. George II and his father were always estranged, and according to Walpole, George I's treatment of Sophia Dorothea was a major cause of this. George II even stated that he intended to bring his mother to England when his father died and have her declared queen dowager. This was something that she would have dearly desired, but she was not destined to survive her husband. The best that George II could do was to preserve, in secret, two portraits of his mother, which he immediately had hung at court when news reached him of his father's death.

Following George Louis's accession to the throne of England in 1714, on the death of Queen Anne, no mention was made of Sophia Dorothea, and there was a great deal of speculation as to her whereabouts and whether a divorce had actually been pronounced. George I was a suspicious man, and whilst he undoubtedly hated Sophia Dorothea and kept her as a prisoner for over thirty years, he also feared her. According to Walpole, 'it is known that in Queen Anne's time there was much noise about French prophets. A female of that vocation (for we know from Scripture that the gift of prophecy is not limited to one gender) warned George the First to take care of his wife, as he would not survive her a year'. Sophia Dorothea spent the years of her imprisonment in her religious devotions and in carrying out acts of charity in the surrounding area, as well as managing, from a distance, her financial affairs. The years of disappointment eventually ground her down, and she died on 13 November 1726, raging in her fever at the cruelty of her husband. George I, who believed the prophecy, was troubled by her death, considering that it presaged his own demise, and he survived her by less than a year, dying on 11 June 1727.

Sophia Dorothea's life was a great tragedy and a terrible waste. She was never queen of England, but she was the wife of one king and mother of a second. She never attained any political influence, and her great folly was in underestimating the fury of her husband and his family, for which she paid a terrible price. Her life was a great contrast to that of her daughter-in-law, Caroline of Ansbach, who was one of the most powerful English queen consorts.

CAROLINE OF ANSBACH (1683-1737) was born on 1 March 1683, the daughter of John Frederick, Margrave of Brandenburg-Ansbach, and his second wife, Eleonore of Saxe-Eisenach. Caroline's father died when she was only three years old, and he was succeeded by his son from his first marriage. Whilst Caroline was still young, her mother made a second, disastrous marriage to the unstable Elector of Saxony, and Caroline passed into the custody of Frederick, Elector of Brandenburg, and his wife, Sophia Charlotte of Hanover. Caroline lived with the couple in Berlin when they became king and queen of Prussia, and she was very close to Sophia Charlotte, who was the sister of George Louis, Elector of Hanover. According to Horace Walpole, Caroline received only a limited education. More attention was paid to her appearance:

Queen Caroline was said to be very handsome at her marriage, soon after which she had the small-pox; but was little marked by it, and retained a most pleasing countenance. It was full of majesty or mildness as she pleased, and her penetrating eyes expressed whatever she had a mind they should. Her voice too was captivating, and her hands beautifully small, plump, and graceful.

Caroline's 'understanding was uncommonly strong', and she was deeply ambitious. By the late 1690s, she was talked of as a possible bride for the Archduke Charles, titular King of Spain and later Holy Roman Emperor, and in 1704, she received a firm proposal from him. This was the grandest match in Europe, and it pricked Caroline's ambition. She was, however, unwilling to abandon her Protestant faith to marry the Catholic archduke and ultimately refused, to the disappointment of her guardians. In January 1705, the Queen of Prussia died, and Caroline wrote to her friend, the philosopher Leibniz, that 'Heaven, jealous of our happiness, has taken away from us our adored and adorable queen. The calamity has overwhelmed me'. With the Queen's death, Caroline returned to live with her half-brother at Ansbach. That summer, George Augustus, the son of George Louis of Hanover passed through Ansbach whilst travelling in disguise, and he immediately fell in love with Caroline. By 1705, he was third in line to the throne of England after his grandmother and father and he was an excellent match for Caroline. The couple were married at Hanover on 2 September 1705.

From the first, Caroline had a powerful hold over her husband, and he was deeply attracted to her. According to Lord Hervey, who was present, when Caroline was on her deathbed, George Augustus assured her that 'he was sure he could have been happy with no other woman upon earth for a wife, and that if she had not been his wife, he had rather have had her for his mistress than any woman he had ever been acquainted with'. In spite of his devotion, he was never faithful to her, but it was noted by his contemporaries that he appeared to commit adultery only because he felt it was expected of him, rather than due to any real desire. George Augustus certainly appears to have had little respect for his longest-standing mistress, Henrietta Howard, Countess of Suffolk, who arrived in Hanover with her husband shortly before the death of Queen Anne in 1714. Caroline, who was always careful to show George Augustus no disapproval, obligingly took his mistress into her service and brought her with her to England shortly after the accession of her father-in-law as George I. According to Horace Walpole, Caroline's superior influence over George Augustus ensured that Henrietta had no political power and received very few rewards. She was also able to regularly humiliate her rival:

From the queen [Caroline] she [Henrietta] tasted more positive vexations. Till she became Countess of Suffolk, she constantly dressed the queen's head, who delighted in subjecting her to such servile offices, though always apologising to her good Howard. Often her majesty had more complete triumph. It happened more than once, that the king, coming into the room while the queen was dressing, has snatched off the handkerchief, and, turning rudely to Mrs Howard, has cried, 'Because you have an ugly neck yourself, you hide the queen's'.

Once Caroline had taken the measure of her husband's mistress and was aware that she was superior to her intellectually, she was determined to keep her in place:

The queen, who, however jealous of Lady Suffolk, had latterly dreaded the king's contracting a new attachment to a younger rival, and had prevented lady Suffolk from leaving the court as early as she had wished to do. 'I don't know' said his majesty, 'why you will not let me part with an old deaf woman, of whom I am weary'.

Caroline always appeared obsequious and willing to her husband, but she used her hold over him and subtle persuasion to ensure that, unbeknownst to him, she was always the dominant partner in their relationship.

With Sophia Dorothea of Celle's continuing imprisonment, Caroline became the highest-ranking woman in England following George I's accession. George I was deeply unpopular in England due both to his obvious partiality for Hanover and his refusal to learn English. George Augustus and Caroline, anxious to be liked in their new home, immediately set about learning English, and whilst both spoke with thick German accents, they were viewed considerably more favourably than the King. The relationship between George Augustus and his father was one of mutual loathing, with Horace Walpole describing it as the 'hereditary enmity in the House of Brunswick between the parents and their eldest sons'. Matters came to a head following the birth of Caroline's third son, George William, in 1717. George Augustus intended that George I and his brother, the Duke of York, should act as the prince's godfathers, and he was furious when the King insisted that the Duke of Newcastle should be godfather instead. The christening took place in Caroline's bedchamber, and as soon as it was over, George Augustus rushed up to the Duke of Newcastle and cried, 'You are a rascal, but I shall find you.' The following morning, Caroline's attendants were amazed to discover that her apartments were guarded and that she and George Augustus had been placed under arrest in the night. The arrest order was soon lifted, but the King insisted that the couple leave St James's Palace immediately, retaining custody of their children himself.

Caroline and George had left their eldest son, Frederick, in Hanover when they came to England in 1714, and they never established a close relationship with him. Their second son had been stillborn in 1716, and their third son died a few months after his birth. Whilst George I lived, he always retained the custody of the couple's three eldest daughters, Anne, Amelia and Caroline, and this may account for the somewhat distant relationships Caroline had with her eldest children. Certainly, she was known for being strict with her children, and the Duchess of Marlborough recorded that she visited Caroline one day to find one of the children crying having just been punished. When the duchess tried to comfort the child, Caroline replied that 'you English are none of you well bred, because you was not whipt when you was young'. Caroline had a better relationship with her youngest son, William, Duke of Cumberland, who was born in 1721, and he was her favourite child. Daughters Mary and Louise followed in 1723 and 1724.

Caroline and George Augustus recovered authority over their children in 1727 when George I died unexpectedly on his way to Hanover. George Augustus was jubilant at his accession and immediately declared his intention to rid himself of his father's Prime Minister, Sir Robert Walpole, in favour of his own candidate, Sir Spencer Compton. According to Horace Walpole, this was the moment that Caroline was finally able to fully assert the dominance that she had obtained over her husband. Caroline, who was a good judge of character, recognised Walpole's abilities as a statesman. She also favoured him because he, unlike most of the other members of the court, had recognised that it was she who held power over the King rather than his mistress, Henrietta Howard.

[Caroline,] who had silently watched for a moment proper for overturning the new designation, did not lose a moment in observing to the king how prejudicial it would be to his affairs, to prefer to the minister in possession a man in whose own judgment his predecessor was the fittest person to execute his office. From that moment there was no more question of Sir Spencer Compton as prime minister.

Caroline and Walpole worked closely together throughout the reign and they effectively managed the King in order to ensure that he acted in accordance with their own wishes. This was always done with the utmost subtlety by Caroline. Horace Walpole related of George that

> though his affection and confidence in her were implicit, he lived in dread of being supposed to be governed by her; and that silly parade was extended even to the most private moments of business with my father [Sir Robert Walpole]. Whenever he entered, the queen rose, curtsied, and retired, or offered to retire. Sometimes the king condescended to bid her stay – on both occasions she and Sir Robert had previously settled the business to be discussed. Sometimes the king would quash the proposal in question, and yield after talking it over with her – but then he boasted to Sir Robert that he himself had better considered it.

George II never suspected the influence that Caroline truly wielded, and according to her friend, Lord Hervey, he was fond of declaring that Charles I was ruled by his wife, Charles II by his mistresses, James II by his priests, William III by his male favourites, Queen Anne by her female favourites and his father by anyone who could get access to him, but that he was his own man. This was not how he was viewed by his contemporaries, and one popular rhyme stated,

> You may strut, dapper George, but 'twill all be in vain;
> We know 'tis Queen Caroline, not you, that reign –
> You govern no more than Don Philip of Spain.
> Then if you would have us fall down and adore you,
> Lock up your fat spouse, as your dad did before you.

George was furious when he heard this and other rhymes highlighting Caroline's prominence, but he always left her as regent when he journeyed to Hanover, to the fury of his eldest son.

George and Caroline's eldest son, Frederick, Prince of Wales, arrived in England shortly after his father's accession. The couple had played little role in his upbringing, and the hereditary enmity between Hanoverian parents and their eldest son soon manifested itself. Frederick greatly resented the fact that his parents gave him little role in government, and this turned to fury on the marriage of his sister, Anne, in 1734, which granted her independence whilst he was still reliant on his parents. Caroline disliked Frederick as much as her husband did, and the relationship turned particularly sour during George's absence in Hanover in 1736. According to Hervey, Frederick involved his wife, Augusta of Saxe-Gotha, in the quarrel, something that caused Caroline to comment, 'Poor creature, if she were to spit in my face, I should only pity her for being under such a fool's direction, and wipe it off.' Matters came to a head when Augusta announced her first pregnancy in the early months of 1737. Both Caroline and George were concerned that Frederick meant to introduce a spurious child, and they were determined that the Queen should be at the birth. Frederick was equally determined that she should not, and when, on 31 July, Augusta went into premature labour whilst the couple were staying at Hampton Court with the King and Queen, he hustled his wife into a coach and drove her to St James's Palace, in spite of the fact that nothing was ready and the princess's bed had to be made with tablecloths instead of sheets. George and Caroline were woken in the early hours of the morning by Mrs Titchburne, one of Caroline's ladies, to be informed that the princess was in labour. The Queen immediately called for her nightgown so that she could go to her and was stunned to be told that she would also need to call her coaches, for the princess was at St James's. 'Are you asleep, my good Titchburne?' Caroline cried out, before being assured that what she was told was true. George turned on his wife in a fury:

> You see, now, with all your wisdom, how they have outwitted you. This is all your fault. There is a false child will be put upon you, and how will you answer it to all your children? This has been fine care and fine management for your son William; he is mightily obliged to you: and for Anne, I hope she will come over and scold you herself; I am sure you deserve anything she can say to you.

Mortified, Caroline hurried to St James's and was relieved to find that, instead of a suspiciously strapping boy, the baby that was presented to her was an 'ugly she-mouse'.

Caroline devoted her whole life to obtaining power over George, and she was constantly worried that she would lose influence. Her concerns appeared to be realised in the summer of 1735, when, whilst he was in Hanover, George fell deeply in love with a young woman called Madame Walmoden (who he eventually created Countess of Yarmouth). George was devoted to his mistress, and when he was finally forced to return to England in the autumn, he was in a foul mood, singling out Caroline for particular censure. During his absence, Caroline had replaced a number of the pictures in the drawing room at Kensington Palace. As soon as he saw this, George furiously demanded that Lord Hervey replace all the pictures, complaining that Caroline 'was pulling my house to pieces and spoiling all my furniture: thank God, at least she has left the walls standing!' The Queen was very upset to hear what George had said, and the following day, he renewed his attack on her; entering the gallery,

> [He] snubbed the queen, who was drinking chocolate, for being always stuffing; the Princess Emily [Amelia] for not hearing him; the Princess Caroline for being grown fat; the Duke [of Cumberland] for standing awkwardly; Lord Hervey for not knowing what relation the Prince of Sultzbach was to the Elector Palatine: and then carried the queen to walk, and be resnubbed, in the garden.

Caroline was hurt by George's actions, and she finally snapped, declaring that 'I see no reason, that made your coming to England necessary; you might have continued there, without coming to torment yourself and us: since your pleasure did not call you, I am sure your business did not, for we could have done that just as well without you as you could have pleased yourself without us'. George said nothing to this, but stormed out of the room. He returned to Hanover the following spring, shortly after Madame Walmoden bore his illegitimate son, and he and Caroline were only reconciled when, on Walpole's advice, she wrote to her husband to request that he do her the 'honour' of bringing his mistress back to England with him.

George returned to England in January 1737, ending Caroline's last period of regency. To Caroline's relief, he did not bring Madame Walmoden with him, and his mood was considerably improved. Caroline's health had never fully recovered from her last pregnancy in 1724, and she suffered from a variety of ailments. She was always aware that, in order to ensure that she remained in power, she needed to maintain a physical hold over George, and she took to soaking her foot, which suffered from painful gout, in cold water, to allow her to accompany him on his walks. For Caroline, physical discomfort was a price worth paying for power, and when, on 9 November 1737, she was suddenly taken ill, it soon became clear that she had concealed a far more serious malady in her attempts to keep her grip on her husband. After collapsing on 9 November, Caroline struggled to attend to her duties at court before retiring to bed. She never left it again, and concerned about her, George spent all night lying on her bed beside her. The following morning, the doctors examined her and discovered that she had suffered an umbilical rupture during the birth of her youngest child, which had always caused her considerable pain. On hearing that it was serious, George was grief-stricken and told Lord Hervey that he had first noticed the rupture after the birth of Princess Louise, but that Caroline had made light of it, telling him that 'it was nothing more than what was common for almost every woman to have after a hard labour, or after having many children'. Caroline was immediately informed that she needed an operation if she was to have any chance of survival, and this was performed. In the early hours of 13 November, the Queen complained that her wound was painful, and when it was examined, it was found to be festering.

When Caroline was told of the state of her wound, she knew she was dying. During her illness, Frederick made repeated attempts to see his mother, but she refused, sending him only a curt message stating that she forgave him. Caroline then took her leave of George, advising him to marry again, to which he replied that he would only have mistresses. Caroline had a brief interview with Walpole, declaring that 'I have nothing to say to you, but to recommend the king, my children, and the kingdom to your care'. George was grief-stricken, and he slept on the floor of Caroline's room whilst her second daughter, Amelia, slept on a couch. During the night on 20 November, they and Lord Hervey, who was also present, were woken by the sound of a rattle in Caroline's throat. She weakly said, 'I have now got an asthma. Open the window,' before whispering 'pray' as she expired.

George was devastated at Caroline's death, and true to his word, he did not remarry, instead bringing Madame Walmoden over to England as his mistress. Frederick was never to become king of England, as he died in 1751, leaving his eldest son, George III, to succeed George II in 1760. George III, like his grandfather, was devoted to his wife, although Charlotte of Mecklenburg-Strelitz never attained the political influence of her predecessor as queen.

CHARLOTTE OF MECKLENBURG-STRELITZ (1744-1818) was queen consort for nearly sixty years. She never attained, nor wanted, the influence of her husband's grandmother, Caroline of Ansbach, and she was expressly chosen by her husband for her docility and ability to give him a happy family life. Sophia Charlotte was the youngest child of Charles Louis Frederick of Mecklenburg-Strelitz and his wife, Elizabeth Albertina of Saxe-Hildburghausen. Charlotte's uncle was the reigning duke of the tiny German duchy of Mecklenburg-Strelitz, and on his death in 1753, her eldest brother, Adolphus Frederick IV, succeeded in place of their father, who had died the previous year. The duchy was both small and poor, and whilst the family could trace their descent back past Charlemagne to a near-legendary king of the Vandals, the marriage prospects for Charlotte and her sole-surviving sister were poor. In recognition of this, Charlotte was enrolled in a Protestant convent in her youth with a view to her spending her life there. She received a conventional education and spoke French reasonably, as well as excelling at music. It was only in 1760 that Charlotte came to any sort of international notice. She was always passionately devoted to the interests of the duchy, and when Frederick II of Prussia, who had involved Mecklenburg-Strelitz in his wars by stationing his troops there and recruiting amongst the local population, won a great victory at the Battle of Torgau, Charlotte wrote to him:

I am at a loss whether I shall congratulate or condole with you on your late victory; since the same success that crowns you with laurels has overspread the country of Mecklenburgh with desolation. I know Sire, that it seems unbecoming in my sex, in this age of viscous refinement, to feel for one's country, to lament the horrors of war, or to wish for the return of peace. I know you may think it more properly my province to study the arts of pleasing, or to turn my thoughts to subjects of a more domestic nature; but however unbecoming it may be in me, I cannot resist the desire of interceding for this unhappy people.

It was but a few years ago that this territory wore the more pleasing appearance; the country was cultivated, the peasants looked cheerful, and the towns abounded with riches and festivity. What an alteration at present from such a charming scene! I am not expert at description, nor can my fancy add any horrors to the picture; but sure even conquerors themselves would weep at the hideous prospect now before me. The whole country, my dear country, lies one frightful waste, presenting only objects to excite pity, terror, and despair. The business of the husbandman and the shepherd is quite discontinued; the husbandman and shepherd are become soldiers themselves, and help to ravage the soil they formerly occupied. The towns are inhabited only by old men, women, and children: perhaps here or there a warrior, by wounds or loss of limbs, rendered unfit for service, left at his door: his little children hang round him, ask a history of every wound, and grow themselves soldiers before they find strength for the field. But this were nothing, did we not feel the alternate insolence of each army, as it happens to advance or retreat. It is impossible to express the confusion which even those who call themselves our friends, excite. Even those from whom we might expect redress, oppress us with new calamities. From your justice, therefore, it is that we hope for relief; to you even children and women may complain, whose humanity stoops to the meanest petition, and whose power is capable of repressing the greatest injustice.

Charlotte's letter was widely circulated, with a copy reaching the new king of England, George III.

George III, the son of Frederick, Prince of Wales, succeeded to the throne on the death of his grandfather, George II. George III was only twenty-two at the time of his accession in October 1760, and he was fully under the influence of his mother, the dowager Princess of Wales, and her favourite, Lord Bute, who George later made his prime minister. Augusta and Bute had been alarmed when, even before he came to the throne, George showed a romantic interest in the beautiful Lady Sarah Lennox, the sister of the Duke of Richmond, and they were determined to marry him to an appropriate princess as soon as possible. George flirted with the idea of marrying Sarah, but his shyness, and his sense of duty, got the better of him, and he allowed a shortlist of appropriate princesses to be drawn up. Charlotte's name featured on the list, but she was not considered a likely choice until the King received a copy of her letter. When he saw it, he turned to Lord Harcourt and declared that 'this is the lady whom I shall secure for my consort. Here are lasting beauties. The man who has any mind may feast and not be satiated. If the disposition of the Princess but equals her refined sense, I shall be the happiest man, as I hope, with my people's concurrence to be the happiest monarch, in Europe.' Whilst Lady Sarah Lennox and her family waited hopefully for a marriage proposal, George allowed an embassy to travel to Mecklenburg-Strelitz with an offer of marriage for Charlotte, something that was readily accepted. George, who intended to share his coronation with his bride, chose duty over love, and in July 1761, he delivered a declaration to his council:

Having nothing so much at heart as to procure the welfare and happiness of my people, and to render the same stable and permanent for posterity, I have ever since my accession to the throne, turned my thoughts towards the choice of a Princess for my consort; and I now with great satisfaction acquaint you, that after the fullest information and mature deliberation, I am come to a resolution to demand in marriage the Princess Charlotte of Mecklenburgh Strelitz; a Princess distinguished by every eminent virtue and amiable endowment; whose illustrious line has constantly shewn the firmest zeal for the Protestant religion, and a particular attachment to my family. I have judged proper to communicate to you these intentions, in order that you may be fully apprised of a matter so highly important to me and to my kingdoms, and which I persuade myself will be most acceptable to all my loving subjects.

For Charlotte, who had faced the prospect of life as a spinster, it was a flattering offer, although it destroyed the hopes of her elder sister, who had intended to marry the Duke of Roxburgh. Charlotte's sister Christiane was, at twenty-five, too old to be considered by the King, and her marriage plans were quietly dropped when it was made clear that it would be impossible for George to marry the sister-in-law of one of his subjects. Charlotte always believed in the need to keep royal blood separate from that of subjects, and she would have considered the match proposed for her sister to be beneath her. She also had more exciting prospects to think about, and on 17 August, she left Mecklenburg-Strelitz, arriving at Harwich on 6 September. Charlotte was always considered to be plain, with her contemporary Horace Walpole describing her as 'not tall, nor a beauty; pale and very thin; but looks sensible and genteel. Her hair is darkish and fine; her forehead low, her nose very well, except the nostrils spreading too wide; her mouth has the same fault, but her teeth are good'. She tried to make the best of herself, dressing in English fashions for her reception in London on 8 September. Charlotte met George for the first time at the entrance to the garden at St James's Palace and she immediately sank to her knees as he raised her up. Some observers noted a brief look of dismay on George's face when she first came into view, but he was nothing but courteous to her on their first meeting. The couple were married that evening in the Chapel Royal.

For Charlotte, the days following her marriage were bewildering, and whilst she started working with an English tutor soon after her marriage, at first, she was unable to communicate with many people at court other than the royal family. She and George were crowned on 22 September in a poorly organised ceremony that was delayed due to the sword of state being lost and conducted in the near-dark at Westminster Abbey. In spite of the difficulties, Charlotte later confessed to her attendant, Fanny Burney, that she had initially revelled in her role as queen, commenting on

how well she had liked at first her jewels and ornaments as queen, - 'But how soon', cried she, 'was that over! Believe me Miss Burney, it is a pleasure of a week, - a fortnight, at most, - and to return no more! I thought, at first, I should always choose to wear them; but the fatigue and trouble of putting them on, and the care they required, and the fear of losing them, - believe me, ma'am, in a fortnight's time I longed again for my own earlier dress, and wished never to see them more!'

Charlotte was very shy, and whilst George was always kind to her, she was aware of his interest in Lady Sarah Lennox, who had tactlessly been appointed as one of her bridesmaids. George was never unfaithful to Charlotte, but their marriage was, at first, no love match. The Princess of Wales was also determined to maintain her control over her son, and both she and George treated Charlotte as a child. George had no intention of allowing Charlotte any role in politics, and the Queen often found that, whilst her husband would take her to Carlton House where he had daily meetings with his mother and Lord Bute, she was pointedly made to wait in another room and allowed to play no part in the discussion. Charlotte had always been obedient to her mother (who had ruled as regent in Mecklenburg-Strelitz) and then her brother, and she never showed any desire to interfere or even discuss politics, something that delighted her husband. She was always dutiful and obedient to George, but she had a troubled relationship with his family. When George's brothers, the Dukes of Cumberland and Gloucester both made marriages to members of the English nobility, Charlotte fully supported George in refusing to recognise the marriages or receive the new duchesses. She always showed a particular dislike for George's eldest sister, Princess Augusta, Duchess of Brunswick. When, in January 1764, the Duchess of Argyll yielded precedence to Lady Gower to allow her to sit next to her old friend, the Duchess of Brunswick, who was visiting England, Charlotte rebuked her:

> I must reprimand you, for letting Lady Gower take place of you, as lady to the Princess of Brunswick. I had a mind to speak to you on the spot but would not, for fear of saying anything I should repent of, though I should have thought it. The Princess of Brunswick has nothing to do here, and I insist on your recovering the precedence you gave up. One day or other my son will be married, and then I shall have his wife's ladies pretending to take place in my palace, which they shall not do.

It was unfortunate for all concerned that Charlotte's son's wife was ultimately to be the Duchess of Brunswick's daughter, and Charlotte transferred her loathing of her mother to her. It was Charlotte who ultimately won in her battle with George's family, and when, in early 1772, the Duchess of Brunswick came to visit her dying mother, she was pointedly informed that there were no rooms available for her at any of the royal palaces in London, in spite of the fact that Charlotte's own brother was staying in an apartment at St James's Palace. Charlotte was always committed to her own birth family to the exclusion of George's, and when, in 1782, she named her youngest child after George's aunt, Princess Amelia, the rumour at court was that this was merely in the hope that the old lady would leave her young namesake her fortune.

Whilst the first few months of her marriage were difficult, Charlotte, by always appearing obedient to George, won his devotion. The couple were determined to live as quietly as possible and build a happy family life. Charlotte was famous for her remarkably strong constitution, and in the twenty-two years following her marriage, she bore fifteen children, thirteen of whom survived to adulthood. Charlotte's eldest, George, Prince of Wales, was born on 12 August 1762 and baptised on his parents' first wedding anniversary. His birth was followed by that of Frederick in August the following year, then by William, Charlotte, Edward, Augusta, Elizabeth, Ernest, Augustus, Adolphus, Mary, Sophia, Octavius, Alfred, and Amelia. According to Holt, one of George III's earliest biographers, by 1774, the royal parents established a daily routine, allowing them to spend as much time with their children as possible:

> Their Majesties were now accustomed to rise at six o'clock in the morning, and enjoy the two succeeding hours, which they called their own: at eight the Prince of Wales, the Bishop of Osnaburgh [Frederick], the Princess Royal [Charlotte], and Princes William and Henry [*sic*, in fact Edward] were brought from their several houses at Kew-house, to breakfast with their illustrious relations. At nine their younger children attended to lisp or smile their good morrows; and while the five eldest were closely applying to their tasks, the little ones and their nurses passed the whole morning in Richmond-gardens. When the weather was unfavourable in the morning, her Majesty entertained herself with needle work.

The king and queen frequently amused themselves by sitting in the room while the children dined; and, once a-week, attended by the whole offspring in pairs, made the little delightful tour of Richmond-gardens. In the afternoon the queen worked, and the king read to her: all the children again paid their duty at Kew-house before they returned to bed, and the same order was presented through each returning day.

Whilst the children were young, the family routine was harmonious. George was responsible for the education of the couples' sons, whilst Charlotte was left in sole control of her six daughters. She raised them expertly, and the princesses were renowned for their kindliness and good manners. In one anecdote, told to Fanny Burney by Charlotte herself, the Queen employed as one of the children's tutors a Mr Webb whose nose had been disfigured in an accident. Charlotte warned her nine-year-old daughter Sophia never to stare at the tutor or mention his disfigurement, something that the princess took so much to heart that, when she was alone with Lady Cremorne and Mr Webb was announced, Sophia rushed over to her and said, 'Lady Cremorne, Mr Webb has got a very great nose, but that is only to be pitied – so mind you don't laugh!' George and Charlotte loved to live quietly in the countryside, and they purchased Buckingham Palace in order to possess a London residence as far out of town as possible. The couple led a particularly abstemious life, and they hoped that their children would follow their virtuous, if dull, existence.

Whilst the children were young, they were happy to obey their parents, but as they grew up, there were tensions in the family. Like all of the Hanoverian monarchs, George had a poor relationship with his eldest son, and both he and Charlotte were grieved by the Prince of Wales's disreputable lifestyle. The prince, like his younger brother Augustus, made an unsuitable marriage to a commoner, and whilst the prince was persuaded to abandon his first wife, Mrs Fitzherbert, Augustus remained with his bride for some years, to his father's anger. George was always particularly fond of his daughters, and he had no wish to let them leave the family group. He therefore took no steps to arrange marriages for them and actively discouraged suitors from visiting. Charlotte, obedient to George in everything, did not help her daughters, and as they aged, they became increasingly unhappy. The Princess Royal attempted to marry the Duke of Bedford, and whilst this was not allowed, she was eventually permitted to marry the King of Wurttemberg at the age of thirty. Her younger sisters were not so lucky, and Mary and Elizabeth both had to wait until their forties to marry. Augusta, the beauty of the family, was given no opportunity to find a husband and always remained with Charlotte. The youngest, Amelia, enjoyed a love affair with an army officer, Charles Fitzroy, whom she was not permitted to marry, and there were rumours, probably true, that Sophia bore an illegitimate child to her lover, General Thomas Garth, in 1800. Charlotte encouraged no particular intimacy with her daughters as they grew up, and she always addressed her eldest daughter formally as the Princess Royal.

As well as assisting in the upbringing of her children, Charlotte's interests were domestic, and she and George enjoyed taking long country walks. Both were charitable, and the Queen paid for the upbringing of one hundred orphaned children of army and naval officers. Charlotte could also be spontaneously charitable, and when, in 1784, she and George were out walking together near Windsor, they were driven by a storm to take refuge in the cottage of a poor woman. Their hostess did not know who her guests were, and whilst the couple waited for the weather to clear, she lamented that she had nothing to offer them but bread, telling them that, in more prosperous times, she had been famous for the quality of her bacon. The woman also informed the King and Queen that her daughter was ill and showed them where she slept, covered in rags. Charlotte took pity on her and said, 'Well, my good woman, I do not despair of seeing your bacon-rack again well stored, and when it is, remember I bespeak a spare-rib of you, as I am remarkably fond of pork.' On her return to Windsor Castle, Charlotte sent the woman both funds to pay for her daughter's treatment and a pig. The woman was so grateful that, when the pig was slaughtered, she walked all the way to London to present Charlotte with her spare rib. She was then sent home on the public coach, at Charlotte's expense. Although often seen as distant and forbidding, Charlotte sympathised with her poorer subjects, and both she and George were particularly interested in agriculture, with the King becoming known by the nickname 'Farmer George'.

In August 1782, Charlotte and George suffered their first family tragedy when their youngest son, Alfred, died shortly before his second birthday. George took the news reasonably, commenting that if it had been his favourite son, Octavius, he should have been heartbroken. To the couple's grief, Octavius died suddenly the following year after an illness of only forty-eight hours duration, and whilst the King transferred his affections to his youngest child, Amelia, who was born shortly after Octavius's death, the tragedy continued to play on his mind. In the summer of 1788, George fell ill, and whilst he seemed to recover, in October, his symptoms suddenly became alarming. On 26 October, Fanny Burney, Charlotte's attendant, recorded an encounter with the King in her diary:

> The king was prevailed upon not to go to chapel this morning. I met him in the passage from the queen's room; he stopped me, and conversed upon his health near half-an-hour, still with that extreme quickness of speech and manner that belongs to fever; and he hardly sleeps, he tells me, one minute all night; indeed, if he recovers not his rest, a most delirious fever seems to threaten him. He is all agitation, all emotion, yet all benevolence and goodness, even to a degree that makes it touching to hear him speak.

To those around the King, it soon became apparent that all was not well, and he continued to speak so rapidly and continuously that he almost-entirely lost his voice. Charlotte was particularly anxious, and by 1 November, Burney recorded that she was so upset that she wept whilst being read to, commenting, 'How nervous I am! I am quite a fool! Don't you think so?' The King continued to grow worse, becoming cloyingly fond of Charlotte and the princesses. Soon afterwards, Burney recorded,

> Nor can I ever forget him in what passed this night. When I came to the queen's dressing-room he was still with her. He constantly conducts her to it before he retires to his own. He was begging her not to speak to him when he got to his room, that he might fall asleep, as he felt great want of that refreshment. He repeated this desire, I believe, at least a hundred times, though, far enough from needing it, the poor queen never uttered one syllable! He then applied to me, saying he was really very well, except in that he could not sleep.

Charlotte was almost paralysed with terror at George's illness. She was not even able to retain her dignity for appearance's sake, and her hair turned grey due to the strain. On 5 November, at dinner, George spoke so deliriously that Charlotte fell into violent hysterics and the princesses wept. The following morning, Burney recorded that the Queen 'looked like death – colourless and wan', and Charlotte, who had always been guided by George's wishes, was unable to act under her own volition, instead surrendering the entire running of the household to her eldest son and shutting herself away. She was also terrified of George himself and moved rooms following a night where the King, candle in hand, walked quietly into her bedroom and pulled back her bed curtains, standing watching her for half an hour in silence.

By the end of 1788, it was well known across England that the King was mad, and he spent Christmas Day with a pillow which he said was his lost son, Octavius. To add to Charlotte's misery, in the early weeks of 1789, George conceived a violent dislike of her, claiming that he had never had any feelings for her and that she had a bad temper and the children were afraid of her. He also tried to take her favourite dog from her, saying that it was fond of him but not of her. To Charlotte's humiliation, George declared that he was deeply in love with one of her ladies, Lady Pembroke, and he was observed to speak about her amorously on a number of occasions. George's condition was baffling to his doctors, and unusually, he had, on occasions, a degree of self-awareness, obtaining a copy of Shakespeare's *King Lear* and summoning his three elder daughters to inform them that 'I am like poor Lear, but thank God I have no Regan, nor Goneril, but three Cordelias'. Whilst Charlotte relied on her eldest son to take the lead, she was disconcerted when he and his friends in the opposition in parliament took steps to try to have him appointed regent. Charlotte, who had no interest in politics, instinctively placed herself behind George's Prime Minister, William Pitt, who opposed the prince's regency, and she was upset to find herself attacked by the opposition. It was a great relief to Charlotte when, in mid-February, George suddenly began to recover his wits and a regency was averted. Although it was not known at the time, George was probably suffering from the hereditary condition Porthyria, which caused the appearance of madness. With the King's recovery, Charlotte was once again able to retreat to her domestic sphere, although there was always a tension in her marriage that the King could relapse, and she was terrified when he again briefly displayed the symptoms of madness in 1804.

Charlotte and George suffered a further family tragedy on 2 November 1810 when their youngest child, Amelia, died after a long illness. Amelia was the King's favourite child, and he tended her constantly during her sickness. His devastation at her death caused his sanity to entirely break down. As she had done before, Charlotte remained in the same residence as George, and in early 1811, she received a deputation from parliament that came to discuss the regency. Once again, Charlotte made no moves to be appointed regent herself, and she consented to her eldest son becoming Prince Regent. Charlotte was appointed as George's guardian, and she spent much time with him at Windsor, issuing intermittent bulletins about his health. At first, both Charlotte and the doctors were optimistic that George would recover, and physically, he appeared in good health. However, as the months and then years passed, all hope was lost, and by the end of his life, he was almost entirely blind and deaf and presented a sad and unkempt figure as, according to his biographer, Holt, he 'wandered amidst the phantoms of his imaginations'.

Charlotte tried to carry on much as before, and with the Prince Regent's estrangement from his wife, Caroline of Brunswick, she remained the first lady in the land. Whilst Charlotte and her eldest son had had disagreements in the past, he always remained her favourite child, and she fully supported him in his battles with his hated wife, who she, in any event, had never liked. In 1812, Charlotte began to hold drawing rooms again, at which members of the court were permitted to approach her, and in May 1814, at her son's request, she wrote to her daughter-in-law, banning her from attending court:

> The Queen considers it to be her duty to lose no time in acquainting the Princess of Wales, that she has received a communication from her son the Prince Regent, in which he states, that her Majesty's intention of holding two drawing-rooms in the ensuing month have been notified to the public, he must declare, that he considers his own presence at her Court cannot be dispensed

with: and that he desires it may be distinctly understood, for reasons of which he alone can be the judge, to be his fixed and unalterable determination, not to meet the Princess of Wales upon any occasion, either in public or private.

The Queen is thus placed under the painful necessity of intimating to the Princess of Wales, the impossibility of her Majesty's receiving her Royal Highness at her drawing-rooms.

Caroline, who had a gift for publicity, ensured that the Queen's letter was widely circulated, and she responded, appealing to Charlotte to ensure that the guests were aware that her banishment was not due to any misconduct on her part. Charlotte continued to insist that Caroline was not welcome at court and stood firmly beside her son, something that made her deeply unpopular in England, where the princess enjoyed considerable support. The Prince Regent was also often on difficult terms with his daughter, Princess Charlotte, the only legitimate grandchild of George and Charlotte, and whilst Charlotte played a part in arranging her namesake's education, they had a troubled relationship. As a result of this, Charlotte travelled to Bath in the autumn of 1817 rather than staying in London to attend her granddaughter's confinement with her first child. On 6 November 1817, Charlotte had just entered a drawing room to receive an address from the representatives of the city of Bath when she was informed that her granddaughter had given birth to a stillborn son. The Queen was extremely agitated by this, but on hearing that the princess seemed well, she stayed to hear the address. Later that day, she was sitting down to dinner when a second messenger arrived. Charlotte immediately exclaimed, 'I know some fatal event has happened,' and she was informed that her granddaughter had died. The death of Princess Charlotte was a national tragedy and left the monarchy perilously exposed. The Queen was also deeply upset, in spite of her poor relationship with her granddaughter, and this cannot have helped her already declining health.

In early February 1818, Charlotte was forced to postpone a drawing room due to her ill health. She was able, however, later that month, to hold a drawing room to celebrate her official birthday, appearing propped up on cushions to support her weight. On 7 April, the Queen attended the marriage of her daughter, Elizabeth, to the Prince of Hesse-Homburg. She held a further drawing room later that month and, on 11 July, was present at the double wedding of two of her sons, William and Edward. She continued to appear frail, and in the summer, she suffered a number of fits, which left her unable to walk. Charlotte moved to Kew with her daughters Augusta and Mary. By November, the elderly queen was barely conscious, and she died on 17 November 1818, just over a year before her husband, George III, followed her to the grave in January 1820.

Charlotte of Mecklenburg-Strelitz played a very limited political role. She and her husband, George III, did, however, have a profound influence on the monarchy and they set a standard of propriety that their own children found impossible to emulate. The secret first marriage of Charlotte's eldest son to Maria Fitzherbert was a demonstration of this, and during George IV's lifetime, Maria was never even recognised as his wife.

MARIA FITZHERBERT (1756-1837) was never queen of England, and her marriage to the Prince of Wales, who later became George IV, remained an open secret throughout her lifetime. Maria was not born to make a royal marriage, and her upbringing as a Roman Catholic, quite apart from her non-royal background, was enough to make such an event particularly unlikely. Maria was born Mary Ann Smythe and was the eldest child of Walter Smythe and his wife, Mary Errington. Her father was the younger son of a baronet, and the family were prominent in Shropshire. Whilst a younger son, Maria's father was fortunate enough to inherit Brambridge Hall in Hampshire in 1763, which the family made their home. Like many wealthy Catholics at the time, Maria was educated in a French convent, beginning her education at around the age of twelve. In her memoirs recorded by her cousin, Lord Stourton, she recalled that her parents accompanied her to France and that they attended the French court to view Louis XV dining in public. Maria was beautiful, and the King noticed her, sending her a dish of sugared plums as a compliment.

Maria returned to England when she was aged around sixteen and made her debut into London society. She soon caught the attention of Edward Weld, a wealthy Catholic landowner who was fifteen years older than her. This was an excellent match for Maria, and the couple married in July 1775 before moving to Weld's seat at Lulworth Castle in Dorset. They were there in October when he suddenly fell ill, dying on 26 October 1775. In her marriage settlement, Maria was entitled to only £800 a year as her widow's pension, and the death was followed by a dispute between Maria and her brother-in-law over some jewellery and other property. She remained at Lulworth Castle for some time after her husband's death, before returning to London in either 1776 or 1777.

Whilst in London, Maria met Thomas Fitzherbert, another wealthy Catholic, who was ten years older than her. He was something of a character, and according to Sir Thomas Clifford, who knew him, 'Mr Fitzherbert was an astonishing pedestrian, and being inclined to corpulency, he endeavoured to counteract that tendency, by the most extraordinary bodily exertions, by which he was supposed greatly to have impaired his constitution'. He was also a brave man and during the anti-Catholic riots in London of 1780, 'his curiosity led him on one occasion to mingle with the mob; and at the close of the day, being much fatigued and overheated, he had the imprudence to throw himself into a cold bath'. Mr Fitzherbert was handsome, and he and Maria made a good-looking couple at their marriage on 24 June 1778. Maria's second marriage proved more lasting than her first, and according to Clifford, she bore her husband a son who lived only a few months. This was her only recorded child. At some point during her second marriage, she abandoned her birth name of 'Mary Ann' in favour of the more cosmopolitan 'Maria'.

Maria and Mr Fitzherbert spent much time at their London residence in Mayfair, and the first time she saw the Prince of Wales was when she was out driving with her husband and he pointed him out. She saw the prince again a few days later, again with her husband, when she noticed that he had been following her. In his youth, George, Prince of Wales, was strikingly handsome, but Maria paid him little attention at the time. George had been nearly sixteen at the time of Maria's second marriage and would have been in his late teens when she first saw him. By that time, the prince already had a reputation for hedonism, being fond of gambling, wine and women. By his sixteenth birthday, he had seduced one of his mother's maids and the wife of a man in the royal household, before becoming infatuated with a young lady, Mary Hamilton, two years later. In December 1779, George embarked on an affair with an actress, Mary Robinson, and he was known for many other lovers over the years. Prone to falling in love, he would bombard the object of his affections with love letters, as Maria was later to find out. When she noticed the prince's interest during her second marriage, however, she is unlikely to have reacted in any other way than amusement. By 1780, Mr Fitzherbert's health was in decline, and the couple travelled to Nice for the warmer climate. He died there on 7 May 1781, and Maria, who appears to have been in love with her second husband, later referred sadly to her 'sufferings at Nice' in a letter to her adopted daughter, Minney Seymour.

Maria was grieved by her second husband's death, and she purchased a chapel in Nice in which to house a memorial to him. Mr Fitzherbert left her wealthy, as she inherited his London house and an annual income of nearly £2,000. Maria had returned to England by the summer of 1782, and she spent some time in the up-and-coming resort of Brighton. She returned to London society in 1784 and that summer accompanied her friend, Lady Sefton, to the opera, sharing her box. Maria caused something of a stir at the opera, and when she was escorted back to her carriage by a friend, Henry Artan, the Prince of Wales came up to her carriage and requested an introduction, asking who the pretty girl was. Maria was undoubtedly flattered by the attention, but she did not take the prince seriously at first. When he was in love, George threw himself wholeheartedly into the pursuit of his object and with Maria he made no exception. When she refused to become his mistress, fearing for her reputation, he began to talk about marriage.

Maria was shocked when George suggested that they marry, as she knew that, according to the law, an heir who married a Roman Catholic would forfeit his right to the throne. Even more immediately, it was doubtful whether a marriage between Maria and George would be valid, as George's father, George III, had passed the Royal Marriages Act in 1772 in response to the clandestine marriages of two of his brothers. This Act invalidated the marriage of any descendant of George II aged under twenty-five, that was made without the consent of the sovereign. If any member of the royal family wished to marry after the age of twenty-five, they were required to apply to the privy council before their marriage could be considered valid. Aware that she could not become the prince's wife and embarrassed by his continued pursuit, Maria resolved to travel to the Continent in the hope that he would lose interest.

According to Maria's own account, preserved by Lord Stourton, the prince was frantic when he heard that she intended to travel abroad, on the night before her departure, he took drastic action:

> Keit, the surgeon, Lord Onslow, Lord Southampton, and Mr Edward Bouverie, arrived at her house in the utmost consternation, informing her, that the life of the Prince was in imminent danger – that he had stabbed himself – and that only her immediate presence would save him. She resisted, in the most peremptory manner, all their importunities, saying that nothing should induce her to enter Carlton House [the Prince's London residence]. She was afterwards brought to share in the alarm, but still, fearful of some stratagem derogatory to her reputation, insisted upon some lady of high character accompanying her, as an indispensible condition; the Duchess of Devonshire was selected. They four drove from Park Street to Devonshire House and took her along with them. She found the Prince pale, and covered with blood. The sight so overpowered her faculties, that she was deprived almost of all consciousness. The Prince told her, that nothing would induce him to live unless she promised to become his wife, and permitted him to put a ring round her finger. I believe a ring from the hand of the Duchess of Devonshire was used upon the occasion, and not one of his own.

George was satisfied with Maria's promise to become his wife and allowed her to leave. Maria was deeply troubled by the prince's apparent suicide attempt, and when Lord Stourton later suggested to her that it might not have been genuine, she maintained that it was, declaring that 'she had frequently seen the scar, and that some brandy-and-water was near his bedside when she was called to him on the day he wounded himself'. Maria was still concerned by all that had happened and, aware that she had been prevailed upon under duress, left for the Continent the next day, in spite of her promise to George.

George's infatuation did not end when Maria left the country, according to the *Memoirs of the Whig Party*:

> In 1784 or early 1785, the Prince of Wales was so deeply enamoured of Mrs Fitzherbert that he was ready to make any sacrifice to obtain from that lady favours which she either from

indifference or scruple persisted in refusing him. He did not conceal his passion, nor his despair at her leaving England for the Continent, Mrs Fox, then Mrs Armitstead, who was living at St Anne's, has repeatedly assured me that he came down thither more than once to converse with her and Mr Fox on the subject, that he cried by the hour, that he testified the sincerity and violence of his passion and his despair by the most extravagant expressions and actions, rolling on the floor, striking his forehead, tearing his hair, falling into hysterics, and swearing that he would abandon the country, forego the crown, sell his jewels and plate, and scrape together a competence to fly with the object of his affection to America.

George was undoubtedly sincere in his affection for Maria, and he bombarded her with love letters wherever she went, with one running to an impressive forty-three pages in length. The letters were so frequent that the French government suspected Maria of being a spy and placed her under observation. When she reached Holland, she found herself in the difficult position of having to talk of the prince to the Princess of Orange, who hoped to marry him. George's pressure had the desired effect, and with the constant proofs of his love, Maria's resolve weakened. Finally, in October 1785, she agreed to return to England to become his wife.

George had confided his plans to his friend, the parliamentarian Charles James Fox, and a letter from Fox to the prince survives from 10 December 1785, warning him against the marriage and pointing out that such a marriage would be illegal and that, even if it were not, it would lead to George being barred from the throne. He finished by saying that 'if I were Mrs Fitzherbert's father or brother, I would advise her not by any means to agree to it, and to prefer any other species of connection with you to one leading to so much misery and mischief'. George, who was a very accomplished liar, replied denying that he intended to marry Maria, but in reality, that December, he could think of nothing else. On the evening of 15 December 1785, he arrived at Maria's London house with only one attendant. He entered the house alone where Maria waited with her uncle, brother and a Protestant clergyman whom George had procured. The ceremony, although performed by a Protestant, was a valid marriage as far as Maria's Catholic faith was concerned, and she later obtained a papal bull to confirm it. After the ceremony, George wrote out the marriage certificate with his own hand, before passing it to Maria for safekeeping. As a further mark of his commitment, he notified his siblings of what had taken place, and Maria was treated with respect by George's many brothers and sisters throughout her life.

Whilst the marriage was conducted in secrecy, it soon became something of an open secret, and the couple appeared together in public regularly. According to Maria's contemporary, Charlotte Bury, George showed all the signs of being in love with his new wife:

I dined with Sir ___. In speaking of Mrs Fitzherbert, he told me that she had a stronger hold over the Regent than any of the other objects of his admiration, and that he always paid her the respect which her conduct commanded. 'She was', said Sir ___, 'the most faultless and honourable mistress that ever a prince had the good fortune to be attached to; and certainly his behaviour to her is one of the most unamiable traits of his character. I remember, in the early days of their courtship, when I used to meet them every night at Sir ___'s at supper. The Prince never forgot to go through the form of saying to Mrs F[itzherbert] with a respectful bow, 'Madame, may I be allowed the honour of seeing you home in my carriage'.

Maria was in love, and there were rumours of a pregnancy during 1786 when the couple were living in Brighton, although there is no evidence that Maria bore the prince a child. Neither

George nor Maria were able to live within their means, and by 1787, George's debts were immense, and he sought a grant of funds from parliament. This led to the first trouble in the marriage, and the prince authorised his friend, Charles James Fox, to make a declaration to parliament on 30 April 1787 that there was no marriage. Maria was furious when she heard what had happened, and she remonstrated with George, threatening to leave him. George was able to persuade Maria that the declaration had been entirely Fox's doing, and Maria never spoke to the politician again. The declaration was the first sign that George was less committed to their marriage than she was.

In 1791, Prince George's younger brother, Frederick, Duke of York, was promised that his debts would be paid if he married a Protestant German princess. By the early 1790s, George owed over £400,000, and in 1793, he also turned to his father for help and was told that he would receive assistance if he married. By that time, there were already tensions between him and Maria, and the prince had taken a new mistress, Lady Jersey. In the summer of 1794, Maria left London for her house in Richmond, expecting George to join her in a few days. She was upset to hear that he had instead gone to Brighton with Lady Jersey, but he sent her an affectionate note on 24 June, and Maria went that evening to dine with his brother William, Duke of Clarence. She was sitting at the table when a note was brought in to her from George, telling her that he would never enter her house again. This was devastating for Maria, and worse news was to come the following year when she heard that her husband had married Caroline of Brunswick. According to Bury, who received her information from Caroline herself, Maria had refused to believe that George would go through with the ceremony:

> The Princess of Wales speaks highly of Mrs Fitzherbert. She always says, 'that is the Prince's true wife; she is an excellent woman; it is a great pity for him he ever broke vid her. Do you know I know de man who was present at his marriage, the late Lord B[radfor]d. He declared to a friend of mine, that when he went to inform Mrs Fitzherbert that the Prince had married me, she would not believe it, for she knew she was herself married to him'.

She certainly had reason to believe that he still thought of her, as, on the night before the ceremony, she looked out of the window of her house to see George passing backwards and forwards on horseback before finally riding away. Maria fainted when she was finally made to believe that George had indeed married someone else. According to Bury, when she was later asked if she would ever become reconciled with the prince, she declared, 'No; the chain once broken, can never be linked together again.'

In spite of her resolution not to be reconciled with George, Maria still regarded herself as his wife, and when George's second marriage proved to be disastrous, he also began to look more fondly on the wife he had abandoned. Shortly after the birth of his and Caroline's only child, Princess Charlotte, in 1786, he believed himself to be dying and wrote his Will, leaving his property to Maria, who he referred to as his wife, and only one shilling to Caroline. Maria at first refused to take George back, but when he fell ill at the rejection, his mother and sisters joined in the pleas that she rekindle the relationship. In 1800, Maria finally agreed to take the prince back, and she later referred to the next eight years as the happiest of her life. George was also able to be of some service to her during that period.

Before her reconciliation with George, Maria had assumed responsibility for the infant daughter of her friend, Lady Horatia Seymour, who had travelled abroad in the hope of regaining her health. Maria was devoted to the child, Mary, whom she nicknamed Minney, and when her friend died in 1801, she was determined to keep her with her. Lady Seymour's husband died in the West Indies soon after his wife, and his executors demanded the return of Minney, who had remained with Maria, so that she could be raised with her elder siblings. Maria always regarded Minney as her own child, and George also became devoted to her, favouring her over his own daughter, Charlotte, with whom he had a troubled relationship. Minney nicknamed George 'Prinny', and the couple took on the role of parents to the young girl, with Maria writing in 1807 to her charge,

> Many thanks, my sweet child, for your letter. I am very glad your cough is better, and I hope when I return I shall have the happiness of finding you quite well. I will deliver your message to Prinny and Wiggy, when I see them, but I am just going out and am afraid if I don't send my letter now I may be late for the post. I shall certainly be with you on Thursday for dinner. I daresay you will be very glad to have your little friend Sophia Keppel at Brighton. Pray send and ask her to dine with you on Christmas day.

George also finished a letter to Maria, writing, 'And now adieu, my dearest Maria, and with a thousand loves and kisses more tender than ever to dearest Minney.' He later wrote tenderly to Minney, assuring her that he 'who whilst he yet lives, never will cease to be, my dearest Child, your ever most affectionate Father by adoption'. Maria refused to hand Minney over, and she and George took the case to court, with the matter eventually reaching the House of Lords. Whilst George petitioned the lords to support Maria, Maria herself went to Lady Hertford, the wife of one of the most prominent members of the lords and Minney's uncle. In 1806, when the case was before the House, Lord Hertford had himself appointed as Minney's guardian, before handing her over to Maria's care. Maria was pleased with this result and settled down to life with her adopted daughter. She was, however, soon to regret the involvement of Lady Hertford.

Lady Hertford first came to George's attention during the Seymour Case, and she quickly became his mistress, to Maria's grief. As he had done with Lady Jersey, George began to ignore his first wife, and matters came to a head in 1811 when he held a dinner in honour of the French King Louis XVIII. For the first time, he insisted that the guests should sit in order of their rank rather than, as was usual, allowing Maria to sit with him at his table. When Maria heard this, she questioned George on the matter, but he merely replied, 'You know, Madam, you have no place,' to which she answered, 'None, sir, but such as you choose to give me.' Maria recognised this for the dismissal it was, and she refused to attend, writing a hurt letter to her husband:

> Sir, After the conversation Your Royal Highness held with me yesterday I am sure you will not be surprised that I have sent my excuses for not obeying your commands for Wednesday next. Much as it has ever been my wish during a period of near thirty years to save you from every embarrassment in my power, yet there are situations when one ought not entirely to forget what is due to oneself. You, Sir, are not aware. In your anxiety to fill your table with persons only of the highest rank, that, by excluding her who now addresses you merely for want of those titles that others possess, you are excluding the person who is not unjustly suspected by the world of possessing in silence unassumed and unsustained a Rank given her by yourself above that of any other person present. Having never forfeited my title to Your Royal Highness's public as well as private consideration by any act of my life, to what could this etiquette be for the first time imputed? No one, my dear Sir, has proved themselves thro' life less solicitous than myself. But I cannot be indifferent to the fair, honourable appearance of consideration from you, which I have hitherto possessed and

which I feel I deserve, and for which reason I can never submit to appear in your house in any place or situation but in that where you yourself first placed me many years ago. Yesterday I was too much surprised, when you informed me that from my want of rank I would not be admitted to your table, to be able to express my feelings in due bounds; and to-day, the impression remaining unabated, I sent my excuse to Colonel Thomas, but on reflection I think it more candid and open to lay my reasons before you, begging you at the same time to believe me.

Maria's humiliation was complete a few days later, when, on a visit to the new Duchess of Devonshire, she came across George enjoying an intimate conversation with Lady Hertford. According to Maria, 'thus terminated this fatal, ill-starred connection', and she never saw George again, playing no role in his reign when he succeeded to the throne as George IV in 1820. The couple still thought of each other however, and when George lay dying in 1830, Maria moved up to London in the hope of seeing him. She received no reply to her letter to him, but he had it placed under his pillow, and George's executor, the Duke of Wellington, later confirmed that, at George's request, he was buried with Maria's picture hanging around his neck.

Maria spent her final years living quietly and raising both Minney and her niece, Marianne Smythe, who also lived with her. Following George's death, Maria had a personal interview with his brother and successor, William IV, and she showed him the papers that she held proving her marriage. William was touched by Maria's loyalty to his brother in never making the marriage public, and he offered to make her a duchess, an honour that she refused, declaring that 'she did not wish for any rank; that she had borne through life the name of Mrs Fitzherbert; that she had never disgraced it, and did not wish to change it'. William recognised Maria as his sister-in-law and allowed her to wear widow's weeds for his brother and use the royal livery. She was also a frequent guest to the Royal Pavilion at Brighton, attending private family occasions with William and his wife. Maria's health gradually failed, and she died on 27 March 1837 from influenza. She had been truly loved, and George's brother, the Duke of Sussex, wrote kindly to Minney to console her on the death of her 'adopted Mother, of whose loss I most deeply deplore'.

Maria Fitzherbert's marriage was never publicly recognised, but she was George IV's companion for a large part of his life and, in his own mind, his true wife. She was greatly lamented at her death, both by her two adopted daughters and by the royal family, which finally accepted her as one of their own. George IV's second and official wife, Caroline of Brunswick, suffered a very different fate, and she died alone and unlamented.

CAROLINE OF BRUNSWICK (1768-1821) was the third child and second daughter of Charles, Hereditary Prince of Brunswick, and his wife Augusta, the sister of George III of England. Caroline was born and raised in the German duchy of Brunswick, which her father inherited on the death of his father in 1780. To her parents' concern, Caroline showed an alarming independence of spirit from her early childhood, a character trait that would remain with her all her life. According to one account, recorded by Caroline's contemporary biographer, Huish, when asked by her tutor 'in what country is the lion found?' she replied boldly, 'In the heart of a Brunswicker.' On another occasion, Caroline's governess refused to let her ride on a carousel for fear that it would make her giddy. Caroline replied that she would ride regardless, for 'a Brunswicker dare do any thing. Fear is a word, of which a Brunswicker is ignorant.'

Whilst Caroline's youthful boldness initially caused amusement, as she grew up, her conduct became positively scandalous. An officer in Caroline's father's guards later recalled that:

a great ball was given, to which the Duchess would not allow her daughter, then aged sixteen, to go. The ball was just begun, when a messenger came to the Duke and Duchess to inform them that Princess Caroline was taken violently ill. Of course, they returned immediately to the palace, all the court following them; the landamman, then on guard, being one among them. When they reached the antechamber of the apartment of the Princess, they found she was on a bed in the next room, screaming in agony; they were told that she was black in the face, &c &c. The doors were all open, when the Duke and Duchess went up to the bed and tenderly enquired what was the matter. The doctors were not yet arrived; the Princess said any attempt at dissimulation would be useless and impossible. 'I am in labour, and I entreat you, madam, to send for an accoucheur immediately'. These words were spoken loud enough to be heard by all those who were waiting in the next room; their astonishment may be conceived. Soon after the accoucheur came: as soon as the Princess saw him, she jumped out of bed, wiped the livid colouring off her face, and with a loud laugh said to the Duchess, 'Now, madam, will you keep me another time from a ball?'

Caroline always had an odd sense of humour, and this was not the only pregnancy she would fake. It was outbursts like this that perhaps account for the fact that the princess remained unmarried at the advanced age of twenty-six. Caroline's actions in Brunswick caused some to doubt her sanity, and her mother later told a friend whilst pointing to her forehead that her daughter 'was not right here'. Caroline's mother was responsible for her daughter's education, but the pair had a poor relationship, and the English envoy at the time of Caroline's engagement commented that she 'had no respect for her mother, and was inattentive to her when she dared'.

By 1794, Caroline knew that she was fast heading towards spinsterhood, and it was therefore with surprise and excitement that she greeted the news that her cousin George, Prince of Wales, wished to marry her. By 1794, George had amassed vast debts and on being informed that parliament would pay them if he married, he immediately looked around for a bride. According to the *Memoirs of the Whig Party*, George was not particularly concerned about whom he married and, when his father offered to send envoys across Europe, saying that '"your wife must be Protestant and a princess: in all other respects your choice is unfettered". "It is made", replied the Prince; "the daughter of the Duke of Brunswick"'. George III confirmed that he was pleased with the selection of his niece, but that he recommended that his son make more substantial enquiries. 'The Prince pretended to have done so; though his brothers, or indeed every young English traveller in Germany would, if asked, have told him that even in that country, where they were not at that period very nice about female delicacy, the character of his intended bride was exceedingly loose.' George simply required a bride as soon as possible and he despatched the Earl of Malmesbury to Brunswick in autumn 1794 with a marriage proposal.

Malmesbury arrived in Brunswick on 20 November 1794 and recorded his initial impressions of Caroline in his diary, commenting that she seemed embarrassed on first being presented to him but had a 'pretty face – not expressive of softness – her figure not graceful – fine eyes – good hand – tolerable teeth, but going – fair hair and light eyebrows, good bust – short'. Caroline seemed pleasing enough on first inspection, and Malmesbury found both the princess and her mother in a state of excitement about the marriage proposal. As the duchess later confided to Malmesbury, it was a very flattering offer, and 'all the young German Princesses, she said, had learnt English in hope of being Princess of Wales – she never would give the idea to Caroline, and she never thought it could happen, as the king had often expressed his dislike to the marriage of cousins-german'.

Malmesbury was pleased to find Caroline cheerful and with good sense, but he had grave concerns about her character and manners, something which he discussed in a conversation with the duke's mistress, Mademoiselle Hertzfeldt. According to his diary, she 'reports to me what the duke had before said – stated the necessity of being very strict with the Princess Caroline – that she was not clever, or ill-disposed, but of a temper easily wrought on, and had no tact'. Malmesbury found Caroline willing to be guided by him, and that evening at dinner, she begged him for advice, receiving the response that 'I recommend perfect silence on all subjects for six months after her arrival'. Malmesbury spent much of December advising Caroline on how she should behave as Princess of Wales. He was disconcerted to discover that she knew the identity of Lady Jersey, Prince George's mistress, and at dinner on 28 December, he found both Caroline and her mother in a state of agitation having received an anonymous letter from England 'abusing the prince, and warning them in the most exaggerated terms against Lady ___ [Jersey], who is represented as the worst and most dangerous of profligate women'. Malmesbury found his work of explaining away the letter more difficult, since 'the Duchess, with her usual indiscretion, had shewn this to the Princess, and mentioned it to everybody'. He later had a difficult conversation with Caroline where he first made her aware that, whilst infidelity was to be expected in the prince, in her, as the Princess of Wales, it was treason and would lead to the deaths of both her and her lover. According to Malmesbury, 'this startled her'.

Malmesbury was relieved to finally set out with Caroline and her mother on 30 December, and they hoped to quickly arrive in England. This proved not to be the case, as, due to the war in Europe, the party were forced to spend some weeks at Hanover. Throughout the journey, Malmesbury's concerns about Caroline's character increased, and on 31 December, he recorded that the 'Princess wanted me to be in the same coach with her – I resisted it as impossible, from its being improper – she disposed to laugh at the matter'. Five days later, Caroline again caused disappointment, and Malmesbury recorded that she was 'very gauche at cards – speaks without thinking – gets too easy – calls the ladies (she never saw) "*Mon couer, ma chere, ma petite*". I notice this and reprove it strongly. The Princess, for the first time, disposed to take amiss.' On 21 January, she had a tooth pulled and shocked Malmesbury by sending him the extracted tooth as a present.

Another major concern was Caroline's personal hygiene. During the journey, Malmesbury had two conversations with her on the subject of washing and on the importance of wearing clean clothes, and whilst, after the first, she appeared the next day 'well washed', she soon reverted to her old habits. Malmesbury recorded his second conversation with Caroline on 6 March:

> I had two conversations with the Princess Caroline. One on the toilette, on cleanliness, and on delicacy of speaking. On these points I endeavoured, as far as was possible for a man, to inculcate the necessity of great and nice attention to every part of dress, as well as to what was hid, as to what was seen. (I knew she wore coarse petticoats, coarse shifts, and thread stockings, and these never well washed, or changed often enough). I observed that a long toilette was necessary and gave her no credit for boasting that hers was a 'short' one.

Caroline took this in good part, but there is no evidence that she obeyed her escort, and her lack of personal hygiene may account for her husband's reaction to her. The second point on which Malmesbury spoke to Caroline was on her treatment of her mother, and the relationship between the two women was tense. The duchess was a very reluctant companion and was desperate to return to Brunswick throughout the journey, whilst Caroline, according to Malmesbury, spoke 'slightingly' to her, as well as 'being peevish towards her, and often laughing at her, or about her'.

Malmesbury was relieved to finally reach Greenwich on 5 April 1795, aware that his duties would soon be over. On arrival, the earl was disconcerted to find that the King's coaches had not arrived and that this was due to Lady Jersey, who had not been ready to leave on time. Caroline was forced to wait for an hour, and when the coaches finally did arrive, Lady Jersey found fault with her dress, forcing Caroline to change into clothes that she herself had provided. The prince's mistress also insisted on sitting beside Caroline in the coach, something that would have implied that the pair were equals, instead of facing backwards as was appropriate for a lady of the bedchamber. By that time, however, Malmesbury had had enough, and to Caroline's relief, he spoke sharply to Lady Jersey, insisting that she sit in her allotted place or ride in a separate carriage.

Once everyone was ready to leave, the party travelled to St James's Palace. Caroline must have been apprehensive about her first meeting with George, and it proved to be disastrous, as Malmesbury reports:

> I, according to the established etiquette, introduced (no one else being in the room) the Princess Caroline to him. She very properly, in consequence of my saying to her it was the right mode of proceeding, attempted to kneel to him. He raised her (gracefully enough), and embraced her, said barely one word, turned round, retired to a distant part of the apartment, and calling me to him, said 'Harris, I am not well; pray get me a glass of brandy'. I said, 'Sir, had you not better have a glass of water?' – upon which he, much out of humour, said, with an oath, 'No; I will go directly to the queen', and way he went.

Malmesbury was once again left alone with Caroline, and he found her 'in a state of astonishment'. Whilst George was undoubtedly disappointed in her appearance, there was also regret on Caroline's part, and she commented to Malmesbury that her fiancé was very fat and not like his portrait. Matters did not improve that evening at dinner, when Caroline forgot everything she had been taught and appeared 'flippant, rattling, affecting raillery and wit, and throwing out coarse vulgar hints about Lady ___ [Jersey], who was present'. This behaviour fixed George's hatred of Caroline, and he later complained to Malmesbury that he had not warned him in advance about his bride.

In spite of the obvious dislike that both Caroline and George had for each other, both knew that they had to go ahead with the marriage. On the day of the ceremony, 8 April 1795, as Malmesbury delicately recorded, the prince had 'manifestly had recourse to wine or spirits' and could barely stand up straight. The ceremony was farcical, and at one point, George stood up abruptly during a prayer, apparently intending to flee. Everyone was also aware that, due to George's earlier marriage to Mrs Fitzherbert, his second wedding was possibly bigamous, and when the Archbishop of Canterbury came to the part of the ceremony where he asked if there were any impediments to the marriage, he repeated the words twice and stared fixedly at the reluctant bridegroom. Nothing was said, and the couple were married. If Caroline had hoped that matters would improve after the ceremony, she was again to be disappointed, and as she later confided to one of her ladies, Lady Charlotte Bury, 'judge what it was to have a drunken husband on one's wedding-day, and one who passed the greatest part of his bridal-night under the grate, where he fell, and where I left him'. According to George, the marriage was only consummated on three occasions and it was therefore a stroke of luck for the couple when Caroline found herself pregnant, bearing a daughter, Princess Charlotte, on 7 January 1796.

Caroline and George spent the year after their wedding living uneasily together at George's London residence, Carlton House. They spent as little time together as possible, and their initial dislike soon turned to deep and embittered enmity. Finally George, who had dismissed his first wife in a similar way, sent a message to Caroline through Lord Cholmondeley, informing her that 'I never was to have de great honour of inhabiting de same room wid my husband again'. Caroline was unconcerned about the loss of George's person, but she was furious with her dismissal and demanded that George set out his demands in writing. George duly complied on 30 April 1796:

> Our inclinations are not in our power, nor should either of us be held answerable to the other, because nature has not made us suitable to each other. Tranquillity and comfortable society are, however, in our power: let our intercourse, therefore, be restricted to that, and I will distinctly subscribe to the condition which you required, through Lady Cholmondelay, that even in the event of any accident happening to my daughter, which I trust Providence in its mercy will avert, I shall not infringe the terms of the restriction by proposing, at any period, a connexion of a more particular nature. I shall now finally close this disagreeable correspondence, trusting that, as we have completely explained ourselves to each other, the rest of our lives will be passed in uninterrupted tranquillity.

Whilst George hoped that he could discard Caroline quietly, she, with her usual flair for drama, was determined that he could not, writing a reply on 6 May:

> The avowal of your conversation with Lord Cholmondeley neither surprises nor offends me: it merely confirmed what you have tacitly insinuated for this twelvemonth. But after this, it would be a want of delicacy, or rather an unworthy meanness in me, were I to complain of those conditions which you impose upon yourself.
>
> I should have retuned no answer to your letter, if it had not been conceived in terms to make it doubtful whether this arrangement proceeds from you or from me; and you are aware that the honour of it belongs to you alone.
>
> The letter which you announce to me as the last, obliges me to communicate to the king [George III], as to my sovereign and my father, both your avowal and my answer. You will find enclosed a copy of my letter to the king. I apprize you of it, that I may not incur the slightest reproach of duplicity from you. As I have at this moment no protector but his majesty, I refer myself solely to him upon this subject: and if my conduct meets his approbation, I shall be in some degree at least consoled I retain every sentiment of gratitude for the situation in which I find myself, as Princess of Wales, enabled by your means to indulge in the free exercise of a virtue dear to my heart – I mean charity.
>
> It will be my duty, likewise to act upon another motive – that of giving an example of patience and resignation under every trial.

By involving the King, Caroline employed a tactic that only inflamed George further, and she knew that her uncle and father-in-law, George III, was her only supporter in the royal family. Over the years of her dispute with George, Caroline often employed the policy of publicising their correspondence, and many of her later letters were published, at her instigation, in the newspapers.

Caroline moved to her own house next to Blackheath following her separation from George. Charlotte remained with her father at Carlton House, but Caroline was able to receive regular visits from her daughter, who spent one day a week with her. According to Huish, it was Caroline herself who determined the amount of time that she spent with Charlotte, and she commented that 'if I were to have the child with me every day, I should be obliged sometimes to speak to her in a tone of displeasure, and even of severity. She would then have less affection for me, and what I said to her would make less impression upon her heart'. Charlotte was used as a weapon by both her warring parents, and as the girl grew, Caroline's relationship with her daughter became troubled. Caroline was able to indulge her love of children more satisfactorily in the poor children that she took under her protection. Most of these, Caroline raised in accordance with their station in life: the boys being prepared for careers in the navy and the girls raised to be housewives. Two children were her particular favourites: the first, a baby girl found on Blackheath, was named Edwardine Kent in honour of her godfather, Caroline's brother-in-law, the Duke of Kent. Caroline was convinced that this child was the daughter of upper-class French refugees, and she paid for her to have an expensive education. The second child, William Austin, who was Caroline's undoubted favourite, caused his foster mother a great deal of trouble.

Early in 1801, Caroline heard that a neighbour, Lady Douglas, to whom she had not been introduced, had given birth to an exceptionally pretty baby girl. In defiance of convention, Caroline rushed round to the house in the snow and paced up and down outside until Lady Douglas saw her from the window and invited her in. Caroline immediately became firm friends with Lady Douglas, and it appears that she later decided to play a little joke with her friend, which Lady Douglas's own account describes:

In May or June following [1802], the Princess came to my house alone; she said she came to tell me something that had happened to her, and desired me to guess. I guessed several things, and at last I said I could not guess any thing more. She then said that she was pregnant, and that the child had come to life. I don't know whether she said on that day, or a few days before, that she was at breakfast at Lady Willoughby's, that the milk flowed up to her breast, and came through her gown; that she threw her napkin over herself, and went with Lady Willoughby into her room and adjusted herself, to prevent its being observed. She never told me who was the father of the child. She said she hoped it would be a boy. She said that if it was discovered, she would give the Prince of Wales the credit of being the father, for she had slept two nights at Carlton House within the year.

Caroline kept up the story of her pregnancy for some months, pretending to suffer from morning sickness at the same time as Lady Douglas, who was pregnant herself. Caroline's interest in children and childbirth extended to her forcing her way into Lady Douglas's bedchamber as she was giving birth, and she insisted that the infant be handed first to her to inspect. She also told Lady Douglas that she intended to disguise her own child as one of the poor children that were brought to her in baskets for her charity. According to Lady Douglas, at the end of October 1802, she saw Caroline 'dressed so as to conceal her pregnancy; she had a long cloak, and a very great muff'. Lady Douglas then went away for a few months, and when she visited Caroline in January, 'upon the sofa a child was lying, covered with a piece of red cloth. The princess got up and took me by the hand; she then led me to the sofa, and said, "There is the child; I had him only two days after I saw you"'. The child was allowed to play with Princess Charlotte when she visited and called Caroline 'Mamma'. Lady Douglas claimed that she did not know who the child's father was, but that 'the Princess of Wales has told me that she got a bedfellow whenever she could; that nothing was more wholesome' and that she suspected it was Sir Sidney Smith, a frequent visitor to the Princess's house.

Although firm friends at first, Caroline soon tired of Lady Douglas, and the pair fell out, with Caroline sending the other woman three anonymous letters suggesting a love affair between Lady Douglas and Sir Sidney Smith. Lady Douglas was furious and went to the

Prince of Wales in 1806 with her information about Caroline. For George, this was the opportunity that he had been looking for, and his father ordered a secret commission of lords to examine the evidence, a process named 'the Delicate Investigation'. Caroline became aware of the investigation following the examination of her servants, and on 8 June, she sent a formal protest to the King about this treatment. The investigation centred on Caroline's alleged love affairs with Sir Sidney Smith and another man, Captain Manby, who was also a regular visitor to her house, as well as the parentage of William Austin, the baby that Lady Douglas claimed was Caroline's. To George's disappointment, and Caroline's jubilation, it soon became clear that the boy, who Caroline nicknamed 'Willikins', was indeed the child of Samuel and Sophia Austin of Deptford and that he had been adopted by the princess when his mother brought him to her house. Whilst no adultery was proved, however, the commissioners' report was damning of Caroline's conduct in entertaining male visitors, and she lost the only friend in the royal family that she had: the King.

Following the Delicate Investigation, Caroline's position in England became even more difficult, and whilst she was always loved by the people, she was ostracised by her husband and the royal family. In 1811, when George became Prince Regent, Caroline's position became intolerable, and the prince let it be known that anyone who visited Caroline would not be welcome at court. Finally, in 1814, she could stand it no more, sailing from Lancing in Sussex on 8 August for a protracted tour of the Continent. She went with royal consent, although, as Caroline's lady in waiting, Lady Charlotte Bury, noted, 'The Prince hates his wife with inveterate malice; and, if she goes out of the kingdom, it will be only on one condition, that she shall never return.' Caroline was certainly in no hurry to return, and she set about enjoying herself as she wandered aimlessly around the Continent.

Throughout her life, Caroline always displayed an independent spirit and a determination not to follow conventions, and her behaviour abroad quickly caused controversy. According to Bury, Caroline's bizarre behaviour first became apparent at Geneva when she attended a ball given in her honour, 'but what was my horror when I beheld the poor princess enter, dressed as Venus, or rather not dressed, further than the waist. I was, as she used to say herself, "all over shock". A more injudicious choice of costume could not be adopted'. Bury, who was fond of Caroline, was 'grieved to see her make herself so utterly ridiculous'. Caroline spent only four days in Geneva, but she made an impression, also insisting that Napoleon's wife, Marie Louise, sing a duet with her, which, as Bury again commented, 'was an event of the 18th century worthy of being recorded. I wonder what Marie Louise thought of the Princess's singing? She must have been astonished'. Caroline continued to make a laughing stock of herself wherever she went. On one occasion, she appeared in public with half a pumpkin on her head. When she was questioned on this, she merely replied that 'the weather was hot, and nothing kept the head so cool and comfortable as a pumpkin'. Caroline's English attendants rapidly deserted her as she moved south into Italy.

Lady Charlotte Bury had remained at Geneva when Caroline moved south, but she joined the princess in Genoa in April 1815. Caroline was staying in a fine palace there, and when Bury arrived, a remarkable-looking man opened the door. He was 'six feet high, a magnificent head of black hair, pale complexion, mustachios which reach from here to London'. This was Bartolomeo Pergami, a courier that Caroline had taken into her employment as her English servants deserted her. Whilst it was never proved, it is likely that Pergami was Caroline's lover, and there was much gossip in her household, with servants reporting the imprint of two bodies on Caroline's bed and the pair being seen sitting closely together on the sofa. Caroline also ordered a bedroom to be prepared for Willikins for the first time, rather than allowing him to sleep in her room as he had done since infancy. Caroline surrounded herself with Pergami's relatives, appointing his sister as her chief lady-in-waiting, and she lavished gifts and affection on him in public.

Caroline was still in Italy when she was rocked by the greatest tragedy of her life. Caroline had always been fond of her daughter, Charlotte, although the relationship had not been close. She had also looked forward to the day when Charlotte became queen, giving Caroline the status of queen mother. In Caroline's absence, Charlotte married, and Caroline excitedly looked forward to the prospect of becoming a grandmother. Disaster struck on 5 November 1817 when Charlotte, after a long and difficult labour, gave birth to a stillborn son. Charlotte at first seemed to recover well from the birth, but in the early hours of 6 November, she woke up screaming in agony and died soon afterwards. Charlotte's death, as the only legitimate grandchild of George III, was devastating to Britain but it was all the more so to Caroline, and George did not even have the courtesy to notify her personally. Caroline found out about her daughter's death from a messenger who was on his way to the Pope to officially announce the news. On 3 December 1817, she wrote a short note to Bury, in response to a letter of condolence, declaring that 'I now trust we shall soon meet in a much better world than the present one'. With Charlotte's death, Caroline had very little reason to return to England, but when she heard of George III's death in January 1820, she was determined to assert her rights as queen.

Caroline travelled slowly across Europe, leaving Pergami and the other Italians in her entourage at Calais before sailing to Dover. She landed on 5 June and was gratified to receive a gun salute from the castle. As she progressed towards London, she was met by cheering crowds everywhere she went, a mark of her great popularity. George was furious when he heard of his wife's arrival, and he immediately ordered an investigation into her conduct, in the hope of securing a divorce. George had paid spies to follow Caroline around on her journey across Europe, and he had no difficulty in locating witnesses who would testify against her, with a party of Italians arriving in England in early July. Once it had become clear that there was sufficient evidence to proceed, a Bill was drafted, setting out that 'a most unbecoming and degrading intimacy commenced between her said Royal Highness and the said Bartolomo Pergami' and bringing into law Caroline's divorce and the loss of her status as queen.

Caroline immediately petitioned the House of Lords when she heard of the Bill's existence, arguing that she should be allowed to defend herself against the accusations. In order to further enlist public support, she published an open letter to George in the newspaper, speaking of 'the unparalleled and unprovoked persecution which, during a series of years, has been carried out against me under the name and authority of your Majesty'. In her letter, she demanded a fair trial, and finally, on 17 August, she set out to the House of Lords surrounded by cheering crowds in order to hear the case against her. Caroline did not attend every day of her trial, but she heard much of the evidence, listening as those who had attended her on the Continent gave their opinion of her relationship with Pergami. Caroline and Pergami almost certainly had been lovers, but whilst the evidence against Caroline was damning, it was also only circumstantial. On 10 November, when there was a third reading of the Bill, the majority in favour of passing it had been reduced to nine and it was adjourned for six months. For Caroline, it was a victory, but, like the Delicate Investigation, a hollow one, as she was very far from being cleared of impropriety.

Whilst the crowds were jubilant at Caroline's acquittal, details of all that had occurred in Italy did not make edifying reading and the mood of the populace began to turn against her, with a contemporary rhyme noting,

Most gracious queen, we thee implore
To go away and sin no more;
But lest this effort be too great,
To go away, at any rate.

Caroline was given a taste of just how unpopular she had become when, on 19 July 1821, she attempted to gatecrash George's coronation, demanding to be crowned beside him. Caroline went on foot from door to door at Westminster Abbey, finding them all locked against her. She finally came to an open door, only for it to be unceremoniously slammed shut in her face by a page. Caroline finally admitted defeat and, humiliated, returned to her house as the crowd turned on her, jeering. Caroline shut herself away weeping. With this final humiliation, she lost the will to live, and her health rapidly declined. She died on 7 August 1821 unloved and unlamented by all but William Austin, who sat weeping at her bedchamber door. Lady Charlotte Bury perhaps provided the best epitaph for Caroline when she said before the Queen's death that 'for certainly, however much she may have been in the wrong, the Prince is fully as much to blame as she is; and however greatly the Princess of Wales deserves censure, she deserves fully as much pity'.

Caroline of Brunswick lived a turbulent and unhappy life. Much of this was of her own making, but her husband's enmity towards her was not her fault, and it blighted her life. Caroline was an eccentric, and her behaviour was outlandish to say the least. Her successor as queen, Adelaide of Saxe-Meiningen, kept a much lower profile than her sister-in-law, and she is little remembered today. Her marriage came about as a direct consequence of the failure of Caroline of Brunswick's marriage and the death of her daughter, as George IV's brothers desperately tried to provide England with an heir.

ADELAIDE OF SAXE-MEININGEN (1792-1849) made little impact on the country of which she was queen. She was the eldest of three children born to George, Duke of Saxe-Meiningen, and his wife Louisa of Hohenlohe-Langenberg. The duchy of Saxe-Meiningen had been created in the seventeenth century when the larger state of Saxony had been divided into seven parts. The area ruled by Adelaide's father was tiny and had a population of only around 140,000 people. Adelaide's father died on 24 December 1803, leaving his three-year-old son as his heir and Adelaide's mother as regent.

Adelaide's mother was determined to raise her children strictly, and her court was famed for its morals. According to one of Adelaide's earliest biographers, Watkins,

> From earliest childhood, the Princess Adelaide, in particular, was remarkable for her sedate disposition, and rather reserved habits. The greatest portion of her time, it is said, was devoted to her studies; and though perfectly cheerful with her intimate companions, she took little pleasure in the gaieties and frivolities of fashion. Even when arrived at more mature years, she manifested a strong dislike to that laxity of morals, and contempt for religious feeling, which had sprung out of the French Revolution, and infected almost all the courts of Germany.

Adelaide and her younger sister, Ida, devoted their time to charity and were involved in the establishment of schools for the poor children of the duchy. The duchy avoided much of the trouble that beset Europe during the first years of the nineteenth century, and Napoleon, who conquered so much of Europe, did not deign to conquer the tiny state, seeing it as too insignificant. Saxe-Meiningen was poor, and Adelaide's contemporary, Charles Greville, later unkindly referred to her homeland as 'her beggarly country'. Adelaide's upbringing was impoverished and Greville recorded that, when she visited

Meiningen with her English attendants after becoming queen, 'she showed them her old bedroom in the palace (as they call it) at Meiningen – a hole that an English housemaid would think it a hardship to sleep in'.

Whilst she had a reputation for goodness, Adelaide was small and very plain, and she was passed over for marriage in favour of her younger and prettier sister, Ida. By 1817, Adelaide was twenty-five years old, and she, like everyone, assumed that she would remain a spinster. In November 1817, however, Princess Charlotte, the only legitimate grandchild of George III died in childbirth. This caused a rush of royal marriages amongst the British royal family, and Adelaide found herself personally selected by Queen Charlotte as a bride for one of her sons.

William, Duke of Clarence, the third son of George III, like most of his brothers, had not bothered to enter into a legitimate marriage and, instead, lived for many years with the actress Dorothea Jordan, by whom he had ten children. Dorothea had died in 1816, and the couple had separated some years before to allow William to make tentative enquiries about matrimony. In 1817, this became considerably more urgent and both the Prince Regent, who was unhappily married to Caroline of Brunswick, and the second brother, Frederick, Duke of York, whose marriage was childless, were unlikely to provide an heir. William was in his fifties and, after service in the navy from a young age, was renowned for his poor manners. He was also heavily in debt and had a large family of illegitimate children to support. He was not a very attractive candidate and more than one woman turned him down before his mother suggested Adelaide, having heard favourable reports of her virtue. Adelaide must have been alarmed at the prospect of her aged bridegroom, but the thought of remaining a spinster did not appeal, and she arrived in London with her mother on 4 July 1818.

Adelaide received visits from both her fiancé and his eldest brother at her hotel on the night of her arrival, and in spite of apprehension on both sides, the meetings went well. A few days later, she was taken to visit her formidable mother-in-law, Queen Charlotte, and this meeting was also satisfactory. William and Adelaide were married in a joint ceremony at Kew Palace with William's brother, the Duke of Kent, and his bride, Victoire of Saxe-Coburg-Saalfeld. After the ceremony, there was a dinner in honour of the couples before William, Adelaide, and her mother returned to St James's Palace. With her mother's presence, Adelaide had little opportunity to get to know her new husband and the next day, they were joined by William's eldest son, George FitzClarence, who had broken his leg. Adelaide was determined to be a mother to William's children, something that endeared her to her husband, but with many of the FitzClarence's around her own age, the relationship was often troubled. As Greville recorded, 'all the Fitzclarences dislike her, and treat her more or less disrespectfully. She is aware of it, but takes no notice. She is very civil and good-humoured to them all, and as long as they keep within the bounds of decency, and do not break out into actual impertinence, she probably will continue so.' William's perilous finances meant that the couple could not afford to live in England, and they left for Hanover three weeks after the wedding, probably to Adelaide's relief.

Adelaide was always aware that her primary purpose was to bear an heir, and soon after her marriage, she was pleased to discover that she was pregnant. Adelaide was never robustly healthy, and according to Watkins, she caught a cold in March 1819 whilst walking in the palace gardens. This led to a more serious illness, and on 21 March, she gave birth to a daughter, Charlotte, two months prematurely. To Adelaide's grief, Charlotte died within hours of her birth, and Adelaide's life was also feared to be in danger. In order to help her recuperate, William took Adelaide to Meiningen, where she was reunited with her family. She soon conceived again and agreed with William that the child should be born in England.

The couple set out from Meiningen in October 1819, but 'the roads had become very bad for travelling. Her Royal Highness, however, knowing the Duke's anxiety to be at home persevered with uncommon resolution, and, after suffering considerable fatigue, reached Dunkirk, where she miscarried, and was again taken seriously ill.' Adelaide was well enough to cross the channel but then relapsed, being forced to spend six weeks at Walmer Castle. Touchingly, William, who had fallen in love with his bride, remained with her throughout her illness, in spite of his hurry to return to London.

Adelaide conceived for a third time soon after her return to London and, on 10 December 1820, gave birth to a second premature daughter. Unlike her first, Adelaide's second child seemed healthy, and she was baptised Elizabeth on the day of her birth. The choice of name was recognition of the fact that Adelaide was unlikely to bear a son to supplant his elder sister and that the princess was therefore likely to become queen one day as Elizabeth II. Adelaide doted on her daughter, and the few short months of Elizabeth's life were her mother's happiest. On 4 March 1821, the princess fell ill and died a few hours later. According to Watkins, 'the Duchess of Clarence was deeply affected by this calamity, and her health, which suffered considerably at the time, was still further impaired by the following year, by another miscarriage, from the effects of which she recovered but slowly'. Adelaide never recovered from the loss of her daughter and she carried a sculpture of her child with her wherever she went. The couple spent a considerable amount of time on the Continent after Elizabeth's death, visiting relatives. In 1827, William's elder brother, Frederick, Duke of York, died, leaving William as heir to the throne and, with George IV's health failing, it became obvious that William would soon inherit the crown.

George IV spent the last years of his life as a virtual recluse, and it was no surprise when he finally died on 26 June 1830. As soon as the King had died, his physician, Sir Henry Halford, rushed to William to bring him the news. When she saw the messenger, Adelaide immediately burst into tears, terrified at the interference to her quiet, domestic life that the crown would bring. She recovered her composure quickly and passed her prayer book to Sir Henry, telling him that it was 'the first gift of the queen of England'. Later that year, William paid Adelaide the compliment of appointing her as regent in the event that she bore a child who inherited the crown as a minor. By 1830, this was recognised as being distinctly unlikely, and of more immediate concern was the provision that the widow of William's younger brother, the Duchess of Kent, would act as regent for her own daughter, Victoria, in the event that she succeeded to the crown. Greville did, however, record rumours that Adelaide was pregnant as late as 1835, although this came to nothing.

In spite of the provisions allowing for her to become regent in the event of William leaving a minor child, in reality, Adelaide played no political role, and she preferred to remain in the domestic sphere. William's reign was characterised by a movement towards political reform, something that the King resented. On 21 September 1831, the Reform Bill, which had been created by the Whig government, was passed in the House of Commons to public jubilation. On 8 October 1831, however, it was rejected by the House of Lords, causing riots across the country. William refused a request from the Prime Minister, Lord Grey, to create sixty new Whig peers. The Reform Bill was again passed by the Commons on 23 March 1832, and it was rejected by the lords the following month. When Grey once again requested that the King create new peers, he told the king that there would be a revolution if the Reform Bill was not brought into law, to which the ever-blunt William replied that he did not care if there was.

Whilst William did not care if there was a revolution, Adelaide was terrified. The failure of the Reform Bill made William deeply unpopular, and he was hissed at in the street. To make matters worse, Adelaide, who was certainly no friend to reform but had no political power, was popularly believed to be behind the King's stance. Public animosity towards her did not end when the Bill was finally passed on 4 June 1832, and that night, when she attempted to go to the theatre, her carriage was mobbed by a crowd crying for reform. Adelaide's footmen were forced to beat back the crowd with their canes, and it was with difficulty that a terrified Adelaide managed to return home. Adelaide's unpopularity continued for some time, and when the new prime minister, Lord Melbourne, was dismissed by William on 15 November 1834, Adelaide was widely, and unfairly, blamed, with *The Times* declaring that 'the Queen has done it'.

Adelaide dearly loved children, and she spent a great deal of time with William's grandchildren and her own nieces and nephews. She also assumed the guardianship of William's nephew, George of Cambridge, who was sent by his parents in Hanover to be educated in England. A letter of Adelaide's to her friend, Baroness von Bulow, shows the pleasure that she took in spending time with children and she wrote that

> I should very much like to go to the children's ball with you. Had I been in town I should certainly have asked for an invitation. I enjoy seeing happy children; their innocent pleasures are so pure and natural; it is refreshing to watch them, and it would be well to follow their example, one too much neglected in the great world. Even the Bible bids us to be like little children. 'Whosoever shall not receive the Kingdom of God as a little child he shall not enter therein'. How deep is the significance of those words and how little they are considered! How rarely you meet a simple man or woman in our great world: they would be hard to find even with Diogenes's lantern.

Adelaide was also deeply fond of William's niece and heiress, Victoria, and it was a source of great grief to her that the child was often kept away from her.

Adelaide had initially been friendly with her sister-in-law, the Duchess of Kent, and had visited her regularly when she was widowed in 1820. Adelaide always showed an interest in Victoria and wrote the first surviving letter addressed to the princess, saying, 'My dear little heart, – I hope you are well and don't forget Aunt Adelaide, who loves you so fondly.' In 1833, on her niece's fourteenth birthday, Adelaide held a children's ball in her honour. This event was marred when the Duchess of Kent insisted on leaving early and taking the guest of honour with her. The following year, Adelaide again staged a ball, only to be told at the last minute, that the duchess would not allow her daughter to attend because she was in mourning for an infant cousin that had died. When Adelaide offered to visit Victoria at Kensington Palace instead, she was told that the princess was not available. Adelaide never criticised the duchess, but she was hurt by the slights done to her. William also grew increasingly angry with the duchess's hostility. In 1836, William invited the duchess and Victoria to Windsor to celebrate Adelaide's birthday on 12 August and William's nine days later. He was furious when the duchess completely ignored the Queen's birthday and arrived on 20 August to celebrate the King's. William, who was deeply fond of Adelaide, resented the duchess's treatment of her, and after his birthday dinner on the following day, he stood up and declared that

> I trust in God that my life may be spared for nine months longer, after which period, in the event of my death, no regency would take place. I should then have the satisfaction of leaving the royal authority to the personal exercise of that young lady, the heiress presumptive of the Crown, and not in the hands of the person now near me, who is surrounded by evil advisers, and is herself incompetent to act with propriety in the station in which she would be placed. I have

no hesitation in saying that I have been insulted – grossly and continuously insulted – by that person, but I am determined to endure no longer a course of behaviour so disrespectful to me. Among many other things I have particularly to complain of the manner in which that young lady has been kept away from my Court; she has been repeatedly kept from my drawing-rooms, at which she ought always to have been present, but I am fully resolved that this shall not happen again. I would have her know that I am King, and I am determined to make my authority respected, and for the future I shall insist and command that the Princess do upon all occasions appear at my Court, as it is her duty to do.

Adelaide was upset by this outburst, and Princess Victoria burst into tears. Ever conciliatory, Adelaide persuaded the furious duchess to wait until the morning before hurrying away with her daughter. The breach between William and the duchess was never healed, although it must have been a satisfaction for William that Adelaide was able to prepare a ball to celebrate Victoria's eighteenth birthday the following May. Unfortunately, he was unable to attend.

In the spring of 1837, Adelaide was called to Meiningen to attend her mother's deathbed. She suffered further grief when she returned to England and discovered that William was dying. Whilst Adelaide and William had seemed an ill-assorted pair at their wedding, they fell in love, and Adelaide was generally felt to have improved her husband, correcting his manners and encouraging him to lead a more sedate life. According to Adelaide's obituary, which was published in the *Gentleman's Magazine*, Adelaide tried to keep up appearances as late as 5 June by attending Ascot. To her grief, when she returned to Windsor later that day, she found William very much worse, and on 8 June, she asked the guests staying at the castle to leave. From that day until William's death twelve days later, Adelaide remained at his side, not even leaving to change her dress and merely taking snatched rests on a couch. She nursed him personally and only cried once, bursting into tears when the Archbishop of Canterbury read the service for the Visitation of the Sick. William was distressed to see Adelaide so unhappy, and he kindly told her to 'bear up, bear up'. The next night, he died in her arms.

Adelaide was grief-stricken at William's death, but she still took the time to write to her niece, the new queen:

> My dearest niece, I feel most grateful for your kind letter full of sympathy with my irreparable loss, and thank you with all my heart for your feeling expressions on this melancholy occasion. I am, as you may suppose, deeply affected by all the sad scenes I have gone through lately; but I have the great comfort to dwell upon the recollection of the perfect resignation, piety, and patience with which the dear King bore his trials and sufferings, and the truly Christian-like manner of his death.
>
> Excuse my writing more at present, my heart is overwhelmed and my head aches very much. Accept the assurance of my most affectionate devotion, and allow me to consider myself always as your Majesty's most affectionate Friend, Aunt, and Subject.

Victoria kindly said that Adelaide could remain at Windsor for as long as she liked and that, when she left, she could take whatever furnishings she wanted. Adelaide took only a silver cup that she had used to give the King his medicine in his final illness and a portrait of her FitzClarence stepchildren.

Adelaide had often suffered from ill health during her marriage, and after William's death, she became a virtual invalid. The British climate did not agree with her, and she spent several winters abroad, including visiting Malta in 1838. Adelaide carried out a great deal of charity work, and she was estimated to have spent over £20,000 a year on good works during her widowhood. One of her projects was the building of an Anglican church in Malta, and she wrote to the Queen from the Island, hoping for government support:

> The English mail going to-day gives me another opportunity to address you, and to name a subject to you which I think deserves your consideration, and about which I feel most anxious. It is the want of a Protestant church in this place which I mean. There are so many English residents here, it is the seat of an English government, and there is not one church belonging to the Church of England.

Adelaide was unable to persuade the Queen to donate any money, and she paid for the church herself. She remained on excellent terms with Victoria for the rest of her life and stood as godmother to the Queen's eldest child. In the spring of 1849, Adelaide's illness took a turn for the worse, and in September, she moved to Bentley Priory in Middlesex. She received many visits from her family during her last illness, including both her sister and her niece, the Queen. Up to 6 October, she was still able to ride in her carriage, but she then became bedridden. She died on 2 December 1849.

Adelaide of Saxe-Meiningen is very little remembered today, and her most lasting legacy is the name of the Australian city of Adelaide. Whilst sometimes unpopular, by the time of her death, she was genuinely loved, and her niece, Queen Victoria, wrote on her death that 'we have lost the kindest and dearest of friends, and the universal feeling of sorrow, of regret, and of real appreciation of her character is very touching and gratifying'. Adelaide loved her niece and she was proud of the queen that she saw Victoria become.

QUEEN VICTORIA (1819-1901) is the longest-reigning English monarch, and her reign of over sixty years saw great changes in Britain and the world. Victoria presided over the peak of Britain's power in the world, and by the end of her life, she was the matriarch of almost all the royal families of Europe. This was all very different at the time of her birth, and whilst a member of the royal family, she was an insignificant one. Victoria was the only child of Edward, Duke of Kent, and his wife, Victoire of Saxe-Coburg-Saalfeld, the widowed Princess of Leiningen. Her father, the fourth son of George III, was fifty when he left a comfortable life with his mistress of over twenty-five years, Madame de St Laurent, to marry Victoire, a widow with two young children. Kent had been told by a fortune-teller that he would be the father of a great queen and, following the death of Princess Charlotte, was determined to take part, along with his brothers, in the race to marry and produce a royal heir. The marriage was soon successful, and the couple's daughter was born on 24 May 1819 at Kensington Palace.

Both the Duke and Duchess of Kent hoped that their daughter, or future sons, would rule, and they chose a grand selection of names for the baby: Georgiana Charlotte Augusta Alexandrina Victoria. Unfortunately, Kent was not on good terms with his eldest brother, and the Prince Regent sent the couple a note the night before the christening informing them that, on no account, was the baby to be named Georgiana after him. At the christening the next day, the Archbishop of Canterbury asked what name had been chosen, and the regent immediately declared 'Alexandrina', after another of the baby's godparents, the Tsar of Russia. Kent then suggested Charlotte, which was vetoed by the regent due to it being the name of his own deceased daughter. Augusta was blocked for being too grand, and with the Duchess of Kent weeping and the guests watching uncomfortably, the baby was eventually christened as simply 'Alexandrina Victoria'. She was known by her family as 'Drina' until she was old enough to declare a preference for 'Victoria'.

Whilst of little significance at the time of her birth, Victoria rapidly moved up the line of succession. Her father died suddenly of pneumonia on 23 January 1820, and he was followed by his father, the unstable George III, a few days later. Kent died whilst the family were staying at Sidmouth in Devon, and according to Victoria's own account, she and her mother 'were so poor at the time of his (the Duke of Kent's) death, that they could not have travelled back to Kensington Palace had it not been for the kind assistance of my dear Uncle, Prince Leopold'. Victoria's maternal uncle, Leopold of Saxe-Coburg-Saalfeld, was the widower of Princess Charlotte and lived mostly in England until he accepted the throne of Belgium in 1831. Leopold was very aware that all that stood between Victoria and the throne in 1820 were the lives of three middle-aged men: George IV, Frederick, Duke of York, and William, Duke of Clarence. Neither the King nor York were likely to produce further legitimate children, and whilst Clarence had taken a young wife a few years before, it was not certain that she would produce a child. Leopold therefore persuaded his sister to raise her child in England, and he became a father figure to Victoria, grooming her for queenship. In one letter, written by Victoria to her uncle in November 1834, she wrote that 'I am much obliged to you, dear Uncle, for the extract about Queen Anne, but must beg you, as you have sent me to show what a Queen ought not to be, that you will send me what a Queen ought to be'. In her journal in September 1836, Victoria also summed up her feelings for her uncle, writing that 'he is indeed '*il mio second padre*', or rather '*solo padre*'! for he is indeed like my real father, as I have none! He is so clever, so mild, and so prudent; he alone can give me good advice on every thing'. With the exception of the interest taken by Leopold, Victoria lived in a very female-dominated environment at Kensington with her mother, her beloved maternal half-sister, Feodore, and her governess, Baroness Lehzen.

With the exception of her aunt, Princess Sophia, who also lived in Kensington Palace, Victoria had little contact with her father's family during her early childhood. According to Victoria's own account, her father's brother, the Duke of Sussex, was used to frighten her into behaving, and she was told 'that if I cried and was naughty my "Uncle Sussex" would hear me and punish me, for which reason I always screamed when I saw him!' Another uncle, the Duke of York, gave Victoria presents and was kind to her, but the 'wicked uncles' as Victoria called her father's brothers were distant figures. Victoria, her mother, and Feodore were finally called for a meeting with George IV in 1826. The visit went well, although, according to Victoria's own account, the King paid so much attention to her beautiful half-sister that there were rumours that he might decide to marry her. For Victoria, this might have been preferable to Feodore's marriage in 1828 to the Prince of Hohenlohe-Langenberg, as she did not see her sister for six years after she left for Germany. Feodore and Victoria were always close, and the separation was devastating. In 1834, following a visit to Kensington by Feodore, Victoria wrote in her journal that

the separation [from Feodora] was indeed dreadful. I clapped her in my arms, and kissed her and cried as if my heart would break, so did she dearest Sister. We then tore ourselves from each other in the deepest grief ... When I came home I was in such a state of grief that I knew not what to do with myself. I sobbed and cried most violently the whole morning ... My dearest best sister was friend, companion, all to me, we agreed so well together in all our feelings and amusements ... I love no one better than her.

Feodore's absence increased Victoria's loneliness, and she had little contact with other children, instead spending time with her over-protective mother.

Victoria always had a troubled relationship with the Duchess of Kent. The duchess was very much under the influence of Sir John Conroy, the comptroller of her household, who was very charming and also numbered Princess Sophia as one of his devoted followers. The duchess and Conroy, who was rumoured to be her lover, were determined to keep Victoria under their control, and she was raised strictly with little contact with the outside world. Victoria was forbidden from even walking downstairs unaccompanied, and she was forced to share a bedroom with her mother until she was finally able to insist on her own on the night following her accession. The duchess and Conroy were determined to allow no other influence on her, and they quarrelled with the King in keeping her away from court. Conroy also invoked the King's ire by implementing a series of annual progresses for Victoria by which she could show herself to her future subjects. Victoria, supported by her governess, the strong-willed Lehzen, loathed Conroy, and she resisted his and the duchess's attempts for her to appoint him her private secretary, a very important royal office. Conroy and the duchess made two attempts to secure Victoria's acquiescence, once in 1835, when she was ill with typhoid, and a second time in 1837, following her eighteenth birthday, when it was clear the King was dying. The pressure exerted on Victoria was intense, and it destroyed her relationship with her mother.

On her eighteenth birthday, the King wrote to Victoria to offer her an independent household, which, to her mother and Conroy's chagrin, she gleefully accepted. The household was destined never to be constituted, as by June 1837, only weeks after Victoria's birthday, it became clear that William IV was dying. Victoria expected her accession imminently, and on 19 June, she wrote to King Leopold to inform him:

> The King's state, I may fairly say, is hopeless; he may perhaps linger a few days, but he cannot recover ultimately. Yesterday the physicians declared he could not live till the morning, but to-day he is a little better; the great fear is his excessive weakness and no pulse at all. Poor old man! I feel sorry for him; he was always personally kind to me, and I should be ungrateful and devoid of feeling if I did not remember this.
>
> I look forward to the event which it seems is likely to occur soon, with calmness and quietness; I am not alarmed at it, and yet I do not suppose myself quite equal to all; I trust, however, that with good-will, honesty, and courage I shall not, at all events, fail. Your advice is most excellent, and you may depend upon it I shall make use of it, and follow it, as also what [Baron] Stockmar [Leopold's emissary to Victoria] says. I never showed myself, openly to belong to any party, and I do not belong to any party. The Administration will undoubtedly be well received by me, the more so as I have real confidence in them, and in particular in Lord Melbourne, who is a straightforward, honest, clever and good man.

Victoria did not have long to wait, and at 6 a.m. the following morning, she was woken by her mother to inform her that the Archbishop of Canterbury and the Lord Chamberlain were there to see her. Victoria went down to them in her dressing gown, refusing, to her mother's anguish, to allow her to accompany her. The two men informed her of her uncle's death earlier that morning before kneeling and kissing her hand. For Victoria, this was a moment of jubilation and, more importantly, liberation, and she saw her Prime Minister, Lord Melbourne, alone, later that morning. According to Charles Greville, who was present, the privy council meeting that was called that morning had an excellent turnout, as the Queen's 'extreme youth and inexperience, and the ignorance of the world concerning her, naturally excited intense curiosity to see how she would act on this trying occasion'. Victoria performed her role perfectly at her first privy council meeting and, once again, refused to let her mother accompany her. That night, for the first time in her life, Victoria slept in her own bedroom.

Victoria moved to Buckingham Palace on 13 July 1837. As an unmarried woman, for appearance's sake, she was forced to take her mother. To the duchess's anger, she was allocated a suite of rooms far away from Victoria's own, whilst Lehzen slept in a room off the Queen's own bedchamber. Victoria also insisted that her mother see her only when granted written permission, and the duchess's requests for access were often met by a curt note saying 'busy'. Victoria was angered by Conroy's continued presence with the duchess and she instructed Lord Melbourne to open negotiations for him to depart, although this took some years to achieve. Victoria rapidly became devoted to Lord Melbourne, and like King Leopold before him, she looked upon him as a father figure, relying heavily on his political advice. The Prime Minister was also fond of the young queen, and the pair spent time together on most days. The early years following Victoria's accession were her most carefree, and she loved the theatre and entertainments, writing to King Leopold on 5 May 1838 that 'I have been dancing till four o'clock this morning'. On 28 June 1838, just over a year after her accession, Victoria was crowned queen.

Whilst she enjoyed herself as queen, the shadow of her mother and Sir John Conroy continued to hang over Victoria at Buckingham Palace, and it was this dispute that led to Victoria involving herself in the biggest scandal of her early years on the throne. Victoria had always disliked her mother's lady-in-waiting, Lady Flora Hastings, who was a friend of Conroy. On 2 February 1839, she recorded in her diary that

> Lady Flora had not been above two days in the house before Lehzen and I discovered how exceedingly suspicious her figure looked – more have since observed this and we have no doubt that she is – to use the plain words – with child!! [Sir James] Clark [Victoria's physician] cannot deny the suspicion; the horrid cause of all this is the Monster and Demon Incarnate whose name I forbear to mention but which is the first word of the 2nd line of this page [Conroy]. Lady Tavistock accordingly with Lehzen's concurrence told Lord Melbourne of it, as it was a matter of serious importance.

Lady Flora was an unmarried woman of thirty-two. Unfortunately, she had once travelled in a carriage alone with Sir John Conroy, and Victoria was determined to believe that she was his mistress. Rumours were soon flying around court and Lehzen instructed Sir James Clark to speak to Lady Flora about the matter, urging him to begin the conversation by declaring that 'you must be secretly married'. Lady Flora indignantly denied that she was pregnant, but Clark was convinced, and on 16 February, Victoria informed her mother that Lady Flora was not to appear at court until her innocence was proved. The following day, Lady Flora submitted to an examination by Sir James and a second doctor, Sir Charles Clarke, at which it was proved that she was still a virgin. This did not satisfy the Queen, and she wrote to her mother that 'Sir C[harles Clarke] had said that though she is a virgin still that it might be possible and one could not tell if such things could not happen. There was an enlargement of the womb like a child'.

Victoria was undoubtedly misled in her view of Lady Flora by the doctors' continuing claims that she could be pregnant and by Lord Melbourne's firm belief that she was indeed with child. However, she was also determined to believe the worst of her mother's lady-in-waiting and Conroy, and she ignored the fact that, as well as being swollen, Lady Flora looked very ill. The Duchess of Kent firmly sided with Lady Flora, and the mood of the population was also with the lady-in-waiting, to Victoria's horror. It was only by the early summer of 1839 that Victoria was finally convinced that Lady Flora was not, in fact, pregnant, and, on being told that she was dying, the Queen visited her on 27 June. According to Victoria's journal, 'I found poor

Lady Flora stretched on a couch looking as thin as anybody can be who is still alive; literally a skeleton, but the body very much swollen like a person who is with child.' Lady Flora died on 5 July and, following a post-mortem that she herself requested, was found to have had a tumour in her liver that had caused her enlarged abdomen. Victoria was mortified by all that had happened, and she found herself deeply unpopular and attacked in the press. 1839 was to prove a difficult year for the Queen because, even before Lady Flora's death, she had undergone the second great crisis of her early reign.

Victoria relied heavily on Lord Melbourne, and she identified firmly with his political party, the Whigs, over the other dominant party, the Tories. In 1839, Melbourne resigned as prime minister when his majority in the House of Commons fell to five and the Tory, Sir Robert Peel, attempted to form a government. Victoria had filled her household with women politically inclined towards the Whig party, and when Peel asked that she dismiss some of these ladies and replace them with Tory ladies, she refused, claiming that they were her personal attendants and not her political advisors. Victoria was not prepared to compromise, and on 10 May 1839, she sent him a note that had been dictated by Lord Melbourne, saying, 'The Queen having considered the proposal made to her yesterday by Sir Robert Peel, to remove the Ladies of her Bedchamber, cannot consent to adopt a course which she conceives to be contrary to usage, and which is repugnant to her feelings.' Without a majority in the House of Commons, Peel was unable to enter into a battle with the sovereign, and he conceded defeat, allowing Lord Melbourne to return as prime minister, an office that he held for a further two years. Victoria was jubilant, but like the Flora Hastings affair, the matter cost her a great deal of popularity, and she was hissed in the streets and insultingly referred to as 'Mrs Melbourne'.

In her journal on 17 April 1839, Victoria wrote that she was concerned at the prospect of many years of having to live under the same roof as her mother but that her mother had sworn never to leave her whilst she was unmarried. In answer to this, Lord Melbourne had declared 'well then, there's that way of settling it', to which Victoria replied 'that was a schocking [sic] alternative'. Victoria was enjoying her freedom too much to marry, although those around her had long been considering who her choice might be. King Leopold had always intended that Victoria should marry his favourite nephew, Prince Albert of Saxe-Coburg-Gotha, who was Victoria's first cousin. The pair had first met when Albert and his elder brother, Ernest, visited England in May 1836. Victoria had been very taken with her cousin, and she had written to her uncle, saying that

> I must thank you, my beloved Uncle, for the prospect of great happiness you have contributed to give me, in the person of dear Albert. Allow me, then, my dearest Uncle, to tell you how delighted I am with him, and how much I like him in every way. He possesses every quality that could be desired to render me perfectly happy. He is so sensible, so kind, and so good, and so amiable too. He has, besides, the most pleasing and delightful exterior and appearance you can possibly see.

She recorded in her journal that Albert, 'who is just as tall as Ernest but stouter, is extremely handsome; his hair is about the same colour as mine; his eyes are large and blue, and he has a beautiful nose and a very sweet mouth with fine teeth'. Victoria, who was tiny, at around five feet tall, and inclined to plumpness, was always attracted to tall, athletic men, and King Leopold was encouraged by the first meeting between his nephew and niece. In spite of Victoria's reservations about marriage, she was persuaded to invite Albert to England in October 1839. According to her journal, 'it was with some emotion that I beheld Albert – who is beautiful'. Within days of his arrival, Victoria, who, as a sovereign, was expected to make any proposal of marriage, had made her decision, and she sent for her cousin on the afternoon of 15 October, the events of which were recorded by Victoria in her journal:

> He came to the Closet where I was alone, and after a few minutes I said to him, that I thought he must be aware why I wished [him] to come here, and that it would make me too happy if he would consent to what I wished (to marry me); we embraced each other over and over again, and he was so kind, so affectionate; Oh! to feel I was, and am, loved by such an Angel as Albert was too great delight to describe! He is perfection; perfection in every way – in beauty, in everything! I told him I was quite unworthy of him and kissed his dear hand – he said he would be very happy and was so kind and seemed so happy, that I really felt it was the happiest brightest moment in my life, which made up for all I had suffered and endured. Oh! how I adore and love him, I cannot say!! how I will strive to make him feel as little as possible the great sacrifice he has made.

Albert had been groomed to become Victoria's consort, and whilst his feelings for her were less intense, he was fond of her and wanted to marry her. To Victoria's intense joy, the couple were married on 10 February 1840.

Victoria was devoted to Albert, but the early years of their marriage were troubled as they negotiated the difficulties caused by Victoria's anomalous position as a reigning queen. Even before Albert's arrival, Victoria had been angered when parliament granted Albert an allowance of £30,000 a year, considerably less than the £50,000 pension granted to Leopold when he had married Princess Charlotte. Victoria was also unable to confer the title of Prince Consort officially on Albert until 1857, and his foreign birth aroused suspicion in Britain. Albert was energetic and hard-working and his lack of a role rankled. He was also angered by the fact that he was not to be master in his own family with Victoria selecting his household attendants for him.

Albert found himself in conflict with Lehzen, who exercised a considerable amount of influence over the Queen, and matters came to a head following the birth of the couple's eldest child, Victoria, or Vicky as she was known in the family, on 21 November 1840. Vicky failed to thrive, and around the time of her first birthday, she began to lose weight. Albert was infuriated by Victoria's insistence on listening to both Lehzen and the doctor, Sir James Clark, over him, and in January 1842, the couple had a furious row. Later that evening, Albert sent Victoria a note saying, 'Doctor Clark has mismanaged the child and poisoned her with calomel and you have starved her. I shall have nothing more to do with it, take the child away and do as you like and if she dies you will have it on your conscience.' Victoria was angered by Albert's note, but she was also deeply in love with him, and she capitulated. On 30 September 1842, Lehzen quietly returned to her native Hanover without even saying a final farewell to the Queen. Victoria also slowly granted Albert a bigger political role, and in September 1841, when Sir Robert Peel finally became prime minister, it was Albert who persuaded Victoria to replace some of her Whig ladies with Tory ones. By the time of his death, Victoria consulted Albert on all political matters, and he was also influential in other spheres, being the orchestrator of the Great Exhibition of 1851. He also brought about a reconciliation between his wife and her mother, which endured until the Duchess of Kent's death in 1861.

Victoria came to rely on Albert more heavily than anyone else, and he dominated her whole life. Albert liked to live quietly, in contrast to Victoria's love of London life, and she quickly began to share his interests, with the couple purchasing two houses, Balmoral in the Scottish Highlands and Osborne House on the Isle of Wight, to use as retreats. Although Victoria disliked pregnancy and was not fond of babies, the couple went on to have nine children, with Vicky's birth being followed by those of Albert Edward (the future Edward VII), Alice, Alfred, Helena, Louise, Arthur, Leopold, and Beatrice. Of these children, Arthur was Victoria's favourite. Victoria's relationship with Vicky, who was Albert's favourite, improved immensely following her eldest daughter's marriage in 1858 to the Crown Prince of Prussia, which allowed Victoria to once again have Albert to herself in the evenings. Victoria and Albert were fortunate in that all nine of their children survived to adulthood, although Leopold, who suffered from haemophilia, was a source of grave concern to his mother throughout his lifetime. Neither Victoria nor Albert had a good relationship with their eldest son, and Albert laid out a strict programme of study for the boy that, temperamentally, he was quite unable to follow. Victoria, who believed that 'Bertie', as her eldest son was known, had inherited all her bad qualities and none of her good, always refused to give him any responsibility, and he received no training from her for his future role as King.

Victoria's relationship with Bertie was nearly destroyed in December 1861 when she blamed him for the death of Prince Albert. By 1861, Albert, who was only forty-two and would certainly be described as a workaholic today, was exhausted and depressed. His health had begun to fail, and he was already ill when he was forced to rush up to Cambridge to visit Bertie, who was studying there, to investigate reports that the prince had had an affair with an actress. When Albert returned, he was very much worse, and by early December, he was believed to be suffering from both rheumatism and influenza. Victoria was not, at first, unduly alarmed, and on 6 December, she wrote to King Leopold to inform him that 'altogether, this nasty, feverish sort of influenza and deranged stomach is on the mend'. As late as 9 December, Victoria was also able to assure her uncle that 'every day however, is bringing us nearer the end of this tiresome illness, which is much what I had at Ramsgate, only that I was much worse, and not at first well attended to'. By 11 December, it was clear that Albert was suffering from typhoid, and whilst Victoria and her second daughter, Princess Alice, tended him diligently, he continued to grow weaker, becoming bedridden and delirious. Victoria was with Albert when the end came on 14 December, and when she realised that her beloved husband had died, she let out one great scream that was heard throughout the palace.

For Victoria, Albert's death was the end of all her happiness, and six days after the event, she wrote to King Leopold to inform him that

> my own dearest, kindest Father, – For as such have I ever loved you! The poor fatherless baby of eight months is now the utterly broken-hearted and crushed widow of forty-two! My life as a happy one is ended! The world is gone for me! If I must live on (and I will do nothing to make me worse than I am), it is henceforth for our poor fatherless children – for my unhappy country, which has lost all in losing him – and in only doing what I know and feel he would wish, for he is near me – his spirit will guide and inspire me! But oh! to be cut off in the prime of life – to see our pure, happy, quiet, domestic life, which alone enabled me to bear my very much disliked position CUT OFF at forty-two – when I had hoped with such instinctive certainty that God never would part us, and would let us grow old together (though he always talked of the shortness of life) – is too awful, too cruel! And yet it must be for his good, his happiness! His purity was too great, his aspiration too high for this poor, miserable world! His great soul is now only enjoying that for which it was worthy! And I will not envy him – only pray that mine may be perfected by it and fit to be with him eternally, for which blessed moments I earnestly long.

Victoria's heart was broken, and she always blamed Bertie, whose indiscretions had caused his father to rush up to see him. Victoria believed that Albert had been almost a living saint, and after his death, she focused all her efforts on her mourning and on immortalising his memory. Within a few years of Albert's death, the weddings of both Alice and Bertie, of which Albert had approved, were allowed to go ahead, but with something of a funereal atmosphere. Victoria insisted on wearing black for the rest of her life, and she kept all of Albert's things exactly as he had left them, continuing to have his clothes laid out for him each evening as she had done in life. Victoria relied heavily on her youngest child, Beatrice, who was only four at the time of her father's death, and this later led to Victoria's refusal to let her go when she was an adult, with the Queen only reluctantly consenting to her marriage on the promise that the princess and her husband would continue to live with her. More damagingly, Victoria retreated into seclusion and, in the decade following Albert's death, made few public appearances, to increasing public discontent. She was even unable to conduct the business of government and privy council meetings were held with Victoria sitting in an adjoining room with the door kept open. Victoria's seclusion brought the monarchy to its lowest level of popularity since the days of the Prince Regent, and there were mutterings of republicanism that it was impossible to contain.

Although she continued to grieve for Albert for the rest of her life and continued with her seclusion as much as possible, Victoria did gradually begin to re-emerge during the mid-1860s due to her relationship with a second man who became dear to her. Victoria's Highland servant John Brown had been in her service before Albert's death, but by the 1860s, it was noticed, both by those who knew her and the population at large, that she had come to rely on him for support. John Brown, who had been born and raised on the Balmoral estate, was tall and handsome, and there is no doubt that Victoria was attracted to him. He was also blunt with her and, with his rough manners, treated her in a familiar way which no one else would have dared to do. Victoria was often alone with Brown, who accompanied her everywhere, and there were soon rumours that he was her lover or that they had gone so far as to contract a secret marriage, with Victoria commonly referred to by the nickname of 'Mrs Brown'. The full details of Victoria and Brown's relationship do not survive, and it is not impossible that they were lovers or, even, secretly married. Certainly, Victoria's children all loathed the blunt Scotsman, and the Queen came to rely on him deeply, referring to him in a letter of October 1874 as her 'darling one'. She always took his side in any dispute, and when, in 1868, he complained that the men in her family kept him up late whilst he waited for them to finish smoking, the Queen immediately sent an order that, for the sake of the servants, the smoking room was to be vacated by midnight at the latest. Victoria also liked the fact that Brown spoke his mind to her and often criticised her dress, commenting 'what's this ye've got on today?' at anything that displeased him. On the balance of probabilities, it appears more likely that Brown was Victoria's friend rather than her lover, but he certainly filled much of the void left by Albert, and she was devastated by his sudden death in April 1883 and, as she herself confessed, reminded terribly of the death of the Prince Consort. In her journal for 20 March 1883, she wrote, 'It is the loss not only of a servant, but of a real friend,' and in a letter to Vicky on 8 April 1883,

I am crushed by the violence of this unexpected blow which was such a shock – the reopening of old wounds and the infliction of a new very deep one. There is no rebound left to recover from it and the one who since 1864 had helped to cheer me, to smooth, ease and facilitate everything for my daily comfort and who was my dearest best friend to whom I could speak quite openly is not here to help me out of it! I feel so stunned and bewildered by this anguish that comes over me like a wave every now and then through the day or at night is terrible! He protected me so, was so powerful and strong – that I felt safe! And now all, all is gone in this world and all seems unhinged again in thousands of ways! – I feel so discouraged that it requires a terrible effort to bear up at all against it.

As with Albert's death, Victoria immediately set about trying to preserve Brown's memory, and she kept his room exactly as he left it. She also laid flowers on his grave and ordered a memorial to be placed close to Prince Albert's tomb. To the disgust of Bertie, who ordered it to he moved as soon as he became king, Victoria erected a statue of Brown in the gardens at Balmoral, and she grieved for him for the rest of her life.

Although Victoria was deeply grieved by John Brown's death and the early deaths of her daughter Alice in 1878 and son Leopold in 1884, they did not send her back into deep seclusion, and she gradually became more of a presence in Britain as the years passed. She presided over a period of great expansion in Britain, with the growth of industry and urbanisation and the extension of the British Empire. By the time of her death, she ruled over much of the globe and was particularly pleased in 1876 to be declared Empress of India. The Queen worked closely with a number of prime ministers, including William Gladstone and Benjamin Disraeli, of whom she was fond. Albert had considered Disraeli not to be a gentleman, and her opinion of the politician was one of the few areas in which Victoria disagreed with her deceased husband. Disraeli himself was always respectful to Albert's memory, and the Queen loved him for it, considering him to be the only other person who truly appreciated her beloved husband. She was saddened when his first ministry ended quickly and she was forced to recall Gladstone, although she ensured that there was no repeat of the earlier 'Bedchamber Crisis'. As she began to appear more in public, her popularity increased, and by the time of her golden jubilee in 1887 and diamond jubilee in 1897, she had become an institution. In 1897, the Queen surpassed the record of her grandfather, George III, and became England's longest-reigning monarch, and this, together with the marriages of her children and grandchildren into most of the ruling houses of Europe, made her almost a legend in her own lifetime. Victoria had always enjoyed good health, and although her eyesight began to fail, she remained active. The last few years of her life were again tinged with sadness when her second son, Alfred, died in July 1900. Victoria was also aware that her eldest daughter, Vicky, was suffering from terminal cancer, although the German Empress survived her mother by some months. Old age finally caught up with Victoria on 22 January 1901, after over sixty-three years on the throne, and she died at Osborne House, surrounded by family and in the arms of her eldest grandchild, Kaiser Wilhelm II of Germany.

The Hanoverian dynasty, which began with the ineffectual and tragic Sophia Dorothea, ended with the triumphant reign of Queen Victoria, who ruled a country at the peak of its power. The Hanoverian queens had mixed fortunes, but the dynasty had a number of influential figures. With Queen Victoria's death, the country saw the accession of a new dynasty of Saxe-Coburg-Gotha, a name that was, within only a few short years, transformed into the more British 'House of Windsor'. Like the Hanoverian queens, the Saxe-Coburg-Gotha and Windsor queens (and, also, the wife of an ex-king) have led varied lives as they took the monarchy into the twentieth century and beyond, and like the Hanoverian dynasty, for now at least, their story ends with a reigning queen.

11

From the House of Hanover to the House of Windsor

The death of Queen Victoria in 1901 ushered in a new dynasty in Britain, as well as a new century. Victoria's son, Edward VII, became the first monarch of the House of Saxe-Coburg-Gotha, Prince Albert's family name, and this was changed to the House of Windsor due to the anti-German feeling created by the First World War. A monarch of the house of Windsor sits on the throne today, and the twentieth and twenty-first centuries have so far seen three queen consorts, a wife of a former king and a reigning queen.

ALEXANDRA OF DENMARK (1844-1925) waited longer than any other queen consort to become queen, and for most of her marriage, she was overshadowed by her formidable mother-in-law, Queen Victoria. Alexandra enjoyed a happy, if impoverished, childhood as the second of the six children born to Prince Christian of Schleswig-Holstein-Sonderburg-Glucksburg and his wife, Louise of Hesse-Cassel. Alexandra was born in Copenhagen on 1 December 1844, and whilst her father was, at the time, only an obscure member of the Danish royal family, in 1852, he was designated as heir to the Danish throne, eventually succeeding in 1863. Alexandra's family was renowned for being close, and the children spent much time with their parents. Neither Christian nor Louise set much store by academic pursuits, but they did ensure that their children were athletic, encouraging them to undergo strenuous gymnastics tuition. All her life, people commented on Alexandra's beauty and personal kindness, and her grandson, Edward VIII, recalled in his memoirs that

> my grandmother, Queen Alexandra, was as usual at the Big House. I used to go to see her nearly every day, walking over in the evening to chat or play patience or do jigsaw puzzles with her. Although she was quite an old lady by then, she still retained much of the beauty of the lovely young woman who had come from Denmark almost fifty years before to marry my grandfather. With her delicately chiselled features, her high coiffure, and the grace of her manner, she was still greatly admired. Her charm was irresistible and overcame such disabilities as a stiff leg, acute deafness, and rebellious unpunctuality in a family determined to be run by clockwork. She was late for everything – meals, church, trains, and, worst of all, big ceremonies. The story is told that she was even late for her Coronation and that my grandfather, exasperated, burst into her room, watch in hand, remonstrating, 'My dear Alix, if you don't come immediately you won't be crowned Queen.'

Throughout her lifetime, Alexandra charmed everyone she met, and her future husband and his mother were no exception.

By the late 1850s, Albert Edward (or Bertie as he was known by his family), the eldest son of Queen Victoria, was the most eligible man in Europe. Bertie was three years older than Alexandra and, in contrast to her, had endured a strict childhood. Neither Queen Victoria nor her beloved consort, Prince Albert, thought much of their son's intelligence, and Albert had imposed a heavy educational programme on his son. Neither the Queen nor the Prince Consort were happy with their son's progress, and both hoped that marriage would settle him. By December 1858, Victoria had enlisted the help of her half-sister, Feodore, Princess of Hohenlohe-Langenburg and her eldest daughter Victoria, or Vicky, Crown Princess of Prussia, in order to find Bertie a bride. A list of suitable princesses was soon drawn up, on which Alexandra was included. She was not the most favoured potential bride, as, by the late 1850s, there was tension between Prussia and Denmark, causing concern for the German-orientated British royal family. Bertie insisted that he wanted a beautiful bride, and by 1860, Alexandra, the most beautiful princess in Europe, was the leading contender. On 29 May 1861, Vicky went to Strelitz to see Alexandra for herself, and she was charmed by her. Alexandra remained oblivious to the planned match, and she was surprised when, on 24 September 1861, her mother told her to wear her best dress for a trip by rail to Speyer. Alexandra did as she was told and, at the cathedral in the city, was met by Vicky and Bertie. The prince was impressed by her but hesitated to commit to the match. Bertie's father, Prince Albert, supported the Danish marriage and wrote to his son strongly urging that he marry. When Albert died suddenly in December 1861, his widow saw it as her duty to ensure that a match that he had favoured was brought about.

Queen Victoria always blamed Bertie for Albert's passing, believing that a trip the Prince Consort had made to Cambridge to see his son had contributed to his death. The visit had been made following revelations about Bertie's relationship with an actress, Nellie Clifden. By April 1862, when negotiations for the marriage were no further advanced, Victoria wrote to Vicky, concerned that Alexandra's parents were having second thoughts:

> Has perhaps Princess Christian [Princess Alexandra's mother] heard of poor wretched Bertie's miserable escapade – and thinks him a regular '*mauvais sujet*'? The Aunt here [the Duchess of Cambridge, aunt of both the Queen and of Princess Christian] may have written in that way? I fear we can say no more. The meeting must be at Laeken, and can't be before the 2nd or 3rd Sept. I will however let Bertie know that she is much sought after; but more we cannot do. Your account of the family is certainly as bad as possible, and that is the weak point in the whole affair, but dearest Papa said we could not help it. Oh! the whole thing is so disheartening to me! Alone! To do all this, and with B.! If he turns obstinate I will withdraw myself altogether and wash my hands of him, for I cannot educate him, and the country must make him feel what they think. Affie [one of Victoria's younger sons] would be ready to take her at once, and really if B. refused I would recommend Affie's engagement to marry her in three years.

Alexandra had a number of suitors, including the heir to the Russian throne, but her parents were eager for the match with Bertie. In September 1862, Victoria went herself to Belgium to view Alexandra, and she was very impressed with what she saw. Soon afterwards, Bertie visited Alexandra at Brussels, and on 9 September, he proposed, with Alexandra accepting at once. It was intended that Alexandra would be moulded into a British princess, and in November, she was taken by her father to spend three weeks with Victoria at Osborne House on the Isle of Wight. Bertie was then absent in the Mediterranean, and Alexandra's father, of whom the Queen did not approve, was not even invited to spend one night at

Osborne. Alexandra was well aware that, during the visit, she would be scrutinised by the Queen. The good effect she had on Victoria was everywhere noted, and she elicited smiles and even laughter from the grieving monarch, who was thoroughly charmed by her.

Alexandra arrived in London in March 1863, accompanied by her parents and siblings. As the court was still in mourning for Prince Albert, it was decreed that the wedding would be held in the relative seclusion of Windsor. For Victoria, thoughts of Albert were very much on her mind as the guests assembled for the wedding, and she wrote in her journal on 24 February that 'all is spoilt; a heavy black cloud overhangs every thing now, and turns pleasure into woe'. Alexandra behaved impeccably towards the Queen, and on 7 March, the day of Alexandra's arrival in London, Victoria wrote,

> The bells began to ring, and at length, in pouring rain and when it was getting dark, the carriages and escort were seen coming.
>
> I went down to the bottom of the staircase, and Bertie appeared, leading dear Alix, looking like a rose. I embraced her warmly, and with her parents, Dagmar [Alexandra's sister], the two sons, Thyra and Waldemar, went upstairs. Alix wore a grey dress, with a violet jacket, trimmed with fur, and a white bonnet. We all went into the White Drawing-room, where we remained a few minutes, and then Vicky took them over to their rooms. I went back to my room, desolate and sad. It seemed so dreadful that all this must take place, strangers arrive, and he, my beloved one, not be there! Vicky and Alice soon came to me and tried to cheer me, and kiss away my tears.
>
> While I was waiting, Vicky returned and was sitting with me, dressed for dinner, when dear gentle Alix knocked on the door, peeped in, and came and knelt before me, with that sweet, loving expression which spoke volumes. I was much moved and kissed her again and again. She said the crowd in London had been quite fearful, and the enthusiasm very great, no end of decorations, etc., but the crush in the City had been quite alarming. Bertie came in for a moment whilst Alix was there. There was a family dinner, I dining alone.

Alexandra always knew how to handle the Queen, and Victoria soon came to love her as a daughter. Alexandra had a further mournful ceremony to endure on 9 March before she could celebrate her wedding, which Victoria recorded in her journal:

> Drove with Alix, Lenchen and Bertie to the Mausoleum where Vicky and Fritz met us. I opened the shrine and took them in. Alix was much moved and so was I. I said, 'He [Albert] gives you his blessing', and joined Alix and Bertie's hands, taking them both in my arms and kissing them. It was a very touching moment and we all felt it.

Bertie and Alexandra were married the following day, and whilst the Queen wept during the ceremony, it was a joyful occasion for the couple, who, whilst not in love, were fond of each other.

Queen Victoria hoped that marriage to Alexandra would improve Bertie, commenting in a letter to Vicky shortly after the marriage that 'she is so quiet, so placid, that it is soothing to one, and I am sure that must do Bertie good'. Upon further acquaintance, she had some complaints about her daughter-in-law, writing to Vicky on 21 March that she was concerned that Alexandra was 'not I fear reasonable or careful of her health'. On 25 March, she added that 'very clever I don't think she is, but she is right-minded and sensible and straightforward'. Victoria's apparent disapproval of Alexandra was due to the princess's interest in socialising, and on 6 May 1863, the Queen further commented on the couple that

I fear there is none [no signs of pregnancy] with Alix and though to be sure, unintellectual children which one might fear with B.'s children, would be a great misfortune, it would be very sad if they had none, and I sometimes fear they won't. Are you aware that Alix has the smallest head ever seen? I dread that – with his small empty brain – very much for future children. The doctor says that Alix's head goes in, in the most extraordinary way just beyond the forehead: I wonder what phrenologists would say.

In spite of Alexandra and Bertie's riotous living, Victoria's fears that they would have no children were unfounded, and within a few months of the wedding, she was pregnant. On 6 January 1864, two months before her baby was due, Alexandra went to watch Bertie play ice hockey near Windsor. Following her return to the castle, she suddenly felt pains, and the town doctor was fetched. Before the Queen, or any of the planned witnesses for the birth could arrive, Alexandra gave birth to a son, who weighed only three and a half pounds, but was otherwise strong and healthy. The sudden birth was a shock to both Alexandra and Bertie, and when Alexandra's lady-in-waiting, Lady Macclesfield, checked on her some hours after the birth, she found the couple crying in each other's arms.

In spite of their fears over their son's premature birth, he thrived. To Bertie's anger, the Queen selected the child's names, informing Alexandra in a letter that 'as regards the names, if others besides Albert Victor are added (which I don't the least object to), you must take dear Uncle Leopold's also. You could not give King Christian's and the Landgrave's without also Uncle Leopold's. I would advise reserving Edward for a second or third son'. Whilst Alexandra and Bertie had no choice over their baby's first two Christian names, they asserted their independence as much as possible, ignoring 'Uncle Leopold's' name entirely and adding Christian and Edward. Their eldest son was always known as Eddy to everyone except the Queen. Most of Alexandra and Bertie's children were premature, and on 3 June 1865, Eddy was followed by a brother, who the couple hurriedly named George before Victoria could intervene. Daughters Louise, Victoria and Maud followed before a final son, Alexander John, in April 1871, who, to his parents' grief, lived only one day. Bertie insisted on placing his infant son in his coffin himself, and Alexandra always remembered him sadly, writing to her son, Prince George, on the eleventh anniversary of the death to say that 'it is sad to think that nothing remains on earth to remind us of him but his little grave'.

Whilst the early years of Alexandra's marriage were personally happy, they were overshadowed by the Prussian invasion of Denmark in 1864. The war was over the disputed duchies of Schleswig and Holstein, and by July, Alexandra's father had been forced to hand them over to Prussia, losing more than half his kingdom. For Alexandra, the conflict led to a lifelong hatred of Germans, which placed her at odds with the British royal family. This bitterness was increased in 1865, when Alexandra discovered that Bertie's younger sister, Princess Helena, was intending to marry the German Prince Christian of Schleswig-Holstein, a move that was a clear recognition of German rights to the duchies. Queen Victoria was unable to understand Alexandra's antipathy towards Germany, and in a letter to Vicky on 3 February 1864, she commented that 'though I blame the haste and violence of the Germans, my feelings and sympathies in the war can only be with them! … Poor Alix is in a terrible state of distress and Bertie frantic, thinking every one wishes to crush Denmark! This is not true.' Whilst the British royal family did, in the main, fully support Prussia, Alexandra did have one ally, as her husband, distressed by her obvious unhappiness, threw his weight behind Denmark, with his mother commenting sadly to Vicky 'oh! if Bertie's wife was only a good German and not a Dane! Not, as regards the influence of the politics but as regards the peace and harmony in the family! It is terrible to have the poor boy on the wrong side, and aggravates my sufferings greatly'. Bertie was usually denied any political role, but he retained a fondness for Denmark throughout his life, always maintaining a suspicion of Prussian aggression, which coloured his relationship with his nephew, Kaiser Wilhelm II.

Whilst Alexandra and Bertie found a common cause in their support for Denmark, the reality was that, after a few years, they began to grow apart. Towards the end of 1866, during her third pregnancy, Alexandra became ill with rheumatic fever, and she was distressed when Bertie continued to attend parties and other social functions without her. On 20 February 1867. she bore her third child, Louise, but her illness continued, and she was soon dangerously unwell. Alexandra was so ill that, in March, her parents came to visit and they found her bedridden. In May, she was well enough to attend her daughter's christening in a wheelchair, but she remained gravely ill. According to a letter written by Queen Victoria in November 1867, Alexandra was, by the end of the year, able to get out and about, but her progress was slow:

> Dearest Alix walks about, and up and down stairs – everywhere with the help of one or two sticks – but of course very slowly. She even gets in and out of a carriage, but it is a sad sight to see her thus and to those who did not see her so ill as we did, when one really did not dare hope she would get better, it is sad and touching to see. She is very thin and looks very frail but very pretty, and is so good and patient under this heavy trial. The poor leg is completely stiff and it remains to be seen whether it will ever get quite right again. I much fear not.

Whilst Alexandra did eventually recover much of her health, her leg always remained a problem and she walked with a limp. For someone who had always been athletic, this was a sore trial, although, as an incident related by her grandson in his memoirs shows, she learned to compensate:

> During the First World War, while visiting wounded soldiers in an orthopaedic hospital, she noted the depressed expression on one patient's face. On her inquiring the reason, the Medical Officer informed her that the man's knee would be permanently stiffened as the result of a gunshot wound. My grandmother went straight to his bed to comfort him. 'Never mind if you have a stiff leg,' she reassured him. 'I have one, and look what I can do.' Whereupon she swung her bad leg easily over the seat of an adjacent chair.

A more significant consequence of Alexandra's illness was that it increased the hearing problems that she had inherited from her mother, and by the end of Queen Victoria's reign, she was almost completely deaf. For a woman as lively and sociable as Alexandra, this was a tragedy, and the difficulties in communicating increased the distance between her and Bertie.

Whilst Bertie was fond of Alexandra, he was never faithful. In spring 1869, Alexandra was informed that an acquaintance of Bertie's, Harriet Mordaunt, had confessed to her husband that she had committed adultery with the prince. Sir Charles Mordaunt immediately announced his intention of divorcing his wife, and Bertie was called as a witness in the divorce case. Alexandra was kept informed of the case by her husband, and she fully supported him when he denied adultery with Lady Mordaunt in the witness box. That night, the Prince and Princess of Wales dined publicly with their friends, the Gladstones, in a show of unity. Whilst on this occasion it appears that Bertie's conduct with Lady Mordaunt had been improper rather than adulterous, Alexandra was well aware that he took lovers.

Alexandra also found herself involved in another divorce case that was connected to Bertie, whilst he was absent in India in 1876. At that time, Lord Aylesford announced his intention to divorce his wife, with whom Bertie had enjoyed an earlier flirtation and to whom he had imprudently written a number of letters. In an attempt to blackmail Bertie into intervening in the case on her behalf, Lady Aylesford, along with her friends, Lord Randolph Churchill and Lord Alington, went to see Alexandra with the letters. Alexandra was already aware of the case and would certainly not have agreed to see Lady Aylesford. However, unfortunately, due to her deafness, when Lady Aylesford was announced, she thought it was her friend, Lady Ailesbury, and hurried down to see her. Once in the presence of Lady Aylesford and her friends, Alexandra was informed that, if the letters were made public, Bertie would never become king. Alexandra was devastated and rushed to the Queen to tell her what had happened. Both Victoria and Bertie were furious at the hurt that had been caused to Alexandra, but whilst the affair eventually petered out with the Aylesfords separating rather than divorcing, it was not the last such case that Bertie was involved with.

In 1877, Bertie became involved with one of his most famous mistresses, the actress, Lillie Langtry, whilst Alexandra was absent on a visit to her brother, the King of Greece. Alexandra was always prepared to ignore Bertie's affairs providing that they did not expose her to public humiliation, and she received Lillie when she visited her husband. By the 1890s, Lillie had been superseded by another mistress, Daisy Brooke, the wife of the heir to the Earl of Warwick. Daisy had earlier had an affair with Lord Beresford and had written him a very damaging letter, which was passed to his wife and lodged with her solicitor. To Alexandra's grief, Bertie attempted to obtain the letter but was turned on by Lord Beresford, who called him a coward and a blackguard to his face. It is possible that Alexandra's decision to attend her sister's silver wedding celebrations in Russia rather than Bertie's own fiftieth birthday party was a mark of her hurt and anger, and by the end of Queen Victoria's reign, the couple led largely separate lives. Alexandra was never unfaithful to Bertie, although she did develop a platonic friendship with an equerry, Oliver Montagu, who was in love with her. Following Montagu's early death, Alexandra sent flowers to his grave every year, so he clearly meant a great deal to her.

One thing that did unite Alexandra and Bertie was their love for their children and grandchildren. In his memoirs, Alexandra's grandson, Edward VIII, recorded that, when his parents were absent on a foreign tour, Alexandra and Bertie spoiled the children and 'encouraged our innate boisterousness'. Lessons were never a priority as far as Alexandra and Bertie were concerned, and Edward VIII recorded that

> I had passed temporarily under the sunny auspices of a grandfather who remembered how dull his own lessons had been, and of a grandmother who believed that lessons were less important to children than their happiness. If my grandparents were not entertaining distinguished company at lunch, they liked to have us romping around in the dining-room.

It was the same with Bertie and Alexandra's own children, and they were noted for their unruly behaviour. One courtier described the couple's three daughters as 'rampaging little girls', and Queen Victoria commented that the two boys were ill-bred. Alexandra had difficulty in accepting that her children had to grow up, and she was particularly reluctant to part with her daughters. Whilst her eldest and youngest daughters married, Alexandra kept her middle daughter, Victoria, with her until her death, to the younger woman's frustration. Alexandra also wrote devotedly to her sons when they were absent from her.

Alexandra and Bertie's second son, George, caused them no concerns, but they were greatly worried about their eldest son, Eddy. Eddy had joined his younger brother as a naval cadet but made no progress and was generally considered to have been slow. There were also concerns about his dissipation, and by 1890, when he was created Duke of Clarence and Avondale, Alexandra was actively looking for a wife for him in the hope that it would steady him. Eddy's first choice was his cousin, Alice of Hesse, but she refused him. He then fell in love with Princess Helene of Orléans, the daughter of a pretender to the French throne. Politically, the match was difficult and Helene's Catholic faith meant that marriage would bar the prince from the throne. In spite of this, Alexandra, who was a romantic at heart, was enthusiastic and pushed the couple together. When they became unofficially engaged in August 1890, she encouraged them to go straight to the Queen and beg for her blessing, knowing that Victoria could not resist such an emotional appeal. Alexandra, who was unaware that, at the same time, her son was writing emotional letters to Lady Sybil St Clair Erskine, was upset when Helene's father refused to countenance the match. Alexandra and Bertie were both relieved when Eddy eventually found another bride, becoming engaged to Princess Mary of Teck. The wedding was fixed for 27 February 1892, but in January 1892, as the family assembled for Eddy's birthday at Sandringham, the prince caught a cold whilst out shooting. This turned into an inflammation of the lungs and Alexandra remained devotedly at her son's side until the end. He died on 14 January. Alexandra was devastated, and she never fully recovered, keeping the hat that Eddy had waved at her as he set out for the shoot hanging in her bedroom for some years.

Alexandra was in her late fifties when she finally became queen on the death of Queen Victoria in January 1901. Bertie, who became king as Edward VII, was deeply involved in an affair with Alice Keppel, and he and Alexandra lived largely separate lives. Alexandra enjoyed being queen, and she shared Bertie's coronation, which had to be postponed by some weeks when the King developed appendicitis. To Alexandra's consternation, Bertie was unwilling to allow her much of a public role, and she instead devoted herself to her charity work. Both Bertie and Alexandra had an interest in health care, and in 1905, Alexandra became the president of the British Red Cross Society. She kept this interest up until the end of her life, making numerous hospital visits during the First World War and receiving considerable praise for her warmth and naturalness with the soldiers. Alexandra was also a major benefactor to the people living near her favourite residence, Sandringham, and she set up a technical school there for local boys. Queen Alexandra's generosity was famous, and according to her grandson, Edward VIII,

[Her] interest and care for the workers and villagers at Sandringham were bountiful. Her generosity was a source of embarrassment to her financial advisers. Whenever she received a letter soliciting money, a cheque would be sent by the next post, regardless of the authenticity of the mendicant and without having the case investigated. She also loved animals, especially horses and dogs. A lame horse or one pulling a heavy load would cause her to stop in the street or on the road to upbraid the driver.

Alexandra was grieved by the death of her husband on 6 May 1910, although she once again showed her kindness in allowing Bertie's mistress, Alice Keppel, to visit him for a final farewell. During the years of her widowhood, Alexandra continued her charity work. She remained living with her daughter, Victoria, at Sandringham and received frequent visits from family, including her sister, the exiled dowager Empress of Russia. She died quietly on 20 November 1925, remaining a popular and much-loved figure until the end.

Alexandra of Denmark was Queen of England for only a short period, and most of her life was spent waiting to take on the role of Queen Consort. She was a warm and popular figure, in contrast to her more severe daughter-in-law, Mary of Teck.

MARY OF TECK (1867-1953), the queen of George V, was born on the fringes of the royal family, and she lived a life devoted to duty and to the preservation of the British monarchy. Victoria Mary Augusta Louise Olga Pauline Claudine Agnes of Teck, or May as she was known throughout her life, was born on 26 May 1867 at Kensington Palace. She was the eldest child and only daughter of Princess Mary Adelaide of Cambridge and her husband Prince Francis, Duke of Teck. At the time of her birth, Mary's mother was thirty-three, and the fact that she had finally found a husband at all had been a cause for rejoicing amongst her family. Mary Adelaide was the daughter of Adolphus, Duke of Cambridge, a younger son of George III, and as such, she was a first cousin of Queen Victoria. Mary Adelaide, who was immensely overweight, was popularly referred to as 'Fat Mary' in London, and more than one potential suitor had rejected her when they saw her. Francis of Teck was undaunted by this, and he proposed to Mary Adelaide in April 1866 during a visit to London. Francis was the son of Duke Alexander of Wurttemberg, who would have eventually become King of Wurttemberg had he not made a morganatic marriage to a beautiful Hungarian countess. Due to the unofficial nature of his parents' marriage, Francis received no inheritance and was denied the title of 'His Royal Highness', always having to accept the lesser title of 'His Serene Highness', something that rankled with him. Mary was raised to be fully aware of her father's morganatic birth and the fact that, amongst the German royal families at least, it meant that she ranked somewhere below a princess, although was far above an ordinary noblewoman.

Mary was three months younger that Princess Louise of Wales, the eldest daughter of the Prince and Princess of Wales, and she often played with her cousins, becoming well acquainted with both Louise's elder brothers, Princes Eddy and George. From her childhood, Mary was cripplingly shy, and she loved reading, receiving a better education than many children of her age and class. Mary was well travelled in childhood, and the family frequently made visits to their German relations. Mary Adelaide and her husband were also notoriously extravagant, and in September 1883, they were forced to move abroad to reduce their living costs. Mary keenly felt the humiliation of their exile, although she came to love Florence, one of the places where they stayed, writing later to a friend of Queen Victoria's own visit to the city,

> You may imagine with what interest we read of the dear Queen's magnificent reception at dear Florence all the well known places came so vividly back to our minds & we seemed to see all the windows gaily decorated with carpets flags etc. how lovely & touching it must have been to hear 'God Save the Queen' struck up at the Piazza del Duomo & San Marco, we howled when we read the account in the Italian Papers. I can quite fancy that you missed us at the beloved I Cedri – oh! how happy those days were, I sometimes long to go back there.

Mary's family had returned to London by May 1885, and she made her debut into society. With her plain looks, crippling shyness and ambiguous status, it was some time before Mary was able to attract a husband.

Throughout 1891, Mary saw her friend, Princess Louise of Wales, who had become Duchess of Fife, regularly. This brought her to Queen Victoria's attention, and in October 1891, she and her brother Adolphus were summoned to visit the Queen at Balmoral. Victoria had already formed the view that Mary would make a good queen, and during the ten days of the visit, she spent much time with her in order to confirm this impression. By 1891, Queen Victoria's grandson, Prince Albert Victor (or Eddy as he was always known) was twenty-seven years old, and his family were much concerned about his apparent backwardness and lethargic nature. He had already been disappointed on several occasions in finding a bride, but he was easily led, and when it was suggested to him that he might like to propose to Mary, he agreed, asking her to marry him at a house party at Luton on 3 December 1891. Whilst Mary was not in love with Eddy, she liked him, and she readily accepted. The marriage was arranged for 27 February 1892, and on 4 January, Mary and her parents travelled to join Eddy and his family at Sandringham. It was with grief and shock that Mary greeted Eddy's death on 14 January, an event rendered all the more tragic by his forthcoming nuptials. In her diary for the day of Eddy's death, Queen Victoria summed up the feelings of many:

> Words are too poor to express one's feelings of grief, horror and distress! Poor, poor parents; poor May to have her whole bright future to be merely a dream! Poor me, in my old age, to see this young promising life cut short! I, who loved him so dearly, and to whom he was so devoted! God help us! This is an awful blow to the country too!

Mary attended her fiancé's funeral on 20 January, arranging for her bridal wreath to be laid on the coffin.

During the days after Eddy's death, Mary's father had caused his family acute embarrassment by declaring on several occasions that 'it must be a Tsarevich, it must be a Tsarevich'. This was in reference to the fact that the Princess of Wales's own sister, Dagmar of Denmark, had been engaged to the Tsarevich Nicholas of Russia, and when he died unexpectedly, she had married his younger brother and successor as heir to the throne. With Eddy's death, the heir apparent became his younger brother, Prince George. George was only a year younger than Eddy, and in spite of their very different characters, the pair had always been close. George was heartbroken at Eddy's death and when it was first suggested that he should marry Mary, he dismissed the idea, insisting that he would choose his bride for himself. Mary also found the idea distasteful, and she and her parents went to Cannes in March 1892 in an attempt to recover from the shock of the death. Whilst in Cannes, George visited Mary, and he continued to do so after she returned to England in July. They soon found that their common grief drew them together, and on 3 May 1893, George proposed and Mary gladly accepted. The couple were married on 6 July 1893. For Mary, who was still painfully shy, it must have been an ordeal to be the focus of so much attention at the wedding, and according to Queen Victoria in her journal, Mary 'though quite self-possessed, spoke very low'. Although never described as beautiful, Mary looked her best at the ceremony, with Victoria describing her as looking 'very sweet':

> Her dress was very simple, of white satin with a silver design of roses, shamrocks, thistles and orange flowers, interwoven. On her head she had a small wreath of orange flowers, myrtle, and white heather surmounted by the diamond necklace I gave her, which can also be worn as a diadem, and her mother's wedding veil.

Whilst the Prince and Princess of Wales were initially unhappy with the marriage, concerned that it suggested that Mary had never cared for their eldest son, Queen Victoria was very happy with the match, recording in her journal 'thank God! Georgie has got such an excellent, useful, and good wife'.

After the wedding ceremony, Mary and George went to Sandringham for their honeymoon, where they set up home in York House on the Sandringham estate. George had been created Duke of York after his brother's death, but the couple soon found that, like his father, he was excluded from any role in government by Queen Victoria. The early years of Mary's marriage were fully taken up with childbearing, and her eldest son was born on 23 June 1894. Queen Victoria always insisted that the eldest son of each of her descendants' families should be called Albert, after her beloved husband, but Mary and George were determined to call their son Edward, in memory of Eddy. They had their way, and their eldest son was christened Edward Albert Christian George Andrew Patrick David. He was always known to the family as David. Mary's second son arrived on the anniversary of the Prince Consort's death in 1895, and bowing to the inevitable, the couple duly named him Albert. Albert's birth was followed by a daughter, Mary, and sons Henry and George. The youngest child, John, was born in 1905.

Whilst they loved their children, Mary and George were strict and distant parents and neither found it easy to relate to small children. Before Eddy's death, George had had a promising career in the navy, and according to his eldest son, David (the future Edward VIII and Duke of Windsor), he retained 'a gruff, blue-water approach to all human situations'. David recalled that his parents were distant figures during his childhood and that his association with them tended to a 'fixed and regulated pattern'. David's memoirs record that his relationship was further damaged by one of his nurses who

> appears to have been to blame for an early unfavourable impression that I made upon my parents. They liked to have the children brought downstairs to be with them at tea-time. I was, after all, their first child, and my father no doubt looked forward to this interlude at the end of the day as an occasion of possible mutual pleasure and understanding. But it seldom turned out that way. Before carrying me into the drawing-room, this dreadful 'Nanny' would pinch and twist my arm – why, no one knew, unless it was to demonstrate, according to some perverse reasoning, that her power over me was greater than that of my parents. The sobbing and bawling this treatment invariably evoked understandably puzzled, worried, and finally annoyed them. It would result in my being peremptorily removed from the room before further embarrassment was inflicted upon them and the other witnesses of this pathetic scene.

It took Mary three years to realise what was happening, and whilst her children were fond of her, her relations with them were never easy. David was, however, able to recall Mary enjoying a joke with her children, and when they commented on a likeness between a bust of Queen Victoria's father, Edward, Duke of Kent, and a footman named Smithson, Mary 'was greatly amused but lectured us gently on the impropriety of making fun of our great-grandfather, and also of holding up a servitor to ridicule'. Mary also took part in a practical joke in which tadpoles were served on toast to the children's French master. The master gathered up the toast too quickly and Mary was only able to cry 'No, no! That special savoury is not meant to be eaten at all' before it had been devoured. She later bade David apologise on the family's behalf. As her children grew up, Mary spent more time with them, and she taught all of her children to crochet.

Mary was present at Queen Victoria's deathbed in January 1901, and in March, she and George sailed for a tour of Australia and New Zealand. On their return in November, George was created Prince of Wales by his father, but as in the previous reign, he was allowed no political role. George and Mary spent much of Edward VII's reign travelling and, in 1905, made a tour of India. They also attended the coronation of George's brother-in-law and sister as king and queen of Norway, as well as the wedding of the King of Spain to George's cousin. Edward VII had spent so long waiting to be king that it was inevitable that his reign would be brief. He died on 6 May 1910 and George succeeded to the throne as George V. George had always hated double names and insisted that Mary, who always signed her name 'Victoria Mary', choose one name by which to be known. She did not feel she could decently become Queen Victoria so soon after the old queen's death and, instead, decided to become Queen Mary.

Mary always had a great interest in family history, believing that she resembled her ancestress and predecessor as queen, Charlotte of Mecklenburg-Strelitz. As a result of this interest, she was determined to help preserve the monarchy at all costs, and in order to appear dignified in public, she often came across as cold, a reputation that she retains to the present day. Mary was, like George, averse to change, but she was not heartless, and much of her time as queen was occupied with charity work. This was particularly apparent during the First World War, which began on 4 August 1914. Within days of the declaration of war, she organised her needlework guild to begin making clothes for the troops. She also inspected the offices of the National Relief Fund and the Red Cross. Mary was greatly occupied during the war in visiting wounded soldiers, and whilst her shyness made this a difficult task for her, she kept it up stoically, insisting on seeing even the worst cases, which the hospitals tried to keep from her. Mary also took on some of George's duties when, in October 1915, he was severely injured whilst visiting the front lines when his horse fell on top of him. To Mary's grief, George never fully recovered, and his pain made him irascible. As the war dragged on, Mary, along with everyone else, longed for peace, and she was overjoyed when the Armistice was declared on 11 November 1918, writing in her journal that it was 'the greatest day in the world's history'.

Once the war was over, Mary and George settled into a more retired routine, rarely socialising or attending entertainments. The couple suffered a personal blow on 18 January 1919 when their youngest son, John, died. He had suffered from epilepsy and appears to have had some learning difficulties, and from 1917, he had lived apart from his family with his devoted nurse. Mary and George were saddened by the death and rushed down to Sandringham as soon as they heard the news. Both also felt it was a release for the boy, however, and Mary commented that she was glad his death had been so gentle. In February 1922, the couple's daughter, Mary, married the son of the Earl of Harewood. Whilst George and Mary approved of the match, they were saddened by their daughter's departure to her own home, and Mary wrote soon afterwards to her son, David, that

the wonderful day has come & gone & Mary is married & has flown from her home leaving a terrible blank behind her as you can well imagine. Papa & I are feeling very low & sad without her especially as Georgie had to return to Malta yesterday while Harry has at last joined the 10th Hussars at Canterbury & Bertie has gone hunting for a few days – Nothing could have gone off better than the wedding did, a fine day, a beautiful pageant from start to finish, a fine service in the Abbey, Mary doing her part to perfection (a very great ordeal before so many people) – & everyone happy & pleased.

Mary suffered a further blow in November 1928 when George fell dangerously ill with septicaemia. The couple had become devoted to each other, and Mary stayed with George during his recuperation at Bognor the following year. By May, George seemed to be improving, but at the end of the month, he developed a dangerous abscess. He never fully recovered and died on 20 January 1936 in the presence of Mary and their children. She wrote in her diary for that day that she was broken-hearted.

With George's death, the couple's eldest son, David, succeeded as Edward VIII. Mary had already been aware of his relationship with a married American, Wallis Simpson, before he became king, but she hoped that he would abandon her following his accession. To Mary, the preservation of the throne was her life's work, and she was adamant that David should do his duty and remain as king above all else. David, however, had other ideas, and on 16 November 1936, he dined with his mother and sister. According to his memoirs, after the meal,

> I told them of my love for Wallis and my determination to marry her; and of the opposition of the Prime Minister and Government to the marriage. The telling was all the harder because until that evening the subject had never been discussed between us. Neither my mother nor Mary reproved me; in fact they sympathised with me. But as I went on and they comprehended that even the alternative of abdication would not deter me from my course, I became conscious of their growing consternation that I could even contemplate giving up the throne of my forbears. My mother had been schooled to put duty, in the stoic Victorian sense, before everything else in life. From her invincible virtue and correctness she looked out as from a fortress upon the rest of humanity, with all its tremulous uncertainties and distractions.

Mary refused absolutely to meet Wallis Simpson. Following David's abdication early in December 1936, Mary did not see him for another nine years, and the relationship remained strained until her death.

Mary could never understand how her son could put love before duty, and she threw her energies into supporting her second son, Albert, who became king as George VI. According to Marion Crawford, the governess to Mary's two granddaughters, Princesses Elizabeth and Margaret, Mary was involved in setting the girls' curriculum, and she showed a great interest in their education. During the Second World War, it was only with difficulty that the King was able to persuade Mary to leave London, as, in spite of her age, she was determined to be of use to the war effort. She finally relented and stayed at Badminton House, the home of her niece, the Duchess of Beaufort, carrying out work for the war effort from there, including organising salvage campaigns. Mary was somewhat overzealous in this, and after she had carried out salvage operations, her attendants were often forced to return farm implements that she, in her eagerness, had collected. Mary also made a point of offering lifts in her car to any servicemen that she passed whilst driving. For Mary, the war was tinged with personal tragedy when her son George, Duke of Kent, was killed in an aircraft accident, but she continued to keep busy, returning to London at the end of the war.

Following the end of the Second World War, Mary's health declined, and she began to use a wheelchair. She was devastated in February 1952 when her second son, the King, died unexpectedly, and she appeared heavily veiled and frail-looking at his funeral. In spite of her grief, Mary was able to attend her granddaughter, Elizabeth II, at her accession, telling her that 'her old Grannie and subject must be the first to kiss her hand'. Mary never recovered from the death of a third son and she aged rapidly. She died suddenly during the evening of 4 March 1953 at the age of eighty-five.

Mary of Teck led a life devoted to the preservation of the monarchy at all costs. This was in direct contrast to her daughter-in-law, the controversial Wallis Simpson, who nearly brought the monarchy to its ruin.

WALLIS SIMPSON (1896-1986) was never queen and has the distinction of being the only woman to marry an ex-king of England. Bessie Wallis Warfield was born on 19 June 1896 at Blue Ridge Summit, Pennsylvania. She was the daughter of Teackle Wallis Warfield and Alice Montague, both of whom were members of prominent and wealthy families. Some mystery surrounds Wallis's birth, and unusually for her family, no announcement was made. This has been taken by one biographer to suggest that there may have been some uncertainty as to the child's gender, something that seems unlikely given that Wallis eventually went on to have three husbands. Alternatively, another biographer has suggested that Wallis was illegitimate. Whether this is true or not is uncertain, but Wallis's parents were certainly married before her father's early death when Wallis was an infant. Teackle's death left Wallis and her mother in financial difficulty, and the pair lived with his mother in Baltimore for some time before moving to stay with Alice's sister, Bessie, after whom Wallis was named. Wallis was always fond of her aunt, but she abandoned her first name as soon as she was able, commenting that 'I always hated the name Bessie, for, as I told my aunt, "So many cows are called Bessie". Eventually I succeeded in persuading everyone but my grandmother to drop it'.

Alice and Wallis's fortunes changed when Wallis was twelve and Alice married John Freeman Raisin, a member of a wealthy Baltimore political family. Wallis liked Raisin and, whilst she was initially upset by the marriage, soon became close to her stepfather, who paid for her to attend an exclusive girls' boarding school. She was deeply upset when, on 4 April 1913, she was called out of her lessons to be told that her stepfather had died. With Raisin's death, the family were once again dependent on relatives, and Solomon Warfield, Wallis's 'Uncle Sol', paid for her to make her debut into Baltimore society. Wallis, who had been a 'poor relation' all her life, was determined to make her way in the world, and in April 1916, she went to stay with relatives at Pensacola Air Station in Florida. Whilst there, she was invited to a lunch with a number of airmen. According to Wallis's own account,

> As the masculine opinions rumbled around the table, I became increasingly aware of lieutenant Spencer. Whenever I turned away to listen to one of the others or to exchange comments with Corinne [Mustin, Wallis's cousin], the gold stripes on his shoulder-boards, glimpsed out of the corner of my eye, acted like a magnet and drew me back to him. His gaiety and sense of fun were continually in play, though a certain undertone of sarcasm hinted at harsher forces working beneath the surface. The eyes were surprisingly intense and bright and quick to flash in response to a quip. Above all, I gained an impression of resolution and courage; I felt here was a man you could rely on in a tight place.

Wallis had never even seen an aeroplane before arriving at Pensacola, and she found the airmen incredibly glamorous. She and Earl Winfield Spencer Jr, who was known as Win, were married on 8 November 1916.

Wallis had been attracted to her husband's glamour, but almost immediately after the wedding, she realised that she knew very little about him. When they arrived for their honeymoon in West Virginia, Win was horrified to find that it was a dry state. According to Wallis, he then took out a bottle of gin from his suitcase, commenting that there was 'just enough left to get up to flying speed until I can locate a local source of supply'. Win's alcoholism rapidly caused the marriage to deteriorate, and he took pleasure in insulting Wallis in public. He also sometimes disappeared overnight, offering no explanation as to his whereabouts. Wallis's own account claims he locked her in a room on a number of occasions whilst he went out. The final straw came in 1921 when he locked her in a bathroom all afternoon. Following this, she and Win separated. In 1924, she travelled to Europe for the first time and, whilst in Paris, received a letter from Win asking for a reconciliation. Wallis, whose family had opposed any divorce, sailed to join him in Hong Kong, where he was stationed, but the reunion was unsuccessful. Wallis spent some time living alone in China before returning to America in 1925 and securing a divorce in 1927.

Even before her divorce from Win Spencer was granted, Wallis had identified her second husband. At Christmas 1926, she was invited by her friend, Mary Raffray, to stay with her in New York. Wallis was introduced by the Raffrays to Ernest Simpson, a businessman of British descent who had been raised in America. Wallis recorded of Ernest that he was 'reserved in manner, yet with a gift of quiet wit, always well dressed, a good dancer, fond of the theatre, and obviously well read, he impressed me as an unusually well-balanced man. I had acquired a taste for cosmopolitan minds, and Ernest obviously had one. I was attracted to him and he to me'. Ernest was married at the time of this meeting but soon obtained a divorce. In 1927, he was transferred to his firm's London office and asked Wallis to marry him. It was no love match on Wallis's part, and shortly before she joined him in London, she wrote to inform her mother that 'I've decided definitely that the best and wisest thing for me to do is to marry Ernest. I am very fond of him and he is kind, which will be a contrast'. For Wallis, Ernest promised stability, and the couple were married on 21 July 1928.

Wallis and Ernest quickly became active in London society. Wallis was always fascinated by royalty and she had her first glimpse of the glamorous Prince of Wales one day when her car passed his near St James's Palace. She was given the opportunity to meet him in the autumn of 1930 when her friend, Connie Thaw, whose sister, Thelma, Lady Furness, was the prince's mistress, invited her and Ernest to a house party at Melton Mowbray. Wallis was thrilled by the invitation and spent the train ride up to the house practising her curtsey. Unfortunately, she also had a bad cold, but the meeting was a success, and she sat next to the prince at lunch the next day. Wallis met the prince for a second time the following spring at a reception held by Lady Furness, and he remembered her, something that pleased Wallis.

The Prince of Wales was always fascinated by Americans, and Wallis had an irreverent manner that attracted him. In June 1931, Wallis was presented at court. As documented in her memoirs, 'as the Prince of Wales walked past, I overheard him mutter to his uncle, the Duke of Connaught, "Uncle Arthur, something ought to be done about the lights. They make all the women look ghastly"'. Following the presentation, Wallis and Ernest went back to Lady Furness's house. When the prince arrived, he spoke admiringly of Wallis's gown, to which she replied, 'But, Sir, I understood that you thought we all looked ghastly.' The prince was startled by this and replied, smiling, 'I had no idea my voice carried so far.' Wallis's words were bold, and the prince was immediately interested in her, offering her and Ernest a lift home that evening in his car. Wallis did not see the prince for another six months; then, out of the blue, she and Ernest received an invitation to a house party at his residence, Fort Belvedere. The Fort was the only place where the prince was truly able to relax, and Wallis was surprised when he opened the door himself, showing them personally to their room. Wallis came to love the Fort, and she and the prince shared an interest in it, viewing it as the most romantic place they had known. The visit was a success, and Wallis and Ernest were invited back for other parties throughout the year, although, as Wallis commented, 'if the Prince was in any way drawn to me, I was unaware of his interest'.

The turning point in Wallis and David's relationship came in January 1934 when the prince's mistress, Lady Furness, left on a visit to her native America. Wallis claims, 'The day before she sailed she asked me for cocktails. We rattled along in our fashion; as we said goodbye she said, laughingly, "I'm afraid the Prince is going to be lonely. Wallis, wont you look after him?" I promised that I would, but privately doubted that he would be in need of solace.' The week that Lady Furness left, David came to Wallis's flat for dinner, and soon afterwards, he telephoned her for the first time, inviting her out for dinner. For Wallis, the dinner was instructive:

> Before, the Prince had never dwelt upon his duties and the particular function that he fulfilled in the imperial scheme of things. In fact, I had formed the impression the times I had seen him that he deliberately kept the conversation from these topics, as if the subject of his working hours was something to be thrust aside in hours of relaxation. But on this particular evening, some chance remark of mine broke through this barrier, and suddenly, while the others, as I recall, were away from the table dancing, he began to talk about his work, the things he hoped to do, and the creative role he thought the Monarchy could play in this new age, and also dropped a hint of the frustrations he was experiencing.

For Wallis, David's candour was illuminating, and the prince also found in her a woman with whom he could share his problems and concerns. According to the prince's friend, Walter Monckton, Wallis was, for David, the perfect woman, and during Lady Furness's absence, he became besotted with her. After the dinner, David asked if he could visit Wallis at her flat, and she, the prince, and Ernest often spent evenings together. As time wore on, Ernest, who often brought work home with him, began to excuse himself, leaving his wife and the prince alone. Wallis was a naturally dominant personality, and David loved the order that she brought to his life. She quickly took control of many of the prince's domestic affairs, writing in one letter,

> David –
> Have the table moved back as far as possible and if the V[ansittart]s are coming there would be far more room for 10 if the Finn could produce chairs without arms. Here is a suggestion for seating. I would also have two sorts of cocktails and white wine offered as well as the vin rose, the servants to serve the wine. Also I didn't see a green vegetable on the menu. Sorry to bother you but I like everyone to think you do things well. Perhaps I'm quite fond of you.

By the time that Thelma Furness returned from the United States in March, Wallis was firmly ensconced as the object of David's affections, and at her first weekend at the Fort, Thelma noticed that 'the Prince and Wallis seemed to have little private jokes. Once he picked up a piece of salad with his fingers; Wallis playfully slapped his hand.' That summer, Wallis went with the prince on his European holiday, with her Aunt Bessie as a chaperone, and they fell in love.

Whilst, during the early months of the relationship, Ernest, who was star-struck by the prince, was happy for Wallis to spend time with him, he soon began to object. According to Wallis, matters came to a head when David invited the couple on a skiing trip to Austria. Wallis accepted the invitation on behalf of both her husband and herself, and she was angered when Ernest refused to go. As Wallis later recalled,

> Later that evening, after a rather silent dinner, he asked me whether my mind was definitely made up to go. I remember answering, 'Of course. Why not? I wouldn't dream of missing it'.
> He got up from his chair and said, 'I rather thought that we might have gone to New York together. I see now that I was wrong'. I asked if he couldn't come out for at least some of the time. He answered that it was quite out of the question.
> With that he went to his room, and for the first time I heard the door bang.

Wallis's attendance on the skiing trip marked a change in Ernest's attitude towards her, and whilst she was always anxious to try to retain Ernest, fearing that she would eventually be forgotten by the prince, her marriage steadily collapsed. Wallis had always viewed Ernest as a stable and lasting influence in her life and as her future. In one letter to the prince, she wrote to complain of his selfishness when he stayed too late with her and Ernest one evening, commenting that 'please understand I am not writing a lecture, only your behaviour last night made me realise how very alone I shall be some day'.

Wallis did not view her affair with the prince as lasting, and she knew that he would never be permitted to marry her. David was also aware of the opposition that their relationship would face, but he was infatuated by her and wrote a number of besotted letters to Wallis when they were apart, in which he referred to himself in the third person and to himself and Wallis as 'WE' for Wallis and Edward. One typical letter reads,

A boy is holding a girl so very tight in his arms tonight. He will miss her more tomorrow because he will have been away from her some hours longer and cannot see her till Wed-y night. A girl knows that not anybody or anything can separate WE – not even the stars – and that WE belong to each other for ever. WE love [twice underlined] each other more than life so God bless WE. Your [twice underlined] David.

Another letter from David reads,

Oh! a boy does miss a girl here so terribly tonight. Will try and sleep now but am not hopeful yet. Have been numbering our pictures. Please, please Wallis don't get scared or loose [*sic*] faith when you are away from me. I love you more every minute and no difficulties or complications can possibly prevent our ultimate happiness. WE are so strong together in our purpose which is our very life that it must not, cannot fail for any reason or obstacle that may confront us. I am sending this up to you in the morning with all the things I want to do and say to you right now. I do hate and loathe the present situation until I can start in to talk more than you do my sweetheart and am just going mad at the mere thought (let alone knowing) that you are alone there with Ernest. God bless WE for ever my Wallis. You know your David will love you and look after you so long as he has breath in his eanum [very emotional] body.

For David, his love for Wallis was the most important thing in his life, and he could not bear to be parted from her, writing in another brief note, 'My own beloved Wallis I love you more & more & more & please come down to say goodnight to David. I haven't seen you once today & I can't take it. I love you.'

Wallis responded lovingly to David, and it is clear from the sheer length of time that their relationship endured that she was also in love with him. She was upset in January 1936 when he became king as Edward VIII. Only a few days after David became king, Wallis wrote to him:

I am sad because I miss you and being near and yet so far seems most unfair. Some day of course I must learn to be always alone for I will be in my heart also I must develop strength to look at papers containing your photographs and accounts of your activities – and perhaps you will miss the eanum in your scheme. One can be awfully alone in crowds – but also perhaps both of us will cease to want what is hardest to have and be content with the simple way. And now I hear your machine which generally was a joyous sound because soon you would be holding me and I would be looking 'up' into your eyes. God bless you and above all make you strong where you have been weak.

Even as king, David was not prepared to abandon Wallis, and shortly after his accession, he began to talk of marriage. Wallis ignored this, believing it to be impossible, and David therefore took the initiative, meeting with Ernest in March and persuading him to give Wallis grounds for a divorce. Ernest had begun an affair with Wallis's friend, Mary Raffray, in 1935, and he agreed to go to a hotel with her in order to be caught in adultery by a member of staff. In return, he asked that David promise to look after Wallis. Wallis was shocked at what David had done, but she agreed to consult his solicitor in June and petition for divorce on the grounds of Ernest's adultery. The divorce hearing was held on 27 October 1936, and Wallis was granted a *decree nisi*, meaning that she had to wait six months for the divorce to become absolute.

Once Wallis's divorce was in hand, David started trying to break the news of his impending marriage to his family and the government. Marion Crawford, the governess of David's two nieces, Princesses Elizabeth and Margaret, recorded that he brought Wallis to tea with his brother and sister-in-law, the Duke and Duchess of York, and it is clear that he was trying to gain their approval of Wallis. The meeting was not a success, and Wallis and the duchess, the future queen, Elizabeth Bowes-Lyon, loathed each other. David also invited the Prime Minister, Stanley Baldwin, to dinner at York House, explaining to Wallis that 'it's got to be done sooner or later; my Prime Minister must meet my future wife'. Wallis was shocked, as this was apparently the first time that David had openly talked of them one day marrying, and she replied that 'you mustn't talk this way. The idea is impossible. They'd never let you'. David merely said 'I'm well aware of all that, but rest assured, I will manage it somehow'. The dinner went ahead, and David was told in no uncertain terms that Wallis, as a divorced woman, could never be queen. As the months went by, the couple investigated the possibility of a morganatic marriage, but this was also denied them. Finally, in early December, David received word that the British press, which had hitherto censored news of the affair, intended to publish, and Wallis fled to France, with a barrage of hate mail following her there.

Even before she left England, David had begun to hint that he would give up his throne, telling her, 'They can't stop me. On the throne or off, I'm going to marry you.' Wallis was in agony, desperate that he should wait and not take so drastic a step. She made a number of frantic telephone calls to England, begging him to do nothing hasty and also wrote on 6 December saying, 'I am sending this by air as I think it important you have it before. I am so anxious for you not to *abdicate* and I think the fact that you do is going to put me in the wrong light to the entire world because they will say that I could have prevented it'. Wallis begged David to wait until the following autumn. For David, however, the thought of being without Wallis was intolerable, and on the morning of 10 December 1936, he abdicated, making a farewell broadcast on the radio the following day. For David, the abdication was a great release, and after being created Duke of Windsor, he left England for Austria. Wallis listened to the broadcast before writing to David on 12 December:

> My heart is so full of love for you and the agony of not being able to see you after all you have been through is pathetic. At the moment we have the whole world against us and our love – so we can't afford to move about very much and must simply sit and face these dreary months ahead and I think I shall have to stay here.

To ensure that Wallis's divorce was not jeopardised, it was necessary for the couple to live apart until it was pronounced, and they spent six months of frustration unable to see each other. Finally, on 3 May 1937, Wallis received word that her divorce had become final, and

David arrived in France the next day. As he bounded up the steps to his beloved, he declared, 'Darling, it's been so long. I can hardly believe that this is you, and I'm here.'

The couple were married in France on 3 June 1937 in a ceremony that was, to David's grief, boycotted by his family. To his fury, a few days before the wedding, David also received a letter from his brother, George VI, informing him that Wallis would not receive the title of 'Her Royal Highness'. The couple had already suspected that this would be the case, with Wallis writing on 12 December 1936 that 'York I don't suppose will make me HRH'. In spite of repeated appeals by David, Wallis never received the title that, constitutionally, she was entitled to, and David never forgave his brother and family for implying that his wife and 'perfect woman' was not good enough for him.

Following their marriage, Wallis and Edward found themselves exiled and without a role. Controversially, in October 1937, they visited Nazi Germany and met with leading members of the Nazi party, including Adolf Hitler himself, who commented that Wallis would have made a good queen. Following the visit, rumours of Nazi sympathies dogged the couple, although it is perhaps fair to say that they, like many others of their time, were not Nazi-supporters but did believe that Germany had some genuine grievances. Certainly, when war broke out in 1939, David was anxious to serve his country, and he accepted a post from his brother in Paris. Following the fall of France, the couple were sent to the Bahamas to take up the governorship there, a post that David viewed as an exile.

The couple spent five years in the Bahamas, a place they hated, before settling permanently in France. They spent the rest of their lives living comfortably, remaining devoted to each other until the end. Whilst still in the Bahamas, Wallis took steps to reconcile David with his mother, Queen Mary, and she wrote to her, giving details about the couple's life together. Queen Mary always refused to listen to any news of her daughter-in-law, but in her next letter to David, she shocked him by saying 'I send a kind message to your wife'. David visited his mother at her death, although it is clear that the reconciliation was incomplete, and he wrote to tell Wallis of his mother's iciness. By the 1960s, relations with the royal family began to thaw somewhat, and when, in 1964, David underwent surgery in Texas, his niece, Elizabeth II, sent flowers. She visited him in hospital in London a few months later. In 1967, both Wallis and David were invited to attend the unveiling of a plaque in honour of Queen Mary, although Wallis caused a stir by refusing to curtsey to the Queen Mother. In late 1971, David was diagnosed with cancer, and he received a visit from his niece in France in May the following year. Only a few days later, on 8 May 1972, he died in Wallis's arms.

Before his death, David had secured a promise from his niece that he and Wallis could be buried side by side at the royal burial ground at Frogmore at Windsor. Wallis was devastated by David's death and always refused to pack away his things, leaving everything exactly as it was during his lifetime. She was able to attend his funeral and was invited to stay at Buckingham Palace, appearing grief-stricken at the window in a photograph published in the press. At the funeral, Wallis commented that Edward had been her whole life, and she never got over his loss. By 1976, she began to show signs of senility, and when the Queen Mother offered to visit her in October of that year, the visit had to be cancelled at the last minute. The Queen Mother instead sent flowers with a note saying 'in friendship, Elizabeth'. Wallis was unable to leave her house after 1981 and spent the last years of her life in seclusion. She died on 24 April 1986, shortly before her ninetieth birthday, and was buried beside David.

Wallis Simpson was never queen and was always held responsible for the abdication of Edward VIII. Through their long years together, Wallis and David proved that theirs truly was a great love affair. In spite of a gradual thaw in relations, Wallis was never accepted by the royal family, and her funeral service at Windsor, whilst attended by the royal family, was remarkable for the fact that the deceased's name was never mentioned. Wallis's sister-in-law, Elizabeth Bowes-Lyon, never forgave her for the part that she played in elevating her husband to an unwanted throne.

ELIZABETH BOWES-LYON (1900-2002) is best remembered as the 'Queen Mother', a position that she held for fifty years. She is also the longest-lived of any English queen, and her life spanned all but eight months of the twentieth century and the first two years of the twenty-first. Elizabeth was born on 4 August 1900, the ninth child of ten born to Claude Bowes-Lyon, Lord Glamis, and his wife, Cecilia Cavendish-Bentinck. Her father became Earl of Strathmore in 1904, and the family spent some time at Glamis Castle in Scotland, although Elizabeth spent most of her childhood at her father's house of St Paul's Walden Bury in Hertfordshire. There was a seven-year age gap between Elizabeth and the youngest of her elder siblings, and she and her younger brother David, who was only fifteen months younger than her, were particularly close. The siblings were so often together that the family nicknamed them the 'two Benjamins'. It was also with David that the young Elizabeth exhibited a mischievous streak, and according to her contemporary, Lady Cynthia Asquith,

> Her brother David tells me that he and his sister once decided to run away, and laid in a store of emergency provisions. But as their mother has no recollection of this incident, I gather that they cannot have run very far. On one occasion, proudly remembered, they gave a chauffeur palpitations by placing a football directly in front of one of the front wheels of the car. As the car started the football burst with a terrific explosion.

Elizabeth enjoyed an idyllic childhood, although her education was limited. She was, however, fluent in French and was taught music, dancing and drawing by her mother. Elizabeth was a precocious child, and her mother recalled to Asquith an occasion when 'two people were talking together, unaware that Lady Elizabeth, then five years old, was in the room. "How sad to think," said one, "that poor X will only be married for his position and money." "Perhaps," said a small voice, faintly tinged with reproach, "perhaps someone will marry him 'cos she loves him"'.

Elizabeth's idyllic childhood abruptly came to an end with the outbreak of the First World War in 1914, and four of her brothers enlisted in the armed forces. Elizabeth played her part, and when Glamis was converted into a hospital for wounded soldiers, she assisted by entertaining the patients and helping to keep their spirits up. According to Asquith, one soldier who spent time at Glamis commented that 'my three weeks at Glamis have been the happiest I ever struck. I love Lady Strathmore so very much on account of her being so very like my dear mother, as was, and as for Lady Elizabeth, why, she and my fiancay [*sic*] are as like as two peas'. A second soldier recalled Elizabeth good-naturedly teasing him when he was scared by a stuffed bear. Elizabeth also helped the war effort in other ways, and according to her own account, once war broke out, 'lessons were neglected, for during these first few months we were so busy knitting and making shirts for the local battalion – the 5th Black Watch. My chief occupation was crumpling up tissue paper until it was so soft that it no longer crackled, to put into the linings of sleeping-bags'. Elizabeth's family suffered a tragedy during the war when her brother, Fergus, was killed at the Battle of Loos in September 1915.

Elizabeth met Prince Albert, the second son of George V for the first time in April 1916, at a tea party, but they made little impression on each other. Once the war was over, Elizabeth was ready to join London society, and she was presented at court in July 1920. On 8 July, she went to a ball at the Ritz, which Albert also attended. Elizabeth was attractive, and Albert, who did not remember their earlier meeting, asked who she was. The couple danced, and whilst, for Elizabeth, this had little significance, Albert fell in love with her. Albert, or Bertie as he was known, was cripplingly shy, with a stammer, but Elizabeth brought out the best in him, increasing his confidence. He proved an ardent suitor, and in the summer of 1920, he invited himself to Glamis whilst Elizabeth was there. Back in London in the autumn, Bertie continued to call on Elizabeth, and early the following year, he obtained his parents' consent to the match, with George V commenting, 'You'll be a lucky fellow if she accepts you.' On 27 February 1921, Bertie proposed to Elizabeth, and to his horror, she refused him. He continued to court her and proposed again in March 1922, only to be refused once more. Finally, on 3 January 1923, he proposed again, and after thinking it over, she accepted. Elizabeth's initial reluctance was due to her fear of losing her independence by marrying into the royal family rather than any ambivalence towards Bertie, and Asquith commented that 'I dare say she was very much afraid of the position, but she just found she couldn't do without him'. Elizabeth had fallen in love, and on 16 January 1923, their engagement was announced to general rejoicing. They were married in a grand royal ceremony at Westminster Abbey on 23 April 1923.

As Elizabeth had feared, her life changed dramatically with her marriage, and she and Bertie were constantly in the public eye. On 21 April 1926, she bore her first child, a daughter named Elizabeth after herself. She was horrified when it was announced soon after the birth that she and Bertie would travel to Australia to open the new Federal Parliament Buildings in Canberra, forcing them to part with their daughter. The couple acquitted themselves well on the tour, which began in January 1927, but the months spent away from their beloved daughter were hard for both Bertie and Elizabeth.

Elizabeth, Bertie and their family were always close, and the younger Elizabeth's birth was followed in August 1930 by the arrival of a second daughter, Margaret. According to the children's governess, Marion Crawford, Elizabeth and Bertie received a visit from the children each morning, right up to the day of Princess Elizabeth's marriage. The family also played games together, with Bertie often joining his daughters for hide and seek in the gardens. The couple enjoyed domesticity, and 'the Duke and the Duchess rarely dined out. In the evening, the happy bath hour over, the children bedded and the day's work done, they would sit one each side of the fireplace like any other young married couple, happy in each other, not requiring any diversion'. Crawford noted that 'rarely was there a dinner party. They were happiest alone. As in those days they had fewer social obligation, they were able to do as they wished'. In one letter to Princess Elizabeth after her marriage, Bertie wrote, 'our family, us four, the "Royal Family" must remain together'.

For Elizabeth, Edward VIII's abdication in December 1936 was a disaster for their family and Bertie succeeded unexpectedly as George VI, taking his father's name to show the continuity in the royal family. Elizabeth always believed that the strain of becoming king eventually killed her husband, and she never forgave his brother or his brother's wife, Wallis Simpson. Soon after the abdication, Elizabeth, Bertie, and their family moved to Buckingham Palace. Elizabeth immediately had to get used to a new routine, which abridged the time she was able to spend with her family. According to Crawford,

> In the evenings there was always something doing. Their Majesties would have to attend a reception, a command performance, or a first night.
> The Queen had her dressmakers. Between eleven and twelve she went through her letters with her lady-in-waiting and made up her engagement book. There was always a little queue of people waiting to see the Queen.

From twelve to one she would meet the ambassadors' wives. Occasionally I would see the Queen in the middle of the morning in full evening dress, wearing her tiara. She would be sitting for one of the various painters who were doing her portrait.

In the afternoon the Queen always had a function of some sort. She never took the customary afternoon rest or nap. Often after the function was over she would come out and join us [Crawford and Princesses Elizabeth and Margaret] in the gardens, glad of a breath of fresh air. She would be enthusiastically welcomed by the dogs.

But no matter how busy the day was to be, the morning sessions with the children began it. The children came first. Only the happy high jinks of the evening bath hour had to be curtailed and often abandoned. There was no longer time.

Crawford felt that Elizabeth and Bertie 'must have thought often, regretfully, of their quiet evenings, one either side of the fire. They who had wanted only a simple life with their children were now besieged by photographers, pursued by Press agents, and harried by officials'. As Elizabeth once noted sadly of her family and herself and the daily grind of duties, 'we aren't supposed to be human'.

In spite of the unexpectedness of their position, Elizabeth and Bertie proved successful, and Elizabeth, who was crowned with her husband, came into her own during the Second World War, which broke out in September 1939. Adolf Hitler is reputed to have called her the most dangerous woman in Europe, and from the first, Elizabeth set out to help improve morale in Britain, declaring when it was suggested that her children be evacuated to Canada for their own safety that 'the children could not go without me, I could not possibly leave the king, and the king would never go'. Within days of war being declared, Elizabeth began visiting institutions such as the London Civil Defence Region Headquarters, and her own regiments. As the Battle of Britain got underway, she visited bombed cities, as well as making frequent visits to devastated areas of London. She took the attacks on London in her stride, declaring, after Buckingham Palace was bombed, that she could 'now look the East End in the face'. According to Crawford, Elizabeth and Bertie also showed considerable bravery following one attack on the palace and '"almost before the wreckage had cooled off," someone told me, "here they were, the two of them. Calmly making their way about it, like people crossing a river on stepping-stones!"' Elizabeth will always be remembered for her efforts during the war, and she became immensely popular. She appeared with her family on the palace balcony on VE Day in May 1945 to celebrate the victory in Europe.

Elizabeth and Bertie always enjoyed an exceptionally happy marriage, and she was distraught when his health began to fail shortly after the war. He was unwell throughout 1948, and the couple were forced to cancel a planned tour of Australia and New Zealand. Bertie's condition deteriorated even further, and in 1951, he was diagnosed with lung cancer. He underwent a dangerous operation on 23 September 1951 and appeared to be making a good recovery, even being well enough to attend a musical with his family at the end of January 1952 and to see Princess Elizabeth off at the airport when she set out on an Antipodean tour the next day. On 5 February, he was well enough to shoot rabbits at the estate at Sandringham, and he appeared well and happy when he went to bed. The following morning, Elizabeth received a message that Bertie's servant was unable to wake him. She rushed down to his room to find that he had died during the night.

Elizabeth, who had always been devoted to Bertie, was devastated by his death. She also immediately lost her public role as queen, increasing her sense of loss. Elizabeth announced that she would be known as 'Queen Elizabeth, the Queen Mother', and whilst she was reluctant to leave Buckingham Palace, she eventually moved to Clarence House in London, which remained her main residence until her death. She also purchased a derelict Scottish castle, the Castle of Mey, on a whim in the summer of 1952, and it soon became a favourite residence.

During her long widowhood, Elizabeth carried out many official engagements, right to the end of her life, and always remained popular. She was the patron of a number of organisations and took her role as chancellors of the Universities of London and Dundee seriously. In private, she had a great interest in steeplechasing and purchased her first horse in 1949. She always tried to attend events at which her own horses were racing, and it was her greatest passion. She also remained close to her family and was dismayed in 1953 when her daughter, Princess Margaret, announced that she wished to marry a divorced member of her household, Peter Townsend. Elizabeth cautioned her daughter not to act too hastily, and she was relieved when, in 1955, Margaret finally broke off the relationship when faced with the loss of her royal status. Elizabeth had enjoyed a long and happy marriage, and she was dismayed later in life by Princess Margaret's own divorce and the divorces of her grandchildren.

The Queen Mother was famous for being as old as the century, but as the years progressed, her life was tinged with sadness as her entire generation died out. Her favourite brother, David, died in 1961, and her last surviving sibling, Rose, Lady Granville, died in 1967. In February 2002, she received the greatest blow when her daughter Margaret died. Elizabeth insisted on attending the funeral, and she remained active almost until the end. She was unable to join the royal family for Easter 2002 in accordance with her usual custom, and on 30 March 2002, at the age of 101, she quietly passed away.

Elizabeth Bowes-Lyon, the first non-royal woman to become queen since Catherine Parr, lived a long and varied life. She was happiest in the early years of her marriage, living quietly with her husband and daughters. Family was very important to her, and she was devoted to her eldest daughter, the current queen, Elizabeth II.

ELIZABETH II (born 1926) is the current reigning queen of England. She was born on 21 April 1926 at the Mayfair home of her grandparents, the Earl and Countess of Strathmore. As the eldest child of the Duke and Duchess of York, it seemed unlikely that she would ever come to the throne. This changed in 1936 with the abdication of her uncle, Edward VIII, and the accession of her father as George VI.

Until her father's accession, Elizabeth enjoyed a contented family life and saw more of her parents than many children of her class. She was nicknamed Lilibet in her infancy, and according to her governess, Marion Crawford, 'she had given herself this name when she found 'Elizabeth' rather difficult to get round, and it had stuck ever since'. She was a precocious child, and Crawford, who arrived to teach Elizabeth just before her sixth birthday, noted that 'from the beginning I had a feeling about Lilibet that she was "special". I had met many children of all sorts in my time, but never one with so much character at so young an age.' Crawford recorded her first meeting with the young Elizabeth:

> The night nursery was decorated in pink and fawn, the Duchess's favourite colour scheme. A small figure with a mop of curls sat up in bed. She wore a nightie with a design of small pink roses on it. She had tied the cords of her dressing gown to the knobs of the old-fashioned bed, and was busy driving her team.
>
> This was my first glimpse of Princess Elizabeth.
>
> 'This is Miss Crawford,' said Alah [Knight, Elizabeth's nanny], in her stern way.
>
> The little girl said, 'How do you do.' She then gave me a long, comprehensive look I had seen once before, and went on, 'Why have you no hair?'

I pulled off my hat to show her. 'I have enough to go on with,' I said. 'It's an Eton crop.'

She picked up her reins again.

'Do you usually drive in bed?' I asked.

'I mostly go once or twice round the park before I go to sleep, you know,' she said. 'It exercises my horses.' She navigated a dangerous and difficult corner, and went on, 'Are you going to stay with us?'

'For a little while, anyway,' I replied.

'Will you play with us tomorrow? Will you come to the Little House with us?' she said eagerly. Alah had by now unhitched the team, and laid her flat. She allowed herself to be tucked away like a small doll. 'Good night. See you tomorrow,' she said to me.

Crawford, or 'Crawfie' as she was nicknamed by the two princesses, found two pleasant little girls who enjoyed games and had a close relationship with their parents. Elizabeth was also always devoted to duty, and she took her responsibilities as a future queen seriously, making her first radio broadcast, to the British evacuated children, in October 1940. In 1945, she further assisted the British war effort by joining the Women's Auxillary Territorial Service, and she was photographed servicing an army lorry. She joined in the celebrations at the end of the Second World War with her parents. Elizabeth also enjoyed personal happiness in the years following the war, and her marriage to Prince Philip of Greece on 20 November 1947 was turned into a great state occasion in an attempt by the government to blow away the dark clouds still hanging over the country.

Elizabeth and Philip first met when Elizabeth was thirteen and went with her parents to visit the Royal Naval College at Dartmouth, at which Philip was a cadet. Philip was five years older than Elizabeth and handsome, and he made an impression on her at their first meeting. Crawford, who was present, described that first meeting in her memoirs:

> The Dalrymple-Hamilton family lived in the Captain's House at Dartmouth College. The house had a very pleasant lived-in feeling, and the children – a boy and a girl rather older than the Princesses – came out to meet us. There was a clockwork railway laid out all over the nursery floor, and we all knelt down to play with it.
>
> We played for ages, and after a time, a fair-haired boy, rather like a Viking, with a sharp face and piercing blue eyes, came in. He was good-looking, though rather off-hand in his manner. He said, 'How do you do' to Lilibet, and for a while they knelt side by side playing with the trains. He soon got bored with that. We had ginger crackers and lemonade, in which he joined, and then he said, 'Let's go to the tennis courts and have some real fun jumping the nets.'
>
> Off they went. At the tennis courts I thought he showed off a good deal, but the little girls were much impressed.
>
> Lilibet said, 'How good he is, Crawfie. How high he can jump.' She never took her eyes off him the whole time. He was quite polite to her, but did not pay her any special attention. He spent a lot of time teasing plump little Margaret.
>
> When we went back to the yacht for lunch, the fair-haired boy was there. He was near Lilibet, and we all sat around and talked and laughed a good deal. After that we went to see the swimming-pool and then it was time to go back to the yacht again. It had started to rain by this time, and we were a bedraggled little party.

The boy who captured Elizabeth's attention was Philip, and he joined the royal party for lunch the following day, with Elizabeth solicitously asking him 'what would you like to eat?

What would you like?' When it was time for the royal party to leave in their yacht, Elizabeth took a long look at Philip through binoculars.

Elizabeth and Philip corresponded throughout the war, and in many ways, Philip, whose family had been exiled from Greece when he was eight, proved to be an ideal choice for her husband. He was educated in Britain, and he was also a descendant of Queen Victoria, through her daughter, Alice, and a relative of most of the royal families of Europe. Elizabeth gave birth to the couple's first child, Charles, in November 1948, and he was followed by three younger children: Anne, Andrew, and Edward. In the early years of their marriage, Philip was posted to Malta, and Elizabeth joined him there, attempting to live as an ordinary officer's wife.

By 1951, Elizabeth's father, George VI, was dying of lung cancer, and Elizabeth began to take on more of the burden of royal duties. On 31 January 1952, the King was well enough to see his daughter and son-in-law off at the airport as they set out on a royal tour in his place. Elizabeth and Philip were in Kenya on 6 February when George VI died, leading to Elizabeth being proclaimed queen as Elizabeth II in her absence. The couple returned quickly to England, and the Queen was crowned the following year.

Elizabeth's accession was hailed romantically as a 'New Elizabethan Age', and there were hopes, which have largely been met, that she would preside over a nation that would leave behind postwar austerity and shortages and become prosperous. The Queen has always devoted herself to her duties as a constitutional monarch. Her role, as head of state, gives her the right to be consulted, to advise and to warn. Throughout her reign, she has met regularly with prime ministers, and whilst her role as queen regnant has few of the political powers of her predecessors, she has performed the constitutional role admirably. Elizabeth II has experienced great difficulties, most notably in 1992, when the marital difficulties of her three eldest children became public news and when Windsor Castle was badly damaged by fire. The Queen was shocked by the public outcry when it was suggested that the public purse should meet the cost of rebuilding the damaged castle. Elizabeth referred to 1992 as her *'annus horribilis'*. Worse was to come in 1997, with the death on 31 August of the Queen's former daughter-in-law, Diana, Princess of Wales. The Queen was publicly criticised for her apparent indifference to the death, for example, in refusing to display the Royal Standard at half-mast over Buckingham Palace. The Royal Standard is only flown when the monarch is in residence at the palace, and the criticism was unfair. Finally, aware of the public anger, she compromised in allowing the Union Jack to be hung at half-mast over the palace in place of the Royal Standard. She also made a short speech to the nation. She and Prince Philip publicly viewed the tributes laid outside the palace in memory of the princess, and the public mood began to soften. Diana's death brought the royal family to the brink of disaster, and Elizabeth II could very well have been the last English queen, but she saved the situation.

Elizabeth II has now ruled Great Britain for nearly sixty years, and she is fast approaching the record for longest-reigning sovereign set by Queen Victoria. Her life has been one of duty, and since she was ten years old, she has been in the public eye. As she fast approaches her diamond jubilee, she remains one of the most popular members of the royal family, and like her predecessor Queen Victoria, she has become something of an institution and, to many, a living symbol of Great Britain. Elizabeth II is the latest in a long line of English queens that stretches back to the Anglo-Saxon period and earlier. Some are remembered fondly, others with horror, and some are barely remembered at all. They all, in their own way, have contributed to the development of the monarchy and the nation, and their voices and actions echo throughout English history.

Genealogical Tables

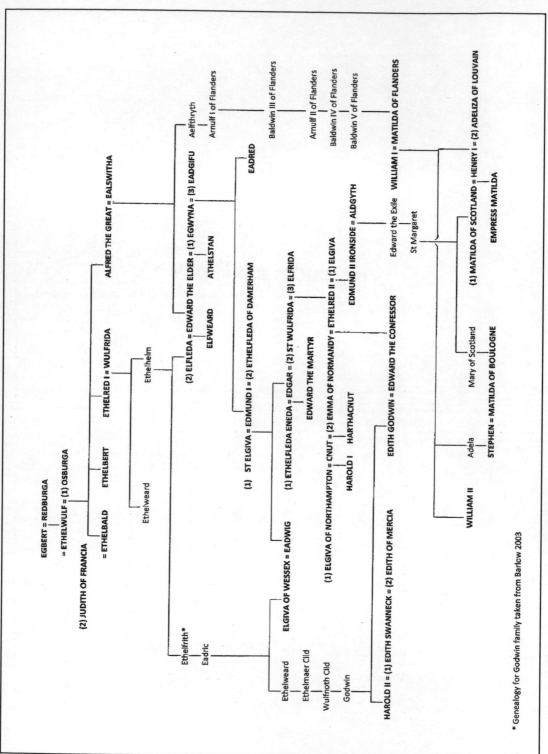

237. The Anglo-Saxon and Norman queens.

* Genealogy for Godwin family taken from Barlow 2003

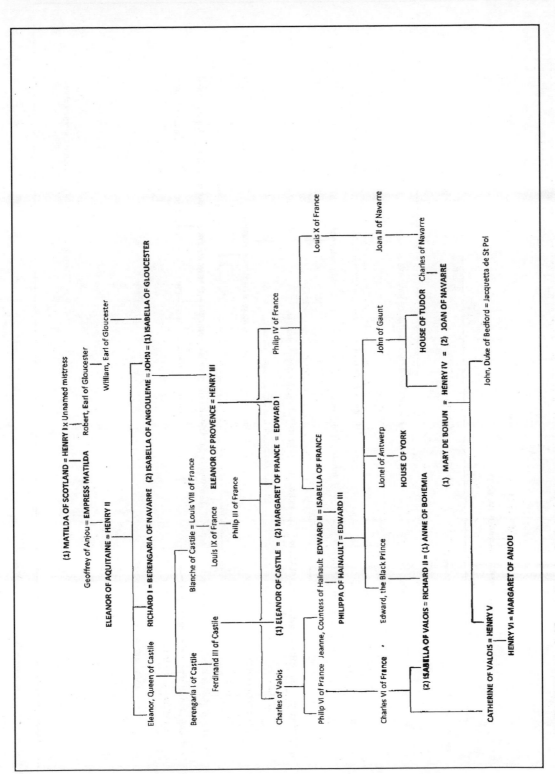

238. The Plantagenet and Lancastrian queens.

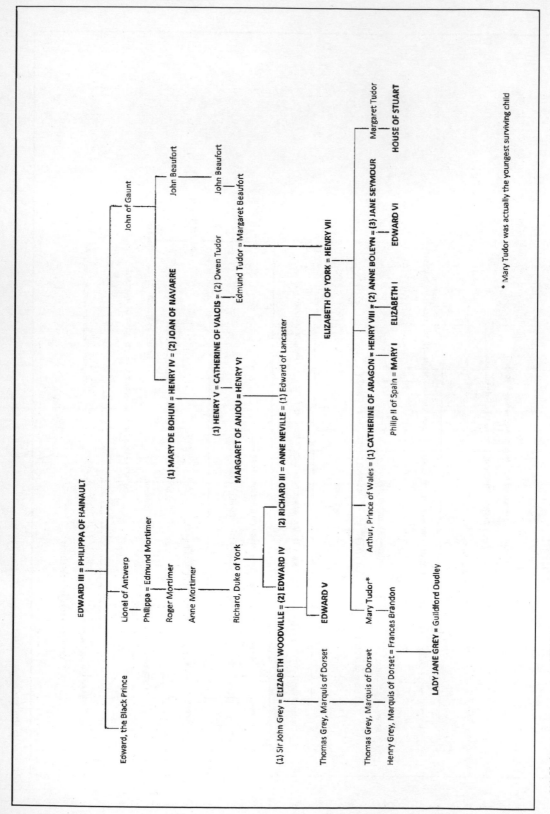

239. Yorkist queen consorts and Tudor queen regnants.

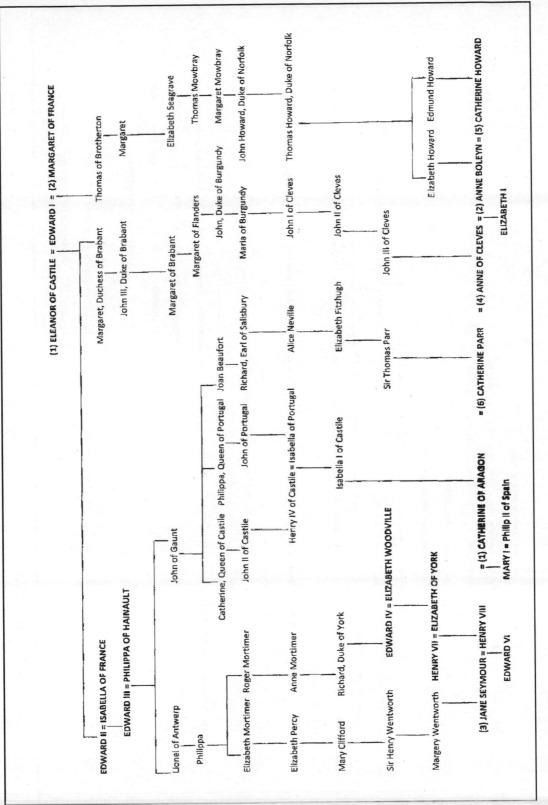

240. The six wives of Henry VIII.

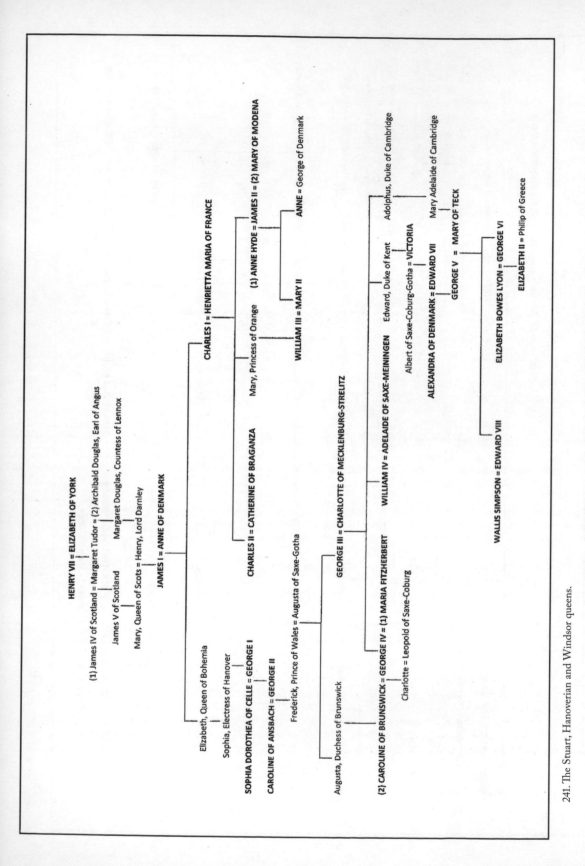

241. The Stuart, Hanoverian and Windsor queens.

Notes & Bibliography

Due to the large scope of this work, it would be impossible to list all primary and secondary sources consulted. The main works used for each queen are listed below. Place of publication is London unless otherwise stated.

1 The Early & Mythical Queens

Sources used include
Bede, *Ecclesiastical History of the English People*, Sherley-Price, L., Latham, R. E., and Farmer, D. H. (eds) (1990).
Dio, C., *Roman History, vol. VIII*, Cary, E. (ed.) (1925).
Fairweather, J. (ed.), *Liber Eliensis: A History of the Isle of Ely* (Woodbridge, 2005).
Giles, J. A. (ed.), *Six Old English Chronicles* (1848) (which includes Geoffrey of Monmouth's *British History*, Nennius and the *Chronicle of Ethelweard*).
Gregory of Tours, *The History of the Franks*, Thorpe, L. (ed.) (1974).
Malory, T., *Morte d'Arthur*, Strachey, E. (ed.) (1868).
Roger of Wendover, *Flowers of History*, Giles, J. A. (ed.) (1849).
Tacitus, *Complete Works*, Hadas, M. (ed.) (New York, 1942).
William of Malmesbury, *The Kings Before the Conquest*, Stephenson, J. (ed.) (1854).

There are short biographies of many early queens in Hall, Mrs M., *The Queens Before the Conquest* (1854). Information on Rowen is from Geoffrey of Monmouth and Nennius. Sexburga is described in the *Chronicle of Ethelweard*. There are a number of works on Boudica, including Hingley, R., and Unwin, C., *Boudica: Iron Age Warrior Queen* (2005) and Bedoyere, G. de la, *Defying Rome* (Stroud, 2003). There is one biography of Cartimandua: Howarth, N., *Cartimandua: Queen of the Brigantes* (Stroud, 2008). Bedoyere 2003 details Caratacus and Venutius. Klein, S. S., *Ruling Women: Queenship and Gender in Anglo-Saxon Literature* (Notre Dame, 2006) discusses Bertha. Pope Gregory's letter is from Hall 1854. Kirby, D. P., *The Earliest English Kings* (2000) discusses Cynethryth.

2 The Anglo-Saxon Queens

The leading sources are
Asser, *Life of King Alfred*, Keynes, S., and Lapidge, M. (eds) (2004).

Douglas, D. C., and Greenaway, G. W. (eds), *English Historical Documents vol. II: 1042–1189* (1981).

Florence of Worcester, *Chronicle*, Stevenson, J. (ed.) (1853).

Sawyer, P. H. (ed.), *Anglo-Saxon Charters* (1968) (charter numbers are abbreviated to S1454, for example).

Sturluson, Snorri, *Heimskringla: History of the Kings of Norway*, Hollander, L. M. (ed.) (Austen, 2002).

Swanton, M. (ed.), *The Anglo Saxon Chronicles* (2001) (*ASC*).

Whitelock, D. (ed.), *English Historical Documents vol. I: 500–1042* (1979).

William of Malmesbury, *The Deeds of the Bishops of England*, Preest, D. (ed.) (Woodbridge, 2002).

Norton, E., *She Wolves: The Notorious Queens of England* (Stroud, 2008) contains short biographies of some Anglo-Saxon and later queens. Where appropriate, spellings of Anglo-Saxon names have been modernised and simplified.

Redburga

Egbert's campaigns are in the *ASC*. Asser describes Queen Edburga. Woodruff, D., *The Life and Times of Alfred the Great* (1974) details Egbert's kingship. The *Annals of St Bertin* are in Whitelock. William of Malmesbury (Preest) comments on Ethelwulf's upbringing.

Osburga

Asser and Florence of Worcester are the main source for Osburga. Woodruff 1974 also describes her.

Judith of Francia

Nelson, J. L., *Charles the Bald* (1992) and Kirby 2000 detail Judith's life. The *Annals of St Bertin* are in Whitelock. Judith's coronation is discussed in Nelson, J. L., *Politics and Ritual in Early Medieval Europe* (1986) and Stafford, P., 'Charles the Bald, Judith and England' in Gibson, M. T. and Nelson, J. L. (ed.), *Charles the Bald: Court and Kingdom* (Aldershot, 1990). William of Malmesbury (Stephenson) discusses Ethelbald's rebellion. A surviving charter of Ethelbald is S151.

Wulfrida

Stenton, F., *Anglo-Saxon England* (Oxford, 1971) discusses the Viking raids. Asser describes Ethelred's kingship and death. Yorke, B., 'Edward as Æthling', in Higham, N. J. and Hill, D. H. (eds), *Edward the Elder* (2001) suggests that Wulfrida may have been crowned. Charter 56 in Pierquin, H. (ed.), *Recueil General Des Chartes Anglo-Saxonnes 604–1061* (Paris, 1912) is witnessed by Wulfrida. Ethelwold's rebellion is in *ASC* Winchester 901.

Ealswitha

The main source for Ealswitha is Asser. The charters attested by Mucil are S340 and S1201. *ASC* Winchester 903 calls Ealswitha's brother an ealdorman. Charter S1442 names him as a member of the Mercian royal family.

Egwyna

The main sources for Egwyna are William of Malmesbury (Stephenson) and Florence of Worcester. Sharp, S., 'The West Saxon Tradition of Dynastic Marriage: with special reference to Edward the Elder' in Higham and Hill 2001 discusses Egwyna.

Elfleda

Stafford, P., 'The King's Wife in Wessex, 800–1066', in Damico, H., and Olsen, A.H. (eds), *New Readings on Women in Old English Literature* (Bloomington, 1990) discusses Elfleda. Nelson 1986 suggests that Elfleda may have been crowned. Coatsworth, E., 'The Embroideries from the Tomb of St Cuthbert' in Higham and Hill 2001 notes Elfleda's commission of the embroidery.

Edgiva

The main source for Edgiva is William of Malmesbury (Stephenson). Hart, C., 'Two Queens of England' (*Ampleforth Journal* 82, 1977) and Stafford, P., *Queens, Concubines and Dowagers* (1983) give information on Edgiva. Charters from Edmund and Eadred's reign are S489, S562 and S1511. Eadred's Will is S1515. The *Life of Dunstan* is in Whitelock. St Ethelwold is described in Ælfric's *Life of St Æthelwold* (Whitelock) and Wulfstan of Winchester, *The Life of St Æthelwold* (Oxford, 1991). Dunstan's exile is in *ASC* 957. The New Minster Charter is in Miller, S. (ed.), *Charters of the New Minster, Winchester* (Oxford, 2001). The *Liber Eliensis* records Edgiva's bequests to Ely Abbey.

St Elgiva

S755 contains a grant made by Edgar to his maternal grandmother, Wynfleda. Florence of Worcester and

William of Malmesbury (Stephenson and Preest) are the main sources for Elgiva. Campbell, A. (ed.), *The Chronicle of Æthelweard* (1962) notes her death.

Ethelfleda of Damerham

ASC Worcester 946 records Ethelfleda's marriage and Edmund's death. Ethelfleda's Will is S1494.

Elgiva of Wessex

Elgiva's Will is S1484. William of Malmesury (Stephenson) and the *Chronicle of Æthelweard* are the main sources for Elgiva. Elgiva's relationship with Bishop Ethelwold is in Yorke, B., 'Æthelwold and the Politics of the Tenth Century', in Yorke, B. (ed.), *Bishop Æthelwold: His Career and Influence* (Woodbridge, 1997). Florence of Worcester, William of Malmesbury (Preest) and *ASC* Worcester 958 describe the attacks on Eadwig, and Elgiva's divorce. The grants to Elgiva are S737 and S738.

Ethelfleda Eneda

Ethelfleda's background is described in William of Malmesbury (Stephenson).

St Wulfrida

Yorke, B., 'The Legitimacy of St Edith' (*The Haskins Society Journal* 11, 1998) describes Wulfrida. Stubbs, W. (ed.), *Memorials of St Dunstan* (Rolls Series, 1874) contains the *Life of St Dunstan*, which describes Edgar's affair with a nun. Elfrida's conflict with Wulfhilde is in '*La Vie de Sainte Vulfhilde Par Goscelin De Cantorbéry*' (*Analecta Bollandiana* 32).

Elfrida

William of Malmesbury (Stephenson) describes Elfrida. Her first marriage is in Gaimar's *Lestoire des Engles Solum*, Hardy, T. D., and Martin, C. T. (eds) (1888), Hart, C., 'Athelstan 'Half-King' and his Family' (*Anglo-Saxon England* 2, 1973) and Macray, W. D. (ed.), *Chronicon Abbatiae Rameseiensis* (1886). Elfrida's dower is S725. Edgar's changes to the monasteries are in Symons, D. T. (ed.), *Regularis Concordia: The Monastic Agreement of Monks and Nuns of the English Nation* (1953). The *Life of St Oswald* is in Whitelock. The earliest account of Edward's murder is in *ASC* 979 (version E). Osbern's *Life of St Dunstan* is in Stubbs 1874. The renewal of the freedom of Taunton is in Robertson, A. J. (ed.), *Anglo-Saxon Charters* (Cambridge, 1939). Elfrida's letter is from Harmer, F. E. (ed.), *Anglo-Saxon Writs* (Manchester, 1952).

Elgiva

Ethelred's reign is described in Lavelle, R., *Aethelred II* (Stroud, 2002) and Williams, A., *Æthelred the Unready: The Ill-Counselled King* (2003). Stafford 1983 comments on Elgiva.

Emma of Normandy

Works on Emma include Stafford, P., *Queen Emma and Queen Edith* (Oxford, 1997), O'Brien, H., *Queen Emma and the Vikings* (2005) and Strachan, I., *Emma the Twice-Crowned Queen* (2004). The leading source is Campbell, A. (ed.), *Encomium Emmae Reginae* (Cambridge, 1998) (the *Encomium*). Emma's background is in Wace, *The History of the Norman People* (Woodbridge, 2004). The letter from Pope John XV is in Whitelock. The quotation suggesting Edward was named as heir is from Barlow, F. (ed.), *The Life of King Edward who Rests at Westminster* (1962) (*King Edward*). *ASC* Peterborough 1013 records Ethelred's exile. *ASC* Peterborough 1017 notes Cnut's marriage to Emma. Archbishop Wulfstan's letter is in Whitelock. The reburial of St Alfheah is in *ASC* 1023 Winchester. Emma's plot to make Harthacnut king of Denmark is in the *Heimskringla*. *ASC* Worcester 1035 records Cnut's death. Emma's letter to her sons is from the *Encomium*. The seizure of Emma's goods by Edward is in *ASC* Peterborough 1042 and William of Malmesbury (Preest).

Aldgyth

William of Malmesbury (Stephenson) is the main source for Aldgyth.

Elgiva of Northampton

Campbell, M. W., 'Queen Emma and Ælfgifu of Northampton: Canute the Great's Women' (*Medieval Scandinavia* 4, 1971) details Elgiva. The main source for Elgiva is the *Heimskringla*. Florence of Worcester describes Elgiva's family background and the rumours about the births of her sons.

Edith Godwin

The main work on Edith is Stafford 1997. Barlow, F., *The Godwins* (2002) and Mason, E., *The House of Godwine* (2004) feature Edith. The main source for Edith is *King Edward*. William of Malmesbury

(Stephenson) describes Edith's education and marriage. Florence of Worcester and William of Malmesbury (Stephenson) recount the attempt to divorce Edith. William of Poitiers (Douglas and Greenaway) states that Edward made William his heir. John of Worcester, *Chronicle*, McGurk, P. (ed.) (Oxford, 1998) notes Edith's death and burial.

Edith Swanneck
Walker, I. W., *Harold: The Last Anglo-Saxon King* (Stroud, 1997) and Barlow detail Edith.

Edith of Mercia
The main work on Edith is Beech, G., 'England and Aquitaine in the Century Before the Norman Conquest' (*Anglo-Saxon England* 19, 1990), which suggests that she died in France. Walker also details Edith's life. Orderic Vitalis, *The Ecclesiastical History, vol. II*, Chibnall, M. (ed.) (Oxford, 1968) describes Edith's family. Edith's father's exiles are in *ASC* Peterborough 1055 and *ASC* Worcester 1058. Gruffydd's death is in *ASC* Peterborough 1063. Florence of Worcester claims that Edith's brothers left Hastings to move her from London. The death of Edwin and the capture of Morcar are in *ASC* Worcester 1072. William of Malmesbury (Stephenson) notes young Harold's role in the King of Norway's campaigns.

3 The Norman Queens

The leading primary sources for the Norman queens are
Orderic Vitalis, *The Ecclesiastical History, vols III-VI*, Chibnall, M. (ed.) (Oxford, 1973-83).
Potter, K. R. (ed.), *Gesta Stephani* (Oxford, 1976).
Van Houts, E. (ed.), *The Normans in Europe* (Manchester, 2000).
William of Malmesbury, *Gesta Regnum Angorum, vol. I*, Mynors, R. A. B. (ed.) (Oxford, 1998).
William of Malmesbury, *Historia Novella*, King, E., and Potter, K. R. (eds) (Oxford, 1998).
Wood, M. A. E. (ed.), *Letters of Royal and Illustrious Ladies, 3 vols* (1846).

There are short biographies of most of the post-Conquest queens in Strickland, A., *Lives of the Queens of England, 12 vols* (1844).

Matilda of Flanders
Fettu, A., *Queen Matilda* (Orep, 2005) details Matilda. William of Poitiers is from Douglas and Greenaway. Orderic Vitalis vol. II details Matilda's background, family and piety. William of Malmesbury (Mynors) comments on Matilda's wisdom. Strickland notes Matilda's love for the English ambassador. Matilda's gift of a flagship to William is in 'The Ship List of William the Conqueror' (Van Houts 2000). The foundation charter for Lewes priory is in Douglas and Greenaway. Matilda's coronation is discussed in Gathagan, L. L., 'The Trappings of Power: the Coronation of Matilda of Flanders' (*The Haskins Society Journal* 13, 1999). The quotation on Matilda's love for Robert is from Orderic Vitalis vol. III.

Matilda of Scotland
The only biography of Matilda is Huneycutt, L. L., *Matilda of Scotland: A Study in Medieval Queenship* (Woodbridge, 2003), which also contains a translation of the *Life of St Margaret*. Menzies, L., *St Margaret, Queen of Scotland* (London, 1925) details Matilda's early life. Orderic Vitalis vol. IV records Matilda's time at Romsey. Eadmer, *History of Recent Events in England*, Bosanquet, G. (ed.) (1964) recounts the controversy over whether Matilda was a nun. William of Malmesbury (Mynors) records that Matilda wore the veil to reject suitors. John of Worcester describes Matilda's coronation. Matilda's letters are from Wood.

Adeliza of Louvain
Thompson, K., 'Queen Adeliza and the Lotharingian Connection' (*Sussex Archaeological Collections* 140, 2002) and Wertheimer, L., 'Adeliza of Louvain and Anglo-Norman Queenship' (*Haskins Society Journal* 7, 1997) contain details of Adeliza. John of Worcester notes Adeliza's parentage. Adeliza's marriage and coronation is in *ASC* Peterborough 1121. William of Malmesbury (King and Potter) notes the visit of the Empress Matilda to Arundel.

Matilda of Boulogne
Tanner, H. J., 'Queenship: Office, Custom, or Ad Hoc? The Case of Queen Matilda III of England (135-1152)', in Wheeler, B., and Parsons, J. C. (eds), *Eleanor of Aquitaine: Lord and Lady* (Basingstoke, 2002) details Matilda. Her activities are described in Green, J. A., *The Aristocracy of Norman England* (Cambridge,

1997), Crouch, D., *The Reign of King Stephen* (Harlow, 2000) and Matthew, D., *King Stephen* (2002). Matilda is prominent in the *Gesta Stephani*. William of Malmesbury (King and Potter) records that Henry I arranged Matilda's marriage and that of her parents. Given-Wilson, C., *The Royal Bastards of Medieval England* (1984) describes Stephen's illegitimate son. Henry of Huntingdon, *Chronicle*, Forester, T. (ed.) (1853) describes Stephen's seizure of the crown. Orderic Vitalis vol. VI records Matilda's siege of Dover. Henry of Huntingdon (Douglas and Greenaway) describes the Battle of Lincoln and its aftermath. The *Gesta Stephani* discusses Matilda of Boulogne's triumphant entry to London after the Empress's expulsion and the siege of Winchester. Robert of Gloucester's capture is from William of Malmesbury (King and Potter).

Empress Matilda
The most detailed biography of Matilda is Chibnall, M., *The Empress Matilda* (Oxford, 1991). Two other biographies are Pain, N., *Empress Matilda: Uncrowned Queen of England* (1978) and Bradbury, J., *Stephen and Matilda* (Stroud, 2005). There is a chapter on Matilda in Fraser, A., *The Warrior Queens* (1988). ASC Peterborough 1109 records the arrangements for Matilda's first marriage. Robert of Torigni is quoted from Van Houts. Details of the Emperor Henry V are from Mommsen, T. E., and Morrison, K. F. (eds), *Imperial Lives and Letters of the Eleventh Century* (New York, 2000). This work includes a translation of the *Life of the Emperor Henry IV*, which describes Henry V's seizure of the Imperial crown and a letter of Henry IV's, which is quoted from. ASC Peterborough 1127 records that Matilda's second marriage was unpopular in England. John of Worcester describes Matilda's landing in England in 1139 and her activities at Bristol. The *Gesta Stephani* and William of Malmesbury (King and Potter) describe the Council at Winchester. Chibnall, M., 'The Charters of the Empress Matilda', in Garnett, G., and Hudson, J. (eds), *Law and Government in Medieval England and Normandy* (Cambridge, 1994) discusses whether Matilda was called Queen. Matilda's letter is from Wood.

4 The Plantagenet Queens

The main sources used are
Capgrave, J., *Chronicle of England*, Hingeston, F. (ed.) (1858).
Crawford, A. (ed.), *Letters of the Queens of England* (Stroud, 2002).
Froissart, J., *Chronicle, 6 vols*, Berners, Lord (trans.) (1901).
John of Salisbury, *The History Pontificalis of John of Salisbury*, Chibnall, M. (ed.) (Oxford, 1986).
Myers, A. R. (ed.), *English Historical Documents, vol. IV: 1327-1485* (1969).
Nicholson, H. (ed.), *Chronicle of the Third Crusade: A Translation of the 'Itinerarium Peregrinorum et Gesta Regis Ricardi* (Aldershot, 1997).
Paris, M., *Monachi Sancti Albani, Chronica Majora, vol. II*, Luard, H. R. (ed.) (1874).
Paris, M., 'The Chronica Majora 1247-1250', in Vaughan, R. (ed.), *Chronicles of Matthew Paris* (Gloucester, 1984).
Richard of Devizes, *The Chronicle of the Time of King Richard the First*, Appleby, J. T. (ed.) (1963).
Roger de Hoveden, *The Annals*, in Riley, H. T. (ed.) (Felinfach, 1997).
Rothwell, H. (ed.), *English Historical Documents, vol. III: 1189-1327* (1975).
William of Newburgh, *The History of English Affairs*, Walsh, P. G. and Kennedy, M. J. (eds), Book I (Warminster, 1988).

Eleanor of Aquitaine
There are a number of works on Eleanor of Aquitaine, including Meade, M., *Eleanor of Aquitaine* (1977), Boyd, D., *Eleanor: April Queen of Aquitaine* (Stroud, 2004), Huneycutt, L. L., 'Alianora Regina Anglorum: Eleanor of Aquitaine and her Anglo-Norman Predecessors as Queen of England', in Wheeler, B., and Parsons, J. C. (eds), *Eleanor of Aquitaine: Lord and Lady* (Basingstoke, 2002), Kelly, A., *Eleanor of Aquitaine and the Four Kings* (Cambridge, 1950), Martindale, J., 'Eleanor of Aquitaine: The Last Years', in Church, S. D. (ed.), *King John: New Interpretations* (Woodbridge, 2003) and Weir, A., *Eleanor of Aquitaine* (1999). Eleanor's comments that she had married a monk are from William of Newburgh. The crusade is described in Odo of Deuil, *De Profectione Ludovici VII in Orientem*, Berry, V. G. (ed.) (New York, 1948) and John of Salisbury. Gerald of Wales (Douglas and Greenaway) describes Henry II and his visit to Paris. Roger de Hoveden describes the death of the Young King. Matthew Paris (Luard) describes Eleanor's release from prison and the early days of Richard's reign. Richard of Devizes records John's conduct during Richard's absence. Richard's imprisonment and release is in Matthew Paris (Luard). Eleanor's letters are from Crawford.

Berengaria of Navarre

There are two biographies of Berengaria: Mitchell, M., *Berengaria: Enigmatic Queen of England* (Burwash Weald, 1986) and Trinidade, A., *Berengaria: In Search of Richard the Lionheart's Queen* (Bodmin, 1999). Berengaria's marriage is described in the *Gesta Regis Ricardi*. Richard of Devizes records Alais's affair with Henry II. The same two sources note the conquest of Cyprus and the crusade. The Bishop of Lincoln's rebuke to Richard is from Douie, D. L., and Farmer, H. (eds), *The Life of St Hugh of Lincoln, vol. II* (1962). Pope Innocent's letters are from Cheney, C. R., and Cheney, M. G. (eds), *The Letters of Pope Innocent III (1198-1216) Concerning England and Wales* (Oxford, 1967). Berengaria's letters are from Wood.

Isabella of Gloucester

Patterson, R. B. (ed.), *Earldom of Gloucester Charters* (Oxford, 1973) describes Isabella's life. Charters referred to are from this source. Richardson, H. G., 'The Marriage and Coronation of Isabelle of Angoulême' (*English Historical Review* 61, 1946) describes Isabella of Gloucester's background and her marriage to John. Roger de Hoveden details the marriage of Isabella and John. Richardson, H. G., 'King John and Isabelle of Angoulême' (*English Historical Review* 65, 1950) claims that no dispensation was sought. Warren, W. L., *King John* (1997) details John's activities during Richard's reign and his attempts to marry Alais of France.

Isabella of Angoulême

Works on Isabella include Cazel, F. A., and Painter, S., 'The Marriage of Isabelle of Angoulême' (*English Historical Review* 63, 1948), Cazel, F. A., and Painter, S., 'The Marriage of Isabelle of Angoulême' (*English Historical Review* 67, 1952), Richardson 1946, Richardson 1950, and Vincent, N., 'Isabella of Angoulême: John's Jezebel' in Church, S. D. (ed.), *King John: New Interpretations* (Woodbridge, 2003). She is described in Snellgrove, H. S., *The Lusignans in England 1247-1258* (Albuquerque, 1950). Matthew Paris (Luard) describes Isabella's marriage and the Dauphin's invasion. Isabella's letters are in Crawford and Wood.

Eleanor of Provence

The leading biography of Eleanor is Howell, M., *Eleanor of Provence* (Oxford, 1998). Other works include Goldstone, N., *Four Queens: The Provençal Sisters who Ruled Europe* (New York, 2007), Howell, M., 'Notes and Documents: The Resources of Eleanor of Provence as Queen Consort' (*English Historical Review* 102, 1987) and Biles, M., 'The Indominable Belle: Eleanor of Provence, Queen of England' in Bowers, R. H. (ed.), *Seven Studies in Medieval English History and Other Historical Essays* (Jackson, 1983). Strickland claims that Eleanor composed a poem about a Cornish hero. Eleanor's letters are from Wood 1846 and Crawford 2002. Ridgeway, H. W., 'Foreign Favourites and Henry III's Problems of Patronage, 1247-1258' (*English Historical Review* 104, 1989) details the favouritism of the Savoyards. Henry III's letter to Alexander III is in Shirley, W. W. (ed.), *Royal and Other Historical Letters Illustrative of the Reigh of Henry III, vol. II* (1866). Matthew Paris (Vaughan) describes the Lusignans. Matthew Paris (Rothwell) records Edward's move toward the Lusignan faction and Louis's refusal to receive them. Stubbs, W., 'Annales Londoniensis' in *Chronicles of the Reigns of Edward I and Edward II, 2 vols* (1882) notes Edward's reconciliation with his father. The *Annals of Dunstable* (Rothwell) describe Edward's raid on the Temple and Eleanor's attempt to leave the Tower. The *Annales Londoniensis* describe Edward's escape from prison.

Eleanor of Castile

Works on Eleanor include Parsons, J. C., *Eleanor of Castile* (New York, 1998), Powrie, J., *Eleanor of Castile* (Studley, 1990), and a collection of essays in Parsons, D., (ed.), *Eleanor of Castile 1290-1990* (Stamford, 1991). Prestwich, M., *Edward I* (1997) also details Eleanor. Eleanor's letters are from Wood 1846. Capgrave describes the assassination attempt. Camden, W., *Britannia,* Piggot, S. (ed.) (Newton Abbott, 1971) recounts that Eleanor sucked poison from Edward's wounds. Parsons, J. C., 'The Court and Household of Eleanor of Castile in 1290' (Pontifical Institute of Medieval Studies 37, 1977) contains Eleanor's household accounts.

Margaret of France

There are no works specifically on Margaret but details of her life are in Prestwich. The *Chronicle of Peter Langcroft* is in Rothwell. The Song of the Scottish Wars is in Wright, T., (ed.), *The Political Songs of England* (1839). Edward's letters are from Chaplais, P., 'Notes and Documents of Some Private Letters of Edward I' (*English Historical Review* 77, 1962). Margaret's letters are from Crawford 2002. Margaret's death is in Stubbs, W., 'Annales Paulini' in *Chronicles of the Reigns of Edward I and Edward II, 2 vols* (1882).

Isabella of France

There are two biographies of Isabella: Doherty, P., *Isabella and the Strange Death of Edward II* (2003) and Weir, A., *Isabella: She-Wolf of France, Queen of England* (2005). Articles on Isabella are Bond, E. A., 'Notices of the Last Days of Isabella, Queen of Edward the Second, Drawn from an Account of the Expenses of her Household' (*Archaeologia* 36, 1853) and Menache, S., 'Isabella of France, Queen of England – A Reconsideration' (*Journal of Medieval History* 10, 1984). The leading primary sources are Froissart and Maxwell, H. (ed.), *The Chronicle of Lanercost* (Glasgow, 1913). Details of Isabella's early life and marriage are from *The Chronicle of Lanercost*. The *Annales Paulini* record that Edward sent his wedding presents to Gaveston. Capgrave records Gaveston's conduct at the coronation. Isabella's letter to Edward is from Crawford. *The Chronicle of Lanercost* describes the murder of Gaveston. Conway Davies, J., *The Baronial Opposition to Edward II* (1967) records Isabella's efforts in securing the see of Durham for her candidate. Capgrave describes the Leeds Castle incident. Fryde, N., *The Tyranny and Fall of Edward II* (Cambridge, 1979) records the invasion of Gascony and the *Annales Paulini* relates the seizure of Isabella's lands. *The Chronicle of Lanercost* and Froissart describe Isabella's time in France. Mortimer's life is described in Mortimer, I., *The Greatest Traitor* (2003). Isabella's proclamation is from Crawford. The *Pipewell Chronicle* (Rothwell 1975) describes Edward II's abdication. The *Chronicle of Geoffrey Le Baker* (Myers 1969) details the execution of Kent and Edward III's attack on Mortimer. The quotation from the Bard is from Gray, T., *The Complete Poems*, Starr, H. W. and Hendrickson, J. R. (eds) (Oxford, 1966).

Philippa of Hainault

The only biography of Philippa is Hardy, B. C., *Philippa of Hainault and Her Times* (1910). Packe, M., *King Edward III* (1983) also details her life. The main source is Froissart, who Philippa knew personally. Le Bel, J., *Chronique de Jean Le Bel*, Viard, J., and Deprez, E. (eds) (Paris, 1904) records Isabella of France's visit to Hainault. The *Pipewell Chronicle* (Rothwell 1975) details parliament's agreement to the marriage. Magrath, J. R., *The Queen's College, vol. I* (Oxford, 1921) details Philippa's foundation of Queen's College, Cambridge. Ormrod, W. M., *The Reign of Edward III* (1990) describes Edward's affair with Alice Perrers.

Anne of Bohemia

There are no works specifically on Anne of Bohemia, although Bevan, B., *King Richard II* (1990) and Saul, N., *The Three Richards* (2005) detail her life. The main sources are Froissart and Hector, L. C., and Harvey, B. F. (eds), *The Westminster Chronicle 1381-1394* (Oxford, 1982). Froissart discusses the Great Schism. Hayward's account of Anne's sea crossing is in Hayward, J., *The Life and Raigne of King Henrie IIII*, Manning, J. J. (ed.) (1991). Anne's books are discussed in Bell, S. G., 'Medieval Women Book Owners: Arbiters of Lay Piety and Ambassadors of Culture', in Erler, M. and Kowaleski, M. (eds), *Women and Power in the Middle Ages* (Athens, 1988). The *Westminster Chronicle* records the favouritism of Bohemians and Anne's death.

Isabella of Valois

Palmer, J. J. N., *England, France and Christendom 1377-99* (1972), Bevan and Saul contain details of Isabella's life. Hayward comments that the marriage was unpopular with Richard's uncles. Philippe de Mézières's letter is in Coopland, G. W. (ed.), *Letter to King Richard II* (Liverpool, 1975). Isabella's entry to London is from Strickland. Froissart describes Gloucester's plot and his murder. Hayward describes Henry IV's seizure of the crown.

5 The Lancastrian Queens

Major sources for the Lancastrians include Froissart, Capgrave, Hayward, and the selected documents in Myers 1969. Further sources include
Dockray, K. (ed.), *Henry VI, Margaret of Anjou and the Wars of the Roses: A Source Book* (Stroud, 2000).
Gairdner, J. (ed.), *The Paston Letters, 3 vols* (Westminster, 1896).
Hall, E., *Chronicle Containing the History of England*, Johnson, J., *et al* (eds) (1809).

Mary de Bohun

Details of Mary's life are in Mortimer, I., *The Fears of Henry IV* (2007) and Weir, A., *Katherine Swynford* (2007). The main sources are Froissart and Hayward.

Joan of Navarre

Strohm, P., 'Joanna of Navarre: That Obscure Object of Desire' in *England's Empty Throne* (1998) describes Joan. Kirby, J. L., *Henry IV of England* (1970) contains details of Joan's life. Joan's childhood and first marriage is discussed in Jones, M., *Ducal Brittany 1364-1399* (Oxford, 1970), Jones, M., *Between France and England* (Aldershot, 2000) and Strickland. Mortimer 2007 discusses Joan and Henry's love match. Joan's letters are from Wood. Henry's illness is noted in the *Eulogium Historiarum* (Myers 1969). Joan's imprisonment is in Myers, A. R., 'The Captivity of a Royal Witch: The Household Accounts of Queen Joan of Navarre' in *Crown, Household and Parliament in Fifteenth-Century England* (1985).

Catherine of Valois
Loades, D., *Tudor Queens of England* (2009) contains a section on Catherine. She is also described in Griffiths, R. A., and Thomas, R. S., *The Making of the Tudor Dynasty* (Stroud, 1985). Strickland details Catherine's troubled childhood. Shakespeare, W., 'Henry V' in Wells, S., and Taylor, G. (eds), *The Oxford Shakespeare: The Complete Works* (Oxford, 1998) is quoted. Henry and Catherine's progress is noted in the *Chronicle of John Strecche* (Myers 1969). The *Chronicle of London* is in Myers 1969. Griffiths, R. A., *King and Country: England and Wales in the Fifteenth Century* (1991) details Catherine's relationship with Edmund Beaufort. *Hall's Chronicle* discusses Catherine's second marriage. Pepys, S., *The Illustrated Pepys*, Latham, R. (ed.) (2000) is quoted.

Margaret of Anjou
Works on Margaret include Archer, R. E., 'Queen Margaret of Anjou, Queen Consort of Henry VI: A Reassessment' in *Crown, Government and People in the Fifteenth Century* (Stroud, 1995), Bagley, J. J., *Margaret of Anjou*, Erlanger, P., *Margaret of Anjou* (1970), Haswell, J., *The Ardent Queen*, and Maurer, H. E., *Margaret of Anjou* (Woodbridge, 2003). There is information on Margaret in Cron, B. M., 'The Duke of Suffolk, the Angevin Marriage, and the Ceding of Maine, 1445' (*Journal of Medieval History* 20, 1994), Laynesmith, J. L., *The Last Medieval Queens* (Oxford, 2004), Lee, P. A., 'Reflections of Power: Margaret of Anjou and the Dark Side of Queenship' (*Renaissance Quarterly* 39, 1986), Griffiths, R. A., *The Reign of King Henry VI* (Stroud, 1998), and Storey, R. L., *The End of the House of Lancaster* (Stroud, 1999). The couple's first meeting is described in Report to Bianca Maria Visconti Duchess of Milan, 24 October 1458 (Dockray). Polydore Vergil and *Wherhamsted's Register* are from Dockray. Warwick's comments on Margaret are from Dockray. Margaret's attempts to secure Henry's recognition of their son are from Paston letters 195 and 226. *Hall's Chronicle* details York's claims to the throne. Margaret's letter is from Wood. Paston letters 385 and 687 detail Margaret's defeat at Towton and captivity.

6 The Yorkist Queens

The main sources for the Yorkist Queens are
Bacon, F., *History of the Reign of King Henry VII*, Lumby, J. R. (ed.) (Cambridge, 1885).
Dockray, K. (ed.), *Edward IV: A Source Book* (Stroud, 1999).
Halliwell, J. O., *Warkworth's Chronicle of the First Thirteen Years of the Reign of King Edward the Fourth* (Llanerch, 1990).
More, T., *The History of King Richard III* (2005).
Mancini, D., *The Usurpation of Richard III*, Armstrong, C. A. J. (ed.) (Gloucester, 1984).
Pronay, N. and Cox, J., *The Crowland Chronicle Continuatios: 1459-1486* (1986).

Elizabeth Woodville
There are two recent works on Elizabeth Woodville: Baldwin, D., *Elizabeth Woodville* (Stroud, 2002) and Okerlund, A., *Elizabeth Wydeville: The Slandered Queen* (Stroud, 2005). Laynesmith also discusses Elizabeth. More recounts that Elizabeth considered herself too good to be Edward's concubine. *Warkworth's Chronicle* records the secret marriage. More and Mancini note Cecily Neville's fury. The *Annales Rerum Anglicarum* is from Dockray. Elizabeth's household is discussed in Myers 1985. Elizabeth's letter is from Wood. Edward and Elizabeth's pilgrimages to Walsingham and Canterbury are in Paston letter 676. The proclamation made by Warwick, Clarence and the Archbishop of York is from Dockray. Paston letter 654 records Elizabeth's move to sanctuary in 1470. More and the *Crowland Chronicle Continuations* relate Richard III's coup. More recounts Elizabeth's surrender of her youngest son. Philippe de Commines is quoted from Dockray.

Anne Neville
The only biography of Anne is Hicks, M., *Anne Neville* (Stroud, 2006). Further details about her are in Laynesmith 2004, Hicks, M., 'Warwick – The Reluctant Kingmaker' (*Medieval History* 1, 1991), Hicks, M., *False, Fleeting, Perjur'd Clarence* (Bangor, 1992), Saul 2005 and Seward, D., *Richard III: England's Black Legend* (1997). The *Crowland Chronicle Continuations* details the feud between Edward and Warwick and Clarence. Anne Beauchamp's petition is from Wood. Hicks, M., 'One Prince or Two? The Family of Richard III'

(*The Ricardian* 9, 1993) details Edward of Middleham's birth. *Hall's Chronicle* describes the coronation. The *Crowland Chronicle Continuations* notes the rivalry between Anne and Elizabeth of York.

Elizabeth of York

There are two biographies of Elizabeth: Okerlund, A., *Elizabeth of York* (Basingstoke, 2009) and Harvey, N. L., *Elizabeth of York* (1973). Nicolas, N. H. (ed.), *Privy Purse Expenses of Elizabeth of York* (1830) contains Elizabeth's expenses as queen and details of her life. Visser-Fuchs, L., 'Where Did Elizabeth of York Find Consolation?' (*The Ricardian* 9, 1993) records Richard III's plan to marry Elizabeth. Bacon describes Henry VII's accession and his marriage to Elizabeth. Elizabeth's letter is from Wood. Elizabeth's death is recorded in *Hall's Chronicle*. Her funeral is described in Baker, R., *A Chronicle of the Kings of England from the time of the Romans unto the Death of King James* (1696).

7 The Six Wives of Henry VIII

The contemporary Hall's Chronicle is a major source. Other sources include
Calendar of State Papers, Spanish vols I-IX, De Gayangos, P., Hume, M. A. S., and Tyler, R. (eds) (L1888-1949) (*CSP*).
Cavendish, G., *Thomas Wolsey Late Cardinal, His Life and Death*, Lockyer, R. (ed.) (1962).
Clifford, H., *The Life of Jane Dormer Duchess of Feria*, Estcourt, E. E., and Stevenson (ed.) (1887).
Ellis, H. (ed.), *Original Letters Illustrative of English History* (1824).
Herbert, E., *The History of England under Henry VIII* (1870).
Letters and Papers, Foreign and Domestic, of the Reign of Henry VIII, vols I-XXI, Brewer, J. S., Gairdner, J., Brodie, R. H. (eds) (1876-1932) (*L&P*).
Sander, N., *Rise and Growth of the Anglican Schism* (1877).
St Clare Byrne, M. (ed.), *The Lisle Letters, 6 vols* (Chicago, 1981).
Strype, J., (ed.), *Ecclesiastical Memorials* (1822).
Williams, C. H. (ed.), *English Historical Documents, vol. V: 1485-1558* (1967).
Wriothesley, C., *A Chronicle of England During the Reigns of the Tudors, 2 vols*, Hamilton, W. D. (ed.) (London, 1875-78).
Wyatt, G., 'Extracts from the Life of the Virtuous Christian and Renowned Queen Anne Boleigne' in Singer, S. W. (ed.), *The Life of Cardinal Wolsey* (Chiswick, 1825).
There are a number of general works on the six wives, including Hume, M., *The Wives of Henry VIII*, Fraser, A., *The Six Wives of Henry VIII* (1992), Weir, A., *The Six Wives of Henry VIII* (2007), Starkey, D., *Six Wives* (2003), Lindsey, K., *Divorced Beheaded Survived* (De Capo, 1995), and Loades, D., *The Six Wives of Henry VIII* (Stroud, 2009).

Catherine of Aragon

Works on Catherine include Dixon, W. H., *History of Two Queens, 4 vols* (1873), Froude, J. A., *The Divorce of Catherine of Aragon* (New York, 1970), Hope, Mrs, *The First Divorce of Henry VIII* (1894), Claremont, F., *Catherine of Aragon* (1939), Luke, M. M., *Catherine the Queen* (London, 1967), Mattingly, G., *Catherine of Aragon* (1944) and Paul, J. E., *Catherine of Aragon and her Friends* (1966). *Hall's Chronicle* describes Catherine's first marriage. Details of Catherine and Arthur's wedding night are from *L&P* IV. Catherine's letters to Ferdinand are from Wood. The report of the Venetian diplomat is from Williams. The Field of the Cloth of Gold and Catherine's regency are described in *Hall's Chronicle*. Catherine's letter to Henry following Flodden is from Ellis. There is a discussion of Catherine's childbearing record in Dewhurst, J., 'The Alleged Miscarriages of Catherine of Aragon and Anne Boleyn' (*Medical History* 28, 1984). Herbert describes the divorce. *L&P* IV contains a number of official documents and letters, some of which are quoted here. Sources for Catherine's death are from *L&P* X. Catherine's last letter is from Crawford.

Anne Boleyn

There are a number of biographies of Anne, including Bengar, E. O., *Memoirs of the Life of Anne Boleyn, 2 vols* (1821), Bruce, M. L., *Anne Boleyn* (1972), Chapman, H. W., *Anne Boleyn* (1974), Denny, J., *Anne Boleyn* (2004), Dixon 1873, Erickson, C., *Anne Boleyn* (1984), Friedmann, P., *Anne Boleyn* (1884), Ives, E. W., *The Life and Death of Anne Boleyn* (Oxford, 2005), Norton, E., *Anne Boleyn, Henry VIII's Obsession* (Stroud, 2008), and Sergeant, P. W., *The Life of Anne Boleyn* (1923). Other works focus on specific periods of Anne's life, such as Weir, A., *The Lady in the Tower* (2009) and Wilkinson, J., *The Early Loves of Anne Boleyn* (Stroud, 2009). Important sources for Anne are Latymer, W., *Chronickille of Anne Bulleyne*, Dowling, M. (ed.) (Camden

Miscellany XXX, Fourth Series, vol. 39, 1990) and Constantine, G., 'Transcript of an Original Manuscript, Containing a Memorial from George Constantyne to Thomas Lord Cromwell', Amyot, T. (ed.) (*Archaeologia* 23, 1831). Anne's early life is discussed in Paget, H., 'The Youth of Anne Boleyn' (*Bulletin of the Institute of Historical Research* 54, 1981) and Round, J. H., *The Early Life of Anne Boleyn* (1886). Margaret of Austria's letter is from Sergeant 1923. The quotations on Anne's appearance are from Wyatt, G., *The Papers of George Wyatt Esquire*, Loades, D. M. (ed.) (1968) and Wyatt 1825. Wyatt's poems are from Wyatt, T., *Collected Poems*, Daalder, J. (ed.) (1975). Anne's letter to Wolsey is from Crawford. Anne's comments on Mary and Catherine and the arguments between Henry and Anne are taken from various sources in the *L&Ps* and were recorded by Chapuys. Wyatt 1825 records Anne's second miscarriage. Anne's fall is discussed in Bernard, G. W., 'The Fall of Anne Boleyn' (*English Historical Review* 106, 1991), Ives, E. W., 'The Fall of Anne Boleyn Reconsidered' (*English Historical Review* 107, 1992), Walker, G., 'Rethinking the Fall of Anne Boleyn' (*The Historical Journal* 45, 2002) and Warnicke, R. M., 'The Fall of Anne Boleyn: A Reassessment' (*History* 70, 1985). Anne's words in the Tower are from the letters of William Kingston (Singer).

Jane Seymour

There are two works on Jane: Norton, E., *Jane Seymour, Henry VIII's True Love* (Stroud, 2009) and Gross, P., *Jane the Quene* (Lewiston, 1999). Further details are in Seymour, W., *Ordeal by Ambition* (1972). Fuller, T., *The Worthies of England*, Freeman, J. (ed.) (1952) contains details on Jane, and the Lisle letters are an important source. Jane's background is described in Locke, A. A., *The Seymour Family: History and Romance* (1911), Jackson, J. E., 'Wulfhall and the Seymours' (*The Wiltshire Archaeological and Natural History Magazine* 15) and St Maur, H., *Annals of the Seymours* (1902). Most documents referred to are from the *L&Ps* and *CSPs*. Cromwell's comments on Jane's death are from Merriman, R. B., *Life and Letters of Thomas Cromwell, 2 vols* (Oxford, 1902).

Anne of Cleves

There are three books on Anne of Cleves: Norton, E., *Anne of Cleves, Henry VIII's Discarded Bride* (Stroud, 2009), Saaler, M., *Anne of Cleves* (1997) and Warnicke, R. M., *The Marrying of Anne of Cleves* (Cambridge, 2000). Documents on Henry's search for a bride are in *L&P* XII and XIII. Anne's family is described in *The History of the Succession of the Countries of Juliers and Berg* (1738), Midelfort, H. C. E., *Mad Princes of Renaissance Germany* (Charlottesville, 1994) and McEntegart, R., *Henry VIII, The League of Schmalkalden and the English Reformation* (Woodbridge, 2002). Wotton's letter concerning Anne's upbringing is from Ellis 1824. Accounts of Anne's first meeting with Henry, her marriage and her divorce are taken from Strype. The Flanders Mare comment is from Smollett, T., *A Complete History of England, vol. II* (1757). Details of Anne's time in England come from the documents in *L&Ps* and *CSPs*. Rutland's account of the divorce is from Rutland Manuscripts: *Historical Manuscripts Commission, Twelfth Report, Appendix, Part IV: The Manuscripts of his Grace the Duke of Rutland, vol. I* (1888). Harst's account is from Bouterwek, A. W., 'Anna Von Cleve' in *Zeitschrift Des Bergischen Geschichtsvereins* 6 (1869) (translated by Stefanie and Renate Worden). Anne's letter to Henry is from Wood. Anne's time at Richmond is described in Norton, E., *Anne of Cleves and Richmond Palace* (*Surrey History* 8, 2009).

Catherine Howard

There are three books on Catherine: Smith, L. B., *Catherine Howard* (Stroud, 2008), Denny, J., *Katherine Howard* (2005) and Glenne, M., *Catherine Howard* (1947). Details of Catherine's childhood come from the later examinations of members of the household (recorded in the *L&Ps*). Catherine's own confession and interrogation are from *Historical Manuscripts Commission: Calendar of Manuscripts of the Marquis of Bath, vol. II* (Dublin, 1907). Catherine's letter is from Crawford. Documents on her time as queen are in the *L&Ps* and *CSPs*.

Catherine Parr

There are several books specifically on Catherine: Gordon, M. A., *Life of Queen Katharine Parr* (Kendal), Martienssen, A., *Queen Katherine Parr* (London, 1975), Kemeys, B., and Raggatt, J., *The Queen who Survived* (London, 1993), James, S., *Catherine Parr* (Stroud, 2008), Withrow, B. G., *Katherine Parr* (Phillipsburg, 2009), and Norton, E., *Catherine Parr* (Stroud, 2010). The *L&Ps* and *CSPs* contain documents relating to Catherine throughout her life. Catherine's background is in Farrer, W. (ed.), *Records Relating to the Barony of Kendale, vol. I* (Kendal, 1923). The correspondence between Maude and Lord Dacre is from Nicholson, C., *The Annals of Kendal* (1861). The Pilgrimage of Grace is described in Dodds, M. H., and Dodds, R., *The Pilgrimage of Grace, 1536-1537, and the Exeter Conspiracy, 1538, 2 vols* (Cambridge, 1915). Details of Thomas Seymour are in MacLean, J., *The Life of Sir Thomas Seymour, Knight* (1869). Catherine's letters are from Crawford 2002.

Elizabeth's letter is from Marcus, L. S., Mueller, J., and Rose, M. B. (eds), *Elizabeth I, Collected Works* (Chicago, 2002). The plot against Catherine is from Foxe, J., *The Acts and Monuments of John Foxe, vols V and VI* (New York, 1965). Sources for Catherine's life after Henry's death include Hayward, J., *The Life and Raigne of King Edward the Sixth*, Beer, B. L. (ed.) (Kent, 1993) and Knighton, C. S., (ed.), *Calendar of State Papers Domestic Series of the Reign of Edward VI 1547-1553* (1992). Sources concerning the relationship between Elizabeth and Seymour are in Marcus. Catherine's death is described in Dent, E., *Annals of Winchcombe and Sudeley* (1877).

8 Tudor Queen Regnants

Major sources include
Falkus, C. (ed.), *The Private Lives of the Tudor Monarchs* (1974).
Johnson, J., *et al* (eds), *Holinshed's Chronicles of England, Scotland and Ireland* (New York, 1965).
Loades, D. (ed.), *The Chronicles of the Tudor Queens* (Stroud, 2002).
MacCulloch, D. (ed.), *The Vita Mariae Angliae Reginae of Robert Wingfield* (Camden Miscellany 28, fourth series, 1984).
Madden, F. (ed.), *Privy Purse Expenses of the Princess Mary* (1831).
Nichols, J. G. (ed.), *The Chronicle of Queen Jane and Two Years of Queen Mary* (Felinfach, 1996).

Lady Jane Grey
There are a number of works on Lady Jane Grey: Chapman, H. W., *Lady Jane Grey* (1962), Davey, R., *The Nine Days Queen* (London, 1910), Ives, E., *Lady Jane Grey* (2009), and Plowden, A., *Lady Jane Grey* (Stroud, 2004) (revised from Plowden, A., *Lady Jane Grey and the House of Suffolk* (New York, 1986)). Jane is featured in Ashdown, D. M., *Tudor Cousins: Rivals for the Throne* (Stroud, 2000), Lisle, L. de, *The Sisters who would be Queen* (2009), and Weir, A., *Children of England* (Pimlico, 1996). Henry VIII's Will is in Williams 1967. Dorset's account of his arrangements with Seymour are from Knighton 1992. Seymour and Dorset's correspondence is in Haynes, S. (ed.), *Collection of State Papers Relating to Affairs in the Reigne of King Henry VIII, King Edward VI, Queen Mary and Queen Elizabeth from the year 1542 to 1570 Transcribed from the Original Letters and Other Authentick Memorials left by William Cecil* (1740). Ascham's visit is in Ascham, R., *The Scholemaster* (1934). Jane's correspondence with Bullinger is in Nicholas, N. H. (ed.), *The Literary Remains of Lady Jane Grey with a Memoir of her Life* (1825). Mary's gift of jewellery to Jane is recorded in Madden. Mary's gift of material for a dress is in Aylmer's *A Harbour of Faithful Subjects* (Falkus). Edward's illness is from North, J. (ed.), *England's Boy King: The Diary of Edward VI, 1547-1553* (Welwyn Garden City, 2005). John Hayward (Kent) describes Edward's plans for the succession. Jane's account of her time as queen is from her letter to Mary in Wood. The *Vita Mariae* describes Mary's rebellion. The *Chronicle of Queen Jane* describes Jane's time in the Tower and Mary's accession. Foxe (Townsend) contains Jane's letter to her father. Jane's death is in the *Chronicle of Queen Jane*. The quote on Jane's turbulent days as queen is from Julius Terentianus to John [Ab Ulmis], 20 November 1553, in Robinson, H. (ed.), *Original Letters Relative to the English Reformation* (Cambridge, 1846).

Mary I
There are many works on Mary, including Erickson, C., *Bloody Mary* (New York, 1978), Loades, D., *Mary Tudor* (Oxford, 1989) and Prescott, M., *Mary Tudor, The Spanish Tudor* (2003). Documents in Knighton 1992 record the persecution of Mary in Edward's reign. The *Vita Mariae* describes much of Mary's reign. The statute repealing Mary's parents is in Loades 2002. Renard's comments on the religious changes are from *CSP* XI. Knighton, C. S. (ed.), *Calendar of State Papers Domestic Series of the Reign of Mary I* (1998) contains an official account of Mary's coronation. *CSP* XI and XII contain documents on Mary's marriage. The *History of Wyat's Rebellion* is in Pollard, A. F., (ed.), *Tudor Tracts* (Westminster, 1903). The *Vita Mariae* claims that Mary panicked when Wyatt entered London. The *Life of Jane Dormer* contains Mary's comments about Elizabeth resembling Smeaton. Philip's arrival and marriage are described in John Elder's letter and the official account (both in Nichols 1996). Mary's 'pregnancy' is described in Foxe (Falkus). Foxe (Townsend) has Mary's quotation on Calais. Feria's dispatch is in Rodriguez-Salgado, M. J., and Adams, S. (eds), *Count of Feria's Dispatch to Philip II of 14 November 1558* (Camden Miscellany 28 fourth series, 1984).

Elizabeth I
There are many works on Elizabeth. These include Rex, R., *Elizabeth* (Stroud, 2009), Somerset, A., *Elizabeth I* (1991), Starkey, D., *Elizabeth* (2001), and Weir, A., *Elizabeth the Queen* (1998). Major sources are Camden, W., *The History of the Most Renowned and Victorious Princess Elizabeth Late Queen of England*, MacCaffrey, W. T. (ed.) (Chicago, 1970), Hayward, J., *Annals of the First Four Years of the Reign of Queen Elizabeth*, Bruce, J. (ed.) (1840) and *Calendar*

of State Papers: Domestic Series, Elizabeth, 5 vols and Addenda, Green, M. A. E., and Lemon, R. (eds) (1865-71). Lady Bryan's letter to Cromwell is in Falkus. The *Chronicle of Queen Jane* records that Elizabeth was implicated in Wyatt's Rebellion. Elizabeth's letters, speeches and poems are from Marcus. Elizabeth's coronation is described in Richard Mulcaster's account (Loades 2002). Elizabeth's rejection of a proposal from the Prince of Sweden is in a document in Knighton 1998. Camden details Elizabeth's English suitors. Dispatches by the Spanish ambassadors contain details of Elizabeth and Dudley's relationship and Elizabeth's illness (Loades 2002). The relationship between Elizabeth and Mary, Queen of Scots, is discussed in Dunn, J., *Elizabeth and Mary* (2003). Camden also details Mary. Documents on Norfolk's treason are from the *CSPs*. Camden records Elizabeth's promise to marry Alençon. He also details the Armada. Documents on Essex's rebellion and Elizabeth's death are in the *CSPs*.

9 The House of Stuart

The main sources are
Brown, B. C. (ed.), *The Letters of Queen Anne* (1935).
Browning, A. (ed.), *English Historical Documents, vol. 8 1660–1714* (1953).
Burnet, G., *Bishop Burnet's History of his own Times, 6 vols* (Oxford, 1833).
Clifford, A., *Diaries*, Clifford, D. J. H. (ed.) (Stroud, 1990).
Evelyn, J., *Diary and Correspondence, 4 vols*, Bray, W. (ed.) (1887).
Halliwell, J. O. (ed.), *Letters of the Kings of England, vol. 2* (1848).
Hamilton, A., *Memoirs of the Court of Charles the Second* (1859).
Pepys, S., *Diary and Correspondence, 4 vols*, Smith, J. (ed.) (Boston).

Anne of Denmark
Williams, E. C., *Anne of Denmark* (1970) is the only full biography of Anne. There is a chapter on Anne in Bevan, B., *King James VI of Scotland and I of England* (1996). Stevenson, S., *Scotland's Last Royal Wedding* (Edinburgh, 1997) details the marriage and contains a Danish contemporary account. Moysie, D., (ed.), *Memoirs of the Affairs of Scotland* (Edinburgh, 1830) contains a Scottish account of the marriage. Klarwill, V. von (ed.), *The Fugger Newsletter* (1926) notes the marriage negotiations. James and Charles's letters are in Halliwell. Anne's letters are in Walker, P. (ed.), *Letters to King James the Sixth* (Edinburgh, 1835). Anne's coronation oath is from Craig, J. T. G. (ed.), *Papers Relating to the Marriage of King James the Sixth of Scotland* (Edinburgh, 1828). Clifford is a useful source.

Henrietta Maria of France
There are a number of works on Henrietta Maria. These include Marshall, R. K., *Henrietta Maria* (1990), Oman, C., *Henrietta Maria* (1951), Taylor, I. A., *The Life of Queen Henrietta Maria* (1905). There is a section on Henrietta Maria in Gray, R., *The King's Wife* (1990). Details of the Civil War are in Bennett, M., *The Civil Wars 1637-1653* (Stroud, 1998), Russell, C., *The Causes of the English Civil War* (Oxford, 1990), and Royle, T., *Civil War* (2004). Important sources are *Memoirs of the Life and Death of that Matchless Mirror of Magnamity and Heroick Virtues Henrietta Maria de Bourbon* (1671) and Evelyn. Charles's letters are in Halliwell. Henrietta Maria's letters are in Green, M. A. E. (ed.), *Letters of Queen Henrietta Maria* (1857). Herbert, E., *A Collection of the Most Instructive and Memorable Lives Ever Published, vol. VIII: Lord Herbert* (1830) details Charles's incognito visit to Paris. A letter of Mr Pory to Sir Thomas Puckering in Ellis 2nd Series vol. IV details Henrietta Maria's participation in court masques. Spalding, J., *The History of the Troubles and Memorable Transactions in Scotland in the Reign of Charles I* (Aberdeen, 1829) details the Burlington Bay attack. Charles II's letter to Prince Henry is from Evelyn vol. IV. Henrietta's visits to England as queen mother are noted in Clifford.

Catherine of Braganza
Mackay, J., *Catherine of Braganza* (1937) and Gray 1990 detail Catherine's life. The main sources are Hyde, E., *The Continuation of the Life of Edward Earl of Clarendon by Himself, vol. III* (Oxford, 1759), Evelyn, Hamilton and Pepys. Charles's decision to marry Catherine is noted in a letter of Sir Edward Nicholas to the Earl of Winchelsea in *Report on the Manuscripts of Allan George Finch, vol. I* (1913). The letters discussing Catherine's pregnancies are from Bickley, F. (ed.), *Report on the Manuscripts of the Late Reginald Rawdon Hastings, vol. II* (1930). There is an account of the Popish Plot in Browning 1953. The French ambassador's account of Charles's death is in the same work.

Anne Hyde
There are no works on Anne Hyde. Details of her life can be found in Craik, H., *The Life of Edward, Earl of*

Clarendon, 2 vols (1911) and Waller, M., *Ungrateful Daughters* (2002). The main sources are Burnet, Evelyn, Hamilton and Pepys. Elizabeth of Bohemia's letters are printed in Evelyn vol. IV. Anne's letter to her father is in Ogle, O. (ed.), *Calendar of Clarendon State Papers Preserved in the Bodleian Library* (1869). The meeting between James and Anne is described in Sells, A. L. (ed.), *The Memoirs of James II: His Campaigns as Duke of York, 1652-1660* (Bloomington, 1962). One account of Anne's marriage is from Burnet. Pepys records that Anne secured Lady Chesterfield's exile from court. Anne's flirtations are recorded by Pepys and Hamilton. The rumours about Clarendon's role in Catherine's infertility are from Pepys. Anne's death is described by Burnet. Anne's funeral is from Clifford.

Mary of Modena

Hopkirk, M., *Queen Over the Water* (1953) is a biography of Mary. Haile, M. (ed.), *Queen Mary of Modena: Her Life and Letters* (1905) is an important source. Details of Mary's early years in England are in Toynbee, M. R., 'An Early Correspondence of Queen Mary of Modena' (*Notes and Queries* 188, 1945) and Toynbee, M. R., 'A Further Note on an Early Correspondence of Queen Mary of Modena' (*Notes and Queries* 193, 1948). Details of Mary's time as queen and exile are from Clarke, J. S. (ed.), *The Life of James the Second, 2 vols* (1816) which is compiled from James's memoirs. Letters and other documents of the reign are from *Calendar of State Papers Domestic Series James II, 2 vols* (1960-64). James's memoirs detail the controversy over his son's birth. Anne's letters are from Brown. The invitation to William is in Browning. The account of Mary's flight is by Francesco Riva who accompanied her (Haile).

Mary II

Chapman, H. W., *Mary II Queen of England* (1953) is a biography of Mary. Waller 2002 and Waller, M., *Sovereign Ladies* (2006) detail Mary's life. The most recent study of Mary is Van Der Kiste, J., *William and Mary* (Stroud, 2003). The main sources for Mary are her letters and memoirs contained in Bowen, M., *The Third Mary Stuart* (1929) and her later memoirs in Doebner, R. (ed.), *Memoirs of Mary, Queen of England, 1689-1693* (Leipzig, 1886). Other sources include Evelyn and Pepys. Some details of Mary's reign are in Ede, M., *Arts and Society in England under William and Mary* (1979). Mary's memoirs and Marlborough, Sarah, Duchess of, *An Account of the Conduct of the Dowager Duchess of Marlborough, From Her First Coming to Court to the Year 1710* (1742) describe the quarrel between Mary and Anne.

Anne

The most comprehensive biography of Anne is Gregg, E., *Queen Anne* (2001). Waller 2002 and Waller 2006 also detail her life. The main sources for Anne are Brown, B. C. (ed.), *The Letters of Queen Anne* (1935), Marlborough, Evelyn and Pepys. Anne's dispute with Mary over the object in the distance is quoted from Gregg. Mary's letter is from Bowen. Anne's discussion with Mary of Modena over the prince's birth is from James II's memoirs.

10 The Hanoverian Queens

Sources for the Hanoverian queens include

Benson, A. C., and Esher, Viscount (eds), *The Letters of Queen Victoria, 3 vols* (1908).
Bury, C., *The Diary of a Lady-in-Waiting, 2 vols*, Steuart, F. (ed.) (1908).
Greville, C., *A Journal of the Reigns of King George IV and King William IV, 2 vols*, Reeve, H. (ed.) (1875).
Hayward, A., *Diaires of a Lady of Quality* (1864).
Greenwood, A. D., *Lives of the Hanoverian Queens of England, 2 vols* (1911), Doran, Dr, *Lives of the Queens of England of the House of Hanover, 2 vols* (1855) and Hichens, M., *Wives of the Kings of England: From Hanover to Windsor* (2006) contain short biographies of most of the Hanoverian queens. Black, J., *The Hanoverians* (2004) provides background information to the dynasty.

Sophia Dorothea of Celle

There are a number of works on Sophia Dorothea. The leading biography is Wilkins, W. H., *The Love of an Uncrowned Queen* (1901). Other works include *Memoirs of Sophia Dorothea, Consort of George I, 2 vols* (1846) and Morand, P., *Sophia Dorothea of Celle: The Captive Princess* (1972). Brown, J. (ed.), *Anecdotes and Characters of the House of Brunswick* (1821) contains a number of important sources, including Walpole and 'An old courtier to a Young Prince'. Sophia Dorothea's letter on her betrothal is from *Memoirs of Sophia Dorothea*. Königsmarck and Sophia Dorothea's letters are from Morand. The discovery of the affair is from *Memoirs of the Love and State Intrigues of the Court of Hanover* in Brown. George II's love for his mother is described in Mrs Smith's *History of England* in Brown.

Caroline of Ansbach

Caroline is the subject of a number of biographies, including Quennell, P., *Caroline of England* (1939). Important sources include Horace Walpole's reminiscences in *Walpoliana* (Chiswick, 1830), Montagu, M. W., *The Letters and Works of Lady Mary Wortley Montagu, vol. I*, Wharncliffe, Lord (ed.) (1861) and Hervey, J., *Memoirs of the Reign of George the Second, 2 vols*, Croker, J. W. (ed.) (1855). Coxe, W., *Memoirs of the Life and Administration of Sir Robert Walpole, Earl of Orford, 2 vols* (1816) details Caroline's relationship with Walpole. Thomson, Mrs, *Memoirs of Viscountess Sundon, Mistress of the Robes to Queen Caroline, 2 vols* (1848) contains important details on the queen. Information on Caroline's proposed marriage to the Archduke Charles is from a letter from Leibniz to Benedicta, Duchess of Brunswick-Luneburg, 8 April 1698 (in Kemble, J. M. (ed.), *State Papers and Correspondence Illustrating of the Social and Political State of Europe from the Revolution to the Accession of the House of Hanover* (1857)). Details of the rivalry between George I and George II are by Walpole in Brown, J. (ed.), *Anecdotes and Characters of the House of Brunswick* (1821). The Duchess of Marlborough's anecdote is from Montagu.

Charlotte of Mecklenburg-Strelitz

The only modern biography of Charlotte is Hedley, O., *Queen Charlotte* (1975). A number of biographies were produced soon after her death, including Craig, W. M., *Memoir of her Majesty Sophia Charlotte of Mecklenburg Strelitz, Queen of Great Britain* (Liverpool, 1818). Details on George III can be found in Black. An excellent recent study of Charlotte's daughters is Fraser, F., *Princesses* (2004). Important sources for Charlotte include Burney, F., *Diary and Letters of Madame D'Arblay, 7 vols* (1854), Galt, J., *George the Third, His Court and Family, 2 vols* (1824) and Holt, E., *The Public and Domestic Life of his Late Most Gracious Majesty, George the Third, 2 vols* (1820). Charlotte's letter to the King of Prussia and George's declaration are from Holt. Walpole's description of Charlotte is from Greenwood. Charlotte's charity is detailed in Holt. Hayward contains details of George's obsession with Lady Pembroke and his comments on King Lear. The correspondence with Caroline of Brunswick is from Holt. Holt also describes Charlotte's reaction to Princess Charlotte's death and her own death.

Maria Fitzherbert

Mrs Fitzherbert is a popular subject for biographies. Recent works include Munson, J., *Maria Fitzherbert* (2001) and Irvine, V., *The King's Wife* (2005). Langdale, C. (ed.), *Memoirs of Mrs Fitzherbert* (1856) contains Lord Stourton's account of Mrs Fitzherbert's life, based on his conversations with her. Other sources are Holland, H. R., *Memoirs of the Whig Party During My Time, vol. 2* (1854) and Bury. Letters to and from Mrs Fitzherbert are in Leslie, S. (ed.), *The Letters of Mrs Fitzherbert* (1940). Details of Maria's marriage to Mr Fitzherbert are from Clifford, T. B., and Clifford, A., *A Topographical and Historical Description of the Parish of Tizall, in the County of Stafford* (Paris, 1817).

Caroline of Brunswick

There are a number of biographies of Caroline. These include Fraser, F., *The Unruly Queen* (1996), Parry, E., *Queen Caroline* (1930), Plowden, A., *Caroline and Charlotte* (Stroud, 2005), and Robins, J., *Rebel Queen* (2006). There is a section on Caroline in Gray. Important sources are Bury, C., *The Diary of a Lady-in-Waiting, 2 vols* (1908), Huish, R., *Memoirs of her Late Majesty Caroline, Queen of Great Britain, 2 vols* (1821) and Holland. The story concerning Caroline's feigned labour is from Hayward. Caroline's engagement and journey to England are described in Harris, J. (ed.), *Diaries and Correspondence of the Earl of Malmesbury, vol. 3* (1844). George and Caroline's letters on their separation and Lady Douglas's testimony are from Huish. Caroline's appearance with a pumpkin on her head is from Hayward. Caroline's trial is described in *The Trial of Her Majesty, Queen Caroline, Consort of George IV for an Alleged Adulterous Intercourse with Bartolomo Bergami* (1820). The rhyme about Caroline is from Bury.

Adelaide of Saxe-Meiningen

The only full-length biography of Adelaide is Hopkirk, M., *Queen Adelaide* (1950). Details of Adelaide's life can also be found in Watkins, J., *The Life and Times of 'England's Patriot King' William IV* (1831). Greville is an important source for Adelaide. Adelaide's Obituary is from *The Gentlemen's Magazine* 188 (1850). Adelaide's letter showing her love of children is quoted from Greenwood. Adelaide's other letters are from Benson and Esher. William's attack on the Duchess of Kent is from Greville vol. II.

Victoria

There are many works on Victoria. The most detailed is Longford, E., *Victoria R.I.* (1998). Others include

De-la-Noy, M., *Queen Victoria at Home* (2003), Marshall, D., *The Life and Times of Victoria* (1992), Strachey, L., *Queen Victoria* (1928) (reprinted as Strachey, L., *The Illustrated Victoria* (1987)), and Thompson, D., *Queen Victoria* (2001). There is a section on Victoria in Waller 2006. A recent life of Victoria's youngest daughter, Dennison, M., *The Last Princess* (2007), also contains many details of the queen's long widowhood. Victoria's letters are from Benson and Esher and Hibbert, C. (ed.), *Queen Victoria in her Letters and Journals* (1984). Letters written to Victoria are from Benson and Esher. Greville vol. II details Victoria's accession. The queen also provided her own account in her journal. Albert's note concerning the Princess Royal is quoted from Longford.

11 From the House of Hanover to the House of Windsor

Important sources include
Crawford, M., *The Little Princesses* (2002).
Windsor, Duke of, *A King's Story* (1950).

Alexandra of Denmark
The only full-length biography of Alexandra is Battiscombe, G., *Queen Alexandra* (1972). Further information can be found in Plumptre, G., *Edward VII* (1995) and Cook, A., *Prince Eddy* (Stroud, 2008). Sources for Alexandra's early life are taken from Hibbert. Details of Alexandra's time as queen and later life are recorded in the memoirs of the Duke of Windsor (Edward VIII).
Mary of Teck
The leading biography of Mary is Pope-Hennessy, J., *Queen Mary* (New York, 1960). There are also sections on Mary in Hichens and Gray. Hibbert contains Queen Victoria's letters and diaries describing Mary. The Duke of Windsor's autobiography is useful and provides details about Mary's family background and the upbringing of her children. Extracts from Mary's letters and diaries are quoted from Pope-Hennessy. Crawford details Mary's old age and interest in her grandchildren.

Wallis Simpson
There are a number of biographies on Wallis. One of the most detailed is Higham, C., *Mrs Simpson: Secret Lives of the Duchess of Windsor*. Bloch, M., *The Duchess of Windsor* (1996) is a highly favourable account, although the author does suggest that Wallis may not have been female. Wallis's autobiography is Windsor, Duchess of, *The Heart Has Its Reasons* (1975). Edward VIII's autobiography is useful. Wallis and Edward's letters are in Bloch, M. (ed.), *Wallis and Edward: Letters 1931-1937* (New York, 1986). Monckton and Lady Furness's comments are from Bloch 1986. Queen Mary's message is related by Wallis in her autobiography.

Elizabeth Bowes-Lyon
The definitive biography of Elizabeth is Shawcross, W., *Queen Elizabeth, The Queen Mother* (2009). Another biography is Mortimer, P., *Queen Elizabeth: A Life of the Queen Mother* (Harmondsworth, 1986). Asquith, C., *The Duchess of York* (1927) is Elizabeth's earliest official biography and a useful source for her early life. Documents for Elizabeth's early life are quoted from Asquith. Details of Elizabeth's family life are from Marion Crawford. Bertie's letter to his daughter is from Mortimer. Interesting details of Elizabeth's old age and household are contained in Burgess, C., *Behind Palace Doors* (2006).

Elizabeth II
As the current reigning monarch, there are a number of books about the queen, and she is also frequently in the news. Biographies include Turner, G., *Elizabeth: The Woman and the Queen* (2002). There are sections on Elizabeth II in both Waller 2006 and Ormrod, W. M. (ed.), *The Kings and Queens of England* (Stroud, 2004). Details of Elizabeth's early life and education are from Crawford. There are also a number of works on the royal household and other areas of the Queen's life, such as Hoey, B., *At Home with the Queen* (2002).

List of Illustrations

98. Stained glass from Wolf Hall in Wiltshire showing Jane Seymour's emblem of a phoenix with a Tudor rose and the feathers of the Prince of Wales. Nothing else now survives of Jane's childhood home. © Elizabeth Norton and the Amberley Archive.

99. Anne Boleyn's execution, 19 May 1536. © Jonathan Reeve JR965b20p921 15001600.

100. The entwined initials of Henry VIII and Jane Seymour (H & I) at Hampton Court. © Elizabeth Norton and the Amberley Archive.

101. Jane Seymour's son, Edward VI. © Elizabeth Norton and the Amberley Archive.

102. Jane Seymour by Hans Holbein. Henry VIII's third wife. Jane was always aware of the dangerous precedent set by her predecessor and was determined not to follow her to the block. © Jonathan Reeve.

103. Anne Zouche, one of Jane Seymour's ladies-in-waiting. © Elizabeth Norton and the Amberley Archive.

104. The Chapel Royal at Hampton Court. Jane's son was christened in the chapel and her body was placed there whilst a solemn vigil was kept. © Elizabeth Norton and the Amberley Archive.

105. Windsor Castle, where Henry VIII is buried longside Jane Seymour. © Elizabeth Norton and the Amberley Archive.

106. Henry VIII. © Elizabeth Norton and the Amberley Archive.

107. The Chapel at Windsor Castle. Jane and Henry are buried together in a vault beneath the choir. © Elizabeth Norton and the Amberley Archive.

108. The gatehouse at Richmond Palace. Little else remains of the great Tudor palace that Anne of Cleves made her home. © Elizabeth Norton and the Amberley Archive.

109. Anne of Cleves' House in Lewes. Anne was granted the house following the annulment of her marriage, and it now houses a museum. © Elizabeth Norton and the Amberley Archive.

110. Anne of Cleves, the painting by Holbein that persuaded Henry she was a beauty. © Amberley Archive.

111. Westminster Abbey where Anne of Cleves is buried. © Jonathan Reeve JR729b46fp16 13001350.

112. Catherine Howard as the Queen of Sheba from a stained-glass window at King's College Chapel, Cambridge. © Elizabeth Norton and the Amberley Archive.

113. Traitor's Gate, through which both Anne Boleyn and Catherine Howard passed on their entry to the Tower of London. © Elizabeth Norton and the Amberley Archive.

114. Catherine Parr depicted in stained glass at Sudeley Castle. © Elizabeth Norton and the Amberley Archive.

115. Catherine Parr's badge as queen showing a maiden emerging from a Tudor rose from stained glass at Sudeley Castle. © Elizabeth Norton and the Amberley Archive.

116. The tomb of Catherine Parr at Sudeley Castle. Catherine was the last queen consort for over fifty years, and the late Tudor period was dominated by queen regnants. © Elizabeth Norton and the Amberley Archive.

117. Catherine Willoughby, Duchess of Suffolk. Court rumour suggested that Henry VIII considered making the widowed duchess his seventh wife. © Elizabeth Norton and the Amberley Archive.

118. Sudeley Castle. Catherine and Thomas saw the castle as the seat of the dynasty that they hoped to found and Catherine died there after giving birth to her only child. © Elizabeth Norton and the Amberley Archive.

119. Henry VIII's will. © Jonathan Reeve.

120. Lady Shelton, Princess Mary's governess, appointed by Anne Boleyn. © Elizabeth Norton and the Amberley Archive.

121. Interior view of Gainsborough Old Hall. The Hall has been reconstructed to be shown as it appeared at the end of the fifteenth century, shortly before it became Catherine Parr's home. © Elizabeth Norton and the Amberley Archive.

122. Henry VIII and Anne Boleyn at Hever Castle in the days of their courtship. © Jonathan Reeve JR959b61p689 15001600.

123. Henry gave Anne Boleyn an elaborate clock during their courtship, as a symbol of his devotion. When she accepted him, she gave him a present designed to represent her troubled state of mind: a jewel fashioned in the image of a maiden in a storm-tossed ship. © Jonathan Reeve JR1162b4p648 15001550.

124. Title page of the first edition of the Great Bible, published in English in 1539. Anne Boleyn promoted the study of the scriptures and she owned a copy of the Bible in French. She also kept an English version on open display for her household to read. Anne had considerable influence over Henry and, some years after her death, an English Bible known as the 'Great Bible' was published with royal support. © Jonathan Reeve JR896b7p161 15001550.

125. The family of Thomas More. Thomas More, who was appointed as Lord Chancellor after Wolsey's fall, and his friend John Fisher, Bishop of Rochester, were the most outspoken critics of the break with Rome and Henry's divorce. When they refused to take the Oath of Succession, swearing to recognise Anne and her children as Henry's legitimate family, they were imprisoned and executed. © Elizabeth Norton & The Amberley Archive.

126. Letter from Anne Boleyn to Cardinal Wolsey. Writing before her marriage to the King, she thanks Wolsey for his great services in her cause, and promises that if, after the attainment of her hopes, there is anything in the world she can do for him, 'you shall fynd me the gladdyst woman in the world to do yt'. © Jonathan Reeve JRCD3b20p899 15001550.

127. A letter from Cranmer at Dunstable (17 May 1533), informing Henry VIII of the date when 'your graces grete matter' will be resolved, and apologising because the liturgical calendar for the week meant it could not happen earlier than Friday. © Jonathan Reeve JR894b7p53 15001550.

128. The coronation procession of Anne Boleyn to Westminster Abbey, 31 May 1533. © Jonathan Reeve JR968b42p404 15001600.

129. The Condemnation of Anne Boleyn. Anne quarrelled with the King's chief minister, Thomas Cromwell early in 1536, declaring that she would have his head. As a result, he joined with Jane Seymour and the supporters of Princess Mary in an attempt to bring about her ruin. © Elizabeth Norton & The Amberley Archive.

130. Pope Clement VII's judgement against Henry. The Pope's 'definitive sentence' issued on 23 March 1534 was in favour of Catherine of Aragon. © Jonathan Reeve JR1171b2p45 15001550.

131. Catherine of Aragon spent the last years of her life in a number of unhealthy and isolated residences. She finally died in January 1536, still declaring her love for the King, her 'husband'. © Jonathan Reeve JR958b61p693 15001600.

132. At Windsor Castle, Anne's ghost has been seen standing at this window in the Dean's Cloister. © Jonathan Reeve JR954b7p45 15501600.

133. The Barn at Wolfhall. Legend claims that Henry and Jane were married in this barn before enjoying their honeymoon at the Seymour family home. © Jonathan Reeve, Elizabeth Norton & The Amberley Archive.

134. Jane's signature as queen. © Elizabeth Norton & The Amberley Archive.

135. Catherine Parr's signature during her time as regent of England. © Elizabeth Norton & The Ambrley Archive.

136. Sybille of Cleves. Anne of Cleves' older sister was a famous beauty, and it was hoped in England that Anne would resemble her. © Elizabeth Norton & The Amberley Archive.

137. Richmond Palace by Hollar *c.* 1650.© Jonathan Reeve JR1112b67plviii 16001650.

138. Oatlands Palace in Surrey, where Henry VIII and Catherine Howard were married in a private ceremony. © Jonathan Reeve JR1149pc 15001550.

139. The coat of arms of the Dudleys carved as graffiti into the wall of the Beauchamp Tower at the Tower of London. The verse carved below refers to Lady Jane Grey's husband, Guildford Dudley, and his brothers. © Elizabeth Norton and the Amberley Archive.

140. The chapel of St Peter ad Vincula in the Tower with the scaffold site in the foreground. Three queens of England – Anne Boleyn, Catherine Howard, and Lady Jane Grey – died on Tower Green and were buried in the chapel. © Elizabeth Norton and the Amberley Archive.

141. Lady Jane Grey depicted in stained glass at Sudeley Castle. Henry VIII's great-niece was surprised to find herself proclaimed queen of England on the death of Edward VI. © Elizabeth Norton and the Amberley Archive.

142. Mary Queen of Scots. © Jonathan Reeve JR1178b2fp440 15001550.

143. Holbein's design for a jewelled pendant for Princess Mary, probably done during his first visit to England (1526-28), when Mary was still in favour and was perhaps even being groomed for possible succession to the throne. © Elizabeth Norton and the Amberley Archive.

144. Mary I as princess. Mary had a happy early childhood, but her parents' divorce blighted her life. © Elizabeth Norton and the Amberley Archive.

145. Mary I as queen. Mary's reign began to popular acclaim, but it quickly proved to be a disaster. Ripon Cathedral.

146. Framlingham Castle. Mary I chose Framlingham as her base from which to launch her attempt to claim the English throne. © Elizabeth Norton and the Amberley Archive.

147. The memorial to John Hooper, Bishop of Gloucester, one of the 'heretics' burned by Mary I. © Elizabeth Norton and the Amberley Archive.

148. Philip II of Spain. Mary I dearly loved her husband, but he was indifferent to her, spending much of their marriage abroad. © Jonathan Reeve JR188b4p823 15001600.

149. Manuscript owned by Mary I. © Jonathan Reeve JR2143b97plate6 13001350.

150. Great Seal of Mary I. © Jonathan Reeve JR2300b4p721 15001600.

151. Hatfield House, the childhood home of Elizabeth I. © Elizabeth Norton and the Amberley Archive.

reluctance to sanction a definitive solution to the problem posed by Mary. © Jonathan Reeve JR204b5p9 15501600.

193. The Spanish Armada off the French coast. From George Carleton's *Thankfull Remembrance* (1627). By the 1620s, when this pamphlet was published, the 'Protestant wind' here shown blowing along the Channel was already a fixture in the national mythology. © Jonathan Reeve JR216b5p148 15501600.

194. Preaching at Paul's Cross, London. Londoners flocked to hear sermons at the open-air pulpit in the cathedral churchyard. On Sunday 24 November 1588, a stately procession escorted Elizabeth to the cathedral for an official service of thanksgiving for victory over the Armada, which included a sermon preached from this pulpit by John Piers, Bishop of Salisbury. © Jonathan Reeve JR209b5p68 15501600.

195. When Elizabeth visited the Earl of Hertford at Elvetham in 1591, he arranged splendid outdoor entertainments around a small ornamental lake in the shape of a half-moon, specially dug for the occasion. The entertainments, including pageants, songs, verses, fireworks and banquets, filled all three days of her visit. In this picture of the scene, Elizabeth is shown seated beside the left horn of the moon on a throne beneath a cloth of estate. © Jonathan Reeve JR211b5p104 15501600.

196. The 'Procession Picture', from Elizabeth's last years, is an idealised representation of one of her formal public appearances. Gentlemen Pensioners (her bodyguard) armed with halberds line the route, while other young gentlemen carry the Queen shoulder high on a litter beneath an exotic canopy. Before her walk senior courtiers, Knights of the Garter, while behind her follow ladies-in-waiting and maids of honour. © Jonathan Reeve JR200b5pii 15501600.

197. Engraved portrait of Elizabeth I by William Rogers *c*. 1595. © Jonathan Reeve JR1016b5fp26 15001600.

198. St James's Palace, London, the arrival of Queen Mary de Medici to visit her daughter, Henrietta Maria. © Jonathan Reeve JR1953b22p1274 16001650.

199. Charles II by Pieter Nason. © Jonathan Reeve JR1903b94fp72 16501700.

200. Lord Mayor's Day 1683 by John Griffier. © Jonathan Reeve JR1911b94fp269 16501700.

201. The Fire of London, 1666, by Lieven Verschuur. © Jonathan Reeve JR1904b94fp130 16501700.

202. Coronation procession of Mary of Modena, Queen of James II. © Jonathan Reeve JR1986b61p1049 16501700.

203. Coronation in Westminster Abbey on 23 April 1685 of James II and Mary of Modena. © Jonathan Reeve JR1959b24p1440 16501700.

204. Coronation in Westminster Abbey on 11 April 1689 of William III and Mary II, from a contemporary ballad, *c*. 1689. They were crowned together by Henry Compton, the Bishop of London. The crowning was normally the duty of the Archbishop of Canterbury, but the Archbishop at the time, William Sancroft, refused to recognise the removal of James II. © Jonathan Reeve JR1960b24p1488 16501700.

205. Contemporary depiction of Queen Anne, who ascended the throne in 1702. © Jonathan Reeve JR1961b24p1569 16501700.

206. Carisbrooke Castle on the Isle of Wight. Charles I was imprisoned in the castle during the Civil War. © Elizabeth Norton and the Amberley Archive.

207. Charles I's chamber at Carisbrooke Castle. The King attempted unsuccessfully to escape from this room. © Elizabeth Norton and the Amberley Archive.

208. Charles I. © Jonathan Reeve JR1722f15 16001700.

209. Henrietta Maria by Van Dyck. © Jonathan Reeve JR1901b94fp4 16001650.

210. Catherine of Braganza, wife of Charles II. © Jonathan Reeve JR1904b94fp80 16501700.

211. Charles II miniature by Samuel Cooper. © Jonathan Reeve JR1900b94frontisC 16501700.

212. St Paul's Cathedral. Catherine of Braganza was consulted on the rebuilding of London following the Great Fire in 1666. Sir Christopher Wren's great cathedral was the most ambitious part of the design. © Elizabeth Norton and the Amberley Archive.

213. Anne Marie Louise D'Orléans. Charles II proposed to her in 1659 but was rejected. © Jonathan Reeve JR1906b94p165T 16501700.

214. Lucy Walters, who had a brief affair with Charles II. © Jonathan Reeve JR1906b94p165BL 16501700.

215. Barbara Villiers, mistress of Charles II, miniature by Samuel Cooper. © Jonathan Reeve JR1907b94p219 16501700.

216. Nell Gwyn, long-standing mistress of Charles II, by Peter Lely. © Jonathan Reeve JR1908b94fp232 16501700.

217. Louise de Kerouaille, mistress of Charles II, by Pierre Mignard. © Jonathan Reeve JR1909b94fp248 16501700.

218. Hortense Mancini, mistress of Charles II, by Pierre Mignard. © Jonathan Reeve JR1910b94fp256 16501700.

219. Anne Hyde, first wife of King James II of England, by Peter Lely. © Jonathan Reeve JR1905b94fp152 16501700.

220. Mary of Modena, wife of King James II of England. © Jonathan Reeve JR1912b94fp264 16501700.

221. Queen Mary II, wife of King William III of England, by Peter Lely. © Jonathan Reeve JR1905b94fp160 16501700.

222. The entrance to the Queen's Apartments at Kensington Palace. Kensington was Mary II's favourite residence, and she died there in 1694. © Elizabeth Norton and the Amberley Archive.

223. A statue of Queen Anne outside St Paul's Cathedral. Although dominated by her female favourites, Anne was a successful monarch and held her throne in spite of the claims of her half-brother, the Old Pretender. © Elizabeth Norton and the Amberley Archive.

224. Caroline of Brunswick and George, Prince of Wales (the future George IV). The couple loathed each other from their first meeting, and George spent their wedding night in a drunken stupor lying in the fire grate. © Elizabeth Norton and the Amberley Archive.

225. Mary II loved gardening and helped to plan the formal gardens at Hampton Court. © Elizabeth Norton and the Amberley Archive.

226. William III and Mary II carried out major building works at Hampton Court in an attempt to rival Louis XIV's Palace of Versailles. © Elizabeth Norton and the Amberley Archive.

227. Queen Victoria's bathing machine at Osborne House. The bathing machine would be wheeled into the sea to allow the Queen to enter the water without being observed in her bathing costume. © Elizabeth Norton and the Amberley Archive.

228. A satirical cartoon depicting the morning after the wedding of Mrs Fitzherbert and Prince George. Although denied by the prince, news of the marriage quickly spread. © Elizabeth Norton and the Amberley Archive.

229. Osborne House on the Isle of Wight. Victoria and Albert bought the house as a place of retreat and they spent as much time as possible there with their children. © Elizabeth Norton and the Amberley Archive.

230. Victoria as queen from stained glass at Canterbury Cathedral. © Elizabeth Norton and the Amberley Archive.

231. Queen Victoria. © Jonathan Reeve JR1714f9 18001900.

232. Elizabeth Bowes-Lyon as Duchess of York. © Elizabeth Norton and the Amberley Archive.

233 Elizabeth Bowes-Lyon with her daughter, the future Elizabeth II. © Elizabeth Norton and the Amberley Archive.

234. Abdication letter from Edward VIII. © Jonathan Reeve JR1721b90p291 16001700.

235. King George VI and Queen Elizabeth, to become better know in the late twentieth century as the Queen Mother. The future Elizabeth II is next to her mother. © Jonathan Reeve JR1722b90fp304 16001700.

236. The procession of Princess Diana's funeral. Courtesy of Jonathan Reeve JR1715f10 19002000. Photo by Neville Elder.

237. The Anglo-Saxon and Norman queens. © Elizabeth Norton.

238. The Plantagenet and Lancastrian queens. © Elizabeth Norton.

239. Yorkist queen consorts and Tudor queen regnants. © Elizabeth Norton.

240. The six wives of Henry VIII. © Elizabeth Norton.

241. The Stuart, Hanoverian and Windsor queens. © Elizabeth Norton.

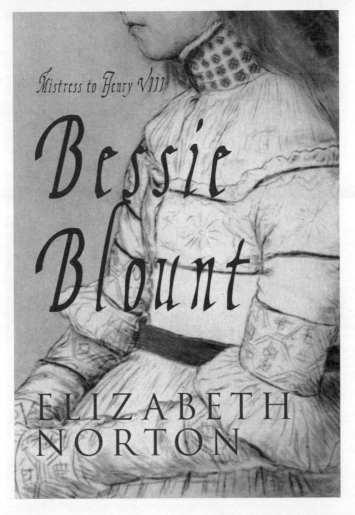

Also available from Amberley Publishing

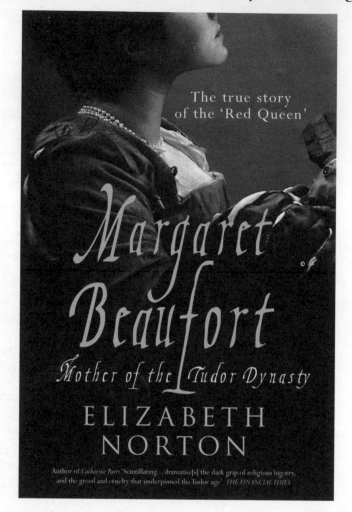

Divorced at ten, a mother at thirteen & three times a widow.
The extraordinary true story of the 'Red Queen', Lady Margaret
Beaufort, matriarch of the Tudors

'Portrait of a medieval matriarch' THE INDEPENDENT

Born in the midst of the Wars of the Roses, Margaret Beaufort became the greatest heiress of her time.
She survived a turbulent life, marrying four times and enduring imprisonment before passing her claim
to the crown of England to her son, Henry VII, the first of the Tudor monarchs.

Henry VII gave his mother unparalleled prominence during his reign and she established herself as an
independent woman.

£9.99 Paperback
63 illustrations (39 col)
272 pages
978-1-4456-0578-4

Available from all good bookshops or to order direct
Please call **01453-847-800**
www.amberleybooks.com

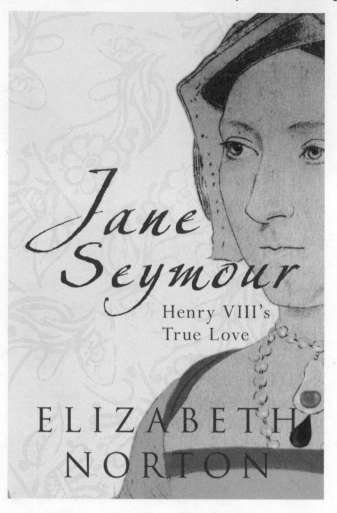

Also available from Amberley Publishing

Wife, widow, mother, survivor, the story of the last queen of Henry VIII

'Scintillating' THE FINANCIAL TIMES

'Norton cuts an admirably clear path through the tangled Tudor intrigues' JENNY UGLOW

'Wonderful, an excellent book, a joy to read' HERSTORIA

The sixth wife of Henry VIII was also the most married queen of England, outliving three husbands before finally marrying for love. Catherine Parr was enjoying her freedom after her first two arranged marriages when she caught the attention of the elderly Henry VIII. She was the most reluctant of all Henry's wives, offering to become his mistress rather than submit herself to the dangers of becoming Henry's queen. This only served to increase Henry's enthusiasm for the young widow and Catherine was forced to abandon her lover for the decrepit king.

£9.99 Paperback
49 illustrations (39 colour)
304 pages
978-1-4456-0383-4

Available from all good bookshops or to order direct
Please call **01453-847-800**
www.amberleybooks.com

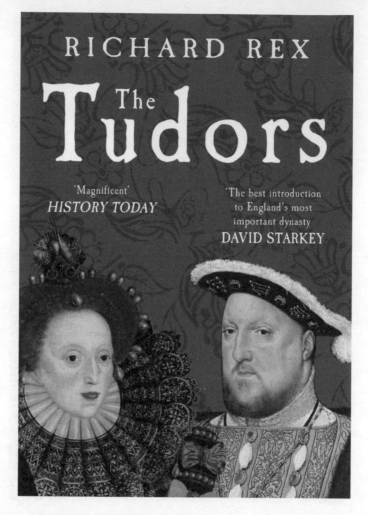

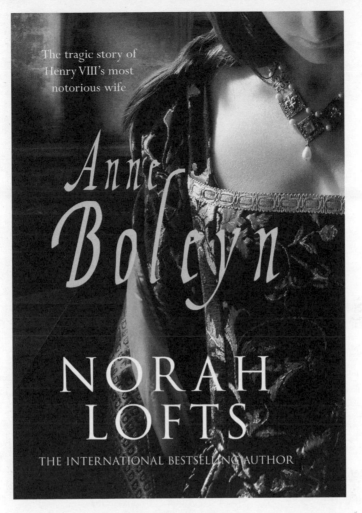

Index